Space Patrol

Space Patrol

Missions of Daring in the Name of Early Television

JEAN-NOEL BASSIOR

McFarland & Company, Inc., Publishers
Jefferson, North Carolina, and London

Library of Congress Cataloguing-in-Publication Data

Bassior, Jean-Noel.
Space patrol : missions of daring in the name of early television / Jean-Noel Bassior.
p.   cm.
Includes bibliographical references and index.

ISBN 0-7864-1911-3 (illustrated case binding : 50# alkaline paper) ∞

1. Space patrol (Television program : 1950–1955)
I. Title.
PN1992.77.S67B37   2005   791.45'72 — dc22   2004015874
British Library cataloguing data are available

On the cover: The *Terra V* rocketship and *Space Patrol* crew on television;
planet image ©2005 PhotoSpin; TV set image ©2005 Photodisc

McFarland & Company, Inc., Publishers
Box 611, Jefferson, North Carolina 28640
www.mcfarlandpub.com

To Virginia Sherwood Fletcher Bach,
who believed in this book and made it possible

And for
Norman Jolley and Lou Huston, who shaped the vision into words,
Dick Darley, who made the words real,
Ed Kemmer, whose portrayal of Corry
gave me inspiration to last a lifetime,
Lyn Osborn, who crashed the dimensional barrier
and wouldn't leave me alone until the *Space Patrol* story was told

Acknowledgments

Author E. L. Doctorow once said that when you commit to doing a book, you become like a magnet, attracting everything you need to complete it. That's exactly what happened as this book emerged from "nowhere" into the "now here." When I posted a notice on the Web that I was seeking *Space Patrol* memories, people contacted me with the most amazing, heartfelt stories—but when I added these to my research files, bursting with over one hundred first-hand interviews with cast and crew plus countless articles about the show, I panicked. I remember one morning when I stared at the cartons of *Space Patrol* research I'd gathered over the years and had a sinking feeling that there would never be time to write the story. And yet, once I committed to doing it, people appeared to supply what I needed to get the job done. Virginia Bach gave me financial backing, making it possible to cut back on my freelance magazine work and focus on the book; then, at various stages along the way, friends stepped in to help bring things to completion.

Writing is a lonely business and brings up all kinds of feelings, but Pamela Madison shared the vision, held the energy and let me talk … and talk … and talk. Nancy Heck volunteered her incredible research, organizing and proofing skills, saving me eons of time and tons of work. Richard Felnagle, English professor and *Space Patrol* fan, reviewed the manuscript and suggested changes that made it a whole lot better. Photographer Alice Su flew from New York to California whenever I panicked about getting the photos right. Terry Drucker, my longtime partner in crime (we can forge any teacher's signature you might need on a report card), proofed the final version at the eleventh hour. David Fryxell showed me how to take control of vast amounts of research material. Ed Kemmer answered endless questions for twenty years; without his contribution, this book would not be possible. Dick Darley soon learned that "one more question" meant twenty-five, but he was always patient, open and honest. Lyn Osborn's sister Beth Flood and her husband, Bill, shared their memories of Lyn and gave me access to his letters, scrapbooks and personal papers, which were invaluable. Alice Akins cheered me on and put me in touch with her former colleagues at ABC. Julie Ann Matheson coached me through overwhelm and martyrhood. Rick Fleishman, my brother, spotted errors in the text that I couldn't see myself and prevented several major disasters. Fran Kemmer offered her loving support, and Mike Guarino urged me to stretch the vision and write the big story—the one I really wanted to tell.

Some people ended up doing more work for this book than they ever expected, namely: Steve Handzo, who created a guide to *Space Patrol* merchandising and tirelessly researched the fate of the Ralston Rockets; Chuck Lassen, who produced the first-ever Space Patrol Radio Log; William F. Drish, Jr., who offered essential additions to the Log;

Jack McKirgan II, who tracked the ships and models of the Space Patrol for future historians and supplied important research for chapter four, "The Right Stuff"; and Elliott Swanson and Nancy Heck, who compiled the index (no small task).

Special thanks to those "cadets" who keep the flame burning for our space opera heroes: Dale Ames, Jeff Berkwits, Bob Burns, Warren Chaney, Rory Coker, Bruce David, Jerry Haendiges, Jack Hagerty, Chris Mason, Ed Pippin, Joe Sarno, Elliott Swanson. And to Don McCroskey, who patiently explained how studio equipment worked in the 1950s until I understood it enough to write about it; Jon Rogers, who always took time to answer my questions and contributed scale drawings of the Terra V; Richard (Dick) Tufeld, whose humorous e-mails always gave me a lift; and Bob Trachinger, who, even when answering technical questions, always spoke from the heart.

Thanks to Ned Comstock, archivist, USC Cinema-Television Library, who took a special interest in this book and went out of his way to steer me toward research gold; Ellen Bailey, Pasadena Playhouse archivist, who communicated the spirit of the Playhouse so well that I could feel what it was like to have been there; the late John Buckley, who didn't sugarcoat his memories (which always adds life to a book); Chuck Barkus, Carol and Michael Hagen, Abigail Shelton Baker, John Feneck and Tyler MacDuff, who, like Buckley, knew Lyn Osborn well and made me feel as if I knew him too; Mark Young, co-author with Steve Duin and Mike Richardson of *Blast Off! Rockets, Robots, Rayguns and Rarities from the Golden Age of Space Toys*, for sharing photos from that great book; Kirk and Lynn Leonhardt of Creative Moments and Steve Werth, director of ASIFA-Hollywood Virtual Archive, who went out of their way to supply photos of Ed Kemmer as Prince Phillip in *Sleeping Beauty*; Michael Stein, publisher and senior editor of *Filmfax* magazine, who boosted my confidence when he ran my story on the show in 1986; James J.J. Wilson, story and managing editor of *Filmfax*, whose thoughtful suggestions and belief in this project lent strength during the final stages; and Kaylan Thornhill, who told me I was a writer when I didn't know how to do this.

My thanks forever to the late Ken Mayer, Virginia Hewitt, Nina Bara, Bela Kovacs, Glen Akins, Rickey Barr, Larry Dobkin, Truck Krone, Tom Mason, Ruth Mayer, and Ben Welden.

And to all the "cadets" and ABC staffers who shared their *Space Patrol* memories and believed that someday (in this century) there really would be a book: Dan Adams, William Adrian, David Alexander, Andy Andersen, Philip Angerhofer, Bobbi Averell, Bill Baldwin, Jr., Dick Beals, Kenneth Berry, Ken Bird, Leonard Bischoff, Steve Blake, John Blakely, Linda Blakely, Red Blanchard, Larry Bloomfield, Dick Bolt, Ron Boucher, William Bourne, Rick Brandon, Frank Bresee, Susan Brickwood, Jim Buchanan, Lonnie Burr, Frank Callaway, David Caplan, Dale and Tysa Carley, Charles Chamberlin, Allan Cohen, Jordan Cohen, John Coleman, Michael Colin, Jerry Cook, Jack Cox, Dr. Paul Crandall, Bob Cremer, Brian Czarnota, Malcolm Dalkoff, Chris Darley, Greg Davis, John Davis, Dr. Ward Dean, Herb Deeks, Kara DeGrazia, Maury (Orr) De Mots, Al Doshna, Charles Drapo, Margo Ehrlich, Bob Eisenhauer, Bob Ekman, Mike Elmo, Joe Emmett, Steve Faessel, John Farabella, Jeff Fenton, Bud Fraze, Guy Fry, Jim Ganley, Doug Gard, John and Sandy Garrity, John Gassman, Larry Gassman, Larry Gelbart, Joel Geoffrey, David Gerrold, Mel Gilden, Wynn Gilligan, Ron Glaze, Dr. Stuart Grant, Cary Griffin, Kathy Griffin, Rich Gronquist, Bob Gurr, Albert Hale, Diana Hale, Marty Halperin, Jerry Hankins, Bill Hanlon, Dr. Allen Joe Harris, Judy Harris, Randy Harris, Ralph Hartnagel, Sr., Ralph Hartnagel III, Tom Hatten, Glen Hawkins, Jimmy Hawkins, Clair Higgins, Maurice Hill, Robert Hill, Joseph Hogg, Eric Hogling, Paul Holbrook, Dick Hovey, Carol Howard, Robert Jennings, Bruce Mason Johnson, Lois Jolley, J. Davey Jones, Thomas Jones, Steve Joyce, Setsuko Kaldor, Kathy Kasten, Ted Katz, Bob Key, Norm Knights, Stan Kohls, Linda Konner, Bator Kovacs, Matt Kovacs, Tor Kovacs, Marta Kovacs-Ruiz, Steve La Vigne, Jodean Lawrence, Judd Lawson, Bob Lee, Rick Lett, Susan Levin, Chuck Lewis, Peter Lind, Ken Linville, Clyde Lyman, Bobb Lynes, John MacMurray, Ken Mader, Roberta Nelson Manning, Mike Marder, Irv Mayer, Stark Maynard, Reparata Mazzola, Rose Marie McDaniel, Penny McFadden, Marty McKee, Bob McKelvey, Roy Miles, Darla Miller, Hank Miller, Kent Miller, Carl Molesworth, Margaret Montreys, Doug Moore, Franklin Mullen, Story Musgrave, Jeanette Nall, David Narz, Jack Narz, Jane Newell, Barry Newman, Marian A. Nickerson, Gary North, Bill O'Connell, Christianne Osborn, Steve Owen, Mike Pahlow, Richard Perea, Les Perkins, Marianne G. Petrino, Chad Phillips, Mark Phillips, Charles Phoenix, Cecillia Pier, Bob Polio, Tom Powers, Shawn Randall, Arie Raymond, Philip Allen Read, Jr., Robert Robinson, Dennis Rose, Gary Rosine, Louis Rugani, Edmund Ryden, Steve Salem, Marg (Clifton) Satchell, Jim Saunders, Jim Scancarelli, Tom Schaad, David Sciacchitano, Mitch Semer, Gary Shusett, Dr. Leon Siegel, Dr. John Simelaro, Leslie Singer, Steve Smith, Doug Souter, Sybil Starr, George Stevens, Paul Subbie, Loren Sutherland, Judy Laws Sutherlin, Robert "Slim" Sweatmon, Tamiko, Alyce Teaney, Frank Thomas, Robert Thomas, Sue Thomas, Roy Trumbull, Ken Viall, Richard Walker, Rick Watkins, Blair White, Virginia White, Brian Williams, Theo Williams, Tom Williams, Wade Williams III, Tom Winegar, Diana Woodruff, Conrad Youngren, Marc Zicree.

And very special thanks and love to Baratta, Torah, Shulanda and, of course, Lazaris.

Contents

Preface

Perhaps you've picked up this book because the words "Space Patrol" stirred childhood memories, or you're interested in the early, hair-raising days of live television when just about anything could happen (and did) before millions of viewers. Or maybe this book just called to you, as some books do.

I'm a journalist off my usual beat (celebrity interviews for magazines) who's spent twenty years researching a television show that was hugely popular in the 1950s. Though I didn't know it at the time, *Space Patrol* did more than help me survive childhood; it gave me a vision on which to build the rest of my life. It modeled courage and compassion, good choices in bad situations, heroic behavior that transcended fact, fiction, space and time. These life lessons stayed with me, though I forgot where they came from — until *Space Patrol* suddenly surfaced in the mid–'80s on cable networks and video tape. It wasn't until then, when I revisited my childhood heroes, that the show's full impact hit home.

Space Patrol was a live, action-adventure saga, or "space opera," set in the 30th century. It began as a local TV show in Los Angeles in March 1950, but was soon picked up by both the ABC radio and television networks. It ran for five years (1950–55) and captured the dawning space-age fantasies of the nation. Though its creator, Mike Moser, thought of it as a children's show, its writers, director and actors didn't, and *Space Patrol* quickly attracted a viewership of all ages.

Why was the show so popular? The magic hinged on the cast: Commander Buzz Corry, Cadet Happy, Major "Robbie" Robertson, Carol Carlisle and Tonga — a band of comrades willing to risk their lives for each other and the greater good on a second's notice. Together they faced a slew of 30th-century threats, from the hazards of space travel, exploding stars and wayward comets to mad scientists, evil robots and sadistic silicon life forms intent on ruling the universe. These imaginative stories took place against a backdrop of special effects never seen before on the newfangled medium called television — an alien technology invading 1950s living rooms at warp speed. Adults, enthralled by this show initially aimed at kids, soon made up over 60 percent of the audience.

For a few years, just about everyone in the country knew about *Space Patrol*. Ed Kemmer and Lyn Osborn, who starred as Commander Corry and Cadet Happy, were pictured on boxes of Wheat Chex, Rice Chex and Hot Ralston cereals, and *Space Patrol* gear was everywhere. Toys, clothing and household items, such as flashlights and emergency kits, flew off mail order and department store shelves. In 1952, *Life* magazine predicted that sales of *Space Patrol* merchandise that year would peak at $40 million. The cast appeared at grand openings and civic ceremonies, raised stellar sums for charity telethons, and was featured in *Look, Life, Collier's* and all the popular TV and film fanzines of the day. Kids and adults alike dreamed of jumping into the cockpit of Buzz Corry's battlecruiser

1

and blasting off alongside the Commander for thrilling adventures in the "wild, vast reaches of space."

But there was something else about *Space Patrol*—something important. For on Earth, in the mid–20th century, the compassionate hero was still revered. It was a time when figures such as The Lone Ranger, Hopalong Cassidy, Captain Video, Sergeant Preston and Buzz Corry served as role models for kids and adults who wanted to be like them. Looking back, that may seem quaint and incredible, but television was new — and if you were a kid who was part of the first TV generation, then perhaps you remember how impressionable we were. We're far too sophisticated now to yearn for those old-fashioned, black-and-white heroes — though if you've picked up this book, you may disagree. I'm with you there. I long for the daring, compassionate hero who risks his or her life to protect others from violence or tyranny, but who doesn't have to crash cars, shoot everyone in sight, or blow up buildings or planets to get the job done. (Chapter 22, "Where Have All the Heroes Gone?" takes a look at what it's like to grow up with heroes who inspire, and the deep longing in some ex-kids for the role models of yesteryear.)

What aspects of the show does this book cover? All of them — technical, emotional, social — and maybe it delves into the personal lives of the key players a little more than it should. I've tried, too, to re-create the heart-stopping excitement of live TV in the 1950s by taking readers onto Stage A at ABC Television Center in Hollywood while *Space Patrol* is kinescoped. What could go wrong often did, as guest actors panicked, special effects fizzled, and players leaned against teetering scenery about to fall. In spite of it all, the fast-paced show usually came off well, and viewers had no idea that the cast and crew — many of them risk-taking vets out of World War II — brought it home on a wing and a prayer.

You've probably got some idea now of how *Space Patrol* fits into television history. But what about its place in the context of science fiction? The space operas of the 1950s brought SF into millions of living rooms, melding it with everyday life in a way that made it seem as if a futuristic society was just around the corner. When science fiction met television, says James J. J. Wilson, managing editor of *Filmfax* magazine, the genre invaded popular culture, "giving kids a vision to hang their space helmets on." The marriage of TV and space-age drama created a powerful force that, launched in the 50s, emerged in the next decade as *Star Trek*, which popularized science fiction as never before. "*Space Patrol*," says author and SF critic David Gerrold, "is the uncredited ancestor of *Star Trek*. It was a brilliant show, deserving of far more credit than it has ever been given because it had such impact on the viewing audience."

The show broke new ground in another genre, too. Few people realize that *Space Patrol* was possibly the first soap opera ever aired on TV. The daily show, which debuted in LA in 1950 and was soon sent by kinescope recording to stations around the country, was a live, cliffhanging drama that got viewers hooked on the characters and tuning in the following day to learn their fate. (The first "official" TV soap opera, *Guiding Light*, which began on radio in 1937, didn't cross over to television until June 30, 1952.)

How did I do my research? First-hand. By getting to know the cast and crew over two decades and recording more than one hundred interviews; by tracking down facts in magazines and newspapers of the day; and by sifting through scripts, letters, schedules, production records and scribbled notes, long-forgotten, when I was granted access to personal files.[1]

---

[1]Quotes without footnoted sources come from personal communications — mostly interviews in person or by phone, but occasionally from e-mails or letters I have received.

Why did I write this book? Well, have you ever had a TV show (book or movie) hit you between the eyes as if it carried some personal message just for you? Did you ever fall in love with a fictional character because he or she embodied everything you wanted to be? When I was a kid, I felt that way about Cadet Happy, played by Lyn Osborn.

Hap was Commander Corry's sidekick. He was light-hearted, funny and cheerful—until he ran into the bad guys, who threatened him and sometimes beat him up. The villains in *Space Patrol* were physically and emotionally abusive—especially Corry's archenemy, Prince Baccarratti—and as a kid I marveled at Hap's amazing resilience as he survived some pretty rough treatment at the hands of these heavies. Hap never held a grudge or bore an emotional scar, and that looked like a pretty good game-plan for handling bullies and other annoyances in my life. It gave me something to hang onto: a vision of how to be in the world, how not to succumb to life's injustices. And though "Hap" was conceived by show creator Mike Moser and developed by writers Norman Jolley and Lou Huston, from all accounts, actor Lyn Osborn deeply merged with the character. The boundaries even blurred for Osborn's friends and family, who at times lost track of where Lyn ended and Hap began. As a child, I saw no boundaries either. I wanted to be like this young "cadet," who, nurtured by Corry's mentoring, gave me a pattern for right action, the blueprint for a positive human being.

When I was nine years old, I met Cadet Happy.

One Sunday, my grandmother, a fashion designer, took me to brunch at the posh Beverly Wilshire Hotel. Suddenly I saw Cadet Happy only a few yards away. I froze—it couldn't be true. Trembling, I edged closer to him. It was as if a real spaceman, a larger-than-life god had descended to Earth. He noticed me staring at him, but instead of doing his upbeat Cadet Happy thing, he quietly stared back. I summoned all my courage and moved closer. He stooped down to my kid level, and for what seemed like an eternal moment, we both stared into each other's eyes. I was transfixed by my hero; he was looking into the eyes of his future biographer and didn't know it. Neither of us knew he'd be dead in less than five years. "You have beautiful eyes," he said softly. I heard that often in those days, but when Cadet Happy said it, it went straight to my soul.

Decades later, when I posted a notice on several Web sites that I was writing about *Space Patrol*, e-mails poured in from fans about the impact of the show on their lives—memories they had carried for *fifty years*. As I read their heartfelt letters and sensed the longing for heroes like Buzz Corry and Hap, I realized that I was not alone; others remembered, too. The show had a much deeper impact than its cast and crew ever knew, and when I tracked down the writers—Norm Jolley (television) and Lou Huston (radio)—it was heartening to deliver this news. I wish they had lived to see this book.

Smokin' rockets, I think I've covered why *Space Patrol* is an important piece of both TV and SF history, so it's time to blast off. As you come along on this journey into the "wild, vast reaches of space," back to a timeline when Earthlings pioneered television and had true heroes, I wish you smooth orbits, soft landings and spaceman's luck.

CHAPTER 1

Countdown

If Paint isn't headed for the last roundup, he's at least pawing the ground in anticipation of the inevitable day. A new supersonic generation is putting its cowboy suits in mothballs and encasing itself in space helmets. The handwriting is on the clouds.
— *Woman's Day*, August 1953

I'm now 60 years old, Chief Engineer for a consumer electronics manufacturer and holder of 14 U.S. patents. Space Patrol fostered my interest in things scientific. It instilled in me the feeling that the future held great promise of marvels to come.
— Doug Moore

GUERNEVILLE, CALIFORNIA: APRIL 1984

The voice was urgent: "Go inside and ask about *Space Patrol*."

I was standing alone — except for the eerie feeling that Someone or Something was at my side — in front of the new nostalgia store in Guerneville, California, a small resort town on the banks of the Russian River. Guerneville makes the national news every few years when the river floods its banks and devastates the town — again. Each time it happens, folks gripe about the reckless expansion of the city of Santa Rosa upstream, a burgeoning bedroom community sixty miles north of San Francisco. In recent years, vineyards and pastures that used to absorb the rainwater have been paved over to make way for housing developments, so the floodwaters rush downstream, ravaging the small communities that dot the river's shores.

It was a crisp spring morning. A block away, a few "river rats," as the year-round residents call themselves, ambled by King's Fish and Tackle on Main Street. Then, impatient, the voice spoke again: "Go inside and ask about *Space Patrol*."

I had not thought about *Space Patrol* in 25 years.

Inside, the store was dimly lit and crammed with memorabilia — a fuzzy twilight zone of comics, record albums, vintage toys, B movie posters and bubble gum cards right out of the 1940s and '50s. The dusty-gold light brought a postwar childhood into soft focus, stirring memories of cap guns, hopscotch, skate keys, erector sets, the Hardy Boys and Nancy Drew, selling lemonade to the neighbors for five cents a glass, blowing my 25-cent allowance on comic books and peppermint sticks, rainy days watching war movies on TV, long summers of street baseball and trespassing in neighbors' yards as my friends and I played hide-and-go-seek in the late afternoon. I ran fast for a girl — faster than any boy on the block — and played hard at handball and dodgeball until 6:40, when I beelined for home. Rush through the unlocked back door, race to the living room, plop down in front of the Hoffman console TV … it's almost time … any moment now… the announcer's voice booms, "This is the ABC Television Network" ... and then it happens...

> SPAAAAAAACE PATROL! *High adventure in the wild, vast reaches of space! Missions of daring in the name of interplanetary justice! Travel into the future with Buzz Corry, commander-in-chief of the —*

"*Space Patrol* memorabilia?" The bearded guy with tinted glasses behind the counter breaks into a smile. "Funny you should ask about *that* show — it was my favorite." His name is David, and we talk about ray guns for a while like two members of the NRA. "Tell you what," he says finally, "I've got a *Space Patrol* tape and a video recorder at home. I'll bring them to the store. Can you come back tomorrow?"

This is cool. It's 1984 and nobody I know actually *owns* a video recorder. It'll be fun to see the show after so many years.

The sun has burned off the mist rolling in from the river the following morning as I enter the pale golden gloom of David's store. True to his word, he's setting up the recorder. Then he turns out the lights, hits the play button, and, calling over his shoulder that he has errands to do in town, leaves me alone in the dark with a huge, raw chunk of my childhood. I steel myself for disappointment. *Space Patrol* was a kid's show; viewing it as an adult is bound to shatter sacred childhood memories. Then suddenly I'm watching Commander Buzz Corry, Cadet Happy, Major Robertson and Carol Carlisle menaced by Agent X — but this is not kiddie fare. The script is not childish and everyone — actors, writer, director — seems to be taking it seriously. As the evil "X" holds the comrades hostage, I'm concerned — and so are they. And there's something else; something I'm struggling to remember...

You see, as kids, my friends and I assumed we'd grow up to become like our heroes — that someday, like them, we'd do great things, make a difference in the nonsensical world that belonged to adults. Now, watching the *Space Patrol* crew resist Agent X, the kid who dreamed of living heroically snaps out of a long, deep sleep. It's like awakening in the middle of the night — or in midlife — remembering something you forgot to do. Something very important.

These feelings flood in like the river overflowing its banks.

When David returns, I leave in a half-dream, stumbling into the glare of the noonday sun. I'm back from the outer galaxies, back on Main Street, but shaken by the magic I've revisited on that black-and-white screen. And something has changed. It's as if some sense of purpose has reawakened. The haunting "*Spaaaaaace Patrol*" intro has stirred echoes of childhood, when life stretched ahead as an endless adventure. For in the pre–Rambo 1950s, a band of superheroes dedicated to the struggle against evil led the first generation of TV kids on thrilling escapades, proving weekly that justice was achieved through strength, compassion and courage. They never drew first blood. They fought the bad guys with fists, revolvers, ray guns and shock rifles, but unlike many celluloid heroes today, they held their tempers in check, using violence only when reason failed. Some of these crimefighters, such as Captain Video, Sky King and the Lone Ranger, were private citizens who got fed up with evil and decided to battle it full-time on their own. Others belonged to official crime-fighting organizations like the Texas Rangers and the Space Patrol. All had pledged their lives to truth and justice, and as a kid it was comforting to know that in the complex world grownups had built (where we would go someday), these watchdogs kept things from getting totally out of hand.

Through the late afternoons of the '50s, in the timeless twilight between school and supper, and on Saturday morning, we rode horses and spaceships alongside our heroes. We patrolled a dimension that stretched from the lawless west to the uncharted outer galaxies, and we helped a lot of people who were victims of foul play. It was an eerie, dangerous black-and-white world, where outlaws could ambush you in a canyon and aliens could trap you in time. But just when you reached the limit of your courage and endurance, your hero-companion — whether Buzz Corry or the Lone Ranger — would come up with a brilliant escape plan and together you'd fight your way out, overpower the bad guys, and justice would prevail. Then you were safe — until the next show; same time, same station.

If you've studied Earth's history, you know that the TV space operas that soared to success from 1949 to 1955 had their roots in the first sci-fi flick, *A Trip to the Moon*, launched by French film pioneer George Méliès in 1902, less than 50 years after the Civil War.[1] It was the first film to show Earthlings encountering aliens — ill-tempered "moon-men" who, fortunately, exploded when struck with umbrellas. In 1926, German filmmaker Fritz Lang stunned audiences with the futuristic *Metropolis*. Set in the far-off 21st century, it focused on the struggle between a ruling class who dwelt in skyscrapers and slave laborers who cowered underground. Lang topped this three years later with *The Woman in the Moon* (*Die Frau im Mond*), the first film to depict real space travel. Hitler banned the film for national security reasons — Wernher von Braun and other top German scientists were rushing to develop a rocket like the one in the film.[2]

Another milestone in the evolution of celluloid sci-fi was Buddy DeSylva's *Just Imagine* (1930), a quirky musical set in a space-age future (1980) where people with names like J-21 and D-6 feast on food pills and procreate via test tubes. The film featured an art deco spaceship later used in the *Flash Gordon* movie serial (the granddaddy of TV space shows) that set the prototype for what a make-believe spaceship *should* look like. Six years later, Alexander Korda's anti-war epic, *Things to Come*, adapted for screen by H. G. Wells from his book *The Shape of Things to Come*, dealt with troubling themes that stalked SF movies and TV space operas for decades to come. The film tracks a place called "Everytown" (obviously London) from 1940 to 2036 as a savage world war bombs civilization back to the Dark Ages. Eventually, a shiny, futuristic (but underground) society emerges from the ruins, along with pressing questions such as, Can science solve every problem? Can we hold onto our humanity in a high-tech society? That same year, the 13-part *Flash Gordon* serial hit theaters, followed three years later, in 1939, by *Buck Rogers in the 25th Century* — the first of twelve cliffhanging episodes. No one seemed bothered by the fact that Buck and Flash were played by the same actor, Olympic swimming champion Buster Crabbe (who bleached his hair blond to play Flash). Both action heroes had been born in comic strips and invaded homes in the 1930s via radio before their big-screen debuts.[3]

---

[1]This section tracks space opera's celluloid roots. In the literary world, E. E. "Doc" Smith is often credited with inventing the genre. His groundbreaking novel, *The Skylark of Space* (1928), and other action-packed books featured larger-than-life heroes (including strong female characters), dark warlords, galactic battles and awesome weaponry.

[2]One of Lang's technical advisers, Willy Ley, later served as consultant for the 1950s space opera *Tom Corbett, Space Cadet*.

[3]It wasn't until 1950 that more sophisticated sci-fi aired on radio when NBC presented *Dimension X* with scripts by giants such as Robert Heinlein, Ray Bradbury, Isaac Asimov and Kurt Vonnegut, but the show only lasted a year. Audiences took better to *X Minus One* ("*Countdown for blast-off: X minus five ... four ... three ... two ... X minus one ... FIRE!*"), which had a three-year run on the same network from 1955 to 1958 and drew many of its stories from popular *Galaxy* magazine.

In the early '40s, World War II flicks muscled out sci-fi and dreams of space exploration were put on hold. But box office hits such as *Flying Tigers, Thirty Seconds over Tokyo* and *A Yank in the RAF* that featured daring pilots pitted against the evil Axis powers set the stage for a new genre just over the horizon: space opera. Take airborne heroes defending a freedom-loving people against tyrants hell-bent on ruling the world, set the story a thousand years in the future, raise the stakes to conquering the solar system (or even the *universe*), and you've got the formula for TV's first space shows—a marriage of World War II heroism and celluloid dreams of space travel dating back to Méliès' *A Trip to the Moon.*

A spirit of hope and expansion swept through America in the postwar '50s, but the West had been tamed. Space was the next frontier. While the big screen had served as a natural venue for westerns with their sweeping landscapes and galloping action, the newfangled television set—a strange and alien technology—was the perfect medium for space operas set in the future. After all, what better way to showcase sci-fi than on a device that was sci-fi itself invading your living room? "All over the air waves, the Wide Open Spaces are being traded in for the Wide Upper Spaces," *Collier's* magazine reported in January 1952.[4] "The trend may be away from horses and up into the heavens for keeps." To prove it, the article cited a rumored $10 million, five-year contract inked by *Captain Video* with Post cereals—a lot of space credits in the 1950s.[5] But not everyone agreed with *Collier's* prediction. Buster Crabbe, who in addition to starring as Buck and Flash had played film roles ranging from Tarzan to Billy the Kid, saw space opera as a fleeting fad. "The cowboy," he insisted, "is the great romantic American hero. He'll never be replaced by the guy in space." Though actor William Shatner might disagree, Crabbe was right in the short term. In 1955, when fickle youngsters fell in love with wild-west warrior Davy Crockett, space opera vanished faster than a streaking comet and space helmets were replaced by coonskin caps.[6]

But from 1950 to 1955, three major shows—*Space Patrol, Captain Video* and *Tom Corbett, Space Cadet*—plus a slew of also-rans held kids and their parents spellbound as a new kind of galactic hero battled evil and challenged the unknown. New wardrobe, new gear and a whole new language were needed to keep up with these champions. Department stores stocked spacesuits and cadet uniforms, rocket dart guns and blasters, while kids baffled their elders with phrases like "Plug your jets!" and "Blast me for a Martian mouse!" Concerned parents wrote letters to magazines asking for advice on how to deal with the juvenile space craze. One columnist tried to ease their fears, but cautioned that if children got too space happy, parents should seek professional help:

> Do I think it's good for children to concentrate so much on spaceships and interplanetary travel TV shows? Probably it is no more harmful to a normal, imaginative child than the stories of giants and ogres so many of us grew up on. But if your child seems unnaturally absorbed with the subject or has bad dreams about being lost in space, I think a doctor should be consulted.[7]

[4]"Planet Parenthood" by Murray Robinson, *Collier's,* January 5, 1952, page 31.

[5]The show didn't last five years; it left the air waves in April 1955.

[6]*Men Into Space* (CBS) starred William Lundigan and tracked "the more-or-less realistic adventures of Colonel Ed McCauley, head of the American space program as he battles saboteurs, budget cuts, defective equipment and other problems in outer space," sums up film critic Marty McKee on the Internet Movie Database (www.IMDb.com). Though critically acclaimed, the show failed to rekindle the space craze sparked by the early '50s space operas. (Trivia: In the pilot for the show, "Moon Probe," Ed Kemmer, star of *Space Patrol*, plays the launch-control team member who does the countdown for the first manned flight around the moon.)

[7]Unidentified magazine, circa 1951, found in the files of Virginia Hewitt, *Space Patrol's* "Carol."

The desperate mother of a two-year-old fan who owned a long-suffering pet turtle (miniature turtles were popular household pets in the '50s) didn't need a doctor; she needed space gear. She pleaded with the producers of *Tom Corbett* to market a space helmet — to protect the turtle, not the two-year-old. Seems that whenever the show came

Space fever sweeps through the country's juvenile population. "A new supersonic generation is putting its cowboy suits in mothballs and encasing itself in space helmets," proclaimed *Woman's Day* in August 1953.

on, the boy made a makeshift helmet out of the turtle's bowl, tipping it upside down on his head.[8]

But beyond the kid-slang and gadgetry, for a brief spell in the 1950s, space opera gave Americans a larger vision — a glimpse of a peaceful solar society where you were as at home on Mars or Jupiter as on Earth. People were weary of westerns where life was cheap and cowboys and Indians slaughtered each other nonstop. In contrast, *Space Patrol's* "United Planets" was a safe and law-abiding place where criminals were rehabilitated, not punished. Not that space opera villains weren't nasty — they had weapons that could blow up your block, your town, and even your planet. The good guys fought back with ray guns, blasters, atomic rifles, thermoid ejectors, nucleamatic pistols and cosmic missiles, but their intent was clearly not to kill. "Only the villains speak of killing — that's why they're villains," a producer for *Captain Video* explained to *Collier's*. Otherwise, with the exception of a handful of maniacs, rogue scientists and alien warlords who wanted to rule the universe, most solar citizens tried to do the right thing, and peace and order prevailed. Eventually, even criminals got with the program. In the utopian *Space Patrol* universe, the most power-mad piece of space scum (with the exception of Commander Corry's nemesis, Prince Baccarratti) could be transformed by that medical marvel, the "Brainograph," into a law-abiding citizen.

In fact, in the society of the future, not only was the solar system a pretty safe place — thanks to the efforts of Buzz Corry, Captain Video and other heroes — but it was a familiar one, too. There were cities on all the planets, but the terrain was a lot like Earth, notes Rory Coker, professor of physics at the University of Texas at Austin:

> Venus was a jungle, Mars a desert, outer moons might be like the North or South Pole, but people could survive on these extraterrestrial locations with not much more equipment than that needed to subsist in similar locations on Earth. Humans were everywhere. The human race, far from putting all its eggs in one basket and polluting that basket, had spread colonies all over its home solar system and into solar systems beyond.

Moreover, adds Coker, space travel was fun:

> Even criminals and private citizens had rockets that could reach Mars or the asteroids. Navigation was by the seat of the pants and dead reckoning, with a bit of sextant work or keypunching on what looked like a 1948 office comptometer. Take-offs and landings were quick and there were never problems with other traffic. Rockets were not much larger than three freight locomotives ganged together, and probably simpler to run. Communication was instantaneous, as if the speed of light were infinite. Rockets could reach their distant destinations in hours or days, not months or years.[9]

All in all, the space opera universe was a well-run, rational place, with ordinary folk from Peoria to Pluto pretty content most of the time. Perhaps the key to this stress-free existence was that the citizens of the 30th century inhabited a friendly analog world devoid of sealed digital devices that drove you mad. Problems with the time-drive mechanism in your starship? Nothing you couldn't repair with the manual and a screwdriver. Because in this futuristic society, points out Coker, the most advanced technology was still user-friendly:

---

[8]"Planet Parenthood," *Collier's*, January 5, 1952, page 31.
[9]"Roaring Rockets" Web page created by Dr. Rory Coker (www.slick-net.com/space/).

Machines and vehicles were not featureless black boxes with no moving parts and no possibility of repair. Like 1940s radios, all equipment and spaceships were robustly built with huge valves, controls, conduits, switches, levers and dials. Anyone could take anything apart, repair it and get it working again with not much else than a few tools and several hours of tedious labor. It was obvious, by inspection, how things worked. Any educated person could repair something if given the time and — in the worst case — one or two replacement parts.

People, like machines, were friendly, too, for though society was technologically advanced, it was not impersonal. Except for the bad guys (who were more intent on conquering your planet than stealing your wallet), the solar system was just one big, extended neighborhood. Automated communication —faxes, e-mails and voice-mails where you might not reach a human being for days— were not part of this futuristic vision born of the neighborly 1940s and '50s. No one had yet envisioned a society where "face time" (meeting with another human being) was just one possible way to interact. *Space Patrol*'s TV writer, Norman Jolley, and radio scribe, Lou Huston, who both hailed from small-town America, brought a down-home humanity to the United Planets— a vast expanse where Buzz Corry, the second most powerful man in the solar system, was as friendly with an old prospector on Asteroid 237 as he was with the governor of Saturn. It made the future seem like a chummy place, where despite the mind-boggling distances between planets, you could jump in your private cruiser and zip over to Mars to call on a friend as easily as you'd hop in your surface-car to visit Aunt Betty in the next town.

This vision of a near-utopian society just around the corner got Americans excited about space exploration. "When the TV space shows were running, the topic of space travel was hot talk," says *Captain Video* aficionado Louis Rugani. "Even everyday objects— appliances, automobiles, homes— took on a Hollywood set designer's idea of a space-age look."

"Those shows were hugely important to the space program," confirms real-life astronaut Story Musgrave, who served on a record-breaking six shuttle missions. "The imagination had to create it when the reality wasn't there."

"Shows like *Space Patrol* gave children the idea they could build a space-age future," adds radio historian Bobb Lynes. "A lot of kids grew up to become rocket scientists." Adults caught space fever too. "The politicians 'selling' space travel and its very large budget had no qualms about spending the huge funds," says Ed Kemmer, who starred as *Space Patrol*'s Commander Corry. "It was what most every voter wanted at that time." TV space operas sparked a powerful vision, agrees producer–film historian Al Doshna, who points out that NASA now names spacecraft after *Star Trek* ships. "What you see in the arts eventually ends up in society. There was a 'reality' to those shows, and the kids who grew up with them thought, 'Hey, let's bring this to pass. We can do this!'"

One of those kids was Jon Rogers, an aerospace engineer who worked on hardware for the Apollo missions and the space shuttle. While visiting the Kennedy Space Center on a winter day in 1999, he paused at the Apollo–Saturn V exhibit to watch a film that described the fledgling days of the space program and credited the TV space operas of the '50s with inspiring kids to pursue aerospace careers. Suddenly, says Rogers, a clip from *Space Patrol* flashed on the screen:

> For the first time in many decades I heard those thrilling words: "*Spaaaaaaace Patrol! High adventure in the wild, vast reaches of space! Missions of daring in the name of interplanetary justice….*" At that moment I knew my old dream was still alive, and I realized

that others had also heard the message. I knew that the show had helped us become NASA engineers and create this first step to the stars.

If you were a space opera kid of the '50s who dreamed of becoming an astronaut, you may wonder why you lost interest in space exploration faster than you can say "Sputnik." Story Musgrave may have the answer: "The space program got stripped of romanticism," he says sadly. The creators of '50s space opera had a stronger and better vision of space flight than the people who *do* space flight. Most astronauts have not expressed the *experience* of space flight — they've only expressed what they *did*. They haven't said what they felt or what it meant to them." And while many ex–Space Patrollers, Solar Guard "cadets" (fans of *Tom Corbett, Space Cadet*) and *Rocky Jones* "rocket rangers" did find their way to NASA, the government bureaucracy that swallowed them seemed to lose touch with the public's desire to seek answers to life's mysteries in the wild, vast reaches of space. The tightly monitored government space program, says Musgrave, has astronauts diligently performing task lists of mission experiments, but rarely gives us news that stirs our spirit of adventure:

> What really excites people is when space exploration becomes a mirror for who we are, for life on Earth. We want to know: What kind of universe have we got? What's our place in it? What does it mean to be a human being? That's what touches people. But that experience is not being communicated. Instead, our experience of space flight is a list of what was done and what happened. [The space operas] caught it better than reality. When you have a reality that doesn't have imagination or exploration, it's dead.

Musgrave, who led the team that repaired the Hubble Space Telescope in 1993, admits that there's nothing he wants more than to see folks inspired once again by the wonder and romanticism of space exploration. If the U.S. government had launched its space program out of curiosity, rather than as a response to Russia's Sputnik satellite, people would be as excited today about space exploration as they were in the 1950s, he maintains. "We went into space for the wrong reason: to compete with the bad guys. That's why we were lost when we came off the moon program and have never had a vision since. It was 'We won the ball game, let's all go home.'" Musgrave sighs. "We never built a long-term vision based on curiosity. That's what the public wants and, unfortunately, they're not getting it."

Though the earliest episodes of *Space Patrol*, which began as a 15-minute daily serial aired locally in Los Angeles, smacked of dull science lessons that would have made NASA proud, the show soon morphed into a fast-paced drama with an action peak every five minutes. No other space opera came close to depicting the suspense and depth of emotion shown on *Space Patrol*— and no other show had such an attractive, sexy cast, featured often in TV and movie fanzines of the day. Commander Buzz Corry, Cadet Happy, Major "Robbie" Robertson, Carol Carlisle and Tonga formed a tight-knit, family-like unit built on caring and mutual respect, each willing to sacrifice his or her life for the others. It was an unbeatable formula: five beautiful people in heroic roles, sadistic villains, imaginative stories heightened by edgy lighting, poignant music, and extreme close-up shots that captured a range of emotions from silliness to sheer terror. Adults looking over their children's shoulders soon made up over 60 percent of the audience. With plots that later showed up on *Star Trek*, *Space Patrol* went where no space opera

The Space Patrol crew blasts off for thrilling adventures in the wild, vast reaches of space. From the left: Lyn Osborn (Cadet Happy), Ken Mayer (Major Robertson), Virginia Hewitt (Carol Carlisle), Ed Kemmer (Commander Buzz Corry) and Nina Bara (Tonga).

had ever gone, long before the starship *Enterprise* got off the launch pad. "*Star Trek* owes a lot to it," says author and SF critic David Gerrold. "*Space Patrol* was one of the first attempts to do serious science fiction on television with continuing characters." Not only that, says Gerrold, but beneath its sci-fi veneer, *Space Patrol* occasionally took a poke at current events. "They went back in time to the Salem witch hunts. When a woman spoke of this spaceship she'd seen, she was going to be tried as a witch—and that was right at the height of the McCarthy era." Gerrold adds that the series had a profound effect on him as a child because it modeled an heroic approach to life that made him believe any obstacle could be conquered:

> *Space Patrol* embodied a courageous way of being, of challenging life, that said: You're not going to be beat, whether you're up against this invisible matrix thing that eats everything or you go to the limbo planet where they replace you when you fall asleep. Whatever it is, you can deal with it. And in my life, when I've had some major thing come up, I've always said, "I will get through this." It's a way of being that got ingrained in me early on.

If you were looking for plenty of action, believable heroes and steadfast camaraderie in the face of death, *Space Patrol* was your show. While fellowship was a key element in other space operas—notably *Tom Corbett, Space Cadet*—nothing came close to the loyalty and trust expressed by Buzz, Hap, Robbie, Carol and Tonga for one another. Chemistry sparked in every scene, as if the characters delighted in each other's presence. Crew members at ABC noticed that the cast seemed to merge with their characters, both on and offscreen. "They made it real — as if it was really happening," says Chuck Lewis, then an audio operator at ABC. "The only shows that had that type of chemistry were *I Love Lucy* and *Ozzie and Harriet*." Of course, given the total number of *Space Patrol* shows, both radio and TV (1,328, by some calculations), few characters have ever been played more thoroughly in the history of broadcasting. So completely did the cast take to their roles that decades later they still called each other by their character names.

But as viewers watched, they had no idea that dramatic as well as galactic peril was taking place on the set. *Space Patrol* was a *live* show. Cameras got tangled in cables and barely made it to the scene, key lights went out, guest actors buckled under the pressure of live TV and forgot their lines, and special effects followed their own evil timetables. Cast and crew members who'd served in the war only a few years earlier were used to this kind of stress and uncertainty; that the show came in on a wing and a prayer was something its millions of viewers never knew. But the sheer energy generated from behind-the-scenes close calls and near misses heightened the drama, adding tension and excitement that glowed off the screen. Day after day, the show's crew met each new challenge by inventing whatever was needed, whether it was a backdrop of stars or a rotating lens that made it look as if people were drifting in space. To the first technical crews, television was a beast they were nudging from one hoop to the next, a genie struggling out of the bottle. Through it all, ABC technical director Bob Trachinger forgot to write anything down. "I'm saddened by the fact that no one I knew kept a journal," he says. "We didn't know we were making history."

LOS ANGELES, CALIFORNIA: MAY 1984

A month after I'd watched the show in David's store, I went to Los Angeles on business. Driving down a dreary street on my way to a meeting, I passed a nostalgia store. Suddenly the voice I'd heard in Guerneville spoke sharply in my ear: "Go inside and ask about *Space Patrol*." I was running late and didn't have time for this nonsense. "Later," I told it. This was ridiculous — and a little scary. But on my way back, I gave in. I worked for a newspaper and that killer instinct to pursue a lead no matter what the source was alive and well. If Someone or Something wanted me to check out that store, so be it. It was a gray afternoon. Inside, the shop seemed even more dismal, steeped in shadowed memories.

"*Space Patrol?*" The wraith of a guy behind the counter, a relic from the '60s, nodded his head. "Funny you should ask about *that* show. The actress who played Tonga was in here two days ago, trying to sell me some memorabilia. Do you want her phone number?"

I called Nina Bara and asked for an interview, saying I'd pitch a story on her to my newspaper. Big white lie. I didn't really think this rural paper in Northern California would give a column inch about Bara's career, but I had to meet her. And I sensed this would be the first of many interviews for a story on the show that I would write someday.

It turned out that this nostalgia store was a long way from where Bara lived. It was also miles from the mecca of memorabilia shops on Hollywood Boulevard, where I would have gone on my own to research *Space Patrol*. That the voice had steered me to this place where Bara had been only two days earlier was exhilarating, yet disturbing. And maybe I needed a reality check, because that sense of an invisible companion by my side was stronger than ever. I even talked to it in my thoughts, like telepathy, as I left the store. "OK," I said, "are you happy?" Happy. There was something familiar about my unseen friend.

Back on the job in Guerneville, I found it hard to concentrate. I was preoccupied by *Space Patrol* and the strange sense of purpose it had awakened. Meanwhile, that pesky Presence — not satisfied that It had reintroduced me to the show and put me in touch with one of the actors — was telegraphing another message: "*Write about the show. Tell the* Space Patrol *story.*" I knew now for certain that this was bigger than the interview with Bara. It meant finding everyone — the whole cast, except for Lyn Osborn, who'd played Cadet Happy and passed away in 1958, three years after the show went off the air. As a child, I'd idolized him. When he died of a brain tumor at the age of 32, I was devastated.

After a few weeks of not much sleep and the feeling — often — that Something was urging me to delve into *Space Patrol*, I quit my day job at the newspaper and went freelance, determined to write my first piece on the show.[10] This was like jumping off a cliff, but at least I wasn't alone. As I set about tracking down cast and crew, I felt my unseen friend at my elbow, gently guiding me to *call this number, not that one*. I'd do it and invariably someone at the other end would say, "Funny you should ask about *Space Patrol*" — and supply the next piece of the puzzle. It was a strange way to work, this partnership with Something I could not see, but, hey, I follow all leads and take any help I can get. Anyway, I was starting to have some ideas about who my invisible companion might be, though it seemed too fantastic to be true.

[10]The story appeared as a two-part series in the first two issues of *Filmfax* magazine (January-February and April, 1986) and was reprinted in issues 9 and 10 (February-March and April-May, 1988). Editor-publisher Michael Stein commissioned a painting of the cast by artist Barbara Fister-Liltz for the cover of the premier issue.

CHAPTER 2

Blast-Off

For many youngsters of the 1950s, Space Patrol had no equal in providing action, adventure, despair, hope and resolution on a weekly basis.

— Jack McKirgan

You played it for real — you had to. Otherwise, it would be condescending and kids wouldn't like that. You never play down to kids— they're generally a little ahead of you.

— Ed Kemmer

Streaking through hyperspace, the *Terra IV*, flagship of the Space Patrol, pursues a vector from the 30th century, backwards in time toward Planet Earth. Target: May Company Department Store, Los Angeles, California. Commander Corry, at the controls, issues an order to Cadet Happy to cut time-drive while Major Robertson checks the astrogation chart. Position: Hovering 3,000 DUs above the city. Timeline: 1951. Carol and Tonga secure all hatches as the Commander lowers the great ship down on repeller ray, docking it on the second floor of the store. Atmosphere check: no spacesuits necessary. The visit to Earth by the Space Patrol crew has been advertised days in advance. In response, on the concrete surface of the planet below, 30,000 fans converge in surface-cars.

The day to avoid that traffic jam in downtown Los Angeles was Tuesday, June 26, 1951. Having blasted off on the ABC network only six months earlier, *Space Patrol* was now clearly headed into stardrive.[1] The magic hinged on the cast: Commander Buzz Corry, Cadet Happy, Carol Carlisle, Major Robertson and Tonga —five totally believable 30th-century personalities whose lives entwined with soap opera strength as they undertook "missions of daring in the name of interplanetary justice" for an organization serving the noblest galactic ideals: the Space Patrol.

The show's creator, director, and leading actor were all real-life World War II pilots, no strangers to panic and danger miles above the Earth. Producer William "Mike" Moser, 35, a cherub-faced movie and radio scriptwriter, told *Time* magazine that he conceived of an interplanetary police force fending off cosmic marauders and keeping the space lanes clear while flying Navy Air Corps missions over the South Pacific. He got to wondering about the universe, and his brain gave birth to the United Planets—a solar confederation devoted to peace but willing to fight when menaced by foes whose morals had not caught up with their technology. Moser only spent three more years on Earth after cre-

[1]The show had debuted locally the previous year on L.A. affiliate KECA.

16

Space Patrol's creator, Mike Moser, 36, pictured in *Life* magazine at the height of the show's success. (Photograph by John Swope, Time Life Pictures/Getty Images)

ating *Space Patrol*. At the height of the show's success, he was hit by a surface-car and killed.

Ten months after its debut on March 9, 1950, as a local show in Los Angeles, *Space Patrol* went network — and captured the dawning space-age fantasies of the nation. A sponsor-conducted survey revealed that adults were hooked along with their kids. In 1952, *Life* magazine reported that a convention of top stellar scientists meeting in California opened with the chairman remarking, "Even though Commander Corry may not agree with me, the moon is...." The article estimated the show's viewership at 7 million.[2]

Space Patrol toys, clothes and gear were everywhere. For a while, says Dick Darley, "It seemed like every flashlight in the world was a *Space Patrol* flashlight." (Photograph © Ed Swift, courtesy Dale Ames)

Paraphernalia deluged department stores: flight suits, boots, space helmets, pup tents. "At one point it seemed," says director Dick Darley, "that every flashlight in the world was a *Space Patrol* flashlight." Once Commander Corry, for reasons best known to himself, removed a two-foot inflatable space bunny named "Cosmo" from some far reach of the galaxy — and that was immediately marketed. Cardboard and plastic cereal box premiums (Cosmic Smoke Guns, Periscopes, Space-o-Phones) were offered weekly by sponsor Ralston Purina, maker of Wheat Chex, Rice Chex, and "good, Hot Ralston," for a boxtop plus "25 cents in coin." In the fall of 1952, *Life* magazine predicted the sale of *Space Patrol* merchandise that year would reach $40 million.[3]

The actors merged deeper and deeper with their characters as they kept pace with the impossible weekly schedule: five 15-minute daily TV segments aired locally in L.A. (then sent to selected affiliates in other cities), the weekly half-hour network show, and two (later cut to one) radio episodes. On weekends the cast toured the country, working telethons, grand openings, promotions and benefits. Ken Mayer, who played Major Robertson, pointed out to Nina Bara (Tonga) that they spent more time in uniform than in civilian clothes. "It was pretty hard to get out of character, we were together so much," recalls Ed Kemmer. "I was Corry even when I wasn't. Not that I ever was a real Buzz Corry who could take on the world; but there were attributes Corry had that I adopted. When you play a running role for a long time, it's not so much that you become that role as that role becomes you."

"I think the characters they developed into weren't there at the beginning — they

[2]*Life* magazine, September 1, 1952.
[3]*Ibid.*

Mike Moser in a script conference with director Dick Darley. (Photograph by David Sutton, courtesy Dick Darley)

found their way as they went," says Dick Darley, who'd made the decision early on to shoot the show from an adult angle. Cast and crew rose to the occasion; no one treated *Space Patrol* as "just" a children's show. "Everybody meant it," says Darley. "If Major Robertson found out that Hap and Buzz had crashed, he would get upset, and I think he really was concerned. It wasn't like, 'Hey, I'm a Hollywood actor and I do better things than this.'"

Character believability weaves back and forth through many memories as the thread holding the show together when guest actors went blank and special effects went berserk. Audio man Chuck Lewis and other ABC crew members recall being swept up at times by an eerie feeling that what was taking place on the set was real. "It was as if it was *really happening*," Lewis marvels, fifty years later. "When the spaceships 'flew,' it was as if they were really up in the air. I'd sit there in the booth and the actors made *me* believe it — and I'm a guy who was grown up, who had been through a war."

Ed Kemmer tries to account for what Lewis and others felt. "We were so familiar with our roles that, to some extent, we became our characters," he says finally. "I made

Ed Kemmer: Commander Buzz Corry.

Virginia Hewitt: Carol Carlisle.

Corry an idealized Ed Kemmer, so the 'emotions' coming through were *my* emotions—more real than if I had 'acted' them. It's hard to explain." But it's not hard for Kemmer to shed light on the show's appeal to all ages. "We were an inner family group fulfilling a need, as soap operas have done for years. If one member didn't get you, the other did." And Kemmer got to most people with his leading-man looks, daring but thoughtful: the perfect hero. Though barely thirty, he melded authority and compassion into a portrait of the quintessential commander-in-chief. Kids related to him as a father or older brother they could trust. No matter how threatening the peril, Commander Corry had a plan. "Or was looking for one or hoping to have one," Kemmer laughs. "Knowing there must be a way out and, by God, we'll find it!" But in the meantime, "playing the fear, playing the unknown — *maybe* something could go wrong ... *maybe* you won't live through it." Still, *Time* magazine pointed out, should a show end with the Commander facing certain death, the camera moved in to reveal a faint smile on the hero's face, a tip-off to young viewers that Corry would prevail. "If we cause a single nightmare," creator Mike Moser told *Time*, "we've failed in our purpose."⁴

Commander Corry's romantic interest was Carol Carlisle (Virginia Hewitt), daughter of the secretary general of the United Planets— but it was unrequited love, forever. Interplanetary pressures being what they were, Buzz barely had time to kiss the cold nose of his spaceship. Carol's dazzling blonde looks radiated right through your black-and-white TV screen, plus she could fly a spaceship and build an atom bomb in less than an hour. Frequently kidnapped, she was resistant yet composed until Buzz could rescue her.

Major Robertson (Ken Mayer) was always there when you needed him. "Without Robbie, we'd have been in big trouble," Kemmer admits. The Major — steady and concerned, like a favorite uncle — gave risk-taking Corry some leeway. If the villains threw a nasty curve, trapping the Commander in a hideout in some remote part of the galaxy, you knew Robbie was on his way. The Major was tough, direct and less controlled than Corry, sometimes recklessly taunting the bad guys — you could feel his anger and frustration building when he did one of his slow burns. As Space Patrol security chief, he sometimes accompanied Buzz and Hap on their missions of daring or undertook a few of his own; otherwise, you'd find him back at headquarters, holding the fort. When Buzz set out on a risky adventure, you knew Robbie's response: "I'll be standing by, Commander."

Ken Mayer: Major Robertson.

Tonga (Nina Bara) was Robbie's assistant, a bizarre state of affairs, since she was a reformed criminal. However, that 30th-century wonder, the Brainograph, which cleansed thoughts as easily as machines used to wash clothes back in the 20th century, had rid her of criminal tendencies — sort of. In a few early shows, she reverted back to her evil ways, like that unpredictable aunt of yours who might be in a snarly mood next time she visited. But Tonga was exotic and it was fun when she was bad (even though you wished she'd be good), and it kept Commander Corry guessing…

And then there was Hap.

Cadet Happy, played by Lyn Osborn, was the indelible character of the show. As Corry's lighthearted sidekick, Hap deflected terror into comedy and asked questions

Nina Bara: Tonga.

that allowed the Commander to deliver informative monologues essential to the show's plot. Osborn's genius was to make kids believe they could be like him. His irrepressible, childlike energy bounced right out at you like a ball you had to catch. Hap was part kid, part adult, caught between two worlds. "You felt," says Jim Buchanan, who at one time sported one of the country's largest collections of *Space Patrol* memorabilia, "that if you got the Membership Kit and joined the Space Patrol, you were one of the cadets — almost like Lyn Osborn — working with the Commander, protecting the universe."

According to most accounts, Osborn was truly, offscreen, like the character he played. "It was just like the part was made for him," says his sister, Beth Flood. Dick Darley

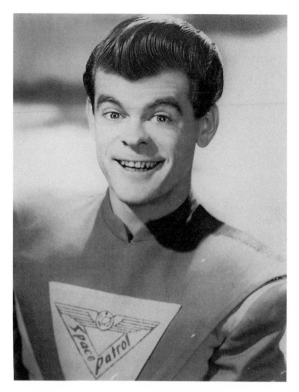

Lyn Osborn: Cadet Happy.

agrees: "Whenever he needed something to feed off of for the character, it was just himself. Other than saying 'Smokin' rockets' and that laugh that developed, he was just playing Lyn. I tried to keep him under control without losing that childlike quality, but he was wild, like a spark in a bottle. He was over the edge, but that was part of his charm."

Ed Kemmer still calls him "Hap."

"He was funny, funny, marvelous!" Kemmer recalls. "But he'd be funny when you wished he wouldn't be — on the show, *on the air.*" Osborn was a nutsy practical joker whose antics pushed cast and crew to the edge of endurance before they dissolved into helpless laughter, and one of his favorite pastimes was putting the Commander on the spot. "The worst thing," Kemmer smiles, "was when Hap would go cold on a line. He'd give his funny little laugh and look at me and say, 'What do *you* say, Commander?' And I had to say *something*. Though I loved him like a brother, I could have gladly broken his neck at that moment — but I got used to it." Kemmer's voice softens. "You could never stay angry at him."

It was the DuMont network that won the TV space race, launching the first space opera, *Captain Video*, in June 1949, with its thrilling intro:

> *Master of space! Hero of science! Captain of the Video Rangers! Operating from his secret mountain headquarters on the planet Earth, Captain Video rallies men of good will and leads them against the forces of evil everywhere!*

From his clandestine hideaway, Captain Video and his teenage sidekick, the Video Ranger, took off in the spaceship *Galaxy* to match wits with "various menaces from outer space and strange situations on distant planets."[5] Set in the late 21st century, Video was a freelance crimefighter, accepting assignments from various planetary governments in the interest of universal peace. You might say the captain had an undercover assignment, too. The show was created so that the DuMont network, operating from its studio hideaway above Wanamaker's Department Store in New York, could unleash schlock westerns on unsuspecting kids.[6] Just when the courageous captain and the Video Ranger were

---

[5]*www.slick-net.com/space/.*

[6]According to *Spaceship Handbook* by Jack Hagerty and Jon C. Rogers (ARA Press, Oct 2001), the DuMont network, owned by Dr. Allen B. DuMont, was the smallest and poorest of the four TV networks. It started in 1946 and folded in 1955. Dr. DuMont also manufactured TV sets as early as 1938.

squaring off against the evil robot Tobor or arch-rival Dr. Pauli, the camera would cut to "Ranger Rogers," who announced it was time to check in on the captain's "agents in California." Suddenly viewers were transported by "remote carrier" to the Wild West and, for the next seven minutes, forced to watch vintage horse operas. It was all a diabolical plot by DuMont's execs to expand programming time by running 1930s westerns that cost them next to nothing and that no one but kids would tolerate. Finally, the producers came to their senses, and in September 1953, the western segment bit the dust.

Al Hodge, as the captain, brought dignity and a true sense of heroism to the role, while Don Hastings was totally believable as the nameless Video Ranger.[7] But the show destroyed Hodge's career. A World War II Navy lieutenant who had starred in the 1940s radio series *The Green Hornet*, he claimed he was so typecast as "Video" that he could no longer make a living as an actor after the show's demise. When he testified at a Senate hearing on juvenile delinquency and TV violence, even the senators addressed him as "Captain."[8]

In October 1950, *Tom Corbett, Space Cadet* burst onto the scene. Set in the year 2350 at Space Academy, U.S.A., a futuristic West Point, it focused on three cadets—straight-arrow unit leader Tom Corbett (Frankie Thomas), earnest Venusian power deck cadet Astro (Al Markim), and snotty radar bridge cadet Roger Manning (Jan Merlin)—officers-in-training for the Solar Guard, an interplanetary peacekeeping force similar to the Space Patrol.[9] Thomas, a ship's navigator trained at the U.S. Merchant Marine Academy, was convincing as Corbett, but the hook was the camaraderie of the cadets (despite Manning's bad attitude, which masked a soft heart and courage) and the challenges they faced as they were put through their paces at school and on training flights. The Space Academy was a little like your high school or junior high—with one big difference, notes Rory Coker: "After you hit the books, the rocket cruiser *Polaris* was waiting just a few feet beyond the classroom for a glorious jaunt through the solar system."

Though the cadets encountered the occasional space pirate or rebel, the *Corbett* universe was short on bad guys. Somehow they'd solved the crime problem that plagued Buzz Corry, Captain Video and other space opera heroes. Thus the main themes of the show, says its star, Frankie Thomas, were man against nature and man against himself ("because it was cheaper," he quips), with the action centering on mishaps and close calls the cadets encountered on training flights. If you liked your sci-fi technically accurate, Corbett was your show. Famed rocket expert Willy Ley served as technical adviser, and nothing escaped his watchful eye. When the show ended, so did Thomas's acting career, but he went on to become a champion bridge player and author of twelve Sherlock Holmes novels. The show's trademark phrase, "Spaceman's luck," used when the *Polaris* crew took off on an adventure, is still a byword for space opera fans today.

While *Space Patrol*, *Captain Video* and *Tom Corbett* were by far the most popular

---

[7]Richard Coogan was the first Captain Video, but he was replaced in 1951 by Al Hodge, who most viewers remember in the role.

[8]*Captain Video* ran live from June 1949 to April 1955. In 1951, Columbia Pictures produced a 15-part movie serial starring Judd Holdren, based on the TV show. But it was Al Hodge who was forever linked to the role. "When he walked into a talent agency, they'd say, 'What can we do for you, Video?'" notes *Captain Video* historian Louis Rugani.

[9]*Tom Corbett* bounced between four networks, at one point running on two simultaneously. It debuted in 1950 on CBS as a 15-minute show, then aired on NBC and ABC. From 1953 to 1954, it ran on DuMont as a 30-minute show, then switched back to NBC from 1954 to 1955. It had a six-month stint as a radio show on the ABC network from January to July 1952.

space shows of the day, a few others slipped in under the radar and drew loyal followings.

Die-hard fans of *Rocky Jones, Space Ranger* will swear on Saturn's rings that this show topped *Corbett* and *Space Patrol*. It starred Richard Crane as Rocky Jones, fighting for law and order in a solar system that may or may not have been our own. That point was never made clear, but if you can't locate Ophiuchus, Fornax and Cryko on your planetary map, it probably wasn't this one. Rocky's entourage included his sidekick Winky, an annoying child named Bobby, doddering scientific adviser Professor Newton, and female pal Vena Ray. Though Jones encountered the usual space rats and mad scientists, his arch-rival was Queen Cleolanthe of Ophiuchus, who wanted to either seduce him or kill him. Crane carried the hero role well, and the show (which survives on video tape) aired on ABC from January 1954 to December 1955.[10]

Meanwhile, back in *our* solar system, former sailor Cliff Robertson starred in *Rod Brown of the Rocket Rangers*, a live weekly show that ran from April 1953 to May 1954. Operating out of a Ranger Port on Earth, Brown and his sidekicks took flight in spaceships that "surged with the power of the atom and gleamed like great silver bullets" as they sought to protect the planet against globe-shaped aliens, shadow creatures and Neptunian stickmen. The series was CBS's attempt to compete with *Space Patrol* and *Tom Corbett*, but despite special effects culled from *Corbett* and imaginative foes reminiscent of *Space Patrol*, it failed to steal fans from those shows and crash-landed after only a year. Guest actors Don Knotts, Jonathan Winters, and stage manager John Frankenheimer, however, went on to big-time careers.

That can't be said of Commando Cody, a low-budget cross between the Lone Ranger and Superman, whose TV career spanned less than three months. Unfortunately, this character is sometimes confused with Commander Corry of the Space Patrol, so let's set the record straight: Cody's roots go back to the 1949 Republic serial *King of the Rocket Men*, whose hero invents an atomic-powered flying suit to battle Dr. Vulcan, a mad scientist who wants to rule the world. Though the Cody character was not in that film, it laid the foundation for the commando, who appeared three years later as a similar jet-propelled hero in *Radar Men from the Moon*. Later that year, using the same production crew, the studio spun the concept into a tacky TV series, *Commando Cody, Sky Marshall of the Universe*, which ran on NBC from July to October 1955. In this show, unlike other space operas, the bad guys sometimes got killed.[11] Fortunately, the carnage ended with the twelfth and last episode where Cody captures his archenemy, the Ruler, who warns, "It isn't over yet. My subjects will tear your world apart to rescue me." So far, they haven't.

Trailing behind in the rocket blast of these six shows were TV remakes of *Buck Rogers* and *Flash Gordon*, two groundbreaking movie serials of the '30s that paved the way for space opera but failed to kick up much meteor dust on the small screen.

One day former World War I pilot Anthony "Buck" Rogers was surveying an abandoned mine when the roof caved in. Knocked unconscious, he stayed that way while radioactive gas preserved him in a state of suspended animation (but didn't kill him). When some fresh air leaked in 500 years later, he awakened in the year 2430.[12] Making the best of a bad situation, he turned the cave into a secret headquarters and science lab

---

[10]*Rocky Jones* was distributed by United Television on 16mm film. There were 39 episodes.

[11]Villains occasionally got offed on *Tom Corbett* too, but since there weren't very many of them, and some died off-screen when they ran into space torpedoes or runaway reactors, no one took much notice.

[12]By the 25th century, scientists had discovered that fresh air is the antidote to radiation.

from which to battle galactic marauders. Rogers first appeared in the August 1928 issue of *Amazing Stories*, picked up the nickname "Buck" in his 1929 comic strip debut, then shot to fame in a 1930s radio series. In April 1950, ABC, eyeing the success of *Captain Video* on the DuMont network, created a live half-hour Tuesday night series, *Buck Rogers in the 25th Century*, starring Kem Dibbs and later Robert Pastene. The network pulled the plug at the end of January 1951, no doubt realizing that *Space Patrol*, which had debuted four weeks earlier, was destined to be its mega-hit space show. But Buck refused to die. In 1979, he returned to NBC-TV in yet another incarnation as a NASA space shuttle pilot. Instead of the cave mishap, his life support systems froze during a mission in deep space; he passed out and awoke in the year 2491. Gil Gerard played Buck and famed voiceover artist Mel Blanc dubbed the part of his wisecracking robot companion, Twiki. The show lasted two seasons.

Like Buck Rogers, Flash Gordon did not soar to stellar heights in his small screen debut. Flash had a long history of fighting intergalactic hoodlums. He first appeared in Alex Raymond's 1934 comic strip as a world-famous polo player forced to parachute from a plane struck by a meteor. When he lands, he meets Dr. Hans Zarkov, who's having problems with the evil planet Mongo, and decides to help him out. In 1936, Universal Pictures brought Flash to the big screen in a serial starring Buster Crabbe, but when the DuMont network aired the first two episodes on TV in 1951, all did not go well. *New York Times* critic Jack Gould felt the films were too violent and called them "an utterly deplorable and irresponsible abuse of television's welcome into the home." DuMont panicked and cancelled the show.[13]

Flash surfaced again in 1954 when space hunk Steve Holland starred in a bargain-basement, syndicated TV series filmed in Germany in which Flash, Zarkov and Dale Arden (whose skirt is even shorter than Carol's or Tonga's in *Space Patrol*) battle bad guys, bad scripts and bad actors. It bombed, but Flash reappeared in an animated series, *The New Adventures of Flash Gordon* (1979–1983), on NBC and returned once more in a hip but short-lived encore (26 episodes) in 1996. Considering that Flash was born as a Sunday comic strip in the 1930s, he may hold the record for longevity among sci-fi characters.

But while these space heroes tried desperately to keep peace and order in the universe, their producers weren't doing the same on Earth. In 1950, *Space Patrol*'s creator, Mike Moser, threatened to sue CBS over *Tom Corbett, Space Cadet*, which, he insisted, was clearly a rip-off of his show. And in 1953, lawyers for *Corbett* sued the creators of *Rod Brown*, citing similarities between characters, space slang and plot.[14] Eventually, everyone cooled their jets.

Depending on who you talk to, Mike Moser — a short, stocky man with a pleasant, open face and curly hair — was either a savvy entrepreneur with a creative streak or a hard-drinking wheeler-dealer who cared only about the bottom line. No one seems to know much about William J. Moser. Even Moser knew little about himself, or at least his heritage. An orphan adopted by a Catholic family, he found out shortly before his death that his birth parents had been Jewish. Moser didn't talk about his personal life,

---

[13]The Universal films were aired a few months later by another New York station, says Rory Coker, "and there was no comment at all."

[14]*Variety*, June 3, 1953.

and few people knew him well. Born in Spokane in 1916, he picked up the nickname "Mike" in Gonzaga, Washington, where he was raised. Armed with a degree in literature and philosophy from Gonzaga University, he set out for Hollywood at age 20 to fulfill a long-held dream of becoming a screenwriter. He found work writing radio and film scripts until 1941, when he joined the Navy as a flier. During World War II, he served with a fleet electronics unit and later took charge of weather training for three hurricane-hunter squadrons based in San Diego. After the war, he returned to Hollywood, where he tried his hand at producing. One of his efforts was *Mr. Do-Good's Castle*, a local children's show for which he invented a carefree character named Happy. "I may be the only person alive who remembers seeing Cadet Happy before *Space Patrol*," says author-publisher Gary North. "An old man went into a youth-machine box — and stepped out as Lyn Osborn! I couldn't forget that face."[15] Though Moser seemed to like creating children's TV shows, he and his wife, Helen, had no children of their own.

Moser launched *Space Patrol* when he was 34 years old, convincing Los Angeles ABC affiliate KECA to run it as a 15-minute daily show at 6:15 P.M.[16] His genius lay more in promoting than writing, but the show was his baby and he penned the scripts for several months before handing the job to Norman Jolley, an actor with writing experience who'd been cast as the villainous "Agent X." Though no Boy Scout morally, Moser was a dreamer, with strong beliefs about the show's setting and values and how the characters should be portrayed. He even helped design the first costumes. When *Tele-Views* magazine compared the ambience of *Space Patrol*'s United Planets to utopias such as James Hilton's Shangri-La, Moser agreed that he'd created a near-perfect society where most problems had been resolved.[17] Of course, power-mad villains constantly threatened his solar alliance, but when captured, they were rehabilitated, not punished. In the society of the future, he told *Tele-Views*, "science will be sufficiently advanced so that it can conquer mental quirks of the individual and correct them."[18]

Moser set his planetary paradise in the 30th century, but if you're currently an Earthling experiencing a 21st-century timeline, you can pinpoint exactly when *Space Patrol* takes place — thanks to a remark Buzz Corry makes when two desperate criminals hijack the top secret stardrive ship he and Hap are testing. During a fistfight, the bad guys smash the control panel, damaging the time-drive mechanism. The ship is stranded in hyperspace — until suddenly the radio picks up a news flash from Earth announcing that planet's first manned moon launch. The "date" is given: October 1972. "That's 1009 years ago," Buzz says, using this info as a time marker to calculate their present position.[19] Do the math (1972 + 1009), and the year is 2981. (Re: Earth's "moon launch": Radio writer Lou Huston was only three years off; Apollo 11 was launched on July 16, 1969. But in October 1954, when Huston penned the episode, Earthlings had no idea that in less than a decade, president John F. Kennedy would inspire a massive effort to reach the moon.)

---

[15]Dick Darley's schedule shows *Mr. Do-Good* running from 6:00 to 6:15 P.M. on KECA in March 1950. And at least one other ex-kid, besides North, remembers the show. In Nina Bara's self-published book, *Space Patrol* (1976), Irene Gizzi recalls the character "Happy" debuting on *Mr. Do-Good*, though she remembers the show airing on local station KHJ. Norm Jolley thinks the show first aired on the Don Lee station, KTSL.

[16]The time of the local show varied during its three-year run. It switched to 6:45 P.M. the following week (March 13, 1950), later moved to a 6:00 time slot, then returned to 6:45.

[17]"Space Patrol" by Gwen Hope, *Tele-Views*, November 1950.

[18]*Ibid.*

[19]"Voice from the Future," radio show, October 2, 1954.

It was Moser who handpicked the cast. When he saw someone who looked or talked like a character he'd conceived, he sprang into action. He spotted Jack Narz announcing on *Queen for a Day* and phoned to say that auditions for *Space Patrol*'s announcer would be held the following week, but never mind, Narz had the job. And Nina Bara recalls the afternoon she was relaxing at Nickodell's, a Hollywood hangout for starving actors, when a voice in the dark yelled, "That's Tonga!" Moser had seen her at the bar, and he *knew*. Riding a wave of success eight months after the show's debut, he was bursting with pride and affection for the cast he'd assembled, telling a reporter from *Tele-Views*:

> I just can't give the players enough credit for the way they're pitching. They constitute an excellent team, are deeply interested in their work, and just about live their parts. They usually don't get their scripts until a few hours before broadcast time, but there's never a complaint.[20]

Moser told *Tele-Views* that he had only two rules on the set: "Never be late for a rehearsal" and "Don't use bad grammar." Failure to comply was punished with a fine. In fact, the producer left cast and crew pretty much alone, and while he *usually* didn't interfere creatively, he knew the characters and setting better than anyone else and was quick to quash anything that didn't follow the formula. Dick Tufeld, who'd been hired to announce the radio shows, can vouch for that. Hoping to pick up an extra 75 bucks, he got permission to write a radio script, but when he turned it in, Moser spotted a fatal flaw.[21] "I had the Earth dragged out of its orbit by a pirate sun — it was going to crash into our own sun and burn up instantly," Tufeld recalls. The script called for a guy "at a place like Cal Tech" to invent the Cycloplex, a magnetic device that would push the hostile sun away from Earth in the nick of time. "I can't put this on the air," Moser told him. "Buzz Corry didn't save the day." Tufeld solved the problem by having Corry invent the Cycloplex.

Veteran radio writer Lou Huston (*Suspense, The Whistler*), who came on board in 1951, had a run-in with Moser over an issue that seemed to trouble the producer for personal reasons. Huston's mistake was writing a script that implied that evolution had taken place somewhere else in the solar system, producing creatures different from the kind found on Earth:

> I wrote about a planet that had its own native, prehistoric animals on it, and Mike called up and said in a very angry, authoritative tone, "*There are no animals in the solar system that never existed on earth.*" He was so didactic that I thought, "Well, gee, maybe he's religious and doesn't believe in evolution." Or maybe he thought somebody at the ad agency or the network would jump on him for offending Creationists.

Huston backed down and suggested that maybe the critters could be giant turtles like those found on Earth's Galapagos Islands. Would that be OK? Fine, said Moser, and gave him the go-ahead. "In the script," says Huston, "I was careful to avoid any reference to *how* the animals came into being."

It was no secret that Moser had a drinking problem and that his moods were unpredictable. At his worst, he made crude remarks to women employees at ABC; other times, he was pleasant, peeking in on *Space Patrol* rehearsals, but usually staying out of the

---

[20]*Tele-Views*, November 1950.
[21]Tufeld was hired in 1951.

way—though outspoken lighting director Truck Krone clashed with him several times. "He was a bastard, a little sonofabitch screaming—" Krone bites his tongue. "Oops, I shouldn't have said that." Moser, says Krone, often got uptight about production time:

> Time is money and he'd love it if you could do it in one-tenth the time. But the only way to do that is with flat lighting: everything bright, high noon in the marketplace. Well, I could do that all day long—you know, when they go to bed and say good night, it's *still* high noon in the marketplace. Moser just cared about the bottom line, but that's what producers are; they're money men. It's OK with *them* if it's bright all the time—it costs less money.[22]

Was Moser tight with money? "Like all producers," Ed Kemmer says carefully, "he had to watch the bottom line, so he never paid us what we thought we should be paid." Writer Norm Jolley is more to the point: "Moser had good business sense and didn't want to give away everything to the actors."

Jack Narz remembers Mike visiting the set, poking here and there, ever curious, but not saying much:

> I can see him flitting around, checking out the rocketship, seeing what's in there. He never made comments about the acting—he left all that up to Dick [Darley]. It was his baby, but everybody else was babysitting it. He was on the periphery. A lot of people might have said, "Who the heck is that guy? What does he have to do with this show?"

Ed Kemmer was one of the few who got on well with the producer. "He was 'hail fellow well met,'" he recalls, "always cheerful and full of energy. He never sat down." Kemmer seems to have encountered Moser's personable side more often than most people:

> He'd stop by and say "Hi, any problems?" and we'd say "No, everything's fine." If there was a problem, we'd discuss it, but I don't remember him ever saying anything about my work except "Good." It was not where you got buddy-buddy, like you were with him every day. So you didn't really end up knowing a helluva lot about him.

No one knew Mike well—not even Jack Narz, who invited him to regular poker games at his house. "He was a shadowy figure, an enigma—a strange little guy with great ideas," Narz recalls. "A lot of people didn't like him, but with me he was easygoing, like 'Anything you want is fine.'" Mike got on well with Jack's poker buddies, too. "He wasn't pretentious. He never came on like 'I'm a big TV producer.'"

The main complaint against Moser was that as *Space Patrol* morphed from a 15-minute kiddie show seen locally in Southern California into a national mega-hit, he cut an enormous slice of the pie for himself, leaving others hungry. Lyn Osborn, who had strong likes and dislikes and let you know exactly what they were, did not take to Moser. "I remember Happy didn't like him at all," Ed Kemmer recalls. "Maybe he suspected Mike was making a lot more than he claimed." In fact, says Norm Jolley, the producer was making $5,000 a week from the show—a hefty sum in the early 1950s and a secret he kept from the cast and crew. But as the show became wildly successful, the actors suspected they weren't getting their due. "At one point," says Jolley, "everyone was mad and

---

[22]According to then–ABC technical director, Bob Trachinger, Moser may have had reason to hassle Krone, who was a talented lighting director but known for straining the budget with too many back-up lights.

Cast members celebrate Mike Moser's birthday, circa 1950. From the left: Lyn Osborn, unidentified actor, Nina Bara, Moser, Virginia Hewitt, Bela Kovacs, Ed Kemmer. (Photograph by David Sutton, courtesy Dick Darley)

organized against him." The irascible Bela Kovacs, who played wily Prince Baccarratti, "took everybody out and had his agent represent the cast — it was like a union," Jolley recalls. After a brief battle, Moser upped everyone's wages and things settled back to normal.

A sore point, says Kemmer, was the dividend Moser promised him and Osborn from the sale of spin-off retail toys and the premiums touted on the show that kids got for a cereal boxtop and a quarter:

> Moser didn't share much of that. We had a percentage of the marketing, but hardly
> earned a penny from it. Of course it's all written in the contract, but it's like in movies—
> the first thing the stars learn is to never accept a piece of the *net* profits, because there
> aren't any — ever. The stars learn fast to demand a piece of the gross. I think Hap felt that
> Moser made a killing. And maybe he did.

It's true that Moser was never short of space credits at chow time — that's when those thousands of quarters sent in by the kids came in handy. Radio historian Frank Bresee, a former child actor who played "Little Beaver" on the *Red Ryder* radio show, had a friend who once met Moser for dinner.[23] Before they entered the restaurant, says Bresee, the producer strolled around to the back of his car:

[23]Bresee was one of five actors who played Ryder's young sidekick between 1942 and 1951.

Mike said, "Just a minute," and opened the trunk—and he had all these bags of quarters in there. He took out a lot of them, enough to pay for the meals, and my friend said, "Where did that money come from?" Well, apparently they were having a contest—you know, you send in a quarter and a boxtop and you get something—and Moser had all that money in the trunk of his car. Bags of quarters. He must have just picked them up that day.[24]

Others besides Kemmer and Osborn were promised 5 percent of the lucrative retail and premium sales, but when Moser's affairs were examined after his death, says a colleague who never got paid, "we found out he'd given away enough '5 percents' to equal 150 percent."

Whether prudent or greedy, Moser was undeniably talented and genuinely concerned about the quality of the show. He wrote the first scripts, in which he defined the main characters, giving them blueprints for their personalities; and he penned "Treachery on Mars," the first half-hour show to air when *Space Patrol* was picked up by the ABC television network. Jolley fleshed out the characters when he took over the writing in the summer of 1950, but he notes that Mike, though fully immersed in the business end of things, never lost touch with his creation. "He had a good sense of the characters; he was not without talent."

For all his flaws, some part of Mike Moser was still an idealist—the philosophy major who'd created the peace-loving United Planets where greed and hunger for power were aberrations, even though in his own life he had not won those battles. *Space Patrol*'s characters were his children—he'd assembled the players, nurtured the show in its struggling days—and though he cared about content and production, most of the time he had the good sense to leave cast and crew alone, allowing the magic to happen.

Like him or not, Moser's death, when he was struck by a car in 1953 at the height of *Space Patrol*'s success, left a hole that was never filled. He'd had the smarts and chutzpah to steer the show through corporate waters, but when he died, no strong personality with vision stepped forward to take his place. *Space Patrol* had soared to stellar heights, but now Mike's driving force was gone and the show was running on sheer momentum. He'd nurtured and promoted his baby, but just as his own birth parents had abandoned him, Moser left his brainchild too soon. "He deserves credit for the show—period," sums up Ed Kemmer. "To start a show on a shoestring isn't easy, and he did it; it wouldn't have been on without him. If Mike was still alive, *Space Patrol* would be on the air today."

---

[24]How did Moser get all those quarters when the commercials told kids to mail their "25 cents in coin" to an address in St. Louis where cereal sponsor Ralston Purina's ad agency was based? Moser's loot probably came from the popular Lunar Fleet Base premium, offered in May 1952, in which quarters and boxtops were sent to a local address: Box 962, Hollywood, CA. "With over 200,000 orders filled, Moser could have had $50,000 in his trunk," points out film historian Stephen Handzo.

CHAPTER 3

Up Ship and Away! Launching the Show in Los Angeles

So I open the door and Muggs [Lyn Osborn] sneaks up behind and zaps me with a rubber mallet. Then he decides I'm being too dramatic with my fall, so he gives me a shove to make it quicker. Well… I miss my mark and hit my head on a stage brace—cut it open and blood is coming out. It's running down my head, but there isn't anything I can do because I'm in this quick transition to the next scene where I enter the big mucky-muck's office…. He looks at the blood coming down my head and blows his line. That really messed up the scene.

— Charles Barkus (Villain "R-6")

In live TV, the technical parts of the staging had to come first because nobody would get to see the interpretation if the image wasn't there.

— Dick Darley

As the Space Patrol archives remind us, it was not all smooth sailing from the 20th to the 30th century. Who can forget the Great Solar System War? As attempts to form a Solar Federation failed, centuries of bitterness came to a head and "the planets were unable to agree upon a form of government and its location. Jurisdictional arguments spread as small interplanetary wars broke out."[1] These wars soon escalated into the Great War. How long the fighting lasted is unclear, since many records were destroyed. But if you've studied your Space Patrol Handbook — the one that came with the Membership Kit when you sent in a Ralston cereal boxtop and 25 cents in coin — you know that when the war ended, reps from all the planets met on Earth and formed the United Planets of the Universe, patterned after that ancient democracy, the United States of America.[2] Though "orbital pride" among the delegates sparked heated debates as to where the capital city should be located, they finally agreed to construct an artificial planet halfway between the orbits of Earth and Mars. The planet was named "Terra" (the Latin word for Earth), and a capsule containing soil from each planet in the Federation was placed at its core.

At last, the solar system was at peace, but there was still widespread devastation from the war. Spaceships and space platforms had been destroyed; debris lay dangerously scattered in the space lanes. And there were other problems: Outlaws and space pirates

---

[1]From Mike Moser's fact sheets, his blueprint for the show.

[2]The official Membership Kit contained a membership card, chart of the universe, plastic insignia badge, Space Patrol Handbook, photo of the cast and letter of welcome from Buzz Corry. (A second version included the red and blue plastic Cosmic Glow Rocket Ring.) About 700,000 kits were produced — by far the most widely distributed premium, according to collectibles sleuth Steve Handzo. If you have the handbook, which was based on Moser's fact sheets, note that it does not mention the Great Solar System War. Did Moser or some other adult think it might scare kids to learn of this cataclysmic event?

a

b

c

Key components of the Space Patrol Membership Kit — a must-have for any Space Patroller: (a) Membership Card, (b) Insignia Badge, (c) Handbook, and (d) Chart of the Universe. (Courtesy Jim Scancarelli)

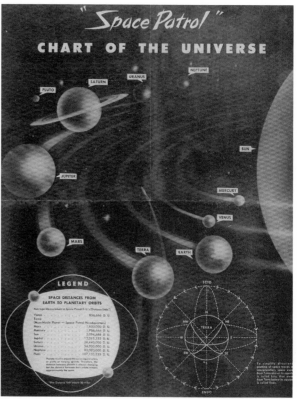

d

staked out remote regions of less-populated planets, setting up hideouts from which they preyed upon innocent travelers. An interplanetary police force was desperately needed; thus the Space Patrol — headquartered on the manmade planet Terra — was formed. Its duties were

To maintain peace.
To defend the rights of free men.

To defend the United Planets against all enemies.
To keep the space lanes clear.
To protect all travelers against the elements.
To aid and assist all space travelers in emergency.
To police the traffic of the space lanes against violations.
To maintain security throughout the United Planets.[3]

Contrary to everything you may know about 30th-century history, Buzz Corry was not the first commander-in-chief of the Space Patrol. His older brother Kit held that honor, but unfortunately his war wounds soon forced him to step down. It was at this time that the younger Corry, who was also an officer in the Space Patrol, distinguished himself in a daring mission that caught the attention of Edward Carlisle, Secretary General of the United Planets.

Captain Buzz Corry, known as much for his invention of Endurium (an indestructible metal used in spaceship hulls) as for leading the first expedition to Pluto, was irked in those days because the revolutionary "super-power space drive" was not yet standard equipment on Space Patrol battlecruisers. This meant that patrol ships could escort transport and passenger carriers only as far as planetary perimeters; then the civilian ships were on their own, fair game for increasing hordes of vicious space pirates. As solar historians will tell you,

> The Space Patrol was not always a powerful instrument of justice. Once its ships clung close to the planets, powerless to combat the bold marauders who terrorized the void. Then, in a universe filled with fear and chaos, there appeared a leader: Buzz Corry, a man whose vision and courage extended to the stars.[4]

One day Corry has a student observer from Earth's Space Academy aboard his ship: Cadet Happy, winner of the coveted Corry Scholarship. Suddenly the space-o-phone crackles and the voice of the Secretary General, head of the United Planets, asks the captain to pick up the escort of a transport ship carrying top secret blueprints for the new super-power space drive. But Prince Baccarratti, evil tyrant of the planet Neptune, is lurking in the space lanes. Before Corry can reach the ship, the Prince uses his null-ray to neutralize its power, weapons and space-o-phone, forces his way onboard and seizes the plans from the helpless crew. When Corry arrives, the damage is done. "C'mon, Hap," he vows, "I'll catch Baccarratti if I have to chase him all the way to Arcturus!"[5]

Catching up with the power-mad Prince, Corry and the cadet magnetize their hull to the tyrant's ship, cut their way in with an atomo-torch and recover the top-secret plans, nearly losing their lives in the process. A few days later, back on the man-made planet Terra, captain and cadet stand in awe before the Secretary General himself:

SECRETARY GENERAL: I wanted to tell you, Corry, that, thanks to you, ships with the new super-power space drive are already in production. That means that all the planets can extend their perimeters considerably. That solves many of our problems, but it creates others. One

---

[3]Space Patrol Handbook.
[4]Decca 78rpm record, *Buzz Corry Becomes Commander-in-Chief*, written by Lou Huston and released in November 1954. It was the first of two "prequels" produced after Mike Moser's death by his widow, Helen, and Lew Spence. The second was *Cadet Happy Joins Commander Corry*. Special music was composed for the records by Sonny Burke, but only a few bars are heard at the beginning as a chorus sings "Space Patrol!" The lead voice is Ed Kemmer's.
[5]*Ibid.*

is to find a man who can organize the individual planet defenses into one operation. I've solved that problem. The other problems, Corry, are up to you.
CAPTAIN CORRY: *To me, sir?*
SECRETARY GENERAL: *Yes. You are now commander-in-chief of the Space Patrol! Well, Corry, haven't you anything to say?*
CORRY: *Well, I... I...*
HAP: (excited) *Congratulations, Captain, I mean Commander, I mean... Oh, smokin' rockets![6]*

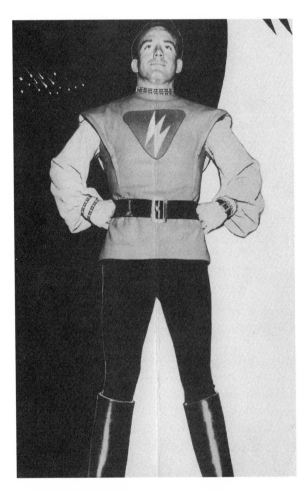

Glen Denning strikes a heroic pose for a brochure put together by the KECA sales staff to help sell the show. (Photograph courtesy Franklin Mullen)

Space Patrol debuted in Los Angeles at 6:15 P.M. on Thursday, March 9, 1950 — a good day to launch a space opera, since newspapers were reporting a strange "flying disc" in the skies over Mexico, causing *Los Angeles Examiner* columnist Pat Hogan to accuse Mike Moser of planting the disc as a publicity stunt.[7] Glen Denning starred as Commander Kit Corry. But the 15-minute "strip show" (as TV serials were called) that aired locally, Monday through Friday, over ABC affiliate KECA was a far cry from the half-hour action-packed saga starring Ed Kemmer as Buzz Corry that captivated the nation a year later.[8]

The show's premier episode was one big, fat science lesson. The minutes dragged by as you watched Kit Corry teach his cadet, Happy, played by Lyn Osborn, "what storms are really made of," that is, how rain freezes and turns to ice. In a primitive attempt at special effects, viewers "see" inside a storm cloud through Hap's "electroscope," a device that magnifies ions and even attaches little plus or minus signs to them to indicate if they're positively or negatively charged. Things get more exciting when the Commander shows Happy how to fly the ship and kids can identify with being a young cadet in the Space Patrol. But when Kit Corry starts talking about the components of Earth's atmosphere — troposphere, tropopause and stratos-

---

[6]*Ibid.*
    [7]Lyn Osborn wrote his parents on March 29, 1950, about Hogan's accusation. The columnist later became a huge fan of the show.
    [8]By the following Monday, according to Dick Darley's schedule, the show had moved to 6:45. It changed time slots several times, airing at 6:00, 6:15 and 6:45 during its three-year stint on KECA.

phere — it's one big yawn. The most dramatic thing that happens is when the pair looks through the "viewscope" and spots some strange explosions on Mars. Concerned, Kit radios Space Patrol headquarters. Not to worry, he's told — the atom power supply unit broke loose from its moorings, but it's "under control." No action here. As the episode ends, Corry takes a few potshots at those pesky guided missiles from Earth's last war that still clutter the space lanes. Cut to a shot of the targets exploding — against faint lettering on the packing-box cardboard used as a backdrop to depict "deep space." Occasionally, Hap's arm and shoulder protrude through the cockpit window. Welcome to live TV.

Glen Denning, whose agent probably thought his real name — Franklin Felch Mullen — lacked star quality, broke into radio at age 16 as a staff announcer at a Phoenix radio station, appeared in several movies, including *Command Decision, Fighter Squadron* and *Beyond Glory*, and guested often on *Lux Radio Theatre*. On *Space Patrol*, he was a competent but unimaginative actor who let it be known to cast and crew that he was just marking time on this kiddie show on his way to greater things. Norm Jolley, who played the villainous Agent X-9 (later shortened to X), had crossed paths with Denning a few years earlier when both were Marines stationed in San Diego. Jolley was producing radio and stage shows for the Corps and hired Denning as an actor on *The Halls of Montezuma*, heard over the Mutual Radio Network. "I used him *once*," he says pointedly. "He was cantankerous, had an inflated opinion of himself."

Franklin Mullen, AKA Glen Denning, who starred as Commander Kit Corry when *Space Patrol* debuted in Los Angeles, does a short-wave newscast in 1946 for the Armed Forces Radio Service while serving as a Marine. (Photograph by Crile Studios, courtesy Franklin Mullen)

Denning played Corry as a straight-arrow military kind of guy with a let's-get-the-job-done approach to life, which included training his cadet. While he radiated mild enthusiasm and came across as a decent mentor, he lacked the emotional range Ed Kemmer later brought to the role. Denning's attitude alienated the other players. There was little chemistry between him and Osborn, and, says Jolley, "there was *no* chemistry between him and *me*. When I played Agent X, I was standing this close to him, watching the guy work — and I didn't like him." In fairness to Denning, let it be said that he was no better than Moser's first scripts, which were dully educational. However, as Moser wrote more action into the series and the show became more saga than science lesson, Denning seemed dramatically challenged. In one episode, he decides to grin at everything: He intercepts a space-o-phone call in which the bad guys (Agent X and Major Sova) congratulate themselves on infiltrating the ground crew of his (Corry's) own unit. Grin. He learns that those explosions on Mars seen through the viewscope spell trouble — there *is* sabotage afoot in the atomic power plant. Grin. It's hard to say whether this detachment came from his disdain for the show or was just plain bad acting, but it doesn't take long to see why Jolley and others found him annoying.

Fifty-three years later, Franklin Mullen (no longer called Denning) is watching a tape of himself as Kit Corry. The stupid grin, he explains, was an attempt to compensate for scripts that bored him silly. At 76, Mullen, a silver fox with hair cropped close in a military cut, steady blue eyes, lithe build and quick smile, cops to being "an angry young man" during the 1950s who probably ticked some people off. Once full of hope that *Space Patrol* would be educational, he quickly lost interest when it swung toward action-adventure, no longer the lofty show that he and Mike Moser had hammered out in "conceptual conversations" over drinks at Nickodell's. "A bunch of us sat around with Mike, and his idea for *Space Patrol* started to gel," he recalls. Mullen adds that it was difficult to have a two-way exchange with the producer, who was usually three sheets to the wind. "Most of the time, it was like talking through mush." He knew that Moser, when sober, had an idealistic streak, but a few weeks into the show, he felt that Mike had sold out. "He had only one purpose: Get it sold to a sponsor —fast. The story content was becoming flat, the dialogue was contrived and mechanical. But the cast accepted it — they read whatever they were given. It was an embarrassment to be on the show — I couldn't hide it." Mullen was a true idealist. To him and a small group of actor friends, TV held great promise. "We were so excited and anxious to get going and do the kind of shows that would inform and inspire people. We thought, 'Can we change them, move them along, help them to grow and become more aware and responsible?'" He did not see that kind of potential in *Space Patrol*.

Sit through a few of the early 15-minute episodes and you see Mullen's point. Perhaps the only thing worse than watching them was being in them. In a few months, Norm Jolley would take over the writing from Moser, punch up the plots and develop the characters, but Mullen, 23 years old in the spring of 1950, had no patience to spare. He saw commercialism glomming onto television, swallowing "clear thinking, good ideas and human values" faster than a black hole. When he left *Space Patrol* after only six weeks (which he insists was by "mutual agreement" with Moser), he never watched an episode; not one. Disillusioned by Hollywood, he reenlisted in the Marine Corps and served in Korea. For a second, a flash of sadness clouds his clear eyes. "I left Hollywood in disgust, bored silly, feeling betrayed by my culture. I probably cared more about *Space Patrol* than anybody, including Mike Moser. Mike was one of my biggest disappointments."

Mike Moser, a Navy pilot, got the idea for the show and its hero from two sources: pulp fiction and a naval base. Between 1940 and 1944, a series of short stories about Captain John Bullard of the Space Patrol appeared in the popular SF pulp magazine *Astounding Science Fiction* (*ASF*). Bullard was born — guess where: On the planet *Terra* in the year 3915. Penned by prolific SF writer Malcolm Jameson, a retired naval officer, the six stories track Bullard's adventures aboard the spaceship *Pollux* as he rises through the ranks to lieutenant, commander and finally acting admiral of the Great Lunar Base. Starting out as "a clever man, not physically outstanding in any way, who passed almost unnoticed from the Patrol Academy into the Service," Bullard "fought in grim [planetary] wars and put down rebellious criminals." Though he lacked the panache of *Space Patrol*'s Commander Buzz Corry, he was steady, with a good officer's instinct for handling people, making the right decisions, and cutting through "the red tape of Terra's bureaucracy." His courage, combined with common sense, won him "a fame unequaled among the mariners of deep space."[9]

Now Moser had the setting, but he needed a name for his hero. "He got it from Corry Field, where he was stationed in Texas during the War," says Franklin Mullen. Corry Field (now Corry Station), a Naval Technical Training Center, was named for Lieutenant Commander William M. Corry, Jr., a World War I hero and aviation pioneer. Corry, one of the first pilots to receive the Navy's Wings of Gold insignia, graduated from the Naval Academy in 1910 and commanded the Air Station at Le Croisic, France. In 1920, he survived a plane crash but rushed back into the flaming wreckage to rescue the pilot. He died of his burns and was awarded the Congressional Medal of Honor.

Unaware that Moser had borrowed the name from Corry Field, ABC staffers Margaret Montreys and Don McCroskey were convinced that the producer had named his hero and other key characters after certain crew members and office workers on the ABC lot at Prospect and Talmadge, where L.A. affiliate KECA was based. After all, you had video operator Ed *Corey*, assistant director Larry *Robertson*, operations manager *Carol* Howard, and technical director Al *Hayward*. ("Captain Hayward," played by actor-writer Maurice Hill, appeared in a number of shows.) "Three out of four people in the control room had last names identical to the character names," points out McCroskey. "What are the chances of that?"[10] With the exception of Corry, it's likely that Moser did, in fact, draw his character names from staffers. After all, says a colleague who disliked the producer, Mike helped himself to a lot of things at KECA. "He was always down in the front office, rifling through people's desks for information that could give him an edge in closing a deal."

Though Moser clearly liked to educate, he liked money better, and it was dawning on him that *Space Patrol* could be a slide-to-the-edge-of-your-seat experience, a cops-and-robbers saga set in space. Overnight, his scripts veered toward action and adventure with maybe 25 percent science thrown in, and by the second week of the show, Kit Corry was facing some nasty heavies whose greedy hearts were set on ruling the universe. You had Agent X and Major Sova, members of a vicious gang led by femme fatale Tonga (AKA "Lady of Diamonds"), who had infiltrated the Secretary General's office and become his trusted assistant. Some of her henchmen, notably Marcol and Major Gorla, were Space Patrol officers gone bad. None of these creeps was big on personal freedom. "These namby pambies," Sova tells X, "everyone choosing their own life, doing what they want to do. Most people are too stupid to enjoy life. The superior people should be running this universe."

This is what Kit Corry was up against, and by week three, he, Hap and Carol were Sova's prisoners, locked in a dungeon. These bad guys meant business, although eventually, Tonga was transformed into a good character, thanks to "dematerialized banishment" (an early form of suspended animation) followed by a course of treatment

---

[9]Jameson's short stories about Bullard were reissued as a book, *Bullard of the Space Patrol* (New York and Cleveland: World Publishing Company, 1951).

[10]In the early credits for the 15-minute show on KECA, Kit Corry's name is spelled "Corey" (erroneously) as in crew member Ed Corey's name — probably an error by a fellow staffer. Moser always spelled it "Corry" in his scripts, but the misspelling was picked up in early articles about the show and persists today.

with the Brainograph that erased her criminal tendencies. One problem: Her evil brother, Prince Baccarratti, had messed with the 'Graph, so whether her genetic predisposition to crime had been totally altered was uncertain. Anyway, with this space scum now on the scene, Kit Corry was starting to lose the stupid grin, and worry less about what a storm cloud looks like inside and more about whether he'd live to see the 31st century.

Moser and his production manager, Dick Vrunnenkant, pulled all-nighters, churning out the next day's story and rushing it to the set. Often the cast had just a few hours—or less—to study the script and walk through the show. When Norm Jolley took over the writing in the summer of 1950, he, too, raced to beat the clock, sometimes dashing in with stacks of mimeographed pages only minutes before airtime. Nina Bara remembers several occasions when he didn't make it, so the actors improvised, working from an outline of the plot. "We got three or four pages and we ad libbed the whole show," she recalls. As the cast struggled to learn their lines (if there were any), director Dick Darley was figuring out how to make it work on the set. From the beginning, the director was bent on realism, says actor Charles Barkus, who played villain "R-6," but sometimes things got a little *too* real:

> Dick called me aside and said, "Look, we're gonna do this scene and it's gonna hurt. Can you take a real slap in the face?" And I said, what the heck, I'll try it. In the scene, I'd done something wrong and my boss was reprimanding me. Well, the guy was pretty strong and he hit me hard, like it was for real. The camera was right up six inches away from my face, so there was no pulling punches. After the show, he said, "My hand is still stinging. How does your face feel?" Well, my face was certainly hurting—and I'd agreed to this, I mean, just for the sake of art.

Another time, Barkus was taking food to a prison cell where Hap and Carol were held captive by him and his cohorts:

> So I open the door and Muggs [Lyn Osborn] sneaks up behind and zaps me with a rubber mallet.[11] Then he decides I'm being too dramatic with my fall, so he gives me a shove to make it quicker. Well, it got me off balance and I miss my mark and hit my head on a stage brace—cut it open and blood is coming out. It's running down my head, but there isn't anything I can do because I'm in this quick transition to the next scene where I enter the big mucky-muck's office, with him behind his fancy desk. He looks at the blood coming down my head and blows his line. That really messed up the scene.

By the end of April, the show was shaping up, but there was one big problem: Kit Corry. Moser solved it by telling Mullen to go kiss a comet. Besides having an attitude problem, says Jolley, the actor just wasn't good at remembering his lines. Retiring from the Space Patrol didn't faze Mullen, who insists that he wanted out. "I excused myself, as you would from a boring conversation," he explains. "His attitude was that he was above all this," says Darley. "He thought the show wasn't going anywhere and he wanted to do bigger things." It was decided that Kit would be kicked upstairs to a consular post by the Secretary General and his younger brother, Buzz, would replace him as commander-in-chief. A search was on for an actor who could carry the crucial role, but in

---

[11]Lyn Osborn was dubbed "Muggsy" by his friends at the Pasadena Playhouse because of his uncanny resemblance to actor Leo Gorcey, who played "Muggs McGinnis" in a series of 1940s films about "The East Side Kids."

the meantime, Buzz (who was on an off-planet mission and only communicated by space-o-phone) was played as an offstage voice by Ken Mayer. During this transition period, Norm Jolley, who had begun to write some of the scripts, indulged his dislike of Mullen by making him stay on for a few more episodes to establish that Buzz was Kit's brother. But Jolley's scheme nearly backfired when Mullen had a senior moment on the air and couldn't remember if he was Kit or Buzz. It happened when he called Buzz on the space-o-phone:

"This is Buzz... Kit? Uh, this is Kit... Buzz?"

As the other actors in the scene try not to lose it, Mullen makes a smooth recovery: "Quite a routine — we've had this going on between the two of us for five years now! Report to me," he tells his kid brother, when he remembers who's who. "I have an idea there's a new assignment coming up for you — and it'll be *big*."

It was Lyn Osborn who phoned Ed Kemmer with the news: The male lead of the TV space opera Lyn was in had received his walking papers in the form of an ambassador-ship to a distant planet. Was Ed interested in auditioning for the part? Kemmer was surprised when he got the call. He'd known Lyn only by sight at the Pasadena Play-house — they were in the same class but had not been friends. Osborn set up a meeting with Moser and Darley. Like Lyn, Kemmer was fresh out of the Playhouse; he had never auditioned — ever.

Osborn had watched Kemmer as leading man in several Playhouse productions and knew he was right for the role. Norm Jolley wasn't so sure. He recommended another actor over Kemmer, but Moser had already offered the part to Warner Bros. contract player Harry Lewis, who later went on to create the popular Hamburger Hamlet chain of restaurants with his wife, Marilyn. "Lewis turned down the role because it didn't pay anything," Ken Mayer recalls. According to the May 1951 issue of *Tele-Views* magazine, 45 actors auditioned for the part, but Osborn had been the first to sense what soon became obvious. "The minute [Ed Kemmer] walked in, we knew he was Commander Corry," recounts Nina Bara in Volume I of her self-published *Space Patrol Memories*.[12] "It was a break," says Kemmer, "coming right out of the Playhouse, not having to starve to death for two years, which my personality couldn't have done."

When Kemmer came aboard in Episode 34 of the daily show, April 25, 1950, it took him a while to get his chops. The rest of the cast had done nearly three dozen live shows by then, so when he went blank, they covered. Kemmer admits he had a tough time at first. "I remember the first show I did — I fell apart, forgot my lines, and boy, I couldn't have told you my name. It was just a blank. And then Hap started talking and got me back into it."

But Osborn was having his problems, too, mainly a tendency to chew the scenery in an effort to resuscitate Moser's dull scripts. His comedy genius was yearning to surface, but no one was writing for it yet. About the only place for Lyn to unleash his natural exuberance was in Hap's wide-eyed eagerness to learn, as a new cadet — but at times

---

[12]*Space Patrol Memories by Tonga* (3 volumes) by Frances Linke (AKA Nina Bara) (Los Angeles: 1966, 1976, 1977). "The book is permanently out of print," says Bara's daughter, Ceci Pier. Note: Linke listed three different copyright dates at the front of the book.

Top and bottom: Nina Bara and Virginia Hewitt mug for the camera. (Photographs by David Sutton, courtesy Dick Darley)

he overdid it. When Norm Jolley took over the writing, he recognized Osborn's comedic potential as well as his capacity to play dead serious, and the "Hap" character fell more in line with Lyn's complex nature. Meanwhile, Kemmer was learning to memorize faster and drawing on his recent war experience as a fighter pilot and P.O.W. to merge his personality with the heroic Corry. Mayer, Hewitt and Bara seemed at ease with their characters early on, but they had fewer lines and didn't bear the huge responsibility of carrying the show that fell to Kemmer and Osborn. Catch Kemmer talking about the "stace spation" in one of the early episodes and it's clear why he's fond of saying, "The first 500 shows are the toughest."

Hap, Carol, and Tonga had been in from the beginning. (Forty-seven actors answered the casting call for Cadet Happy.) Ken Mayer was recruited a few weeks later to do offstage voices when he dropped by the set to visit his friend Don Gordon, who was playing the then-evil Tonga's henchman, Marcol. Years later, Mayer confessed that when Mullen left he'd had his eye on the part of Buzz Corry, but when Kemmer walked in "with that Steve Canyon look," he had to admit he was a ringer for the role.[13] By that time, Moser had spotted Mayer's talent and wrote him in for two weeks as Major Robertson. The mail was favorable, so "Robbie" stayed.

They were Moser's characters and he knew what he wanted. "[Mike] gambled on our acting ability and endurance," Nina Bara wrote in a column for *Tele-News.* She added that the cast, in turn, had gambled on the show's success, turning down "many a lucrative job during those early years." Ed Kemmer smiles when he hears this, years later: No one was beating down his door at the time. The cast hung on during the first six months, he says, because "we fully believed we would go network sooner or later." Preferably sooner, since he and Osborn were top paid at $8.00 a show, while Mayer, Hewitt and Bara drew only $5.00. On that salary, Kemmer points out, he was too poor

---

[13]Steve Canyon was a dashing aviator hero who appeared in comics, television and novels in the '40s and '50s.

to own a television set. "In the early days," recalls Lyn's sister, Beth Flood, "the cast would gather at Nickodell's, where two would order soup and the others would stretch it out with ketchup. They were really struggling then, with not enough to eat." From a budget scribbled by someone on an early script, it appears that after a few months Kemmer and Osborn's pay was upped to $20 per show while Mayer, Hewitt and Bara got $12.50. But the Space Patrol was a solid organization, issuing regular raises. In 1954, Hap mentioned to *TV Guide* that his cadet pay had skyrocketed to $45,000 a year.[14]

Shortly after Kemmer was hired, he ran into Bela Kovacs, a classmate from the Playhouse who was working at a Hollywood radio shop to make ends meet. "Do you think I could get a part on the show?" Kovacs asked. Ed intro-

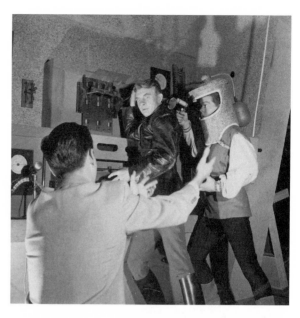

Darley directs a tense moment between Osborn and Bela Kovacs (Prince Baccarratti). (Photograph by David Sutton, courtesy Dick Darley)

duced Bela to Moser, who transformed the former theology student into Prince Baccarratti, evil ruler of Planet X. Kovacs played the role to the hilt and it wasn't long before Commander Corry was deluged with mail. "Please be careful," the kids wrote, citing a number of bad deeds the Prince might be plotting. Kovacs was versatile; when he wasn't Baccarratti, he played a number of character roles, ranging from mad scientist to mild-mannered professor. He craved more involvement with the show and was constantly looking for a niche to fill. Finally, Moser, who knew Dick Darley was stretched to the limit dealing with technical hurdles, put Kovacs in charge of casting.

By June, with Kit Corry gone, the show was on track. Kemmer's dashing looks and sensitive acting turned Buzz Corry into a hero both kids and adults admired and women swooned over, while Osborn's spirited energy won the hearts of the "juves." Things were taking off. But on August 6, Kemmer received an urgent call from a friend of Osborn's who said the actor was gravely ill. Kemmer rushed to his apartment.

SCENE: Commander Corry and his cadet, Happy, are on a routine training flight. Suddenly the ship coughs and sputters— probably a minor problem with the cosmic mass reaction generator.

HAPPY: (EAGER) *Want me to try and fix it, sir? I'm on a training flight— and that's part of my training...* [15]

BUZZ: *If you want to, Happy. Check the main power cable for a short. I think that's what's wrong.*

[14]"Space Happy," *TV Guide*, December 25, 1954.
[15]Stage directions *IN CAPS* are Norm Jolley's.

To the best mother in the whole Universe!! Love always Buddy (Cadet Happy)

Chemistry sparked between Kemmer and Osborn when Kemmer came aboard as Buzz Corry — and the show took off. Osborn, high on his sudden success, sent this photo to his mother, signing his nickname, Buddy, and his new handle, Cadet Happy. (Photograph courtesy Beth Flood)

HAPPY: (*REACHES INTO GENERATOR*) *Yes, sir.*
BUZZ: *It's beginning to sound better, Hap… Be careful you don't touch that open wire — you can get a nasty cosmic ray burn…*
HAPPY: *Oh, don't worry, sir. I won't touch that wi —* (*GETS IT*)
    I… Yi… Yi… Yi! O-ooo-oh, Commander!

BUZZ: Let go of the wire, Happy!
HAPPY: I... c-c-a-a-a-an-t-t-t... S-i-i-r-r-
BUZZ: (THROWS SWITCH ON GENERATOR) There you are!
HAPPY: (RELIEF) Whew! Smokin' Rockets! That was hot!
BUZZ: Let me see your hand... (IT'S ALL BLACK ... HE'S IN PAIN) We've got to get you to Med-
ical Science Center and get that hand treated.
HAPPY: Is it a bad burn, sir?
BUZZ: Any cosmic burn is bad, Happy... They can be fatal. I'll call Medical Science Center and
tell them we're on our way. Let's go...
HAPPY: (SWAYS DIZZILY)
BUZZ: (STEADIES HIM) What's the matter, Hap? Getting dizzy? Grit your teeth, boy. Hang on.
We'll get you to Terra in no time. Here, I'll give you a hand...
—"Race Against Radurium," TV Episode 15, April 7, 1951

When Kemmer arrived at Osborn's apartment, he found him doubled up in pain:

I insisted on calling the ambulance and getting him to the hospital. He couldn't
straighten up and he wanted to know if I thought it was serious. I remembered reading
something about appendicitis and I knew that he'd waited kind of long. When we got to
the hospital, the doctor said it was just in time because it was ready to burst. If it had,
that would have been bad.

Osborn underwent an emergency appendectomy at Cedars of Lebanon Hospital
(now Cedars-Sinai), and Moser hastily rewrote the next day's script to explain that Cadet
Happy had been taken ill while visiting his parents on Earth. With a touch of realism
(and the innocence of the '50s), the show gave the hospital's actual address and the name
of Osborn's doctor. Within hours, several hundred children had jammed the corridors,
and the next day a special plea was broadcast urging Osborn's fans not to phone or visit.
Over the next two days, 700 letters addressed to "Cadet Happy, Cedars of Lebanon Hospital, Los Angeles, California, North American Continent, Western Hemisphere, Planet
Earth" arrived. Looking back on the incident, Kemmer is pleased that Lyn relied on him.
"It gives me a good feeling that in a real time of need Hap called on me," he says, years
later.

By mid-summer 1950, Moser had convinced ABC to run *Space Patrol* twice a week
on its nationwide radio network. It debuted the first week of August in a half-hour format with Moser writing and radio veteran Larry Robertson directing, making it one of
the few shows that crossed over from TV to radio (rather than the other way around). It
was a heady victory for Moser, who now became obsessed with getting *Space Patrol* on
the ABC television network in a weekly half-hour time-slot. To do that, he needed to let
go of the writing chores and focus full-time on what he did best: promotion. It was time
to implement his secret plan of handing the writing to Norman Jolley, the actor he'd hired
to play Agent X.

He'd pegged Jolley early on for the job when the actor's then-wife, Alberta, had talked
up a storm about her husband's writing skills. Norm had done radio dramas and comedy routines, she bragged, not to mention scripting *The Don Lee Music Hall*, a popular
variety show he'd hosted with longtime comedy partner Archie Leonard. Moser invited
Jolley to write several scripts. They were good. He knew the show, understood the char-

acters. Now the producer offered him $250 a week — ten times what he was making as an actor — to write the daily TV scripts plus the two weekly radio shows. Jolley loved acting more than writing, but he couldn't resist that kind of money. Besides, he had a background in engineering — enough to help him spin credible sci-fi plots. When he took over, he focused on action and the show picked up pace. Director Dick Darley liked this new format. "Moser's scripts tended to be educational, with lots of tedious military and scientific references," he recalls. Jolley's shows were exciting. What's more, he, Darley, and leading man Ed Kemmer were on the same page: They saw *Space Patrol* as a straight dramatic show, not limited to youngsters.

It was Darley, Jolley and Kemmer's determination to play *Space Patrol* straight that made it a sleeper hit with age groups across the board. Darley, who resented being assigned to a children's show, knew that TV was young and no one was sure yet where to draw the line between "juve" and adult fare, so he let the boundaries blur:

> I said, OK, I've gotta do this damn show, so I'm gonna make it as adult as I can, get a broader audience and satisfy myself. I didn't 'kid' the show because you don't talk down to children. I'd learned that children loved *Dragnet* — shows like that had a very large children's audience, so I figured they did understand adult shows. In those days, you weren't allowed to get too sophisticated, so an "adult" show was one that appealed to people's intelligence.

Top: Ken Mayer, Lyn Osborn and Ed Kemmer look up from examining a 30th-century gizmo. *Bottom:* Osborn and Kemmer share a laugh. (Both photographs by David Sutton, courtesy Dick Darley)

Radio director Larry Robertson held the same vision, and in November 1950, *Tele-Views* magazine confirmed that the show had crashed the age barrier in both its TV and radio formats:

In the comparatively brief time since it went on KECA-TV (last March) the adventure series called "Space Patrol" has won tremendous acclaim, and it's also on radio twice a week. It's on TV every day, at an hour calculated to attract adults and children, since the series is designed for both.[16]

When I mention the show's early radio success to Ed Kemmer, he denies it. Not only that, he's angry. "There is *no* possibility that we went to radio before the network TV show — it just didn't happen," he says testily. "I'd remember because of the money — we would have had a big raise, maybe $200 a week." He wants broadcast historians to know that *Tele-Views* made a mistake. "If we did radio shows before network TV, then I did them in my sleep and deposited the money in a dream bank." At 82, he still has Corry's stubbornness. He's not backing down — not even when confronted with a column written by Mike Moser in *The Los Angeles Examiner* on August 29, 1950, in which he talks about the radio production. "The radio show," Moser wrote, "does not offer quite as many problems as the [local] TV version."[17]

"He meant *future* radio shows," Kemmer says, thinking fast like Buzz Corry. "Moser was always talking about future plans. Look, I feel strongly about this — I'd stake my life on it. I want my feelings known."

The November 1950 *Tele-Views* story that reported *Space Patrol*'s radio success went on to describe what happened that fall when Kemmer visited an LA department store:

> You should have been at the May Company recently when Ed Kemmer made a personal appearance. The crowd swamped Commander Corry, knocking over furniture and everything else around, until they were quieted only when Ed Kemmer, I mean Commander Corry, spoke to them forcefully, in character. A hush fell over the place and the riotous tumult dissolved into meek acquiescence.[18]

Kemmer doesn't dispute that incident. It was a taste of things to come.

Though Moser wrote the TV scripts for only the first few months (and the radio show for just a few weeks) before handing both jobs to Norm Jolley, he set a true course, defining the main characters and mood of the show. His villains were nasty — you saw that by the brutal way they treated each other (as R-6 can tell you). They were up close and personal with a sadistic streak, and usually a grudge against Corry; and most of them had an irresistible urge to enslave the freedom-loving citizens of the United Planets. When Jolley took over, he revved up the action and deepened the characters, but it was Moser who first brought Buzz, Hap, Carol, Robbie and Tonga to life, patiently sketching their backgrounds in character fact sheets. He knew them better than anyone else — their origins, childhood, and the significant life events that led each of them to the Space Patrol.[19]

According to Moser's fact sheets, Edward "Buzz" Corry, the younger of two brothers, hailed from Bakersfield, California, Earth. Early in life, he showed remarkable skill in space astrogation and followed his older brother, Kit, into the Space Patrol. After the

[16]"Space Patrol" by Gwen Hope, *Tele-Views*, November 1950.
[17]"Stop-Look-Listen," Pat Hogan's column in the *Los Angeles Examiner*, August 29, 1950. (Mike Moser filled in for Hogan, who was on vacation.)
[18]"Space Patrol" by Gwen Hope, *Tele-Views*, November 1950.
[19]Moser's fact sheets were supplied by collector Warren Chaney. Phrases in quotes are Moser's words.

Left: The camera moves in for a close-up of Ken Mayer flanked by Osborn, Kemmer and an unidentified actor. *Right:* Baccarratti forcibly takes command of Corry's battlecruiser. (Both photographs by David Sutton, courtesy Dick Darley)

Great Solar System War, when a new planetary government was formed, it was Captain Corry who flew the first daring solo mission to Pluto to secure soil to place at the core of the man-made planet Terra. An equally remarkable achievement was his invention of the Brainograph shortly after he discovered an indestructible, silvery metal, Endurium. Buzz was promoted to commander-in-chief of the Space Patrol when his brother Kit stepped down from the post. Under his strong leadership, it quickly became an organization revered and trusted by the 6 billion citizens of the United Planets.

Lyn "Happy" Osborn[20] was "typical of the thousands of men and women who serve as cadets in the Space Patrol and who, in the years ahead, will become the leaders in maintaining interplanetary justice." Hap grew up an only child in Chicago, Illinois, on Planet Earth. During high school he excelled in astrophysics, math and sports and won a rare scholarship to the famed Space Patrol Academy, where he majored in interplanetary operations. Because of his hard work and dedication, the young cadet received an internship to Space Patrol Headquarters on Terra and won the coveted Corry Scholarship, which caught Buzz Corry's attention. After several daring adventures together where Hap showed exceptional courage, Corry chose him as his permanent co-pilot and cadet.

Carol Carlisle, daughter of the Secretary General of the United Planets, earned an astrophysics degree from a prestigious university on Earth. Upon graduation she went straight into the Research and Development Branch of the Space Patrol, where she invented "many important materials and devices used in space travel." Carol's special interest was the development of alloys used in Space Patrol ships. Because of her quick mind and grasp of political issues, she served as liaison officer between her father's office and Space Patrol Headquarters. To her credit, she never took advantage of her dad's post to gain perks for the Space Patrol. Occasionally she was given special assignments where she faced "imminent danger," but in these situations she demonstrated "exemplary determination, resourcefulness and courage."

---

[20]For the male leads, Moser integrated the actor's real first name — and in Happy's case, both first and last name — with the character name.

Major Ken "Robbie" Robertson began his career as an enlisted man in Earth's armed forces before receiving his commission as a Space Patrol officer. During the War Between the Planets (AKA the Great Solar System War), he cracked many enemy secret codes. After the war, the young sergeant was commissioned as a lieutenant in the newly formed Space Patrol. Robertson developed many security code systems that ensured the safety of the United Planets and helped set up "Space Control," a ship-tracking system that facilitated safe travel between the planets. Because of his many contributions, he was promoted to captain, then to major, and appointed security chief of the United Planets.

Tonga, the daughter of a royal family on Neptune, was raised and educated on Saturn. Bitter following her family's fall from power, she blamed government officials and conspired with her nefarious brother, Prince Baccarratti, to do away with Commander Corry. A notorious criminal known as the "Lady of Diamonds," she plotted against the United Planets until she was defeated by Corry himself, who personally supervised her rehabilitation. It was during this rocky period that Major Robertson offered her a job as his assistant. Tonga's skill as a pilot, coupled with her background in chemistry, led to special assignments in the Space Patrol Chemical Research and Development Program, where she pioneered many secret advances in galactic crime detection.

Major Robertson subdues the "bad" Tonga, who, despite a series of Brainograph treatments, has relapsed into her evil ways. (Courtesy Bob Burns)

Dick Darley, beset by technical hurdles, worried that he had too little time to work with the actors, but he noticed that they seemed to be finding their way on their own. Day by day, he saw "the written characters become real people," and he relaxed as he realized that, in most cases, the actors instinctively knew what to do. "We knew our characters," confirms Ken Mayer. "I'd change my dialogue if I felt 'Robbie wouldn't say that.'" But Darley noticed something else. A magic was brewing:

> It wasn't just a job — they all believed in it. It might have started out as a job, as wanting exposure, wanting it to lead to other things. But they got caught up in it without knowing why, because when you're in it, you don't see the mystique. As the cast began to work as a unit and play off of each other, they became a family. They would kid each other, push each other around. Sometimes there was rancor or little feuds, but there was a loyalty and a love between them, too.

What sparked the magic was the cast's belief in the show, but there was something more: an uncanny resemblance between the characters Moser had created and the real-life people who played them. "There was a meeting of character and actor," says writer-producer Marc Zicree, a veteran of many SF shows, including *Star Trek — The Next Generation* and *Babylon 5*. "Ed Kemmer really was a World War II flying hero. He seems real, like someone who'd actually be in the job of commander-in-chief. You believe him." And, in fact, it was true right down the line: Lyn Osborn (Cadet Happy) was a happy-go-lucky practical joker; Ken Mayer (Major Robertson) was a steady, dependable guy who'd enlisted in the Army, known struggle, and worked hard to get to his station in life; Virginia Hewitt (Carol) came from a well-to-do background and her father (like the Secretary General) held a supervisory position in a large organization;[21] Nina Bara (Tonga) hailed from Argentina, a far-off country that seemed, in the '50s, as distant as Saturn and Neptune, and her childhood was touched by political strife.

Kemmer, Osborn and Bela Kovacs (Prince Baccarratti) shared a special connection. They were grads of the prestigious Pasadena Playhouse, which had produced such stars as Robert Young, William Holden, Barbara Rush and Victor Mature.[22] Attending the Playhouse, says its archivist, Ellen Bailey, was an intense experience that forged a life-long bond. "It was a magical place. You opened yourself up completely when you went there. Later on, when you were out in the world, if you met someone from the Playhouse who'd been through the same thing, you hugged them because there was a rapport. It was like a family."

Kemmer whizzed through the school in less than two years, emerging serious and professional. Between his Playhouse training and experience as a fighter pilot, he stayed cool under fire during the constant crisis that was live TV. "Ed didn't clown around as much as the others," Darley recalls, "which was fine for his character." Audio man Chuck Lewis remembers that the young actor was always prepared. "He was a perfectionist. He'd have his dialogue down."

In contrast, Osborn was a loose cannon. From the first day of the show, it was as if Lyn disappeared and "Hap" was born. "You couldn't tell Lyn and Hap apart," says announcer Dick Tufeld. Osborn fired off a constant barrage of jokes and antics that broke the tension on the set, but could also increase it as cast and crew rushed headlong toward airtime with major problems still unresolved. At these times, Osborn's innocent but raucous behavior bordered on sabotage, as far as Darley was concerned, but he stifled his anger. He couldn't risk dampening Osborn's natural exuberance, which powered the show. Tufeld remembers the director quietly taking Osborn aside. "He'd say, 'C'mon, Hap, get serious. This is serious stuff.'"

Ken Mayer attended broadcasting school on the G.I. bill and honed his acting in theater workshops. Like his character, Robbie, he had a comforting presence. "He was warm and open, like a big huggy bear," says Darley. But the actor had a problem remembering his lines and a tendency to blow them — on the air. "He faked a lot of stuff. But as soon as he got lost, he'd bumble around until he bailed himself out, or somebody else did," the director recalls. "Nobody gave up on Kenny," says Norm Jolley. "He'd screw up a line and stutter and sometimes go blank, but the others would help him, get him over the edge and gradually bring him back." The cast was intensely loyal and forgiving, since Mayer's solid presence was indispensable. "Nobody ever suggested we replace him," says

---

[21]He was a supervisor for Panhandle Eastern Pipe Line Company.

[22]Famous Playhouse alumni who attended the school at the same time as Kemmer, Osborn and Kovacs include Carolyn Jones, who appeared in *King Creole* and *Invasion of the Body Snatchers* and starred as "Morticia" in *The Addams Family* (1964), and Leonard Nimoy, of *Star Trek* fame.

Darley. Decades later, Mayer confessed that at times he'd been frustrated by playing the third leading man. "That's normal," says Darley. "When somebody else is the hero, you're written to make bad decisions while he makes good ones. Robbie was that kind of part."

Virginia Hewitt left Kansas City, Missouri, for Hollywood in 1947 with dreams of becoming a writer, but her stunning looks soon landed her modeling jobs that she parlayed into an acting career. Hewitt was reserved. She was pleasant enough to everyone, but it was hard to tell if she was shy, aloof, or both. "She was very ladylike," recalls Ken Mayer's wife, Ruth. "She didn't like anybody swearing around her or using street talk." Says Tufeld, "She was not a 'one of the guys'–type lady."

Dark-haired Nina Bara was the opposite — earthy and unpredictable with an alluring Argentinean accent that enhanced her mystique. "She would have been at home in burlesque," says Darley. Bara, whose real name was Frances Bauer, was a child actor in Argentina and Germany, then honed her skill in summer stock after moving to the States. Like "Tonga," she carried an aura of mystery. "You could tell she had a dark side," says Tufeld. Bara was savvy about publicity, plugging the show nonstop in the chatty gossip columns she wrote for several film magazines. This was priceless promotion and boosted the show, though sometimes Ken Mayer caught himself wondering if Nina's priorities were out of whack. He recalls the time they were speeding to a public appearance and nearly collided with a fire truck. Bara turned to him excitedly. "Can you see the headlines tomorrow? 'Robbie and Tonga killed by a fire engine!'" For her, says Mayer, "publicity was sometimes more important than doing the show."

Bela Kovacs, though born in the States, grew up in Czechoslovakia. His Hungarian parents pushed him to be a minister, but he rebelled and pursued an acting career. Like his character, Prince Baccarratti, he was hot and unpredictable. "He was a raw nerve," says Darley. "He'd have violent tantrums, get terribly moody and depressed. And he was so emotional — my God, he'd break down and cry right in the middle of what you thought was a small argument!"

Though the cast had bonded, the pressure of getting the daily show on the air pushed everyone to the limit — even Kemmer, who was slow to anger. What bugged him most, says Darley, was when guest actors hadn't learned their lines. "That really got him upset because if an actor isn't prepared in rehearsal, the others have to go over and over the scene to get him through it — and then, on the air, they're not sure he'll come through." When Kemmer boiled over, "he'd say what he thought very bluntly," Darley recalls. "All of us were under pressure. We had to let off steam, and we did. But we realized it wasn't the end of the world; it was just that afternoon."

It didn't take Norm Jolley long to slip into overwhelm, once he took over the writing from Moser. Juggling seven shows (five TV plus two radio), he was aware of the turmoil he caused cast and crew when he delivered the scripts at the eleventh hour, but he couldn't help it. He had never written a daily TV show before. Like Moser, sometimes he'd deliver the scripts only minutes before air time. "We got 'em on onion-skin paper, hot from the typewriter," Kemmer recalls, "with no time to even read them before we went on the air." Other times, Jolley managed to turn the scripts in a full day in advance, and in that case, wrote *Los Angeles Examiner* columnist Pat Hogan, the cast arrived at the studio at 3 P.M., lines memorized, ready to rehearse for that evening's show. After the live broadcast, the cycle repeated. Hogan zeroed in on the enormous pressure:

They take time for a quick dinner, usually with their next day's script before them. Then they memorize all the way from 20 to 50 sides before calling it a night. Next morning it's eggs and script again. That script is never out of their minds until airtime. After each night's performance, the [process] starts all over again.[23]

The pressure didn't let up until the daily show folded in 1953, but in the meantime, TV history was being made. *Space Patrol*, debuting in March 1950, was television's first real soap opera — a live, daily cliffhanging drama where you cared about the characters and tuned in the next day to know their fate. (*Guiding Light*, which began on radio in 1937, didn't cross over to TV until June 30, 1952.) It was the first time in television's short history that actors had to memorize so much material on such short notice, day after day. "Memorizing a script five days a week was certainly unique in those days," confirms Kemmer, "and we learned six a week when the network show was added. Later, when I did shows like *Lux Video Theatre* and we had a whole week to rehearse, it was like a vacation." Photos of Lyn Osborn relaxing offscreen usually reveal a script tucked in his jacket pocket.

To ease the enormous pressure, the cast, egged on by Osborn, teased each other nonstop and played practical jokes — and Kemmer, more serious than the others, was an irresistible target. The TelePrompTer had not been invented yet, so the commander (who was always explaining technical things about hyperspace, time warps and magnetic force control) had a habit of pasting cue cards all over the spaceship. "So," recalls Ken Mayer, "one day Hap and I just went in after rehearsal and moved Ed's dialogue to different parts of the ship, just mixed it up" — resulting, no doubt, in an interesting show.

Actor-writer Maurice Hill watched the cast's frantic rush to learn their lines. "They'd get the script so late — sometimes at 4:30 for a 6:45 show, so they *had* to have lines all over the place." (Dick Darley jokes that dialogue was plastered everywhere — even on the backs of hands.) Hill came onboard at the end of 1951 to assist Norm Jolley who, he says, "was about to go off into space himself," hammering out 83,000 words a week.[24] Once Hill submitted a story where the ship caught fire — but he noted that cue cards went up all over the ship's walls, just the same. "The rehearsal went fine," he recalls, "but when the real show went on, real smoke obliterated all the lines. They were desperately trying to clear it away so they could read what they had to say next." Hill earned $15 per script. When he needed extra money to pay the rent, he wrote himself in as "Captain Hayward." When his friends needed money to pay their rent, he went to casting director Bela Kovacs. "I'd say, 'I've got a new villain. He's middle-aged and he looks like this — and I happen to know a guy who'd be fine for the part.' And Bela would say, 'Send him in.' I got a big kick out of hiring lots of my friends," Hill laughs.

It was good for Hill's friends, but not for the show. If *Space Patrol* has a weak link, it's the villains who flub or forget their lines or turn in a wooden performance. While some guest actors were superb — notably Lee Van Cleef, Ben Welden, Tom McKee, Larry

---

[23]Pat Hogan's column in the *Los Angeles Examiner*. No date on the clipping, but probably circa 1951. (Hogan was a little off on his calculations. For the fifteen-minute daily show, the cast would have had no more than fifteen pages of script to memorize per night.)

[24]By mid–1951, Jolley knew he needed help. He hired G. Gordon Dewey, a teacher and sometime sci-fi writer, to write the daily shows; Dewey was quickly replaced by Dick Morgan, who didn't last long. Finally Maury Hill got the job. Jolley liked Hill the best, though he insisted that he always edited and frequently rewrote every show penned by an assistant.

Dobkin and Marvin Miller — others panicked during the live performance.[25] Dick Darley, wrestling with technical problems, admits that he didn't have time to cast guest players and coach them, so the task fell to Kovacs, who was highly emotional and let his feelings cloud his judgment. As a result, he often hired weak or inexperienced actors. Of course, even seasoned players, veterans of stage and film, could go into meltdown when faced with the triple whammy of last-minute scripts, not enough rehearsal time and a live performance. Others, says Darley, were "fragile, insecure, or live TV moved too fast for them." The director never knew what to expect from these actors, who could be passable in rehearsal, but unpredictable on the air. "They'd give you a wooden performance in the camera rehearsal; then, when the light went on, they'd ham it up, chew the scenery. They'd surprise you that way — but once you're on the air, there's not a damn thing you can do about it."

But imaginative storylines and strong performances by the regular cast overrode

OUT OF THIS WORLD

Space Patrol, of course. This is a live production that really gives the actor a chance. The leads are set, but character parts are frequently open. These parts often become an integral part of the show if the actor is versatile and his work of a high caliber. Bela Kovacs, Casting Director, holds open auditions every Thursday at 1:00 P.M. Kovacs is also an actor and really understands an actor's problems. "Space Patrol" does five local shows each week and one national Saturday. The Saturday show uses an average of two character parts in addition to the regular cast. And here's a tip . . . 95 percent of his casting is for villain types. It is also suggested that you take a picture with you to the readings, as they are kept on file for frequent referral. "Space Patrol" is a Mike Moser Production, 6404 Hollywood Blvd., HI. 5188. Dik Darly directs. Norm Jolly writes the script. One last word from casting director Kovacs, "Learn to read intelligently and learn to concentrate."

Space Patrol casting call. "Bela Kovacs, Casting Director, holds open auditions every Thursday at 1:00 P.M.," *Television Casting Magazine* announced on August 17, 1951. "95 percent of his casting is for villain types."

Left and right: Nina Bara drives home a point to Ken Mayer as they rehearse; she wins. (Photographs by David Sutton, courtesy Dick Darley)

[25]In addition to his villainous roles on the TV show, Larry Dobkin appeared as Prince Baccarratti's henchman "Malengro" on the Decca record, *Buzz Corry Becomes Commander-in-Chief* (1954).

Virginia Hewitt and Ed Kemmer give the script and each other their full attention. (Photographs by David Sutton, courtesy Dick Darley)

bumbling heavies, incorrigible special effects and a variety of technical snafus. Viewers got hooked on the lead characters and the chance to dream about the endless adventures that awaited in the wild, vast reaches of space. Kids and teens basked in the kinship between Buzz Corry and his favorite cadet, and adults picked up on the three-musketeer camaraderie between Buzz, Hap and Major Robertson — not to mention the subtle romance between Buzz and Carol, and (less obvious) Robbie and Tonga. It was clear that the Space Patrol gang cared deeply about one another, so the audience cared about them. And once they were hooked on the characters, daily cliffhangers stoked the addiction.

Dick Darley grew up on cliffhangers, but he hated it when the Saturday afternoon movie serials teased you, then failed to deliver the following week. "It bugged me that the guy on a cliff galloped off into thin air, but then next week, when it picked up again, the horse stops before it gets to the edge. I hated those cheats, but I saw the value of the suspense — wanting kids to be concerned as to whether the hero made it or not."

Moser (and later Norm Jolley) scripted uncertainty into the end of each daily show. (For example, at the close of the episode that aired on Tuesday, May 30, 1950, Hap and Buzz lose their horizontal stabilizer and the ship dives toward Terra on an out-of-control collision course.)[26] Darley, recalling how suspense had thrilled him as a child, made these final moments as hair-raising as possible, so that the audience would come back tomorrow. It worked. Surveys showed that most viewers tuned in several times a week. An ABC press release proclaimed that the Hooper ratings for August-September 1950 ranked *Space Patrol* as "the most popular TV strip [serial] show in Los Angeles." Virginia Hewitt told reporter Tom Danson that even she was on edge, waiting to know what would happen next. "At the end of the week, I can hardly wait until Monday to find out how I get out of the situation," she purred, adding, "We don't get our scripts until the

[26]Cadets keeping track of Corry's ships, take note: In this script, his ship is referred to as *Terra the Third*, a rare model mentioned only in shows penned by Mike Moser, including his half-hour demo, "Secret of Terra," which aired as network episode 47. The ship was also featured in Moser's first radio scripts, written in the summer of 1950.

night before a show, so it's almost right up to the last moment before I know my fate."
Danson conveyed the excitement to readers of *TV Radio Logic*:

> Some of the stories in the *Space Patrol* series get very complicated with many of the end-
> ings similar to the old-time Pearl White serial thrillers. On a weekend, Space Patrollers
> find themselves right in the middle of an exciting sequence with bombs about to burst or
> the spaceship completely out of control, racing toward certain doom.[27]

Like Ed Kemmer, who flew P-51 Mustangs in the European theater during the war,
Darley had served as a Navy fighter pilot in the South Pacific and knew danger up close.
To him, excitement was what life was about. When World War II ended, he wondered
what in the universe he could do to equal the thrill of flying off aircraft carriers, but when
he stepped into the control booth of a live TV show in progress and felt the heart-pound-
ing adrenaline rush, "I knew in ten seconds, 'This was it.' It was doing strategy, having
near misses and close calls. There was excitement to it."

The best way to start out in broadcasting, he'd heard, was to become a page at one
of the networks. You had access to any office, from the president to the mailroom. So
Darley took his skills in visual arts and creative writing, garnered at prestigious USC, to
the Don Lee–Mutual Broadcasting Network, where he ran errands, emptied wastebas-
kets and tried to type, but, most important, hung around the TV office at 1313 N. Vine
Street in Hollywood.

It wasn't long before he attracted a mentor among the higher-ups: E. Carlton Winckler, who put him to work as a stage manager at W6XAO on Mount Lee, the network's
fledgling TV station.[28] Soon he was directing, driving up to the top of the mountain, doing
five shows a night, five times a week. Then, suddenly, the network laid off 10 percent of
its work force and Darley got hit. Winckler promptly got him a job launching a new TV
station in San Diego where, for the next six months, he honed both his directing and cri-
sis-management skills, learning every aspect of the business, including how to fill air
time when a live studio broadcast crashed and burned. In a pinch, he'd send a camera on
a long cable up the stairs from the station's basement studio to the sidewalk above, grab-
bing passers-by for spontaneous "Man on the Street" interviews until regular programming was back on track. He worked his way up to senior director-producer, but when
he heard about an opening at ABC-TV in Hollywood, he demoted himself back to stage
manager to grab it. Within a month, he was directing again, and in the winter of 1950,
ABC assigned him *Space Patrol*.

"I didn't want any part of it," Darley sighs. "I was on my way up in dramatic shows,
and I figured I'd get stuck. But somebody told me to do it, and I was on the staff at ABC
and had to do what they gave me." His fear was that "other directors would get the plum
stuff and I'd be stuck on this kid's show." But once *Space Patrol* got under way, he got
into it. "I tried to make it believable," he says, "make it look like it was really happening." He bonded with Kemmer, a fellow fighter pilot with whom he felt instant rapport.
"We were comrades from that experience, because whether you're over the ocean or
Europe, you're on your own." Before long, he'd made other friends among the cast and
crew and had to admit that the show was "creative fun." As with everything else in his

---

[27]"Involved Story Endings Excite Virginia Hewitt," by Tom E. Danson, *TV Radio Logic*, month unknown, 1952.
[28]Licensed in May 1931, by the end of the year W6XAO was broadcasting one hour a day to five television sets in
Los Angeles. Now known as CBS 2, the pioneer station aired the first full-length motion picture ever presented on
television: *The Crooked Circle*, March 10, 1933.

life, he made it a challenge. "I tried to make it look like a movie every time, as best I could with live cameras—tried to get a lot of close-ups, reactions." That was a new concept for television. Reaction shots were used in movies, but hardly anyone was doing them on live TV. At times he'd "get in super-close on the face and read the eyes." It gave viewers an intimacy with the characters that was heightened by the fact that they were coming right into your living room. "You felt," says Slim Sweatmon, who grew up with *Space Patrol* and plays "Mr. Boyd" on *Barney & Friends*, "that you were right there, looking over the actors' shoulders."

Though *Space Patrol* was a hit by mid-summer, it didn't attract a sponsor until September—six months after its March debut. Backing a show at the dawn of television was a risky commitment for advertisers because most people didn't own a TV set. Finally, four high-profile companies took the leap and signed on. Good Humor Ice Cream, whose merrily jingling trucks rolled down the nation's streets in the late afternoon, came aboard in early September, followed by Dr. Ross pet food ("Dr. Ross dog food is doggone good!"), the local show's longest-running sponsor. Leslie Salt occasionally ran spots and so did Reddi-wip, who proved the truth of that age-old adage: Mix a can of pressurized whipped cream with live TV and something bad is bound to happen.

Sue Thomas' father was general sales manager for Reddi-wip. Her dad was excited about advertising on *Space Patrol*—until one day when things went terribly wrong. Sue, then six, and her younger brother were watching:

> A blonde model was standing at a table showing how you could frost a cake with Reddi-wip. She was doing great until a huge horsefly found the whipped cream. In the background, you could see shadows of the crew trying to get the black fly off the white cake—of course, it was stuck—but the model never missed a beat. Whatever they paid her, it wasn't enough, because she just went on with her script, burying the fly in a big glob of whipped cream. You could see the camera jiggle as the cameraman went into hysterics. My brother and I, being little kids, were absolutely gone—we were gasping for breath.

Thomas's father knew that his boss, the president of Reddi-wip, was prone to "fits" and waited tensely for the phone to ring. This, he knew, was the end of his job. Fortunately, the chief exec had stepped out for a moment and missed the fiasco.

By fall, cast and crew had learned by doing, and many rough edges had been smoothed. In early episodes, there had been obvious blunders. In one scene, Carol has a heart-to-heart talk with her father, the Secretary General of the United Planets, but the camera focuses on the empty space between them, leaving the Secretary almost totally offscreen. Another time, Carol and Hap sit down for a lengthy conversation, but there's so little camera movement that it looks like the operator went out for a smoke. When Jolley took over the writing, long sit-down talks ceased; meanwhile, Darley had realized that he needed to get the actors on their feet and moving as they talked to generate excitement.

Jolley's scripts, livelier than Moser's, gave the director much more to work with. He started shooting the show like a movie, going for tight shots that heightened the drama. His liberal use of close-ups was groundbreaking for television. It was also practical, says assistant director Maury Orr (De Mots), filling the void left by dazzling special effects that did not yet exist. "We didn't have the scope or the money to build a giant spaceship like the *Enterprise* where the actors could walk around and push buttons. You had to imagine half of what was going on." The sets, adds Orr, though imaginative for their time, were primitive by today's standards, so Darley focused on the characters, moving in close to read their thoughts. "It was TV soap opera before it was invented—close-ups and expressions: 'What's he thinking? What's she thinking? What's he going to do next?' People didn't realize that Dick was ahead of his time."

Darley was itching for ways to make the show more visually dramatic. He experimented with wide-angle shots, camera cuts and his soon-to-be-trademark close-ups, but, he says, "when I got my hands on a crane, there were all sorts of fun things to do that had never been done on TV before." Sometimes he sent a camera up to the rafters, searching for ways to get a more powerful shot. Shooting down with a wide-angle lens gave him the striking angles he wanted. They heightened excitement, creating an edgy, futuristic feeling. He soon learned that actors could move toward the 600-pound camera more easily than it could move toward them, so he had people walk forward for close-ups as they delivered important lines. But as much as he craved close shots, sometimes he hung back. It was live TV and he never knew what a guest actor might say or do next. "I wanted to get in as close as I could to some of the people and, in other instances, I tried to protect them by not getting too close." There were no rules, no precedents, because no one had ever done any of this before. "It was 'make it up as you go along,'" he explains. "Nobody knew how to do anything; but we knew more than anybody else."

For all the headaches, at least that promise of excitement he'd felt when he'd first stepped into a TV control booth had been fulfilled. Live TV, where anything could go wrong at any moment, took stamina and nerves of steel. More and more, Darley was feeling that the strategy it took to bring off a show was indeed like wartime piloting, demanding intense focus and split-second decisions:

> I was always preparing for mistakes. That's part of carrier flying, and thank God I'd had that kind of training. Instant reactions—always trying to think a step or two ahead, just in case the engine stopped or the navigation equipment went out and you didn't know where the hell the ship was.

The only difference between live TV and his war experience, he realized, was that "this wasn't going to kill me. But," he adds quickly, "it would kill me inside if I screwed up." The closest thing to losing an engine was losing a camera. He used two cameras on the daily show, but worried about what would happen if one of them failed. Lacking funds, ABC was known as "the poor sister network." It didn't have the budget or personnel to keep its equipment in top shape.[29] He tested himself by shooting a show with one camera, just to see if he could survive. Between scenes, when he would normally switch cameras, he went to a shot of miniature set models or to black, spinning the camera and fading up on the next scene. He was in his element: problem solving; that was what live TV was about. "The technical parts of the staging had to come first," he points out, "because nobody would get to see the interpretation if the image wasn't there."

---

[29]ABC was an offshoot of NBC, which at one time controlled two radio networks known as the Red and Blue networks. In 1943, fearing a monopoly of the airwaves, the Federal Communications Commission forced NBC to give up one of them. The Blue network was sold to Edward J. Noble, who'd made his fortune with the popular "Lifesavers" candy packs. He named his new network the American Broadcasting Company, but was unable to fund it properly through the transition into television. "At CBS, they had three people doing what one person did at ABC," says *Space Patrol*'s technical director Bob Trachinger.

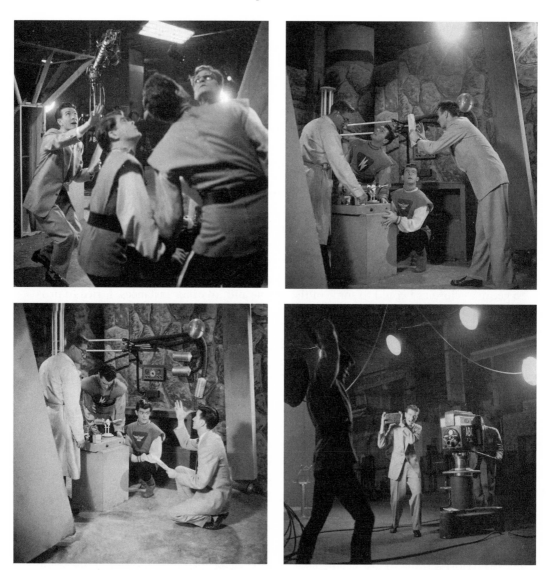

Top and bottom: Hands-on director Darley gets into the scene to give Kemmer, Osborn and an unidentified actor some tips. (Photographs by David Sutton, courtesy Dick Darley)

Two major problems clung like Martian lichen through the entire run of the local show: not enough time and not enough money. When Jolley came racing in with the scripts at the last-minute, Darley swung into action, pulling props and special effects out of thin air:

> I'd get to one of the art directors fast, we'd talk about [the script], then go out to the scene dock and pull pieces that would fill the bill. Then I'd figure out how to shoot some scenes minimally against flats with signs like "Space Patrol Headquarters" on them, just to avoid [building] another set. Sometimes the sets were still being taped and painted when the cast came in. We'd go into a staging rehearsal with the actors still learning their lines, then try to get a stop-and-go camera rehearsal, but there would be no time for a continuity run-through from top to bottom. Thus everyone knew what they were

supposed to do, but hadn't really run through it. The crew was savvy — they'd worked the show enough times to know what was going on…. We were always under the gun.

Property master Al Teaney, a kid at heart who'd been inventing weird gizmos since high school, was in charge of models and special effects. Teaney could create almost anything out of nothing. "He had a budget of 50 cents a week," his wife Alyce jokes. "When they gave him a script, they didn't say *how* this gun or ship was supposed to look. It was all his imagination. At night he'd get real quiet and smoke, thinking about what he had to do the next day and how he'd do it. He'd draw things on napkins. He was constantly creating."

Darley and Teaney combed junkyards and war surplus and hardware stores for peculiar objects— especially

Property master Al Teaney tests a space helmet crafted from hardware and war surplus store parts on Darley in the ABC prop room. (Photographs by David Sutton, courtesy Dick Darley)

plumbing fixtures— that could be transformed into weapons, space helmets, space-o-phones, complex astrogation devices and 30th-century technology like magnetic force

Dick Darley, shopping for futuristic props and trying to figure out what he just bought at a war surplus store. "I never ask clerks what these things really are," he told an interviewer. "It might distract me." (Photographs by David Sutton, courtesy Dick Darley)

Terra City Spaceport. Designed by prop master Al Teaney, this futuristic wooden model shown at the opening of the show inspired dreams of space travel. "As the show progressed," says model maker Jack McKirgan, "more pieces were added and Terra City seemed to grow up around the spaceport." (Courtesy Joe Sarno)

control. "I never asked the clerks what the things were *really* for," says Darley. "The answer might have distracted me." While Teaney labored long hours to construct props and models used regularly on the show, meeting the demands of each day's script was often a last-minute deal. "Unless it called for something really 'design-y,' we were just faking it," Darley admits. "We got the scripts so late that sometimes it would be *me* running out to the warehouse for a pillar or column."

Lumir Mathauser was the first art director, followed by Herbert O. Phillips, but it wasn't long before easygoing Carl Macauley took over, spelled by ABC staffers Seymour Klate and Al Goodman.[30] Using paint, cardboard, papier-mâché, rented backdrops, an assortment of 1950s furniture and Teaney's ingenious props, they struggled on meager budgets to capture the grandeur of the 30th century. The sets varied in size, but Alex Quiroga, and later Truck Krone, created ominous lighting that gave depth and perspective, making things look large and surreal — the way they *should* look in a space-age society. To enhance this "larger-than-life" ambience, Macauley decorated Corry's sparse office with huge plants — two decades before monster houseplants became trendy in the

---

[30]Many ABC staffers worked on the show during its five-year run, but since records are no longer available, it's not possible to list everyone.

'70s. Prop master Teaney added high-tech details, such as doors that slid open at the touch of a button (a stagehand pulling a flat sandwiched between two other flats), but there was no time or money to design futuristic furniture. Thus, the Brainograph Room at Space Patrol Headquarters, the hub of an advanced technology where a subject's thoughts could be viewed on a movie screen, looked like a dentist's office circa 1950. The gauges and dials in Corry's spaceship were all analog; no one had envisioned the digital revolution.

Fortunately, Macauley and Teaney were wizards who could operate on a shoestring. They built and constantly upgraded the miniature models of Terra City and its space-port that flash across the screen in the show's fast-paced opening as announcer Dick Tufeld yells, "*Spaaaaaace Patrol!*" "Those models were crafted with superb detail," notes Jack McKirgan, a *Space Patrol* fan and model maker who worked on the first two *Star Wars* films:

> The rooftops of many buildings were adorned with spaceships and launch ramps. In one version, a monorail track can be seen winding through the buildings and a multi-lane freeway system, complete with entry and exit ramps, appears to be handling a high volume of ground transportation. Many buildings were skyscrapers with spinning radar antennae and blinking lights on their roofs. Other structures were made from a wide range of shapes, some of which seemed whimsical yet conveyed a sense of purpose.[31]

Teaney fashioned a miniature superhighway with cars traveling at different speeds. The tiny autos were glued to gray elastic, motorized belts. Beneath the belts were flywheels of varying sizes, so that some lanes moved faster than others. "That's what made it look so real," Dick Darley explains. Perhaps the most-remembered part of the show's spirited intro is a ship with teardrop fins, smoke billowing from its tail, blasting off into space as Dick Tufeld shouts, "Travel into the future with Buzz Corry...." The ship's realistic rocket blast was achieved with a hose hidden under the fuselage, one end lined up with its tail, the other attached to a portable fire extinguisher. "When you wanted it to look like the rockets were blowing out the back," says Darley, "you'd turn on the extinguisher and the CO_2 would come out. We used a special light on it to make it look like a rocket blast." These were sophisticated special effects for the day. They had never been done on television.

McKirgan adds that some pieces used in the model of Terra City, such as a trio of fuel tanks and a domed power plant, inspired components of Marx playsets, which were popular toys at the time. (Newsflash: If you ever get the urge to play Space Patrol, they're still available.[32])

A big problem in the studio was the growing rat population at ABC. Not human rats, though you'd hear stories about those a few years later when management clamped down on the free and easy spirit of creativity that had overrun its soundstages. No, says technical director Bob Trachinger, we're talking *real* rats:

> If you had visited one of those stages then, you'd be astonished at what we did. I'm talking about camera work, because the floors were waffled and splintered, there were holes in the ceiling, and there were mice and rats in the building. The way we approached the

---

[31]McKirgan tracks the evolution of the show's model ships and miniature sets in Appendix 4.

[32]Marx's "Cape Canaveral Space Center," Limited Collector's Edition, still contains several pieces used in their 1952 *Space Patrol* Rocket Port playset.

rodent problem is that somebody brought in a cat who looked very husky and fat. Her name was Jenny and she was our extreme mouser. Then, suddenly, she had nine kittens and we had cats all over the studio.

Which could explain the mystery of the kittens in outer space. According to Darley, the first model spaceship was a tiny, 2½-inch miniature attached to a black nylon string. A crew member drew the ship-on-a-string across a swatch of black velour to show Buzz Corry's battlecruiser streaking through space. Ever dangle a string in front of a kitten? One day, on the air (so the story goes), one of Jenny's offspring, chasing the string, leaped onto the special effects table — and suddenly viewers saw a giant paw knock Corry's ship off course. Another time, Jenny and her kittens scrambled onto the huge set that was the hull of the spaceship and could be seen padding through "outer space." When Jenny died, says Trachinger, the crew dedicated a plaque to her which they placed at the studio's front gate.

If it wasn't cats, it was pigeons or planes. "We had a lot of pigeons up in the rafters and they created sound problems, damn birds," grumbles Darley. Raccoons were up in the eaves too. "We had the world's oldest, fattest raccoon up there," says Maury Orr. "When we were doing live shows and there was an open mike, you could hear him either scratching or procreating."

A worse problem was air traffic, which drowned out both the birds and raccoons. The ABC studios, on the east end of Hollywood at Prospect and Talmadge, were not adequately soundproofed to block out aircraft noise, but fortunately, *Space Patrol* was a noisy show with plenty of aviation sound effects. Still, the sound of a prop plane from Earth's 20th century could be a problem if Buzz and Hap were deep in the Cydonia jungle on Venus, far from a spaceport. But it was all part of live TV — things happened that you couldn't control, as Dick Darley knew all too well:

> We made a recording of the introspective thoughts of a guy who'd been set adrift in space by the villains. The actor was good-looking, but not one of your stellar performers. I needed some emotion from him — he was helpless and going to die unless somebody could get to him in time. I figured if I could get a quiver in his voice, I'd settle for that, so I had him hang from a light tower with his feet off the floor until his arms started to shake. Then I recorded the lines. Well, they were very emotional and I was really proud of myself. In my mind, for that afternoon, I was Irving Thalberg. I figured we had it made.

Airtime. The bad guys dump their victim out in space and make a getaway in their ship with Corry and Hap in hot pursuit. Darley remembers the cam shots as if it were yesterday: Cut to the actor helplessly adrift in space; to the bad guys; to Buzz and Hap racing after them. "I kept going back and forth," he recalls, "building … building…." He'd carefully planned the audio track: Chase music as Buzz and Hap rush after the villains; quiet, stellar music — or silence — for the poor guy marooned in space. Darley moved in closer with each shot of the victim, building tension until finally he had a full head-shot rotating slowly onscreen. Time for the pre-recorded thoughts of this man about to die. He cued the recording. "Well, the audio guy had mixed up two tapes — and suddenly on the air goes the full orchestra and chorus of *The Dinah Shore Show* singing 'See the USA in your Chevrolet.'" Darley fell off his chair, laughing uncontrollably.

By June 1950 — only three months after the show debuted in Los Angeles — Moser was thinking "network." He penned an imaginative half-hour script in which the usual

Dick Darley shows Kemmer how to use a space-age thing-a-ma-jig, then makes sure he gets it right. (Photographs by David Sutton, courtesy Dick Darley)

suspects—the "bad" Tonga, Agent X and Major Sova—plot to steal the Secretary General's locket, which contains the secret element that holds together the man-made planet Terra.[33] The story featured some cool technology, such as the "vacuum locator," a handy gadget that can tell you who's been in a room by analyzing electromagnetic imprints left in the air (a great boon to crimefighters). Moser called the episode "The Secret of Terra," and even gave himself a part as one of the offstage voices manning "Space Control." In late August, special rehearsals were called and the show was kinescoped.[34] The demo was sent to ABC execs in New York, says Dick Darley, "to show the network what we could do."

But on October 2, as ABC was considering *Space Patrol* for its network line-up, *Tom Corbett, Space Cadet,* blasted off on CBS. Mike Moser was furious. Though *Corbett* focused on the adventures of cadets at a Space Academy, he felt that the concept of an interplanetary peacekeeping force had been lifted from *Space Patrol*—right down to the space slang. Somehow, he convinced the network execs at ABC to share his outrage, pointing out that *Corbett* must have been "stolen" from the show being aired by their very own Los Angeles affiliate, KECA. With that brilliant move, says Ed Kemmer, the producer turned a setback into a victory:

> Mike Moser and ABC threatened to sue CBS, so *Space Cadet* switched to ABC, hoping to avoid the suit.[35] The result was that Mike now had ABC in the uncomfortable position of suing itself. At that point, he demanded that *our* show be on the ABC network. We got on without a sponsor, though we picked one up in no time. I don't know how Mike got ABC to join in the original suit, but it was a master move.

---

[33]This script was later rewritten by Jolley and ran as network Episode 47 with the character "Major Sova" replaced by "Major Gruell." Tonga, by this time, had morphed into a "good" character, so she appeared as Major Robertson's trusted assistant security chief.

[34]A kinescope is a film made with a special camera that records a live show from the output seen on a monitor screen. See Chapter 8.

[35]How or why *Corbett* was able to jump over to ABC is unclear—but it happened.

The tables had been turned. Though the cost of his victory was that *Corbett* was now part of ABC's line-up, too, Moser had piggybacked *Space Patrol* in right along with it, forcing the network to give his local show a chance. *Space Patrol* beat *Corbett* to the launch pad by two days, debuting on Saturday, December 30, 1950. It had taken Moser's chutzpah to push his baby into the big time, but as it turned out, ABC couldn't have been happier.

CHAPTER 4

The Right Stuff

Much like the martial arts master who does not need to brag about his skills and exploits, a true hero is often a common man swept up in uncommon — and sometimes surreal — circumstances.

— Jack McKirgan

I wanted to grow up to be just like Commander Corry — cool under fire, brave in the face of danger, inventive when the need arose, caring of others' feelings, hopes and dreams, and willing to stand up for what he believed in.

— Jon Rogers

NEW YORK CITY: JULY 1984

A soft, gray mist cradles Riverside Park across the street from the 654-unit brick co-op apartment complex where Ed and Fran Kemmer live. The park hugs the shore of the Hudson River and the late afternoon sun transforms the water into a glistening sheet of liquid crystal. Though the day is fading, you can still smell fresh-cut grass. Thick, green boughs shadow bicycle paths, and stone arches frame the river. If Commander Corry ever retires, he'd do well to check out this magical strip of Earth in Manhattan called Riverside Drive. From Kemmer's apartment you can see a slice of the river rippling across to the New Jersey shore.

There's plenty of bustle and background noise the first time I visit Kemmer in New York. The console TV opposite his easy chair is tuned to the 1984 Olympics. He later turns it down, but never off— images of athletes in their prime flicker across the screen during the entire interview. From behind closed doors come crashes, clangs and shouts of "Mom!" as Kemmer's wife, actress Fran Sharon, tries to keep their three kids out of the living room where her husband, then 63, is giving yet another interview about a part of his life that no one in this household has shared. Only his seven-year-old daughter Kim — the child he delivered himself — wanders in and out, climbing into his lap where he wraps her in his arms.

Kemmer's voice, deepened by the years, is still melodious but wistful as he delves into *Space Patrol* and the real-life drama of his war experience. At times he slips into "actor" mode, voice rising and falling dramatically from shout to whisper. A fast thinker, he crunches words on his rush to the next thought, sometimes finishing sentences inaudibly under his breath. I decide that interviews with Kemmer should be conducted under the Brainograph so you can retrieve the parts you're missing.

What made his portrayal of Buzz Corry so believable, perhaps, was that he was a real-life war hero. A fighter pilot shot down over German-occupied France during World

War II, he was captured and held prisoner for 11 months. But like *Space Patrol*'s Corry, who (thanks to the writers) could find a way out of any prison, from dungeon to deadly radiation chamber, he risked a daring escape. It's a safe bet that if Kemmer and Corry ever had a drink together, they'd find some common ground.

Model of Kemmer's P-51 Mustang, built by Jack McKirgan II. Kemmer finally received his own plane in 1944, christened it "Damn Yankee"—and was shot down the first time he flew it. The model brought back memories. "When I presented it to him," says McKirgan, "he looked like he wanted to climb into the cockpit." (Courtesy Ed Kemmer)

On this summer evening, trim in jeans, plaid shirt, square western belt buckle (and still-square jaw), Ed Kemmer is reliving the worst day of his life.

June 17, 1944: Earth's Second World War. German artillery knocks Kemmer's P-51 Mustang out of the sky, and he's faced with the kind of life-and-death peril Buzz Corry met weekly. His steel-blue eyes are steady. "I thought I was too low to bail out, but it caught fire and the flames came through, real hot; I had no choice." He leans forward and the lamplight plays with Buzz Corry's trademark curls, now handsome shades of dark and light gray Endurium. "I'd bail out at ten feet, rather than face burning. You just don't burn."

He'd taken off at 8:30 that morning from Maidstone, southeast of London, as part of a dive-bombing mission by the Army Air Corps' 381st Fighter Bomber Squadron, 363rd Fighter Bomber Group, 9th Air Force. There were eighteen P-51s on the flight, twelve with bombs and six as top cover. "P-51 Mustang, World War II fighter," he says tersely, slipping into military mode:

> Fastest long-range, propeller-driven fighter ever built. Most maneuverable — you could go from England to Berlin and back. Göring said — in one of his interviews shortly before he killed himself — that when he saw P-51 fighters over Berlin, that was the turning point of the war.

The squadron headed toward a target area in German-occupied France, four miles south of Saint-Lô, seeking to destroy freight cars and a railroad bridge at Condé-sur-Vire. But the weather report had been wrong — the target area was overcast, making dive-bombing impossible. They went in under the cloud cover, flying at 2000 feet, "looking for something to bomb." But at that level, the planes themselves were easy targets.

As he went down, Kemmer jettisoned his bombs — unarmed. "They might bounce up and get me with the explosion, and I didn't want to hit anyone on the ground. I didn't want them angry, in case I was captured." Then he jumped. The speed of the falling aircraft twisted his parachute and he hit the ground flat on his back, "harder than hell." He takes a deep breath, remembering:

> It just knocked me silly — I felt it in every bone in my body, but I was happy to be alive. The first thing I remember is coming to — I wasn't really "out" but I didn't quite know what was going on. You think of your E and E lectures — Escape and Evade. First thing is, get out of the chute, hide the chute, and get the hell out of there.

Kemmer started struggling out of the parachute. Someone shot him in the leg. "There were Germans all around. I guess they'd been yelling at me — I didn't hear them." No one moved the scenery or cut to a commercial. There was no space-o-phone at hand to radio Hap or Major Robertson for help. Kemmer raised his hands above his head.

Back at home base in England, Lt. Byron Gentry filed this official Mission Summary Report:

> 2nd Lieutenant Edward W. Kemmerer, 0-694166, was hit by flak over Saint-Lô, his engine caught fire, he bailed out at T-3842, 0930 hours.[1] His chute was seen to open at 2,000 feet.[2]

It was his twenty-ninth mission (forty-seventh sortie).

Edward William Kemmerer was born to Aaron, a roofer, and Lillian, a factory worker, on October 29, 1920, in Reading, Pennsylvania. It was Lillian's second marriage. Her first husband had died and she brought two children — June, four, and Lloyd, two — to the union. A year later, Ed was born. Lillian was an orphan who had worked from the age of nine, and Ed remembers peering through a factory window when he was small, watching her make silk stockings. She was a "topper," he says proudly, describing how she'd slip a piece of silk with unerring precision under a bar with protruding needles. "The last holes in that square piece would be right on every needle and every loop. It was amazing." Aaron, too, was a skilled craftsman, specializing in expensive slate roofing that required special tools. But a few years before the Depression hit, construction slowed, jobs slacked off, and many people could no longer afford the best. The family struggled. "We went through some hard times," Kemmer admits. When there were no more roofing jobs, his father found work in a steel plant. "It was rough for everyone, but particularly for the adults," he recalls. "We kids somehow always got enough to eat, but it was hard on our parents — imagine what *they* went through."

Ed Kemmer, 20 months old. "Obviously my mother had a problem cutting my curls," he explains. (Courtesy Ed Kemmer)

He remembers Christmas Eve, 1926, when he was six years old. That night, he and his nine-year-old half-brother, Lloyd, crept to the top of the stairs and looked down on the living room where their parents were putting up the tree. Their mother was crying:

[1]He shortened his name to Kemmer when he was graduated from the Pasadena Playhouse.

[2]From *Fighter Pilots in Aerial Combat* magazine, Issue 9. A further account of this mission appears in *Seven Months over Europe: The 363rd Fighter Group in World War II* by Kent D. Miller: "Captain Dalgish led 18 aircraft of the 381st on a dive-bombing mission from 0825 to 1040. The pilots crossed in at 0916 near Cap Levy and hit targets south of St. Lo and near Condé-sur-Vire. Claims 2-0 locomotives, 2-1 rail cars, and 0-1 bridge, but three pilots were lost: Lt. Edward Kemmerer was hit by ground fire and bailed out near Cerisy-la-Salle (captured), Lt. Virgil T. Johnson was lost in the Tessy area, and T/Sgt. Walter H. Yochim simply disappeared (MIA)." Researched by Jack McKirgan.

They were saying that they just wished they had some money to buy us nicer gifts. And my brother and I sneaked back to bed. We never told them we saw that—we felt so sorry for them. And in the morning we made a big splash about what we did get, believe me! It was small and inexpensive, but we acted like it was the best stuff in the world. It was just a bad year, you know?

Kemmer taught himself guitar, bass and piano, and at 16, while in high school, he was working local clubs at night and earning more than his teachers. Often he slept through class the next day. Still, he got good grades ("I don't remember ever taking a book home") and even made the National Honor Society. But college was not in the cards. "I had friends who went to college who were more fortunate than me," he says matter-of-factly. "Their families had more money and better jobs—they weren't affected by the Depression." Instead he took typing, shorthand and business—commercial courses "to prepare for making a living" as an office worker.

But not yet. After graduation, he worked as a musician. By that time, World War II was raging in Europe, and eligible men were disappearing from the job market, drafted into the service in case the U.S. got involved. He got an announcing job at a local radio station and at night played music in neighborhood bars—one of them a popular hangout for pilots flying out of the Reading airport. He'd always wanted to fly and bugged them for lessons. Soon he was soloing in a two-seater, single engine Piper Cub.

Meanwhile, his half-brother Lloyd, also a musician, had attracted the attention of publishing giant Southern Music, who wanted him to record a catchy new tune called "You Are My Sunshine." Lloyd threw together a trio with Ed on rhythm guitar, himself on bass, and a cheerful, chubby friend of theirs rounding out the vocals. Singing tight three-part harmony, the group (dubbed "The Airport Boys" by Mr. Joy at Southern Music) cut what Kemmer believes was the first recording of "Sunshine," released by Victor Blue-bird Records.[3] When the vocalist left, the Kemmer brothers were joined by jazz guitarist Johnny Smith.[4] Riding on the airplay of "Sunshine," they toured nightclubs, theaters and county fairs, even appearing on the same bill as Count Basie in Boston. Then the Japanese bombed Pearl Harbor and the trio broke up as all three men went into the service, putting Kemmer's musical career on hold.

He enlisted in the Army Air Corps and passed the test for cadet training, but there was a six-month wait to start classes in Texas. Impatient, he hounded his recruiting officer, asking, "When am I gonna get my chance?" The man, aware of Kemmer's work as an announcer, tapped him to do radio spots for the Air Corps while he waited. Later he asked Kemmer to assist with entrance exams in eastern Pennsylvania. Sworn in and in uniform, he visited colleges, testing recruits. When at last the call came, the officer put him in charge of 30 future cadets heading from Pennsylvania to San Antonio. He laughs, remembering. "I was just hoping they'd behave themselves!"

During primary training, his flight experience at the Reading airport kicked in. "I was the first one to solo in my class," he says excitedly, "which was a big deal because when you took lessons in the service as an Air Corps cadet, you'd come in from the flight and immediately pull off your helmet and goggles and carry them—that meant you didn't

[3]Two songs by the Airport Boys exist on tape. "You Are My Sunshine" (by Jimmy Davis and Charles Mitchell) and "Bad Girl" (penned by Kemmer's half brother, Lloyd "Slim" West) are available from American Gramophone and Wireless Co.

[4]Smith shot to fame in 1952 with his hit rendition of "Moonlight in Vermont," which received *Downbeat* magazine's Jazz Record of the Year award.

The Airport Boys, 1941. From left to right: Ed Kemmer, half brother Lloyd "Slim" West, and jazz guitarist Johnny Smith, who later shot to fame with the 1952 hit instrumental "Moonlight in Vermont." (Courtesy Ed Kemmer)

solo. But I was the first one to wear my goggles and helmet into the flight room. And everyone looked…"

But while flying came naturally, physics didn't. "You work like the devil in ground school," Kemmer remembers, noting that some basic physics was required. His buddies came to the rescue, coaching him at night in the only place there was light — the latrine. In primary training, he flew an open cockpit monoplane (PT-19), then the basic training "Bucket of Bolts" (BT-13), and finally an AT-6 (Advanced Trainer) — sometimes used in war movies because it resembled Japanese fighters. Pilot training lasted one year. In February 1944, he was shipped overseas.

SCENE: Commander Corry, Hap and Tonga are speeding 1,000 years back in time to the year 1953 on Earth, on an errand of mercy. Their cargo: Precious blood from 30th-century donors for soldiers wounded in the Korean War. It's a gift to replenish blood banks in the United States, an ancient, freedom-loving culture that some historians believe was the prototype for the United Planets.

But the ship meanders off course, timewise, and instead of touching down on Earth in

1953, it misses the mark and lands behind German lines in the midst of World War II. Leaving the ship, Corry and Hap spot a soldier in Nazi garb. Behind Corry's demeanor, you can sense Kemmer's wariness as he relives a nasty slice of real-life experience.

CORRY: (watching the guard) *He's wearing a Nazi uniform.*
HAP: *Nazi?*
CORRY: *A nation of aggressors who tried to conquer Earth in the 20th century.*
    (Two guards overpower Buzz and Hap and haul them before the German commandant, played with gusto by Bela Kovacs.)
NAZI: *What is your name?*
CORRY: *Buzz Corry.*
NAZI: *What is your rank?*
CORRY: *My rank would mean nothing to you.*
NAZI: (infuriated) *WHAT IS YOUR RANK?* (Grabs Buzz's tunic. Hap moves to protect the Commander but a second Nazi slugs him and drags him away.)
NAZI: *What army are you with?*
CORRY: *I'm not with any army.*
NAZI: (hits Corry in the mouth) *Now, answer me! Your rank, name, unit, serial number!*
CORRY: (puts hand to mouth) *Don't try that again.*
NAZI: *Answer me!*
CORRY: *I'm Buzz Corry, Commander-in-Chief of the Space Patrol. We're from another planet, another time period. We got mixed up in your war quite by accident.*
NAZI: *Why don't you admit you are spies?*
CORRY: *Because we're not!*
NAZI: *Where is your parachute hidden?*
CORRY: *We didn't use parachutes.*
NAZI: (frustrated) *You must have bailed out. There are no landing strips around here.*
CORRY: *We landed by repeller ray...*
NAZI: (furious) *I told you to tell me the truth!* (raises fist)
CORRY: *And I told you not to try that again!* (As the Nazi swings, Corry ducks and gains the advantage, but another Nazi subdues him with a blow to the head.)

—"Errand of Mercy," TV Episode 94, October 11, 1952

The main air officers' camp, Stalag Luft III, near Sagan, Germany, housing 8,000 P.O.W.s, had three compounds: American, British and Russian-French. The American section was full, so Kemmer was placed in the British compound with 3,000 prisoners, all officers. The airmen — pilots, bombardiers, navigators — were guarded by Luftwaffe (German air force) personnel. For that reason, says Kemmer, they were "treated straight," not baited or mistreated. There was a faint sense of brotherhood among these men, guards and prisoners, who shared the bond of being airmen:

> They were doing their job like an American flier or soldier would. The idiotic side would be if the S.S. or the Gestapo got ahold of you — the fanatics. Then logic can go out the window. That was the fear behind everything.

In fact, the Gestapo had seized control of the camp for a brief time earlier that year after the famed "Great Escape" attempt, which took place in the very compound where Kemmer was held.[5] A daring group of men had dug a network of tunnels from their barracks to the woods beyond the barbed wire. On a spring night, a number of P.O.W.s

---

[5]The incident was memorialized in *The Great Escape* (1963), a movie based on the book by Paul Brickhill (1950) with an all-star cast headed up by Steve McQueen.

escaped — but just as they emerged from the underground passageway, snow began to fall. Knowing it would be an easy matter to track their footprints, some turned back, but many men forged on. Kemmer learned of their fate from fellow prisoners:

> When they found out at roll call the next morning that a hundred guys were missing, there's hell to pay. The Gestapo moved right in and tracked down just about every one of them — maybe two or three got away. And half of those that they recaptured, they shot. Just shot. When I arrived, the Luftwaffe had taken over again. They were allowing work parties to go out and build tombstones for those men.

Barring incidents like that, for which the punishment was death, life went on in the camp, but the pressing problem, day-in, day-out, was not enough food. "You dreamt of food, planned food — some guys wrote menus that would cover almost a year, at three meals a day," he says, remembering. "I'll tell you, women came in a very poor second, at that time." His weight dropped from 185 to 133.

To keep busy and forget about hunger, some of the men staged plays, and Kemmer won the role of Hildy Johnson in *The Front Page*. It was his first acting experience. Someday, he thought, he might give it a whirl. He joined the band, playing bass and piano ("It took a lot of time, thank God — you forget how hungry you are") and noted the well-oiled organizational structure of the camp. Besides acting, music, and other food-free pastimes, there was the Escape Committee:

> If you had an idea for escape, you had to figure it all out — I mean every bit of it — and present it to the Escape Committee and get their blessing. If they thought it had a chance of working and that you wouldn't be killing yourself, they'd help. If they said no, you didn't try it.

Once a horse-drawn wagon, loaded with trash, left the camp. The driver paused at the main gate, under a catwalk, while a guard jabbed a steel spike repeatedly into the trash. From a distance, Kemmer watched while the head of the Escape Committee informed him that a man was concealed in the refuse...

> The odds were with him — it was maybe three to one that he wouldn't get hit, but I didn't want that spike jammed into *me*. Someone took a chance that day. I think he got away, because there was no yell ... nothing. The wagon went on.

Kemmer acknowledges that observing this kind of daring fed into the creation of Buzz Corry. "We go back to experience," he explains. "The more you experience life of any kind — wartime if you're going to play an action character — can only add to what you draw on, instead of just imagination."

The "gutsiest escape" he ever witnessed involved a cast of several thousand prisoners, who took a risk for two men:

> It was January, I mean, snow all over the place. The American compound is right next door to ours. You have barbed wire. First, a warning wire, about a foot off the ground. Don't cross it: a guard will shoot you. Then the first barbed wire fence, then tangled barbed wire for about 10 yards, then a second fence — that's what kept you in.

There were goon towers about 30 feet high at intervals, manned with armed guards.

Every morning and evening the men were counted. On this freezing morning, word was passed that when signaled during roll call, they were to start a snowball fight. Kemmer lights another cigarette, body tense:

> Now we knew it was to mask something, so I'm throwing snowballs — we're all throwing like mad — and I'm wondering what's going on. And all the guards in the goon boxes are watching 3,000 men throwing snowballs. It's a sight — you couldn't get it in a movie! Well. Over in the compound next door, two American guys with wire cutters walked right underneath a goon tower — and they kept right on going. Not one guard was looking down there — in broad daylight. That took guts!

Kemmer started thinking about escape.

> *SCENE*: Commander Corry and Cadet Happy approach the mysterious hideaway which is base of operations for Manza, an evil, invisible being who holds Major Robertson and other Space Patrolmen captive.
>
> CORRY: *Hap, as we landed, I got a quick look at Manza's structure. As I remember, it was a square, walled area, with another square wall surrounding that one, and another square wall surrounding that one, and so on. Must be about five or six of them — each one enclosing the other.*
> HAP: *Now I get it! We can use the Space Patrol Periscope to look over each wall as we come to it, and work our way to the center.* (Watches Buzz use the periscope to peer over the first wall.) *Any guards?*
> CORRY: *No... I don't see any. Wait! There's some kind of guard — a robot. Take a look, but be careful.*
> HAP: *Smokin' rockets, Commander! It looks like a tank. It's got a gun turret and everything...What's the matter, sir?*
> CORRY: *That's the only opening, but the robot guard's sitting right in front of it.*
> HAP: *Oh, great. That's all we need. What are we gonna do?*
> CORRY: *We've come this far. No point in turning back now.*
> HAP: *Yeah, but how are we gonna get around that robot?*
> CORRY: *Make a run for it... Right now, that first robot — it'll take a couple of seconds for him to sight in on us. If we're fast enough, maybe... maybe we can take advantage of those few seconds, get past him and through that door before he can shoot at us.*
> HAP: *Uh, just maybe, sir?*
> CORRY: *Just maybe, Hap...*
> —"Space Patrol Periscope," TV Episode 186, September 11, 1954

In January 1945, Russian troops came too close to the prison camp, and the men were marched out in freezing weather, headed for another camp near Nuremberg. "It was a miserable time, cold as hell," Kemmer recalls. "You wore every piece of clothing you owned and built fires to melt whatever food you had, because it was all frozen. Even the guards didn't have food." They arrived at the new camp in late February, and one night, from the outskirts of Nuremberg, watched the sky light up as the British bombed the hell out of the city. "God, what an emotional thing that was," he says softly. A few weeks later, General Patton came too close, and the prisoners were marched out again, this time bound for a camp in Moosburg.

On the march, they slept in barns along the route, with guards at each door. Some guards had dogs. Kemmer and two other men studied the layout, looking for a possible way out. They noticed that some barns had a low animal door about two feet high, secured with wire. Kemmer had a friend with wire cutters.

"Ever since you were captured, you thought of escape," he says, but risking it meant "adding up the pros and cons"—and there were a lot of negatives. For one thing, the war could be over soon. "The Germans were taking a beating and couldn't last much longer. It would have been safer to sit it out until we were freed." Plus, you couldn't take much, if any, food with you—so why risk that extra discomfort? Most important, he cautions, "You had to have a decent plan. Otherwise, you were committing suicide." If you were recaptured, there were worse things than the P.O.W. camp.

> The danger was who got ahold of you—that's the risk. You didn't want the S.S. troopers, you didn't want Gestapo, and you didn't want civilians. They were all baby-killers. When we flew missions into Germany or in occupied [territory], we carried a .45. It was to protect against civilians. A lot of guys were killed with pitchforks.

Still, there were reasons why escape made sense. When he was captured, Kemmer was sure the war would end shortly. Ten months later, he was still a P.O.W.:

> It's hard to describe being a prisoner—the lack of freedom. It's not a flag-waving thing at all; it takes a toll. There's not enough food—it's hunger, hunger, hunger—and the boredom of it. You can't wait to get out—you just can't wait! And you'll take chances to change it.

A man could squeeze through one of those low animal doors in the barns.

He doesn't remember who thought up the plan, but it hinged on a certain set of conditions. If those were right, maybe—just maybe—it might work.

> The barn couldn't be in a bunch of other buildings with a lot of people around. There had to be nice flat ground that you could cross on your hands, knees and elbows and get far enough away where you could get up and run. We were anxious, yeah... You wanted it all to go right, that's for sure.

Though downplaying what courage it might take to escape, Kemmer concedes that any attempt was a risk.

"What would happen if they spotted you crawling out through the door?" I ask.

"They might have fired some shots. They would have yelled to halt."

"And if you didn't?"

"Well, then they would shoot you—but at times, you *must* take those chances. Hopefully, the odds are in your favor. Look," he bursts out suddenly, "I wanted to get the hell out of there! I wanted to *change* it—*do* something!"

SCENE: The Nazi shoves Corry into a windowless room with a dirt floor, where Hap is held prisoner. Corry takes it in.

CORRY: *Any way out of here?*

HAP: *I don't think so, sir. I've looked over every inch of this place. There is one loose stone over here, Commander, but it'd take a lot of digging to get it out—and we don't have anything to dig with.*

CORRY: Maybe we have... Belt buckles! (Rips off his belt)
HAP: Commander, that would take forever...
CORRY: (tersely) Then we'd better get started! (Using the buckles, they chip away earth from
a stone that blocks an opening about two feet high.)

— "Errand of Mercy," TV Episode 94, October 11, 1952

The wire cutters that Kemmer and
two buddies used to escape during the
forced P.O.W. march to Moosburg.
"They're framed above my desk," he
says, "as a reminder that 'things could
be worse.'" (Courtesy Ed Kemmer)

Miraculously, the next night the P.O.W.s were confined in the "right" barn. "It was a gift, a golden opportunity," Kemmer says with emotion. He and two other men — one was the camp interpreter — cut the wire and crawled through the animal door, hugging the ground while the rest of the prisoners broke into song to distract the guards and cover any sounds.

We crawled until we got far enough away, then got up and ran for it. The main thing was, stay out of sight — not above the horizon — and don't get near a dog that could smell you.

The man who gave them the wire cutters did not come with them. "His name was Ike and he looked Jewish," Kemmer recalls. "He knew he'd probably be killed [on the outside]." But Ike pressed something into Kemmer's hand. "He gave me a little box of cubed sugar. It didn't last long, 'cause we had no food with us at all. But it was worth more than its weight in gold." For years, on the anniversary of the Liberation, he and Ike mailed the wire cutters to each other, back and forth.

The three P.O.W.s headed toward Switzerland, but Kemmer, weak, kept falling behind. The terrain was rough and the men had to stay off every path or road to avoid being seen. They traveled at night and holed up during the day. It was April, cold and wet. They dug up seed potatoes for food. But Kemmer was growing weaker by the hour.

I was holding them up. They'd been prisoners for much less time than I, so they were stronger, and though they insisted I keep going, I said, "No, you go on." They could make much better time without me. I'd just had it — I was hurting then, I couldn't go on. I gave them a night's start in case anyone thought to look for other people — if they found me.

He was suddenly alone, roaming the woods, a fugitive P.O.W. He came to an isolated house, and from a distance observed an elderly man, some women, and very young children. At dusk he approached.

SCENE: Commander Corry, Cadet Happy, and Major Robertson have apprehended Arachna, the "Space Spider"—merciless human ruler of a ring-shaped planet, who operates like his insect counterpart by snaring unwary space travelers in a "web" of force rays. But as the Space Patrolmen prepare to take the tyrant's debilitated prisoners back to Terra for medical attention, Arachna escapes, taking with him a neutronium component from the planet's delicate anti-gravity booster.

CORRY: *That neutronium capsule's gone!*
HAP: *Arachna must have taken it with him!*
CORRY: *The power's still on.* (A menacing rumble sounds in the distance.)
HAP: *What's that?*
CORRY: *That's what I mean! There are seven other neutronium deposits still generating gravity, but with that one gone, it'll set up stresses.*
MAJOR ROBERTSON: *That means it's just a matter of time before the gravity booster pulls this planet apart!*
CORRY: *You two get aboard the* Terra V *and blast off. With that one neutronium capsule gone, there'll be a gap in the gravity field—but you can get through it in the* Terra V.
HAP: *But Commander, what about you?*
CORRY: *You've got to get those prisoners to safety. I'll follow in that decoy ship as soon as I find Arachna.*
MAJOR: *But Commander...*
HAP: *Commander, you can't...*
CORRY: *Blast off. That's an order!*
HAP, MAJOR: *Yes, sir!*

(Aboard the *Terra V* a few minutes later...)

HAP: *But Major, we can't just blast off and leave the Commander here!*
MAJOR: *We've got an order, Hap.*
HAP: *Yes, sir.*
MAJOR: (lays hand on Hap's shoulder) *Besides, he knows what he's doing.*
                                    —"Collapse of the Spider's Web," TV Episode 204, January 15, 1955

Kemmer walked out of the woods and approached the German family. They were sympathetic.

By that time, the war was "nicht gut," Hitler was "nicht gut." The year before, they would have said the opposite and kicked you in the face. That was one of the signs peculiar to the Germans: If they were losing, they'd lick your boots; if they were winning, they'd kick you in the head. I told them in broken German: "Prisoner of war. Sick." And I didn't look so good, either. I was so cold—God, I'd been wet for a week. I sat by their kitchen stove and they gave me a piece of bread, which tasted like angel food cake, and some warm milk. And that was heaven—it was truly heaven.

Then a friend of the family appeared, a loyal member of the People's Army, sporting an armband and a sidearm.

He was kind enough, but he made it plain he had a duty to turn me over to a military outfit nearby. I tried to argue and he started to reach for his gun, to force me ... so, of course, I went.

("Some things you don't discuss," says Virginia Hewitt, "and Buzz would not talk about the P.O.W. experience, at least to me, and I don't think to the rest of the cast. Especially then — it was still too close. But I knew he had not been treated ... beautifully." Asked if she thought there was some quality in Kemmer akin to the heroic Buzz Corry, Hewitt answered, "Yes. He was stoic enough to want to escape. I think he must have been a very brave man.")

It was early in the morning when Kemmer was turned over to a Luftwaffe group. The sergeant who received him into custody ordered him to sweep up the office. "When I didn't leap to attention," says Kemmer, "he pushed me around. I was in pretty bad shape and I wanted to just sit down, but he shoved that broom at me and he *meant* it. So I started to sweep."

Suddenly a voice said, "You look like you shouldn't be doing anything." It was a German colonel — a former judge who'd been educated in England, spoke perfect English and was aware that the Germans were on the verge of defeat. "He was marvelous," Kemmer says, his body seeming to relax as he remembers. "And there was food!" Big German women fed him in the warm mess hall, and he stuffed as much bread as he could into his shirt, just in case.

Though an Allied victory would most certainly be declared within days, the colonel, concerned for Kemmer's safety, sent him back to Moosburg to rejoin the P.O.W.s he was with when he escaped. "You're safer there than you are as a lonely prisoner here," he told him. "If retreating S.S. troops come through here, my rank won't protect you." An old man with a rifle was assigned to take him back to Moosburg. They hitched a ride on a truck carrying wounded German soldiers. Kemmer prayed his guard would not divulge his identity because "I could pass as a French laborer." They reached Moosburg without incident. On April 29, Patton's tanks came through, heralding liberation.

Silence. Kemmer hands himself another cigarette.

When he seems ready to go on, I ask to what extent the war experience shaped the heroic make-up of Buzz Corry, daring galactic hero of the 30th century — an almost perfect commander-in-chief.

> I think it all helped — any experience of life and death, of fear, of physical manipulation: doing what you have to do to accomplish something you think maybe you can't. As an actor, you draw on everything. The more you've done, the better.

"Anything else?"

> The sense memory of real fear. One time they threatened to shoot me in the morning. We'd had lectures saying, "If you get shot down and captured, they'll threaten, but don't worry, they *probably* won't." It was a way of getting you to talk. I didn't know anything that could help them; they knew more than I did.

There was some quality, I tell him, that seemed to spill over from real experience — some magic, some depth in the character of Corry that fulfilled the heroic fantasies of the nation, contributing to the enormous popularity of the show.

Well, I like to think that it came off well, that you're right. I suppose there was an experience there that a lot of young guys didn't have — true. If I brought something to it, I'm happy with that... I'm happy with that. I don't know how some other actor would have done — as well, or worse, or better...

Kemmer sighs. "It's a moot thing. I'm the one who did it."

CHAPTER 5

Stardrive: Going Network

"Even the insignias on their uniforms — the lightning bolt on Corry, Hap's wings and Robbie's exploding star — were just perfect. They communicated that this person is magnetic and charismatic, this person is light-hearted and ethereal, this person is as stable as the sun. As a kid, it hit me that these were powerful elements — the forces of sun, air and electricity. And the characters all seemed to pretty much live up to them."

— Mike Guarino

"We knew the show was doing well because Mike Moser kept taking us out to dinner at better and better places."

— Truck Krone

You could cut the tension on the ABC soundstage with an atomo-torch as announcer Dick Tufeld's thrilling call "*Spaaaaaace Patrol!*" bent the air waves, followed by the urgent summons to "travel into the future with Buzz Corry, Commander-in-Chief of the Space Patrol!"

Director Dick Darley: "Everything was happening fast, the equipment was whirling around…. You just had to ignore all that and be where you were supposed to be and talk when you were supposed to talk."

But even if you were where you were supposed to be, maybe the camera wasn't. "Cameras can get tied up where they can't make it to the scene; they run over cable and someone has to rush over and get the pedestal off the cable, so they get there late," says Ed Kemmer:

So instead of making the cross you're supposed to make to the camera that isn't there, you don't *go* there. You have to be aware if a boom gets tied up — you can't look up at it, but you're aware of it. If it hasn't gotten to you yet, you hold your line. The same with the sets — you can see them start to go. If it's a rock, you let it fall, but if it's a wall, you go over and lean against it. If a key light goes out, you get to a lighted part of the set; otherwise, no one can see you.

It took fast footwork to compensate for blown bulbs and absentee cameras. To the men, says Kemmer, it became second nature. "Hap could do it, Robbie could do it. Carol and Tonga didn't seem to be quite that logical about it." ("Really?" says Virginia Hewitt, when told how Kemmer, Osborn and Mayer made split-second blocking changes and shored up teetering scenery. "I was never aware of any of that.")

But the hyperalertness generated by tackling missions of daring on the set as well as in the name of interplanetary justice imbued the show with an eerie reality that glows off the kinescopes fifty years later. "You won't get the same thing in a filmed show," says

Kemmer and Osborn, guided by a starchart, plot some fancy navigation. (Courtesy *Filmfax* magazine)

Kemmer. "Energy can come from total fear, but, boy, is it energy! I mean, the adrenaline's going. In the early shows, I'm sure I come off as knowing what I'm doing, but underneath I was sweating like mad, wondering what I was going to say next."

"Part of why *Space Patrol* had what it had was because it was live," says Darley. "If it had been pre-taped and canned and cleaned up and made perfect, it would have been different. You were wrung out at the end of it. If everything came off well, I had a euphoric situation."

You can bet your Jupiter emeralds that when 30,000 fans showed up at the May Company department store in downtown Los Angeles on June 26, 1951, to catch a glimpse of the *Space Patrol* cast at a personal appearance, some ABC execs in New York yelled "Smokin' rockets!" Moser's half-hour demo, "Secret of Terra," had convinced them to add the show to the network's lineup at the end of December 1950. By the following May, Ralston Purina had signed on to sponsor, and plans were already in the works to feature Buzz Corry and Cadet Happy on boxes of Wheat Chex and Rice Chex.[1] Now, only six months after launching the series nationwide, ABC had a mega-hit on its hands.

As traffic screeched to a halt in front of the May Company, police rushed to the scene, relieving store employees and Boy Scouts who'd been desperately trying to keep order. Three city blocks were cordoned off for five hours as Space Patrollers—both kids and adults—stormed the store. Eventually the cops got things under control, and an orderly line snaked down from the second floor, spilling onto the street and around the block. Virginia Hewitt remembers that day:

> We all piled into one car—I think for comfort and courage more than anything else—and when we got there, we saw this huge crowd that wrapped around the block as far as the eye could see. Later, when we stood for so long, autographing, we were exhausted but also relieved. That morning we'd thought, "This will be a fiasco. Who dreamed this up?"

As the show soared, the magic deepened. Because the cast had merged so thoroughly with their characters, they handled last-minute script changes and blocking with an ease that astounded the ABC crew. "Those five kids were incredible. They could do things that people today who are paid the big bucks can't do," says audio operator Chuck Lewis:

> You could give them new dialogue, change it, move where they had to be on a certain spot or under a certain light, and with everything they had to worry about—and they had more than anyone else to worry about—they were there. That doesn't happen today. That's why there's tape.

Not so guest actors. All too often, they buckled under the pressure of the fast-paced, live show, blowing lines, going blank or skipping scenes entirely. "You could see that curtain—it's actually like a curtain—come down in front of them," recalls Ed Kemmer:

> I'd look at their faces and know they couldn't tell me their own names; I mean, they didn't know what to say next if their lives depended on it. Often the whole scene had to be finished by Hap and me because they were "gone"—totally gone—or had jumped to another scene, three scenes later. You had to jump right in on top of them and bring them back. It happened many, many times.

The regulars got used to covering. It meant learning not only their own lines, but everyone else's. When an actor faltered, "you'd pick up their dialogue and give them part of their speech," says Kemmer:

---

[1]Ralston Purina began sponsoring the network show with Episode 22, "Dangerous Intrigue," Saturday, May 26, 1951. Nestlé (the second sponsor) didn't come aboard until January 16, 1954, Episode 160, "The Pirate's Escape."

Hap hands Corry a supply of oxygen as he prepares for a dangerous mission on the other side of the set panel. (Courtesy Bob Burns)

And you'd better know what they're going to say because the show can't stop. Put it in the form of a question if they're supposed to tell you something: "Well, how far away from Mars could we be — about 20 million DU's?" They'd generally pick it up: "Yeah, that's right! Just about 20 million."

But one time the lead heavy went totally blank and didn't recover. "We had to ad lib twenty-six minutes," says Ken Mayer, "so we made him into a telepathist." Another time, Mayer was powerless to bail out a panicked actor:

I'd done the play *What Price Glory?* with this guy and I'd noticed that when he had trouble with his lines, he'd bust out in perspiration — you'd see little beads of sweat begin to form. Well, I got him a job on *Space Patrol*, and we're doing this scene where I'm under the influence of the Z-ray, so I can't say anything. And he's speaking to me when all of a sudden, I see these little beads of perspiration start to come out. As I "pass out" from the Z-ray, I'm thinking, "I can't help you now, you son of a gun" — and away I go.

The cast stood by again and again as shaken actors stalked off the set. Kemmer mimics a typical exit line: "'I will never, ever, in my *life* — EVER — do another live TV show. This is my first and last!' They were sweating blood and meaning it."

Some guest actors, notably Lee Van Cleef, Marvin Miller and Gene Barry, went on to big careers. "It was interesting, seeing them move on," says Dick Darley. "Occasionally, a peripheral character would let you know he had other jobs that were more important. But years later, they were proud to say they'd been on *Space Patrol*."

By the fall of 1952, the network TV show was drawing a weekly audience of 7 million, according to *Life* magazine; by year's end, some estimates were as high as 10 million.[2] The radio show was booming too — 3.5 million fans tuned in to the weekly broadcast over 344 ABC affiliates.[3] Suddenly the country seemed seized with the burning need to dream about space travel, thanks to TV space operas, realistic SF movies such as *Destination Moon*, and radio dramas for grownups such as *X Minus One*. At times, in the naïve clime of the early '50s, a space-age society seemed just around the corner — and *Space Patrol* made it look so easy. No worries about weightlessness, waste disposal or defective o-rings — you just jumped in your ship, which propelled you in comfort to exotic places and fantastic adventures. Buzz, Hap, Robbie, Carol and Tonga put a human face on the future. They were role models for the coming space age where brave people would challenge the unknown and battle new forms of evil never seen on Earth. These 30th-century comrades did all that, yet they were still normal people — so human, yet so extraordinary. They were people you felt you knew, and people you never would know.

Television reviewer Hal Humphrey credited writer Norman Jolley's blend of "high tension science fiction and plain old cops-and-robbers action" for *Space Patrol's* success among all age groups and noted that the show was drawing an enthusiastic — if slightly embarrassed — adult following. He cited a recent guest appearance by "the Hedy Lamarrish-looking Nina Bara" as the Mystery Voice on a radio quiz show. A male contestant of "mature age" immediately identified her as Tonga from *Space Patrol*. The emcee asked how he'd recognized Bara's voice so quickly. "Because it's my kid's favorite show," the man explained. "And how old is your child?" the emcee asked. "Six weeks," the contestant replied.[4]

As the transcontinental cable, completed in August 1951, and a growing network of microwave towers brought the weekly show to thousands of new viewers, the press tuned in, too. *Life* magazine ran a three-page spread featuring a large photo of Kemmer in a

[2]*Life* magazine, September 1, 1952, reported a viewership of 7 million, but Howard McClay's column in the *Los Angeles Daily News*, December 24, 1952, lists an audience "in excess of ten million."

[3]Radio stats from an ABC promotional flyer. A week after the debut of the network TV show on December 30, 1950, the twice-weekly radio show went on a seven-month hiatus, according to *On the Air: The Encyclopedia of Old-Time Radio* by John Dunning (New York: Oxford University Press, 1998). When it returned in August 1951, it aired once a week until March 1955.

[4]*Los Angeles Mirror*, March 17, 1952.

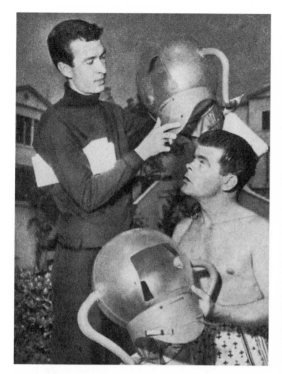

"Poolside Patrol," *TV Star Parade*, October 1953. *Left:* Dick Darley shows Lyn Osborn space-age swim gear. *Right:* Ed Kemmer keeps Virginia Hewitt safe from Venusian crocodiles.

bubble helmet (a customized version of the Outer Space Plastic Helmet, which had debuted as a toy for kids that spring) and the cast became fodder for TV and film magazines, proving they were as popular with adults as with kids.[5] In the 'zines, they rubbed shoulders with huge stars of the day—Elizabeth Taylor, Alan Ladd, Robert Mitchum, Irene Dunne—and these stories weren't written for the "juves." Out of the kiddies' earshot, the implied romance between Buzz and Carol and the less obvious one between Robbie and Tonga were played up. *TV Star Parade* featured a two-page spread of the cast cavorting in swimsuits, while a staged photo in *Tele-Views* showed Kemmer and Hewitt locked in a passionate embrace with the caption "Here's a picture you'll never see on *Space Patrol*."[6] *Look* magazine spotlighted cast members several times in its "Photocrime" spread, where popular celebs of the day posed as characters in a fictional crime drama depicted in photos. In the first, which appeared in October 1950, Kemmer is "photographer Bill Bentley," torn between his current girlfriend, "fencer Linda Loring" (Nina Bara), and his new squeeze, "ballet dancer Maureen LaBouvie" (Virginia Hewitt). Needless to say, though Bara threatens Kemmer, he ends up in Hewitt's arms.[7] While Cadet Happy was jokingly odd man out in stories that dealt with the romances on the show, in real life

[5]*Life*, September 1, 1952—the issue with Ernest Hemingway on the cover that contained the complete text of his new book, *The Old Man and the Sea*.

[6]*TV Star Parade*, October 1953; *Tele-Views*, November 1950.

[7]*Look* magazine. Virginia Hewitt's copy is hand-dated October 10, 1950—before the first network TV show aired on December 30th. If this date is correct, then this issue featured the cast because of the popularity of the network radio show. *Look* did two more "Photocrime" picture essays with the cast in the January 2, 1951, and December 2, 1952, issues.

The cast on the cover of *TV-Radio Life*, January 18, 1952. From lower left, clockwise: Ed Kemmer (Commander Buzz Corry), Nina Bara (Tonga), Ken Mayer (Major Robertson), Virginia Hewitt (Carol Carlisle) and Lyn Osborn (Cadet Happy). (Author's collection)

he had the last laugh. Gossip columnists reported that Osborn and Hewitt were hitting hot nightspots such as Ciro's together, and photographers snapped enough shots of him with his arm around her to confirm that they were indeed an item.

Lyn loved the nightlife but was chastened when Mike Moser saw one too many press photos of the cadet with a drink and a cigarette. The producer warned him to cut it out or his pay would be docked. Osborn obeyed. From then on, says his sister, Beth Flood, Lyn was careful about his public image. "He'd order a drink with orange juice or soda. He didn't want the kids to see him drinking liquor." And he didn't want to jeopardize his job. "We had a morals clause in our contracts," says Jack Narz. "If you were seen drunk in a public place, you could be fired. You didn't get by with the things that people do today." But as wild and fun-loving as Osborn could be, he took the role of Hap seriously and assured friends and reporters that he wouldn't do anything to disillusion the kids who had made him their hero. When he noticed that the children who waited at the studio gate each day to catch a glimpse of the cast were crestfallen when he drove up in a 20th-century automobile, he parked around the corner and walked to the lot, explaining that his "rocket car" was in the garage for an oil change.[8]

But while adults on Earth might fantasize about the romantic relationships among the characters, life was platonic as ever on the man-made planet Terra, observed *Los Angeles Mirror* columnist Hal Humphrey:

> Although a couple of comely dolls by the name of Tonga and Carol are very much in evidence, adult followers of *Space Patrol* have to assume that they have learned to control some of their most basic urges to the point of com-

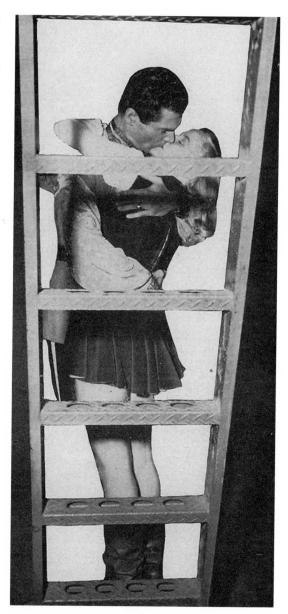

"Here's a picture you'll never see on *Space Patrol*," read the caption to this photograph that ran in *Tele-Views*, November 1950, in which Carol literally sweeps Buzz off his feet. Since there were no kisses, births or deaths on the man-made planet Terra, home of Space Patrol Headquarters, this was as close as viewers ever got to seeing Corry and Carol steal a kiss. (Author's collection)

[8]Bill Kennedy's column, *Los Angeles Herald Express*, June 17, 1952.

Captain Jack Narz gives the Space Patrol salute. (Courtesy Jack Narz)

plete abstinence. Both gals wear 30th century tunics which strike their legs at finger-tip length. These uniforms, coupled with occasional subtle glances at Commander Corry, are as far as anyone goes in suggesting that life on Terra is anything but platonic.[9]

The fact that there were no births, no deaths and no kisses on Terra delighted the National Parents and Teachers Association (PTA), which gave the show its stamp of approval and "Best Live Video Show for Children" award in 1950 and 1951.[10] Even so, magazines demanded fluffy features and self-help tips from the *Space Patrol* cast about dating and other problems that didn't seem to exist in the lives of the characters they played. Hewitt and Osborn obliged. She wrote "So You Want to Be Sexy!" and he penned "Don't Be a Problem Pal."[11] Both actors did, in fact, have writing aspirations. Hewitt had already had one article published before she auditioned for *Space Patrol*, and Osborn's papers, saved by his mother after his death, revealed several short stories and poems. When Kemmer, whose drop-dead good looks did not go unnoticed by the 'zines, was asked by *TV Time* magazine what Buzz Corry's ideal "Girl of Tomorrow" would look like, he offered this:

> She'll wear less clothes and shorter dresses because the climate will be controllable, making bundlesome clothes unnecessary. She will probably wear short boots too, as she will be flying spaceships on a moment's notice.... With good climate, diet and improved living conditions, she might easily have the special beauties of all our beauty queens.[12]

"I said *that*?" he exclaims fifty years later. "What nonsense!"
So how would he answer the question today?
"Like this," he says quickly:

> She'd have a sense of humor and a sense of self. She'd be compassionate, generous, fun-loving, politically aware — and she certainly would *not* have to be a beauty queen! As for clothes, whatever's comfortable and, hopefully, attractive. And boots? For riding horses, maybe, but for flying spaceships... *why*?

The fact that many grownups were fans of the cast did not escape a few sharp juves. "I'd appreciate it if you'd send an autographed photo of yourself for my scrapbook," a young boy named Bob wrote to Virginia Hewitt. "Confidentially, I think my dad will like the photo, too, because he seems to watch *Space Patrol* quite often." That the show was

[9]*Los Angeles Mirror*, March 17, 1952.
[10]*Los Angeles Herald Express*, April 8, 1952.
[11]"So You Want to Be Sexy!" by Virginia Hewitt, *TV People*, June 1954. "Don't Be a Problem Pal," by Lyn Osborn, *TV Fan*, June 1954.
[12]*TV Time* magazine, February 1953.

Ed Kemmer (in dress uniform) and Virginia Hewitt sign autographs — free — for young fans. (Courtesy Beth Flood)

attracting all age groups defeated a theory Kemmer and Osborn had developed early on. "We've found that the real young girls first are attracted to Cadet Happy, but as they grow older, their allegiance switches to the character of Commander Corry," Kemmer told a columnist in one of his first interviews. But in 1953, Lyn confided to *The Hollywood Reporter* that 90 percent of his fan mail came from adults.[13]

Suddenly it seemed as if everyone in the universe wanted to meet the cast, who appeared on telethons and toured schools, supermarkets, department stores, air shows, county fairs, taffy pulls and community sings. Weekends were frantic. For two years, the network show was shot at 8:00 on Saturday morning. "We'd finish at 8:30 and be on our

[13]*The Hollywood Reporter*, February 12, 1953.

way to pick up a 9:15 plane for a telethon in New York," recalls Ken Mayer. Lyn Osborn did more telethons than anyone else — a total of 40 during the show's five-year run. It was these junkets around the country that alerted the ABC crew back home to the show's phenomenal impact. "You could get a feeling that we were doing well from the mail and the ratings," says Dick Darley, "but it was when the cast came back and reported how many people showed up at a personal appearance that the reality of the show's success sank in."

When cast members appeared at a TV telethon — usually for cerebral palsy or muscular dystrophy — they worked sheer magic. Inspired by their *Space Patrol* heroes, brigades of kids trudged door-to-door, collecting coffee cans full of cash. Jordan Cohen was one of those kids. Sure, he cared about less fortunate children with cerebral palsy, but to him and his friends there was something more:

> Another reason for our dedication was that Ed Kemmer gave us a character we could identify with and idolize. The *Space Patrol* cast once came to Pittsburgh for a telethon appearance and I forced my dad to take me down there so I could donate $2.00 and shake Commander Corry's hand. I got to do that, and I wasn't the same.

At a telethon sponsored by the City of Hope, the *Space Patrol* cast was credited with raising one-third of the $150,000 donated. These off hours spent fund-raising did not go unnoticed by *Los Angeles Examiner* columnist Jack Lait, Jr.:

> Ed Kemmer of the *Space Patrol* crew helped raise $365,000 for cerebral palsy at a Philadelphia telethon last weekend, and tomorrow Lyn Osborn hosts 50 hospitalized children from the charity ward of Glendale Community Hospital at the Moulin Rouge. These Space Patrollers are so active in charitable work, you wonder where they find time to save the universe every week.[14]

Wherever the cast appeared, they created a frenzy — except once, when Kemmer flew to Philadelphia for a solo appearance at Wanamaker's Department Store. The event had been planned for a school holiday, but only a few dozen kids straggled in. "We were always greeted by crowds," says Kemmer, who knew right away that something was wrong:

> After some frantic investigation, the person in charge found out that the "holiday" they'd counted on wasn't important enough to close the schools, so the kids who did show up were playing hooky! I pretended to chide them but said they could make up for it by working extra hard the next school week. That brought groans. Then — with the organizers standing nearby — I said in a loud stage whisper that the real blame for their playing hooky belonged to the grownups who'd chosen the wrong date. That brought sounds of total agreement. The sponsor group went along with it and overreacted with great shame.

As the show raced into stardrive, thousands of letters poured in from the juves demanding photos of the cast, suggesting ways to handle the villains, and presenting top-secret plans for Venusian spaceships, rocket disintegrators and various contraptions their heroes might need. In the summer of 1951, *Daily News* columnist Paul Price was chatting with Virginia Hewitt about fandom when she pulled the day's mail out of her

---

[14]"Stop-Look-Listen," *Los Angeles Examiner*, December 4, 1954.

Lyn Osborn (right) cracks Ken Mayer up at a personal appearance (probaby a telethon). (Courtesy Beth Flood)

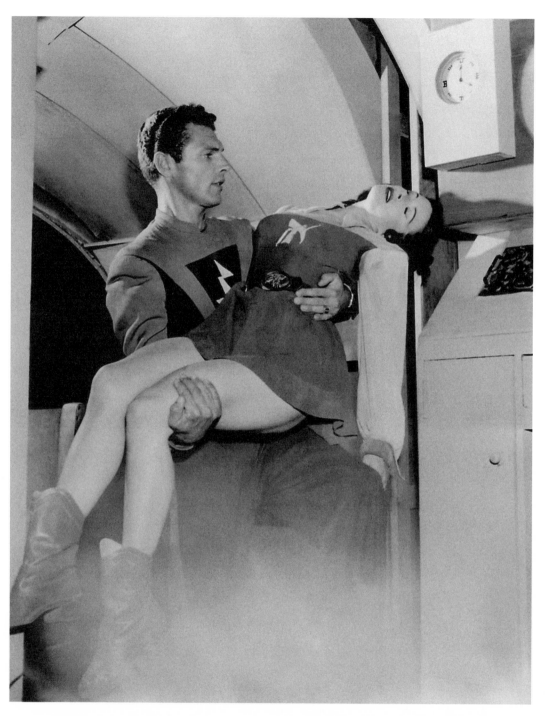

Buzz carries Tonga to safety as poison gas engulfs them both. (Courtesy Bob Burns)

purse. A boy named Harleigh had sent a chart of an atomic rocket propulsion max-hetrometric propeller powered by a gravity generator.

But didn't young male fans like Harleigh want her photo? Price wondered.

"They ask for pictures, but mostly they *send* me pictures," Hewitt replied, "like plans for a new version of a spaceship to be launched from a man-made planet somewhere between Earth and the moon. And they like to discuss atomic rocket propulsion and get my opinion on all kinds of technical points."

What points?

"Oh, they like to know what I think of the feasibility of establishment of an outer-space satellite for the de-oxygenation of atmosphere on warring planets by a cathode tube. Stuff like that."[15]

You can't blame the kids. After all, Hewitt's character, Carol, had been known to whip up an atom bomb in less than an hour, and in "Test Flight of the Galaxy" (Episode 51) she designs a magnetically powered, spherical interstellar spaceship. (She's kidnapped and the ship is stolen.)

It seemed, at times, as if the line between fantasy and reality blurred as the *Space Patrol* cast became symbols for the space age just over the horizon. In 1953, when Los Angeles officials decided to bury a 225-pound steel time capsule under 20 tons of concrete for the *real* inhabitants of the 30th century to open a thousand years later, they called on the stars of *Space Patrol* to be present. "The imagination of children and adults alike has been captured by the program's make-believe but realistic glimpses into the future," the *Los Angeles Times* explained.[16]

Doug Moore can vouch for that. "*Space Patrol* instilled in me the feeling that the future held great promise of marvels to come," he recalls. Moore, chief engineer for a consumer electronics manufacturer and holder of 14 U.S. patents, still can't forget the time the cast visited his local community center in Los Angeles:

> There were probably 100 of us crammed into the building that night, waiting for the appearance of the Space Patrol crew. After what seemed like a long wait, Commander Corry burst through the back door, followed by Happy, Carol, Tonga and Major Robertson. All of them ran up the aisle and leaped onto the stage. Major Robertson appeared to not quite make it and landed face down. He then feigned disgust at his inept entrance. The whole thing was planned, of course.
>
> As Buzz introduced the other members of the crew, a side door opened and Prince Baccarratti entered. He backed the Space Patrol crew up against a wall and took over the microphone. He told us he was taking over our school and we were going to have to stay for 12 hours every day, including weekends—the whole year. Of course, the Space Patrol crew said that this was the most sinister and diabolical plot he'd ever come up with. Some of us in the audience started to boo the villain and, as if on cue, Major Robertson used this distraction to disarm him. As he was being marched off, Buzz told us, "That was a close call, space cadets. Now you won't have to go to school for 12 hours every day, but you will still need to go to school the usual hours on Monday."

"It was hokey, but I still vividly remember it after 50 years," says Moore, who adds that Buzz Corry is still one of his heroes. He's trying to work up the courage to write to Ed Kemmer, but "it's not as easy as I thought. I feel like I'm writing to God."

Rehearsals were never dull, says audio man Chuck Lewis, thanks to Lyn Osborn, "who was always doing something crazy." Osborn's sense of fun was contagious. Lewis recalls that "the cast was always breaking each other up, needling each other, but in a loving way." Egged on by Cadet Happy, "they'd do things backwards to screw up Dar-

[15]Los Angeles *Daily News*, August 14, 1951.
[16]*Los Angeles Times*, April 8, 1952, page A-10.

General Nardo (Carleton Young), leader of the Icarians, joins forces with Corry to battle Manza, a ruthless silicon being determined to rule the univese. (Courtesy Joe Sarno)

ley," says Jack Narz. Lyn's antics, notes announcer Dick Tufeld, "were such a contrast to Ed Kemmer, who was always a true gentleman, reserved and very polite. Lyn was the diametric opposite." And the cadet, adds Tufeld, had "the most endearing way" with off-color material:

> He had this lewd side. At rehearsal one day he brought in something he'd gotten at some burlesque house. It was a piece of paper with some illegible, black scribbling on it. But if you put lemon juice on it and held it over a flame, an obscene photograph came into focus. He loved that kind of subject matter — but what was better than his material was the enthusiasm and joy he got from delivering it.

Osborn was irrepressible and didn't know when to quit. "He could make a joke that might be very funny, but it could throw someone off," says Kemmer. "He'd do it just for the laugh, but oh, God, in the meantime, people are dying." Kemmer remembers how Lyn would mess with critical sound effects:

> We had this sound man — jolly, marvelous guy — but Hap would make him look bad. In a fight scene, you swing and, of course, you miss. As the other guy throws his head back, the sound man does THIS with a piece of leather [*Kemmer smacks fist into palm*]. He times it. Well, Hap would time his moves so that the sound would happen *before* or *after* he threw his punch, and the sound man would say, "You son of a bitch," because he needs

Osborn (center) hosts a dinner party but serves up 30th-century food pills instead of real cuisine. Not too happy, from left, are Ken Mayer, Virginia Hewitt and Ed Kemmer, whose then-wife Elaine Edwards (seated) doesn't seem to mind. (Author's collection)

a rehearsal as much as we do. Or we'd be in a hollow tunnel where you were supposed to hear sound reverberating and Hap would do a little dance and not put his foot down — but you'd hear the sound.

"Lyn was like an accident waiting to happen, the smart-aleck of all time," says Dick Darley, "and I really had a problem because it was his magic that kept a lot of the humanness in the show. I didn't want to drown that. On the other hand, I had to get the show on."

Kemmer and Hewitt discuss plans for a new lunar fleet base at Osborn's party. (Author's collection)

When cast and crew had had enough, they conspired to turn the tables on the cadet. Once Dick Tufeld, wearing a scary Frankenstein mask, burst out of a mummy case that Hap had to open. Another time, the cast broke for lunch, pretending to forget Cadet Happy adrift in a spacesuit, dangling by piano wire from the rafters. And one time, Dick Darley, with the aid of the piqued sound man, *really* got even. "We were rehearsing an episode where they'd found some artifacts from the 20th century — old-time Earth weapons, pistols. So Hap is screwing around, sticking a gun in his mouth, his ear, horsing around." Darley told the sound man: "I've got to settle him down. Next time he points it anywhere near his head, fire off a gun."

Ed Kemmer was watching. "He's doing a dumb thing, looking down the barrel. And the sound man sneaks up and fires a shot right close behind him. Well! Hap was really flipped on that one."

"The kid was scared to death," says Darley. "It straightened him out for the rest of the day. Those were the kinds of things you had to do. I'd argue with him. He was strong in his way, I was strong in mine. Later on, as he developed discipline, he was able to appreciate the need for it and still keep that marvelous character he had going. We worked it out."

Ed Kemmer got even with Lyn *off* the set. There was a party one night at Kemmer's home. In his off-hours, the Commander had been boning up on hypnosis, so he hypnotized four or five people, having fun with post-hypnotic suggestion, "simple, harmless things. I hypnotized Hap, but he never believed he was under." Everyone went home at 2:00 A.M. Kemmer sat up waiting:

> Well, about an hour later, he pulls into the driveway. I open the door. He says, "You son of a gun," goes into my den, opens my desk drawer, pulls out a deck of cards, gets out the ace and says, "There, damn it!" — and goes home. I'd suggested he'd have to come back, do all that, and *then* he could go home and sleep. That's the biggest trick I ever played on him, and he never forgot it.

By the spring of 1953, the network show had hit warp speed. Then, late Thursday evening, April 23, *Space Patrol's* creator, Mike Moser, and his secretary were struck by a car and killed as they stepped into what the *Los Angeles Times* called a "very dark" intersection in West Hollywood at La Cienega Boulevard and Horner Street. Suddenly, the driving force behind the show was gone. Whatever you thought of Moser, his death was a shock, plunging cast and crew into uncertainty.

Moser made enemies both before and after his death, and as the news spread, there was more shock than grief among those who knew him. There are four versions of what happened that night: Mike and his pretty, dark-haired assistant were working late and the accident occurred as they left the office; they were leaving Tail o' the Cock (a restaurant) in West Hollywood; they had just left a motel ("at least they were *leaving*," cracked one crew member); or the official version that ABC gave to the *Los Angeles Times*: The two had just left a meeting of the United Cerebral Palsy Association, of which Moser was honorary chairman.[17]

Moser was hurled 66 feet by the impact, but the 47-year-old studio grip who was driving the car that slammed into the couple was not held. Mike was a lush, says an ABC staffer, which is probably why he never saw it coming. Dick Darley says it was either

[17]"TV Pair's Death Witnesses Sought," *Los Angeles Times*, April 25, 1953.

Kemmer or Osborn who called him at 3:00 A.M. with the news that Mike was dead. "Who killed him?" was Darley's first response. Though he respected Moser for conceiving *Space Patrol* and getting it on the air, he knew the producer had made more promises than he'd kept along the way. Darley's son, Chris, eight years old at the time, recalls the commotion when the call came in. "I remember this hustling and bustling as my parents got up. Then Dad dashed out of the house."

For a while, says Jack Narz, "everyone thought, 'Mike's gone. What will happen now?'"

What happened, says writer Norm Jolley, is that for the next two years, the show ran itself. Mike's widow, Helen, took over the accounting, but she'd been doing the payroll anyway, before his death. Then, inexplicably, Mike Devery, a tall, good-looking man who'd been in charge of *Space Patrol* merchandising, became producer. That no one remembers why Devery was chosen points up how little the cast and crew concerned themselves with the business end of the show. While Devery had been pleasant enough before he took charge, a little power made him much less so. "He wasn't really showbiz," recalls Dick Darley. "He started laying down the law and everyone rebelled. We felt, 'If we're going to keep this afloat, we'll keep doing it the way we've been doing it.'" Everyone ignored Devery and by the end of May, Helen Moser came to her senses and appointed Darley producer.

On Wednesday, April 28, 1953, only six days after Mike Moser's death, the *Space Patrol* cast took part in what was billed as a groundbreaking experiment that would take television to the next astounding level: 3-D broadcasting. Cameron Pierce, Glen Akins, Bob Springer and Alex Quiroga, ABC engineers, had led the way in developing this startling technology, which was touted as the wave of the future. Soon, news stories promised, viewers could don a special pair of Polaroid glasses at home to watch the many shows that would be broadcast in lifelike 3-D. The first demonstration of this revolutionary process that was about to change TV forever would take place for industry insiders and reporters who had gathered at the Biltmore Hotel in downtown L.A.—and what better way to showcase the new technology than with a segment of the futuristic *Space Patrol*? A five-minute episode, shot with cameras equipped with a special adapter that broke images into three-dimensional phases, would be broadcast live over ABC affiliate KECA. One problem: You needed a special TV receiver to translate the signal into a 3-D format and a pair of "Polaroid light glasses" to view it. At the moment, the only people who had those things were the group at the Biltmore. If you were watching at home, all *you* had was an annoying blur of images on your TV screen. But at least you got to witness this grand experiment, because everyone knew that 3-D TV was the Next New Thing.

The studio cameras at KECA, fitted with strange rotating disks and mirrors to create the 3-D effect, were intimidating, says Nina Bara. "It was the only *Space Patrol* show we did in which the entire cast was scared to death. We did not know exactly how to stand in relation to the rotating mirror. To us, it appeared as a giant monster eye, maliciously staring at us!"[18]

Ed Kemmer was more concerned than scared. Paying attention, as usual, to all things technical, he glanced at the fancy 3-D equipment and saw something that troubled him as he waited for the live broadcast to begin:

---

[18]*Space Patrol Memories by Tonga*, 1966 and 1976, Volume I (no page numbers).

The camera in the studio had an attachment in front of the lens. This consisted of a round glass plate — half plain glass and half mirror. This plate would spin and the lens would pick up an alternating straight view and an offset view, one for each eye. At the Biltmore, the receiving TV set had the same type of contraption, and of course it had to be in exact synchronization with the camera at the studio.

It took a bit of time to sync them, and while they were doing that I noticed the power cord hanging down from the camera — just hanging free and not anchored to the camera pedestal. I suggested that perhaps it should be fastened so that it wouldn't accidentally become unplugged. The idea was ignored and the preparation went on. Sometime later, when the camera was moved, the power line snagged on something and it became unplugged. So they had to start the sync process all over again, causing some hair-pulling and an aggravating delay.

Once the equipment was plugged in again and resynched, things went great, but the delay, says Kemmer, lasted an hour or two and seemed like forever. "It was like the old adage: 'For want of a nail, a shoe was lost.'"

Unfortunately, 3-D TV fizzled like a rocket whose booster fails to function. Viewers had little or no desire to have it in their living rooms, and the idea fell on the scrap heap next to the Edsel and other bright ideas of the day. After all, sums up Kemmer, "Who wants to put on a pair of mandatory eyeglasses to watch TV?"

That summer, the 15-minute local show — still airing Monday through Friday in Southern California — bit the dust. Kinescopes had been playing around the country and doing well, but when it was canceled, the cast shed no tears.[19] For two years, they'd been doing seven shows a week (counting radio) plus personal appearances, print interviews and guest spots on other TV and radio programs. Weekends were crammed with telethons and more appearances. It was just too much. To not have to memorize a script overnight — or just minutes before airtime — five days a week was a huge relief. "We'd prayed for it to go off the air," says Kemmer. "Now we could finally have a life."

Ironically, the cast had the network sponsor, Ralston Purina, to thank for the death of the daily show, if a story in *The Hollywood Reporter* is true. According to the paper, Ralston wanted to be the exclusive sponsor of all *Space Patrol* shows, and they'd wangled a contract that gave them "sponsor approval" for the local show.[20] Thus, when current sponsors Dr. Ross Dog Food and Leslie Salt wanted to renew, Ralston said no. The game plan (you'd think) was for Ralston to then take their place, but for some reason not adequately explained by the *Reporter*, that didn't happen. The story said only that KECA-TV (the Los Angeles station that aired the show) had decided to "drop it altogether rather than make a deal with Ralston Purina." This left many questions unanswered, but in any case, the show was abruptly canceled.

Ed Kemmer offers another explanation for why the show was dropped. The newly formed TV actors' union, TvA (Television Authority), which later merged with the American Federation of Radio Artists to become AFTRA, was demanding more money for actors and establishing pay scales. Kemmer, who helped form the union, speculates that KECA and Helen Moser may have decided to kill the daily show "when they found out they'd have to pay us quite a bit more money." Ken Mayer believes this was true. "When the

[19]As early as the fall of 1950, when ABC execs decided to launch a weekly, half-hour version of *Space Patrol*, the 15-minute daily show began to appear in selected markets around the country. On October 16, 1950, Lyn Osborn's mother scribbled "Bud on TV for the first time in Detroit" next to the 5:30 P.M. listing for station WXYZ.

[20]"'Space Patrol' Being Cut to Half-hour Weekly Show," *The Hollywood Reporter*, June 9, 1953.

union came in, the actors had to get paid $200 a week, so for $700–800 a week, they dropped the show," he says. A spokesman for KECA told *The Reporter* that the station was looking for another space show, but in fact *Space Patrol* was replaced by *Comedy Carnival*.

Though the cast was space-happy about the show's cancellation, kids and adults alike were devastated. During its three-year run, the daily Los Angeles broadcast had morphed from a choppy poster child for fledgling TV to a slick, quick fix of *Space Patrol* for fans who craved more than the weekly half-hour adventure. When the news broke in early June that soon the 15-minute show would be history, Commandant May King, a member of the bell-ringing brigade of the Salvation Army, set down her donation bucket and penned a letter to the cast:

> Dear members of Space Patrol:
>   I feel like I have lost some dear friends after hearing the announcement today that we shall no longer enjoy your program every night. I am a Salvation Army Officer with a keen imagination and I just loved your program. I looked forward to 6:45 P.M. as regularly as I did my meals, and when the creator of this program was killed, I feared something like this would happen sooner or later.... A whole week between shows is a long time to have to wait. Sometimes when I take care of a Christmas kettle on Broadway in Los Angeles, I have asked myself the question, "Would I know Major Robertson and Buzz and Happy and Tonga and Carol if they passed my kettle?" and assure myself that I surely would. I saw Happy out of uniform on TV one night and I knew him right away. Who wouldn't know that delightful fellow with his eagerness to serve as a cadet? (I was a cadet once long ago in the Army I belong to.)
>   There is a young boy of fifteen who is in and out of the hospital most of the time and often in bed at home with that dread "Hemiophelia" [sic]. This lad is going to be heart-broken at this news. He lived for that program, and I know what a blow this is to him....
>   I am going to miss you at that particular time more than I can tell. Should you ever come down Broadway in LA, in December, I am the only one at a kettle who plays a Flexatone in front of a Woolworth Store and you couldn't miss me. I am not young, but am a pensioned Officer of this Army, having joined it in Wisconsin in 1905, but I'll never be too old to enjoy everything I can get hold of about space progress, for you see, I am headed toward the skies.

To add insult to injury, the daily show ended smack in the middle of a cliffhanger and viewers never got to see if things turned out OK. "Happy and I were being threatened by something and there was no resolution," Kemmer recalls. Mail poured in demanding to know the outcome. But the fans weren't the only ones suffering withdrawal from their daily *Space Patrol* fix. In early July, Virginia Hewitt told *Los Angeles Daily News* columnist Paul Price that the cast felt it too. "It's strange how we all miss each other. We used to always do things together — meet for lunch, go to dinner, have parties at each other's house or apartment; but now we only see each other occasionally." And while Hewitt hinted mysteriously that "maybe we'll be back with the daily show on another station," chances are that nothing solid was in the works. Had Mike Moser been alive, he would have fought to get the show back on the air — somehow, some way. But then, if Moser had been around, he'd never have allowed Ralston's hissy-fit over sponsorship — much less a union dispute over wages— to knock the show off the air in the first place.[21]

[21]The date the daily show actually left the air is unclear. According to *TV-Radio Mirror* magazine, the last daily Los Angeles show was broadcast on Friday, August 7, 1953 (researched by Don McCroskey), but this is probably a misprint. *The Hollywood Reporter* states that the show was slated to be pulled in mid–June, and when Osborn and Hewitt did the interview with Paul Price that appeared on July 3, 1953, Price noted that the local show was no longer running. (Kinescopes continued to air on some network affiliates, however, even after production ceased.)

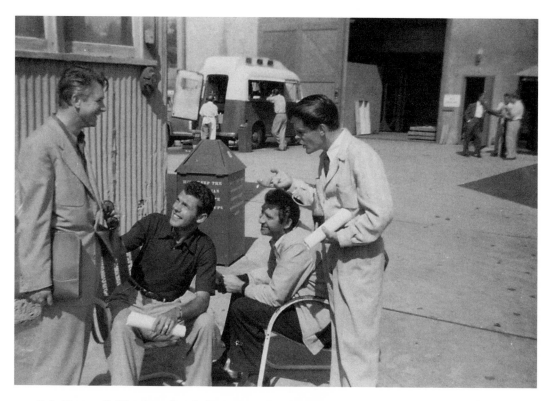

Bela Kovacs (left) takes a break from menacing Kemmer as the two archenemies relax on the set with Mayer and Osborn (right). (Author's collection)

With the 15-minute show gone, the cast and production crew could devote more energy to the network half-hour, which was getting more sophisticated each week in terms of technical tricks and special effects. Music was added, which boosted dramatic moments and quickened the pace. In those days, most background or "underscore" music came from the Mutel (Music for Television) Library, assembled by David Chudnow. That's why when you watch Superman deal with the Mole People you may have flashbacks to *Space Patrol* or *Ramar of the Jungle*: same music.[22] Darley chose the tracks himself, using them to heighten sentiment as well as suspense. *Space Patrol* has many poignant moments, often centered on Happy or Carol in a tight spot with Buzz rushing to the rescue, and Darley had a genius for intensifying those with the right sound track. Ask him about it and he clears his throat, acknowledging that, yes, the music "got more sentiment into those scenes." He chose the lively, ethereal piece "Stratosphere" by British composer Eric Spear to play at the end of the show as the credits rolled.[23] It became the unofficial *Space Patrol* theme.

As the network show gained popularity, it was closely monitored for accuracy by

[22]You can hear this familiar background music on *Adventures of Superman*, Varése Sarabande Records, 2000. Writer Jeff Berkwits reports that some of these same cuts can be heard on *Racket Squad, Sky King, Captain Midnight, Ramar of the Jungle* and, of course, *Space Patrol*. They were used on radio dramas too, such as *Yours Truly, Johnny Dollar* and *Dimension X*.

[23]"Stratosphere," from the Francis, Day and Hunter Music Library (a collection of British production music), is available on CD in *The Sci-Fi Channel Presents Sci-Fi's Greatest Hits*, Volume 4, "Defenders of Justice" (TVT Records, 1998). Researched by Jeff Berkwits.

Left: When Corry suspects that Loren, played by Lee Van Cleef, is an alien masquerading as a Space Patrol officer, Carol, outraged, rushes to Loren's defense. (This was possibly Van Cleef's first television role, according to the Internet Movie Database.) *Center:* A tense scene between Lee Van Cleef and Ed Kemmer. Corry, believing that Van Cleef is a Thormanoid (alien invader), asks him to remove his tunic to reveal his thermo-insulator — gear every Thormanoid needs to keep warm. *Right:* Aha! Van Cleef *is* a Thormanoid. He and Kemmer duke it out as he tries to escape. (Author's collection)

both kids and scientists, who did not hesitate to let writer Norm Jolley know when he made the slightest error. The juves were his toughest critics. When he mixed up Io and Callisto, two of Jupiter's moons, he got letters calling him a "stupid Earthling." And when Commander Corry remarked that there was one planet, Saturn, beyond Pluto, youngsters rushed to set him straight.[24]

But the stupid Earthlings were doing OK, financially. By 1952, *Space Patrol*'s budget had soared to more than $10,000 a week, but, says Dick Darley, more money was funneled into salaries than production, where it could have improved the look of the show. And while some of the skyrocketing profits did trickle down, it was never enough to hire more supporting players or create the elaborate sets seen on other hit shows of the day. Only two guest actors were allowed per episode, which ticked off Norm Jolley. He was well paid now, but forced to limit the number of characters used in a story. He juggled like crazy, writing in only one villain this week so he could have three the next. In one script he notes: "The spaceport is nearly empty—*because we can't afford any extras.*"

Tongues wagged in Hollywood about the astronomical earnings of Kemmer and Osborn, two industry "no-names." "Those wheels of fortune go spinning around, and as a result a couple of unknowns earning $40 a week in television last year, today are drawing approximately $25,000 each per annum," reported *Variety:*

> Lyn Osborn and Ed Kemmer, no names in the accepted Hollywood sense, are the beneficiaries of TV's terrific impact.... Atop their $25,000 income each, the duo will get 5% of merchandising, such as *Space Patrol* uniforms, comic books and other gimmicks.... [Recently] Osborn was reminded by the Internal Revenue Department of his climb in TV. In 1950 he grossed $4,000; for 1951 he paid Uncle Sam $3,500 in income taxes.[25]

It wasn't long before Kemmer and Osborn's pay had shot to $45,000. (More like $60,000, if he got his cut of the merchandising, Lyn confided to close pal Chuck Barkus.) These were unbelievable sums for the early 1950s, and people were talking, confirms Jack Narz. "The rumor was out in town that Ed and Lyn were the two highest-paid actors in Hollywood. They were riding high. In those days, $40,000 a year was a lot of money—

[24]Columnist Barney Glazer, *The Beverly Hills Bulletin*, December 14, 1952.
[25]*Variety*, April 29, 1952.

$125 a week was a good salary."[26] Norm Jolley, knowing that his scripts were the backbone of the show's success and feeling that he should get no less than Ed and Lyn, demanded that Moser pay him as much as the stars. To his surprise, the producer readily agreed.

Mayer, Hewitt and Bara were satisfied with $185 per show, but they had no idea what Kemmer and Osborn were making until the trade papers tattled. Still, their salaries were 37 times the $5.00 per episode they'd drawn when the show began. Meanwhile, writer Lou Huston faithfully churned out the radio show for just $75 a week, with no pay raise in sight. (When Huston penned a half-hour script for *Suspense* or *Phillip Morris Playhouse*, it fetched $400.) He waxes philosophical when he hears, years later, what the others were paid. "I never let myself worry about it. If you're going to do the work, do it and accept the deal, and don't be envious and resentful. There's enough of that in the business anyway." The loyal crew, who were staff employees at ABC, didn't profit hugely from *Space Patrol's* rising star either, except in overtime pay. Lighting director Truck Krone's extra hours boosted his yearly take to $8,000 — pretty good, considering his friends outside the industry averaged around $2,000. Krone gauged *Space Patrol's* success in a culinary way. "We knew the show was doing well," he cracks, "because Moser kept taking us out to dinner at better and better places."

The merchandising folks were raking in space credits, too. Over 80 *Space Patrol* items, from ray guns and space helmets to pajamas and charm bracelets, leapt off the shelves of selected stores. And kids who could eat enough Wheat Chex or Rice Chex could accumulate an arsenal of *Space Patrol* gear — binoculars, space-o-phones, official Membership Kits — offered by sponsor Ralston Purina for a cereal boxtop and "25 cents in coin." These premiums were promoted heavily on the show, and The Gardner Advertising Company, who repped Ralston Purina, was caught unprepared more than once by the overwhelming response to these offers. When Jack Narz told kids on January 12, 1952, that they could own the very same Cosmic Smoke Gun that Commander Corry had used to save the day ("Cosmic Smoke Guns," Episode 55), 500,000 quarters poured in like a meteor shower to "Space Patrol, Box 812, St. Louis, Missouri." But after producing 147,456 guns, the ad agency, overwhelmed by the response, dropped the offer, leaving two-thirds of the orders unfulfilled. (In 1954, the gun was modified and offered again.)

You'd think the marketing guys would have figured out by now that if they touted an item on *Space Patrol*, they'd be buried under an avalanche of orders. Just a few months earlier, in 1951, ABC had run a promotion offering autographed photos of the cast. A staffer stockpiled 300 photos, but on the first day, 4000 requests poured in. Since photos are expensive, the network decided to drop the offer, calling it "too costly," but the requests didn't stop.[27] Finally, someone in the promotions department suggested sending a cheap sketch of the photo to fans instead of the real thing — but no one had reckoned with the cast. "We objected," says Ed Kemmer:

> We didn't want kids getting some kind of little sketch of a photograph. We insisted on the photograph — and we got it. Then they wanted to print our autographs on it, and we said, "No, we will do the autographing." So every night after the [daily] show, we put in a couple hours signing them. We spent many hours, but, by God, we did it! We didn't want it to be phony.

[26]But even at $900 a week, Kemmer and Osborn weren't topping Sid Caesar, who was rumored to rake in $15,000 a week, according to *TV Show* magazine, November, 1953.

[27]*Variety*, April 29, 1952.

Despite the attempt to cut corners on some fronts, other things, notably the costumes, improved. In the early shows, Buzz and Hap wore sleeveless tunics over puffy troubadour shirts with poet's sleeves and gaudy trim at the wrists and neck. These early costumes were effeminate, inspiring the irrepressible Osborn, armed with a felt-tip pen, to transform a photo of Kemmer dressed in the blouse and tunic into a woman.[28] Major Robertson never suffered the billowy shirt; he got a hand-me-down costume from Republic's *Captain Marvel* serial.

Carol and Tonga fared better. Their costumes, which featured perhaps the first micro-mini skirts ever seen on television, were elegant and utterly outrageous for the early 1950s. How these 30th-century "uniforms" got past the watchdogs in what ABC euphemistically called its "Continuity Acceptance Department" (read censorship) or failed to upset the decent people in organizations such as the National PTA (which lauded the show for its wholesomeness) is a mystery that rivals the missing Ralston Rocket.[29] You can only assume that whoever was supposed to police these things was either looking the other way — or maybe *not* looking the other way. Only once, says Virginia Hewitt, can she remember any complaint:

> I was climbing the ladder on one of the network shows. And the cameraman — I think he was just trying to get me in trouble — shot up.... And the ad agency that handled Ralston Purina got on the phone immediately from St. Louis, saying, "Don't ever let a shot like that of Carol be shown again!" And oh, they were emphatic, and they were angry. They said, "We could see under her skirt." Well, under my little red uniform, I had matching red panty hose. By today's standard, I was fully clothed all the way to the ankle, practically. Good Lord, by *today's* standard, it was practically a maternity dress!

In fact, the sci-fi mini-skirt, featured in other space operas and genre films of the day, was strangely predictive. In September 1950, *Tele-Views* ran a photo of Tonga in her uniform, noting, "Should television continue in ever-growing influence, this may well be milady's costume of tomorrow."[30] And though "tomorrow" may have seemed centuries away to the midcalf hem–wearers of the '50s, in fact the mini-skirt craze — a major fashion revolution — exploded in 1966. In the meantime, Tonga and Carol's futuristic attire did not go unnoticed by adults who tuned into the daily show during the dinner hour. "I remember people saying that we had two women in very short skirts for that time," says Dick Darley. Years later, people asked me, "Whatever happened to that blonde and brunette?"

Perhaps the worst fashion statement in *Space Patrol* was the villains' costumes, which were a cross between medieval garb and bad bellhops' uniforms. The insignias were cryptic — often an upside-down pineapple or twisted mollusk. Engineering supervisor Tom Mason, who worked at ABC after *Space Patrol* ended, notes that some costumes in the early episodes were borrowed from the movie serials *Captain Marvel, The Purple Monster Strikes* and *Flash Gordon*. Even Prince Baccarratti's distinctive leather jacket with its sinister black falcon emblem was not designed for *Space Patrol*. It first appeared in the 1939 Columbia serial *Flying G-Men.*

---

[28]The drawing was stored in Virginia Hewitt's mementos, along with Lyn's cards and notes from the time of their affair.

[29]"The word 'censor' or 'censorship' was taboo," says Alice Akins, who worked for a time in the Continuity Acceptance Department for radio during her career at ABC. Nonetheless, "We blue-pencilled every sexual innuendo, curse and racial or religious slur," she recalls.

[30]"Will Television Costume Become Custom?" *Tele-Views,* September 1950.

By the summer of 1951, Buzz, Hap, and Robbie's costumes had evolved into hand-somely tailored, space-age military garb with clean lines and powerful emblems of rank. These symbols made a lasting impression on Mike Guarino, though he was only three years old:

> Even the insignias on their uniforms— the lightning bolt on Corry, Hap's wings and Rob-bie's exploding star — were just so perfect. They communicated that this person is mag-netic and charismatic, this person is light-hearted and ethereal, this person is as stable as the sun. As a kid, it hit me that these were powerful elements— the forces of sun, air and electricity. And the characters all seemed to pretty much live up to them.

If you've been immersed in the grayscale *Space Patrol* universe, seeing the uniforms in color may come as a shock. The tomato-red tunic and forest-green slacks may seem, well, *wrong*. Why not more military blues and grays? "Everything we brought in was camera-tested so we could have sufficient contrast," explains Darley, who adds that those precise colors fit the bill.[31]

Ed Kemmer remembers the feel of the costumes, wool lined with silk and comfort-able most of the time, but hot as hell during action scenes— especially at the end of the show when he raced from a climactic fistfight, which sometimes took place on the cat-walk high above the stage, to the set below for a live commercial:

> The uniforms had to be made of strong stuff because we rolled around on the floor quite a bit in fights. [Their warmth] wasn't a big problem if the scene wasn't too active, but they could be hot when we did the live commercials. We'd usually end the show with a fight — you get the heavy and you're out of breath. Then you run over and do a live commercial, and you're sweaty, sometimes bloody, sometimes very dirty from being on the floor or up in the rafters.

If the uniforms weren't hot enough, try donning a spacesuit over them. The suits were well-crafted copies of the costumes from George Pal's *Destination Moon*, and though they looked great, they lacked one thing every spacesuit needs: temperature control. "They weren't especially heavy but, zipped up, there was no air circulation," Kemmer recalls. "And they were hot because we wore them over our uniforms for quick changes." Fortunately, the suits were big and roomy, but the actors still struggled frantically to get in and out of them fast between scenes.

Space Patrol T-shirts and pullovers with the same emblems Corry and Hap wore were sold through catalogues and selected retail stores so that kids could dress like their heroes. Thus, on a recent winter morning when Mike Guarino went down to the laun-dry room of his Oakland, California, home to fetch a longsleeve pullover from the dryer, he was ambushed by a childhood memory:

> As I was putting it on, I flashed on the Commander Corry longsleeve T-shirt my mother got me when I was three years old. It looked exactly like Corry's lightning-bolt uni-form — it had the emblem and the different-colored shoulders. It was really cool. I used to get up early in the morning and put that thing on because it was like becoming invulnera-ble. I wore it until, after a hundred washings, it literally fell apart.

---

[31]Color photos of the cast in uniform survive in transparencies which came with a rare collectible toy, the Stori-View 3-D viewer.

Ed Kemmer, Lyn Osborn and Ken Mayer, clad in knock-offs of spacesuits from *Destination Moon*, repair the ship's hull — which looks more like wood than Endurium. (Courtesy *Filmfax* magazine)

When the cast had a problem, says Nina Bara, they looked to Ed Kemmer to resolve it. More serious than everyone else, he seemed, like Buzz Corry, to be a natural leader, strong and stable. "Maybe," says Kemmer, sounding a little uncertain. "Underneath I don't know whether that was the character or me *appearing* to be more solid." Despite his doubts, everyone agrees that he projected the image of Corry offscreen, as if part of it never left him, and he admits that "often the cast thought I could mediate some problem or explain something to the producer." In 1952, more in touch with the magic, he told a reporter that playing the charismatic Commander-in-Chief had rubbed off on him. "I've gotten to know the guy so well, he seems like another me," he explained.[32]

But the pressure of live TV was so intense that occasionally even Kemmer cracked. He remembers one time when, at the end of a show, he and Osborn came off a fight scene, dashed to another set to do a live commercial, then on to another one to do the teaser for next week's show. It was one of those hectic transitions:

[32]"Out of This World" by Ellen Crane, *TV Show* magazine, February 1952. Kemmer carried this quality with him throughout his career. The producer of the soap opera *Somerset* told him he was "the leveling factor in the cast."

In the teaser, Hap says, "Where are we going now, Commander?" And my answer was, "Well, first we're going to go..." And I had a long, long phrase, a complicated bunch of foreign-sounding names of planets—it was like using medical language.

Kemmer suddenly had no idea where they were going.

So I said, authoritatively: "Well, first we're going to SNANTOGOVANISNODOURNOW." I just double-talked. And I looked very serious. Well, it *could* have fit, but Hap just wouldn't let it go—he *had* to react. So, instead of playing it straight, he gave me this s-l-o-w take, like *"Where the hell is that?"* I stayed very serious until we went to black. And then I died, Hap died, the cameraman died, and Darley boomed out over the bullhorn: *"WHERE ARE YOU GOING, CORRY?"*

Though focused and serious, Kemmer delighted in playing a prank now and then. "I scared Dick Darley to death once," he admits fiendishly. "I planted some 'blood'—a thick red liquid—in a makeup cap behind a rock where I knew I was going to roll after being hit very hard in the face." Kemmer didn't waste this one on a rehearsal; he saved it for the show. "I took the hit and did a real good roll back to that rock, and behind the rock, I smeared the 'blood' on my face." When he reappeared, the director was shocked, but there was nothing he could do about it. Hey, it was live TV.

While the attractiveness of the cast and alluring costumes worn by Carol and Tonga hooked many teens and adults, *Space Patrol* had something else—an addictive quality that made you want more. For some viewers, it was the fast-paced stories that fed the fantasy of challenging the Unknown. For others, it was the characters. Everyone found someone to identify with—the secret of soap and space operas. You had the brave, compassionate Commander, his cheerful, vulnerable cadet, the loyal Major and two smart, gorgeous heroines—a stunning blonde and a sultry brunette.

But the real secret of *Space Patrol* was its sheer, raw emotion. Writer Norm Jolley built elements of courage and compassion into every script, usually by placing one or more of the regular cast in jeopardy while the others fought impossible odds to come to the rescue. That loyal camaraderie was the big, emotional hook in *Space Patrol*, and Jolley knew what he wanted, how it should play out. Occasionally, he inserted notes in the script that suggested exactly how a character should react. In "The Space Doctor" (Episode 119), Carol is injured, but two desperate criminals have kidnapped the only doctor who can save her life. As Durk, the lead heavy, drags the doctor away, a furious Buzz confronts him, and Jolley scripts not only what the Commander says but how he should say it:

DOC: *Give me one more second and I can save this girl's life!*
DURK: *The boss didn't say anything about that.*
CORRY: (*STEPS UP BEHIND HIM, SO ANGRY HE'S TREMBLING, AND HIS VOICE IS HUSKY AND LOW—AND DEADLY.*) *Let go of the doctor.*

A huge amount of Norm Jolley flowed into the character of Buzz Corry. If it was Kemmer who gave it heart, it was Jolley, like an invisible force, who gave it soul. Kemmer had a genius for flashing between strength and vulnerability, but it was Jolley who gave him the chance, occasionally suggesting how a scene might be staged to spotlight Corry's heroic nature. It was the triangle of Jolley, Darley and Kemmer that created Buzz

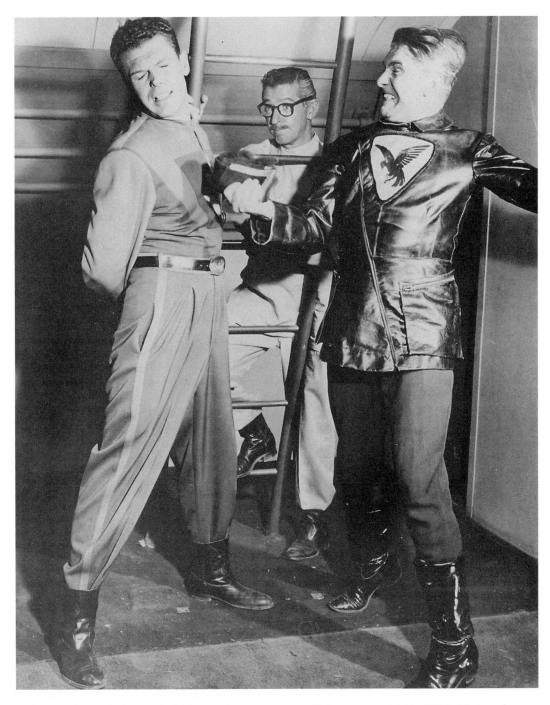

Corry takes his licks from a furious Prince Baccarratti (Bela Kovacs) as actor Bill Baldwin, who plays the Prince's assistant, Barti, looks on. (Courtesy Joe Sarno)

Corry, and Kemmer's talent for playing the hero that ignited the magic. In Episode 183, "The Giant Marine Clam"—a show where Jolley himself plays the sadistic Agent X — he writes a heroic scene for Corry, adding notes that spell out the specific impact he wants this scene to have on viewers.

In this episode, Buzz, Hap, Carol and Robbie track Agent X to his underwater hideout, deep in Venus's Caloric Ocean. But X overpowers Buzz and Robbie and binds their hands tightly to a ring above their heads; then he and his mean-tempered robot, Junior, set out after Happy and Carol.[33] Unable to free themselves, Buzz and Robbie stare helplessly at a monitor screen in the hideout that shows Junior closing in on the two Space Patrollers. Suddenly, Buzz spots a remote control panel a few feet away that operates the robot. If he can free himself and get to it in time, he may be able to prevent Junior from mauling Hap and Carol. He tries desperately to work his hands free, and Jolley makes it plain through copious notes in the script (below in parentheses) that this has got to be a highly charged scene:

> *CORRY:* (With great determination, spurred to super-human strength by the picture on the monitor.) *We've got to help them!* (Then gives it everything he's got.... A close-up of Buzz's hands with the rope really cutting into his wrists as he tries to work loose. Make it pull the skin, so it hurts the viewer. Since we're not using any "tricks" to get out of the ropes, this must be for "real." We've got to believe that any less courage and determination than Buzz Corry's would not have done the job. We see Buzz's face strain, we see the ropes around his wrists wrinkling the skin as he tries through sheer strength and determination to free his hands. Work this bit for all it's worth.... As Buzz finally succeeds in pulling his hands loose, he registers pain.)

You weren't getting this kind of intensity on other kiddie shows of the day, but then, says Jolley, he wasn't writing just for kids. After all, he was getting phone calls from guys at Douglas Aircraft — engineers who were fans of the show and praised its technical accuracy. "I never saw it as a kid's show — 'youth' show, maybe. But the network told us we had a 60 percent adult audience, so I wrote it for anybody who wanted to see it."[34]

"It all began with the script," says Dick Darley, who made the scenes come to life and was just as bent on intensity as Jolley. "The kind of storylines Norm wrote allowed the humanness to come into it." Darley, always under the gun for time, had to focus on staging first; then he worked with the actors, if necessary, to heighten the impact:

> My concern was in developing each week's plot and what the characters' reactions would be to that story. If it didn't originate from them, I tried to help. But [in overall characterization] they found their ways individually. What I did was turn the volume up or down, sharper or softer, to emotionally feature with the camera what should be featured to make it stronger dramatically. I was helped by the terrible thing of being a perfectionist (the bane of most people who've worked with me). I beat everybody to death to make it perfect. I ran a tight ship in regard to rehearsals and staging and action, but the people got through all that, I mean, they got past me.

The cast was aware that their power as an ensemble had propelled them to stardom, and it was that glue that held things together when egos got snarly. Though a love and loyalty had developed among them, there were flashes of anger too, as in any close family. Osborn frustrated Kemmer and Darley with his nonstop antics that ate up rehearsal time, and Darley could tell when Lyn and Virginia, who were dating, were also not speaking. "You had to figure something heavy was going on between them because the faces, the eyes, got very deadly. And it wasn't just the two of them," he notes. "You could see

[33]That's Bela Kovacs as Junior in the robot suit.
[34]As late as November 1954 — three months before it was canceled — *Radio-Film-Television* magazine reported that *Space Patrol* had a "near 60 percent adult audience share."

it occasionally with the others." If you're hooked on the actors and characters of *Space Patrol*, you may have picked up on the intensity of their relationships, both on and off screen. Half in, half out of character, swept up by success with thousands of fans showing up at personal appearances, it was a heady time. There was friendship, fighting and, as one insider put it, "romantic touches." "It was all normal," says Darley. "As an actor, you lay yourself out so vulnerably." When I met the cast in the mid–'80s, three decades after the show had ended, they were still calling each other by their character names. I asked actor-director Larry Dobkin, who guest-starred on many TV series, including *Space Patrol*, if that was common. "*Decades* later?" he said, surprised. "I'd say that's unusual."

But no matter what conflicts were going on in real life, the actors protected their characters' relationships. It wasn't always easy. Virginia Hewitt, who had been through some major traumas with Osborn but hid that well onscreen, also had a few tiffs with Bara just minutes before airtime. And, says Darley, the cast had actors' egos. "I'm sure they all felt they should have their own shows, starring them," he points out. Yet he knew that the cast was fiercely loyal to the show and that, at least for this moment in time, *Space Patrol* had swallowed their separate ambitions. Osborn proved that point when he turned down the role of "Hotshot Charlie" in Dougfair's new TV series, *Terry and the Pirates*.[35] Whenever Lyn was asked about future plans, he brushed the question aside. "This show comes first," he told reporters. Riding a tidal wave of success, he had no doubt that the future would always be bright, that offers would continually pour in. "The movies can wait," he told *TV* magazine in 1954.[36] The previous year, he'd assured syndicated columnist Barney Glazer that he was in no danger of being typecast:

> Playing an established role such as mine absolutely does not convince casting directors that I am not able to handle another characterization. I've been offered movie roles that are far removed from the comedy stint I do on *Space Patrol*.[37]

Like Lyn Osborn, Virginia Hewitt had no fears that playing Carol day in, day out, would hurt her future acting career. Besides, doing live TV was *so* much more interesting than movies, she told reporter Tom Danson. "It's much more like the stage, with complete continuity, and far more challenging than pictures." She was just as certain about Lyn's future and told *Los Angeles Daily News* columnist Paul Price over lunch one day that Osborn would make "a wonderful villain" because he was so versatile. "I don't think any of us are typed," she added confidently.[38]

In January 1954, Nestlé signed on as a second sponsor, touting "wholesome" Ever-Ready Cocoa and chocolate bars. That summer, *Variety* reported that both Ralston and Nestlé had renewed their contracts for another year.[39] In early fall, Kemmer and Osborn, leading a chorus of singers, pressed two tunes for Decca Records: "Space Patrol," a peppy, military-style march; and "Up Ship and Away," a whimsical ditty about peculiar life forms on other planets. The opening bars of the march were used in two Decca "pre-

[35]*Variety*, April 29, 1953.
[36]*TV* magazine, September, 1954.
[37]*The Wilshire Press*, May 21, 1953.
[38]*Los Angeles Daily News*, July 3, 1953.
[39]On January 16, 2001, the Nestlé corporation swallowed Ralston Purina for $10 billion in cash. (Ralston had sold its cereal operation to General Mills in 1997.)

quel" records released six weeks before Christmas. Written by Lou Huston, they explained how Corry became commander-in-chief and how Hap became his cadet. Decca planned to release the songs on a separate album in early 1955.[40] The show was riding a wave of stellar success with all systems go. The future seemed as bright as a blue giant star.

[40]*The Hollywood Reporter*, November 10, 1954. The two songs that Decca planned to release (but didn't because the show was canceled three months later) featured Kemmer singing lead in "a full baritone — my best Nelson Eddy imitation" and Osborn struggling to carry a tune. Lyn didn't have a musical ear, but he did what he could to compensate by studying with Hollywood vocal coach Glenn Raikes, who tutored Lucille Ball and other stars (and two decades later, this author).

CHAPTER 6

Norman Jolley:
The Soul of Space Patrol

Actors love to say, "When I created that character..." But unless it's an improv, they didn't create that character—they interpreted that character. That character was created by some jerk sitting at a typewriter in a room all alone.

— Norman Jolley

Jolley was one of those fascinating guys who could sit down at a typewriter and just keep it rolling.

— Lou Huston

INDIO, CALIFORNIA: MARCH 2000

Norman Jolley is having the time of his life. Robust, energetic, less threatening than when he menaced Corry as "Agent X" (his evil, black mustache now snowy white), he can hardly believe he's just turned 84. He and his wife, Lois, spend half the year touring the country in their 40-foot, wide-body Vogue motor home, and they're taking off again next week. With Agent X's panache, Jolley navigates the mammoth RV anywhere, even through the congested heart of San Francisco, where the risk of collision is greater than flying through the Asteroid Belt. Passing through Orlando, Florida, one summer, he, Lois and a friend visited the Kennedy Space Center at Cape Canaveral. Waiting to enter the popular Apollo exhibit, they found themselves in a darkened theater where visitors are shown a film about the history of space travel before filing into a huge hangar to see the hardware that went to the moon. What happened next, says Jolley, sent a jolt through his being:

> Three screens lit up and the voiceover said, "Early television was responsible for informing and educating the American people about space travel." Bang! *Space Patrol* is on the screen, and there's a shot of Ed Kemmer as Buzz Corry sitting in the cockpit of his ship. I almost fainted. It told me that whoever was in charge of that film had been a Space Patroller when he was young. And then I wondered: How many more aerospace people are there who may have been influenced by the show?

"How did it feel to see that image from *Space Patrol* linked to the *real* space program at Cape Canaveral?" I ask. Jolley is coughing a lot, choking up. "Like I feel right now. I can hardly talk."

Though he's an ex–Marine, he doesn't apologize for showing emotion. His voice is warm and personal and sounds exactly like it did 50 years ago when, besides writing up to eight *Space Patrol* scripts a week, he played the villainous Agent X on the TV show, plus a slew of characters—from heavies to Space Patrol officers—on the radio broadcast.

As the crowd of tourists filed out of the theater, Jolley's friend, bursting with excitement, rushed up to an usher to inform him that the writer of the very show featured in the film — the show that had inspired countless astronauts and engineers—was *here*, right in their midst. "And the guy said, 'Oh, really?'" Jolley recalls. "He didn't know what the hell she was talking about, and didn't care."

It's a clear, hot day in Indio, California, where Norm and Lois spend six months of the year in a trailer park. "That's *mobile home* park," he says sternly, leading you up the stairs into their elegant house on wheels appointed with white leather couches, walnut cabinets and leaded glass windows. He has a forceful presence and his deep-set eyes flash back and forth between mirth and determination. The temperature in this desert enclave rivals the hot side of Mercury — and it's only late March. But the Jolleys don't hang around for the blistering summer; by the end of the month, they'll hit the road, traveling cross-country to a round of reunions with family and friends.

The Jolleymobile is snug inside, if you're not used to living in what you drive. But Norm, six feet tall, doesn't mind cozy places. He wrote the scripts for *Space Patrol* holed up in an office over the garage of his home in Manhattan Beach. "It had a lot of windows looking north over the backyard," remembers Jerry Hankins, a neighborhood chum of Jolley's son, Val. "We couldn't be noisy when Val's dad was writing." Sometimes Jolley wrote all night long (as Moser had done before him), the radio tuned to classical music and Mitzi, his beloved boxer, curled up under the desk as a footrest. There, until dawn, he hung out with Buzz, Hap, Robbie, Carol and Tonga. "I was alone a lot, but I was never lonely," he smiles.

> They were my friends—I don't mean the actors, I mean the characters. I never thought about them as Ed Kemmer and Lyn Osborn; I thought about them as Commander Corry and Cadet Happy. I knew who they were, what they would and would not do. Actors love to say, "When I created that character…" But unless it's an improv, they didn't *create* that character — they *interpreted* that character. That character was created by some jerk sitting at a typewriter in a room all alone.

In the summer of 1950, when he began writing *Space Patrol*, the show aired Monday through Friday in Los Angeles. That fall, the ABC radio network picked it up, adding two more episodes a week to his workload. Three months later, the half-hour TV show debuted, and Jolley found himself writing eight scripts a week — over 1.5 million words a year — until Lou Huston was hired in 1951 to take the radio shows off his back. Even so, Jolley was still writing six shows a week. He was busier than *Lone Ranger* writer Fran Striker, who was churning out three weekly radio shows plus a daily comic strip.

If, as a kid, you couldn't wait to take off on the next daring adventure with the *Space Patrol* gang; if you worried that the bad guys would do something awful to Corry and Hap and that the Commander wouldn't find a way out in time; if you laughed at Hap's jokes and identified with his vulnerability or Corry's strength; if you wanted to grow up to be one of the good guys and fight for truth and justice forever — you can thank Norm Jolley. Those plots and characters came from his brain. And Jolley kept you riveted to the screen with one secret ingredient: conflict. It was the basis of every scene he wrote:

> I had two rules of writing posted above my desk. The first was: "Conflict and story are synonymous." First, there's conflict — your story comes out of that. If there's no conflict

in a scene, don't write it. If you can't go to the bathroom when a show is on, it's because there's strong conflict in every damn scene. No matter what you're writing, that should always be at the back of your mind. Always ask: "Where can I put some conflict in this?" Love is loaded with conflict. It's a different kind than in war, but it's conflict. Without two opposing forces, there is no story. The other rule: "You've got to make people care about the characters." In so many shows I've seen, I didn't care about anybody. But if you don't care who wins the ballgame, why the hell go to the park?

"*Space Patrol* was all conflict," he explains. "Without it, you can't hold the audience. I pass this on to other writers, but I don't know if they listen."

There was one other essential ingredient in *Space Patrol*: Norm Jolley's inviolable sense of right and wrong.

For his strong moral foundation, he credits a small-town childhood in Adel, Iowa (pop. 1,700), and the example and influence of his hardworking parents. His great-grandfather homesteaded a farm, and his father — known as "the best judge of horse flesh in the Midwest" — inherited it, raising 250 head of Hereford cattle, hogs, oats and wheat, until his sudden death from a brain tumor at age 37. Jolley was seven when he saw his father die. He remembers a line of cars stretching two miles long at the funeral. "I never heard anything but good things said about him," he says of his dad, who became his hero.

Though he no longer had a male role model, his mother gave Norm and his two brothers a strong moral code. "She didn't take any crap from us. She was a good disciplinarian and teacher." It was against this backdrop of small-town America, where the best way to keep a boy out of trouble was to keep him busy, that Jolley came of age. Marijuana grew wild along the railroad tracks and farm fences, but he never touched it or any other drug. "In that town, if you stepped out of line, everybody knew it — hell, you were related to half the people anyway!" he jokes. Delivering newspapers, working at the post office and grocery store, and spending summers laboring on a neighbor's farm gave him a strong work ethic. "Basic values were inherent in a small town in the Midwest, and I automatically projected them into *Space Patrol*," he admits. "My environment taught me to behave myself, that good triumphed over evil. And I lived through the Depression, where we had less money but more of each other. I'm sure that motivated much of the show."

"You brought a strong sense of morality to the series — a powerful message to do what's right," I tell him.

"That's the way I feel, and that's what I wrote about," he says tersely.

"You got that into the scripts."

"I hope I did."

Though steeped in the work ethic, he jokes that following the family tradition of farming was *really* hard work, so he set out to find something easier. Since the age of 13, he'd sung and played banjo at the local movie theater while the reels were changed. But he didn't head straight to performing. At 19, he worked as night foreman at a company making radio volume controls; two years later he was building stone crushers. At night school, he studied engineering, found he had a talent for it, and invented two improvements for mining equipment that his boss at the stone crushing plant stole and patented.[1]

---

[1]Jolley displayed his stone-crushing expertise in *Space Patrol* Episode 130, "Gigantic Space Knife," June 20, 1953, notes physicist and mathematician William F. Drish, Jr. "A rock-crushing prop was featured consisting of two counter-rotating cylinders fitted with spikes. Raw ore, falling between the cylinders, was pulverized. Of course, the villains tried to send Buzz and Happy through the crusher."

Above: Norman Jolley as a young Marine. *Left:* Corporal Norman Jolley entertains troops in 1943 during one of the 350 variety shows he wrote and hosted while stationed in San Diego.

Enraged, he quit the job and enrolled in the Drama and Radio School at Drake University in Des Moines. Today Jolley thanks the man who ripped off his inventions because "he was responsible for my having pursued the career I'd secretly dreamed of."

At Drake, he formed a comedy team with fellow student Archie Leonard. They worked nightclubs, with Jolley as straight man. Now he knew that his destiny was to be a performer. In 1940, he joined radio station KOME in Tulsa, then moved to KADA in Ada, Oklahoma, where he wrote and directed live dramatic shows. Returning to Iowa, he worked at a string of stations as staff announcer and DJ, learning the trade, until he enlisted in the Marine Corps in 1942. But the Corps did not interrupt his radio career. Stationed in San Diego, he was assigned to the Radio Unit, where he and other enlisted men produced stage and radio shows, including *The Halls of Montezuma*—sagas of the Marines in action broadcast weekly over the Mutual Radio Network. The show gained fame as "the voice of the Marine Corps."[2]

After the war, he reunited with Leonard in Hollywood to create and headline *The Don Lee Music Hall*, a live comedy-variety TV show that introduced many top performers to America, including Liberace, Sarah Vaughan and Mel Tormé. The show was done live from KTSL (formerly Don Lee's W6XAO), a pioneer station housed in a small, square building with an antenna in the hills above the famed Hollywood sign. Inside those walls, guys like Jolley were having a blast building inventive sets and doing "all kinds of experimental television." There were no rules because no one knew whether to take this maverick medium seriously, so for a halcyon period, the inmates ran the asylum. "We just had a ball," he recalls of television's fledgling days. "Who knew?"

---

[2]*The Halls of Montezuma* was heard over the ABC Radio Network. Says Jolley: "We'd go to the naval hospital, find shot-up Marines, get their personal stories and dramatize them."

Jolley (right) and longtime comedy partner Archie Leonard (left) ham it up in 1948 with an unidentified actress on their weekly variety show, *The Don Lee Music Hall*, aired on KTSL (W6XAO) in Los Angeles. (Courtesy Lois Jolley)

Producer Mike Moser first spotted him there in 1949, saving the day during one of live TV's frequent fiascoes. Jolley was emceeing a fashion show when the projector broke down. "The director hollered, 'Don't leave! We've got 35 minutes to fill and you're it!'" he recalls. "He told me to improvise, and I said, 'How?'" In a panic, Jolley looked directly into the camera and addressed the viewers at home: "Ya wanna see something funny?" Standing up, he revealed his legs sticking out of the ridiculous tux he'd rented from Western Costume that was four sizes too small. *More time to fill...* He looked desperately around and spotted the fashion models. "Uh, maybe you'd like to meet some of these girls, folks..." *More time to fill...* "You know, television is a very new medium and not many people know much about it, so I want to show you how it works." He motioned to a cameraman, asking him to roll his camera over. "It's not a 'camera,' it's a 'televisor,'" the man corrected. Jolley had him open it up and explain how it worked. *Still need more time...* "You know, folks," he said, glancing around wildly, "these sets sure look beautiful, but they're really a bunch of junk." Then he got an idea. "I walked through the sets, tearing them apart, saying, 'Look how these things are made.' I was just showing them television — and all of a sudden I heard 'cut,' and the time was up. I'd filled 35 minutes!"

Moser, impressed, cornered him at once, offering a job in an audience-participa-

From the left: John Rodney, Norman Jolley and Robert Mitchum film *Pursued* (1947) on location in New Mexico. (Courtesy Lois Jolley)

tion show to be broadcast from the Ambassador Hotel. That fell through, but instead, the producer tapped him to play the vicious Agent X in a youth show he was launching called *Space Patrol*. In retrospect, Jolley realized that it was all a diabolical plot:

> Mike had an ulterior motive — he double-crossed me! He found out from my ex-wife, What's-Her-Name, that I'd done some writing along the way.[3] I didn't seek it as a career

[3]Jolley married Alberta Bird in 1941 when he was working at radio station KADA in Ada, Oklahoma. They had three children. After a bitter divorce in 1960, during which she disposed of his *Space Patrol* scripts by donating them to a paper drive, he always referred to her as "What's-Her-Name."

In this early publicity still, Jolley as Agent X (third from left) is menaced by Cadet Happy, who seems to have mixed up the good guys and bad guys. From left: Hewitt, Bara, Jolley, Glen Dixon ("Major Gruell"), Mayer, Kemmer. (Collectors take note: Osborn is packing the first gun used on the show.) (Courtesy Beth Flood)

'cause it's very hard work. But it was a conspiracy, a plot. Mike was writing all the scripts for the series and wanted relief. He hooked me as an actor, then gradually conned me into writing some of the shows. He'd say, "You want to write one of these?" And I'd say, "Yeah, OK." "Wanna write another one?" "OK." The next thing you know, I'm doing *all* of them. But that's what he'd had in mind from the beginning.

What sealed the deal was money. Jolley was making $25 a week as straight man to Leonard on the *Music Hall* and five dollars a day for playing Agent X; Moser was offering $250 a week to write *Space Patrol*. In the summer of 1950, Jolley gave in. At that time, the show was still local in Los Angeles, but six months later, it went network — and that,

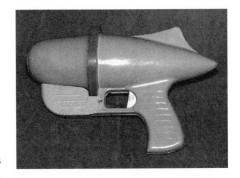

Early weapon. This so-called "paralyzer ray" (as it was tagged in the scripts) was actually a smoke gun made by Nu-Age Products, says Elliott Swanson. (Courtesy Elliott Swanson)

he knew, was where he needed to focus his energy. He hired assistants to write the daily shows, which continued to air in L.A. Dick Morgan ("a neophyte") and G. Gordon Dewey (a teacher who'd published several SF short stories) didn't last long; finally, he settled on actor-writer Maurice Hill, who occasionally appeared as "Captain Hayward." Hill understood *Space Patrol* and did a decent job, but Jolley insists that he edited and often rewrote every script — except one. He was behind the eight-ball, up against the deadline for the network show one afternoon, when he received a frantic call from a friend in the mimeograph room at ABC:

> He said that Maury Hill had written a hospital scene with blood and guts all over the place — strictly unacceptable, in those days. I raced to the studio and made some changes before the script got distributed. It was the only time I'd let an assistant's script go to the studio before I'd seen it.

With the passing of 50 years, memory blurred and he came to believe that not one word he wrote for the series was ever changed. But in fact, Dick Darley's personal set of scripts reveals that the director was forced to cut or chop a scene here and there to come in on time. Jolley has forgotten this, but considering he wrote over 5 million words for *Space Patrol*, it's just a blip on the viewscope. As he likes to tell it (with a touch of menace, Agent X-style), "I had only one incident where somebody on the show tried to get 'cute' with the lines. We had a face-to-face confrontation and we never had *that* problem again." He still loves playing the tough guy, though he can't conceal the twinkle in his eye. In Norm Jolley's world, there are good guys and bad guys, issues are clear-cut, people either do the right thing or they don't. He's conscious of principles: who has them, who doesn't. It's ingrained in his being; nothing has changed.

He was 35 when he began writing *Space Patrol* and "quite slender," but soon he was packing on pounds as he wrestled with procrastination and (as every writer knows) its good buddy, the refrigerator:

> *Space Patrol* is what put the weight on me, because it was very hard work, very easy to put off to just a little bit later — and I was always procrastinating. I'd take five more minutes at the refrigerator before I went up to the office. I'd get it done, but it was getting later and later — a lot of push at the last minute. Many times it was midnight before I'd start writing, and then I'd write all night long, and all the next day, and the next — just writing around the clock.

He delivered the scripts for the daily show just under the wire, racing to the studio (a 45-minute drive) — sometimes arriving just minutes before airtime, leaving the cast barely enough time for a walk-through. Ed Kemmer remembers the last-minute crunch. "It was tough. Norm would come in five minutes before the show and hand us the scripts. We'd glance at them, then talk our way through it."

Jolley was not oblivious to the trouble he was causing cast and crew, but he'd never written full time before; he was overwhelmed by the pressure, the daily deadlines. Sometimes he still hadn't finished the script when he arrived at the studio, so he'd sit at a typewriter outside the mimeograph room, banging out pages, handing them to a secretary who'd cut stencils as soon as she got them. He was deeply ashamed of this back-to-the-wall routine; finally, one day he cornered himself and laid down the law:

> I said, "This procrastination is nonsense — you can't keep doing it." Then I wrote myself a letter, saying: "This is what you wanted to do for a living, isn't it? So why don't you *do* it?

Quit making excuses—you've got to write it, so *sit down and write*! Just get to work and get it done." I did a whole psychotherapeutical number on myself—and it worked! The scripts were in on time after that.

It set the tone for the rest of his career. "*Space Patrol*," he says, "is where I learned to become a writer."

Another thing that helped him set regular hours was falling in love. In 1960, following a bitter divorce from "What's-Her-Name" (Alberta Bird), he married Lois Pearson. Now he wanted to spend evenings with his new wife, so he *had* to keep regular daytime hours. If the Muse didn't show up between nine and six, it was too damn bad:

> Waiting for inspiration to strike is nonsense. You prime the pump. You get a clipboard and pencil or pen and you start noodling, doodling, and pretty soon you get a line and you keep going—and the first thing you know, you're writing as fast as you can. I'd break for lunch, then go back to the office—and at six o'clock I'd quit. I got more done than I used to, when I put it off till midnight.

Lois Jolley remembers her husband's deep and personal bond with the characters he created. One afternoon, she looked in on him in his study as he sat hunched over the typewriter. There were tears running down his face. "You're feeling pretty emotional about this, aren't you?" she asked gently. "That's the only way to do it," he replied.

He knew *Space Patrol's* characters inside-out, but it was important to place them in a scientifically accurate setting, which made them even more real. The rival show, *Tom Corbett, Space Cadet*, boasted famed German rocket authority Willy Ley as technical adviser. Against this expertise, Jolley pitted his night school background in engineering, plus a huge amount of reading and research. As soon as he got a story idea, he'd dig for facts to back it up. His bible was the single-volume *Columbia Encyclopedia*. "It had everything in it—the most valuable book I ever had." He subscribed to *Scientific American*, boned up on hard science, studied Einstein's Theory of Relativity. Though *Space Patrol* was rich in fantasy, its roots in science were true. If a character said that magnetic lines of force could exceed the speed of light, that was fact. "The only way we 'cheated,'" says Jolley, "was to put people on other planets—but we had to do that." Looking back, he's proud that the hard facts in *Space Patrol* were accurate, so that when America really did venture into space, he had "done it right."

The *Columbia Encyclopedia* was a gold mine. In addition to scientific facts, it told him about history, time travel, crystals, telepathy, ancient legends, and mythical beings such as Proteus, who could assume a variety of disguises. He used this knowledge as a springboard for fantasy, making *Space Patrol* the most imaginative of the three leading space operas. But if his brain was roaming the clouds, his feet were still planted on Earth. In Episode 130, "The Gigantic Space Knife," he drew on his patents for mining equipment for a plot where two thugs hijack monazite ore and process it through a rock crusher to extract thorium, a 30th-century spaceship fuel.[4] Often when a story demanded special effects (in this case, the crusher), he revisited his engineering background, inserting notes in the script that described in detail how to build whatever gizmo was needed.[5] "If a crew member said, 'We can't do that,' I'd say, 'Sure you can. Here's how,'" he recalls.

---

[4]Monazite is, in fact, a strongly radioactive mineral that contains the silver-white metal thorium — though whether this was used as spaceship fuel in the 30th century is uncertain.

[5]Bill Drish notes that not only did Jolley design a realistic rock crusher for Episode 130, but his "space knife," described in the script as a force beam, is not unlike the U.S. Army's Tactical High Energy Laser (THEL).

But his painstaking research and inventive plots were eclipsed by the characters. Even Jolley himself was stunned at how, under Darley's direction, they came so perfectly to life. "Never has it happened so completely in anything else I've written — and we're talking thousands of scripts," he confides. "The actors were all incredible, so real — they never let me down. It was every writer's dream." In most shows, he explains, the writer's intent gets diluted as the actors and director filter it through their own interpretations. But with *Space Patrol*, what he wrote was what viewers got — euphoria for a screenwriter. He shakes his head, still in disbelief. Kemmer's shading was superb; Carol came across "just as she was supposed to." What more could you ask?

Well, maybe for more money — at least as much as Kemmer and Osborn were getting. To his astonishment, Moser yielded without a fight. For a while, he says, it made him the highest-paid writer in television.

After *Space Patrol*, Jolley wrote for a string of prime-time shows, including *Science Fiction Theater, Highway Patrol, The Virginian, Laramie,* and *I Led Three Lives.* He was head writer for *Wagon Train, Ironside, Cimarron City, The FBI, Barnaby Jones* and others. He produced five television series and wrote five feature films, including *I've Lived Before* (1956) and *Joe Dakota* (1957).

His career was on course, cruising along, until, in the late '60s, he ran into turbulence.

If you were writing TV crime dramas in the pre–*Sopranos* 1960s, you kept two things in mind: "There is no such thing as the Mafia or *La Cosa Nostra*," and "A criminal never has an Italian name" (think Al Jones, not Capone). Heritage groups like the Sons of Italy, says Jolley, put pressure on sponsors and their ad agencies to make sure no one spoke the word "Mafia" in any TV drama.[6] But in 1967, Jolley wrote "The Executioners," a two-part story for *The FBI*, in which he called the Mafia by name.[7] He did it because the script was true-to-life — he'd based it on fifteen case histories involving the Mob, culled from F.B.I. files. And ABC did a remarkable thing: They gave him permission to use one Italian name in the script.

> This was a shock to me. The rule was to always use WASP — White Anglo Saxon Protestant — names for the heavies to avoid backlash from an ethnic or religious group. Now I was being told I could use an Italian name for a Mafioso! Telly Savalas had been cast in the part of a *capo* named Clement. I added an "i" and he became "Clementi."

The last time a writer had dared to do that was on *The Untouchables* (1959-1963), unleashing a firestorm of protests from the Sons and other Italian watchgroups. Teamster boss Jimmy Hoffa threatened to stop transporting sponsor Liggett-Meyers' cigarettes. The producers (Desilu) backed down and promised it wouldn't happen again. So how could all that have changed overnight?

---

[6]The mission of the Order Sons of Italy in America (OSIA), according to its Website (*www.osia.org*), is "encouraging the study of Italian language and culture in American schools and universities; preserving Italian American traditions, culture, history and heritage; and promoting closer cultural relations between the United States and Italy." In May 2001, the Commission for Social Justice (CSJ), the anti-defamation arm of the Order Sons of Italy, endorsed a resolution brought by Rep. Marge S. Roukema (R–NJ) and 16 colleagues urging the entertainment industry to "stop the negative and unfair stereotyping of Italian-Americans, particularly as profane criminals as portrayed on the television show *The Sopranos*." Representative Bill Pascrell, Jr. (D–NJ), who signed Roukema's measure, had this message for *Sopranos* creator David Chase and the show's producers: "I hope you choke on your money." ("'Sopranos' Under Fire on the Hill, Roukema Resolution Gains," Laurence Arnold [AP], May 24, 2001, *The Record* [Bergen County, NJ].)

[7]The two-part TV drama aired on March 12 and 19, 1967, and was later released as a movie: *Cosa Nostra, Arch Enemy of the FBI* (1967).

Agent X meets J. Edgar Hoover (right). "Thought you might like to have this photograph," Hoover wrote Jolley after their meeting in March 1966. Jolley was allowed access to FBI files so he could write plots based on real case histories for the TV series *The FBI* (1965–74). (Courtesy Lois Jolley)

It hadn't. When Part 1 of "The Executioners" aired in March 1967, all hell broke loose. The American-Italian Anti-Defamation League, whose national chairman was Frank Sinatra, demanded that Part 2 be canceled, accusing Jolley and producer Quinn Martin of maligning 22.5 million Italian-Americans. The League lost that round, but by applying pressure on the show's sponsor, Ford Motor Company (then headed by Lee Iacocca) and its ad agency, they successfully blocked the two episodes from reruns that summer. Jolley was stunned. He couldn't believe that the Mob still had so much power over TV programming:

> I was disappointed — and angry. Angry enough to consider resigning from the series for which I had created the format and into which I had put as much effort as any series I'd ever worked on. But at that moment I got a wire from my alma mater, Iowa Wesleyan College, inviting me to speak during commencement exercises at the alumni-faculty banquet. I called them back and said that it just so happened I had something to say.

At 4:00 one morning, the speech poured out. "I got up and wrote as fast as I could. I just told the truth. Let the chips fall." He wrote in longhand about Mafia censorship, how groups like the Sons of Italy pressured advertisers to never allow any reference to the Mob on a TV program they sponsored. You didn't find this kind of suppression in print media, he pointed out, because advertisers weren't strongly identified with the newspapers and magazines in which they appeared. But TV — where a sponsor's name often became linked with a show — was a different story: Accusations of "discrimination" could trigger a product boycott — and this discouraged TV writers from creating true-to-life, believable characters. The threat to freedom of speech was grave, he warned:

> Any individual, any country that is afraid of a collision with the truth is already vulnerable to the lie.... Historically, it has been the writer's role to hold a mirror to society. I can tell you that restrictions and censorship resulting from the pressure of special interests are helping to stifle the quality and truth right out of television drama.... Is the television writer, who functions in the greatest medium of communications yet devised by man, to be the only writer denied this role?[8]

But speaking out about how the industry yielded to pressure groups was both a personal and professional risk:

> I knew the Mafia played for keeps, and I was going public with names, dates, places— biting the hand that fed me. I made the speech, ending it with a public challenge to the American-Italian Anti-Defamation League and its national chairman, Frank Sinatra, to take a stand against the Mafia because it was vilifying the good name of Italians all over the world. Of course I knew none of them could possibly do such a thing.

The speech got national press coverage, and Jolley (not unlike Buzz Corry) backed up his words with action: He resigned from the show in protest of "the censorship imposed on my work by the Mafia." Producer Quinn Martin stood behind him with full-page ads in *Variety* and *The Hollywood Reporter*. Then Jolley heard that Sinatra, who belonged to the same Palm Desert country club as he did, had been told about the speech and was furious. Sitting at the club's bar one day, he felt eyes boring into his head. He turned and Sinatra quickly looked away. His one fear was that Ol' Blue Eyes would sic his bodyguards on him — he'd heard wild rumors about what had happened to others who had enraged the singer. One guy who'd been beat up, so the story went, was still a vegetable. As he was thinking about this, his wife, Lois, brushed past Sinatra, who pointed at her and whispered loudly to the goon at his side, "That's Norm Jolley's wife." Lois, frightened, panicked and left the bar. "He had us pegged," says Jolley, though the threats went no further. He wanted to deck Sinatra, but he knew that "I'd get the hell beat out of me."

Over the next couple of years, stress took its toll, and in 1970, Jolley had a massive heart attack that (for three minutes) left him dead:

> I was wired up in the hospital, and they could see on the instruments that I was ready to shove off. This nurse was standing over me with a couple of paddles and she said, "How do you feel?" I said, "Pretty good," and she said, "Are you sure you don't feel light-headed or dizzy?" I said, "No." She said, "Are you *sure*?" And then I said, "Oh, yes I do..." Left to right, fade to black: Dead. A split second later — to me — I was right back. And I said, "Maybe you'd like to know that there was an explosion in my chest," and she said, "There were three of them." The doctor told me I was clinically dead for three minutes, but to me there was no passage of time. Dying, by the way, is highly overrated — there's nothing to it.

[8]"[Writer] Tells How Pressure Censors TV," *Des Moines Sunday Register*, June 4, 1967, page 9-L.

He credits a strict exercise regimen with helping him regain his health. At first, he could barely take a step, but a few weeks later, he was walking three miles a day. It made him a believer, and he exercised religiously for the next three decades.

When he returned to work in the early '70s, the face of management had changed. Taking a meeting with a network executive meant pitching projects to a kid barely 20 years old. "It was like sitting down with a fetus in a business suit," he complained, but he stuck it out for another decade. In 1980, he was on a roll, winding up *Barnaby Jones* and feeling at the top of his game, but disheartened about the future of television:

> It just wasn't fun anymore. I'd seen television go down the tubes. If you don't believe me, watch it — if you've got the courage. Morning through night, all you see is one sitcom after another full of brats, and all they do is screw and face-suck. I told one of these [young] writers, "You know, if we didn't know how to do that, you wouldn't have been born. Why are you giving us lessons?"

The new, youthful industry execs sought out young writers who did not have the life experience of those who had pioneered television. Jolley was 34 when he began writing *Space Patrol*, an ex–Marine with an engineering background and over a decade of experience in broadcasting. But by the '80s it seemed to him that not only was the old-fashioned morality of the space and horse operas missing in action, but this new breed of writer lacked the skill it took to craft intricate plots and subtle emotions. "The movies of the week are full of holes," he complains. "It just bugs the hell out of me. I never wrote a hole. When I hit a block in a story, I'd wrestle with it for hours, days, a week — if I had time. I worked my way through it honestly. Now they say the hell with it and just go around it." He's troubled, too, by the death of subtlety across the board:

> Excessive violence, excessive sex, excessive obscenities— it's what the damn business is made of these days. I learned a long time ago that when you do a romantic scene, you can bring the two people into it, bring them right up to what you know is going to happen — and then go away. Let the audience imagine it; let them feel it.

Toward the end of his life, the biggest surprise was what he saw as his legacy shaping up. "I always thought it would be *Wagon Train*," he says, half to himself, "and it turns out that what people remember most is *Space Patrol*." He sits down in the driver's seat of the motor home — the dashboard doubles as a desk when he's off

Norm Jolley in front of his motor home, February 2002. (Photograph by Jean-Noel Bassior)

the road—and swivels to face me. "I can't imagine the feelings people still have for this show after all these years! It's maybe the most important thing I wrote because of the effect it had on people who didn't—and haven't yet—forgotten it." He stares out the window at the sea of RVs moored in the park. "Do you know what it means to me to realize that something I did back then has had this effect on people? It blows my mind." He rummages through a box that serves as a desk drawer and pulls out a worn piece of paper. "I got this letter from an aerospace engineer. We talked and he said that many of his colleagues were motivated by the show." Jolley coughs—that lump in his throat again. When he finds his voice, he reads aloud:

> Please allow me to introduce myself: My name is Jon C. Rogers. For the last 25 years, I was an aerospace microwave engineer. I've had the pleasure and the responsibility of working on hardware that went on numerous communications satellites, Apollo missions, and the space shuttle.... My interest in aerospace stems from having seen many episodes of *Space Patrol* and from having read science fiction novels of the era. You helped give me the vision of the future that I have held most dear and have worked diligently to bring into reality. I'd just like you to know that here's one Space Patroller whose life your work affected deeply, and who did his best to live up to the images you helped me believe in early in life—a world where reason, understanding and harmony won out over ignorance, poverty and brutality. I can only hope that mankind never gives up that dream of a bright future, full of hope. To get to anywhere on Earth, the planets or the stars, first you must go there in your dreams.
>
> Thank you, Norm, for my dreams.

CHAPTER 7

In Search of Heroes

Although a trifle young to have all the burdens of the universe on his slim shoulders, Kemmer's intelligence, gravitas and physical grace elevated a cardboard character from a kiddie series into a hero of Homeric stature.

— Stephen Handzo

I'm sure there are people like me who owe a debt to Commander Corry that we can never repay.

— Doug Moore

NEW YORK CITY: FEBRUARY 1988

Four years after our first visit, Kemmer relaxes in his favorite easy chair as the late afternoon sun streams into the penthouse apartment through the window that fronts the river. His face is thinner; his body seems more fragile than slim. Eight months earlier, he'd passed out and was rushed to the hospital: bleeding ulcers. "Not from worry or fretting," he says quickly, but from following his doctor's advice to take two aspirin a day. He's fully recovered, but admits that in the hospital it was touch and go. "It's borrowed time, anyway," he told himself during the worst of it. "I guess that's my war experience," he explains. "I felt sure I was dead then, so it's all a bonus."

Kids, dogs and kitchen clatter are again the backdrop as we talk about *Space Patrol*. It's winter. Across the street, the trees in the park are etched with frost; the river has faded from blue to gray. Right now, though, Kemmer is remembering a warm summer night eleven years ago when he raced to get his wife Fran to the hospital in time for the birth of their third child, Kim.

Speeding down Broadway, he realized they might not make it in time, so he swung onto 59th Street, lined with hotels, where he knew he could flag down a police car. "I got one cop to sit in back with Fran and the other to beat the parade with his car," he recalls. The police escort cleared the way down Fifth Avenue, but after just a few blocks time ran out. "Fran said, 'It's coming,' and I said, 'Don't push!' And she said, '*You don't understand — it's coming!*' I pulled over across from Tiffany's and honked for the police car to stop. I was in perfect position, just kneeling on the front seat, leaning right over the back."

Delivering the baby was something he had to do himself as the two policemen stood guard by the car:

There was a cop on each door. They were young and a bit excited. I had Kim out, holding her up by the ankles, when a big hand came in. The cop was going to do what he'd seen in the movies — a big slap to get her crying, but I said, "No, no!" and got rid of the hand.

Then I noticed that the baby's lips were sealed tight, so I flipped them a little and she started to breathe and cry right away.

For the next few days, Ed Kemmer was the happiest man in the universe…

> I was on cloud nine. I guess it was like the way someone hopes to feel when they take drugs, only this was for real — an honest-to-God, real McCoy elation! I had a big court-room scene the next day on *As the World Turns* with pages of dialogue, and I didn't get any sleep, but it was a breeze!

Kemmer, it seems, does share some qualities with the take-charge Buzz Corry, but it's a subject he talks about reluctantly. He'll admit that he drew on his war experience to make Corry believable in threatening situations. He'll concede that he's a keen observer who (like Corry) can watch something done and then do it himself — but dwell on these things and he takes evasive action. Delivering Kim without help from the cops was "a rational decision," he says curtly. After all, he'd watched his two sons being born, so "I knew the procedure pretty well." If pressed, he'll agree that maybe not everyone has this kind of self-confidence. "There are some guys you talk to who say, 'The cops would have to do it — I couldn't.' Hell, I didn't want those cops doing it —*I* wanted to do it! It didn't take a world of courage or anything; I just didn't see any choice."

"But it was a risk," I point out.

"That's right. I didn't have any doubts as long as it was a natural birth, but there was always that fear in the back of my mind that something could go wrong. Then the thing would be to get to the hospital fast."

"So does Ed Kemmer share a few qualities with Corry, such as the ability to analyze a situation, make a split-second decision, and act?"

Kemmer in 1977 with the child he delivered himself: Kim, age 3 months. (Courtesy Ed Kemmer)

"To a degree. But you can't act without knowing what the hell you're doing — you don't want to be rash. If I'm not confident about something, I approach it very carefully, analyzing it so that I know it can be done and I can do it. Almost anything that's broken, I can fix. I open it up and see why it's not working; then I fix it." He once watched some builders rip out a wall and install a picture window; then he did it himself. "It's all common sense," he explains.

Kemmer's "can-do" approach to life gave Corry an air of certainty when he had to think fast and act faster, something that didn't escape *Space Patrol's* writers. "Norm Jolley wrote for the characters," says actor Ben Welden, whose specialty was playing smirking villains who got under Corry's skin. Welden quickly picked up on the fact that the regular cast had merged with their characters. "They'd *become* them," he recalls. "Whatever they did was right because they were playing themselves." Kemmer, adds Welden, maintained the air of a commander-in-chief both on and off the screen. "He knew he was the leading man and took it for granted, but he wasn't obnoxious. He never threw his weight around."

Lighting director Truck Krone noticed too that Kemmer had merged so completely with the character of Corry that it clung to him after the cameras stopped rolling. "It was his intensity. He believed he *was* that character, like George C. Scott believed he was Patton. When you work on a show, you bust your ass; then all of a sudden it's over and you get back to who you are. It seemed as though he never got back." Years later, Krone hears of Kemmer's daring escape during the march to Moosburg. "I've never heard that until now," he says slowly. "He never talked about it. That would make it a lot more serious to him than to anybody else on the stage, you know?"

Like Jolley and Darley, Kemmer had made the decision early on to treat *Space Patrol* as a dramatic show, not kiddie fare. "We played it for an adult audience," he says, "we played it for real. That's the only way to approach any part." The result was an intensity that — if you can get beyond the primitive special effects of the era — stands up today. As one ex-kid put it in a thank-you note written half a century later: "Your straightforward, serious portrayal made fantasy seem like reality."

English professor Richard Felnagle wrote Kemmer that it was his ability to radiate concern that made *Space Patrol* so believable:

> I remember one episode in which the Terra V landed on a planet on which rust was accelerated. If repairs were not completed in time, the ship would dissolve into iron oxide. Corry seemed to be taking this threat seriously. I have the most vivid memory of sitting on the edge of the sofa and worrying that the Terra V would rust away before the half hour was over. I was worried because I believed *you* were worried.

Kemmer accepts the heartfelt fan letters, which never stop coming, with silent amazement. He doesn't talk about them easily. Either modesty won't let him acknowledge the impact he had as Corry, or he can't come to terms with his influence on so many lives. Not only did he inspire viewers with the believability he brought to the role, but he dazzled them with his physical strength and endurance. Of course, points out a crew member who was there, camera angles and staging are crucial to making an action hero look good — and Kemmer had plenty of help. In fight scenes, director Dick Darley would carefully position the actors and cameras "within the context of conflict, of fighting, to polish and improve the basic action." Darley recalls that Kemmer sometimes helped coach the actors. "If somebody was struggling too hard or too little — not giving him enough to push against — Ed worked with them." That the action scenes — shot *live* with no retakes—came off so effectively is a testament to careful staging. "We all worked together to make it as real as possible," says Darley. To viewers, this behind-the-scenes teamwork was invisible, making Kemmer, who was fit and had an intuitive understanding of how to play a heroic role, appear larger-than-life. The end result wowed Rory Coker:

> The physical stamina of Ed Kemmer is incredible. The scripts and direction often require him to engage in an extended, violent physical stunt, then immediately run from one set to another — sometimes while frantically changing costume — and then deliver dialogue at the beginning of the new sequence. You can often see him fighting to regularize his breathing when he first appears, but the astonishing thing is that it usually takes him only

a few seconds to regain normal respiration. It was Kemmer himself who choreographed the realistic fistfights and wrestling matches that frequently climaxed Corry's adventures as he subdued the bad guy with bare hands. He rarely spares himself in these sequences. The fights go on for unexpectedly long times and involve continuous, extreme physical exertion. He always gives the kids a "payoff" for their faithful viewing, even though he himself pays the full price in the next scene, having to hit his mark and remember and deliver dialogue while completely exhausted.

"My 'physical strength and endurance' are quite a bit exaggerated," Kemmer responds. Perhaps. But though he insists that nothing he did physically was extraordinary, in one episode the evil Prince Baccarratti traps Corry, dangling from a rope, above a pool of acid and the Commander must desperately shimmy up the rope (attached to a pulley which constantly lowers him) to avoid falling into the fatal brew. If you've climbed a rope lately, you'll notice it takes a lot of upper body strength. In another episode, after a strenuous fight against two opponents, he dives into a pool of water to save Hap from drowning, then slings the waterlogged cadet over his shoulder and carries him to safety. Kemmer downplays it all. The fight scenes, he says, usually weren't very long, but he admits they were "chancy" because he had to depend on the other actors:

> The actors have to remember every move in a fight scene and not let nervousness interrupt the routine. The most important consideration is the camera angle. It must look like the punches hit the target, which of course they don't—at least not on purpose! We had a few "grazings," but no hard hits. In blocking the fight I could usually tell if the actor was the excitable type and not dependable. If so, it would be a short fight.

Kemmer did not work out during *Space Patrol*, but he was "in good shape" and played tennis whenever he could with a neighbor. As a kid, he'd been physically active, lettering in basketball and soccer.

In 1988, as we talk of Buzz Corry, he's still not ready to acknowledge his impact on a generation of baby boomers, still downplaying the shading, depth and believability he brought to the role. Whether out of modesty, denial or reluctance to face the fact that his very first job was the pinnacle of his career, this is not safe ground. He insists that Corry was a simple hero, not challenging to play. "I don't think I added a helluva lot because they wrote him in such a way that he had very few faults."

Not true, says Mike Guarino, former dean of the law school at John F. Kennedy University and a prosecutor used to analyzing good guys and bad guys:

> Corry is complex because Ed Kemmer is complex. Kemmer has all kinds of warring characteristics—he's a bundle of contradictions, and that makes Corry interesting. A true hero isn't some all-perfect, completely controlled, immaculate entity without imperfections—that's not what Corry was supposed to be. Changes in voice, gestures, moods—those little things Kemmer brought to Corry transcended script and plot. They made the show come alive.

When I'd talked with Kemmer four years earlier, he'd admitted that he drew on his war experience for "the sense memory of real fear." That in real life he had been both fighter pilot and prisoner of war, escaped during the march to Moosburg and been recaptured, may have helped him make Corry believable when the script called for strength one moment and vulnerability the next. And nobody brought out these qualities in Kemmer better than Bela Kovacs, who played his archenemy, Prince Baccarratti.

SCENE: Prince Baccarratti, holding Buzz and Happy captive, decides to let a dark period in the history of Planet Earth eliminate Corry and his cadet from the universe once and for all. Using Corry's own ship to journey back in time to the year 1692, Baccarratti plans to abandon the Space Patrollers in witch-hunting New England, where he is confident they will meet a fiery death at the stake as "sorcerers from outer space." As the ship lands, Corry, thinking fast, realizes his only hope is to pull an essential transistor from the ship's firing mechanism so that Baccarratti can't blast off again. To do that, he'll have to goad the Prince into striking a blow that will land him underneath the instrument panel — probably not too difficult. As Hap is forced by the Prince's henchman to leave the ship, Corry stalls.

CORRY: (deliberately) *No matter where you go in time, Baccarratti, I'm coming after you. Remember that.*

PRINCE B: *Oh, don't make me laugh, Corry! How are you going to get off Earth, out of this time line, back to the 30th century? Or are you forgetting that there are no spaceships in the year 1692?*

CORRY: (mocking) *The great Prince Baccarratti. His ego's so great that he's blinded to his own vulnerability.*

PRINCE B: *Why, you...!* (Hauls off, hitting Corry hard across the face. Buzz falls dramatically, lingering under the instrument panel where the Prince fails to see he has swiped the tiny transistor.) *All right, Corry, get up! This is where you get out.* (Shakily, Buzz stumbles down the ladder, off the ship.)

PRINCE B: (screams after him) *All right, Corry! Let me see you get out of this!*

HAP: (gently) *We'd better move back a little, Commander. We might get caught in the rocket blast.*

CORRY: *There isn't going to be a rocket blast, Happy.* (He opens his hand to reveal the transistor.)

—"Defeat of Baccarratti," TV Episode 200, December 18, 1954

"Bela gave you a lot to play off of, and you could play it subtly," Kemmer had told me in 1984, recalling the intensity of the scenes that pit Corry against the violent Prince. "His part demanded he go pretty far with it, so it gave me a lot to work with, work against."

"You flashed so quickly from strength and certainty one moment to extreme vulnerability the next," I remind him now.

He sighs heavily. "I think real-life experience helped me there a great deal, because in any kind of threatening situation you are vulnerable. Unless there's vulnerability, there's no threat — and if there's no threat, there's no story." Another key, he suggests, to his portrayal of Corry was harnessing the power of thought:

In any kind of close-up, screen or TV, whatever you think comes through your eyes, your face — so you have to think the right thought at the right time. You can't pretend. You think the thought of being afraid: "I may die in the next minute; *I may be dead the next minute!*" It doesn't have to be that literal, but it must be specific, not scattered. The thought will come through the face, the eyes. You don't do it by making faces. That goes for love scenes— anything. An actor strives for that.

Kemmer didn't keep the grateful letters that poured in, thanking him for portraying a hero that — decades later — was still not forgotten. When they filled several cartons, he threw them out. ("I didn't 'throw them out,'" he snaps. "I just didn't save them.") As more came in, he read them, savored them, tossed them — until Fran Kemmer discovered what he was doing. "I said, 'Oh, no, you can't do that!'" she recalls. "He was getting rid of everything and it was heartbreaking. I mean, these letters are beautiful, and that part of me that works on intuition and emotion can feel the energy coming from these people. They're amazing letters. They make him feel good, but they make me feel better." There was something else about the letters. Eloquent and heartfelt, sometimes they made him uncomfortable. He knew it wasn't easy for the men who wrote them to dig so deep, to express so clearly what they felt about his work:

> You know, as grown men we don't really like to show these feelings. It could be construed as a kind of "weakness" to state some of this stuff—like how could we be so innocent? But they still say it — they say what they feel and have no qualms about it. A lot of people wouldn't say it; it would be too personal. It never ceases to amaze me.

Perhaps Kemmer's reluctance to talk about the impact he had as Corry (unless pressed) and the artistry he brought to the role stems from a belief that talking may kill the magic, says high school teacher Allan Cohen, who plays *Space Patrol* tapes for his students:

> A man doesn't like to dwell on these things. When there's something he thinks was really good, that he's very proud of, somehow talking about it makes it unmanly. Women can be more emotional, talk more; but a man instinctively doesn't want to say anything 'cause he's afraid it'll disappear or it'll lessen it, if you talk that way. It's enough to know these things but not express them.

In the mid–1990s, as Earthlings moved into cyberspace, the letters to Kemmer from aging fans increased as Web pages sprang up devoted to the space operas of the '50s. He was revered there, forever Corry. Baby boomers, searching the Web for their childhood heroes, reconnected with *Space Patrol*. Finally, 40 years later, his impact as hero and role model began to hit home.

But that hadn't happened yet. Right now, in 1988, as twilight fills the seventeenth-floor apartment, he's 67 and wanting to let you know that while Corry was an important role, he played other parts, too. I brush those aside for the moment, still after his take on how he created the perfect hero. Patient but wary when you tread on this ground, he struggles for words, then clams up. But Fran Kemmer, listening to the conversation, jumps in. "Yes, honey, we've never talked about that," she prompts. "How *did* you do it?"

He circles around it, admitting that, as Welden and Krone suspected, he "was" Corry most of the time in those days, staying in character at personal appearances, careful not to smoke in front of the kids, pushing himself to be as outgoing as possible. He recalls long hours spent signing autograph books. (Believe it or not, on Earth in the 1950s, kids could ask their heroes for autographs and get them for free.) "It was hard work and I could have walked away from it," he says, "but it was important to those kids, so you did it."

"Did 'being' Corry in public bring out your best qualities?" I ask.

"It demands better qualities. If you're going to play a better person and be in public with that character, you can't be a Jekyll-Hyde and get away with it. I couldn't be cruel to kids. I can't see anyone playing that kind of role and saying, 'Go away, I don't have time to sign autographs.' I mean, you could look into their little faces and you'd know how hurt they would be."

"You became an idol to so many people," Fran says quietly, pressing for more. Kemmer falls silent. He can't explain the magic he brought to Corry. I try this: "You seemed to totally merge with the role. What part of yourself did you draw on to make it so real?"

"You play your idealized self," he says slowly. "There's some of it in everybody — right on the surface in many, hidden more deeply in others. That's what playing the hero is."

"How do you tap that 'idealized self'?"

"You have to believe that maybe you're better than what you think you are. You look for that better part of yourself — at what you really can do if you *believe* you can do it. Corry couldn't have too many faults — not as many as Ed Kemmer — but playing an idealized image of myself was easier to do than trying to take on another personality or character. Ed Kemmer wanted to be a good guy and do the right thing, so I didn't have to think 'What would Corry do?' because I *knew* what he'd do. I knew how big and small he'd react to things."

Kemmer manages to change the subject, and we move on to talk about television and how social values have changed. The violence on TV disturbs him:

> Oh, God, the shooting and the gun battles — they're sickening and frightening because they have tremendous power. We get so sickened when our kids want to watch this garbage of killing and destroying. It still hurts me to see them wreck new cars for no damn good reason except that the kids like to watch it. And it's gotten much more violent. I mean, the blood is still make-believe blood, but most people get deadened somewhat, just watching the destruction of human beings time after time. It's watched by too many people, too many hours. That's the dangerous part — the violence becomes an everyday thing; we're used to seeing it all the time. If the real thing happened in front of someone, it would change their perspective in a hurry.

On *Space Patrol*, adds Kemmer, he'd always have a fistfight with the bad guys, but no one ever died. "We'd paralyze them temporarily with a ray gun, then put them in a place where they could get help, correct their wrong thinking. That was an Orwellian idea."

Fran Kemmer sighs. "There aren't many good role models around anymore."

He leaps in, passionate: "That's the point! A lot of them are antiheroes. They have some qualities that are fine, but the dark side is there too. Unfortunately, most of what's on the tube is not something you'd want to emulate."

"Could you play a character like Corry today?" I ask.

"Oh, yes!" he says quickly. "But it would have to be more subtle to be believable."

"Is Corry still a part of you?"

He doesn't answer immediately. "Well, the part of me that was there to begin with is still there. Whatever good I gave to Corry, I feel I have today — staying on top of something that's problematic or helping someone who direly needs it. But any decent person would do that. So whatever part I took of Corry and adapted to me is there — or maybe I adapted some of me to Corry ... I'm not sure."

"Is the line fuzzy?"

"Yeah."

Kemmer was only 29 when he assumed the duties of commander-in-chief of the Space Patrol. Five years earlier he'd been starving in a P.O.W. camp, acting in plays to forget about hunger. Back in the States, TV stardom awaited. But first, he had to come home from the war.

In the early morning hours of April 29, 1945, the day Patton's tanks rolled through the prison camp outside Moosburg, Germany, liberating Kemmer and thousands of P.O.W.s, the men heard small arms fire in the distance. As spent bullets hit the barracks, they knew the battle was near. Most of the German guards had fled as the prisoners sat tight, waiting for what would happen next. Kemmer remembers:

> A tank came down the dirt road going into the camp, and they didn't open the gate—they came right *over* the gate, went right through it. I climbed up on the roof to watch, along with some others. The tank went down the main street of the camp, and the commander was throwing .45 caliber bullets for souvenirs. I tried to catch one—I didn't, but my buddy did. You never saw thousands of guys more happy in your life. Deliriously happy. Believe me, you can't get happier than that.

The liberating G.I.s tossed K rations to the starving men, but the word went around: "Don't eat them." After months of starvation, their stomachs had shrunk. Seeing some of the men get sick from stuffing down food, he exercised all the self-control he could, only cheating with a candy bar or two. Kitchens were set up, but the men were warned to take it slow. "It took about a week of limitation on the food before they said, 'Go ahead, the mess tent is open 24 hours a day,'" he recalls.

He sailed for home from Le Havre, France, the last week of May 1945. For his service, he was awarded the Air Medal with three oak leaf clusters, the ETO (European Theater of Operations) Campaign Ribbon with two battle stars, and the Purple Heart. He left the Air Corps as a second lieutenant, though friends in other units had been promoted to first lieutenant for flying the same kind of missions. His commanding officer did not hand out promotions easily. "It's the way he wanted to run it," Kemmer says matter-of-factly. "It was his prerogative."

Home from the war, September 1945. "I'd gained most of my weight back in those five months from late April to September," says Kemmer. (Courtesy Ed Kemmer)

Back in the States, a chance meeting with actor Percy Kilbride, best-known for his role as Pa Kettle in the Ma and Pa Kettle films, put Kemmer on the road to an acting career.[1] He and a pilot friend had gone to New York to pick up some civilian clothes—in short supply after the war. In the dining room of their hotel, Kilbride, then 57, spotted their uniforms and asked, "May I join you?" When Kemmer mentioned he'd tried acting in the P.O.W. camp and liked it, Kilbride urged him to travel to California and study at the famed Pasadena Playhouse because it was next door to Hollywood, the heart of the film industry. But despite Kilbride's encouragement, Kemmer put acting on hold and returned to what he'd done before the war: playing music. He hit the road with trios and quartets, working nightclubs and hotels. Waiting for the elevator at a hotel in Washington, D.C., one day, he met Elaine Edwards, a tall, auburn-haired model and actress.[2] They wed in 1945 and split in 1964. Kemmer won't talk about the marriage.

Finally tired of life on the road, Kemmer took Kilbride's advice, and he and Elaine moved to California, where he enrolled at the Pasadena Playhouse on the G.I. bill in the fall of 1948. There he found a mentor in outspoken director George Phelps, a veteran of vaudeville and musical comedy, who noticed that he spoke from his throat and could not be heard in the back of the theater. Phelps prescribed vocal lessons and within a year, says Kemmer, his voice was transformed. "If you're onstage doing a love scene and you have to shout 'I love you' to the beautiful girl, it takes away from it. But I learned to speak in an entirely different way, and after a while it was the only way I could talk. Even today I can speak in a normal voice and be heard quite a distance."

But Phelps did even more. "If you were a leading man-type actor in Ed Kemmerer's class at the Playhouse, forget it," recalls fellow student John Buckley.[3] Phelps directed many plays on the prestigious Main Stage, but everyone knew who would get the lead in most of *those* productions. Kemmer was clearly Phelps' protégé. His classmates fully expected that in a few years he'd be a major star, but in the meantime, says Buckley, he was pretty annoying competition:

> There was resentment among other people contending for the parts. They said, "Ed Kemmerer is Phelps's fair-haired boy and he's gonna cast him in everything he can." A Main Stage performance was a plum and Ed consistently got the male leads in those plays. Not weird character parts, but straight leading man parts. He wasn't any John Barrymore, but he did them pretty well.

"How many good roles did Buckley have?" Kemmer asks with a flash of anger. "Whatever was going on, I wasn't aware of it." But Playhouse archivist Ellen Bailey, a former instructor at the school, confirms that Phelps had his favorites "and if you weren't one of them, he ignored you." Kemmer later backs down and admits that Phelps did single him out. "He liked my work, thank God. I got a lot of experience I wouldn't have gained otherwise." And Buckley concedes that, despite his advantage, Kemmer "didn't get a swelled head." Though he was pleasant to everyone, the handsome actor didn't hang out much with the other students. "A lot of girls had their eye on him, but he didn't pur-

---

[1]Kilbride became known for playing Pa Kettle opposite Marjorie Main (Ma Kettle) in *The Egg and I* (1947), the first in a series of eleven Ma and Pa Kettle films. Kilbride did nine of them.

[2]Edwards made eleven films between 1949 and 1961, including *The Bat* (1959), *Inside the Mafia* (1959) and *You Have to Run Fast* (1961), in which Ken Mayer also appeared. She guested on popular TV shows, too, including *Perry Mason* (4-11-59), *Colt .45* (5-10-60), and *The Lone Ranger* (8-18-55).

[3]He was still using his real name, Kemmerer, because he couldn't legally shorten it while he was studying on the G.I. bill.

Space hero showdown: Ed Kemmer (center), who plays the flight engineer in "Nightmare at 20,000 Feet" (*Twilight Zone*, October 11, 1963), strains to see a hairy gremlin that mental patient Bob Wilson (William Shatner) insists is tampering with the plane's engine. Chris White, left, plays Shatner's wife in this episode that some critics call the best in the series. (Courtesy Marc Zicree)

sue any of them," Buckley recalls. "He was already married. When school was out, Ed went home to Elaine. He wouldn't do the social scene like Lyn Osborn, who was at Nardi's getting drunk and socializing." Kemmer buckled down and completed his studies in less than two years, with no vacations. The $65 a month he got from the G.I. bill was not enough to live on, so Elaine got work as a movie extra and he took odd jobs on weekends. "The hardest was construction," he recalls, "mostly hauling concrete in a wheelbarrow, pouring foundations. Murder!" Two months after he graduated in January 1950, Osborn called, urging him to audition for *Space Patrol* and launching what Kemmer calls "five very important years of my life."

When *Space Patrol* ended in February 1955, he appeared on a slew of prime-time shows, including *Gunsmoke, Maverick, Perry Mason, 77 Sunset Strip, The Virginian, Wanted: Dead or Alive, Lux Video Theatre, The Twilight Zone,* and many more. In the surreal realm of TV Land, he crossed paths with others who, like him, would wear the mantle of superhero at some point in their lives. In a classic *Twilight Zone* episode, "Nightmare at 20,000 Feet" (October 11, 1963), he played opposite William Shatner, who later gained fame as *Star Trek*'s Captain Kirk. Shatner plays a mentally disturbed passenger on a plane who insists he sees an ape-like beast on the wing tampering with an engine. Kemmer, as the flight engineer, pretends to believe him, but clearly thinks he's crazy. "I remember the particular moment when [Kemmer] is trying to reassure him, saying 'We see it, too,' and the look that crossed [Shatner's] face when he realized they were putting him on," says Richard Matheson, who wrote the episode.[4] It's a prized scene for space opera buffs—a face-off between galactic heroes "Kirk" and "Corry." Another chance to see two icons meet up is in *Mara of the Wilderness* (1966), in which Kemmer plays a pilot and Adam West, star of the 1960s *Batman* series, heads up the cast as "Ken Williams."

In July 1960, Kemmer landed a co-starring role opposite Phyllis Avery in CBS's West Coast soap *The Clear Horizon*, playing Signal Corps officer Roy Selby, assigned to Cape Canaveral. The show, originally titled *Army Wife*, focused on "the private suffering of yet another housewife," according to *TV Guide*.[5] It ran from July 1960 to March 1961, and was reprised from February to June of 1962. Kemmer doesn't talk much about the series, though he was the male

Kemmer co-starred with Phyllis Avery in *The Clear Horizon*, a space-age soap set in Cape Canaveral but shot on the West Coast. (Photograph by Gabor Rona, courtesy Phyllis Avery)

lead and *TV Guide* featured him and Avery in a two-page spread. "It was a good show, one of the best-written daytime shows I've ever been on," he sums up. He'd rather talk about playing heavies, like the scoundrel who tries to victimize a rich old man by impersonating his son in "The Inheritance," a 1960 episode of *Wanted Dead or Alive*.[6] He wants you to know that he's not just Buzz Corry.

"I played murderers."

"How did that feel?" I ask.

"Great!" He likes this. "It's fun to be nasty, to not be a goody-two-shoes all the time. I've always played pretty nice people, so to play a killer is fun."

If you're hooked on Kemmer as Corry, you may have some problems with that. Unlike Clayton Moore (the Lone Ranger), William Boyd (Hopalong Cassidy) and Richard Webb (Captain Midnight), who willingly merged with the roles that made them famous, Kemmer thinks of himself as an actor first, not an icon or hero. In contrast to Moore, who said, "I like playing the good guy," Boyd, who swore that playing Hoppy had transformed him from a party animal into an upstanding citizen, and Webb, who declared, "I *was* Captain Midnight," Kemmer, in 1988, had no desire to be linked to Buzz Corry for the rest of his life. The actor in him loved to stretch in villainous roles. Occasionally,

[4]*The Twilight Zone Companion* by Marc Scott Zicree (Los Angeles: Silman-James Press, 1992).
[5]"Missiles and Miseries," *TV Guide*, February 25, 1961.
[6]"The Inheritance," April 30, 1960.

In his first feature film, *Sierra Stranger*, a low-budget western (Columbia Pictures, 1957), Kemmer plays Sonny Grover, a guy you want to trust but shouldn't. "He was a nasty character," Kemmer admits. (Author's collection)

he'd had the chance to play snide and nasty on *Space Patrol*, too, when the villains drugged Buzz or somehow got control of his mind. You can get a taste of this in TV episode 143, "The Hate Machine of Planet X," as he struggles against Baccarratti's "hate machine," an evil device that arouses hatred in even the noblest soul.[7] When the Prince drops the machine off in space, aimed at Terra City, Corry rushes to disable it before its bad vibes cause the good citizens to destroy one another. But as he approaches the vile contraption, it works its evil on him, awakening his dark side. With the aid of a prerecorded sound track for the "bad" Corry, he fights a battle against a sinister part of himself that urges him not to thwart the machine:

No, wait. Why should you turn it off?
The people. The people of Terra —
    they'll be doomed to self-destruction.
What do you care for the people?
I'm Commander-in-Chief of the Space
    Patrol. It's my duty to protect them.
*Duty! What do you care for duty? What
    did the people of Terra ever do for you?*
It's my duty — they're good people.
You risk your life for them every day but they don't appreciate it!
It's my duty. It's the only right thing to do.
The people wouldn't care if you lost your life doing their dirty work.
It's my duty... it's right.
Forget the machine.
It's right...
Forget the machine!
It's right... Right!! (With superhuman effort, he switches it off.)

Kemmer has an edge to his personality that gave Corry grit and depth, making scenes like this and confrontations with the bad guys — especially Baccarratti — burn with white-hot intensity. Yet for the most part, the occasional villains (cowpokes and gangsters) he played after *Space Patrol* lacked fire. While no one denies Kemmer's skill as an actor, most fans of his work agree that he's more believable as the good guy. "After *Space Patrol*, he was sometimes cast against type," says radio historian Frank Bresee, "but he was such a good-looking guy — he was one of a kind. It was as if somebody said, 'Let's take Cary Grant and make him an evil character in a movie.' You wouldn't buy it." A few years after *Space Patrol* ended, the wife of a crew member caught Kemmer playing a villain on a detective show. "You watched it wondering, 'What's come over Commander Corry?'"

[7]September 9, 1953.

she recalls. A decade later, Kemmer still had not shaken the role. In the late '60s, a friend told Bresee that "Commander Corry" was a regular on an East Coast soap. "*Space Patrol* was one of the most popular shows on the air for a long, long time," says Bresee, "and Kemmer's face was plastered everywhere — on cereal boxes, trading cards, toys. Everyone knew who he was. He just couldn't get out of it."

That "Kemmer" was synonymous with "Corry" was understood by everyone except Kemmer himself. Say the word "typecasting" and he bristles. He vehemently denies that his bond with Corry ever gave him a moment's trouble or created a single obstacle during the course of his career. After all, he points out, he kept working. True. Unlike Al Hodge, who played "Captain Video," he never sold shoes or real estate. Hodge, who worked a number of odd jobs before he died nearly destitute, railed against typecasting, claiming that directors refused to hire him because they feared "the Captain Video identification will destroy character illusion." In contrast, Kemmer says that when he was cast as a villain in *Wanted Dead or Alive*, the producer was pleased to have "Corry" aboard because he would draw a new audience. But given that nearly everyone else involved with *Space Patrol* concedes they were typecast because of the show, it's likely that Kemmer's brilliance as Corry and the indelible impression he made in the role — whether he admits it or not — was a double-edged sword that may have barred him from starring in another action series. He didn't know it, but in 1964, his name was submitted along with 39 other leading man types to Gene Roddenberry, who was searching for a starship captain for *Star Trek*. Others on the list included Sterling Hayden, Robert Stack, Efrem Zimbalist, Jr., Rod Taylor, Jason Robards, Jr., Hugh O'Brian and William Shatner.[8] Though Kemmer made it into this elite group, it's all too likely that at some point during the selection process someone whispered, "But he's Commander Corry."

And speaking of typecasting, here's a little-known fact: In 1958, Kemmer was the artists' model for "Prince Phillip" in the Walt Disney animated classic *Sleeping Beauty*. Limited editions of the video and DVD contain a "making of" segment that shows him wielding "the sword of truth and the shield of virtue" as he slashes at a pole that represents a fire-breathing dragon.[9] Clad in medieval garb — tunic, tights and feathered cap — he moves with a dancer's grace, again portraying the perfect hero. It was grueling physical work, he recalls, and "you had to look good doing it," since the animators were watching every muscle, every facial expression:

> I was on a saddle on a "wooden horse," which was a long plank with a couple of guys on each end who made all sorts of gyrations while I sliced at the dragon with a sword. Physically, it had to be right, because the animators traced all your movements and it had to be done well, athletically, to come out right on the screen. The important thing was in the sword work — the physicality of fighting the "dragon" and looking decent doing it.

Though he downplays the fact that he was chosen to model the archetypal prince, others don't. Renowned Disney animator Milt Kahl told attorney and *Space Patrol* fan Mike Guarino in 1981 that he had struggled for several years to create a credible Prince Phillip, but it was not until Kemmer was picked to model the character that the prince

[8]*Star Trek Creator: The Authorized Biography of Gene Roddenberry* by David Alexander (New York: Penguin, 1994), p. 209.
[9]*Sleeping Beauty*, Fully Restored Limited Edition (Buena Vista Home Video, 1997); released for a limited time in 2003 as a "Special Edition" DVD.

Kemmer (left) models for the Prince Phillip character in Disney's animated classic, *Sleeping Beauty*; an artist's sketch from the scene (right). (Courtesy Kirk and Lynn Leonhardt, Creative Moments, Inc., West Hills, California)

came to life.[10] "I got a lot of good stuff because the way he moved was so princely," Kahl said, adding, "Walt liked that guy." Kahl confided that Disney had been unhappy with the prince character in *Snow White*, whom he felt was "a stranger to the plot." He saw Prince Phillip as another chance to create the perfect male hero and this time get it right. Disney was well aware of the difficulties his artists faced. "If there's anything really tough to animate, it's the male hero," he often remarked. Whenever an animator griped about his job, Walt snapped, "All right, *you* can draw the prince!"[11]

"It never occurred to me that Disney would give it that much importance, but if he did and chose me, I'm flattered," Kemmer responds. As with Corry, he's modest about the Kemmeresque force and grace he brought to the character, insisting that "if you're coordinated, you can do these things." Playing baseball as a kid, he says, taught him to "move a bit," but except for "some dueling stuff at the Playhouse," he never studied dance or movement. He gets little credit for modeling the prince. His name is not mentioned in the video; the only recognition he receives is in

Ed Kemmer in full costume as Prince Phillip. (© Disney Enterprises, Inc.)

[10]Guarino, then working in the Los Angeles city attorney's office, had contacted Kahl to serve as an expert witness in a case involving artwork.

[11]*Walt Disney: The Art of Animation* by Bob Thomas (Racine WI: Golden Press, 1958), p.129. Note: This rare book has photos of Kemmer in costume modeling the Prince Phillip character.

In *Giant from the Unknown* (Astor Pictures 1958), Kemmer battles a giant who wakes up in a bad mood after 500 years in suspended animation. (Probably something a few Brainograph treatments could have fixed.) From the left: Morris Ankrum, Kemmer, Sally Fraser. (Author's collection)

Bob Thomas's book *Walt Disney: The Art of Animation*, where he's sloppily identified as "Ed Kimmer, a handsome young actor noted as commander of a space patrol on a television show."[12]

Between 1956 and 1966, Kemmer made a string of movies, ranging from the B cult classics *Giant from the Unknown* and *Earth vs. the Spider* in 1958 to the better-crafted *Too Much Too Soon* (1958) and *The Crowded Sky* (1960). He soon learned that the fly-by-the-seat-of-your-pants B-movie world had a few things in common with low-budget live TV, such as never enough time or money to do it right. Once, he recalls, a writer came on the set to apologize for a mediocre script, saying, "They only paid for a first draft." Kemmer made the best of it, always turning in a sensitive performance despite poor scripts and chintzy special effects. With five grueling years of live TV under his belt, he was a quick study, able to deal with technical disasters and last-minute script changes without a fuss. His primary goal was to keep working. "We used to say, 'This is shit, but we'll make it the best shit we can,'" he jokes. *Giant* and *Spider*, in which he starred, were

[12]*Ibid*, p.132.

Kemmer starred as pilot Chuck Lawson in *The Hot Angel* (1958) and did his own flying in most of the film. "A big part of the plot was to rescue a pilot who'd crash-landed in the Grand Canyon," he recalls. (The Internet Movie Database had a different take: "Teenage gangs rip highways and skies with thrills and terror" reads the tagline.) "It was a B movie," Kemmer admits. (Courtesy Ed Kemmer)

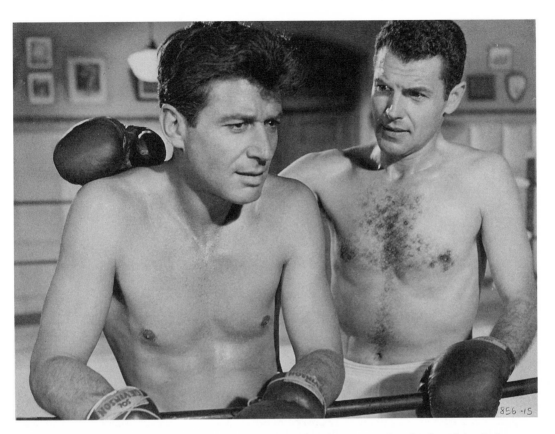

Efrem Zimbalist, Jr. (left, as Dale Heath), spars with Kemmer, who plays his best friend, Caesar, in *The Crowded Sky* (Warner Bros. 1961). (Courtesy Ed Kemmer)

big hits in drive-ins and on the neighborhood theater circuit and brought him a new following of horror movie aficionados.[13] In the late '90s, I showed him a Web page honoring B-movie heroes, and he was pleased that he topped the list.

Too Much Too Soon, which chronicles the life of Diana Barrymore (played by Dorothy Malone), lifted him out of the B world of giants and spiders and was his most prestigious film. He plays Barrymore's third husband, Robert Wilcox, who morphs from a nice guy with eight months' sobriety into a nasty, besotted mess who drinks himself to death. In one scene, Kemmer and Malone argue and he throws a drink in her face, shedding, for once, all remnants of Buzz Corry and, as *Space Patrol* fan Steve Handzo puts it, "portraying weakness as convincingly as he once exuded strength." As the dueling couple bottom out in a sleazy hotel room, there's a knock at the door. By this time, Kemmer, in his underwear, is nearly passed out on the bed, so Malone answers. Heads up, cadets: It's Lyn Osborn, delivering a telegram, and though he doesn't exchange any words with Kemmer in the scene, he throws a knowing glance past Malone into the darkened room. Kemmer says he had no idea that Osborn was in the film. "I didn't see him before that — not until we did the scene. We laughed a lot about it afterwards. Maybe he'd told everyone, 'Don't tell Ed,' because I was quite surprised when I saw him."

---

[13]In a TV remake of *Earth vs. the Spider* (Creature Feature Productions, 2001), the main character is "Quentin Kemmer," reports writer Jeff Berkwits.

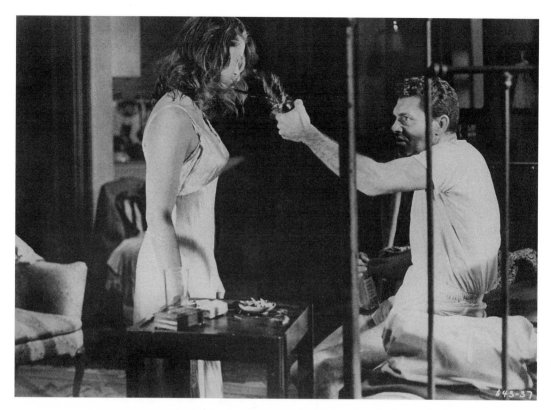

Kemmer sheds any trace of nice-guy Corry and throws a drink in Dorothy Malone's face in *Too Much Too Soon* (Warner Bros. 1958). (Author's collection)

Though Kemmer is convincing as Wilcox, the film, careerwise, proved a stepping stone to nowhere. A-movie offers were not pouring in. He'd heard rumors that Warner Bros. was considering him as a contract player, but he wasn't interested. The pay was steady—about $750 a week—but he'd be tied up for seven years as part of their stable, and even if he ended up in a hit TV series or feature film, the salary stayed the same. "You sell your soul to the studio and they could just beat the hell out of you and sour you on the industry," he says hotly. He was happier freelancing, "earning a good living and free to do what I wanted." In 1960, he appeared in another A film, *The Crowded Sky*, but his movie career failed to ignite and from then on—with the exception of *Mara of the Wilderness* in 1966 (a B film)—he focused exclusively on television.

In the mid–'60s, he saw roles for Hollywood freelancers dwindling as hour-long shows replaced half-hour formats and many series relied on contract players. So when the producers of the East Coast soap *The Edge of Night* came west shopping for actors in 1964, Kemmer, then 43, auditioned for—and landed—the part of alcoholic news reporter Malcolm Thomas. His marriage to actress Elaine Edwards was ending, and he pulled up stakes and moved to New York. Actor Barry Newman, who played John Barnes on *Edge* from 1964 to 1965 and later starred in the mid–'70s detective series *Petrocelli*, remembers Kemmer on the set:

> He was a quiet guy, low-key, soft-spoken, not an extrovert by any stretch of the imagination, not a talker or a "How ya doin'?" kind of guy. He was a man of action, but never

threw his weight around—he just did what he had to do and did it quietly and well. He had that Gary Cooper quality, like "You want me to do it this way? Absolutely. Nope. Yep. See ya later." Very professional, very nice. He wasn't a schmoozer, but if you got to know him, he got to you.

On *Edge*, Kemmer met Fran Sharon, 25, who played Cookie Pollock, and the two fell in love. In the script, Malcolm and Cookie are sweethearts who later marry, but their romance ends tragically when Kemmer's character is stabbed in the back with scissors by a jealous lover played by Connie Ford. (Viewers were outraged. For days afterward, Ford needed a police escort to go to and from the studio.) In real life, Kemmer and Sharon tied the knot in 1969 and have three children: Jonathan, Todd and Kim.

"Do your kids ever watch *Space Patrol* tapes?" I ask.

"They watched once and thought it was pretty corny," he says quietly. "They never play them."

Kemmer in *Edge of Night*, 1965, as news reporter Malcolm Thomas. (Courtesy Ed Kemmer)

Other soaps followed, including *As the World Turns, All My Children, The Doctors, Ryan's Hope, Guiding Light,* and *Love of Life*. In 1970, he kicked off *Somerset* by playing the family patriarch, attorney Ben Grant, but he admits that his soap opera roles were not challenging:

> It's factory work. There's nothing new about anything you do on a soap—it's such mundane stuff. You seldom see things happen, but people talk about them. That's the way you make cheap movies: You don't see the car go over the cliff—someone tells you about it, so it costs less. Maybe once a year you get a scene that, hey, this is gonna be fun because the writers wrote it very well, or it's an interesting part of the plot coming up. But those scenes don't happen very often.

"I can't watch soaps," I tell him.

"I can't either," he says quickly. "It was hard enough doing them. Oh, God, they're such garbage—but probably no worse than

Fran and Ed Kemmer, summer 2000. (Photograph by Jonathan Kemmer, courtesy Ed Kemmer)

most of the stuff that's on TV. They do serve a purpose, I guess. And they pay well." He did "nineteen solid years of soaps" in New York until he retired in 1983. His last television appearance — a military role — was as Admiral Burke in the TV mini-series *Kennedy*, starring Martin Sheen. He doesn't explain or justify the course his career took after *Space Patrol*; he's proud that he worked steadily, an impressive feat for any actor. He sighs. "It was making a living."

A good living, says Barry Newman, who got out of Dodge as fast as he could when his contract with *Edge of Night* expired. Stay in the soaps for more than two or three years, he warns, and you may stay forever. "Suddenly you're a little older and the guys who are making it are the same age as you — and they're movie stars. And where have you been? You haven't been out in the marketplace doing a picture or two; you've been in the soap world." Newman, then single and career-oriented, left for more creative pastures. He'd seen friends sucked into the soap opera whirlpool, from which, it seemed, there was no escape:

> You know what happens: You do the show and your contract is over, and another show wants you — and there's more money. And you say, "Well, that's pretty good." And then you do the other show for three years, and you hate doing it and you say, "God, I'm finished with this!" And they say, "Look, there's another show, but you're going to be the lead and it's double the money." It's a trap for actors.

But to Kemmer, the soaps offered a steady living and a schedule that gave him what he wanted most at this point in life: time with his family. "Ed is perfectly happy doing soaps and nothing else," reported Herbert Fishberg in the December 1977 issue of *Afternoon TV Stars*. Kemmer made it clear to Fishberg that family came first, before his career:

> I prefer to do soaps because it gives me more time to be with my family. It's day work! If I were to do something else, like a play, it would take up a lot more of my time. For me to consider doing a play now, it would have to offer a really good part. When you do a play, you're on the run. If I did the soap and a play at the same time, I wouldn't get to see my kids at all.

"For Ed," summed up Fishberg, "soaps are a way of life."

"A lot of Space Patrollers were in high school and college in the '60s and '70s," I tell Kemmer at the end of our visit. "We lost track of your career because we weren't watching daytime soaps."

"I hope not," he says. "I hope you were busier than that."

In 1988, though aware that Corry was still of interest to many, Kemmer had staked out some distance from the character, still slightly wary. In that year, Earth was on the cusp of a cyberspace revolution. Within a decade, many who remembered Buzz Corry and *Space Patrol* would connect through the Internet, rekindle childhood memories, and seek out their heroes of long ago. But that was still in the future. For the time being, Kemmer had politely answered my questions, delving a little deeper than he wanted, but it was unclear how much of an emotional tie he felt to the hero who had inspired millions of baby boomers and their parents. Unlike actors Boyd, Moore and Webb, he never spoke about his most famous role unless asked. I left it at that, for the moment, still wondering if he realized the impact he'd had as Corry; knowing I'd ask him that question again when the time was right.

CHAPTER 8

Houston, We've Got a Problem

On a particular day on Planet X, Commander Corry, from the safety of the space-ship, was explaining to Cadet Happy that not even the most primitive form of life could exist on X. But as the camera ranged over the X-scape, we saw that the Commander was wrong. Across the forbidding wastes tramped a studio carpenter carrying a ladder. Behind him, an assistant with a tool box.
— TV columnist William O'Hallaren

When television started, the geeks were in charge because nobody else knew how to get a picture out of a camera and onto the screen.
— Dick Darley

It was 4:30 on Saturday morning when Lyn Osborn left his apartment overlooking the Sunset Strip to drive to ABC Television Center in the dark, misty hours before dawn, when even Hollywood slept.

Stumbling onto the set in the chilly blackness, cast and crew had three hours to wake up and whip the show into shape. For two years, *Space Patrol* was shot live in Hollywood at 8:00 A.M. in order to air in the East at 11:00. "It *had* to be live because the East Coast was spoiled," says technical director Bob Trachinger. "They were used to good quality. If they'd seen a kinescope recording, the value of the show would have plummeted."[1] With the transcontinental cable plus a series of microwave relay towers now making live broadcasts possible, there was no way you could give the sophisticated New York audience a noisy, grainy kinescope recording, Trachinger explains. But West Coast viewers, considered less discriminating, were fed a "hot" kinnie later that day.[2]

Making a kinescope is like pointing a Camcorder at your TV screen and shooting a home movie. As *Space Patrol* was performed live, the final edit was fed into a high-resolution monitor that looked like your TV set, except the screen was much smaller and the picture more intense. A special kinescope camera loaded with 35mm film was aimed at the monitor screen, recording the show from the live broadcast.[3] "Think of the out-

---

[1] This chapter describes the *Space Patrol* set during the period when the show was shot on Saturday morning at 8:00 A.M. Pacific Time. According to Dick Darley's ABC schedule, news clips, other documents (including Lyn Osborn's letters) and heroic research by Steve Handzo, the network show was shot at 6:00 P.M. on Saturday from December 30, 1950, to January 5, 1952, then at 3:00 P.M. on Sunday for the next six months (January 13–June 1, 1952)—though some cast and crew members insist it was always shot at 8:00 on Saturday morning so that it would air at 11:00 A.M. on the East Coast. Not true. Darley's schedule confirms the early morning shoot for two years (June 7, 1952–June 12, 1954). Then, following a summer hiatus, the show was shot on weekdays, usually Wednesday or Friday (no time listed), and it appears that all markets got kinescopes for weekend air play. The last show, #210, was shot on Wednesday, February 2, 1955, though it aired on Saturday, February 26.

[2] A "hot" kinescope, says master control engineer Don McCroskey, was processed in less than two hours.

[3] "A 16 mm negative with optical sound was always recorded, processed and played back as the protection source," says McCroskey, who believes that 16 mm distribution copies were struck from this negative.

Cast and crew take a break from rehearsing "The Mystery of the Flying Pirate Ship," aired August 2, 1952. From the left: Mike Moser with art director Carl Macauley in foreground; behind Moser: Ed Kemmer, Dick Darley, technical director Irwin Stanton, and Lyn Osborn. The cameraman is John De Mos. In the back: Ken Mayer flanked by "pirates" Bela Kovacs (left) and Glenn Strange. (Courtesy Dick Darley)

put from the studio as a 'Y,'" says Trachinger. "One leg goes to the kinescope department at ABC; the other to cities in the East via the cable and microwave network." The kinescope of the show, shot by the special camera, was speedily processed, dried and waxed. The West Coast saw it within hours; then copies were sent (or "bicycled") to affiliates that were out of range of the cable and microwave networks or chose not to carry the show live.[4]

By 5:00 A.M. Studio A was alive and bustling with activity. "It seemed like you'd been there all day," recalls lighting director Truck Krone. As the sun rose over the Hollywood Hills, "things were happening all over the place," says assistant director Marg Clifton

[4]It should be noted, points out Steve Handzo, that when the show first went network, California audiences enjoyed a live broadcast for 18 months (December 30, 1950–June 1, 1952), first at 6:00 P.M. on Saturday (until January 5, 1952) and later at 3:00 P.M. on Sunday (January 13–June 1, 1952.) When early morning shooting began on June 7, 1952, with episode 76, "The Scheming Sibling," so that East Coast viewers could get the show live at 11 A.M. on Saturday, the West Coast saw a kinnie later that day at 6:30 P.M. Then, on November 15, 1952, *Space Patrol* became a Saturday morning show for West Coast viewers (as many remember it), when it switched to 11:00 A.M.—but that only lasted four months. On March 21, 1953, it returned to an early evening Saturday time slot, this time at 5:30 P.M.

(Satchell). Jack Narz was standing at one end of the rocketship going over a Chex commercial, while Kemmer and Osborn rehearsed at the other, piloting the ship. Sometimes Kemmer and Kovacs would retreat into a corner, scripts in hand, where Krone overheard them "trying to get themselves to remember the lines." As the lights warmed the cavernous soundstage, everyone shook off fatigue. Most of the crew had set their alarms for 3:00 A.M. "Every week we'd lose sleep, waiting for that alarm to go off," audio man Chuck Lewis's wife recalls. "I don't know how bright *you* are at 4:00 in the morning," says Krone, "but during the first run-through, everyone was half-asleep. The camera ran into the spaceship and shook it a lot. We were like a bunch of little kids."

Dick Darley's stomach was always queasy — he knew that jury-rigged special effects and last-minute script changes for guest actors baffled and panicked by live TV could blow up in his face. Marg Clifton tried to keep things on track, making sure everyone knew about changes in dialogue, blocking, or camera moves. By 6:30, the cast was in costume and makeup; by 7:00, they were onstage for the dress rehearsal — even if not every technical problem had been solved. Clifton recalls that often the cameramen were still figuring out how to swing around from one scene to the next without tangling their cables, and more problems were sure to crop up during the dress rehearsal itself. By 7:30 A.M. — a half-hour before air time — tension ran high as the crew huddled around ornery special effects and actors wrestled with last-minute script changes. At this point, cast and crew had only minutes to make things work because, says Clifton, "at 8:00 A.M. the clock came on and we were doing it live."

Though edgy inside, Darley radiated a certainty that both cast and crew relied on. "He wasn't a hunt-shoot-and-fish kind of guy, but he had presence and authority and knew exactly what he wanted," says Maury Orr (De Mots), who filled in occasionally for assistant director Marge Rotunda. As Darley directed the dress rehearsal from the booth above the stage, he took notes, then came down and gathered the cast. "We'd meet before going on the air and I'd do a critique of the scenes. I called this routine 'The Notes,'" he says with a hint of menace. "Some of it had to do with interpretation, some with staging. If I was trying to set up a dramatic close-up and I wanted Carol to turn into it for visual impact, that's a technical thing. If someone was not connecting with the character they were talking to, I'd say, 'Stop reading the lines.'" Hopefully, there had been time on Friday for a camera rehearsal with the scenes in sequence. "That was ideal," says Darley. But often, the first — and only — run-through in sequence was the dress rehearsal less than an hour before the live broadcast, where the script was nipped and tucked one last time. Announcer Jack Narz was watching:

> About a half-hour before airtime, Dick would come down with stretches and cuts. He'd say, "This line is cut, we're substituting that line for this one." Sometimes they'd have to paste the changes on the walls. It was tough. I would have been up all night, worrying about my lines.

The role of adult fell to Darley. Together with Kemmer, who seemed to never quite shed the aura of Corry when the cameras stopped rolling, you had a team at the helm who could bring the show home. Serious, goal-oriented, steeped in military discipline, both men were hell-bent on surmounting all obstacles. Ed Kemmer, says Darley, was his right-hand man on the set:

> I had a friend in Ed. We were the most nearly alike — both had been in the war as pilots, both rather straight. We concentrated on what we were doing in a business-like way —

not always the most fun-to-do showbiz. Somebody had to be a bastard, so I was elected, but I needed all the control help I could get, and I could count on Ed. He'd have studied his lines, he'd know his stuff. If somebody in the cast was acting up, we'd talk to them in concert. I could depend on him in terms of getting the damn thing on and off the air; I was grateful he was in the cast.

"I think when they cast the part of Corry they were looking for someone solid who could hold things together," Kemmer acknowledges, "and I accepted a big chunk of that responsibility. It wouldn't have taken much for any of those shows to fall in and Dick would have had nothing to photograph."

Truck Krone beat the early morning commute by spending the night in a dressing room — not only on the eve of the live broadcast, but occasionally during the week when sets, effects, sound and lighting were created on impossible deadlines. At 4:00 A.M. on Saturday, he fired up the equipment:

> In those days in television, it was unbelievable, the amount of hours you were there. The weekly show was put together in a day and a half. You'd stay until 12 o'clock at night and the next morning you're in at 4 or 5 A.M. It damn near caused a divorce, because nobody in their right mind would go to work on Thursday and not get home till Saturday.

It was often during the last-minute dress rehearsal, Marg Clifton recalls, that you found out "things didn't always work"; then you had 15 or 20 minutes before airtime to solve the problem — if you could. She watched Ed Kemmer grow anxious as crew members troubleshot obstinate special effects:

> There were lots of explosions and anything could go wrong. If some effect wasn't working right, they were all there checking it, making sure they knew what the problem was, that it wouldn't happen again. Ed would get in on it because if it involved him, he wanted to be sure it wouldn't hurt him. Everybody was concerned, but he was especially concerned. He wanted to know how it worked, what it was doing. But you never knew. You just crossed your fingers and hoped it would work.

But if it worked safely, that didn't mean it worked *right*. Though checked and triple-checked, some stubborn effects just failed to function properly during the live broadcast. The crew learned to expect it. "We'd say, 'This is a special effect and you're lucky if it works,'" says Clifton. Both human and mechanical errors triggered major disasters that the actors had to cover or ignore. Say a tunnel is supposed to cave in at a dramatic peak in the show, but doesn't. "That's when you'd get knots in your stomach," Clifton recalls.

"We worried about special effects all the time," confirms Jack Narz:

> You had sound men dealing with records and turntables, and we're going, "Jesus Christ, let's hope they get it right." It's like in a murder drama when a guy picks up a knife and a gun goes off. We knew how things were held together with strings and safety pins. Of course, it didn't look like that on the air, but we were too busy worrying about the nuts and bolts to see the glamour of it. We were going, "How the hell are we going to get this rocket to fly across the stage without falling off the string?" At the time we were sweating bullets, practically wetting our pants.

Despite the chance that effects could go south, Darley (egged on by Jolley's scripts), continued to push the envelope. In "The Giant of Planet X" (episode 148, October 24, 1953), Prince Baccarratti turns his Diminisher Machine on Corry and Hap, reducing them in size to only a few inches tall. In a risky feat for live television, Darley shot Kemmer and Osborn on one set and superimposed the action on another. One contained the furniture in Baccarratti's castle (which appeared huge in relation to the "diminished" Buzz and Hap); the other only had "levels" that matched the furniture. That set was totally dark, recalls Ed Kemmer:

> Hap and I worked in a completely black set so that only our bodies were visible; we were photographed from a distance so that, when superimposed, we looked much smaller than the objects on the [other] set. The camera on the main set was locked in position so it couldn't move and stayed exactly the same throughout the scene. The other camera (on Hap and me) had to adjust and lock its position so that the levels Hap and I worked on matched the levels in the main set, i.e. the floor, the chair seat, the table top. Once everything was "matched," both cameras were locked off and couldn't move. If either camera moved, the levels wouldn't match and Hap and I might look like we were standing in mid-air instead of on the table top.

The show, admits Kemmer, "did stretch the risk factor a bit. But everything was risky in live TV."

And in case of a disaster — if things had gone horribly wrong?

"I'm sure Dick Darley would have thought of something," Kemmer says quickly.

As he climbed the steps to the control booth minutes before the live broadcast, Dick Darley was the best actor on the set. He knew everyone was watching him, gauging his level of confidence. Just a few years earlier, he'd been a page at the Don Lee Network; now *Los Angeles Examiner* columnist Pat Hogan was calling him "one of the top TV directors in the business."[5] Darley was 5 feet 11 and lean. "I'd swear he weighed 120 pounds soaking wet," says Bob Trachinger, who knew Dick had been a pilot during the war and could feign coolness on the outside. But Trachinger wasn't fooled — he could tell the director's stress level was high because of the mashed potatoes. "Ask him about that," he says, chuckling. "He'd eat them to stabilize his stomach." But right before airtime, everyone's stress level was off the chart. "The most tension came," admits Darley, "when you were headed for the booth and [the show] wasn't ready." You flew by the seat of your pants, hoping to pull it out of a dive. Darley's quiet confidence impressed AD Maury Orr. "It was Dick's show — he had a Mr. Full Charge aura about him. And he was positive, which is what production people love, because when a guy comes out there and says, 'Well, I don't know if we should do it this way or that way,' you've got no faith in him. We had a lot of those kinds of directors at ABC over the years."

If he'd learned one thing in officer training, says Darley, it was to never let anyone sense you're afraid. "You can be panicking inside, but you don't panic before the crew or the actors because they pick up on it. You keep it to yourself, pretend you know what you're doing." But inside he was wracked by nerves:

> Just seconds before we went on the air, you were in such a state of anxiety, ready to pull the trigger. And it was my job to calm everybody down, even if I thought we were going in the toilet. They picked up off me, so I learned early on: Just hold your cool, no matter what.

---

[5]Pat Hogan's "Stop-Look-Listen" column, *Los Angeles Examiner*, March 30, 1950.

But that, says Darley, was the excitement of it, the fun and challenge of doing it. You were tight, on edge — and so were the actors before the first scene. But when the clock went on, you shifted into concentration mode. "You're rolling and there's no tomorrow. You can't go back."

How do you fight off a mean-tempered, man-eating vine that wants to kill you because it's guarding Prince Baccarratti's castle on Planet X?

"*You* grab it and *you* pull it around your neck," says Ed Kemmer, whipping around in his chair during one of our early interviews. He's in actor mode now, straining against an invisible killer vine that has invaded his penthouse domain. "You're 'fighting it,' see? It looks like I'm pushing it away, when actually I'm pulling it toward me. It looks," he gasps, "*as if it's going around my neck and I can't stop it.*" Losing the battle, he slumps in the chair. "So, you see, *you* supply the power to the vine."

Space Patrol had an action peak every five minutes. "Most [adventure] shows do," Kemmer explains. "A fight, some kind of threatening action — it's all built into the formula." And if fending off man-eating plants, Thormanoids, evil robots and crazed humans wasn't enough to worry about, there were other pressures. "Believe me, I was going on several levels. Dick depended on me for timing. He'd send the stage manager over while I was off camera and boy, when he'd hand me that headset, I knew what was coming."

It was Darley: "*Ed, please. I need three minutes.*" Kemmer knew it was up to him to tell the rest of the players to speed up their lines...

> See, some actors stretch like mad during a show. During rehearsal they do it snap, snap, snap [*with fingers*], and then, during the show, they start A-C-T-I-N-G — really overplaying. They take twice as long to say the line. Instead of "I'm going to kill you," they say "I ... am ... go ... ing ... to ... kill ... you." Well, right there, that's double or triple the time. So I'd get to each actor and tell them, "I'm going to cut into your lines, not let you finish. Just stay with plot, plot, plot, and don't worry about it. Pick up the cues, talk fast, and I'll cut you off." It ended up, I was talking like a shotgun. But we never went over; and we never went off before we should have.

Stir in one more hazardous element: live commercials, in which Kemmer and Osborn had to convince kids that the sponsors' products gave them the get-up-and-go to defeat the bad guys. "For months, I was after [Nestlé and Ralston Purina] to film the commercials," Kemmer recalls. "Hap and I would finish a fight scene way up on the catwalks, out of breath, dirty. You could be a little bloody — real blood — a scratch here and there, and sweaty as hell, wiping yourself with a towel and trying to look at a script." If they were lucky, sometimes they had a few seconds to calm down enough to eat the cereal or sip the cocoa. But sometimes they didn't:

> *SCENE:* Commander Corry, at ease, lifts a steaming-hot cup of Nestlé's EverReady Cocoa to smiling lips and, breathless, simulates a contented sigh.
>
> *CORRY: Yes, Nestlé's Cocoa is really a sensational treat — rich with whole milk and sugar, so easy to fix, too. "Look!"* (cues Hap, whose hands are shaking)...
> *HAP: Just one, two, three spoonfuls in the cup, add hot water, and there, Commander, it's made! What a way to start the day!*
> *CORRY: That's right, Hap. So kids, ask Mom to start fixing you the delicious, modern cocoa for all the strength and power a Space Patroller needs: Nestlé's EverReady Instant Cocoa in the bright red can. It's out of this universe!*

"Finally—*finally*, I guess they saw one too many spots with a sweaty, dirty, bloody guy trying to talk through no breath, so they agreed to do a bunch on film and we shot ten in one day." Kemmer sighs, for real:

> The whole thing was rough, but the more you did it, thank God, the easier it became. You didn't have the rehearsals. You had the script overnight, and that's it. You did it because you had to, and you didn't know how tough it was. You try and make it believable; that's all you can do.

But even if you do all *you* can do, somebody else may not. Everyone agrees that one of the worst moments was when a stagehand from Earth, hauling a plank, strolled through a set depicting "outer space"—right between actors and camera—during the live network broadcast. "The stage crew was a bunch of lovable guys, but in those days television got what was left at the bottom of the union barrel," Darley explains:

> The best guys were doing motion pictures, so we got a few who were past retirement and didn't know it. One of them, Henry, never quite got the concept of continuity in live TV. So you'd be on the air in the middle of some kind of tense dialogue scene taking place in the ship—which is flying along light years fast in outer space—and here comes this little wizened-up stage guy wearing a World War I veteran's cap, carrying a plank over his shoulder, walking right through the scene. There was nothing you could do about it. You went right on with the show and paid no attention to it, as if it was a seagull in outer space.

Ed Kemmer: "I didn't believe my eyes, but right between us and the camera is a grip with a 2 × 4 over his shoulder. So Hap and I were talking, and I totally ignore it, but Hap just couldn't let it go—he *had* to react." Kemmer mimics Osborn, opening his eyes wide with astonishment. "If anything unusual happened, he'd give you a reaction that didn't belong in the show but was funnier than hell."

The only thing you could bank on was that there was never enough time.

Ideally, the actors picked up their scripts on Wednesday for the Saturday network broadcast and studied them overnight before the walk-through on Thursday afternoon—but sometimes the scripts weren't available until the day before the show. By Tuesday, Darley was hustling to corral art director Carl Macauley and prop master Al Teaney to confer about set design and special effects.[6] On Thursday, he needed at least three key staffers—technical director, lighting director and head audio man, if he could grab them—plus a stage manager to accompany him as he plotted the staging.

The show was shot with three cameras, so that Corry and Hap, for example, could take off in their battlecruiser in one scene, then race to another set and confront the villains in their Saturn hideout seconds later. During the first rehearsal, Darley walked the cameramen through their moves, scene by scene, showing them when to cut away to miniatures and special effects. "They were thinking guys, real stalwarts and into the show. Jimmy Morris and Johnny De Mos were always making suggestions," he recalls. In a live broadcast, split-second timing is crucial—it has to work—and the men made copious notes which they clipped to their cameras, listing their shots and plotting the fastest way to push the 600-pound machines from set to set through a snake nest of cables without colliding. A few crack cameramen paid rapt attention to the storyline and never wrote

---

[6]Jimmy Angel was Teaney's assistant for a while. He later became a camera operator.

Al Teaney (center) fashions a spaceship in 1952 in the prop room at ABC with assistants Bob Waugh (left) and Cliff (whose last name could not be remembered). Teaney used wood, pipes, wires and sugar to replicate the 30th century. (Photograph by Richard Loeb, courtesy Alyce Teaney)

anything down. "They got into the sequence, what was going on," says boom man and camera operator Clair Higgins. "Not only did Jimmy Morris not write down his shots, he knew *your* shots," recalls Bob Trachinger. He could look at your camera while you were moving into a shot and alert you if you had the wrong lens up. He was a genius."[7]

"Only the best guys worked on Space Patrol," says Higgins. "You couldn't wait to get on it. Once I was on my day off and they called and asked me to fill in for someone — I was really excited. Then before I left the house, they called back to say the guy had shown up. I was broken-hearted." A lot of camera work on other shows was just "standing by and flipping lenses," Higgins explains. "It didn't mean much. But Space Patrol was exciting and much more complex. On that show, you had to be in the right place at the right time, every shot."

On the walk-through, cast and crew learned where the cameras were supposed to be — *if* they made it in time. Everyone made notes as Darley ran through it. "The lighting director has to know all the moves people make so he can place his lights where the boom won't throw shadows across the set," he explains. When audio man Chuck Lewis

[7]Jack Denton and lighting director Alex Quiroga also worked on the show as camera operators.

was present, he'd be figuring out how many extra mikes he could steal from another stage to soup up the sound. Like Darley, Krone and Kemmer, he was a perfectionist—cantankerous at times, but hell-bent on making *Space Patrol* the best it could be:

> I wanted to do something extra, but there wasn't a lot of time or money, so I'd go to another studio and "borrow" a mike. I wasn't stealing it—I'd put it back. I hid mikes behind the instruments on the control panel of the spaceship—we had so many mikes in that ship! The TD [technical director] got upset with me because he didn't think there were enough holes for them in the board. But there was a three-position switch [in the audio booth] so as the actors were talking and moving around, I was switching that key back and forth between mikes and adjusting the sound on three different faders. That made it very pre-carious—that's why he was concerned. He thought there would be a screw-up on the air. I never screwed up.

Audio operator Chuck Lewis at Army Air Corps flying school in 1942. Lewis "borrowed" as many mikes as he could from other stages to enhance the sound on *Space Patrol.* (Courtesy Chuck Lewis)

On Friday, just one day before the live broadcast, the one and only major rehearsal took place, working around other shows that needed the stage— *You Asked For It, Mysteries of Chinatown,* and *Korla Pandit,* a turbaned organist the crew dubbed "The Korean Bandit," who mesmerized housewives without uttering a word.[8] "Sometimes the other shows built sets within our sets," says Darley, who watched actors on *Mysteries of Chinatown* get confused during their live broadcast and wander onto the *Space Patrol* set by mistake.

During the crucial Friday rehearsal, scenes were timed to the second, says AD Maury Orr. "The stopwatch was part of my body. We had to stretch or cut to make it fit the time." Today, explains Orr, you'd simply edit the video tape, "but back then, it was live— we just had the actors to work with. We'd cut scenes or pad dialogue, then add up the minutes and seconds. Sometimes, we'd chop a whole scene." In that case, Darley and Kem-mer would disappear into a corner to rewrite a section of the script. "They were close," says Orr. "You could feel the bond between them."

A day and a half was not enough time to get everything done. "There were always several scenes we didn't have time to light properly," says Truck Krone. "There was never enough time," says Darley flatly. "We always skidded onto the air."

That was nothing new to the crew, many of whom, just a few years earlier, had been skidding planes onto makeshift runways and dodging bullets overseas. "A lot of them

[8]Social Security records obtained by retired broadcast engineer Roy Trumbull reveal that Pandit's real name was John Redd and he hailed from St. Louis, Missouri. In his pre–Pandit days, say Trumbull and Larry Bloomfield in Tech-Note #41 at www.tech-notes.tv, he also used the name Juan Rolando. Trumbull believes that Redd initially began passing himself off as a Latino to avoid race discrimination. "Being a black musician meant working out of the black local musician's union," says Trumbull, noting that Latinos could join the white union and enjoyed better prospects. Pandit's relatives maintain he was born in India.

were gung-ho guys out of the war," says announcer Dick Tufeld, who was younger than the rest. Risk-taking was all in a day's work for these vets, who brought a can-do spirit to live TV. "It was a bunch of brash, young guys inventing television out of necessity and having fun," says Bob Trachinger, who started out as a cameraman at ABC and ended up as vice president in charge of West Coast operations. "Most of us were under 30. You had to be that young and stupid to take the risks we did." Or have been through the war. No one talked much about the war, and only a few knew of Kemmer's fighter pilot experience, though Chuck Lewis, who'd been a member of a B-17 bomber crew, sensed that he and Ed had a few things in common. "We both fought our way back 500 miles from the target," he says quietly. Sometimes he'd see Kemmer "sit off to the side somewhere. He was probably memorizing things, but I have an idea he was thinking back. He used to talk with Ken Manson, another pilot who went down. Bunch of German farmers grabbed him."

Not that everyone was always heroic. While most of the time an air of easygoing cooperation reigned during rehearsal, a combo of special effects misfiring and guest actors stumbling over their lines could make tempers boil. "When things weren't going right," says Marg Clifton, "everyone was on edge." Fifty years later, Clifton (whose strongest expletive is "Cheese and crackers!") doesn't want to offend anyone by "naming names," but it's clear that at times Studio A felt like the hot side of Mercury. When Darley sensed mutiny brewing, he held his ground, knowing that without a strong hand, everything would cave in. "Somebody had to draw the line — someone that everyone could get mad at or blame. You're psychiatrist, mother, father, brother, bastard. My credo was: "I don't have to be loved. I have to have respect to get this show done."

On a bad day, says Darley, the cameramen would "moan and groan" about having to race between sets with the heavy cameras while other crew members insisted that a shot, lighting, or special effect he wanted couldn't be done. When that happened, says Clifton, the director dug in his heels and said that it could. "He knew so much about light, sound and special effects that the crew knew better than to tell him it was impossible," she recalls. When the set was tense, Darley said little if anyone made a mistake. "He just corrected it nicely," says Clifton. "He was in control. He never let them know it was giving him knots inside." Tougher words sped down the chain of command from technical director Irwin Stanton, an ex-wrestler who didn't hesitate to verbally beat up crew members in his quest for perfection. "When you screwed up, you got chewed out," says Clair Higgins, "but in the days of live TV, when it was over, everybody would forget. Today, when you make a mistake, they look at it a hundred times and reshoot it, so it's a different attitude." The thing that bugged crew members most, he adds, was taking flak during the live show:

> The one thing we came up with was that we shouldn't get chewed out too much on the air because one mistake will lead to three. If they start yelling at you while the show's going on, you'll make two or three more mistakes real quick 'cause you're all freaked out. It really shook you up. So we made a kind of unwritten law that they stop doing that because you had a hard time getting your act together again.

Cast members occasionally boiled over and threatened to walk, "but you get that in any production," says Dick Darley. "You can't put a show on without conflicts, and crises came up constantly. At one time or another, everyone was mad at everybody else; everyone was quitting. But that's normal. People not in the business don't understand, but it's

Assistant director Maury Orr (center) and technical director Irwin Stanton (right) work the Academy Awards with director Dick Dunlap (left; he did not work on *Space Patrol*) circa 1965. Dunlap insisted that all ABC crew members dress in formal attire for the Awards, and the tradition continues until this day, says Orr. (Courtesy Maury Orr)

par for the course. We went through so much together." The actors knew how right they were for their parts and drew security from that — enough to push to the limit to get their way. On the other hand, this was showbiz: Push too hard and you could be replaced. But when the red light went on, people dropped their attitudes and snapped into their roles, says Marg Clifton. "On the air, they could cover it."

One morning before reporting to work, Clifton glanced at a copy of the *Los Angeles Times.* A headline predicted that someday planes would take off and land vertically. "Big deal," she thought. "Why are they making such a fuss about that? We do vertical flight all the time." For a few seconds, Clifton's reality had blurred — then she remembered that vertical flight took place *on the set,* in the 30th century. "What you're doing every day is a *model,*" she reminded herself. "It's not the real thing. But," she adds softly, "you could believe it so easily."

The crew, too — despite their occasional grumbling — was swept up in the magic, says Chuck Lewis:

> Every sound mixer, cameraman and lighting director loved that show and contributed to it. We'd think about things we could do to make it better: How to fly the ship in, what kind of sound effect would make a boot clink on the hull, where to hide the microphones so there was good sound. I think we cared because of the characters. Ed Kemmer as the commander was good-looking, lithe, good build on him — and he had a good way about him in mannerisms and talk. And the playoff between Buzz and Happy, and the two of them with Robbie — it was something that was unusual.

Marg Clifton agrees. As assistant director and "script girl," she was in close proximity to the actors and could feel a powerful transformation take place as they slipped into character. "They would forget who they really were — you could see it happening." Kemmer and Osborn were particularly intense. "I don't think they ever divorced themselves from those characters. I don't know what they did when they left there, but it was like they were still a part of it."

Maury Orr thinks that Norm Jolley's scripts fueled the chemistry among the cast because the characters seemed to mirror their real-life personalities and relationships. She sensed that a bond had developed between the actors that was near-telepathic. "It was a tight-knit unit, like a troupe that does Shakespeare and goes on tour. Pretty soon you know what the other guy's going to say before he says it — offstage as well as on."

"They believed it each moment," says Clifton. "It wasn't hokey."

To some crew members at ABC in the 1950s, when television was, in turn, a magical child full of promise or an unruly adolescent, the soundstage was a place where they could solve a problem, make a difference. "I couldn't wait to get to work in the morning," recalls Clair Higgins. "Everybody put out a lot of energy, everyone really cared. We had a whole new industry competing with the film world, and you felt a part of it." And while to some of the ABC crew, a job was a job and wrestling with the technical problems of live TV was a pain, others were fascinated by the challenges that cropped up, and they plied Darley with suggestions about how to solve them. In those days, creativity was unchecked by management, who had the wisdom to stay out of the way and allow everyone's genius to surface. The industry was young, defiant, without rules. "If there was a problem, you'd sit down and figure it out," says Higgins, recalling the "just do it" spirit that permeated the soundstage. This free and easy climate on the set produced innovations that became the backbone of television, though in a few years all that would change, says Bob Trachinger, as "the business, instead of being run by production people, was run by accountants and lawyers." Dick Darley agrees. "When television started, the geeks were in charge because nobody else knew how to get a picture out of a camera and onto the screen."

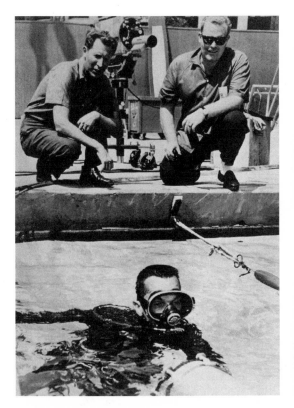

Left: Bob Trachinger (left) and Roone Arledge watch as cameraman Dale Barringer employs Trachinger's latest invention — the underwater camera — at the AAU swim meet in Los Angeles, circa 1964. *Right:* Trachinger, in 1994, displays another one of his gadgets that revolutionized TV broadcasting — the first successful electronic hand-held camera. (Both photographs courtesy Bob Trachinger)

When a crew member came up with a way to do something that had never been done before, Darley listened. He needed ways to shoot people floating upside down in space and to show a spaceship out of control. Lighting director Alex Quiroga produced the answer — a revolving lens the crew dubbed the "Quirogascope." It did everything Darley wanted and more. Turning the lens made objects appear to be sideways or upside down; twisting it back and forth made the set look like it was rocking violently. Now, if the ship was "hit" by a torpedo or meteor, the camera lens revolved and the actors swayed from side to side, but nothing else really moved. *That* was innovative. Before, says Ken Mayer, a bunch of guys had to rock the ship back and forth.

To capture the sense of moving backward or forward through time, Bob Trachinger created the video waver, which filled the screen with surreal pulsations. It had other uses, too. When Agent X retreated to his hideout beneath the Caloric Ocean, Darley shot scenes on the ocean floor through an aquarium stocked with fish, then added the pulsating effect of the waver for that "underwater" feeling.[9]

---

[9]Trachinger also had a part in inventing the hand-held video camera and the underwater camera, but is best known (or should be) for the device that enables "instant replay" at sports games. According to Roone Arledge, in 1960, he and "Trach" were having a beer when Arledge, then producer of *ABC's Wide World of Sports*, asked if it would be possible to replay something in slow motion. "Trach immediately began sketching on napkins," Arledge   →

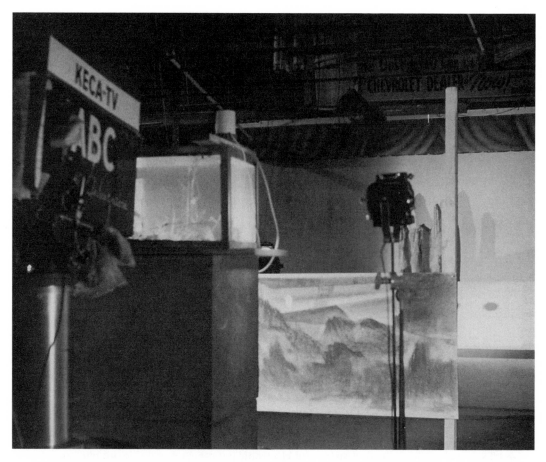

Shooting through an aquarium in June 1954 for "Underwater Spaceship Graveyard," in which Agent X has set up a fishy hideout beneath the Caloric Ocean on Venus. (Courtesy Dick Darley)

Meanwhile, Truck Krone figured out how to make light suddenly flood the set when a character entered a room and flipped a light switch. "Before that, the difference between the light being 'on' and 'off' in a room was just terrible," Krone sighs. Thus when Buzz Corry walked into Space Patrol headquarters and turned on the lights, he was making TV history.

Maury Orr remembers when the freewheeling spirit of early television began to change. By the mid-'50s, people were starting to realize that this bastard cousin of radio was here to stay, and everyone wanted a piece of the action. Hotshot writers and directors from New York and Chicago invaded Hollywood, displacing many talented directors who had pioneered the early days. Gradually the maverick atmosphere on the stage at ABC "evolved" into a more businesslike workplace with management peering over everyone's shoulder. The easy "let's see if this works" approach to problem-solving gave

told *Playboy* in October 1976. "We talked and sketched and drank beer that whole afternoon and when we were finished, we had the plans for the first instant replay device." Trachinger (despite resistance from ABC) developed the system, causing NFL commissioner Pete Rozelle to reportedly say, "I wish the son-of-a-gun who invented instant replay never had."

way to tighter supervisory control, and when CBS led the stampede to video tape recording in 1956, there wasn't the same need for ingenious, spur-of-the-moment solutions to technical problems. No longer did you lean against scenery to keep it from falling or pray that when you fired a cosmic smoke gun it would really puff smoke. Now when things fell or failed, you just did another take.

Production got easier, but Bob Trachinger was troubled. He saw the quirky humanness of television overrun by the quest for perfection. "When video tape first came in, we breathed a sigh of relief because we thought we'd get a better performance and be able, generally, to do a better job," he recalls. "But what we got instead was this sleekness— this push and urgency to do it over again because somebody did not have what he or she considered a 'perfect' take."

With the advent of video tape, live programming virtually disappeared — and along with it the mystical, unpredictable essence of television. Production grew slick and perfect as more and more people bought TV sets — but by the time everyone had a set, the live era was over and TV had outgrown its crazy adolescence. Missions of daring in the name of live television were no longer necessary.

Never again, for example, would you have to worry that the vicious piranha waiting for its close-up would fall asleep before its big moment. Orr remembers the time the production crew of *You Asked for It* had a piranha in a tank backstage because a contestant had, well, *asked* for it. Only one problem: A maintenance man fed the fish a hearty meal just before air time, so it dozed off, sinking blissfully to the bottom of the tank where nobody could — or would — wake it up. Such were the pitfalls of live TV, but you learned to talk fast and ad lib your way out of anything.

Some situations were trickier than others, however, like when your product burst into flames on camera. In those days, explains Orr, commercials were often shot live because sponsors didn't want to pay big bucks for film. It was a lot cheaper to come down to the studio and pitch your product than pay for a filmed commercial that had to be shot and processed and was much more expensive — though Orr knew at least one advertiser who probably had second thoughts about that:

> It was a live car commercial. The dealer, Fletcher Jones, was extolling the virtues of this wonderful used car behind him, the camera zoomed in — and it's madly on fire. You could see flames underneath it and coming out of the engine, but Fletcher never noticed. Finally two stagehands pushed the car off camera as Fletcher moved on to the next car. Up in the booth, we were falling on the floor, we were laughing so hard.

Fifty years later, Orr, relaxing in the locker room of the posh Riviera Country Club in Pacific Palisades, California, where she teaches golf to the rich and famous, is laughing so hard she can barely finish the story. Girlish and fit in her early 70s, she's reliving the perils of live TV. She began as a secretary at CBS and ended up a director at ABC. In the early days, she points out, live commercials were accidents waiting to happen. "I mean, your odds were that something was going to happen that wasn't right," she says wryly.

While most on-air fiascoes weren't as dangerous as car fires, many were just plain annoying. Like those Skippy peanut butter commercials where Margaret, a nice woman who worked in the production department at ABC, got paid twenty-five dollars a week to come over to the studio and spread peanut butter on a slice of toast. But first she had to catch the toast. Unfortunately, there was a faulty spring in the toaster, so often the slices flew up to the studio rafters and Margaret dashed off to look for them, leaving the camera to focus on an empty set. Once, says Orr, the toast never did come down — it just vanished. Other times, the camera caught Margaret trying to pry the bread out of the toaster when it didn't come up at all. How did the crew handle this kind of disaster? "Easy," says Orr. "We giggled our heads off and got on with our lives." So did viewers, who'd had their belly laugh for the day. But that was the fun of watching, says Dick Darley:

> People wanted to tune in and see the dumb gaps and bloopers and if anyone blew their lines. For the actors, it was like walking a tightrope. There was the chance of mishap — but that was the excitement of live TV. People were fascinated by the fact that "This is actually going on this minute — and oh my God, look what happened!" It didn't hurt the shows at all.

Darley sighs. "Now it's 90 percent canned." What "live" means today, famed L.A. talk show host Michael Jackson once remarked, is "pre-recorded for broadcast at this time."[10]

Surviving these daily disasters gave the crew a sense of camaraderie. When ex-staffers speak of the early days at ABC Television Center, a 23-acre studio lot nestled in the midst of a leafy residential neighborhood, they use the term "one big family." It's not just memory softening the rough edges — they dredge up the personal conflicts too. But through it all, everyone pulled together to birth this upstart medium, television, that few people thought would amount to much. "There was more camaraderie than competition," says Bob Trachinger. "The older crew members — I mean the 26 year olds — were willing to share with us 22 year olds what wisdom they had about doing shows." This creative spirit floated out from the soundstages to the administrative offices, housed in California-style bungalows surrounded by grass and shrubbery, where people were sorting mail, planning production schedules, selling ad time and balancing the books. Like toast-maven Margaret, an office staffer might be frantically summoned to the studio when the crew needed an extra hand. One minute you're filing production schedules; the next you're onstage *in* the production. It happened at all the networks. One day in 1952, Maury Orr, just starting out at CBS, looked up from her desk to see a production assistant approaching fast. "He said, 'The director's sick. We need someone to direct the commercial. Can you do it?' And I said, 'Sure!' You were an idiot if you said no. They didn't question if you had any ability or not — nobody knew very much anyway. In those days, it was just being in the right place at the right time. We were all in it together."

Orr decided she preferred the studio to the office and moved to ABC, where she became an assistant director. Women in production were rare, but both Orr and Marg Clifton say they were treated as equals by the crew. "I felt like one of the mob," says Orr, who moved up to director in the early '60s. "I never felt any resentment or had a moment's trouble with any of the guys. It was just a matter of whether you had any ability and if you got along."

But though treated as equals, neither woman was allowed by management to have her name appear in the credits. "I don't want to call it discrimination because nobody looked down on me," says Clifton, "but women couldn't get credit unless someone went to bat for you." Unlike *Space Patrol*'s Carol and Tonga, who hailed from the more enlightened 30th century, women studio employees found that the primitive customs of Earth

---

[10]Jackson, a legendary Los Angeles–based interviewer (*not* the singer), began his broadcasting career in the 1960s.

prevailed. It was comedian George Jessel's personal manager who finally insisted that Clifton be included in the credits when she worked on Jessel's show. "He made a big fuss about it," she says shyly, "but usually you'd just let it ride." Clifton considered it a privilege to work in this field she loved, and a good idea not to make waves. It was enough, she says, that "you were doing something you enjoyed, and you were doing a good job."

The tension on the stage before the live Saturday morning broadcast was something like you might get at, say, an Apollo launch — but that, Dick Darley reminded himself, was why he got into television in the first place. Like his wartime missions, nothing was certain. For one thing, you could never be sure a camera would get to the next set on time. A big problem — besides pushing the weighty cameras over uneven, splintered floors and through puddles where rain had leaked in through the roof of the soundstage — was that cameras got tangled in cable as they raced between sets. That's not cable as in your anemic hi-fi cable; it's cable twice the size of a heavy-duty garden hose, and you needed a cable boy to clear it out of the camera's path. "Equipment moves had to be planned carefully," says master control engineer Don McCroskey, "or you could wind up with a tangle of cables before the end of a show." If another camera got mired in cable, you gave up your camera position to run over and help clear it, says Bob Trachinger — or you hoped Arch Griffin, a one-eyed cameraman, could get there first. "He had the strength of two men," Trachinger says admiringly. "He'd pick up the edge of the camera and we'd pull the cable out and go on shooting." If the cable guy dropped the lines, they made loud slaps, causing Darley to hit the roof if they got on the air. "It was nerve-wracking because it destroyed the illusion," he says, still upset. "Those cables made a terrible noise on the wooden floor," confirms Clair Higgins, who started out as a truck driver at ABC and pulled cables before moving up to cameraman.[11] "I dropped one during rehearsal and Darley yelled, 'One more like that, Higgins, and you're back on the truck!'" To avoid cable tangles and make life easier for the cameramen, Darley worked with the art director to place sets in sequence so the cameras wouldn't have to travel long distances, but it wasn't always possible. He knew what the men were up against:

> They'd break from one scene and rush to the other end of the stage to cover a set that couldn't be put anywhere else. They'd plan it with the cable guys, and somehow they'd make that damn scene, running at top speed with these heavy, heavy cameras 'cause we were shooting very fast — I mean, fast cuts. The cameras would be in such a rush that they ran into each other and you'd hear a crash. Hopefully, it wasn't on the air.

If they got to the scene in one piece, the cameramen faced a new set of problems: the pans and close-ups Darley needed to create the dramatic "motion picture" quality he was after. Ready for your close-up? Better make sure the camera is too. In the early '50s, there were no zoom lenses, so either the lumbering behemoth camera moved toward you, or you moved toward it. It was hard to get it exactly right. Truck Krone remembers Darley urging Arch Griffin to push the camera in for a close-up. "Dick would say, 'Closer, closer!' and he'd run into the spaceship and shake it all over the place." That worked, says Krone, "if the ship was supposed to be moving anyway." But without zoom lenses, says Bob Trachinger, it took muscle and fancy footwork to move in and out for the shots Darley wanted. "When the camera moved in or across a shot, all of the movement was the

---

[11]Crew member Phil Studwell also pulled cable.

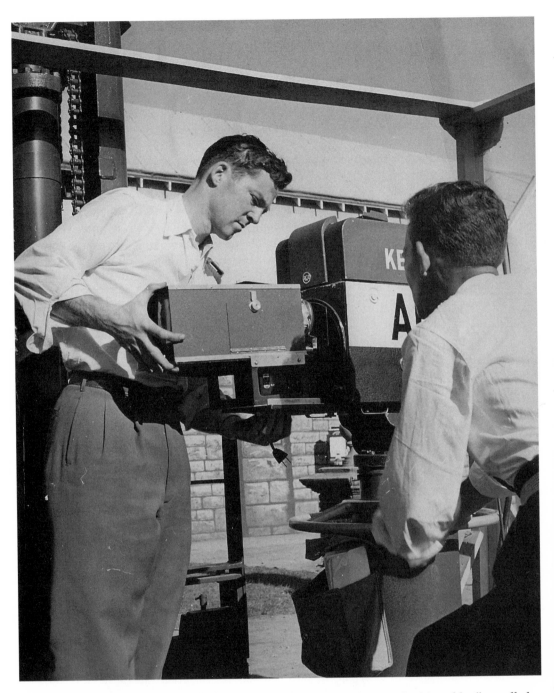

Arch Griffin loads a KECA camera circa 1952. When a camera got mired in cable, "we called Arch," says Bob Trachinger. "He'd lift the camera and we'd pull the cable out and go on shooting. He had the strength of two men." (Courtesy Kathy Griffin)

cameraman pulling the camera as smoothly and rhythmically as he could, but he had to focus at the same time. Dick expected a great deal of us: You had to focus, compose, move in, move out, travel sideways, tilt up and tilt down — all in the same motion."

"You had to learn how to move your body to get the thing going," says Higgins. "It took a lot of energy."

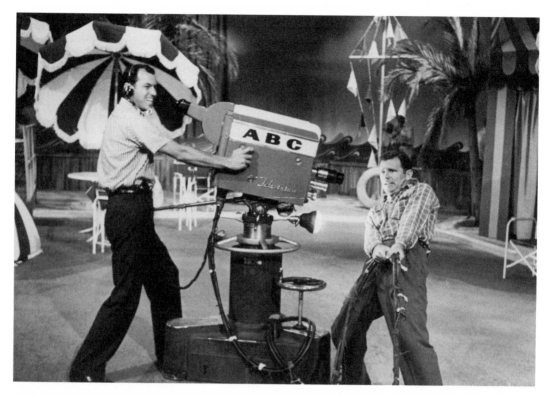

Clair Higgins moves in for a close-up of fellow cameraman John Walsh pretending to struggle with camera cable. (Courtesy Clair Higgins)

Given these problems, it was a good idea when you started a scene, says Ed Kemmer, to make sure a camera and mike were somewhere in sight. If they weren't, you made split-second blocking changes:

> If a camera got stuck on a cable, you didn't do your regular blocking — you stayed there until you were aware that it was off its cable. Same thing if the boom with the microphone ran up on something and they couldn't move it fast enough: You didn't go to your next spot right away — you waited until it got free. You noticed all this without paying attention to it. It was like learning lines; it was part of the job. Of course, it might interfere with dialogue or interpretation at times, but it just became the natural thing to do.

Sometimes Kemmer had to lead the camera to a lighted area.

> A key light would burn out during the show, which makes for a lousy picture, so instead of keeping to the original blocking, you'd just calmly, slowly, walk over to an area that *did* have a key light and do the scene there. The camera would follow you — he'd realize what you were doing. You just took care of these things as they happened, without getting too excited about it.

Kemmer functioned on more levels than most of the actors, expanding his awareness to include the technical workings of the show and assuming responsibility in an uncanny way that meshed with his fictional role of Commander-in-Chief. Ever reluctant to admit that he did anything memorable or extraordinary during *Space Patrol*, he'll allow that maybe it was a feat to stay in character while dealing with problems that actors today blithely leave to engineers and technicians. "It's amazing that you could do anything besides your own part, like worry about microphones, cameras and lighting," he concedes, "but you took care of those things without consciously thinking about it." He also admits that he had a few tricks up his sleeve to help him remember his lines. For tough parts, such as technical explanations, he used his trained pilot's eyes to glance at a script on Corry's desk or hidden beneath the spaceship's control panel:

> In the cockpit scenes, I rigged a clipboard [with the script] just below the throttle handles so it looked like I was checking the instruments. There was plenty of light down there, and if I needed to pick up something, I'd see it. When you're cheating like that, you don't look at something in a steady manner — you keep looking around, like in flying, where you're checking the instruments all the time. If anything's out of place, you notice it — that's beaten into you as a cadet. If some needle is in a bad position, you pick it up when you scan, without looking directly at it.

These things piled up into an overload that made him "pretty nervous," he admits. He psyched himself up before each live performance, knowing that there was no going back:

> You had to be keyed up, ready for it, but not so much that you were shaking. Your knees were kinda weak — it took its toll. You're hoping you know your lines and remember your blocking and where the director said, "Don't answer right away. Wait there because I have to take an extra camera cut." But anyone who did live TV in those days knew the maxim: "You can't stop and do it again." Whatever happens, happens in front of millions of people.

In the booth above the soundstage, facing six video monitors, sat (from left to right) assistant director Marg Clifton, Marge Rotunda or Larry Robertson (or Maury Orr filling in), Dick Darley, technical director Irwin Stanton or Bob Trachinger, lighting director Truck Krone, and a video shader (often Gene Lukowski).[12] In a smaller booth behind them, separated by a glass window, the audio operator — Chuck Lewis, Tom Ashton, Jim Banks, or Ken Grinde — mixed the sound and played underscore music, using turntables and tape machines, following the script and taking cues from Darley. As many as 20 or more musical cuts might be used in a single show. ("The Iron Fist," Episode 81, uses 26.) In the main booth, there were at least three active monitor screens (one for each camera), and two or three more if Darley had a camera outdoors or up on the catwalks, or if special effects on film were to be inserted into the live show. If you think six monitor screens is a lot to watch at once, try dozens more. When he worked on *ABC's Wide World of Sports* in the '60s, says Truck Krone, they had 62 monitors. Then and now, he adds, the production crew learned by trial and error. "Try looking at 62 cameras and figuring out which one you're on. You screw up, is how you do it."[13]

"It's a whole different world in the booth," says Bob Trachinger. He or Irwin Stanton served as technical director, depending on their schedules. Stanton fretted over every detail like a mother hen. Trachinger was more easygoing, and Darley was grateful for his

---

[12]The line-up in the booth changed according to ABC staffers' schedules. Al Hayward was one of the first technical directors; sometimes Charles Coleman or Ted Hurley replaced Trachinger or Stanton. (Hurley was also an audio operator, and Trachinger had been both cameraman and video shader.) Bill Zeck sometimes served as AD.

[13]Today, says Bob Trachinger, as many as 80 monitors might be used for events like the Olympics or the Super Bowl.

"It's a whole different world in the booth," says Bob Trachinger. From lower right: Marg Clifton consults her stopwatch, Dick Darley calls a camera shot, and technical director Al Hayward, lighting director Truck Krone and video shader Gene Lukowski do their thing. (Courtesy Dick Darley)

reassuring presence. "The TD is in charge of the stage and all the equipment. He's responsible for getting the picture and sound onto the kinescope," Darley explains. From the booth, the director and TD could look out over the stage and spot disasters about to happen. "If a camera went out or got tangled up in cable, Trach stayed calm," says Darley. "He understood that there was a life-and-death problem, but he would convey it in such a way that gave us security that he could bail us out."

In those days, says Darley, ABC was very "Hollywood-conscious," so any motion picture director who wanted a peek into the maverick world of television could sit in the booth and observe during a show. "They'd come up and watch for a while and just shake their heads, then run back to their cozy little stage where everything was repeated twelve times. They could not comprehend how it came together. But that was OK, 'cause neither could we."

As Darley called the camera shots, lighting director Truck Krone, with one eye on the script and the other on the monitors, barked commands like "Bring it up to 8" through a headset to a guy on the stage at a dimmer board who brought the lights up and down. You had to be careful: If you dimmed too much, the camera got "noisy" as the lights approached the infrared spectrum, creating a grainy look on the kinescope. When *Space Patrol* began as a 15-minute local show in 1950, featuring more talk than action, the lighting was pretty basic. But as the scripts grew more sophisticated and action-packed, the lighting was constantly adjusted to produce the right dramatic effect. "All of a sudden you had bigger sets and a helluva lot more to do," says Krone. Now you had chases and fight scenes, not to mention villains prowling shadowed passageways in Baccarratti's castle or setting up hideouts in gloomy Martian caves. "Each show had a million cues," says Krone. "It was becoming a bigger goddamn deal."

Meanwhile, ahead in the 30th century, the animate space junk was getting a little out of hand. You had mild-mannered professors intent on ruling the universe, advanced civilizations gone power-mad, underwater spaceship pirates, masters of deception exporting evil into the past and future via time-machines, spacey androids, crazed scientists with Z-rays and Detectoscopes, space spiders and other low-life, and invisible beings up to no good in general. All of them clamored for state-of-the-art special effects, but in the lean days before the ABC network picked up the show, you had to make do with what was on hand. "Everything was B-24 surplus—all the spaceship controls came from old World War II bombers. You couldn't buy a knob for the *Enterprise* with what they did for five or ten dollars a show," says Ken Mayer appreciatively.

With the advent of the network show, the budget increased, but now you had a new problem: If a special effect misfired, blew up or fell off the string, it did so before millions of viewers. "We were learning," points out Kemmer. "Remember, nobody had ten years' experience in TV yet — it just wasn't there." Few shows had risked doing "effects" on live TV — ships coupling in space, futuristic weapons and devices, earthquakes, explosions, living rocks that wanted to eat you for dinner. Though primitive, they were groundbreaking, paving the way for the sophisticated "FX" of today. At best, they were obstinate and unpredictable; at worst, they were laughable. Combined with human error, it was anyone's guess what might happen. When the camera focused on the model of Corry's ship coming in for a landing, says Darley, you prayed that no one opened the stage door, causing the nylon wire to jerk back and forth. "But that's why live TV was so exciting," he adds. "You never knew what would happen next."

Kemmer learned that the hard way in an episode where he and Hap were taken prisoner by a tribe of Amazon women who inhabit the Cydonia jungle on Venus:

> They tied me to a tree and had a crossbow aimed at me. I remember telling the special effects man to *safety* it since they hadn't shot it before. He said, "Oh, no one's going to touch the trigger, and also, it's not going to shoot hard." And then, by God, someone *did* bump that thing and the arrow went sailing and it hit me — not my head, but about three feet below. I was more surprised than anything else. It wasn't that painful, but it was an embarrassing shot.

Looking back, says Kemmer, he took some risks for the sake of the live action show that were pushing his luck:

> We'd do a fight scene on the catwalk, 30 or 40 feet above the floor, and I'd roll to the edge, grab hold of the railing and swing by one arm. I'd check to make sure the stud was strong, that I could hook my arm around and swing from it. And it was a controlled roll — I didn't roll at a tremendous speed and grab wildly. The railing never gave way, but it was a little chancy.

But there were chances he didn't take. Later, after *Space Patrol*, that caution paid off when, in a detective drama, he refused to have a gun loaded with blanks fired near his head. "The director yelled, 'You're foolish,' grabbed the gun, turned on his first assistant and fired. A wad hit him in the skull; they had to cut it out," he recalls.[14]

What with effects gone south, Lyn Osborn's pranks, and last-minute technical snafus, you had a slew of mishaps — all aired — like Endurium door handles coming off in your hand, a butterfly flitting in "deep space" between Hap and Corry, and Lyn (being funny as usual) unzipping Tonga's uniform from behind so that she had to back off the set. Once when Corry wrestled Baccarratti into the Brainograph chair and clamped the helmet over his head to reveal his thoughts on the device's screen, viewers found out, much to their surprise, that the prince was thinking about the crew at ABC-TV back in the 20th century.[15] You had double-take moments too, like when Corry, knocked unconscious, says "Ouch!" when he bumps his head as a bad guy drags him through a doorway. And while you never got a blooper as good as that classic when the staid BBC announcer intoned, "This is the British Broadcorping Castration," you did get Kovacs talking about the "spaceshit" a few times. And everyone cracked up at least once on camera and had to turn their backs until they regained their composure.

Before some shows, the set was like a minefield. If the script called for an earthquake or explosion, scenery was rigged to a trip wire. When an actor (often Kemmer) set it off, huge balsa wood rocks and "debris" came crashing down on the stage. The biggest worry, says Truck Krone, was that someone would stumble into the wire and bring everything down before the cue. Krone explains how a trip wire is *supposed* to work:

> It's catgut, like a piece of string, that attaches to the bottom of a set if you want the whole thing to cave in on you. The actor hits it with his foot when he walks to that spot and

---

[14]Actor-director Larry Dobkin, who played villains in several *Space Patrol* episodes, was not so lucky. One day in a *Gunsmoke* rehearsal, the director set up a shot in which Dobkin and James Arness squared off in a gunfight. "The shot had Arness firing at me from only twenty feet away," Dobkin recalls. "I got the wad in my left eye; I was bleeding and couldn't see out of it for three days." The director said, "Sorry that happened," and wanted to shoot from the other side. "I hit him in the jaw and knocked him down."

[15]"The Resonance Impeller," Episode 145, September 19, 1953. Catch the guy from Earth in a shirt and tie stumbling through the reflection of Baccarratti's castle.

boom!—down comes the ceiling. Then the sound man, the mixer, puts in a bunch of noise. I can't tell you how many times some prop man got in there by mistake and hit the trip wire accidentally. All of a sudden the actors would have to change the dialogue to "Gee, someone must have blown up the planet!"

When Krone joined ABC in 1950, fresh from Columbia Pictures, he brought with him what you might call "advanced technology," which vastly improved the special effects on *Space Patrol*. He created bountiful fields of stars (much better than painted ones) by projecting light from a mirrored ball onto a black backdrop—just like they did in your favorite dance hall or at your high school prom. And he got rid of the wires that suspended the model of Corry's battlecruiser and attached the ship instead to a rod that could be maneuvered by hand. That solved the tacky ship-on-a-string problem. When Darley asked, "How'd you think of that?" he delighted in saying, "They've done it in motion pictures for 20 years." Why hadn't these things been tried before in television? "Because they'd never seen it," Krone shoots back. "Most of the crew were radio people."

But even people with TV experience messed up on occasion, sometimes with disastrous results—like the time cast and crew were forced to flee the stage during the live network broadcast. It happened during *Space Patrol*'s trademark opening: misty clouds depicting the "wild, vast reaches of space." In the early days, before the intro was put on film, a special effects man would set up dry ice on a table or on the floor and sprinkle room-temperature water over it, causing billows of mist to rise. Then he'd either blow on it or use a fan to get the swirling effect of the "clouds." One day prop master Al Teaney replaced the ice with a new kind of chemical smoke, a much more efficient way (so he thought) to create the clouds. Clair Higgins remembers:

> Usually we checked everything out, but not this time. So we go on the air at 8:00 A.M. and Al's guy starts spraying this smoke. At 8:04, we're into the first scene and I guess the smoke was toxic because we all had to run off the stage—the whole cast and crew—it was that bad. And we were on the network, live to the East Coast! The crew upstairs in the booth thought we were all nuts. They had to use a standby slide because that show had a 10-minute hold in it.

Audio man Chuck Lewis says Tufeld recorded his famous "*Spaaaaaace Patrol!*" call in a small bathroom off the soundstage because that was the best way to get an echo behind his voice. "Honestly, I don't remember that," says Tufeld. "If I ever yelled '*Spaaaaaace Patrol*' in the bathroom, it was probably because I'd had a successful experience in there." But Lewis stands by his story, and Tufeld admits that he has, in fact, broadcast live from a bathroom. It happened the first time he announced the Grammy Awards from the Hollywood Palladium:

> The director had nowhere to set up an announcer's booth with a microphone and monitor, except in the men's room. I'll never forget it—tile walls and floor, hard plaster ceiling—the greatest reverberating acoustic venue I've ever worked in. One problem: In the middle of the show—just before I was about to announce something—a guy walks in to use the facilities. I yelled out, "Hold it—I'm turning on my microphone!" Well, he *didn't* hold it, and in the middle of the Grammy Awards you heard me announcing my heart out—and you also heard the very loud flush of a toilet. I've always felt it was part of television history.

If that makes you wonder about the numerous rocket whooshes on *Space Patrol*, you're right: In the early '50s, the best way to get that ship-blasting-off sound was with a toilet flush. Lewis remembers "Tiny" Lamb, a heavyset sound effects guy, planting a mike in a toilet bowl. "Any time we needed a rocket whoosh, he'd cue someone who would push the handle down." Dick Darley confirms the tale. "If a rocket was taking off, they could use the toilet flush and blend into something else, another kind of whoosh. They were inventive — they used some very screwy things. But when you found a sound, you grabbed it."

Sound effects men Lamb and Bob Holmes, two of the best in the business, would arrive on the lot in big trucks loaded with gadgets and turntables, and set up in a corner of the stage. "They had their own kingdom over there," says Darley, adding that "to do live effects on stage was very primitive. But that's how they did it in radio, and since there was no post-production to speak of, that's how we had to do it." The sound men were glued to the script for their cues. "If somebody walked across the metal hull of the ship, Bobby Holmes was doing the [boot] clanks in synch with him," Darley explains. "It was live, and he had to be right on — and sometimes he was."

The dry ice used in the intro to create the clouds could also provide the misty atmosphere of a cave or exotic planet. But like other special effects, recalls Maury Orr, this one often went awry. "Sometimes the prop man got a little carried away and you couldn't see your hand in front of your face. The actors would try to go in or out of the 'cave' but they couldn't see where they were going. Even the camera couldn't find them." And speaking of cameras, any extra ice on hand for the "clouds" came in handy to cool them, says Bob Trachinger:

> We actually used to put dry ice under the intake system that blew cool air into the camera to keep it from overheating. We kept changing the ice in hot weather. In cold weather, the studio didn't warm up until the lights were on for quite a while, so we kept the cameras moving all the time. If your camera was still, the last image in it stuck there for half a minute.

The dry ice vapor often combined with smoke used in "explosions" to create a thick haze that made it nearly impossible for the actors to find their way as they rushed between sets, says Orr. Getting to scenes in the ship's cockpit was especially challenging. Often the preceding scene showed cast members climbing a ladder to the entry hatch of the spaceship above — though viewers never saw the ship. That's because it wasn't there. The ladder, says Kemmer, led to a 5 × 8 foot platform — railed so you didn't fall off. As soon as the actors reached the top, they clambered down an off-camera "escape" ladder at warp speed, tripping over anything in the way as they dashed to the next set, which was the ship's interior. The crew got used to seeing them stumble at the bottom of the ladder as they rushed to beat the camera. "There wasn't much light for descending ladders in a big hurry," Kemmer recalls. The stage manager — the eyes and ears of the director — guided the actors through these maneuvers, getting them to the right place at the right time, cueing them when to start speaking and when to stop (so dialogue from one scene didn't run into the next), signaling exits and letting them know when they were clear of the camera and could dash to another set. Connected to Darley by earphones, he cued the sound effects men and relayed messages from Darley to Kemmer about timing. "He would move around the stage like a ballet dancer," recalls Chuck Lewis. "He was everywhere."[16]

[16]Jim Johnson, Jimmy Baker, George Flournoy, Tommy Thompson, Bob Sheldon, Bill Zeck and Jerry Franks worked as stage managers on *Space Patrol*.

The outer hull of Corry's ship with an unidentified Earthling on the fin — a huge set that stretched nearly the length of the sound stage. (Courtesy Dick Darley)

Today Bob Trachinger marvels at how "ingenious but shabby" the sets were, compared to other hit shows of the day. But they looked impressive and huge on your TV screen, conveying the feeling that the 30th century was a grand place, larger than life. Wide-angle lenses created distance and depth, and the cameramen, who had four lenses on the turrets, flipped to 28 millimeters for wide shots, careful not to move in too close lest they warp or distort the perspective or show stage equipment. "Sometimes you were dangerously close to the edge," says Darley, who could switch a monitor in the booth to "underscan" mode to warn him if crew members or equipment were about to show up in millions of living rooms unless the camera backed off.

Darley wanted "spectacular" shots to contrast with his close-ups and he got them by shooting some fights and chase scenes on the catwalks high above the stage or on the studio's outdoor stairwells. He got dramatic shots, too, when people walked across the ship's hull — a set that really *was* big, stretching nearly the length of the soundstage. The right lighting against a gray cyclorama (a taut backdrop encircling the stage area) could make it look as if infinity stretched beyond the ship. Rented backdrops of jungles, deserts or countryside gave him shots of "wide vistas," making a small set look huge. And when a large set really was needed, no problem. "Unlike shows done in New York," points out

Kemmer, "we had a full soundstage with plenty of room. You could have several sets that connected, going from a room to a hallway or another room — a continuous scene."

Majestic shadows made things look large, too, and Truck Krone used them to create grand spaceports, threatening landscapes and stately corridors in Space Patrol Headquarters. They gave the show an edgy, brooding look that concealed a number of flaws. "*Space Patrol*'s dream-like 'noir' atmosphere, which its low budget mandated, kept you from seeing the sets too well," notes librarian and longtime fan Elliott Swanson. "As with radio, there were a lot of dark, empty places for one's imagination to fill in."[17]

Darley experimented with outdoor shots for variety and soon found he got "great-looking angles" by shooting on the lawn right next to the administrative bungalows on the studio lot. When that happened, TV operations coordinator Maggie Montreys knew the drill. "They'd phone us and say, 'Get under your desks and draw the shades!' Then they'd run right up on the porch, shooting, and we'd get under our desks to stay out of the way."

"I got asked, 'How did you make it look so big?' all the time," says Clarence Frederick "Truck" Krone, Jr. (He picked up the nickname playing football for USC), relaxing over a drink at his favorite restaurant in Thousand Oaks, California.[18] An hour earlier, he'd shown off his 996 Porsche in the parking lot. "Isn't it a beauty? It's my eighth one — my last one. They're gonna put handles on this one and bury me in the sonofabitch." Krone, 76, says this chariot — sleeker than the Terra V — can do 240 mph, though he claims to take it no faster than 170 on the ribbon of road between L.A. and Las Vegas. During his years as a lighting director at ABC, he collected three Emmys and did lighting for Frank Sinatra, Barbra Streisand, Lawrence Welk and "every big show known to man." Full of nervous energy with a big voice, thick glasses, forest of gray hair and boyish giggle, Krone doesn't look a day over 50. He jumps on your questions before you finish the sentence.

He was "a young kid" working at Columbia Pictures when he moved to ABC. His friends said he was nuts, that television would never amount to much, but he reckoned this new medium was hungry for people who knew something about photography. Sound men

Truck Krone finally gets time off to relax in Marina del Rey, California (1973). When *Space Patrol* was shot, he recalled, "it was unbelievable, the amount of hours you were there. It damn near caused a divorce, because nobody in their right mind would go to work on Thursday and not get home till Saturday." (Courtesy Setsuko Kaldor)

---

[17]Roaring Rockets web page (*www.slick-net.com/space/*).

[18]Writer Norm Jolley occasionally slipped crew members' names into the script. Episode 128, "The Fraud of Titan," features a character named "Truck" after Krone; in Episode 59, "Hit by a Meteorite," a reference is made to "Trachinger's Comet."

from radio were trying to do the job, but they knew nothing about visual effects. At Columbia, he'd been wet behind the ears, but at ABC he was looked up to by men twice his age who knew less than he did. He started out as a boom man on *Mysteries of Chinatown* and *The Charlie Ruggles Show*; he was 28 when he was assigned to *Space Patrol*, first as a boom man, later moving up to lighting director. The boom operator stood high on a moving platform, guiding the mike to where the actors were and keeping both mike and boom out of the frame. "They were having a terrible problem with boom shadows, when the light's in the wrong place," Krone recalls. "Suddenly you're talking and there's a black duck on your head. That takes away from what you're saying because viewers go, 'What's that?'"

Another problem boom operators had was finding the actors, says Dick Darley:

> The boom man was often faking it because he couldn't see past the stage lights and wasn't exactly sure where the performers were. And the lights couldn't always be where they needed to be — on the performers — because the boom man had to move in and pick up the sound. It was really tough, but these guys were super-hard workers. They developed ways to pick up the sound from different angles — come in low below the lights, tilt the mike and shoot up, things like that. They developed skills that had never existed before because we were inventing as we went along. There were few boom shadows because there was a lot of swearing.

"Being a good boom man was an art form all its own," says Bob Trachinger, adding that Krone was considered "extraordinary." But Krone was tired of battling black ducks from the boom platform. He wanted to be lighting director and banish them for good. One day he saw his chance:

> There were two lighting directors at ABC who were like kids with their first camera — they had no idea what the hell lighting was all about. They thought that getting rid of shadows was a boom man's job, but that's not true: They're caused by how the show is lit in the first place, which I told them. They said, "Then *you* light it. Do you know how?" And I said, "I know more than *this*." I'd worked on some pretty big pictures at Columbia and I kind of knew what they were doing. And that's how I became a lighting director.

Lighting expert Alex Quiroga took Krone under his wing and taught him all he knew. "I want to speak about Alex," says Bob Trachinger, who remembers Quiroga with affection. Darley wanted mood lighting on *Space Patrol*, Trachinger explains, and Quiroga — a Mexican-born genius from an aristocratic family — transformed the flat lighting of the day into quality, high-contrast lighting. "We called it 'Rembrandt lighting,'" Trachinger recalls. "It had shadows, highlights, texture and tone, and it turned lighting in the industry around. Before that, we had an engineer whose method was to put as much light on the set as possible. The stages used to be very hot." Quiroga was warm, classy and explosive. "He was very emotional," says Trachinger, who remembers Alex bursting into the control room, spitting epithets in Spanish when the equipment misbehaved.

Together, Quiroga and Krone waged a battle against flooding the stage with light. The problem, Krone says angrily, was those ex-radio guys — engineers fleeing from radio to TV — who knew all about sound and nothing about light. "They wanted full light on the face — total, washed-out, flat light — and the hell with where [the light source] was really coming from." Eventually, a mental light went on and, says Krone, "People started saying, 'We're going to make this side dark and this side bright.'" But in those days, he notes, equipment didn't have memory, so dimmers were used to preset lighting. "You'd jot down the numbers and watch your back, because if you left for a moment to do something else, someone might monkey with your settings."

With dimmers and cross-lighting, Quiroga, and later Krone, created the vast, shadowy world of the 30th century. Though some sets were small (Corry's office was about 8 × 10 feet, recalls Ed Kemmer), edgy lighting coupled with Darley's wide shots and simple yet imaginative designs by art director Carl Macauley, Seymour Klate or Al Goodman made them look huge. Krone knew he'd succeeded when, like Darley, he got feedback about how large the sets looked. The secret was making sure black was black. "When you make enough black, it looks like infinity — it looks huge," he explains. To make sure black *stayed* black, he worked with the video control engineer to balance the settings, using the "telephone trick" he'd learned at Columbia:

> One of the most important things in any kind of lighting is to make black *black* and white *white*. If you overlight, the black tends to gray. In film it's totally controlled — you have so many foot-candles in a scene. But in television, you had a video control engineer twisting knobs all the time, so when you rehearsed, that chair was black, but by the time you're on the air, this guy has twisted a couple of knobs and now it's gray. So I told him, "I'm going to put a white telephone and a black telephone on a desk in the scene [during rehearsal] and you balance to those — and then *don't touch it!* If they want it brighter, I'll do it with lights." That's how they did it in pictures.

Krone says he had a helluva time convincing the engineer guys that this little trick really worked, "but once we did it, for the first time in television we had black blacks and white whites."

Improved lighting gave the show both a mystical and moral quality. Flat light on the good guys made them look good, while shadows on villains painted them ominous. You could imply a lot with lighting, says Krone; you could nudge viewers to draw conclusions. "It's like when an actor says, 'The murderer must have gone through that window!' and you cut to the window with a hidden fan behind it ruffling the curtains. You can do similar things with lights." For a flattering shot of a hero like Corry, he'd shoot for a "golden triangle" on the face, a technique pioneered in the 1937 film classic *Lost Horizon*. It was easy to light Buzz and Hap because they were straightforward good guys: Put them both in one key light and "let their faces do what they were supposed to." (Kemmer didn't know it, but Krone watched out for "that crazy, funny end of his nose, like a button," and adjusted accordingly.) But complex characters like Nina Bara's "Tonga," who (in the early shows) was good one day and evil the next, presented a challenge. He tried, through lighting, to telegraph to viewers which side of the law she was on "without her opening her mouth."

But she did. Bara chattered nonstop about the "good" and "bad" sides of her face until it drove Krone over the edge. "Are you shooting my best side?" she wanted to know one day. "No," he replied, "because you're sitting on it." After that, he says, Bara realized the power of the lighting director and "became more kind because she knew I could screw it up." The rest of the cast left the lighting to him. "In the early days of TV," says Krone, "you didn't have a lot of stars with huge egos who pulled emotional stuff, like in motion pictures. Later, it became that way."

After taking so much care to get things right, Krone adds, he had to steel himself to watch the final product because viewing the kinescope could make you lose your rockets:

> Kinescope recording was not accurate — it was harsh black and white, so no matter what you did, you got tremendous contrast. A guy named Fred Atkins ran the kinescope department at ABC. I can't tell you how many times I went down there and said, "This doesn't look anything like the way we did it," and he'd say, "Well, that's your problem, not mine." It's as if you shot some stuff in your camera and when it's developed it comes out all blue. Kinescope recording was so primitive. You had to fight like hell to make it anywhere near what you originally had done.

Krone orders another drink and sighs. "It would look 10,000 times better today because of the grayscales. In those days you had a range of one to ten, from black to white. Now you have two or three hundred steps of gray, so it's gradual."[19]

But millions of viewers found no fault with the kinescopes, which were broadcast by stations that didn't get the show live. *Space Patrol's* popularity was growing fast, though Krone says that he and other crew members were too busy to notice — until *Life* magazine came calling in the summer of 1952 to photograph cast and crew for a three-page spread.[20] "At the time, I had no concept of the show's popularity," Krone recalls. Sure, he'd noticed that you argued less with the production manager about overtime, "but as far as I was concerned," he quips, "it never got past Anaheim." Caught up in the weekly scramble to get the show on the air, the crew paid little attention to its impact. "We didn't realize how big it was. The cast goofed up on the lines, cameras ran into sets, people tripped over things, working all night long, all day. It was like, 'Jesus! Let's get home. Where do I get a martini?'"

Like many ABC staffers, Krone delights in reliving these days when you couldn't wait to get to work in the morning; when maybe you'd solve a technical problem that would allow you to do something totally new. Later, in the restaurant parking lot, he slaps me on the back, saying, "See you around the pool hall, Tiger," and speeds off in his silver road demon. When he died the following year, Blair White, a camera operator for 34 years, sent a note to ABC staffers who still keep in touch:

> Truck fell heavy into that category of one-of-a-kind. He was healthy as a horse, but one day didn't feel so hot. Went to the hospital: cancer. He had a parrot that didn't talk much, but he'd taught it to swear some. When Truck died, the bird started swearing and went on all that day.

When the live broadcast was over, Dick Darley, wrung out but sounding composed, flipped the audio key and signaled "All clear" to cast and crew, adding "That was a good show, and I thank you." Then he headed downstairs to thank each person individually and shake hands. "I tried to say something specific to each one because unless they'd done their job — and it might only be pulling cable — the show wouldn't have gotten on. I did it quietly. It wasn't a grandstanding thing; it came from my heart." He was often in a euphoric state, the way a pilot might feel after a perilous carrier landing. "There would be such a tension release for having survived it. Your adrenaline was pumped up, you

---

[19]"While the grayscale chart used to adjust cameras had 10 steps (reflectance values from black to white), the cameras were easily capable of 100 gradations," notes Don McCroskey.
[20]*Life*, September 1, 1952.

were exhausted mentally and your nervous system was shot — but you were grateful for getting off the air in one piece."

Marg Clifton watched, amused, as many of the men beelined for the restroom. "They'd say, 'See you in a minute,' and make a mad dash," she recalls. "Doing a live show was like walking on the edge carrying a big rock," says Ed Kemmer, who admits he needed some time to return to "normal" when it was over.

His round of cast and crew completed, Darley would slip away to Pickwick Book-store on Hollywood Boulevard and climb the stairs to the second floor used book sec-tion, where he would lose himself in the stacks, allowing the hushed atmosphere to soothe his adrenaline rush.

Over the years, Darley got letters from film school students, intrigued by how he'd made *Space Patrol* so real, how he'd overcome the technical obstacles he faced. Like Kem-mer, Darley deflects any attempt to throw credit his way, but he'll concede that aspiring filmmakers "appreciated what went into it." He laughs self-consciously. "It was head and shoulders above what it was," he says cryptically. "Go figure that out. *I* know what I mean."

Ed Kemmer: "If you can look at it today, knowing it was done fifty years ago, know-ing it was done live, knowing that you had none of the things you have today — it'll still stand up under those conditions. But, my God, you get into a multimillion-dollar pro-duction with all sorts of special effects that were unknown then, and by those standards we were very crude, very simple."

Bob Trachinger remembers Maury Orr telling him once that he ought to "memori-alize" some of his inventions — keep a record or journal, track the history of his contri-butions to TV, like the video waver and the underwater camera. "But I never did. I mean, the next day, there was a new problem." Besides, life was too full, too exciting, and much too pressured to stop and look back — even to celebrate your successes. Trachinger, who retired as a vice president of ABC, had been raised in poverty. "I didn't think I'd amount to anything — I thought I'd be some sort of bum." Enter television. Suddenly he was in the right place at the right time, with other ex-servicemen like himself:

> Those were absolutely golden days when we unbelievably spun out these stories. A lot of us were World War II vets. We were like the early days of flying — we could crash at any time. And yet, when the clock went up, we went up, and we did it show after show. We were so sure of ourselves. If a piece of equipment went down or something went wrong, we knew what needed to be done. We were pros and we didn't know it.

Trachinger is a warm person who wears his heart on his sleeve, and right now he's going through some deep emotion, thinking back to those days. "The whole thing was like a dream," he says slowly. "We had a vision and we kept to it. We didn't reflect on it, we didn't deliberate about it. Shit, we just did it."

CHAPTER 9

Hap

I'd see him and just automatically start smiling. And he'd do something to make me smile more.

— Dick Tufeld

There's more unpleasantness in the world than there should be, so in every situation I face, I try to be happy and pleasant. That's my philosophy of life, and I learned it from Cadet Happy.

— Joe Sarno

When Lyn Osborn was four, he asked his playmate Raymond, who lived next door, if he'd like some candy from the box on his mother's dresser. Of course the boy said yes. Lyn, or "Bud," as his family called him, watched Raymond gobble a handful of the chocolate-covered mints and then devour the rest of the box. Later that night, Bess Osborn wrote in her diary, she discovered that all her Feenamints — a chocolate-coated laxative — were gone. After questioning her son, she rushed next door to tell Raymond's mom to call a doctor, but the hearty German immigrant seemed unconcerned. Unable to sleep, Mrs. Osborn sat up late, watching her neighbor's house for signs of distress.

"Well, things did happen at their house that night," Bess wrote. "There was a light there most all night and the next morning the clotheslines were full of bedding and pajamas. Poor Raymond. I bet he never ate *that* kind of candy again." The next day Raymond's mom wondered why little Bud hadn't eaten the "candy" too. Bess replied that her son had "already been initiated" and knew perfectly well what laxatives could do. "I punished him," she sighed.

Though Bess anguished over Lyn's pranks, the truth was that he took after his mother, who in her youth had been no angel. Once she and a girlfriend — both pregnant — sneaked into a neighbor's chicken house, snapped the necks of five pigeons, and whipped up two tasty pigeon pies. "There never was two young pregnant gals who enjoyed a dinner more than we did," she told her diary, which she called "All the Days of My Life."

Clois Lynn Osborn was born on a turbulent night during a blizzard in Wichita Falls, Texas, on January 21, 1926.[1] He was a large baby — 9½ pounds — and his father named him after his boss at the refinery where he worked. "He hated the name Clois and never went by it," says his sister, Maebeth, who was two years older. "I called him 'my little brother boy,' only it came out 'Buddy.'" The name stuck. Maebeth doesn't know where his middle name, Lynn, came from. Buddy was adorable but full of mischief. "He got into more things than any little boy I ever seen," his mother complained to her diary.

---

[1] He dropped the second "n" in Lyn in 1950, shortly after *Space Patrol* began. His name appears as Lynn Osborn in the early credits.

The Osborn family in 1933. From left: Maebeth, age 9, Bess, Bill and Buddy (Lyn), 7. (Courtesy Beth Flood)

From the time he was an infant, Osborn had both a caring and mischievous side — traits that stayed with him for the rest of his life. When he was 1½, he was so upset when his father shot a skunk and buried it in the orchard that he cried for days, then dug it up and carried it back to the house.

Bess doted on Buddy because she'd lost her first son, who died at birth. Then too, says Maebeth, her baby brother developed "summer complaint" — a worrisome condition where no food agreed with him, so he got extra attention. Though he recovered, he never grew into a large child, despite his birth weight. It was the bane of his life. "He was always short," wrote Bess, "and he wanted to be tall so bad."

There was no question that Lyn got his feisty spirit from Bess, whose roots went back to pioneer days. Her parents traveled by covered wagon from Indian territory in Oklahoma to Paluxy, Texas. At 16, she married Bill Osborn, who bought a truck and went into the oil hauling business. Bess's diary chronicles a hardscrabble existence of traveling with Bill, who sought work in wild and woolly towns that were "no fit place for a woman." It's a detailed account of life in a world where, when your car got stuck in a mud-hole, instead of calling the auto club, you found a mule to pull you out.

The Depression years: William Osborn moved the family from Wichita Falls, Texas, to California in search of work, then east to Muskegon, Michigan, where a friend got him a job in an oil refinery. The Osborns settled in nearby Wolf Lake, where Bud and Maebeth attended a one-room school. When Bill was promoted to refinery superintendent, they moved to southwest Detroit, where Bud ran into some problems. "He was very small for his age and got beat up by the bigger kids," recalls Maebeth. "Finally my Dad

Above: Osborn, stationed in Hawaii, sent this photograph to Bess for Mother's Day, circa 1944. *Left:* Lyn Osborn and his sister play dress-up in 1933. "He was already showing signs of acting," says Beth. (Photographs courtesy Beth Flood)

said, 'Why don't you hit them back?' And Lyn, who'd always been told not to fight, replied 'You mean, you'd *let* me?' He began to defend himself and very soon the kids stopped picking on him."

It wasn't long before Osborn discovered he could gain acceptance, despite his small stature, by becoming the class clown, and when outgoing Bess enrolled him and Maebeth in a children's theater group, his confidence soared. A natural cut-up, he made the other kids laugh with monologues such as "Sister and Her Beau," embarrassing shy Maebeth no end. "He was always wisecracking, making faces," she remembers. "He had people in stitches all the time." At 16, Lyn was still only five feet tall, but in the next few years he shot up another seven inches. He graduated from Lincoln Park High School in June 1943 and enlisted in the Navy in September, when he was 17½ years old. Assigned to a naval air group, he trained in Hawaii as an aerial gunner and radio operator but never saw combat.

"Burlesque people are the greatest people in the world," Osborn informed his family in the fall of 1945. His father didn't think so. "My brother was just out of the Navy," Beth (as she's called now) says forty years later, "and for a while he didn't do anything. Then he started dating a burlesque comedienne. She inspired him — they used to play off each other." The future cadet became a fixture in Detroit bars, mesmerized by his girlfriend and her zany cabaret crowd as they worked the club circuit night after night. "He'd come home in the wee hours of the morning and sleep late, not wanting to even look for a job," says Beth. "He'd found his home among those people. I think that's where he first got the idea he wanted to be a comedian." Instead, Bill Osborn put Lyn to work slinging heavy oil drums around the refinery. "He wasn't cut out for that," muses Beth's husband, Bill Flood, "but when he first started wanting to be an actor, his father was dead set against it. That's what Lyn had to fight." Beth stares out the window of the 33-foot motor home that she and Bill are about to take on the road in search of retirement adventure. "My brother was kind of ... a bum ... during that period. My Dad had no faith in him at all; he never thought he'd amount to anything."

"Lyn's father was not an outgoing man," recalls Ed Kemmer. "He had a wall around him — that was his way of getting through life. And probably Lyn needed more than that."

> SCENE: Major Robertson is off on a mission to a far corner of the galaxy when he spots a phenomenon never seen before: a mysterious ring-shaped planet orbiting the distant sun Algol. Grabbing the hyperspace-o-phone, he radios Buzz and Hap in the Terra V, millions of DUs away, giving a play-by-play as he flies through the planet's strange "ring." Suddenly, a powerful force hits his ship and the Major groans as his rockets roar out of control. Buzz yells into the receiver in vain, then puts down the dead space-o-phone and restlessly paces the cockpit.

CORRY: *Happy.*
HAP: *Yes, sir?*
CORRY: *What would Robbie do if we were the ones who were lost, and he was searching for us?*
HAP: *Well, he'd turn this part of space upside down until he found us. He wouldn't stop until he did.*
CORRY: *You wouldn't expect us to do any less, would you?*
HAP: *Well... no, sir!*

> (Buzz is lost in thought. Finally, he leans over Hap's shoulder as the cadet keeps the ship on course.)

CORRY: *Glad you said that, Happy. Because what we've got to do is going to leave us wide open.*
HAP: (worried) *What do you mean, sir?*
CORRY: *Whatever happened to Robbie happened as he was flying through the center of that planet.*
HAP: *You — you — y-you mean we're going to do the same thing ... sir?*
CORRY: *That's the only way we can find him.* (Pause. Buzz looks expectant, waiting.)
HAP: (bites his lip) *Let's go.*
CORRY: (hand on his cadet's shoulder) *Good boy.*
> — "Web of Arachna," TV Episode 203, January 8, 1955

"My father never touched or hugged us— you never knew how he felt," Beth Flood recalls. "Of course, after Lyn made it big, he was proud of him and sorry he hadn't helped him more when he was struggling. But at the time, he thought he'd be throwing money away."

On the heels of his love affair with burlesque, Lyn struck out for Chicago— no one quite remembers why — where he worked as a candy butcher in the Rialto Burlesque Theater and a busboy at the posh Pump Room in the Ambassador East Hotel. When he soared to success several years later, he delighted in reminding certain fellow celebrities he had cleared their dirty dishes.

Hollywood, at last! "Well, I'm still alive. I start work tomorrow," Osborn wrote his mom on the back of a postcard of Hollywood Blvd., shortly after arriving in Los Angeles in 1947. (Courtesy Beth Flood)

The Pasadena Playhouse. Founded in 1917 by Gilmor Brown, it's known worldwide for giving many top stars their start, including Victor Mature, Robert Young, William Holden, Carolyn Jones, Raymond Burr, Barbara Rush and Leonard Nimoy. (Courtesy Ellen Bailey, Pasadena Playhouse Archivist)

Nobody knows for sure what transformed Osborn's lighthearted fling with burlesque into a serious passion for the theater; but suddenly the busboy journeyed west in the summer of 1947 to cash in his G.I. bill at one of the country's premier acting schools, the Pasadena Playhouse. "He drove a cab, he did restaurant work, he wrote sad letters to my parents asking for $10 to pull him through when the G.I. payment was late—how he must have hated that!" says Beth, who disposed of most of the letters because they were so depressing. But a few survived:

December 25, 1947
Dear Folks,
    ...The way it stands now is this: I have exactly sixty-one dollars.... I register for school January 2nd.... I bought a carton of cigarettes today so I will at least have smokes and I can make out until school starts on that buck if I don't go anyplace or do anything that costs money.... So you see, if I watch myself, I can do it OK.... Have you got an old pillow laying around that you don't need? I could use one. They want seven dollars for them in a store.
Lots of love,
Bud

Osborn (left) as "the King's Marshall" with friend Chuck Barkus in a Pasadena Playhouse production of *Richard II*. "I made the beard myself," Lyn wrote to his mom on the back of the photograph.

> P.S. Don't send me any money. I can get along without it. I'll let you know when I absolutely need it.

Osborn found several roommates to share an apartment in Pasadena and later a house in an orange grove in nearby Duarte. Chuck Barkus, who roomed with Lyn from the beginning, became a close friend. "We just bonded," says Barkus. "You'd seldom see one of us when the other wasn't pretty close at hand." Chuck soon discovered that "Muggsy," as Lyn was dubbed at the Playhouse because of his striking resemblance to actor Leo Gorcey, saw humor in everything and could turn life's everyday chores into a comedy routine.[2]

> Muggs and I bought a two-seat bicycle for transportation to and from school. One day I'm in the front, guiding, and he's on the back of the bike. As I start up a hill, I'm thinking, "Boy, this is tough going." As we passed a storefront, I glanced over at our reflection

[2]Gorcey played "Muggs McGinnis" in a series of 1940s films about "The East Side Kids."

in the big window—and what's this guy doing? *He's sitting back there with his feet up on the handlebars!* I'm doing all the peddling and he's just laying back—and all these people on the sidewalk are laughing. Here I am working my fanny off, and he's putting on this show! I almost killed him. That was Muggs, always the showman.

But beneath Osborn's light-hearted exterior was the constant struggle to make ends meet. Down to his last dollar, he took a job as a cab driver.

> Dear Mom,
>   ...I have been driving a cab every night from four P.M. until two in the morning, plus going to school every day. I have just about decided that it is a little too rough to keep it up, on account of it isn't paying well at all.... I have lost ten or twelve pounds in the past month and it's beginning to show, But now that I have moved in with these fellows I may be able to eat a little more regular....

Despite money woes, Lyn was in his element and he knew it. He'd found his calling, and though he clowned and joked his way through the Playhouse, he hit the books hard. Never an A student—he pulled a few C's in acting—he kept a B average. But no matter what his grades, he scored high in attitude. Though Dick Darley might find it hard to believe, his instructors rated him "Excellent" to "Superior" in his cooperation with the director, stage manager and fellow students.

In letters home, he told Bess excitedly of his progress:

> When I first got to school, I made a recording of my voice and just two days ago I made another, in order to see the improvement. It's really terrific, doesn't sound like the same person.... I now possess an authentic Irish accent, Cockney, English, Scottish, Russian, Jewish, Slavic, and also a deep Shakespearean voice. I'm finally learning how to tap dance.... A couple of the directors at school have taken an interest in me and think I have talent, so who knows, you may be seeing me in a movie before long....

Chuck Barkus watched in awe as Lyn submitted homework peppered with jokes and potshots aimed at his instructors. "My God, he would turn in his paper and it would have some funny bit, you know? He was always 'on.'" One teacher was greeted with the following:

> I am being held prisoner by a mad History professor, and am forced to write this report. As I sit here in this dungeon amid filth and darkness, I sometimes doubt if I shall ever see the light of day again.... There are quite a number of us down here, all writing this material so that our tormenter may compile it into a historical volume and reap the benefits of our labor. If this should happen to get to the outside world, I beg of you to please send some assistance to the few of us broken souls that are left...."

Fortunately, this instructor had a sense of humor and scribbled in the margin: "*We only escaped a short time ago! Will try to get help.*"

You get the feeling, rifling through Osborn's schoolwork, that despite his cracks about being overworked at the Playhouse, he loved every minute of it. Though the courses were grueling, he was learning the technique he needed to unleash his talent, and he was finally perceived for what he was: an actor. People knew it. Women knew it. In fact, some women thought he was a pretty big man, despite his height—especially some high school girls who hung around the exotic Playhouse crowd to meet actors. He became close to one of them, Elizabeth, whom everyone called "Honey." They'd talk as he walked her home from school; then he'd meet her later at her babysitting job. When Lyn died ten years later, Honey's sister, Geraldine, wrote Bill and Bess Osborn that a child had come from that relationship.

Besides attention from women, there were other perks, too. The Playhouse had opened a window on a whole new world. He met people with ideas he'd never heard before. Chuck Barkus's father talked to him for hours about theosophy, a spiritual system of thought based on the concept that life is multi-dimensional and continues in other realms after death. "It's really fascinating and deep," Lyn wrote Bess, "and deals in facts instead of faith. I think this is what I have been looking for." In the winter of 1949, he told her how profoundly the Playhouse had changed him. For the first time, instead of signing the letter "Bud," he used his new nickname, "Muggsy."

> …I think that the best thing that ever happened to me was when I enrolled in this school, I've got rid of my inferiority complex, and most of my self-consceisness (You spell it, I can't). Even if I never do very good in show business, I will be a much better man on account of this school….
> Lots of love and stuff,
> "Muggsy"

Osborn's grades were improving, and at least one teacher glimpsed what the future held. "This student will succeed," he wrote on a grade sheet in April 1949. "In my opinion, he is at a professional level already." Still, when he graduated in 1950, Osborn pulled a C in Radio Production — not what you'd expect from someone who, just six months later, would co-star in a radio show on the ABC network. The Playhouse invited Osborn back for graduate work, but at the same time a more prestigious institution beckoned: In March 1950 (thanks to an audition), he won the much-coveted "Corry Scholarship," awarded yearly to one promising cadet by the commander-in-chief of the Space Patrol.

> March 5, 1950
> Dear Folks,
> …In about a week I graduate from the Playhouse, but I don't think I'll have to worry about a job. Last Thursday I received a call from my agent to go to ABC Television Center for a reading. I went, read a script and got the part. The first show is this coming Thursday…. I'll get $8 per show (5 shows a week) until we get a sponsor & then the money goes up to ??…. The show will be television's answer to Buck Rogers, complete with spaceship & all. It is called "Space Patrol." The star is Kit Corry, Commander-in-Chief of the interplanetary Space Patrol, & I am his co-pilot and buddy. Mine is the second lead and comedy part — just the kind of part I love. So far as I know, there is nothing like it on television yet & it's a natural for the kids! Imagine I'll be moving to Hollywood soon…. I may become an American institution yet! … I'm feeling great about it all & praying that it goes over OK! The whole American Broadcasting Co. is behind it, so I don't know how it can miss!!!
> Love & Stuff
> "Buddy"
> P.S. My new name on the show is "Happy"

When he read for the part, he was so right for it that Mike Moser was stunned. Osborn later wrote about that moment:

> I hustled over and read for the producer, and in the long pause that followed I imagined all sorts of things, including the thought that maybe I should have stood in bed…. Said

[Moser], "You're exactly what I had in mind for Cadet Happy in this script I've written. The part's yours if you want it." It took me a fast two seconds to stammer out my answer....[3]

Lyn held his breath, hoping that this incredible good fortune would not evaporate. But a week later, he wrote his folks that the show was a "go." After scraping by on $65 a month plus the occasional $10 or $25 Bess sent, $40 a week was a windfall. The future looked bright:

> March 13, 1950
> Dear Folks,
>   Well, we did the third show today and everything is going great.... There seems to be no doubt that it will be a big success. I have just found out that they are kinescoping (filming) every show as it goes on the air and sending copies to N.Y., Chicago, Detroit, Dallas, Kansas City, etc. on a 7-week trial basis, so watch for it on ABC.... The sustaining budget has been extended to 26 weeks & we are sure to have a sponsor in about a month! This all seems too good to be true!!

By the end of March, Osborn felt like a Hollywood insider, hanging out on the sets of ABC's hit shows, schmoozing with veteran actors and newsmen:

> March 29, 1950
> Dear Folks,
>   Just a line to let you know that everything is OK and the show is still going fine.... The writer and producer has told me that, as far as he is concerned, I have a good part in any show that he produces in the future. That sounds pretty good, huh? ... I can hang around the studio all day if I want to and watch all the shows— Ruggles, Mama Rosa, Mysteries of Chinatown, etc.... I have all my debts paid off and $100 in the bank.... Do you remember Roscoe Ates, who used to play in all the westerns? I have lunch with him once in a while.... Had dinner a couple of times with Pat Hogan, the radio and TV columnist for the LA Examiner....

A few days later, he wrote, exhilarated:

> ...I have just been thinking, you know, it's been just about three years since I left Detroit, and now I have the second lead on a television show, living in Hollywood, and making a living. That's not bad progress, eh?

During his years at the Playhouse, most of his letters had been addressed to Bess, but now, with success in his pocket, they began "Dear Folks." Perhaps the sweetest reward was that he had proved to Bill Osborn, who'd never had any faith in him, that he was worth something after all.

When *Space Patrol* went network at the end of 1950, Osborn's life whipped into warp speed — a whirlwind of personal appearances, autographs and interviews. He later told newspaper columnist Allen Rich that as a youngster, he had dreamed of showbiz stardom, and now he'd stepped into that dream.[4] When Ralston Purina picked up the show, Lyn's face beamed out from Chex cereal boxes in markets across the country. He even made his film debut with a small part as "Moore" in *Up Front* (1951), a wartime comedy based on the work of famed Army cartoonist Bill Mauldin.

[3]"Why I'm Unhappy" by Lyn Osborn, *TV-Radio Life*, June 27, 1952.
[4]*Valley Times*, August 26, 1952.

As his salary skyrocketed, his letters home tapered off. He could afford to call now.

Those close to Osborn agree that the role of "Hap" fit him like a glove. "I think that in his own life, he wasn't just an actor, he was now Cadet Happy, a public personality," says Dick Darley. Sometimes it was hard to tell where Lyn ended and Hap began. Even Bess, in a friendly note to Virginia Hewitt, referred to her son as Hap instead of Bud. "Cadet Happy *was* Lyn," sums up announcer Dick Tufeld. "He was 'Cadet Lyn Osborn.'" Ed Kemmer agrees: "In playing that role, he tended to live it."

As Hollywood embraced Osborn, so did a number of young starlets, including Piper Laurie, Rita Moreno and Barbara Whiting — if you believe the gossip columnists, who spotted them on his arm at nightspots like Ciro's and Mocambo. He hired a clipping service, which reporters kept busy as they tracked his comings and goings:

> Lyn Osborn, Cadet Happy on Space Patrol, begins first vacation from show next week with a motor trip through West Coast states … Lyn Osborn is taking tennis lessons from Keith Larsen … Lyn Osborn and lovely Powers model Christine Marlowe a twosome at the Hollywood Derby.

TV magazine caught him and Barbara Whiting frolicking at an amusement park; paparazzi snapped him with Virginia Hewitt, enjoying a romantic dinner at Cyrano's on the Sunset Strip.

But despite his active nightlife — and, say friends, a slew of one-night stands — Lyn honored his commitment to the kids who idolized him as Cadet Happy. He was careful not to smoke in public if youngsters were around. If he drank, he used orange juice as a mixer. Sometimes he even passed up a drink. "Success has its little problems," quipped *The Hollywood Reporter*, noting that Osborn was afraid a young fan might see him in public "with an innocent glass of beer in his hand."[5] But success could also be sweet. When the now-famous cadet met Roy Rogers and Dale Evans at a star-studded Hollywood bash, he asked if they had enjoyed their duck dinner at the Pump Room back in 1947. "How did you know about *that*?" asked the couple. "Easy," said Lyn. "I was your busboy."

It was obvious to star-watchers that Hewitt and Osborn were an item. "Since Virginia is the only [cast member] besides me who isn't married, we've naturally gotten pretty well acquainted," he told *L.A. Mirror* columnist Hal Humphrey. "It's suspected that they also have dates together now and then — when they are out of uniform, of course," Humphrey added. "Moser probably takes a dim view of this practice, but has refrained thus far from taking any dire measures to stop it."[6] "Virginia Hewitt and Lyn Osborn of *Space Patrol* are in the clouds in more ways than one," hinted *The Hollywood Reporter*.[7]

In fact, Lyn fell in love with Hewitt, but that was a one-way street. They dated for over a year, but at the end of 1953, she was swept off her feet by Austrian-born interior designer Ernst Meer, who created color schemes to soothe the nerves of L.A.'s socially prominent. Meer offered a passport into that world, and the two became engaged. Osborn was devastated. Hewitt withdrew behind an icy façade, and Lyn, hurt beyond words and out of control, slung insults in a desperate attempt to break through it. But on *Space Patrol*, "Hap" and "Carol" were loyal comrades, so both masked their pain when the

---

[5]*The Hollywood Reporter*, January 31, 1952.
[6]*L.A. Mirror*, April 13, 1953.
[7]*The Hollywood Reporter*, October 6, 1953.

Lyn and Virginia, on a date, can't resist a stop at a photograph machine. (Author's collection)

cameras rolled, escaping into the illusion of what might have been — though Dick Darley, sensitive to the actors' moods, saw looks that could kill pass between them.

To their credit, both Osborn and Hewitt eventually got past the bitterness and remained friends. When Lyn became ill several years later, he turned to Virginia and Ernst for emotional support. Hewitt saved all of Lyn's notes to her, along with snapshots of the two of them out on dates, in dusty boxes of *Space Patrol* memorabilia tucked away in her basement. Strips of photos from a 25-cent self-service machine catch them cuddling and delighting in each other's company. She looks happier and more relaxed than in any other photographs before or since.

In the throes of the breakup, he buried the hurt in the full-time job of being Cadet Happy, joking his way out of heartbreak. Not finding the right woman became part of his schtick. He complained in interviews that his love life would "bore an elderly mollusk" and listed his marital status as "None." When reporters kidded him that on the show Buzz and Carol were an item, and Robbie and Tonga probably were, it gave Osborn a perfect excuse to defend his single status. It was a well-known fact, he told *The Wilshire Press*, that Space Patrol cadets in training are forbidden to marry until they graduate into the commissioned ranks. The interviewer played along. "If wedding bells should ring," he wrote, "Cadet Happy would have to hunt himself a new career." Besides, Lyn told another reporter, he was holding out for "a luscious dish from Venus."[8]

In the meantime, he moved to the posh Sunset Plaza Apartments, overlooking the Sunset Strip. And he bought his dream car — a white '53 Buick Skylark convertible with jazzy hubcaps and "Customized for Lyn Osborn" engraved in gold on the steering wheel. Frank Bresee watched him showing it off one day in front of Schwab's Drug Store in Hollywood. "People walked by and whispered, *'It's Lyn Osborn ... Space Patrol!'* He was letting them admire him and the car at the same time."

But though he was a TV star now — a celebrity with access to Hollywood's glamour — he joked that he still felt like an outsider. Despite *Space Patrol's* popularity, he wasn't rubbing shoulders with the likes of Joan Crawford or Jack Benny — even though he'd gained entry into many stars' homes via their TV screens. In a tongue-in-cheek, "poor me" article, he complained that stardom was not all it's cracked up to be:

> My plunge into the glittering life as an actor took place on March 9, 1950, the day Cadet Happy was born in television, and I waited for the fabulous fireworks to begin. Any moment, I expected the photographers to show up and beg me for my picture. Pretty girls, I knew, would soon begin to swoon over me, and autograph fans would cluster ten-deep around me. And, although I'd be covered with fame, I'd take it all in stride.
>
> Now, 700 TV shows and 250 radio broadcasts later, I'm still waiting... No screen or television siren has threatened to do herself in because of love for me. Hollywood hostesses don't particularly clamor for me to attend their soirees. What hurts even more is to have my out-of-town friends say, "Well, Lyn, you're a celebrity now. How does it feel to be invited to Joan Crawford's for dinner, and what's Shelley Winters like?" Smokin' rockets! I once drove past Joan Crawford on the Sunset Strip and one day Shelley Winters stepped on my toe while I was waiting for a table at a restaurant.[9]

To add insult to injury, parents complained to him that *Space Patrol* was disrupting their household routine:

> They say, in injured tones, "You realize, of course, that you've ruined the dining habits at our house.... The children won't eat unless they're looking at a screen. We might as well rent out our dining rooms, for all the use they're getting!"

And though many of Hollywood's biggest names were *Space Patrol* fans, he rarely met them face to face:

[8]"A Romance for Happy," *TV Time*, March 7, 1953
[9]Osborn's essay appeared in Allen Rich's syndicated column in the *Valley Times*, August 26, 1952.

Osborn's pride and joy: His '53 Buick Skylark convertible with "Customized for Lyn Osborn" engraved in gold on the steering wheel. "All the new Cad drivers stop to look at it," Osborn wrote his mom on the back of the photograph. "He used to show it off in front of Schwab's Drug Store," recalls Frank Bresee. (Courtesy Beth Flood)

> Here are some more of my troubles: Jack Benny, one of my idols, is a regular viewer of our show, but the nearest I've ever gotten to him is my TV or radio dial. Ethel and Lionel Barrymore watch the program [but] it's like asking for the moon to meet them.[10]

Lyn admitted to UP correspondent Vernon Scott that despite his own fame, he was still starstruck. "I get terrifically excited every time I meet a star," he confided. But when he did meet celebs such as Red Skelton, Alice Faye or Tex Ritter, they were cordial enough — then vanished, leaving him alone with their kids to sign autographs.[11] It was a great angle for columnists, and there was always another story about how Lyn Osborn, shackled to the role of a teenage space cadet, couldn't act his age (that is, smoke or drink) in public, or get women to take him seriously. "He's in a fix," wrote Scott. "Just at an age when most young Hollywood bachelors are touring the Sunset Strip with glamour girls, Lyn has to lead an exemplary life." But Osborn said he didn't mind. "I owe it to all

[10]*Ibid.*
[11]Tex Ritter's son, John, grew up to become a television star himself. He passed away in 2003 at age 54.

the kids that watch the show." He said he got thousands of letters from children who guessed he was somewhere between 16 and 21 years old and wanted to know what school he attended. "I can't answer them," he explained. "I've been out of school for longer than I like to think about, and I can't disappoint my fans."[12]

He meant that. Lyn didn't want to disappoint anyone, an angst rooted in the fact that he'd been one huge disappointment to his father until he'd vindicated himself by becoming a TV star. He hid that pain and other insecurities (like being short) beneath his ebullient personality. "It seemed like nothing would bother Lyn Osborn," says Ed Kemmer. "But that's the story of the clown, and he was a very funny one." Osborn could poke you with his sharp wit or make you laugh until tears ran down your face, but you *always* had a reaction to him. "He took great joy in making statements to shock you," says Chuck Barkus. "He did it just to get your attention."

But underneath his brash façade, Osborn was more serious than he wanted to let on. When he wasn't partying hard, he studied the metaphysical tomes of theosophy or his favorite philosopher, Immanuel Velikovsky.[13] Kemmer glimpsed Lyn's deeper side, but he was too busy holding the show together to relate to it much:

> I always felt that Hap was a deep thinker, but he didn't want you to know it. He was very bright and it would shine through now and then when he'd bring you up short with some insightful remark. When he wasn't playing the buffoon, there was that deep, intelligent side of him, but he didn't show it a helluva lot. He wanted to play the comic most of the time. But underneath it all, he was very capable and very bright.

Riding a wave of sudden success and fame, on the set he could spiral out of control. "He was a young guy feeling his oats, and everyone in the world was telling him he had great talent," says Dick Darley, who did his best to get the show on and off the air despite Lyn's antics. "He'd just say whatever came into his head without thinking," adds Kemmer, who got on his case when he threw playful, off-color jibes at Nina or Virginia. "He had a smart mouth and he was very cocky, but if he hadn't been, I don't think he could have done that part," says Darley, his frustration mellowed by the years. "He felt he was indispensable, which — for this show — he probably was."

Dick Tufeld, who didn't carry the burdens that lay on Darley and Kemmer's shoulders, had more time and patience to appreciate Lyn. "He was brash, over-the-top, and he delighted in pushing your buttons. He'd say something outrageous and he'd always get a response from me," Tufeld laughs. "He knew that I liked him because I'd see him and just automatically start smiling, and he'd do something to make me smile more. He was great at lifting your spirits."

Despite his constant clowning, Lyn cared deeply about the show and bragged that he could still recite his lines from the very first episode. He confided to his sister, Beth, that he was honored to be in *Space Patrol*, and told *L.A. Times* columnist Walter Ames that he was content to remain an ageless cadet:

> All the kids want to know when I'm going to step up a grade in the Space Patrol force. I have a hard time convincing them that if I ever make lieutenant or something, I'm out of a job. I just want to remain Cadet Happy.[14]

[12]August 14, 1953, news story by Vernon Scott, UP wire service.

[13]Velikovsky, author of the controversial 1950 bestseller *Worlds in Collision*, believed that in 2700 B.C. a giant comet entered our solar system and became the planet Venus. This event altered Earth's orbit, slowed its rotation and reversed its polarity, giving credence to reports of floods and other natural disasters in ancient times.

[14]*Los Angeles Times*, July 17, 1952.

Perhaps Osborn had an inkling that it was his destiny to be linked with "Hap" forever. "I don't mind being careful of the way I behave in public," he told UP reporter Vernon Scott. When he hit the clubs on the Sunset Strip, he was always on his best behavior. He knew people were watching, that Cadet Happy was admired by adults as well as kids, and he wasn't about to let them down. Besides, he'd made a promise to Bess. In a letter written in February 1949, after describing the new horizons he'd glimpsed at the Playhouse, he told her:

> All this hasn't hurt my sense of right and wrong or affected my morals. You did a pretty good job of teaching me all about that, and I intend to abide by it always. Every so often I sit down by myself and think about the way you brought me up and taught me right from wrong, and I always end up deciding that you did a wonderful job. Thanks a million!!!

Osborn at the height of his success in *Space Patrol*. "I just want to remain Cadet Happy," he told a reporter when asked if he would leave the show for a better role. (Courtesy Beth Flood)

And while some might argue that his partying and womanizing were not in keeping with that vow to his mom to stick to a high moral code, those who knew him will tell you that, at his core, Osborn was both compassionate and generous. "He cared about people," says John Buckley, recalling how Lyn got parts on *Space Patrol* for the starving actors who frequented Nardi's, a Playhouse hangout. "They wouldn't have gotten *anything*, if it weren't for Lyn Osborn." Ed Kemmer agrees:

> He was a very caring person, but he would hide it well. I remember one actor — my God, he's probably still out there trying to get work! He hung around Hap a lot, got bit parts on the show; and I'm sure Hap saw he had a place to sleep and food to eat.

In a 1954 column, *Los Angeles Herald & Express* writer Jimmy Starr revealed the tender side that Osborn kept under wraps:

> There's a side to Lyn Osborn that even his avid televiewers don't know about.... The other night, he was driving along Sunset Boulevard, thinking about his color television set ("This is a better gimmick than having etchings in your apartment," he says) when he saw a wet, half-dead kitten in the middle of the busy street. Obviously someone had tried to drown it. With much screeching of brakes and at the risk of his life, Lyn stopped his car and rescued the scared and frantic kitten. He rushed it to a pet hospital, where a kindly veterinarian stayed up all night and nursed the kitten back to health. Lyn now has a very grateful pet on his hands.... Actually, Lyn is a trifle embarrassed about being a hero — a real one.[15]

---

[15]*Los Angeles Herald & Express*, November 11, 1954.

Lyn, relaxed with his mother, Bess (left), and less so with his father, Bill (right), in October 1952 when they visited him in Los Angeles at the height of his *Space Patrol* success. (Courtesy Beth Flood)

He named the kitten "Rover." Nothing had changed since, as a child, he'd dug up the skunk his father killed and carried it back to the house in his arms.

As *Space Patrol* continued to climb with no end in sight, Lyn took it in stride:

> Dear Folks,
>   Nothing new here. Still doing the show and dickering with the boss for a raise, and maybe a five-year contract.... Have quite a bit of fan mail to answer.... I'm thinking about buying a house and signing with a business manager to take care of my money. Like I said, nothing new, bye for now.

He got the pay raise. In 1953, at age 27, he was making over $30,000 a year. (In the early '50s, you could buy a three-bedroom house on L.A.'s tony west side for $18,000 and a Porsche to go with it for $3,000.) By the following year, he was making $45,000, according to *TV Guide*.[16] When Beth and her husband Bill came out from Michigan to visit, they caught a glimpse of his glamorous life. He took them backstage at a telethon, where they mingled with stars, then to trendy Mocambo, where the owner greeted him like a long-lost friend. Wherever they went, he signed autographs. "He said he had the greatest life, and we were really impressed with how important he was," Beth smiles. But as early as 1952, when Osborn's career was soaring fast, the *Hollywood Reporter* warned of turbulence ahead:

> Lyn Osborn, who plays Cadet Happy on KECA-TV's very successful "Space Patrol," is up against a problem that is peculiarly television's—being typed through appearing six times a week as the same character. The longer he stays with the role, the less chance he's going

[16]*TV Guide*, December 25, 1954.

to have to shake the type; yet if he quits to free-lance and do the many other things any actor naturally wants to do, he gives up a steady and an increasing income.[17]

But Osborn was more worried about his signature than the proverbial handwriting on the wall. He practiced signing his name different ways for autographs and didn't like any of them. The "r" in Osborn was the biggest problem. He wrote a string of them on a scratch pad, never satisfied. "I write such a messy hand that I can't even read it!" he complained in a note beneath them.

Kids trailed him like a Pied Piper. By this time, Chuck Barkus, who wasn't finding much work as an actor, had taken a day job as a hair stylist in Pasadena. Sometimes Lyn would meet him for lunch. "We'd walk down the street, and my gosh, we'd have about fifteen or twenty kids following us," Barkus recalls. "They were thrilled to be in the same place he was." Osborn took it in stride. "Fame never went to his head," says Chuck. "I didn't notice any change in him — he handled it very well."

But by late 1954, Lyn was nervous about how long his good fortune could last. "Osborn's great worry," reported *TV Guide*, "is his inability to break away from the role by which millions of kids know him." For the first time, he expressed doubts about his future:

> Happy is the only role I've ever had and I don't know whether producers will take a chance with me. With this face, how could I be mistaken for anyone else? Eventually, I want to be a comic. A good one. But I look around and see young guys like Donald O'Connor and Sammy Davis, Jr., and I figure I'd better get started.[18]

When the reporter asked if he was seeking other roles on the side, Lyn said, "Yes, but no villains. Nothing that might hurt *Space Patrol*. That show comes first."

Two months later, like a ship knocked out of the space lanes by a torpedo, *Space Patrol* was dropped from the ABC lineup. Of all the cast members, says Dick Darley, Osborn took the hardest fall:

> When you've achieved being recognized by everybody, you're known all over the country and you hear the ratings— how many millions of people watched you last week— and then you drop from that to, say, checking the racing form over coffee at Schwab's Drug Store all day long, that's a helluva drop.

He took physical falls, too.

Everyone has a story about how Lyn Osborn fell and cracked his head, which some say led to his illness. "There used to be a restaurant on Sunset Boulevard with flagstone steps, and he slipped on one of those and hit the back of his head a pretty lick," says actor friend Tyler MacDuff, a veteran of *The Lone Ranger* and other westerns. John Feneck, who'd roomed with Lyn during their Playhouse days, had been out on the town with him that nightin November 1957 when Osborn, no longer in Cadet Happy mode, let his public behavior lapse:

> We had a few drinks, then aced our way to Frascati's on the Sunset Strip and had a few more blasts. As we were leaving, Muggsy walked — or staggered — ahead of me, tripped over something (possibly his own feet), did a sort of somersault over the front stairs, and

[17]*The Hollywood Reporter*, January 31, 1952.
[18]*TV Guide*, December 25, 1954.

landed on his back on the sidewalk, banging his head on the cement. I stumbled down the steps and bent down to see if he was conscious or even alive. His eyes were closed and a small pool of blood started forming behind his head on the pavement.

Feneck raced back into the restaurant to call an ambulance. When he dashed outside again, the police had arrived, wrapped Osborn's head in a towel, and were leading him to a squad car. "I said 'What are you doing? He needs an ambulance!'" Feneck recalls. "But they said, 'He's drunk—we're taking him to the station.'" Feneck followed, pleading with the officers to get Lyn treatment. "They said, 'Get out of here or we'll book you too.' I left."[19]

Rickey Barr, who dated Lyn and later became his agent, remembers the time he fell off a bench onstage during a little theater production in Hollywood:

> He hit the stage so hard it scared everybody in the audience, but he went on with the performance. He almost couldn't make it through the play, but being what he was, he did make it through. I think that's when it happened, because he really hurt his head and had headaches. And it was shortly after that when he started to have the attacks.

Lyn didn't complain, adds Barr, because "he never complained about anything. He said it didn't hurt, but I knew it did."

Even Osborn had his own story about a fall he believed might have triggered his problems. He confided to John Buckley that one night he got pretty drunk and piled into a car with some strangers who were on their way to a party. Rattling off jokes—without thinking, as usual—he said something that was construed as a racial slur. He didn't mean it that way, but two African American men, irate, pushed him out of the car. It wasn't moving fast, but he got a nasty crack on the head. Shortly after that, he told Buckley, he had the first blackout.

---

[19]According to a receipt found in Osborn's files dated November 28, 1957, he was charged with intoxication and posted $20 bail. He appeared in court the next day but, luckily, the incident was not reported by the press.

CHAPTER 10

Hey, Kids!

When I moved out of the house, my mother asked what she should do with the two large drawers full of comic books and other "junk" from my childhood. I said, "Might as well get rid of it." Boy, had I only known.

— Bob Lee

Do you remember the little hand-held ray gun that used to freeze people in their tracks? It made a buzzing sound. Here I am, 53 years of age, having been to three county fairs, one war and a hanging — and I'm still intrigued by that sound I heard when I was four years old.

— Robert "Slim" Sweatmon

Slim Sweatmon can tell you about the power of a simple ray gun:

In the early 1950s, my father was recalled into the U.S. Marine Corps to fly dive-bombers in the Korean conflict. In the short weeks before his departure to combat, my mother and I accompanied him to El Toro Marine Base in California to have as much time with him as we could. It could possibly have been our last.

We had come from the dry ranch country of West Texas, where there was no television. When we got to the promised land of California, my father bought us a used television set. It was pure magic to a four-year-old, and the images on that silver screen gave me something to occupy my time while my parents spent some quiet moments together before he was forced to leave us. Suddenly my life became filled with new and wondrous friends, but none were quite as formidable and dear to me as Happy, Buzz and the whole gang on Space Patrol. As I sat in a darkened room and witnessed them take off into uncertain adventure, I was hooked.

I guess my father knew it, for the present he gave me as he boarded the plane for Korea was a black plastic Space Patrol ray gun. My mother tells me that I held it all the way home to Texas on the train. She put me to bed with it each night since I insisted that I was the man of the house now and I needed it to protect her.

One of the best things about *Space Patrol* was that you could look and act like your heroes. You could actually get the gear that the Space Patrol gang used in their adventures — the uniforms, caps and boots they wore, the weapons, gadgetry and communications devices that saved their lives. You could own these things for only 25 cents and a boxtop from a package of Wheat Chex or Rice Chex. This seemed too good to be true. It was like "carrying an object out of a dream," says Elliott Swanson, who watched as a child in San Francisco. "That you could buy and own the objects used by Corry and Happy created a powerful psychological link to that imaginary world. I know of no other television show that did this to that degree."

The Gardner Advertising Company, with offices in St. Louis and New York, who repped Ralston Purina (maker of Wheat Chex, Rice Chex and "good, Hot Ralston"), was equally pleased. In fact, they were just as excited as the "juves" about these cardboard and plastic premiums that yielded a bundle of space credits. To maximize their gains, Gardner insisted that entire half-hour episodes be built around these toys. The profits offset their advertising costs and forged a strong bond between kids and the show.

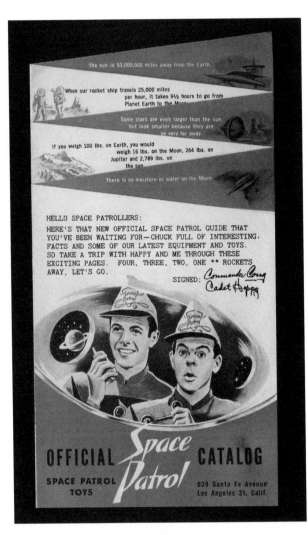

Official *Space Patrol* Catalog, chock-full of must-have gear for every young Space Patroller. You could get everything from a Flying Saucer Gun ($1.00) to *Space Patrol* pajamas ($3.98). (Author's collection)

Space Patrol merchandise fell into four categories: boxtop premiums; in-the-box items (cards or plastic coins buried in cereal); catalogue items; and merchandise sold in retail stores.[1] In September 1952, *Life* magazine ran a photo of most of the 80 *Space Patrol* items then available. If you were a kid of that era, you could dress like a Space Patroller (T-shirt or uniform, cap, boots, flight scarf), carry Space Patrol weapons, save your allowance in a Space Patrol bank ("Now is the time to start saving for that first trip into outer space"), build cardboard models of 30th-century spaceports and cities, sleep in Space Patrol pajamas and throw a party for fellow cadets with Space Patrol paper tablecloths and napkins. And when you weren't protecting the universe with your Rocket Gun or Auto-Sonic Rifle, you could peer into your Space Patrol Microscope and see "a spectacular view of a grasshopper," "hair that looks like a dangerous python snake," or "the tiny details on bugs or your pet turtle." It seemed like there was always a new, exciting offer touted on television by "Captain" Jack Narz or George Barclay, or on radio by Dick Tufeld, Dick Wesson or Lee Zimmer.[2] And often the Commander and Cadet Happy would chime in, assuring you that the box-

---

[1]For a great survey of vintage space opera toys, including full-color photos of many *Space Patrol* collectibles, see *Blast Off! Rockets, Robots, Rayguns and Rarities from the Golden Age of Space Toys* (Dark Horse Books, 2001) by S. Mark Young, Steve Duin and Mike Richardson. "There's something about the shapes, colors and imaginative (but often campy) designs of pre–Sputnik toys that appeals to me," says Young, who spent 15 years amassing material for the book. "I can de-stress just by looking at them."

[2]Narz was, in fact, a real-life captain, having attained the rank in the Army Air Corps. Barclay's full name was George Barclay Hodgkin. He declined to be interviewed for this book.

"From Space Patrol Headquarters to your living room comes the entire Space Patrol gang," promised this flyer for the Space Patrol City of Terra and Cast. This 50-piece plastic and cardboard set sold for $1.00 in the mid–'50s and was recently spotted on eBay for $4,000+. (Author's collection)

top premium was exactly the same as the "official" Space Patrol gear they used on their adventures—which was true. And that, says Ed Kemmer, was the problem:

> We used the real [premiums], but we felt we were kind of cheating people. It was crappy, cardboard stuff, but you *had* to take it seriously—otherwise it would come off twice as bad. It was a damned nuisance and it didn't help the show; it just helped sell the premiums, if they looked good on the air. We hated doing it, unless it was something worthwhile—but it's pretty hard to take a phony cardboard cockpit and make it look good. And that was yucky, making something look better than it was.

Despite Kemmer's guilt, he did the job well. And anyway, the gear looked pretty good on that magic screen in the living room. When your own official gear arrived from "Space Patrol Headquarters" in St. Louis, Missouri, it made you feel like a cadet in the Space Patrol. And if you didn't live too many DUs from a department store like May Company, or you could get your hands on a *Space Patrol* catalogue, you'd lose your rockets over the cadet shirts, flight suits, uniform boots, dress caps, space cars, watches, emergency kits, space helmets, monorails, and elaborate Marx playsets full of miniature space-age buildings and tiny plastic action figures with helmets and weapons.

Of course, for some kids, sighting a Marx playset was as likely as spotting a Venusian buffalo. "Neither I nor any other kid I knew even heard of the playsets, much less owned one," says space opera buff Rory Coker. "Ditto for the uniforms and spacesuits, complete with clear plastic bubble helmets." Greg Davis didn't have any of this fancy gear either, but he improvised his own, as kids did in the '50s, crafting a space helmet from a grocery bag, a spaceship from the boxes that held his father's shirts when they came back from the cleaner's. "I built a cockpit with little switches and levers that moved and wheels that turned—all out of cardboard," he recalls. "Every time I saw something new

Martian Totem Head Mask. "You can see out, Space Patrollers, but nobody can see in!" Even your own parents couldn't recognize you when you morphed into a scary Martian with this fancy headgear. (*Top:* Courtesy Judd Lawson; *bottom:* Photograph © Ed Swift, courtesy Dale Ames)

on the show, I'd add it to my spaceship. Thank God for cardboard, Scotch tape, staples, and my grandmother's straight pins."

But even if you never got to wear a shirt with Corry's lightning insignia on your chest or pitch a Space Patrol pup tent in the backyard, still—for just 25 cents and a cereal boxtop—you could get a pair of Space-o-Phones or Space Binoculars, a Martian Totem Head Mask and many other keen things. In fact, with a weekly allowance of 25 or 50 cents, points out Coker, a kid could do quite well, building a stash of boxtop premiums that "fueled our dreams and provided the necessary hardware for play sessions at prices we could afford." You could set up a base of operations—your Space Patrol "clubhouse"—in a corner of the garage (hang a few blankets for privacy), the backyard, the woods, or that secret space between your house and the neighbor's. Or, like Mike Pahlow, you could turn your entire bedroom into a rocketship control cabin:

> I had all sorts of paper dials, gauges and "control levers" attached to my two bureaus and small writing desk, on which I displayed the beautiful Rocket Cockpit. It was awesome! I played Space Patrol for hours in there. During the summer, my dad took off the storm windows and allowed me and my friends to climb in and out of the "rocket ship" without having to go through the main part of the house.

In the '50s, with the long, unstructured days of summer stretching ahead, there was no limit to the imaginative adventures a kid could think up between breakfast and supper, and you didn't even need Norm

 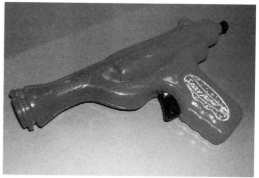

Rocket Dart Gun. "A thrilling, guided-missile gun, just like the one Commander Corry uses," screamed the toy catalogue. It was called a "paralyzer ray gun" on the show and was clearly the regulation weapon of the Space Patrol, although the retail version came with two plastic darts. One had a "Captomatic" warhead ("loud and pleasantly effective as a real guided missile") into which a paper cap could be inserted to detonate on impact. (*Black gun, left:* Photograph © Ed Swift, courtesy Dale Ames; *red gun, right:* Courtesy Chuck Lassen)

Jolley or Lou Huston to write the scripts. Just one boxtop premium fueled endless fantasies, and you could hardly wait to see what would be offered next:

> JACK NARZ: *This is it, boys and girls! Your last chance to examine coins to see if they're counterfeit. Your last chance to examine your miniature pet turtle and other interesting life. Your last chance to own the official Space Patrol Microscope, just like Buzz Corry himself uses every day. You get four transparent slides, plus the mystery slide with an atomic particle on it that glows in the dark! So don't wait! Send 25 cents in coin and a Rice Chex or Wheat Chex boxtop to Space Patrol, Box 987, St. Louis, Missouri. Get your Space Patrol Microscope today!*

Maybe the "atomic particle" that came with *your* microscope wasn't radioactive, like the kind Buzz and Hap might run into, but your Rocket Dart Gun was exactly the same weapon they used — another problem, says Kemmer. "The ray gun that shot darts was a pretty good weapon and it looked fine — until a heavy told you to drop it. When it fell, it sounded like plastic." That didn't cut it for Kemmer, who had his heart in the show and wanted it to be as real as possible. "I had the special effects man put something inside the guns to give them weight so that when they hit the floor they didn't sound like the lightweight plastic toys they were," he recalls. High-tech tricks like that made the gear you got for choking down yet another box of Ralston cereal seem more substantial onscreen than it was when it arrived at your door.

> SCENE: COMMERCIAL
>
> CAPTAIN BARCLAY: *It's a top secret known only to Commander Corry and Cadet Happy, guarded carefully night and day by the Space Patrol. But now it can be revealed: The Commander's new super-colossal, super-stupendous surprise — and it's for you, Space Patrollers: the sensational new Space Patrol Periscope! This honest-to-goodness periscope works magic for you. See around corners, over fences, through windows — and nobody can see you!*
>
> HAP: *Jumping Jupiter, can you ever have a lot of fun peering through your periscope! You can spy on your friends from behind big bushes! Get your pencils ready, boys and girls, 'cause in just a few minutes Captain Barclay will tell you how you can get one!*
>
> BARCLAY: *It's a big, big 24 inches high and it's specially tapered to give you wide-angle vision. It's got a mirror on the top and a mirror on the bottom — and printed on the front of your periscope is a complete identification chart of outer-space citizens!*

HAP: Now watch real close, Space Patrollers, and see how Commander Corry and I use our periscopes today!

If you sent in that quarter, and your mother didn't throw out your *Space Patrol* premiums when she tossed the Dell comic book collection that could have made both you and her millionaires, you could be having a *lot* of fun with the $500–600 that 25-cent cardboard periscope would net you today. Even if there are no citizens from outer space begging to be identified in your neighborhood, *Space Patrol* gear is definitely a good investment. Take the plastic Cosmic Glow Rocket Ring — remember the one from the Membership Kit? That's right. The one that recently sold for $1,400.

"I don't know who this individual is, but he's crazier than I am!" says collector Jim Buchanan in his slow, pleasing drawl. "I had to drop off on the bidding for that ring, but whoever bought it — I call him 'the Big Spender.' I've since been told that it's now worth $1,500." In the early '80s, Buchanan built one of the largest collections of *Space Patrol* memorabilia this side of Arcturus. "It's a childhood love, something you like to rekindle and hold on to. And it's a real challenge because a lot of it is extremely scarce to rare."

Both Kemmer and Osborn appeared on boxes of Wheat Chex, Rice Chex and "good, Hot Ralston," usually touting a boxtop offer or premium inside the package. (Courtesy Judd Lawson)

"The problem with *Space Patrol* stuff is that it was practically all paper or plastic," says collector-historian Andy Andersen. "It either got thrown out or broken, whereas *Flash Gordon* things are like steel. You can run over them with a truck, so they're still around."

"A friend of mine was offered $5,000 for his monorail," says Buchanan, "and he turned it down. Possessing the premiums and memorabilia is like regaining some of your childhood. That's why I collect — it's strictly out of love for the show." But it takes more than love — you'd better have a shipload of space credits, if you're prospecting for *Space Patrol* memorabilia. The plastic badge and official ID card that came with the Membership Kit are worth $250 today, notes grown-up "cadet" Clyde Lyman. A Space Patrol Code Belt might go for $350, adds Warren Chaney, who, as a kid, spent hours learning to sign "Chaney" the way Ed Kemmer signed "Corry" on the Space Patrol Membership Cards. When he was ten years old, Chaney, desperate for a boxtop premium, stuffed so much change into an envelope that his mother had to rescue it from the post office, realizing it would never arrive at "Space Patrol Headquarters" intact.

Carrying this kind of obsession into adulthood can make some collectors "weird," acknowledges Andy Andersen, though he insists he's not one of them. But Andersen, congenial yet wary, strikes you as a man looking over his shoulder for Thormanoids or evil humans about to plunder his toys. He denies it. "Jim [Buchanan] and I aren't 'weird' like you find at the *Star Trek* conventions—you know, 35- and 40-year-old adults running around in spacesuits with ray guns and antennae coming out of their heads. I mean, I haven't gotten *that* far off the beaten track yet."

With The Gardner Advertising Company demanding that entire half-hour episodes be built around the box-top premium *du jour*, it fell to writers Norm Jolley and Lou Huston to come up with clever, action-packed plots that revolved around a two-bit toy yet held the interest of *Space Patrol's* sizable adult audience. Huston resented the edicts that came down from the agency's "creative committee," a gaggle of ad men who ordered up plots to match premiums. They more or less dictated what he

Space helmet offer on Ralston box. (Courtesy Judd Lawson)

wrote, but he made the best of it, crafting skillful radio storylines such as the one where Buzz and Hap save the day by using the Space Patrol Microscope to decipher code messages the bad guys have hidden on bees' wings. In the end, after much hair-pulling, food, booze, and whatever else it took to get the creative juices flowing, both writers came up with plots that were light years beyond the simple adventures the folks at the ad agency had in mind. Jolley even managed to build a four-part TV storyline around the Space Patrol Periscope, a flimsy, cardboard device that enabled Buzz, Hap and Robbie to defeat Manza, a sadistic, silicon-based life form determined to conquer the universe.

In the spring of 1953, Ralston offered a set of black-and-white Magic Space Pictures, one to a box of Wheat Chex and Rice Chex. You could collect the entire set if you could eat 24 boxes of cereal without dying. (Actually more, since you'd need a lot of luck to get a different card in 24 consecutive boxes.) If you stared at the card's reverse black-on-white image for 40 seconds while it burned its way into your brain, then shifted your gaze to the sky or a clear surface like a wall or ceiling—presto!—you'd see a life-like image floating in air.[3] Huston and Jolley, forced as usual to work this cardboard into the

---

[3]How did the Magic Space Pictures work? "Light changes or 'bleaches' chemicals in the retina, causing a temporary after-image," says Dr. Stuart Grant, who along with Dr. Charles May pioneered orthokeratology (the use of contact lenses to reshape the cornea). So was it safe to stare at the cards or did kids damage their eyes for →

No. 1 (24 in Series)

Space Patrol
MAGIC SPACE PICTURE

COMMANDER BUZZ CORRY!

STARE AT SMALL SPOT in center of picture. Count to 30 slowly. *Then stare at one spot on* light-colored wall or in sky for 10 seconds. *Huge Magic Space Picture* will appear and reappear before your eyes!

(over)

No. 2 (24 in Series)

Space Patrol
MAGIC SPACE PICTURE

CADET HAPPY!

STARE AT SMALL SPOT in center of picture. Count to 30 slowly. *Then stare at one spot on* light-colored wall or in sky for 10 seconds. *Huge Magic Space Picture* will appear and reappear before your eyes!

(over)

No. 3 (24 in Series)

Space Patrol
MAGIC SPACE PICTURE

MAJOR ROBERTSON!

STARE AT SMALL SPOT in center of picture. Count to 30 slowly. *Then stare at one spot on* light-colored wall or in sky for 10 seconds. *Huge Magic Space Picture* will appear and reappear before your eyes!

(over)

No. 4 (24 in Series)

Space Patrol
MAGIC SPACE PICTURE

TONGA!

STARE AT SMALL SPOT in center of picture. Count to 30 slowly. *Then stare at one spot on* light-colored wall or in sky for 10 seconds. *Huge Magic Space Picture* will appear and reappear before your eyes!

(over)

Magic Space Pictures. Stare at the "reverse" image and count slowly to 30, then look at a light-colored wall or the sky and — Jumpin' Jupiter!— you'll see the image magically floating in the air. (Courtesy Jim Scancarelli)

life? "You could look at them forever," says Grant, "and they won't hurt your eyes." Next time you play with your Space Pix, cadets, take note: Grant says that the farther away you look after staring at the card for 40 seconds, the bigger the image you'll see floating in midair.

show, came up with the requisite plots. In "The Magic Space Pictures" (radio), March 13, 1953, Corry explains to Hap that studying the pictures is now part of his cadet training because it will teach him to hold images in his mind — a skill needed to fly the XR-51, an experimental ship guided by the pilot's thoughts. Since the two writers always worked independently, Jolley invented an entirely different scenario for "The Laughing Alien" (TV), Episode 118, March 28, 1953. Suddenly Buzz has alarming visions — pictures suspended in midair that invariably show Hap in danger. To unravel this strange phenomenon — and prove his sanity — Corry must track these images to their evil source.

Top and bottom: Space Patrol coin and stamp albums. Believe it or not, on Earth, before the Nintendo Era, kids actually pasted coins and stamps into albums. (Author's collection)

It was Ovaltine that pioneered premium offers in the early 1930s on the radio show *Little Orphan Annie.* That you could own the very same Silver Star Member Secret Message Ring as Annie was a staggering concept. The idea caught fire, and before long Ralston introduced an array of must-have items on its hit radio show, *Tom Mix* — rings, membership kits, belts, badges and pistols. "Heroes had to use the premiums offered in the current episode to escape death or a fate worse than," notes Rory Coker. In 1936, Cream of Wheat introduced the Buck Rogers Solar Scouts Member Badge on the *Buck Rogers* radio show, and a decade later *The Lone Ranger* got into the act with a range of items, including the 1947 Atom Bomb Ring — which looked suspiciously like *Space Patrol*'s Hydrogen Ray Gun Ring, offered a few years later. (Could the Masked Man have time-traveled from the Old West into the future to aid the inventors of the atom bomb?) With these rings you really *did* get a radioactive particle, although it emitted fewer rads than some luminescent watch dials of the day, says Coker, who happens to be a nuclear physicist. Both rings contained a tiny "spinthariscope" — a handy device invented by William Crookes in 1903 for counting alpha particles emitted by radium. Here's how it worked: A speck of radioactive material was enclosed in a metal tube with a phosphorescent screen at one end, and when the heavy alpha nuclei bounced against the screen, there was a visible flash of light. As a kid, Coker was fascinated by this slice of real science:

I would shut myself in the closet with the ring, let my eyes dark-adapt for five minutes, then put my eye to the lens of the spinthariscope. And there would be a magical sight — tiny, brilliant explosions of ghostly blue-white light, like short-lived supernovae. It made your hair stand on end.

Such was the science-in-your-living-room innocence of the 1940s and '50s, when placing a radioactive particle in a toy was neither a risk to homeland security nor cause for a lawsuit. It was a halcyon time when "Be the first kid to blow up your block" was a joke, not a threat. It's doubtful, muses space opera fan Chuck Lassen, that toys like the Space Patrol dart gun could be sold today. "It packed quite a wallop, and no doubt young Space Patrollers broke more than a few windows," he says, noting that when that happened, it was usually accidental, not malicious. "Today, that gun would be considered a 'potential safety hazard,'" he adds, "but kids of the '50s were generally smart enough to handle it with respect."

In the late 20th century, Earth's expansion into cyberspace opened an unexpected portal into the world of premiums via eBay and other Internet auction sites. Suddenly the toys your mother had thrown away were emerging from the attics and basements of strangers, whose parents—out of either wisdom or laziness—had not tossed *their* children's treasures. Thus, when Ron Boucher logged onto eBay, hoping to find the Space Patrol Cosmic Rocket Launcher his mom had confiscated four decades earlier "because I was using it as a weapon," he hit pay dirt. He won the online auction and anxiously checked the mail every day, waiting for the box to arrive, just as he had as a kid. When it finally came, Boucher had a flashback:

> I paused and opened the package gently, realizing that I was doing the same thing I'd done 46 years ago. Inside was the Cosmic Rocket Launcher in its original mailing box! It was the same color as the one I'd had—in fact, I still remember where I was in the kitchen when I pried open the flap on the box with a butter knife so long ago…. But this one cost 800 times more.

Is that all? You might say Boucher got a steal. Consider the red-and-blue plastic Cosmic Glow Rocket Ring that Jim Buchanan spotted for $1,400—that's more than *five thousand times* the original price. "When I left home, my mom threw away all my *Space Patrol* toys because, since I was grown up, why would I need them?" says Rick Brandon "Then, a couple of years ago, I came across a book on collectibles. I made a list of all the stuff I'd sent off for with 25 cents and a boxtop. Going by the list prices, I had $1,350 worth of toys. Geesh!"

To young Slim Sweatmon, still waiting for his dad to come home from Korea in 1952, the memories linked to *Space Patrol* and its premiums bore no price tag. Back in west Texas, he clung to the episodes he'd seen in California for solace. But by December, things looked pretty bleak:

> On Christmas Eve, my uncles and some family friends came over to keep us company, since my father was still in the war zone. After I was in bed, they stayed up all night putting together a Space Patrol space station, complete with all the little space-helmeted characters from the show. In the morning, when I awoke, I was convinced that my father had been to the house and brought it himself. I really couldn't understand why my mother was crying.

When Sweatmon's father did finally make it home from the war, "he often stepped on one of those little space characters in his bare feet and let out more than a 'roaring rockets' type of epithet," Slim recalls. "I never saw *Space Patrol* again, but it was a kind friend at a time in a small boy's life when there was much uncertainty."

Uncertainty stalked Jack Narz as he waited tensely on the *Space Patrol* set for the AD to cue him for the next live spot. Narz, a freelance announcer, was flitting between 30 TV shows — *Queen for a Day, The Bob Crosby Show, Life with Elizabeth* — and hawking White King detergent and Folger's coffee, seven days a week. Exhausted, he fell asleep once during *Space Patrol*, but was awakened in the nick of time by an "explosion" in the teaser for the following week's show that sent shards of papier-mâché flying through the air, hitting him in the face.

Since childhood, he'd wanted to be an announcer. In fact, there were only two things he wanted in life: to fly a plane and to break into radio and movies. "I used to sit in theaters all day, watching the same movie over and over," he says on a crisp, California morning, speeding a golf cart over the rolling green of the Riviera Country Club, ignoring the "No Carts Beyond This Point" sign. His voice has aged well — more resonant than ever and with a hint of the Southern drawl that he tried so hard to suppress when he was breaking into the business. As a kid, he was glued to the radio, "marveling at the fact that I was in Louisville, Kentucky, listening to someone speaking in Chicago." Like Darley and Kemmer, Narz had been a pilot during the war, but he didn't talk about it. "No one did. The war was over," he says tersely. One day, 40 years after *Space Patrol* ended, Narz and Kemmer were having a drink. "And Ed said, 'You flew?' And I said, 'Yeah. You too?' And he said, 'That's where I learned to act — in a P.O.W. camp in Germany.' So that's when we got to know each other."

Narz broke into radio at 250-watt KXO in El Centro, California, on the midnight to 6 A.M. shift:

> We called them "coffee pot" stations. You did everything — news, sports, disc jockey, man on the street, ad copy — and then you swept out the studio. In those days, right after the war, there were a lot of itinerant announcers who went from town to town. Most of them were alcoholics who earned enough money to get drunk and move on. But I was in it for life — I loved it. It was great fun.

But it was stressful too, especially on *Space Patrol* where you had the Gardner agency breathing down your neck. The creative committee wrote the Ralston cereal spots and policed every syllable. "It had to be word for word," Narz recalls. "You couldn't say, 'A breakfast *of* Wheat Chex and Rice Chex will get you going.' You had to say, 'A breakfast *with* Wheat Chex and Rice Chex.'"[4] He got the script the day before the show and memorized frantically, but what if he messed up? There were no TelePrompTers. Finally, he hit on a solution. "When they showed me what deep shit I'd be in if I transposed a word, I went to the art store and bought huge sheets of paper, about 2½ by 4 feet." He wrote out key sentences from the script in big letters and as Darley cut to the commercial, he ran to meet the camera as it rolled toward him, hastily sticking the paper beneath the lens with Scotch tape. Then he raced back to his mark and delivered the spot. "That was my backup," he recalls. After his stint on *Space Patrol*, Narz rocketed to stardom hosting a string of game shows, most notably *The Price Is Right* (guest host), *Beat the Clock*, *Concentration* and *Seven Keys*.

---

[4]The famed military test pilots that the Gardner agency paid to endorse Ralston cereals on *Space Patrol* were careful of their language, too. Flying ace Chuck Yeager would only own up to eating "a good breakfast." It was left to announcer Dick Tufeld to add "like Wheat Chex and Rice Chex." Pilot Bob Love was one of the few who said he actually ate the cereal.

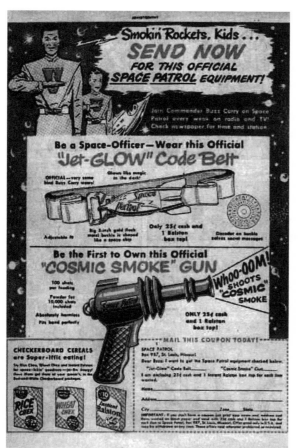

Ad for Cosmic Smoke Gun. (Courtesy Judd Lawson)

Want to play a round of *The Price Is Right* right now? Let's guess some more 21st-century prices of *Space Patrol* gear from the 1950s. How much would you expect to pay today for the 25-cent Lunar Fleet Base, a cardboard and plastic concoction? If you said $3,500, you guessed right, according to collector Warren Chaney, who tracked it on eBay recently. Chaney reports that the City of Terra, a similar toy that sold for a dollar, zoomed to $4,210 before the seller removed it from auction (maybe figuring that if he hung onto it for a few more years, he could send his kids through college). "The battery-powered Monorail Train [priced at $7.95 and later $12.95 in 1952] can go for as much as $5,000," says Jack McKirgan, confirming collector Jim Buchanan's stats. "It seems so sad that I could have funded my retirement by purchasing $300 worth of Monorail sets in the 1950s," he sighs. "Who knew?"

On a budget? Consider a Space Patrol Periscope ($600) or pair of Space Binoculars ($250) if you'd like to bond with your childhood.

"People are nuts!" says Chuck Lassen, who spied the plastic badge from the Membership Kit on eBay for $175 — and that wasn't the final bid. For a mere $1,000, Lassen knows he could own the Cosmic Smoke Gun that delighted him as a child, but he isn't biting. "A puff of 'cosmic smoke' (talcum powder) from the barrel put a villain into a harmless sleep for several hours, allowing Commander Corry and Cadet Happy to elude capture or worse," he explains.[5] But Lassen, who jokingly calls himself "an old space dog," did get his hands on a Rocket Dart Gun for $40, which he asked Ed Kemmer to autograph. It came without the darts or original box, but to snag those would have been an additional $1,340. To Lassen, the gun itself is valuable enough. "If the house caught fire, I'd carry out that gun before the computer!" he maintains.

Ron Boucher remembers the surge of excitement that came from knowing "Buzz Corry sent me this" when a premium arrived in the mail. Steve Handzo felt the same way — until the commander deserted him in 1953:

---

[5]"Old-fashioned guns don't have a chance against this," the catalogue promised.

Just before Christmas, my parents placed a whopping order for *Space Patrol* catalogue merchandise. Nothing came. My mother wrote to them, and after many months she got an official-looking communication. She'd worked as a legal secretary and understood that not only would there never be any more *Space Patrol* merchandise, but we were at the end of a long line of creditors and would never get our money back. I kept the dog-eared, discolored catalogue for years.

Cosmic Smoke Gun. A pretty handy weapon that can put bad guys to sleep instantly with talcum powder smoke. First issued in 1952 in red; two years later, a green gun with a longer barrel was offered. (Photograph © Ed Swift, courtesy Dale Ames)

Signs of trouble at "Space Patrol Headquarters" in St. Louis first surfaced in mid–1953. Sometimes Jack Narz had to apologize to kids who had waited months for their boxtop premiums, explaining that Headquarters was swamped with orders and the gear was on its way. The *Space Patrol* catalogue division seemed equally overwhelmed. "Please place your order early so that those favorite youngsters of yours will not be disappointed on Christmas morning," the 1953 winter edition warned. Handzo's parents received that advice in a catalogue that arrived on December 16. Unless you ordered immediately, that didn't leave much time for the goods to make it to Earth by Christmas Eve, even if shipped on the Terra Express.

Handzo was heartbroken that Christmas morning when his presents failed to arrive. "Buzz Corry betrayed me," he says, 50 years later. To make matters worse, the school bully tore up his paper model of the *Terra V* that had come with the Lunar Fleet Base. That did it. "*Space Patrol* taught me early on that the world is a cruel place with a lot of rotten people in it," he says, trying to

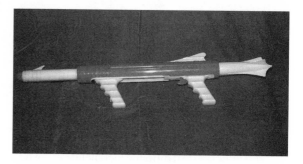

Auto-Sonic Rifle. Still waiting for yours? "Made of sturdy impact material that has withstood the most rigid tests, here's a rifle that will bring joy to any Space Patroller," promised the ad. "Unfortunately, kids who ordered it from the last catalogue never received it," says researcher Stephen Handzo. If you did get it, you could look through your "exclusive telescopic-type aiming sight" and shoot up to six sponge rubber balls at your parents, friends and the dog. (Courtesy Elliott Swanson)

sound serious. But in a great demonstration of that old Earth proverb, "Use lemons to make lemonade," Handzo overcame his trauma by becoming an expert on *Space Patrol* toys. (In Appendix 1 of this book, he offers a rundown on everything from cereal box premiums to selected retail and catalogue merchandise. While it may not include every

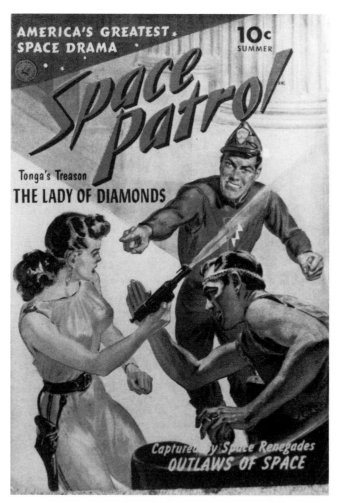

Space Patrol comic book. Looks like Tonga was in her "bad" phase. So was the artist, whose drawings did not resemble the cast; ditto the merchandisers, who promised "12 big issues" but produced only two. (The kids who paid $1.25 for a year's subscription learned the meaning of "rip off" early in life.) (Courtesy Joe Sarno)

item of *Space Patrol* gear ever manufactured, since some, like the Cosmic Rayn Protector [a rain hat], quickly vanished, and others, like the pup tent ["Pitch it on any planet — rain, shine or snow"], coloring books and clothing, were self-explanatory, it's the most complete survey ever compiled — at least in this part of the galaxy.)[6]

Most of those cardboard and plastic artifacts have turned to space dust, but if they hadn't, could they — or similar items — be marketed today? Probably not, says Chuck Lassen. Just think about it:

> The cannon that shot projectiles would have to go — might put someone's eye out. The clear space helmets were neat, but oops! — choking hazard. Some plastic parts in the playsets, like the spaceship ladder, were thin and could break and splinter — a kid could swallow them and puncture his intestine. Not good. That big tin building in the playset — you have to put sharp-edged metal tabs into slots to assemble it. Not only might someone cut his finger, but the little darling might get frustrated if unable to successfully assemble it. After all, you have to read the instruction sheet, and many kids today are unable to read at the age where they might enjoy this playset.

Lassen pauses. "Welcome to the 21st century."

Mike Pahlow managed somehow, over the years, not to shatter or swallow his Space Patrol watch (worth up to $400), which keeps both Earth and universal star time. He put it away when he was 15 and got interested in girls and cars, but took it with him when

---

[6]Note to collectors in other parts of the universe: Every effort has been made to present reliable data, but sources sometimes disagree, and Earthlings are fallible.

he joined the U.S. Air Force and was stationed overseas. "I had it with me on all my tours of duty, for 20 years," he reports. "It still keeps good time."

Dr. John Simelaro no longer has his Outer Space Plastic Helmet, but that's OK with him:

> On September 26, 1954, I was riding with my grandfather. It was a dark night and I was in the front seat wearing my Space Patrol plastic space helmet. It was my pride and joy — I'd saved up the whole summer to get the same helmet my hero, Buzz Corry, wore. My grandfather fell asleep at the wheel and slammed into a high curb at 35 miles per hour. It was like hitting a brick wall. The top portion of my helmet cracked into two pieces as I punched a hole in the windshield and was knocked unconscious — but it totally protected my head. The inflatable blue and white air-filled collar rested on my shoulders, intact.

Outer Space Plastic Helmet — the gear that saved Dr. John Similaro's life in a surface-car accident when he was thrown through the windshield. Designed to protect you in outer space, too, although you might lose oxygen through the 6-inch openings in front and back. (Courtesy Joe Sarno)

Simelaro, who became an osteopathic physician, knows enough about medicine now to better understand what happened that night. "If I hadn't been wearing that toy, I would have suffered neurological trauma and terrible facial lacerations — or worse. I guess you could say that *Space Patrol* saved my life."

CHAPTER 11

Robbie

Without Robbie, we'd have been in big trouble.

— Ed Kemmer

Ken was street savvy — it was part of his persona. He didn't bless it or kick it. He took life like, "There it is."

— Irv Mayer

WEST HOLLYWOOD, CALIFORNIA: MAY 1984

I'd seen a photo of Ken Mayer taken in the 1970s, 20 years after *Space Patrol* ended, so I knew he'd gained weight; but when the 6 foot 2 actor strolled into The Melting Pot, a West Hollywood café, I wasn't prepared for the mountain of a man he'd become. But Mayer sets you instantly at ease with his relaxed manner and twinkling eyes. He still talks like Robbie — tough and streetwise, more Brooklyn than his native San Francisco.[1] Those extra pounds might slow him down if you were in a tight spot and counting on Robbie to get there in time, but his comfortable presence inspires confidence. It's still steady, dependable Major Robertson.

Mayer likes talking about the show — the camaraderie, the bloopers, a few things that rankled him then but don't anymore. Recalling how he got his start as an actor, he glances affectionately at his wife, Ruth, a small, curly-haired woman in sweats and tennis shoes, and they share a laugh about their struggling days and the ups and downs of a career still-in-progress. "She's his biggest fan — it's like they just met yesterday," Virginia Hewitt had told me. "They've been married for years, but she acts as though it's their first date and they've just fallen madly in love." True. I catch Ruth glancing adoringly at Ken throughout our meeting. ("She was Nancy Reagan before there *was* a Nancy Reagan," says Mayer's brother, Irv.)

Mayer looks back on *Space Patrol* with bittersweet nostalgia. Though he has warm memories of the show, he hit the roof when he learned that Ed and Lyn were making stellar salaries compared to his own. For a while, he was angry, but because he was fond of Kemmer and close to Osborn, he let it go. "I'm a bad businessman," he explains, lighting up his first cigarette. "I wasn't looking out for myself at the time." Truth is, he was glad to have a job. "I was working, I didn't care." But, like other cast members, he was bugged that Moser's promise of big dividends from retail toys and cereal-box premiums never materialized:

[1]Mayer could also speak "stage English," which he picked up during his drama studies. He used it in several *Space Patrol* radio shows when he played an erudite villain.

Ken Mayer studies his lines on the set. (Photographs by David Sutton, courtesy Dick Darley)

They cheated us on merchandising, owed us several thousand dollars when the show went off the air — that was Mike Moser. I learned the real story many years later when I ran into a merchandiser. I said, "You guys must have taken a bath because I only got x number of dollars." And he said, "Are you kidding? We sold several million dollars' worth." And that was only *one item*.

For a moment, Mayer looks like he's about to do one of Robbie's slow burns. "I dunno," he says in tough guy mode. "Maybe I should have asked for more, maybe I should have walked." But before we go any further, he wants to put me at ease by acknowledging his weight gain.

MAYER: What really bothers me is seeing myself in *Space Patrol* episodes from thirty years ago, at 178 pounds…
RUTH: [*quickly*] You're still handsome, Honey.

I assure him the weight gain doesn't matter. That out of the way, his voice softens as he recalls the glory days of the show. He's still Robbie, tough and tender.

MAYER: I know the show touched a lot of lives — people in the space program today…
RUTH: We're often in the supermarket and people recognize him.
MAYER: …and there were a lot of things about Robbie — he was the most human of them all. He could be a hero, a dolt, he could run the gamut…

He was, above all, I suggest, reliable. It was almost as if Robbie *had* to be there.

RUTH: That's right!
MAYER: I wish I had known how really important I was to the show at the time.

Breakfast arrives and Mayer shoves aside his Pall Malls and digs in.

Ruth Mayer adoring Ken in 1953 — and adoring him three decades later in 1984. (*Left:* Author's collection; *right:* Courtesy Jeanette Nall)

> MAYER: I'm a reacting actor. I don't really plan what I do; I play off what you do. We brought this along... [*Ruth pulls out a review of his recent performance in* The Odd Couple *at a local dinner theater.*]
>
> RUTH: [*reading*] "Ken Mayer, a skilled veteran of theater, is a natural for the role of 'Oscar'.... Chances are he's a natural for any role he essays." [*Looking up.*] That's from *Dramalogue*, one of the biggest papers here.

Suddenly Mayer, still thinking about *Space Patrol*, sets his fork down and laughs, remembering a prank he played on Kemmer long ago:

> I was taller than Ed, but one day I walked in and looked at him — and found myself looking straight ahead, instead of down. I couldn't figure out why until I saw he had new boots with lifts in them. So I went back to my dressing room and stuffed paper in the back of my boots. When we did the show, he looked up at me and couldn't figure out how I became taller again!

As third leading man, it was not really fitting that he be taller than Kemmer, the star of the show. And in fact, before Kemmer was hired to replace Glen Denning, Mayer had his eye on the starring role. He was already playing the offstage voice of Buzz Corry, who was away on a secret mission and communicated only by space-o-phone — and yet there was Mike Moser searching frantically for a leading man while Mayer was right under his nose. He smiles wistfully. "If they'd gone another week without finding someone ... If Ed hadn't walked in, I probably would have gotten the role."

At last, in one episode, he got to be the star. It was number 93, "The Code Breakers," shot on October 4, 1952. Kemmer's father had passed away and he rushed back east for the funeral. Jolley hastily rewrote the opening of the show to explain that the Commander had blasted off for the outer galaxies to test a new magnetic space car and Major Robertson was acting commander-in-chief until his return. "They didn't change the basic script," says Mayer. "The Commander's dialogue was the same, except Robbie was doing it instead.[2] After the show, I went over to Mike Moser's house, and he got a call from the sponsor asking, 'Why don't they write scripts like that for Ed Kemmer?'"

Of course, Mayer adds quickly, don't get him wrong. There were a lot of things he liked about playing Robbie:

> He was more of a human being, so I didn't have to be as sure of myself as the commander. I could say, "This may work," whereas with Ed Kemmer, it was "This *will* work." I could make a mistake, while he had more limitations. I only had one fight with Ed. It was over a character thing, where someone wanted to take out something sort of heroic that I did. And I wondered, "What's happening? Why am I not getting stronger parts?" And then somebody said, "You're not on the cereal box, see?" That's when you begin to realize you're a secondary character.

Tonga and Major Robertson handle an urgent security call. (Author's collection)

With that off his chest, Mayer wants you to know that he and Kemmer got along well. "If I can remember only one argument after all these years, you know how close we were." Thinking back, he recalls how, early on in the show, he got Bell's Palsy and was sure his acting career was over. He'd gone to the dentist to have some teeth pulled. The next day his mouth was swollen and he couldn't talk. Then a nerve in his ear swelled up and paralyzed one side of his face. He and Ruth panicked. This was it: He could be out of a job. Norm Jolley rushed to the rescue by scripting a paralyzer ray going off accidentally in Robbie's face, while Darley protected him by shooting only from his good side. The ordeal lasted two weeks. "I was lucky," Mayer says. "People have had Bell's Palsy for years."

Mayer was no stranger to overcoming obstacles. "He had a tough time, growing up," says his brother, Irv, who was two years younger. The oldest of four boys, red-haired, freckled Ken was — like "Robbie" — a scrapper. When he was 11, he beat up the school bully, who was bigger than he was. Irv never forgot it. "The whole neighborhood came out to watch. It was a long fight — seven or eight minutes — but Ken took him down." Irv remembers a grateful roar surging up from the crowd. After their parents divorced, Ken, then 12, and Irv were sent to Los Angeles to live with their father, who put them up in a skid row hotel. Ken became streetwise, hanging out on the Sunset Strip and in downtown L.A. He quit school during the Depression and joined the Civilian Conservation Corps, sending $20 of his $25 monthly pay to his mother to help support her and his two younger

---

[2]Actor-writer Maury Hill was brought in as "Captain Hayward" to do the dialogue written for Robbie in the original script.

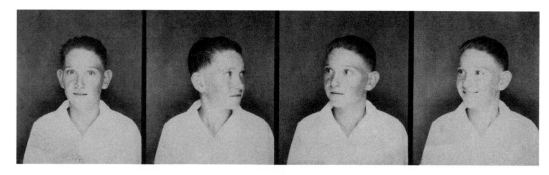

Ken Mayer, age 13, an eighth grader at Hollenbeck Jr. High in East Los Angeles. (Courtesy Jeanette Nall)

brothers. Though a down-to-earth guy, Mayer often amazed his family with knowledge they never knew he had about everything from classical music to golf. He seemed to mysteriously acquire skills that came out of the blue, but he never put on airs—even when he soared to fame in *Space Patrol*. "He treated everybody equally," Irv recalls. As an actor, his income peaked and plummeted, but Mayer took it all in stride. The street smarts he'd learned long ago, says Irv, were part of his persona. "He didn't bless it or kick it. He took life like, 'There it is.'"

Now, as he cleans his plate, Mayer waxes philosophical, living up to his brother's words. "I guess I'm the kind of guy who goes along with the breeze. When the time comes, this or that will happen. I'm a big believer in the Boy Upstairs, and I've been lucky in a lot of ways." He returns Ruth's tender gaze. "We've been up and down together for 42 years, but we've made it."

Beginnings were tough. Ruth worked as a waitress at a place on Hollywood and Vine, while Ken parked cars at NBC and struggled through broadcasting school. "I never planned to be an actor," he says. Instead, in his early twenties, he worked as a delicatessen counterman and truck driver before he was drafted into the Army and assigned to the Air Corps in December 1942. But then a jeep he was riding in at Blythe Air Force Base in California rolled over, killing the driver and leaving Mayer with a broken back, some memory loss, and a speech impediment. As part of rehab, the Army sent him to broadcasting school. There he discovered a talent for radio announcing, but when he was offered a job where he had to ad lib, he froze up in fear. "I was tongue-tied away from a script," he admits, so he enrolled in Gellar's Theatre Workshop to learn to improvise. Suddenly, he was drawing praise, winning awards and falling in love with the stage. It was that passion for acting that sustained him when *Space Patrol* ended.

"We had some starving days after *Space Patrol*," Ruth says candidly.

Mayer nods his head. "I got lost for two years. It was very difficult to get a job. I'd be talking to someone and they'd say, 'Fine,' and then someone else would walk in and say, 'Hey, Robbie, what are *you* doing here?' It took me a long time to break the mold."

But he did. TV comedian Pinky Lee hired him to do skits, announcing and audience warm-up for his popular show on NBC. Then Norm Jolley, who was writing for *Wagon Train* and *Cimarron City*, wrote him into both shows, and "all of a sudden, I was a western actor. I've been every sheriff and every heavy. And the closest I'd ever been to a horse until that time was a donkey in Golden Gate Park." He struck gold on *Bonanza* in a regular part as the foreman on the ranch. "I was the only guy who could tell Lorne

Green he didn't know his ass from his elbow," Mayer jokes, slipping into a western drawl. More windfalls followed, including the lucrative role of "Tex," spokesman for Monroe shock absorbers, and a stint as pitchman for Stroh's beer. He worked steadily, appearing in hundreds of TV shows, commercials and films, including *Spencer's Mountain* (1963), *Bonnie and Clyde* (1967) and *Little Big Man* (1970). He's credited in nearly 100 TV westerns, including *Gunsmoke*, *Maverick*, *Bat Masterson*, *The Big Valley*, and *Rawhide*.

Mayer flips a cigarette out of the pack, leans back and reflects on his career. "Friends of mine have become stars. They're all divorced, have lost their families. I look at it this way: You go in, you do a show, you know maybe you're a better actor than the lead and it kind of eats at you. But the reason *you're* not a star is because that's not your big thing in life."

In the early '80s, he went to New York to see if he could salvage his dream of doing what he

Ken Mayer as "Tex"—spokesman for Monroe Shocks. "Ken loved the job," says his brother, Irv, "and he invented a persona to match it." Mayer pitched the shock absorbers for six years and got plenty of perks, including seats in the pit at the Indy 500 and Daytona Speedway. (Courtesy Irv Mayer)

loves to do best: stage plays. This is a charged subject, close to his heart. He coughs nervously, tugs at his ear, then runs his hands through his hair — just like Robbie did when he faced a dilemma:

> I went back for six weeks to scope out the New York scene. But if we moved there, my career wouldn't count — I'd have to start over again. We'd have to give up our house in L.A., take a cold-water flat, and I'd have to find an agent, go to readings, interviews, auditions. I'd have to start from the ground up, and it would take a long time to adjust. I don't know whether I can make that scene. Who knows what would happen? But if they came to me today and said, "Come on back and do an off–Broadway play," and I liked the role — even if it would cost me more to live there than they could pay me — I'd take that flier, yeah. I'd take that chance.

> RUTH: [*not wincing at the cold-water flat*] That would be fun! A lot of actors want to do a Broadway play. He dreams about that. He's so colorful. When he's on stage, I don't know how he does it. He's not Ken Mayer.

> MAYER: I've come close a lot of times. Years ago, I was offered a play in New York. We needed money then, so when I found out how little they were paying, I declined. I didn't take the chance. That opportunity would have fulfilled a dream.

RUTH: That's *still* one of your dreams.

MAYER (excited): I've been offered the role of Tevye in *Fiddler on the Roof*. I've just started singing lessons...

RUTH: He can do anything, really.

MAYER: I'd love to be in theater every night.

Mayer succumbed to a fatal heart attack eight months later on January 30, 1985.

CHAPTER 12

On the Beam: Lou Huston and the Radio Shows

> In radio, everybody did everything. Specialization was rare. There were people who did announcing and then went out on the street and sold shoes.
>
> — Lou Huston

On a weekday afternoon, at the ABC studio on Vine Street (which used to be a bowling alley) in the heart of Hollywood, Kemmer, Osborn, Mayer, Kovacs, Tufeld, Jolley and Hewitt were sitting around a circular table, reading through the script for the transcribed Saturday morning radio show. Compared to the heart-stopping excitement of doing live TV, this was "the simplest thing in the world," says Kemmer:

> TV is loaded with problems, but with radio you have great freedom. There's a thousand percent difference in the amount of sweat you put into it, the fear and everything else. You don't have to worry about sets, lighting and equipment; there's no rock over your head about lines or special effects not working. You don't have makeup or costumes or get out of breath running between sets. You don't have to worry about anything, so you can concentrate solely on the show itself. Very seldom did anyone blow up. You might say a word a little wrong, but you went right on and most of the time no one caught it.

Characterization was never a problem either, even though Mayer, Jolley, Kovacs and Hewitt stepped out of their TV roles to play an array of nasty radio heavies. Mayer (doing his best not to sound like Robbie) used accents to disguise his voice, ranging from tough Brooklynese to sinister Transylvanian; he even played a cerebral thug with a slight British accent on occasion. Sometimes he played two parts on the same show, as did Norm Jolley, who could double as bad guy and Space Patrol officer. Virginia Hewitt, who appeared less often, played characters ranging from noble entrepreneur to evil scientist; Nina Bara (who could not disguise her voice) appeared occasionally as a heavy, but mostly as Tonga.

The use of the regular cast and doubling-up of characters was done chiefly to save money, says Kemmer, and to keep the work in the family, giving the secondary actors who didn't appear in every TV show a few extra bucks. That was fine with Norm Jolley, who relished the chance to keep his hand in acting, which he loved. Radio was often low budget, confirms actor and voiceover artist Dick Beals, then in his mid-twenties, who played many of the characters you thought were real children in *The Lone Ranger*, *Gunsmoke*, *The Six Shooter* and other popular shows of the day. At 4 foot 6, weighing 65 pounds, "he looked like a nine-year-old kid," recalls Kemmer. Beals, who never grew to full size, had also suffered an illness in childhood that prevented his voice from changing,

Radio director Larry Robertson (left, seated) stirs his coffee as the cast takes a break. From the left: at counter — Robertson, TV director Dick Darley, Kemmer, Bara; standing — Kovacs, Hewitt, Jolley and Mayer. (Hewitt opted for her favorite, Coke, instead of coffee.) (Author's collection)

but it turned out to be his passport into the exciting world of broadcasting, where he impersonated children of all ages—both boys and girls. On the *Space Patrol* radio spots, he played the hyped-up kids who gobbled the cereal, downed the cocoa and gee-whizzed over the premiums. Beals, best known for his "Speedy Alka-Seltzer" character, had plenty of work in those days and hasn't quit yet. "Directors love me because they don't have to deal with a real kid's mother, which is a pain," he laughs. A thoughtful man, now in his mid-seventies, he remembers that "the *Space Patrol* cast was in character the minute they walked into the studio, but they joked around a lot, especially Lyn; if anyone messed up, it would be him. Kemmer never made a mistake — he was just such a pro."

So were the others. The cast took to radio as if they'd been doing it all their lives, developing the special skills needed almost overnight. "Radio actors are a select group," says actor-director Larry Dobkin, a veteran of thousands of radio and TV dramas, including several *Space Patrol* TV episodes:

> Radio people read differently. At school you're taught to read slowly, making an inner sound in your head with every word, every syllable. But radio actors read at a grasp — they lift the words off the page and make choices immediately about *how* to read the lines,

based on an intuitive response to the script. And if somebody asked, "Why did you read it like that?" they'd say, "I don't know. It seemed the thing to do."

Not only could these radio players instantly interpret a line, but, says Dick Beals, they seldom blew up. "On a lot of shows of the '40s and '50s, such as *The Lone Ranger*, *The Green Hornet* and *Challenge of the Yukon* (*Sergeant Preston*)— done by the same actors and directors in the same studio, week after week — the expectation was that you *didn't* make a mistake. If you did, you didn't work for several months," he recalls.

As soon as he'd yelled "*Spaaaaaace Patrol!!!*" for the spine-tingling opening of the radio show, announcer Dick Tufeld rushed back to studying his lines for the next commercial break "so I didn't screw up." He remembers suiting up for the weekly studio session, as actors did in the 1950s. "I'm not sure I didn't wear a suit in my *house*," he jokes. "That's the way it was in those days." (Later in his career, when he announced the *Tom Jones* show for TV, he noticed that the British director and crew showed up in tuxedos for every taping. "We *always* dress for transmission," they told him.)[1]

Though taping the radio shows was a pretty straightforward affair, Lyn Osborn was present, so things were never uneventful. "Of course we heard Lyn's humor, every chance he got," smiles Jolley. Even Kemmer, relieved of the burdens he carried during the TV show, often relaxed and joined in the fun. "A lot of fooling around would go on, and it was mainly Buzz and Hap creating it," recalls Virginia Hewitt. "Once

Radio actor and voiceover artist Dick Beals, who fooled you into thinking those were real children you heard on dramas like *The Lone Ranger* and *The Six Shooter*. Best known as the voice of "Speedy Alka-Seltzer." (Courtesy Dick Beals)

Actor-director Larry Dobkin, a veteran of thousands of TV and radio dramas. (Courtesy Kaela Dobkin)

[1]When Tufeld left ABC in the summer of 1954, staff announcers Lee Zimmer and Dick Wesson covered *Space Patrol*.

Announcer Dick Tufeld, who yelled *"Spaaaaaaace Patrol!!"* like nobody else and promised "high adventure in the wild, vast reaches of space." (Courtesy Dick Tufeld)

Buzz tore out a page of the script and fashioned a pair of lace panties out of it. He wrote 'CAROL' in great big letters and passed it to Hap, who drew a big Coke bottle on the other side because I used to drink Cokes a lot."

Clowning aside, the session usually went like clockwork: a "table" (first-time) reading, then a stop-and-go reading so the sound-effects man could pick up his cues (steps on wood, steps on rock, fight scenes) and the actors could make the changes they wanted. "You'd make the dialogue more comfortable," explains Kemmer. "I'd say, 'I don't think Buzz Corry would say it that way,' and I'd paraphrase the line instead."

Timing was crucial. "Once we had the script set, we'd do a straight-through reading for time," says Kemmer. "If it didn't come out right, [director] Larry Robertson made cuts. You'd pencil in changes: slow here, stretch there." The early radio shows were done live, and thus lost forever to Earthlings (though the citizens of Arcturus are no doubt enjoying them as we speak), but from a set of transcription discs that turned up, it appears that the first recorded program was aired on Saturday, October 4, 1952.[2] Fortunately, ABC had begun using ¼ inch audio tape earlier that year, says engineer Don McCroskey, so if an actor committed a serious error, a correction could be spliced in or the scene repeated. Surprisingly, tape splicing was pretty accurate back then — the early Ampex 200 tape recorders had a speed of 30 inches per second, which made for easy, precise editing. If there were sound effects in the background, however, a splice could throw those out of synch (there were no separate tracks in those days), so the actors would redo the scene. But that rarely happened. "Radio actors are trained to keep reading, even when someone commits an error," says Beals, "unless the director stops you. You know the line is wrong, but you keep on going. The minute we'd get to the last line and 'Up theme, out,' the director would say, 'OK, let's pick up that line on page 16.' If there was music

[2]In this set of transcription discs, the episode numbers leap from 52 to 105. According to audio engineer and collector Jerry Haendiges, this "re-numbering" was sometimes done *arbitrarily* to compensate for unrecorded shows made prior to the disc labeled "1" — and, in fact, this *does* account for the *Space Patrol* broadcasts done live (twice weekly) between the show's radio debut on August 1, 1950, and January 8, 1951, when it went on hiatus for seven months. But it doesn't account for the broadcasts from August 15, 1951, when it returned to the air (now once a week) to October 4, 1952, the date of the disc labeled "1." Either these shows were never recorded or the discs or tapes were lost. Could they be stored in a forgotten warehouse somewhere in Hollywood — or on Arcturus?

Hewitt divides her attention between the script and Kemmer during the radio show. (Author's collection)

in the background, you'd go back to where the music comes in, so it would be a clean take."

When an actor made a *major* mistake, says Dick Tufeld, the director yelled "Cut!" and sometimes everyone lost it, dissolving in laughter. "You *do* know," Tufeld continues, straight-faced, "that radio actors—in rehearsal and even on the air—deliberately tried to break each other up, setting fire to an actor's script, taking his pants off during a monologue or emotional scene. It happened on a lot of shows—and with Lyn there, you *know* it happened on *Space Patrol*." But most screw-ups were minor, he adds. "You had blips and bad readings in lots of the shows, but we kept going because listeners don't notice those things."

"We did catch a few," I tell him. "Like the time you informed us that lichen was 'crapetting' the Martian desert for miles."[3]

"I always did have a way with words," Tufeld responds. "You're talking to the announcer who once said "Peter Pan peter butter" on national TV."

You could say that the radio shows were uneventful, like when you're piloting a ship through millions of DUs of boredom until some little emergency, like the loss of your air supply, catches you off guard. That happened to Ed Kemmer one day when he lit up a cigarette and later wished he hadn't. He was smoking and reading his lines during a run-through for timing. "We all smoked in those days," he recalls, "so when Tonga was ready to light up, she took my cigarette to light hers—but she put it back in my fingers facing the wrong way. Still concentrating on the script, I took a drag—and hit the ceiling! That was a shock, let me tell you!" His lips were singed for several days.

From late summer 1950 to January 1951, *Space Patrol* aired twice weekly on the ABC radio network, preceding the national TV show by five months. A week after the network TV show debuted on December 30, 1950, the radio show went on hiatus, surfacing again the following August.[4] Mike Moser wrote the first radio scripts, then dumped the task on Norm Jolley, who was already writing five 15-minute TV shows a week. As with those shows, Jolley remembers snatching the pages of the radio drama from his typewriter and racing to the studio to deliver it in the nick of time.

During the early, live shows, the United Nations was meeting in San Francisco—a momentous event back then—and breaking news bulletins could interrupt the *Space Patrol* broadcast at any time. If that happened, the show had to be shortened at a moment's notice, so the actors penciled cuts and alternate lines into the script—just in case. These changes became a jumble of illegible notes, nearly impossible to follow. It was hair-raising, says Kemmer, recalling that you never knew if you'd be using the "alternate" version until the very last minute, in which case you hoped you could read it:

> You wouldn't believe what the scripts looked like. You'd be jumping around, trying to read the changes you'd made—a speech out here, two speeches out there, a little write-in here. You couldn't cross out a line entirely because maybe you had to do it, but you had a replacement line written next to it. And yet you couldn't take *that* as gospel because you might have to go back to the way it had been before [the tentative cut]. It was a mess.

---

[3]Tufeld committed the *Space Patrol* radio blooper in the teaser at the end of "The Giant Bubble," 11-22-52.

[4]The radio show probably began on August 1, 1950, though some sources list its debut as September 18. I have a script labeled "Space Patrol Radio Script Number Four," dated Thursday, August 10, in my possession. Since there were two shows a week at first, according to cast members I interviewed and newspapers of the day, this would put the start date at Tuesday, August 1. The shows were probably done live for two years, since Kemmer remembers interruptions by bulletins from the United Nations, and there are no transcription discs until October 1952. They ran twice a week until January 8, 1951, went on hiatus, and resumed on August 18, 1951, airing once a week, on Saturday, until March 19, 1955. (Dates compiled from *The Encyclopedia of Old-Time Radio* by John Dunning [Oxford University Press, 1998]; articles in *Tele-Views* and other newspapers and magazines of the day; research by film historian Stephen Handzo; and data from old-time radio expert Jerry Haendiges, who owns a set of *Space Patrol* transcription discs with dates.)

Director Larry Robertson, tall, slim and laid back, steered everyone through this chaos. "He was very calm," Jolley recalls. "He didn't get nasty or harsh with the actors, like some directors did." Robertson, says Ed Kemmer, "kept us sane and focused. He was the most gentle, compassionate person I've ever met in the business. He'd say, 'Don't worry, it'll work out.'"

In the summer of 1951, Mike Moser hired Lou Huston to write the radio shows and relieve Norm Jolley, who was now churning out the weekly network TV show in addition to the five daily local shows. Huston, a gentle giant at 6 foot 1, was a fan of the TV show and familiar with the characters.[5] His credits included *Phillip Morris Playhouse* and the acclaimed *Whistler* episode "Brief Pause for Murder" (written with his good pal Bill Forman, the voice of "The Whistler"). Huston knew how to craft sophisticated plots, and his *Space Patrol* radio episodes, like Jolley's TV scripts, were aimed at both kids and adults. Though he was careful to keep the show scientifically credible, once in a while he veered off into fantasy or metaphysics, inspired by his favorite writers for the popular SF pulp magazine *Amazing Stories*, "people who were far greater predictors and imaginers than me." Thus he created the Lumens, a race of spiritually evolved beings who thumbed their chakras at the evil Prince Baccarratti; and he once had some conniving crystals attempt to enslave the solar system.

Huston is quick-witted but self-effacing, with merry blue-green eyes, a kind smile and genuine self-doubt.[6] His father was a telegrapher for the railroad, and the family lived in the back rooms of lonely depots next to the tracks. As a small boy, he learned to read from the letters on box cars, but he didn't mind the isolation:

> To a kid, it was paradise. Your dad runs the depot. He can make trains stop and send messages up and down the line with this wonderful telegraph instrument. And you can look out your backyard and see coyotes frolicking in the setting sun on the hillside. That's great for a boy.

He remembers train journeys he took as a child, falling asleep to the swaying of the coach, the click of the wheels. His father, known as a fair man who risked his life as a union organizer, was his hero. "He disliked cruelty and oppression of all kinds," says Huston, "and in those days, you could hire a goon for three bucks to get rid of a union organizer."

Huston's idyllic childhood ended when the family moved to Long Beach, California. His mother, weary of keeping the depot free of soot from coal-burning engines that clattered by 20 times a day, was glad to be in a city again, but Lou hated it. A skinny kid, he got teased and beat up in school. By high school graduation, he'd shot up to over six feet, but he was scrawny and ashamed of his physique — a poster boy for the weakling who gets sand kicked in his face by bullies. Then he discovered the writings of Bernarr McFadden, who popularized body-building during the 1920s and '30s. Huston was hooked. Working out with dumbbells in a garage down the alley from the family's cheap apartment, he built himself up to a muscular 190 pounds and gained enough confidence

---

[5]Jolley recalls writing eight TV and radio shows a week at one point with *four* separate storylines.
[6]Strange trivia: *Space Patrol*'s writers, Lou Huston and Norman Jolley, had similar birthdates and hailed from small towns in Iowa less than 50 miles apart. (Huston was born on February 24, 1914, in Indianola; Jolley on February 21, 1916, in Adel.)

Lou Huston shows off his strength to Air Corps buddies. A scrawny kid, he discovered body-building guru Bernarr McFadden and worked out with dumbbells, building himself up to a muscular 190 pounds by age 20. (Courtesy Darla Miller)

by the time he turned 20 in 1934 to land a job at Long Beach radio station KFOX. Eager to learn, he dusted and filed phonograph records, did a four-hour announcing shift, and churned out several scripts a day for live dramas, including *Married Life with Al and Molly*, a ten-minute soap opera starring the station's manager and a woman employee as husband and wife. One day he talked his boss into letting his buddy, Bill Conrad, hang out at the station. Conrad seemed to have a special knack for radio. "He learned more in ten minutes than I could in six months," Huston says of his close friend, who later soared to fame as "Marshall Matt Dillon" in the radio series *Gunsmoke*.[7]

Huston recalls the creative climate of radio in the 1930s and the family feeling at stations where everyone pitched in and became a jack-of-all-trades. It was a mecca for creative types who would work for low pay, juggling several jobs if need be for the thrill of being on the air:

> Everybody did everything. There were people who only announced, and then there were people who did announcing and went out on the street and sold shoes. We had a secretary who sang, played piano and acted in skits. That was during the Big Depression. Jobs of any kind were hard to get, so we were also driven with the idea that writing scripts and doing long announce shifts was a lot better than digging ditches — if you could find a ditch to dig and someone to pay you for it.

It was at once a frantic yet forgiving time when you could learn on the job, free from the unrelenting pressure to climb to the top of the ratings. In those days, says Huston,

[7]Conrad also starred in the 1970s TV series, *Cannon*.

Top: Lou Huston in his mid–20s — still having a good time. *Bottom:* Huston horsing around at 1000 watt KFOX in 1934. He was once fired from a job for "clowning around and acting juvenile," he admits. (All photographs courtesy Darla Miller)

you focused on getting something on the air, and there wasn't much time for people to criticize your work:

> I've been in a situation where I'd type a page and hand it to somebody, and they'd take it into the studio and put it on the air. All of our energy was in it. We were not calculating markets or demographics; we were just trying to get something entertaining on the air.

After a stint in the Air Corps, Huston got a job at KMPC in Los Angeles, where he wrote a West Coast version of the popular Detroit radio horror drama *The Hermit's Cave*. He roomed for a while with Bill Conrad; a few years later, he moved in with Bill Forman's family, paying his way with the $75 a week he got for writing the *Space Patrol* radio episodes. During this period, he penned the radio classic "Drop Dead" for *Suspense*.

The first time I speak to Huston about *Space Patrol*, our talk turns to the cast members I'd interviewed.

"How is Bela Kovacs?" he wants to know.

"Kovacs," I tell him, "is still an artist in every fiber of his being. But he's drinking himself to death."

"So was the radio writer," Huston says, dropping a bombshell.

He hit the bottle at age 20 and didn't get sober until 23 years later when he joined AA in 1957. He wants you to know this and also that he's been sober now for over 40 years. Was he drunk when he wrote the *Space Patrol* shows? He says no, but admits he often had a helluva hangover. Looking back, he can joke about the many scripts he delivered while drunk. "The continuity person at ABC would probably say, 'I'm trying to remember if Huston ever brought one in sober.'" His battle and hard-won victory over alcoholism became the cornerstone of his life, and he later used his talent to write award-winning films about addiction, including *The Secret Love of Sandra Blain*, which depicts the gradual descent of a suburban housewife into alcoholism.

Now that I know this, a few things make sense. In the TV shows, Buzz and Hap get cracked on the head a lot by the bad guys but make speedy recoveries. Not so in some of the radio shows, written when the writer's head was exploding. "My head feels like a meteor hit it," Hap complains after getting walloped by a nasty heavy. "We'll exchange symptoms later," Buzz tells him curtly. But in another episode, after the two get knocked out by a couple of bad guys who hit and run, Buzz admits that he's hurting too. "Let's get to Medical Science Center," he tells Hap (uncharacteristically). "We're in no shape to go after them."

It took Huston about two days to pen an episode, he says, adding quickly that there were faster writers on other hit shows "who could turn out a script in three to four hours." Once he had an evil purpose for the bad guys—"something that got Buzz Corry's attention"—he pored through scientific journals, looking for "some little paradox I could work into it." He read magazines such as *Popular Science* and "loads of books on astronomy," trying to imagine what would happen if theory became reality. In "The Giant Space Bubble" he created a plastic that remains liquid under a magnetic field, but solidifies when that field is removed. "That's how liquid crystal displays operate," says space opera fan Jack McKirgan admiringly, "except the field is electrical, rather than magnetic."

But Huston's scientifically plausible plots took place in Mike Moser's strictly defined universe, which was a maze of contradictions. For one thing, all the planets were inhabited, thanks to atmosphere domes that sealed in breathable air. Even so, Huston points out, "it would be hard to live on Jupiter because it's gaseous, without a surface; a human being would spread out into a kind of pancake under its gravitational pull." That didn't trouble Moser, however, who had no problem departing from fact when it came to populating the solar system with humans. Animals were another story. When Huston wrote a script that placed prehistoric animals on Venus, the producer went through the roof— perhaps, Huston figured, because of strict Creationist beliefs. Huston backed down, but after Moser died, he created a hybrid beast on Planet X that had (according to Hap) "the jaws of an alligator and the body of a tiger." Fortunately, Corry destroyed it with a shock rifle.[8] Huston liked giant animals and used them in several shows. How did the sound guys get these creatures to bellow and roar? They took a baby's cry and slowed it down from 78 rpm to 33⅓, producing a moan that curdled your blood.

Of course, there were bad guys on all the planets, and Huston delighted in giving them sinister-syllabled, "hard-sounding Anglo-Saxon names" such as Pax Targol, Clayton Slake and Slag Cronin. But even with Moser gone, he did not have total creative control. A constant thorn in his side was the Gardner agency's "creative committee." ("Just what the hell did they 'create'?" he asks with a flash of anger.) He noticed that the ad men on the committee, who demanded that plots be built around the latest boxtop premium,[9] were seldom troubled by accuracy. This bothered Huston, who, like Jolley, took pains to base his stories—at least loosely—on scientific fact:

> There was no communication between the ad people and the script creators about consistency in such problems as gravity and the speed of light. If the promoters wanted a planet 5,000 times the size of Earth [to appear] a billion miles beyond Pluto, lo, the planet was there. Did the ad men care if it yanked Jupiter out of orbit or put a wobble in the sun, or that the gravity of Planet X would spread Baccarratti out into an ice-cold pool of reddish mush? Hell, no.

Another problem was the size of gadgets—computers, calculators and the like. While the Space Patrol did have miniature space-o-phones (the cell phone of today), the concept of personal computerized devices was considered farfetched—more fantasy than science—so he steered away from shrinking equipment down to portable size:

> Back then, computers took up huge amounts of space and used tremendous electric power. If Buzz and Happy had a calculator portable enough to be put in a spaceship, kids wouldn't have believed it, so I was afraid to suggest the communications devices we have today. Everyone thought that was impossible—including a lot of scientists who were writing about them.

But while there were inconsistencies in *Space Patrol*'s physical universe, morality was clearly defined. "There were good guys and bad guys," says Huston, "but the good guys never killed the bad guys. Even the bad guys didn't actually kill anybody, though what they did was potentially fatal." Also, he points out, the heavies watched their language. "They threatened to do unspeakable things, like blowing up Jupiter City and killing millions, but they didn't say, 'People's guts will be spread all over Jupiter.'" Huston sighs. "Today, on the screen, they show it."

As nasty as the villains were, he admits to taking a "paternal interest" in a few of them but suppressing the urge to give them more depth. In the psychological Dark Ages of the '50s, a villain could never express self-doubt. "When he's got Buzz up against the wall with an ax in his hand, you can't have him say, 'Aw, shucks, I can't do this!'" Huston explains. But while he couldn't allow the bad guys any second thoughts, the writer was plagued with his own. "I'd watch the TV version—Norm's stuff—and think, 'By golly, those guys look real! Why the hell can't I get that in the radio thing?'" He felt he

---

[8]"Valley of Dread," September 5, 1953.
[9]In one episode, Buzz and Hap, in the Terra V, use their Space Patrol Periscope to peer into an office building on a planet thousands of DU's away. Bet *your* Periscope couldn't do that. (And if you believe the Commander's could, I've got some rings on Saturn I'd like to sell you.)

wasn't developing the characters enough, especially Buzz and Hap. "I told myself, 'I've got so much pseudo-scientific crap in here... Where are the people?'"[10] But back then, all he could afford to think about was delivering an acceptable script on time. "My chief concern was making the deadline at the ABC studio acceptance office with a script that did not have any violations of the broadcasting code," he jokes. And though he hints that at times, during his hangovers, he may have come close to crossing that line, the finished product lived up to ABC's code of decency. "I do not recall their censor — who was not called that — ever asking me to delete objectionable material, such as Buzz or Happy cursing or making sexually aggressive comments to Tonga. And as evil as Baccarratti was, he never said, 'Kill that S.O.B. Corry.'"

Huston, ever plagued by self-doubt, figured that the scripts he was turning in were *probably* OK because nobody said they weren't. He bumped into Larry Robertson once in a while, but the director never had much to say about his work, and that fed his anxiety. He was the first to admit there were problems. For one thing, because it was radio, Buzz often had to give a play-by-play of the action while in the midst of it, remaining heroic and grammatical at the same time. "I felt the dialogue was cumbersome, that I was having this cadet or Buzz Corry give long explanations of things when there should be more action," Huston recalls. "For years I had the impression that there were two or three guys just standing around jabbering." Not true, says Rory Coker, who hosts the "Roaring Rockets" Web page devoted to space opera: "The *Space Patrol* radio shows never lose momentum; they move like lightning."

Hearing the shows 50 years later, Huston admits that maybe he did a decent job after all. When he finally got up the nerve to listen to a few tapes, he was surprised to find "a lot more action than I remember putting in." And though he'd been preoccupied with plot, action and scientific accuracy, the character relationships had developed "unconsciously," in spite of it all. "Somehow I managed to keep the radio Buzz and Happy consistent enough with Norm Jolley's TV characters so that listeners accepted them," he concedes, adding, "I'm proud of that." But while he finally learned, toward the end of his life, that his shows had held up over time, he couldn't explain why, except to say that there was "a good spirit" that carried the show along, a force much larger than its participants. What touched him most was the loyalty of fans more than half a century later. "To find out that your audience is still with you, even though the show is gone — that's a wonderful feeling!" he told me.

When *Space Patrol* ended in the winter of 1955, Huston sold storylines to *Father Knows Best* and wrote scripts for many TV shows, including Ivan Tor's *Science Fiction Theatre*, *Highway Patrol*, *Petticoat Junction*, *Gilligan's Island*, *The Addams Family*, *The Beverly Hillbillies* and *Green Acres*.[11] In the mid-'50s, he married briefly. He drank, she drank, they drank together and the union ended. At age 43, he finally joined Alcoholics Anonymous. Getting sober turned out to be the most significant event of his life. After a stint writing documentary and industrial scripts for the Los Angeles County Motion Picture Unit, including two award-winning films on alcoholism, he left Hollywood for Colorado and then New York, where he wrote sales aids for several corporations.

---

[10]English professor Richard Felnagle, a *Space Patrol* fan, thinks that Huston's anxiety over character development was a natural (if unconscious) response to the omission of Robbie, Carol and Tonga from most of the radio episodes — a cost-cutting maneuver that deprived radio audiences of the interaction between Buzz and Hap and the three main sub-characters.

[11]The *Space Patrol* radio broadcasts appear to have ended on March 19, 1955, according to Jerry Haendiges's set of dated transcription discs.

In his mid-sixties, a new chapter in his life opened when he took a post as a counselor at Fellowship Hall, a famed rehab center in Greensboro, North Carolina. It was a job he'd hold for the next 22 years. There, in 1999, he met Darla Miller, a 36-year-old openly gay woman who was battling addiction. The two became friends and decided to cut expenses by sharing a house together. "Some people considered it an odd relationship," says Miller. "I mean, I'm gay and he was an older man. But he took me just as I am and I did the same for him." Her voice breaks, remembering Lou. "He loved me so much. That I'm sober today and love my life and myself is due in tremendous part to him. It was the first example of unconditional love that I'd seen in my entire life. And I don't know if I'll ever see it again."

In return, she did small things to make his life easier and brighten his day.

Radio writer Lou Huston, circa 1998. (Courtesy Darla Miller)

"I'll find my shoes shined, my shirts washed and ironed, my messy desk tidied up, a long-stemmed rose on my bedside stand," Huston reported by phone in the summer of 2000. But the following year, liver disease caught up with him, despite 45 years of sobriety. "I'm not expected to live," he told me in July 2001, his voice weak but still resonant.

As he lay dying a week later, Darla crawled into bed with him. "I lay on my side and put my head on his shoulder and held his hand. And I felt when he took his last breath, when his last heartbeat was … and I just lay there next to him for a while." At dawn, she got up, went to the window and opened the curtains. "And I was talking to him about the flowers, you know, like it was just another day." Suddenly she felt Lou's presence behind her, looking over her shoulder, gently teasing. "And he was like, '*What are you doing? Talking to a dead man!*'"

Bill Woodson, a close friend of Huston's since 1934 when they broke into radio together at KFOX, summed up his life in a letter he sent to be read at the memorial service: "He devoted the closing years of his life to helping others combat alcoholism. His material means were scant, but he was the most successful man I have ever known."

CHAPTER 13

Dick Darley:
Making It Real

Right before we went on the air, there was a countdown before we faded up from black — and it was the same feeling I had when I took off from the carrier and the plane dropped a bit before you got up enough air speed. Your heart was in your mouth.

— Dick Darley

It took a lot of courage to do what they were doing, especially in light of the way we do it now.

— Chris Darley

He had three rules: (1) Focus on the illusion, the suspension of disbelief; (2) Stay invisible: Quietly solve technical problems behind the scenes so that nothing mechanical intrudes to shatter the illusion; (3) Don't let it get flat — if it does, goose it up.

Dick Darley likes to say that the Navy missions he flew off aircraft carriers in the South Pacific prepared him for the perils of live TV, but he leaves it at that. The war stuff, he says, is "a whole other book." His voice is young, more like a baby boomer's than one of the Greatest Generation. Darley is open and easy to talk to, but he telegraphs that there are some places he'd rather not go. "He doesn't talk about the war," says his son, Chris, who directs the perennial hit show *Hollywood Squares*.

Dick grew up in Los Angeles, where his stepfather, who worked for the district attorney's office, later hung out his shingle as a private investigator. After attending Los Angeles High School, Darley joined the Navy in 1943. Home from the war, he majored in radio production and writing at USC, then went to work for Don Lee–Mutual Broadcasting. After a stint in public relations, he moved to production, working his way up from stage manager to director at the company's experimental TV station, W6XAO. He polished his skills at KFMB in San Diego, then landed a job at ABC-TV in Hollywood.

Darley wraps whatever conflict he feels about *Space Patrol* and its impact on his career in a wry sense of humor. He returns a call one day with a playful "Space Patroller Dick Darley reporting in!" Though he dreaded getting stuck on a kiddie show when he was handed the series in 1950, he soon realized the enormous creative freedom that came with the assignment. "It was a yeasty period for me. We started out with spit and made up the sets, models and special effects as we went along. It was pretty much free rein — and that was wonderful for a creative person. I recognized it as a terrific experimental ground."

In *Space Patrol*, he dealt with the technical problems first because if he didn't, noth-

Dick Darley with his son, Chris, and daughter, Carol, in the late '50s. (Courtesy Dick Darley)

ing would get out on the air. Once he'd figured out the camera moves, understood the special effects and lighting problems for the upcoming episode, and maybe made a frantic dash to a hardware or surplus store for a prop, he could get to the actual directing. That's when he thought of the people he cared about, imagining how they would react to the story. He thought of people from different age groups: his wife, his two younger brothers, and his six-year-old son, Chris.[1]

As a child, Chris hung out on the set with his dad, playing in the cockpit of Corry's ship, fiddling with the knobs and gadgets on the control panel. "It was the most wonderful playground — too good to be true," he recalls. As Dick's son, he was treated like royalty by cast and crew. Carl Macauley and Al Teaney made him a rocket they dubbed the "Space Patrol Sea-Air Division," but that only whetted his appetite for the real props he saw on the stage. He wanted one of the miniature models of Corry's ship, the *Terra V*, and he felt that, as the director's son, he was entitled to the grand prize in the Name the Planet Contest — the gigantic Ralston Rocket. He threw a tantrum when he didn't get either one.

The only thing more important than these toys was the inspiration he soaked up as

[1]Darley's daughter, Carol, born later, was too young to watch the show.

Chris Darley in the booth, directing *Hollywood Squares*, August 2003. (Kingworld/JPI/Jesse Grant)

he watched his dad work. A few years later, when he was twelve, he'd sit behind Dick as he directed *The Rosemary Clooney Show*. Later that night, watching the broadcast in his room, he cried. "I was so emotionally involved in what he had done, how they had put it together. It was something so wonderful, and I thought: 'I have to do this.'"

When Chris broke into the business, his father was a tough taskmaster. Once, when they worked together, with Chris as stage manager, Dick chewed him out so severely that fellow crew members asked, "Are you OK?" But Chris understood. He admired his dad's uncompromising attention to detail. "He was terribly disciplined — maybe that came from the wartime experience. I've tried to carry it into what I do."

Dick Darley admits he's a perfectionist, approaching each assignment like a wartime challenge. "Coming out of the Navy, I was a 'can-do' guy; now it's 'have-done,'" he cracks. A colleague once called him "unyielding," but he prefers "bastard." No one I talked to on the *Space Patrol* crew remembers him that way, but he claims the label. Surmounting challenges has always driven him; back then, fresh from the war, his fighter pilot experience flying Grumman Wildcats added a dash of recklessness, a go-for-broke style that was unstoppable. "Navy carrier fighter pilots are the cream of the elite," says author Joe Pierre:

> Air combat is only the beginning for them: They are also required to find their ship on a trackless ocean and then land their hurtling aircraft on a rolling, pitching flight deck, often at night in adverse weather conditions. If the situation deteriorates and they must

eject from their craft, the best they can hope for is a chance to survive in the cruel sea. Not a trade recommended for the faint-hearted.[2]

Which accounts for Darley's attitude: "If they gave you a script and an impossible set of circumstances, like an incomplete cast, not enough equipment and not enough time, you didn't say, 'This can't be done.' You said, 'When do you want it—by Tuesday?'"

He knew he was a hard driver, a pain at times, always pushing the envelope, but his can-do approach was contagious, inspiring the *Space Patrol* crew to offer ideas that could make the show better. In one episode, a boy was supposed to "accidentally" drop a letter, but no one could figure out how he should do it until boom man Ralph Elmore suggested he let the paper slip from his hand as he turned a doorknob. It worked. Darley was always open to input from crew members because "I'd been in the position where I wanted to be heard and nobody listened." He made it a point to shake everyone's hand at the end of each network broadcast because he knew it mattered. "The crew felt appreciated—that was part of their pay. We were close. We boosted each other."

To be there in the late 1940s when television was being born was like hitching a ride on a starship bound for the outer galaxies. "We were the upstarts, young and blood-thirsty," he says, recalling the days when he was heralded as one of the youngest and best directors in the business. A video family had begun to form, a fraternity of people in live TV who shared the bond of ephemeral creation and knew that, in television, time was everything. Motion picture people didn't understand this, and they certainly didn't know how to do it. Some of them scoffed at TV because it was just black and white, not even in color. But nobody in the new, maverick industry gave that a thought. "You were thrilled to have a picture at all and an audience to view it," says Darley. "If anybody even *had* a set in 1948, that was amazing." But often the early pioneers of TV had nothing to show for their efforts. "There was no good recording system," Darley explains. "Many shows weren't even kinescoped. What went on, went off—and that was it. Nobody ever saw it again."

In one of the early reviews of *Space Patrol*, someone misspelled his name 'Dik.' He was about to phone in a correction, recalls ABC staffer Alice Akins, but production manager E. Carleton Winckler said, "No, keep it. If it's 'Dik,' people will remember you.'" In those days, Darley liked to point out that Dik was 'kid' spelled backward, but as the innocence of the '50s gave way to the brashness of the '60s, he had second thoughts. "My wife doesn't want me to continue spelling it like that," he told Akins one day.

Though he was not fond of Mike Moser and had doubts about whether the producer had really conceived *Space Patrol* ("I'm sure he stole it from someplace," Darley quips), the fact that the nation had just survived another world war made the concept—a band of comrades protecting the universe, risking their lives for the common good and a greater cause—solid and believable. Occasionally Jolley's scripts seemed childish, and some of the Ralston premiums that had to be worked into the stories were just plain dumb. But there was something brewing between the scripted lines, a quality that transcended all the flaws:

> There was an essence there—a naiveté. I felt it when we were doing it. *Space Patrol* was pure adventure with people who were fond and protective of each other, and because we

[2]*www.joepierre.com*. Pierre, a Navy man, has authored *Handguns and Freedom: Their Care and Maintenance* (Writer's Club Press, 2002).

Darley makes some last-minute script changes. (Photograph by David Sutton, courtesy Dick Darley)

were coming out of the war, you believed it — you really did. It was before the "me, me, me" era. There was a wide-eyed innocence; it was a different world.

It was also a pre–space age world. No one had been in space yet; no one knew what it was really like. You could still dream about the mystery. That gave him a lot of latitude.

Despite the frantic rush to get the network show on the air, he allowed his subconscious mind to work on the script overnight and "get the whole picture." (He had no such luxury with the daily shows, where the script often arrived at the last minute.) And though he was, as he had feared, "stuck" on this kiddie show, a huge adult audience was tuning in and his work was attracting attention. A film magazine called him "one of the outstanding creative directors in a highly competitive Hollywood."[3]

[3]Magazine story titled "Props for Interplanetary Travel," probably 1950-51, from Virginia Hewitt's files; no source on clipping.

Like Kemmer, Darley downplays his role in the show's success. "All I tried to do was translate it, make it as real as possible; not look down on it or 'kid' it, but go for broke, as if every scene was the most important scene ever shot," he explains. What brought him down hard was when, after tedious preparation and testing, the technical snafus won out in the end. "When the models didn't work, it killed me because it killed the believability. The actors were trying so hard to make it real." And though he wanted to stay in the background, invisible, at least one person was watching. "Dick was the cohesive force," says Chris, still in awe. "Those actors were so diverse, so different, but he brought them together and molded them into a unit. I don't know how he did it, and I'll never know because he won't talk about it. But it took a lot of courage to do what they were doing, compared to the way we do it now."

After *Space Patrol*, Darley directed the first year of *The Mickey Mouse Club* and a slew of TV classics including episodes of *Lassie*, *The Millionaire* and *The Newlyweds*, plus numerous sports shows, game shows and musical-variety specials featuring such stars as Sammy Davis, Jr., Carol Burnett, Jack Benny, Debbie Reynolds and Frank Zappa. He did big-ticket commercials, too, for Chevrolet, Hallmark, Tide, Mattel — over 5,000 in all — plus the mid–'60s daytime soap *Paradise Bay* and the short-lived *It's About Time*, a fantasy about astronauts traveling back to Earth's prehistoric era. (The show was panned by critics and adored by kids.) But what he likes to talk about most is "A Tale of Two Cities," a two-part special based on the Charles Dickens novel that he directed for ABC's *Plymouth Playhouse* in the spring of 1953.[4] ABC had just merged with the United Paramount Theatres chain, and the struggling network suddenly had a windfall of cash. New programming was planned for the 1953-54 season, and *Plymouth Playhouse* was the network's showcase for impressive live dramas. "Tale," sporting elaborate sets and 85 extras, challenged Darley to the max. "You have to be so alert to do something like that on a live basis— you can't miss anything." This was his dream, where he hoped his future would go. It was rollercoaster excitement

Dick Darley demonstrates how he really didn't do much directing at all. (Photographs by David Sutton, courtesy Dick Darley)

[4]"A Tale of Two Cities" aired on consecutive Sundays, May 3 and 10, 1953. While Darley was working on it, Larry Robertson directed *Space Patrol*.

Darley confers on the set with lighting director Truck Krone (left). (Photograph by Richard Loeb, author's collection)

even more intense than *Space Patrol*, and it satisfied his deep need to push himself to the limit with a serious dramatic show. "When we finished the first episode," he recalls, "I just started crying for no reason." He talks about the production with great fondness and intensity. It showed him what he could do, if given the chance.

In 1962, he was back in "space" again with *Space Angel*, a cartoon series he created for Cambria Studios. The first animated series to use an outer space scenario and the groundbreaking "Synchro-Vox" technique that superimposed live-action moving lips over the mouths of animated characters, *Space Angel* tracked the adventures of "Commander Scott McCloud," a secret agent for the Interplanetary Space Force.[5] This time it was Darley, instead of Moser, who created a space-age world and filled it with colorful characters. It's rumored that Gene Roddenberry was a huge fan of the show and patterned *Star Trek*'s engineer, "Mr. Scott," after McCloud's Scottish sidekick, "Taurus."

---

[5]Synchro-Vox, invented by Edwin Gillette, cut the cost of TV animation from as much as $11,000 per minute to $500 because by projecting the lips of the voiceover artist onto the animated character, far fewer frames were needed to show lip movement.

Dick and Chris Darley in the early '90s. (Courtesy Dick Darley)

But what Dick Darley really wanted to do was remake *Space Patrol*.

"There was a period when I thought I could resurrect the show. I had miniatures being made, scripts being written." He ran smack into a maze of legal hurdles set up by Helen Moser's second husband, Henry ("Greg") Rhinelander, but that didn't stop him. It was the debut of a new film by George Lucas that finally crushed his plans. One night in 1977, he went to a special screening of *Star Wars* at the Directors Guild:

> This tremendous opening scene came on — and that was it. The reincarnation of *Space Patrol* I'd had in mind was blown away when I saw it. I knew there was no way I could get together the backing I needed to top that. It was just so good that I went, "My God, why am I messing around with this?"

After 40-plus years in the business, he retired in 1990.

There is a sense about Dick Darley that he could have faced bigger, tougher challenges that never came. Like Kemmer, he worked steadily after *Space Patrol*, but perhaps, in an alternate universe somewhere, both he and Kemmer may have surpassed themselves in a way that didn't quite happen in this one. These days, he doesn't talk much about *Space Patrol* because it often evokes blank stares. "When it comes up that I've been a director and people want to know what I've done, I ask, 'What year were you born?' I've learned not to mention *Space Patrol*, or even *The Mickey Mouse Club*, because a lot of people have no clue what I'm talking about."

"People don't realize that what those folks did was exceptional, whether it was *Playhouse 90* or *Space Patrol*," says Chris Darley. "The way he put all those pieces together in terms of the production, the actors, the special effects, is amazing — and so unappreciated. To tie all that together was very hard to do — and he did it! I'm not even sure that he appreciates what he did." For a long time, adds Chris, his father felt typecast by *Space Patrol* and wanted to put it behind him. But in recent years, there has been a change:

> It's come full circle now, and the show means a great deal to him. He'd never say that, but I know in my heart of hearts that it does. He cares about this. All of us who do this for a living do it because we care, but we never think that somewhere down the line somebody's going to say, "You know what? That show really meant a great deal to me, and here's why...." That's such a wonderful bonus, and when he hears it, I know it means a lot to him, though he hasn't said anything — and won't. But it does; I can tell.

Still, Dick Darley resists praise. He reminds you that he was so preoccupied with solving technical problems on *Space Patrol* that he didn't have enough time to work with the actors. All he did, he explains, was some emotional "fine-tuning." Unfortunately for Darley, a set of photos survives that shows him right in the actors' faces, arms flailing, passionately directing a rehearsal. "If I had any problems with a line or the blocking, I would go to Dick and he'd take care of it," recalls Ed Kemmer. "Even though the rest of us were a bit shaky, you could count on Dick to be in control." Darley deflects it all. *Space Patrol*'s success, he insists, had little to do with him and a lot to do with that moment in history, the 1950s, and with the innocence of the times.

But though he won't take credit for making *Space Patrol* so intense that it hooked a huge adult audience, once in a while Dick Darley forgets that he likes to stay in the background, invisible, and admits that maybe he did make some small contribution to TV history:

> A lot of people put down the "Golden Years" of television. They say, "Oh my God, there's no color, no fluidity in the cameras, no close-ups, no this, no that." But they're judging it against what has happened since — the sophistication, the technical advances that make things so slick now. What they're using as their yardstick would not have existed without going through this Golden Age of early TV.

He hesitates, then puts himself in the picture. "We were giving birth to television — and I'm so happy to have been part of that."

CHAPTER 14

"That's My Cadet!"

Corry never seemed to hesitate to throw himself in harm's way to protect Happy or Robbie or Carol. Would the Lone Ranger have laid his life on the line for Tonto? We could argue that one; but more to the point, I don't recall the writers of that show ever calling upon the Lone Ranger to make that decision.
— Richard Felnagle

Ed Kemmer was only five years older than Lyn Osborn, yet the two actors managed to warp time, creating the illusion that the age gap was a decade or more. Perhaps Kemmer's maturity came from the war. Though Lyn had served as a Navy gunner, he'd never seen combat. In contrast, Kemmer's brushes with death had given him experience that, he admits, "a lot of young guys didn't have." In real life, both were complex people. Kemmer has a brusqueness that co-exists with his warmth, while Osborn had a thoughtful side that he hid in public but poured into short stories, poems, letters to his family and notes to himself. Both men brought these shadow sides of their personalities to "Buzz" and "Hap," giving the characters unexpected depth.

It was this phenomenal hero-sidekick chemistry that rocketed the show into stardrive. Unlike Glen Denning, who starred as the first Commander Corry, Kemmer responded readily to Osborn's edginess and unpredictability. It was a perfect match. As an actor, says Kemmer, "you play off what you get, and Hap gave lots of opportunities for good reactions. We played off each other." That spark between Kemmer and Osborn drove the show when the storyline was weak, guest actors fumbled lines, or special effects fizzled and died — and it's the prime reason the show holds up today. The sensitive camaraderie between Buzz and Hap was such a key element in *Space Patrol* that even the villains picked up on it. When evil Gart Stanger takes Carol Carlisle hostage, he tells her what Buzz Corry's priorities will be when he discovers both she and Hap are missing:

Buzz Corry, ha! I can see him now. He'll spend a week looking for the daughter of the Secretary General — and the rest of his life searching all space and time for his cadet![1]

"The real love affair that's going on in that show is not between Corry and the women — it's a father-son thing going on between Corry and Happy. That's huge," says lawyer-educator Mike Guarino. It was. For many kids of the first, impressionable TV generation, the bond between Corry and Hap was like a dream come true — the child who is schooled and protected by the perfect father, brother, buddy or mentor. However you saw it, the relationship filled a deep need in many postwar kids searching for role mod-

[1]Episode 192 "The Theft of the Rocket Cockpit" (AKA "Mystery of the Stolen Rocket Ship"), October 23, 1954.

Osborn and Kemmer rehearse a scene.
(Courtesy Joe Sarno)

els in a world changing at warp speed, thanks to TV and jet planes. It was easy to identify with Hap, jump into his skin and *become* him, imagining that you had Corry's protection and strength to guide you on the perilous road to adulthood. That, says Arie Raymond, is exactly what happened to him:

> Buzz Corry became a father figure — in him I saw an image of what I wanted to grow up to be. He was calm and cool under unearthly stress; he had faith that good would always prevail, no matter how dire the circumstances; he was fair and just; he was always a gentleman to women; he was dashing, courageous and strong — the epitome of reason and manly virtues. But while Corry was my hero, I identified with Cadet Happy. I was the cadet, a junior, a man-in-the-making. I was young, silly, and immature. My desires and feelings often overcame what was reasonable. I suffered from impulsiveness. Sometimes I made my commander laugh, just as Happy did. But sometimes, at my best, I was able to help him or to serve him.

In fact, as Raymond notes, the writers did turn the tables once in a while, having Hap rescue Corry from a tight spot — or even save his life — proving that the cadet could help or serve the Commander. In these scenes, Osborn showed his skill as an actor. Despite his comedic bent, he could play dead serious — and he got the chance, for there were many tense moments on *Space Patrol*. Don't be fooled by the fact that the show received numerous awards for nonviolence from the PTA and other groups who monitored children's TV. What these watchdogs were applauding was that, unlike TV westerns, where good guys and outlaws gunned each other down faster than you could say "Davy Crockett," on *Space Patrol* there was no blood and gore, no cheap death. There was the *threat* of death, but it never happened — even when the bad guys got hold of weapons that could really hurt you, like blasters and Kato guns, not to mention heat rays and mutation bombs that could end your life in a most unpleasant way. On *Space Patrol* the bad guys were dangerous and people got threatened and pushed around a lot, but a good fistfight always straightened things out in the nick of time. Violence happened for a reason. Confronting it brought out the best in the characters and played up the bond between them — a trait shared with other action-adventure shows of the day. (Of course, this was during television's primitive era, before a new breed of hero blew up or gunned down everything in sight in the name of truth and justice.)

A formula used often by both Huston and Jolley was that the bad guys capture Corry and Hap, then try to force Buzz to do something to further their plans, such as giving them top-secret information — something the Commander would never do. They slap him around, but when he resists it doesn't take long to figure out that the way to make

Corry crack is to threaten to harm his favorite cadet. Norm Jolley used this scenario in Episode 34, "Underwater Hideout," where, while one thug presses a deadly Kato gun into Corry's back to keep him in check, the other beats up Hap. Lou Huston wrote a similar scene in the radio show, "The Forbidden Planet," where the vicious "Dakoja" (played by Jolley) threatens to kill Hap in front of Corry if he doesn't make a space-o-phone call that could create an "inter-stellar incident," forcing the United Planets into a war with the evil Arctronian solar system:

> *Perhaps I shall destroy the cadet and let you live, Corry. And you can always remember that you saw Happy crumple at your feet when you could have saved him.*[2]

These tense scenes played up the loyalty and affection between Commander and cadet, and Kemmer and Osborn made them believable, never melodramatic. The writers discovered early on that Osborn could turn on a dime from funny to serious, just as Kemmer could flash in an instant from strength to vulnerability. This stretched the dramatic possibilities, giving both characters the chance to be at once human and heroic. Assistant director Marg Clifton remembers how the two actors played off each other. "They were realistic — they weren't hamming it up. I didn't have a feeling like, 'Oh, come off it.'"

Loyalty, says Norm Jolley, was a value he built into many a plot. It was understood that Corry would give up his life for his cadet, and Hap would do the same for him. Jolley took that theme to the limit in Episode 50, "The Sacrifice," where both men are so intent on dying for each other that they come to blows.[3] It happened on a routine patrol near the Pluto orbit, when a meteoric particle tore a hole in the ship.

With their space-o-phones dead, Corry realizes that their only hope is for one person to escape in a spacesuit while the other stays aboard and blows up the ship by activating the atomic pile that powers it. With luck, the huge explosion will attract help for the man who has escaped but remains adrift in space. Of course, whoever destroys the ship will almost certainly not survive. Here's an excerpt from Jolley's script, along with his stage directions:

> HAPPY: *Pull the damper... rods... on the atomic... pile... sir? That'd be almost suicide! Why the radiation would burn you so badly that...*
> BUZZ: *That's what I meant when I said there'd be a chance for one of us. The one who doesn't pull the rods.*
> HAPPY: *(LETS IT SOAK IN... THEN, VERY SERIOUSLY) I see, sir. (PAUSES... THINKS... THEN TURNS TO BUZZ.) Commander... I'll do it. You can leave the ship first. (SWALLOWS) I'll pull the rods.*
> BUZZ: *(SMILES WARMLY) I knew you'd say that, Happy. But I've already made the decision. You're going to get in your spacesuit and jet pack away from the ship. I'll take care of blowing up the ship.*
> HAPPY: *But... but, sir. You're the Commander-in-Chief... The Space Patrol... the United Planets needs you, sir. They'll never miss a cadet. And besides... I can probably get out of here fast enough to keep from getting burned.*
> BUZZ: *(SMILES AT HIM, BUT SHAKES HIS HEAD) No, Happy. I've made up my mind. Get into your spacesuit.*
> HAPPY: *But, sir...*
> BUZZ: *(STERNLY) That's an order!*

[2]"The Forbidden Planet," radio, circa 1954.
[3]Episode 50, "The Sacrifice," December 8, 1951.

But as Corry turns his back, Hap spies a heavy wrench lying on a counter. He picks it up, struggling with the unthinkable. The only way to keep the Commander from sacrificing his life for him is to knock him out and set him adrift in space, where he might have a chance. "I've never disobeyed an order — until now!" he says, bringing the wrench down on Corry's head. But before it connects, Buzz — expecting it — whirls around and delivers a right to Hap's jaw, knocking him down and out. Then he puts the cadet in a spacesuit, carries him to the outer hull of the ship, opens the valve on his jet pack, and releases him into space.

When I ask Norm Jolley about that compelling hook in *Space Patrol* — the protectiveness of the characters toward one another — he clears his throat repeatedly. It's hard to talk about these things, particularly when it's dawning on you in the ninth decade of your life that you may have done something extraordinary that touched millions of impressionable kids, not to mention adults. In fact, it's almost as difficult for Jolley to deal with the impact of the many TV series he wrote (including classics like *Wagon Train*) on a generation of boomers as it is for Kemmer to talk about playing the hero. While Jolley, who used to write over a million words a year, struggles to find a few of them, his wife, Lois, who's been listening, steps in. "But that's the way he *is*," she says quietly, glancing affectionately at her husband. "He's very protective of people."

Jolley avoided senseless violence in all the shows he wrote — even the westerns. It's something he can't stand to this day:

> If there's violence for a reason, that's different; but today, it's excessive and it doesn't mean anything. I don't remember ever having a gunfight in *Wagon Train*. Very occasionally a gun was drawn for a reason, but I did not believe in excessive violence, and I still don't. Violence at the right time, and a little obscenity — an "Oh, shit" — is all right, at the right moment. But you don't need excessive violence; good drama is better.

Sometimes Jolley's attempts to deepen the characters were cut from the script because Darley was up against the clock and had to slice any dialogue that didn't move the story along. For example, in Episode 188, "Defeat of Manza," as Corry and Hap wait for General Nardo's deadly heat ray to end their lives, they have this exchange as the show resumes from the commercial break — or they would have, if time had permitted:

> BUZZ: *Only another 30 seconds, Happy...*
> HAPPY: *I'm sorry, Commander.*
> BUZZ: *Sorry?*
> HAPPY: *Sorry I doubted you a while ago when I thought you'd given up. Just wanted you to know, sir... I didn't really doubt you... I was just confused.*
> BUZZ: *(SMILES AT HIM, MAKES A FRIENDLY GESTURE LIKE A PAT ON THE SHOULDER' OR RUMPLES HIS HAIR...)*[4]

There are two versions in the Space Patrol archives of how Cadet Happy became Commander Corry's co-pilot and cadet, but keep in mind that in the 30th century, where scientists used hyper-dimensional physics to pierce the time-space continuum, parallel universes were known to exist — so both versions may be true.

According to "Treachery on Mars," the first half-hour episode of *Space Patrol* to air on Earth, Hap saves Corry's life and is rewarded with the assignment as his cadet.[5] Writ-

---

[4]Excerpt from uncut script, Episode 188, "Defeat of Manza," September 25, 1954. Stage directions *IN CAPS* are Norm Jolley's.

[5]Episode 1, "Treachery on Mars," December 30, 1950.

ten by Mike Moser, it tells how Hap, who has just won the prestigious Corry Scholarship, is hitching a ride to Earth with the Commander himself, where he will enroll in the Space Patrol Academy. But in midflight, they're ambushed by Major Gorla, "fierce enemy of universal peace," who fires a deadly cosmic bomb at Corry's ship. Skillfully evading it, Buzz changes course and pursues Gorla and his slimy sidekick, Pasko, to their hide-out on Mars. Once inside, the villains get the drop on the Space Patrollers, but just as Pasko is about to shoot Buzz with a deadly shock-ray, Hap kicks the gun out of his hand and tackles him to the ground. Noting the future cadet's quick thinking—which has just saved his life—and his ability to act in a crisis, the Commander decides to make him his co-pilot.

Others say that's not the way it happened at all, citing Part 2 of the "Space Patrol Adventures" series released by Decca Records in 1954.[6] In this version, penned by Lou Huston, Happy has nearly completed his cadet training at the academy on Earth, but has been on emergency leave on Terra. Corry, headed to Earth to inspect a new spaceport, offers Hap a lift on the swift *Terra I* so he'll make it back in time for graduation. Suddenly a bulletin comes over the space-o-phone: Ruthless criminal Gaff Carter has escaped from the Venus City Rehab Center, stolen a ship and taken Carol Carlisle hostage. Corry changes course to pursue Carter, who crash lands on a robot space station orbiting Mars. As Carter lobs torpedoes at Corry's ship, Hap bravely volunteers to sneak aboard the space station and disable its weapons with an atomo torch. It's a daring plan—and it works. But when Corry boards the space station to capture Carter, he's too late to prevent the villain from blasting Hap with a ray gun. As Happy comes to, he realizes he'll be flunked out of the academy for missing graduation ceremonies. "I think I can fix it up with your CO," Corry tells him. "And I've got an assignment in mind for you, after you graduate. How would you like to be assigned to permanent duty aboard the *Terra I*?"

Hap reacts with amazement: "You mean with *you*, Commander? Smokin' rockets!"

"That's my cadet!" Corry chuckles. It's a phrase the Commander would utter many times over the years.

There are two versions, too, of Kemmer and Osborn's offscreen relationship. After work, they hung out with different crowds. Lyn loved nights out on the town, while Ed had a home life with then-wife actress Elaine Edwards. "We didn't socialize together," says Kemmer. "Hap was of a different genre—young, gadabout, on the go all the time—and I had the house and more mundane things to do. I'd sowed my wild oats—he still had his going for him."

On the set, says announcer Jack Narz, the two actors teased each other nonstop:

> It was like Ed was the father figure and Hap was the playful little brat. Ed had notes all over the place and Hap would take them down or move them. They'd pull tricks on each other—hide each other's scripts. I remember some prop, a gun, that Ed was supposed to pick up but Hap had nailed it down—things like that. Ed was the rock and Hap would bounce off of him—boom, boom, boom.

"Hap was a practical joker—wacky and fun, but never too serious about anything—while I was a very staid, straight young guy," Kemmer admits. Osborn took advantage

[6]*Cadet Happy Joins Commander Corry*, the second in a two-part "pre-quel" series released by Decca Records in November 1954. The first record was titled *Buzz Corry Becomes Commander-in-Chief*.

Osborn shows off his super-strength and "attacks" Kemmer with a giant prop rock; Ken Mayer (left) flaunts his strength, too, while Bela Kovacs (white suit) looks on. (Author's collection)

of Kemmer's diligence, knowing that if he went blank during the live performance, he could count on the Commander to bail him out. "Hap worked hard and studied his lines, but I learned fast to work harder than he did," Kemmer recalls. "When he'd blow a line, he'd say, 'What'll we do now, Commander?' — and turn it over to me. And boy, I'd better know what he's supposed to say, what my reaction is, what the hell the plot is, and what's going to happen next!" Assistant director Marg Clifton witnessed it many times. "When Lyn went blank," she confirms, "he'd throw Ed a hot potato."

But director Dick Darley, who doesn't gloss over the difficult moments on *Space Patrol*, says that Kemmer was often angry at Osborn for his nonstop antics that wasted valuable rehearsal time:

> Ed was very goal-oriented and wanted to make the best showing he could, while Hap was just cocky and screwing around. I don't know how fond they really were of each other, but I think they were comrades, in the best sense of the word, because they had the same vested interest in the show and they respected what each other had to go through to get the damn thing on.

"Dick thought I was a little more angry than I was," says Kemmer. "There were times when I was annoyed at Hap, when you had to sit on him hard to get things done. But he had talent and he was funny, and I enjoyed the jokes as much as anyone. We were good friends." The problem was that Osborn couldn't pass up the opportunity for a gag — and he saw humor in everything. "If he saw a joke, he'd bring it out," says Kemmer, who admits that under the gun, his patience ran thin — especially when Osborn clowned around during the crucial dress rehearsal, throwing everyone off. "There were times when I could have hauled off and really given him one, because that rehearsal was just too damn important," he says heatedly. Instead, he called time out:

> I'd pull him aside and talk to him like a Dutch uncle. I'd say, "Now you've got to cut it out. We have this show. Maybe *you* don't mind if you look like a fool, but *I do mind,* so knock it off!" I'd say it in no uncertain terms, and he knew that I meant it. And he'd say, "Oh, sorry," and we'd go back in and do the show.

At times, this real-life, push-pull relationship mimicked the *Space Patrol* scripts. Norm Jolley recalls how he allowed Hap to bend the rules — until Corry issued an order. "I played Hap's humor against the authority of the Commander, letting him get away with a little of it. But when the Commander turned and said 'Do it!' he did it." Both Jolley and Lou Huston picked up on the spark between the two actors. "It was there, and I used it," says Jolley, who adds that even he was impressed with the subtleties of the hero-sidekick relationship he'd built between Corry and Hap:

> It was extraordinary — and in spite of the rank difference! But they knew who they were. They maintained that difference, and they were still good friends. It was easy to write for the two of them. You could see that here's the serious guy, the boss, and there's the guy who makes the jokes on the side — and gets away with it! It worked because it was real between them, and I just wrote it.

Lou Huston echoed Jolley's words:

> There was something real between them that got through to the writers and the audience. Aside from the fact that they were supposed to be a young cadet and his very competent mentor, their personal relationship fed through that. If you had any common sense, as a writer, you tried to keep that up and expand on it.

It was the chemistry between Kemmer and Osborn, adds Huston, that made the plots believable:

> It was certainly a good motivator for a dangerous situation. If the writer and the audience believe that these people are really important to each other, aside from their jobs, then you try to justify it with a situation and dialogue that carries it out. A lot of it was unconscious. I didn't think, "Boy, those guys sure have got a meaningful relationship and I'll build on that for the show." It was just that if you noticed it at all, you used it without thinking too much about it.

Watching the two actors play off each other could hook you on *Space Patrol* in no time at all. When Osborn was troubled or vulnerable, Kemmer could radiate concern that went straight to your heart. It was a memory Virginia Hewitt carried for decades.

When I first met Hewitt, she did not want to talk about *Space Patrol.* It was something she'd done in her youth before she became a respectable society matron. But as I asked questions about the show's most memorable quality — the caring and concern for one another that the actors conveyed — she nodded her head faster and faster. Suddenly, she was "Carol" again. To Hewitt, the relationship between Kemmer and Osborn was as real offscreen as you hoped it might be. "They had an awful lot of affection and respect for each other, they truly did," she said softly:

They were close and they had a sense of fun, which is terribly important. I traveled with them on personal appearances, and believe me, practically living with each other for five years, you knew what was going on, if you were the least observant. Hap was very strong about his feelings. Whenever he thought someone had done something underhanded or wrong, he'd let them know it in no uncertain terms. He could express his anger completely. But I never did once, in all those years, know of him saying anything to Buzz except in terms of friendship. We'd go to the projection room, in those days, and watch the shows at the end of the week. Buzz, to me, came across as very warm and caring. He'd look at his cadet, for instance, and see that he was upset about something — seriously upset — and I'd see great compassion in his eyes, in his face.

Lyn's sister, Beth Flood, saw it too. "There was a magic between them," she says simply.

If, as a kid, it freaked you out when the villains acted so threatening and mean, *Space Patrol*'s creator, Mike Moser, understood. Though he was totally focused on profits and the bottom line, he really did try to keep the promise he'd made to kids when he told *Time* magazine that he didn't want *Space Patrol* to ever cause a single nightmare.[7] That took some doing, considering the rough stuff that Buzz, Hap, Robbie, Carol and Tonga survived, but early on, when Moser was writing the scripts, he used a gimmick (employed by a long line of cowboy sidekicks) guaranteed to leave a smile on your face. At the end of the show, he had Hap clown around, sending Corry and the other good guys into peals of laughter. (If there were villains present, they'd have been captured, so they just scowled.) Then Corry would give Hap a fatherly look or lay a hand on his shoulder and exclaim, "That's my cadet!" To a child, it was reassuring beyond words. Hap's antics and Corry's easy smile told you that the brutal treatment at the hands of the villains had left no scars and that everyone had come through OK. Norm Jolley continued the tradition, giving Hap a comedy schtick in the final scene that put a sunny face on whatever dark moments had gone before. When he wrote these scenes, Jolley had a dual purpose in mind. "'That's my cadet!' gave the otherwise serious story some light relief," he explains. "And it told the audience that while Commander Corry enjoyed Happy's humor, at the same time he trusted him to carry out serious orders."

It was Bob Lee's favorite part of the show. "We'd leave with a smile and good feelings after watching a half-hour of mayhem on the screen each week," says Lee, who grew up to become a TV broadcaster:

> Buzz Corry was a father figure for us kids. We expected him to excel as a leader and overcome evil while at the same time providing guidance and being a mentor to his young sidekick. After all, we kids were in the same situation as Cadet Happy, hoping to be "good guys" and great leaders someday. But we were still in learning mode, getting into scrapes our parents had to bail us out of — yet giving them a laugh from time to time. And just as our parents forgave our childhood transgressions, so, too, did Buzz Corry forgive his awkward cadet. As exasperated fathers were known to say, "That's my boy!" Commander Corry was saying essentially the same thing with "That's my cadet!" He meant: "He's not perfect, he created a mess for me, but I love him just the same." There was a reassurance there that it's OK to be a kid and make kid mistakes.

In real life, Kemmer seems to have felt fatherly toward Osborn. It's 1988, and I'm visiting him in New York for the second time. When he speaks of Hap (as he still calls

<hr />

[7]*Time*, August 11, 1952.

him), he grows wistful. Looking back, he admits that maybe Osborn's fun-loving approach to life carried a valuable lesson. "You could start feeling a little too self-important once in a while, and boy, he could prick you with a pin and bring you down to earth! He never took anything too seriously; there was a lesson to be learned there for all of us."

I tell Kemmer that nothing I've seen on TV matches the camaraderie that sparked between him and Lyn. He nods. "It was easy to fall into those two characters," he says, "especially with Hap's great sense of humor." For a moment, he's silent, then smiles, remembering his "favorite cadet":

> I treated him like a wayward son at times, but with love, with care, with understanding. We got so used to each other — 1400 shows! He was a lovable minx. He could always get you off that high, too-serious attitude. *Space Patrol* was a sweaty, ditch-digging job at times, and I'd be plugging away.... Hap pulled me back to reality. He'd see me shouldering what I felt I had to shoulder and he'd say, "Tomorrow's another day. There'll be another show next week."

For some reason, at this moment, I decide to tell Kemmer about the mysterious voice that, four years earlier, had urged me to enter the nostalgia store in Guerneville and ask about *Space Patrol*. The same voice that, one month later, guided me to the gloomy, out-of-the-way shop in West Los Angeles where Nina Bara had tried to hawk her *Space Patrol* memorabilia. He listens politely. I should have stopped there, but I want him to know the rest of the story. It's almost as if that playful, unseen friend is at my side again, egging me on. Telling Kemmer is a risk — he may decide I'm a kook instead of a credible journalist. And yet somehow I feel he's supposed to know what happened. He listens without saying a word as I describe the invisible "presence" that drove me to write about the show in the spring of 1984, then segue into the strange event that took place the following December....

It was winter in Guerneville. The strange, vibrant energy I'd felt by my side on and off since I'd watched the *Space Patrol* tape in David's store last April was still with me from time to time, like an invisible sidekick. It didn't feel bad — in fact, it had a kind of playful, teasing quality; but it's wasn't *my* energy — and that was unsettling. Whenever I felt its presence, the message was always the same: "Write about *Space Patrol*."

In fact, I was preparing to do just that — researching the show, reading about live TV in the '50s, boning up on behind-the-scenes lore of programs I'd enjoyed as a child. As I fed all this data into my crowded brain (I'd never had the slightest interest in early television), I still had the feeling — as I'd had from the beginning — that my unseen friend "felt" a lot like Lyn Osborn. I found myself thinking about Osborn a lot — and OK, I'll lay my cards on the table: Having delved into books on quantum physics, string theory and other systems that seek to unravel the space-time continuum and nature of physical reality, I was open to the idea that we live in a multi-dimensional universe; that at the cutting-edge frontier where particle physics meets metaphysics, "death" may be a doorway to other dimensions. If I'd had the ghost of Napoleon stalking me, I'd have sought professional help. But it did not seem too far-fetched to theorize that Osborn, whose short life on Earth was forever linked to *Space Patrol*, might want to connect with someone who could tell the story of the show and secure its place in television history. On some level, it made sense. After all, why was I suddenly driven to research the show, locate the actors and write the story? And why was I thinking so much about Osborn? I had a friend who taught classes in psychic awareness and I decided to see her for a private consultation or "reading." By now, I was used to my invisible companion, who came and went, but it was annoying to not know who or what "it" was. A reading may not have been scientific or space-age, but this was a case of "whatever works." I didn't need expensive therapy; I needed to know what the hell was going on.

Alene had a second-floor office on Main Street, a block from the Russian River. The skeptical part of me decided not to tell her the reason I was there. I'd let her get that herself—if she could. It was a cold, gray afternoon as I climbed the steps to her office. An icy, northern wind was blowing in from the ocean and across the river, so Alene shut the window. She lit three candles on a table in the corner and dimmed the lights.

As we faced each other in straight-backed chairs, she explained that she was seeing my "aura"—an energy field around me—in her mind's eye, and was looking for colors, symbols or pictures that would give clues to what I was experiencing. I didn't help her out. I just sat quietly, wondering if she'd get anything remotely connected to *Space Patrol*. Five minutes passed.

"I don't know what this means," she said finally, "but I see stars and planets. It's like the universe... like space."

Not bad.

"You may be picking up on *Space Patrol*," I told her. I explained that I'd watched the show as a child and especially loved the "Cadet Happy" character. Then I described the strange energy that had been with me, on and off, since the previous spring. "I feel," I said tentatively, "that this 'energy' I've sensed around me may have something to do with Lyn Osborn." As soon as I said it, the skeptic within me woke up screaming, horrified that I could suggest such a thing, and I went into vehement denial. "But it *can't* be Lyn Osborn," I added quickly, "because he's been dead for 25 years."

As if to protest that last statement, slowly the three candles across the room extinguished themselves one by one. They were tall, new candles, snuffed out in their prime. Alene and I froze, staring through the gloom. "I've never seen anything like *that* before," she said, visibly shaken.

When I'd interviewed Ed Kemmer in 1984, I'd seen a book about famous American psychic Edgar Cayce on the coffee table. His wife, Fran, he'd explained, was into spiritual exploration, and he had an open mind. But right now, Kemmer, lost in thought, wasn't saying anything, and both intuition and common sense told me I'd just made a fool of myself, that I shouldn't have told this story. For a long moment, silence hung in the room. Then Kemmer started to chuckle. "I'm surprised he didn't *break* the candles," he said softly. And though he didn't say it, it was as if the silence spoke it: "That's my cadet!"

Chapter 15

Bela

I was always conscious of what kind of impression my character was making on the audience. I was always asking myself, "What is this going to make them feel?"

— Bela Kovacs

He was an extraordinary person who unfortunately never reached his potential.

— Marta Kovacs-Ruiz

NEW YORK CITY: JULY 1984

SCENE: In his huge, gaudy castle on Planet X, Prince Baccarratti paces the floor and berates his chief adviser, Dr. Malengro, whose scientific knowledge is used by the Prince in his attempts to conquer the United Planets.

PRINCE BACCARRATTI: Just look at these production figures, Malengro. We're eight spaceships behind schedule! I ordered a speed-up, didn't I?
MALENGRO: Yes, Your Highness.
PRINCE B: If we are going to attack the United Planets, we've got to have ships. Isn't that right?
MALENGRO: Absolutely, Your Highness.
PRINCE B: (flying into a rage) THEN WHY DON'T I HAVE SHIPS? TELL ME THAT!
MALENGRO: (calmly) First, Illustrious One, there's the shortage of material. We can't make Endurium for the ships unless we have Arctite, and, as you know, Arctite is very difficult to obtain.
PRINCE B: Excuses, excuses — I don't want excuses! I want RESULTS! Ships! Weapons! I want to drive Commander Corry out of the universe!

—"Valley of Dread" (radio), September 5, 1953

But still sharing the universe with Corry — in fact, less than three miles from the Commander's Riverside Drive base of operations—"Prince Baccarratti" paces his headquarters fronting Central Park.

"How many tables have you seen like this one, with wood from all over the world?" he asks.

"It's truly original, Illustrious One," I say jokingly.

Bela Kovacs chuckles warmly. When he turned to sculpting and woodwork after his acting career evaporated in 1955, the results defied space and time. "You don't know how I have to hunt to find this wood," he confides, citing lumber shortages on Earth as grave as the Arctite deficit on Planet X.

It's a sweltering day and the big windows in Kovacs' apartment on the east side of Central Park are thrown open, letting in the deafening roar of trucks and buses on Fifth Avenue. Kovacs doesn't seem to mind as he sips a drink — not his first — in the soft mid-morning light. He looks fabulous—ice-blue eyes framed by bushy brows, ruddy skin, trim figure, strands of gold in his white hair and mustache. Despite the alcohol, his mind is keen. His voice, with its familiar Hungarian accent, sounds exactly as it did on *Space Patrol*. Back then, it seemed too old for his years, but now it fits.

I'm edgy. As a kid, I was terrified of the maniacal villains he portrayed. If I say the wrong thing, will he fly into a rage? But sit with Kovacs for a while and a sort of peace comes over you. No need to speak — in fact, it's as if time holds its breath as he loses himself in the booze and memories of his brush with fame. We sit together in comfortable silence punctuated by the clank and bang of traffic on the Avenue. The whitewashed living room is crammed with his sculptures; they hang from the ceiling, fill shelves on the walls. When Kovacs finally speaks, he's passionate about his acting, his artwork and his loneliness, which he doesn't hide. His artistic success is "very odd," he says, "because I never was trained for this." He waves a hand at his wooden subjects:

> I've been fortunate. Anything I've tried in my life, I've been successful at. Everything in this house comes from me, everything you see…. Prince Baccarratti came out of me, like these things. It wasn't that somebody told me, "This is the way you should do it." I figured things out. I had a pair of leather gloves, so I asked Mike Moser, "Can I use these gloves to hit people?" Because I knew that it doesn't hurt, but it looked very mean! And the audience loved it, in an odd sort of way. I don't know what it was; I can't figure it out. The meaner I acted, the more mail flowed in. It was building up the show. I've done many more pleasant, rewarding things, as an actor; but I felt very good when I sensed that Baccarratti was making the show better and better.

To oppose a character as noble and true as Buzz Corry took a powerful force — something or someone so evil that it would challenge the Commander on every level. That scumsucker was Prince Baccarratti. For while Corry's sharp mind and physical strength outwitted most run-of-the-mill villains and even brilliant scientists who'd had a psychotic break and wanted to rule the universe; and while all these bad guys were violent and vicious, the ruler of Planet X was different. No one hated Corry as passionately as Prince Baccarratti.

SCENE: Having landed on Planet X and survived the deadly jungle surrounding Baccarratti's castle, Commander Corry and Cadet Happy now seek to infiltrate the Prince's fortress, high atop a rocky spire. Overpowering the castle guards and de-activating their ray guns, they force the sentries to bring them before the evil Prince while posing as "prisoners."

PRINCE BACCARRATTI: *Well, well… My friend Commander Corry, and the stupid cadet. So we meet again.*
CORRY: *I said we'd be inside your castle within the hour. We're right on schedule.*
PRINCE B: *Oh, yes. But you neglected to say you would enter as my prisoners.*
CORRY: (deliberately) *Well, maybe that's because we're not your prisoners!* (He and Hap draw ray guns.)
PRINCE B: *You're not taking me, Corry! I'm not through yet…* (Pushes a button, setting off a molecular altering device. Suddenly, the floor dissolves, and Buzz and Hap fall through to a dungeon below. Standing over them a few moments later, the Prince turns to his assistant, Dr. Malengro.)

PRINCE B: Look at them, Malengro! Their attitude has decidedly changed from a few moments
   ago.
HAP: (struggling to his feet) *Hey, Commander… They're not armed! What are we waiting for?*
CORRY: Not a thing, Hap! (Rushes forward; then staggers back, clutching his head as Bac-
   carratti activates the "sonic barrier," a wall of high-frequency sound waves.)
PRINCE B: Ha, ha! You want to try it again, Corry? Or is the pain too much, even for the great
   Commander-in-Chief of the Space Patrol?
                                    —"The Hate Machine of Planet X," Episode 143, September 9, 1953

The kids took it all seriously. Urgent letters poured in, advising Commander Corry of tactics to use against the prince that he, well … wasn't thinking of himself. After 80 shows, says Kovacs, "Mike Moser told me, 'I can't keep you in. Corry looks like a fool.'" Kovacs assumed production duties, becoming casting director and, when Moser died, associate producer. He soon stepped back in as an actor, too, playing over one hundred character parts on both the TV and radio shows. But his juiciest role was that of Corry's archenemy, Baccarratti, a thorn in the Commander's side as annoying as Moriarty was to Sherlock Holmes.

Kovacs is proud that the evil prince drew letters and boosted the viewership. In 1950, Mike Moser had hired him for a four-week stint on the local show, with no idea that "Baccarratti" would prove such a huge success. The more mail that poured in, "the more I hammed it up," Kovacs recalls. Well, maybe a little too much, says Dick Darley:

Bela Kovacs as Prince Baccarratti, AKA the evil "Black Falcon," sports his leather jacket with the falcon emblem (evidently the only jacket in his closet). It was actually a hand-me-down from the 1939 Columbia serial *Flying G-Men*, in which the Black Falcon (Robert Paige) was a good guy fighting enemy spies. (Author's collection)

In my opinion, Bela overacted tremendously — he chewed the scenery and it got in the way of his acting. If you deliver a menace line, there are ways of doing it quietly — so steely or so coldly that it's much more threatening than somebody grinding his teeth and tensing all his muscles and forcing the words out. And that's what Bela always did. He had two gears: high and low. And when he got into a situation where he thought he should be menacing or sinister, he generally overplayed it. But we were bigger than life anyhow, so that never knocked me out of shape, because at least if you overact, people know what you mean. And in a good guy–bad guy, white hat–black hat kind of show, it wasn't that painful.

The way Kovacs sees it, he wasn't overacting at all. In fact, he confides, he craved even more intensity between Baccarratti and Corry. "I think," he says slowly, "there could have been more *wildness* between the two of us, you know?" But all that was back in the 30th century. Right now, he settles harmlessly into a couch he coaxed from a block of wood.

"Is there any similarity in real life," I ask, "between you and Baccarratti?"

"Oh, yes, I get angry, occasionally. But I think my real nature is sort of ... timid. With Baccarratti, I was able to show what I *could* be."

"You were the antithesis of everything Commander Corry stood for."

"Yes, we used that angle. As the role went on, it opened up. It was made obvious that Prince Baccarratti was the son of the King of Neptune, that he was a *royal* person. So he had to act like a big shot, not just a guy who's beating everybody up." Kovacs laughs now, recalling how, when the cast made personal appearances, "the kids were afraid to come close to me. But then, after ten minutes, they were all around, pulling my coat." (When I mention this to Ed Kemmer, years later, he smiles, remembering Kovacs. "He played it to the hilt — the villain you loved to hate. And the kids *loved* it! They knew he meant bad things, but that he wouldn't get away with them. On personal appearances they'd boo and say nasty things, but they were laughing through it all — and he was laughing with them.")

Kovacs was born in Youngstown, Ohio, on August 1, 1915, but his Hungarian parents, struggling to save enough money to return to the homeland, sent him to Czechoslovakia to live with relatives when he was five. He grew up there, but to save his U.S. citizenship, he returned to the States before his twenty-first birthday. As a child, he fell in love with the theater and acted in many Hungarian productions, where he crossed paths with Bela Lugosi. But his parents had other plans. At their insistence, he enrolled in a Presbyterian seminary in Ontario, Canada, to become a minister — until one day Lugosi, touring with a play, sent an urgent telegram from the road. An actor was needed. Could Kovacs get there in two days? "I had to make up a really bad lie to get out of ministry school," he laughs. He never went back. After a wartime stint as a translator for U.S. military intelligence, he set out for California to enroll in the Pasadena Playhouse.

Like other cast members, Kovacs has stories to tell of the perils of live TV, and like Kemmer and Osborn, he learned everyone else's lines as well as his own — just in case. If he saw a guest actor go blank, he'd pick up their part, prefacing it with, "As you told me, sir...." He recalls the time the staircase in Baccarratti's castle collapsed as he made a princely entrance and he picked himself up from the wreckage, ad libbing, "What fool is responsible for this?" Yes, he really did slip and say "spaceshit" in an early show, cracking up both Hap and the commander. And once he got hurt pretty bad during a fight scene:

> We had a lot of fights, but we were always hitting in front of the face, never actually hitting each other. And there was this guy — he was a horrible actor to begin with — and he was supposed to punch me. And he did — I mean, *he did*! Blood started running out of my face all over, and Happy started laughing. The director cut away to something else...

Kovacs can barely finish the story, he's laughing so hard.

By 1954, Kovacs' marriage was failing due to his drinking, and when *Space Patrol* ended, he slid into a tailspin, his personal and professional life shattering around him.

Prince Baccarratti waits in the shadows to ambush Major Robertson and Hap. (Photograph by David Sutton, courtesy Dick Darley)

What he wanted more than anything was to remain an actor, but he found himself trapped in a Hollywood typecasting prison as escape-proof as Baccarratti's castle. The intensity with which he'd portrayed the crazed prince was now working against him. "We can't do very much," casting directors told him. "Everyone thinks you're Baccarratti." He'd done a few movies—*Park Row* and, oddly, three films with "desert" in the title[1]—but all he could get with his thick accent, says his son, Tor, was "evil foreigner" roles. So Kovacs

---

[1]*Desert Fox* (1951), *Desert Rats* (1953) and *Desert Sands* (1955). His meatiest film role was as Ottmar Mergenthaler in *Park Row* (1952).

gave up on Hollywood, tossed a few belongings in the car, and drove to New York. "He left California to make a clean start," says second wife Marta Kovacs-Ruiz, who met him in 1957 at Manhattan's famed Chelsea Hotel, a hangout for artists.

He directed *The Detective*, an off–Broadway play that quickly fizzled. Then, in 1956, the Hungarian Revolution broke out and he went to Austria, where he helped survivors in refugee camps get resettled. Back in the States the following year, he tried to resurrect his acting career.[2] "I didn't do too well," he admits, pouring himself another drink. That was fine with his parents, he adds, who never got over the fact that he'd left divinity school to become an actor — even when he won fame on *Space Patrol*.

"What did they think of the evil Prince Baccarratti?" I ask.

"Not much," he says quietly, still feeling the hurt.

A true Renaissance man, Kovacs— artist, sculptor and musician (he'd worked as a café violinist while attending the Playhouse)— landed a job in 1959 teaching art and acting at Manhattan's prestigious Dalton School. He taught for the next 22 years, but finally his alcoholism forced him to quit, and in 1984, he told me he felt alone and forgotten. For a moment, he lets self-pity take over. "I suppose," he says softly, "we're selfish enough to hope for appreciation."[3]

Bela Kovacs, circa 1974. (Courtesy Marta Kovacs-Ruiz)

He brightens when I mention that a remake of *Space Patrol* may be on the horizon.[4] Suddenly, he sets down his drink and, flushed with excitement, rattles off ideas for the producer, working himself into the storyline as an aged version of the prince...

> Maybe Baccarratti has an evil son. And the old man says, "Oh, this stupid boy is doing the same things I did!" I mean, can you imagine Baccarratti admitting how wrong he was and trying to prevent him from doing those things? It would be quite important, not only for the show, but for humanity, right? You could bring him out of someplace where he's been punished and show that even a villain can change as time comes, as he gets older — which I think would be quite influential on kids.

Kovacs grins. He's just come up with a thought that would delight his late parents. "I am going to think of a very odd thing: Maybe Prince Baccarratti became an old man in, what the hell, a ministry or something. And he's living in an old people's home and he's doing nice things. Can you imagine that?"

---

[2]Ken Mayer believed for 20 years that Kovacs had been killed in the Hungarian Revolution. That was the rumor — which is why many actor friends (including Jamie Farr of *M*A*S*H*) were shocked when he showed up years later at a Pasadena Playhouse reunion.

[3]His life had more impact than he knew. When he died a year later, in 1985, hundreds of people — including many former students— attended the funeral, says his son, Tor.

[4]Wade Williams III attempted to remake *Space Patrol* with a new cast, but the product was so bad that he incorporated the footage into another project, *Midnight Movie Massacre* (1988), in which theater-goers watching "Space Patrol" (footage from the failed re-make) are terrorized and eaten by an octopus-like alien monster. After scathing reviews, the film was renamed *Attack from Mars*.

His second wife, Marta, can't. Nearly two decades later, she listens in disbelief as I describe the lucid, razor-sharp Kovacs I met that morning who remembered every nuance of *Space Patrol*. By the time of my visit, she says, his mind was gone. "He'd reached the highest stage of alcoholism. His brain cells were destroyed." In another example of life imitating art (as it seems to have done frequently in the lives of the cast), it turns out that Kovacs, a functioning alcoholic for decades, had finally lost his grip and, by 1984, was acting as crazy and violent as Baccarratti himself. "He was delirious most of the time," says Marta, "and everyone was his enemy. When I'd come home from work, he'd greet me at the door with a kitchen knife behind his back. He was angry that I was working and he couldn't — but one of us had to pay the bills." For protection, she slept in her son's room. "The kids put a lock on the door." The last ten years, she says softly, were "horrendous." But for Marta, a good-hearted woman who has since remarried, time has dulled some of the pain, and she still has fond memories of the passionate artist who swept her off her feet when she was only 19. "Thank you for thinking kindly of him," she writes in a follow-up note to our talk. "He was an extraordinary person who unfortunately never reached his potential."

Had I known that the version of Kovacs sitting just a few feet away from me was a kind of android stand-in for a man who, like Baccarratti, had descended into violence and despair, I might have been scared or distracted. But on that gentle morning, the evil prince was nowhere to be found.

At the close of our visit, the mild-mannered Kovacs leans forward and runs his fingers lightly along a carved coffee table inlaid with wood from distant parts of Planet Earth — Africa, Asia, Australia. "I think I was a very good actor," he says slowly, "but sculpting is more satisfying. Here I do what I want. In acting, so many other people have influence over you." He sits silently for a moment, then: "Do you see this table? This is not veneer; it goes all the way through. You can sand it down, do anything. I will leave these things, and they will last for a long, long time. A table like this will last forever."

CHAPTER 16

The Search for
the Ralston Rocket

Though I didn't realize it until recently, many of my adolescent dreams of wandering about in search of adventure were fueled by that hope of winning the Ralston Rocket.

— Roy Miles

It's an impressive prize, an outlandish prize — but what happens when it dawns on the winner and his friends that it can't move an inch under its own power?

— Lou Huston

SCENE: *Corry's office, dark. A prowler heads for the Commander's safe.*

ANNOUNCER JACK NARZ: (alarmed) *Hey, someone's going through the Commander's papers — and now he's opening the safe! Who is this ominous intruder and what is he searching for in the quarters of the Commander-in-Chief of the Space Patrol?*

Corry enters, surprising… his cadet!

CORRY: *Happy!*
HAP: (sheepishly) *Hello, Commander.*
CORRY: *Opening the safe?*
HAP: *I-I-I'm sorry, Commander, but I heard you tell Major Robertson that the key to the biggest surprise ever told on Space Patrol was in that safe — and I just had to know what it was… and I can't find it!*
CORRY: *Can't you, Happy? Well, maybe I'd better show you. And you, too, Space Patrollers. Believe me, it's an exciting secret, a secret prize — the biggest prize ever given to any boy or girl! And here's the key…* (Pulls a cereal box from the safe and hands it to Hap, who opens the package and pulls out a plastic space coin.)
CORRY: *That coin is the key to the secret prize, Space Patrollers. A gigantic prize that no other boy or girl on Earth has ever owned…*

In early 1951, The Gardner Advertising Company, a powerful agency whose clients included John Deere, Pet Milk and Anheuser-Busch, was searching desperately for an outlet to replace *Tom Mix.* The radio adventure series had been a gold mine for their client, Ralston Purina, whose cereal division had reaped hefty profits from the boxtop toy premiums touted on the show. Now, after a 17-year run that began in 1933, *Mix* had finally bit the dust — but with the new genre of TV space operas bursting onto the scene, Gardner saw a chance to go back to the future and recreate its mail-in marketing success. So in May 1951, they picked up *Space Patrol* for Ralston Purina.[1]

At first, it looked like a match made in heaven, remembers 95-year-old Ralph Hartnagel, Sr., then vice president of sales and promotion at Gardner. The infatuation would wane by 1954, when the agency sensed that they weren't going to get the long-term results they'd had with *Mix* from this upstart TV show. But in 1953, still hopeful that *Space Patrol* could rocket Ralston to the stars, Gardner pulled out all the stops and launched what was billed as the biggest TV promotion ever — the Name the Planet Contest. All you had to do was name Planet X, the mysterious orb ruled by Commander Corry's nemesis, Prince Baccarratti, that had suddenly invaded the solar system. The grand prize was staggering: Buzz Corry's very own battlecruiser, the *Terra IV*.

A year after Gardner picked up the show, Hartnagel, known as a "good idea man," had made advertising history by commissioning a 35-foot rocketship, billed as Corry's own ship, to tour the country promoting Ralston cereals and *Space Patrol*. He got the idea when he saw a huge spaceship set up in the boys' section of Marshall Field's department store in Chicago where kids could watch movies that depicted space flight. Since *Space Patrol* was all about spaceships, he reasoned, why not have Standard Carriage Works in Los Angeles (who built anything for anybody) fashion a mammoth ship that would descend on fairgrounds and market parking lots from coast to coast? Kids and their parents would be allowed onboard when they presented a boxtop from a package of Ralston cereal. It was a mindboggling concept. "Never before had a manufacturer used store parking lots for promotional devices," notes Beatrice Adams in *Let's Not Mince Any Bones*, a history of The Gardner Advertising Company.[2] The promotion proved so successful that Gardner authorized Hartnagel to commission a second Ralston Rocket. Now some execs at Ralston Purina wanted to take Hartnagel's concept one step further. Why not give one of the ships away in a contest to some lucky kid — a prize so outlandish it was sure to draw media attention? The ad men at Gardner liked the idea. When the Name the Planet Contest was announced on September 19, 1953, during *Space Patrol* episode 143, "The Hate Machine of Planet X," kids and their parents were stunned.

It was a dark day for the United Planets when the mysterious Planet X — 5000 times bigger than Earth and orbiting one billion miles beyond Pluto — invaded the solar system from another dimension, thanks to one of Prince Baccarratti's evil inventions that dissolved the space-time barrier.[3] It was Corry who dubbed it "X," but obviously it needed a better name, so he turned to us kids. The announcement that the Commander would give his own sleek ship to the kid who came up with the best name for the planet was too good to be true. That night, children on Earth fell asleep dreaming they had slipped into the pilot's seat of the *Terra IV* to go where no kid had gone before. Roy Miles could hardly contain his excitement:

---

[1]It wasn't long before some *Tom Mix* premiums — toys, guns, rings, membership badges and periscopes — showed up, redesigned and relabeled, as *Space Patrol* gear.

[2]*Let's Not Mince Any Bones* by Beatrice Adams (Racine WI: Western Publishing Company, 1972), courtesy Ralph Hartnagel III. Adams, vice president of ad copy, worked for the Gardner agency for 30 years.

[3]On October 13, 1999, the BBC reported a story about an "object" on the edge of the solar system — 3 trillion miles from Earth — that some media outlets dubbed "Planet X": "A UK astronomer may have discovered a new and bizarre planet orbiting the Sun, 1,000 times further away than the most distant known planet, Pluto. This new body would be 30,000 times more distant from the Sun than the Earth [is].... It may be a planet that was born elsewhere and roamed throughout the galaxy, only to be captured on the outskirts of our Solar System" (*www.bbc.co.uk*).

The Ralston Rocket was a powerful fantasy for me as a young boy, and the thought of having a vehicle that would allow me to live independently, cruising the galaxy, was significant in later years. Though I didn't realize it until recently, many of my adolescent dreams of wandering about in search of adventure were fueled by that hope of winning the Ralston Rocket. Years later, in college, I exchanged the rocket for a fantasy sailboat, putting a navigational chart of the South Pacific on my dormitory wall. Eventually, I built a cruising sailboat and lived that dream. The need for a "space vehicle" which held my tools (toys) for exploration had not been outgrown.

The Planet X saga pit Corry against the diabolical Prince Baccarratti in a brutal battle of wills that spanned 14 weeks. It was the longest continuing storyline ever run on *Space Patrol*, and it featured the kind of intense interaction between Kemmer and Kovacs that gave the show its adult appeal. Things got pretty serious on Planet X. Baccarratti had a castle full of evil devices that he unleashed on the commander, Hap and Major Robertson, and by the time Corry gained the upper hand, his anger had turned to cold fury. These dark episodes, full of emotional and physical abuse by the evil prince, were set against a backdrop of sunny commercials that plopped you right back into the world of kid stuff when things got scary. Just when Baccarratti had taken Corry and Hap prisoner and thrown them into a tesseract chamber (which trapped them in the fourth dimension) or shoved them in front of a firing squad, "Captain" Jack Narz would cut in with a Name the Planet promo. Suddenly a shot of carefree kids at the controls of the Ralston Rocket replaced the jungles and dungeons of Planet X:

> Look, Space Patrollers! That's where you can be sitting almost before you know it — right at the controls of Commander Corry's own rocketship. (Shot of kids playing in the ship's protective shadow.) And there it goes!— a huge silver and scarlet space rocket, transformed into a clubhouse on wheels. Imagine owning a rolling clubhouse 35 feet long — big as an airplane! And along with it, a huge White truck so you and your pals can be taken anywhere you want to go. It's got built-in bunks, lights and cooking equipment — everything you need to live like a real Space Patroller in your own giant rocket clubhouse. Think of camping out in it with your gang. Think of taking this great rocketship on sight-seeing trips and overnight hikes...

Think of the look of horror on your parents' faces should you actually win this huge piece of space junk that would block their driveway forever. Narz was pretty excited now:

> And hey, what's this? Dollar bills falling right out of space? You betcha! The one thousand five hundred dollars you can win as first prize, along with the rocket clubhouse. Golly, I'll bet you never heard of a contest like this...

Seven hundred and fifty Schwinn Varsity bicycles would be awarded as second prizes, plus 250 Autosonic Rifles, Outer Space Helmets, Emergency Kits and Space Patrol Wrist Watches totaling 1,000 third prizes. Of course, if you won the Rocket and the $1,500, you might consider donating the cash to your parents so they could flee to the outer galaxies before the neighbors went ballistic over the mammoth eyesore obstructing their view. "Will you win Buzz Corry's rocket as your own clubhouse?" Narz wanted to know. "It

Opposite, top: **The man who started it all. Ralph Hartnagel, Sr., who conceived of a gigantic rocketship touring the country touting Ralston cereals and *Space Patrol*, relaxes in Colorado in 1964;** *bottom:* **nearly four decades later, he celebrates his 94th birthday with family in 2002. (Courtesy Ralph Hartnagel, III)**

COOKS IN
10 SECONDS

NET WT.
LB. OZ.

Instant
Ralston

**WHOLE WHEAT
CEREAL**
with added Wheat Germ

KIDS ! SURPRISE INSIDE
Space Patrol Interplanetary Coin

BUZZ CORRY
Commander-in-Chief
SPACE PATROL

RALSTON PURINA COMPANY, MANUFACTURER, ST. LOUIS 2, MISSOURI

Commander Corry beams from a package of pasty hot Ralston that contains one of the Interplanetary Space Coins needed to enter the Name the Planet Contest. (From the Bob Burns collection, courtesy S. Mark Young, Steve Duin, and Mike Richardson, authors of *Blast Off! Rockets, Robots, Rayguns and Rarities from the Golden Age of Space Toys*, Dark Horse Books, 2001, Milwaukie, Oregon)

takes just one word to win," he promised, ordering kids to stay tuned until the end of the show when he would reveal how to enter.

It turned out that entering the contest was no spacewalk. The folks at the Gardner agency had devised a diabolical scheme to force you to scarf down tons of "good, hot Ralston" in order to get the Sun Gold, Midnight Blue or Jet Black Interplanetary Space Coins buried at the bottom of cereal boxes. ("I always suspected," cracks announcer Dick Tufeld, who pitched the cereal on the Saturday radio show, "that Ralston Purina later repackaged hot Ralston and labeled it 'Puppy Chow.'") You had to send in six plastic space coins along with your entry blank. That took a lot of eating, but to cut your cereal consumption in half, you could drag your parents to a Weather-Bird shoe store, where they'd give you three Starlight Silver coins plus an album, in case you ever swallowed enough cereal to collect all 36 coins in the set. (Somehow Weather-Bird — possibly repped by Gardner — had jumped on the contest bandwagon alongside Ralston.[4]) If there was no Weather-Bird store in your area, you could write to Buzz Corry, who sent you six Starlight Silver coins (only three could be used for the contest) and a letter ordering you to eat your cereal to obtain the rest of the coins you'd need. If you did get some coins at a Weather-Bird store, you had to go back a second time to get a shoe salesman to "validate" your entry. Gardner quickly dispatched a flyer to store owners describing this brilliant marketing ploy designed to steer business their way:

EXTRA BONUS! KIDS MUST GO TO YOUR STORE *TWICE!*
YOU GET NOT ONE, BUT TWO CHANCES TO SELL!

1. Kids go to your store to get album and 3 coins they need to enter contest.
2. They then collect 3 more coins from Ralston cereal packages.
3. When they have 6 coins, they name the planet on official entry blank in the album.

[4]Ralph Hartnagel believes that Weather-Bird was not a Gardner client.

Official *Space Patrol* Interplanetary Coin Album, contest rules, prizes and entry blank for the Name the Planet Contest, available from Ralston Purina and at Weather-Bird shoe stores. (What do shoes have to do with birds? "The company's advertising campaign featured a bird that stalked around in rain boots," recalls Steve Handzo.) The six-coin album kids needed to enter the Name the Planet Contest detached from the main album. (From the Bob Burns collection, courtesy S. Mark Young, Steve Duin, and Mike Richardson, authors of *Blast Off! Rockets, Robots, Rayguns and Rarities from the Golden Age of Space Toys*, Dark Horse Books, 2001, Milwaukie, Oregon)

4. Then they must return to your store again so you can sign their entry!
5. Kids then mail validated entry to contest headquarters and keep rest of album.

Despite the hassle of collecting the coins, most kids— when you talk to them half a century later — recall they were thrilled by the contest and *knew* that their name for Planet X would win. Jack Narz made it sound so easy: All you needed was "one magic word." Cadet Chuck Lassen reported for duty on the day of the announcement. "I ate Hot Ralston until I choked to get enough space coins to enter. And I researched Latin and Greek names that had meanings relative to the Planet X plots." Lassen finally submitted "Abiel," which means "Father of Strength."

To seven-year-old Jack McKirgan, the contest was "the first challenge I faced as a child." McKirgan was already reading books far above his age level on space travel, rocketry and aeronautics, but he learned about the contest through a comic book:

> One day on the playground, Bobby Seymour offered to trade me a comic book for some "space marbles"— the ones with air bubbles in them that looked like planets suspended in the cosmos. We made the deal in secret because comic books were forbidden in school. When I got home, I started leafing through my newly acquired booty with the enthusiasm of a teenager who had purloined his father's *Playboy* magazine. There, on the inside of the back cover, was a color rendition of the Ralston Rocket! The words "WIN" and "YOURS" stabbed me in the eyes and lodged in my brain with such force that I couldn't sleep that night. I knew that it would be mine!

After all, McKirgan figured, how many kids could force down enough cereal to get the Space Coins *and* think of a great name for Planet X? Probably no more than ten in the entire country. McKirgan doesn't recall his "winning" entry, but he remembers "gleefully chowing down the paste-like Instant Ralston every breakfast for two weeks. Oh, for a bowl of Cheerios! Every day, for months, I checked the mail for the official announcement that I had won."

But he'd underestimated the competition. Thousands of entries poured into the contest command post in Chicago. Then one day he received a communication from "Space Patrol Headquarters"...

> This was it! I couldn't believe my eyes! I ripped open the envelope and began to read the letter that was printed on official Space Patrol stationery. My eyes scanned farther down, only to find a number of silver-colored space coins enclosed. My heart sank as I discovered that my name, while "excellent," had not been chosen the winner. The coins were enclosed to commemorate my participation in the contest and as thanks for being a dedicated Space Patroller. I was furious! Not at Commander Corry or the Space Patrol — I was mad at the kid who won. This interloper into my universe had a lot of gall!

Chuck Lassen received better news...

> The letter said I was being considered for a "major prize" in the contest and that it would be necessary for my parents to sign and return the enclosed parental consent form, which said they would agree to accept any prize I may win. Well, they did sign it, and for three or four weeks I was 98 percent certain that the rocket would soon be parked in my driveway.

Fortunately, Lassen's parents were spared the fate of John and Evelyn Walker, whose ten-year-old son, Ricky, submitted the winning entry — are you ready? — *Caesaria.*

It's Ricky Walker Day in Washington, Illinois, Tuesday, January 12, 1954, as temps plunge to 14 degrees. Reps from Ralston-Purina passed out Mono-View Outer Space Helmets (the latest cereal boxtop premium) to everyone under four feet tall. "Some kids in the band still hate me," says Walker, 50 years later. "They remember how their lips froze to their instruments." (Photograph by Yale Joel, Time Life Pictures/Getty Images)

It was a freezing day in Washington, Illinois (population 4300), on Tuesday, January 12, 1954, when the White truck tractor carrying the eight-ton Ralston Rocket pulled into the center of town.[5] The city fathers had declared it "Ricky Walker Day" and closed the schools. Bundled up in overcoats, the whole town turned out to honor the red-haired, freckled kid who'd won the Name the Planet Contest. Colder than anyone was "Captain Don," the truck driver who delivered the Rocket—in the line of duty, he went without a coat so the crowd could see his red and green Space Patrol uniform.[6] Busy reps from Ralston Purina bustled among the crowd, passing out cardboard space helmets to every kid as a mob of reporters snapped people shivering under the bare trees that lined the town square. A silent newsreel of the event shows the truck driver presenting the Rocket to Ricky; then the camera follows the tractor as it pulls up to the Walkers' modest white

[5]Some news reports list January 8th or 14th as the day of the ceremony, but a poster from 1954 reads: "Our own Ricky won it! Ricky Walker Day, Tuesday, January 12. Presentation at Town Square at 3:15 P.M."
[6]In real life, Don Jacobsmeyer, according to the *Tazewell County Reporter*, January 14, 1954.

frame home and seals off their driveway. It captures the look of panic on Mrs. Walker's face as she stares at the family's new 35-foot possession and Mr. Walker's stunned realization that he will never again get into his garage. Through the ceremony, young Richard Brian Walker looks on, peering through his "official" bubble space helmet, both dazed and ecstatic. Chuck Lassen, brooding at home, was crushed:

> Imagine my disappointment when I received a letter notifying me I had won one of the "second prize" Schwinn bicycles—and imagine my father's great and thankful relief! I don't think he relished the idea of having a 35-foot spaceship, complete with tractor-trailer rig, dumped at our doorstep. I felt great animosity toward Ricky Walker because the name he won with, "Caesaria," was not as good as any of my three well-researched entries—and his parents [eventually] sold the rocket. Had *I* won it, I feel certain I would still be the proud owner today of a carefully maintained and near-mint condition Ralston Rocket.

Tracked down at his Michigan home nearly half a century later, the much-hated Walker (who now goes by "Rick") recalls the night that he and his mom, brother and sister pored over books and maps in their living room, in search of a name for Planet X. Someone called out "Caesaria" and Walker liked it immediately. "It sounded neat, that's all. 'Caesaria' was a town named after Caesar, over in the Mideast," he explains.

Walker, retired now from his job as a telephone switchman, punctuates his sen-

Left: Ricky Walker, age 11, in a class photograph — still space happy a year after he won the Rocket. "I guess the ink line was Mom's way of remembering which one I was," he quips. *Right:* Rick Walker in 2001, retired from his job as a telephone switchman, with wife, Mary. (Both courtesy Rick Walker)

tences with a wry, resonant laugh as he recalls his brush with fame. Coming up with the winning name was the easy part; the killer was jumping through the hoops the Gardner agency had set up to "qualify" your entry. Deadline day, December 1, 1953, found Ricky and his dad on the road, frantically searching for a Weather-Bird shoe store to hustle up some Space Coins and a last-minute entry blank. "We darn near missed the deadline," he recalls. No, he did not enter more than once. In fact (brace yourselves, cadets), Walker was not really an ardent *Space Patrol* fan. "It was just a program I liked," he says. "As far as anything standing out, geez, it really didn't. I have dimmer memories of *Space Patrol* than of *Captain Video*."[7]

I'm talking to Walker on the phone. He's an affable guy with a laid-back midwestern twang. I like him, but the child in me is outraged at what I'm hearing. I really want to believe that the kid who won the Rocket lived and breathed the show, but Walker is not a particularly loyal Space Patroller.

"The show had a huge effect on a lot of people," I tell him, "but it doesn't sound like you were one of them."

"No."

"Do any episodes stick in your mind?"

"No."

"Did the Buzz Corry character mean anything to you?" I ask.

"I don't remember. I guess not outstanding."

You can say this for ex–Cadet Walker: He's honest. He explains that he was more into the technical side of space travel than the characters and dramatic elements of *Space Patrol*. But one thing Walker had in common with Lassen, McKirgan and a zillion other kids: He *knew* he would win the Rocket. And one day, sure enough, a letter arrived from Space Patrol Headquarters. "They said a 'private investigator' was coming to the house — something to do with the contest," he recalls. A rep from The Gardner Advertising Company, who wanted to make sure nothing was seriously wrong with the Walker family, appeared a few days later. "He talked mostly to the folks and a little bit to me," says Rick. Next came a squad of reps from Ralston Purina. One was a company VP who asked young Ricky what he'd do if he won the Rocket. When Walker didn't say anything psychotic, like "Blow up my block," the man said, "Well, you've won first prize."

Our conversation stalls. While it's true that Walker is reaching back nearly five decades to retrieve these memories, they're curiously devoid of emotion. At this point, in my mind, he has two strikes against him: He got the Rocket, and he doesn't seem to care. "I guess I'm not so fanatical about it," he says suddenly, as if reading my thoughts, "because I *won* it. I'm kind of fulfilled."

Good point. I tell him that there are adult "cadets" who still want to know what it felt like to win, and Walker obligingly delves deeper into the past than he'd like and admits that, at first, he didn't believe all this was happening to him "until they came rolling down the road with that thing. I'd have to say that the world was changed for a long, long time afterwards." He recalls "freezing our tails off at the presentation — it was the middle of January, near zero and blowing hard." And though he insists he never got "overly worked up," he admits it was all pretty overwhelming for a ten-year-old boy. He remembers quietly "taking it in, seeing what's coming next." But there was one big disappointment: Though the truck driver who delivered the Rocket was nice enough, young Ricky (though

[7]To Ricky's delight, Captain Video (Al Hodge) borrowed the Ralston Rocket once for an appearance in Peoria.

The Ralston Rocket wows 20th-century Earthlings as it lands in a market parking lot. (From the collection of Bill Hanlon. Used with permission of S. Mark Young, Steve Duin, and Mike Richardson, authors of ***Blast Off! Rockets, Robots, Rayguns and Rarities from the Golden Age of Space Toys***, Dark Horse Books, 2001, Milwaukie, Oregon)

not a huge Buzz Corry fan) felt that Corry himself should have made the presentation. ("Omigod, yes—I *should* have been there," Ed Kemmer responds when told of Walker's disappointment. "A big prize like that—why wasn't I there? They were saving a couple of bucks after all that hype? Someone wasn't thinking.")

The next day, when reality sank in, Rick Walker admits he was one smug kid. "I certainly had a neat toy in the yard to fool around with," he recalls. But the Rocket's interior was not what he'd expected. In the cockpit, instead of controls, was a dining room table flanked by a circular bench. "The Rocket I got was fixed up like a camper," he explains. "It didn't have any space gear at all." Instead, it had eight bunk beds, a kitchen compartment, a pantry with shelves, and a locker in the back. Lights and utilities ran off a generator. There were dishes and silverware, cooking utensils, four axes, four canteens, two sheath knives and a snakebite kit. That was it.

Of course, the Rocket had been touted as a "clubhouse on wheels with camping equipment" in TV spots and on Ralston cereal boxes, but it never occurred to Walker (or to the kids who entered the contest) that it wouldn't have one iota of space gear inside. Walker was disappointed, but despite this oversight by adults who should have known that a kid needs dials, gauges, a viewscope and stardrive to get through the day, Rick says that he and his friends "played in it for some time." But by the following winter, the play had tapered off "and the thing was still in the driveway. We fooled with it some, but it wasn't like when I first got it."

Contrary to rumor, Mr. and Mrs. Walker did not sell the Rocket shortly after their son won it, but loaned it to an amusement park when they saw his interest wane. The park returned the ship a few months later with some interesting changes. They'd replaced two of the bunk beds with hokey space gear — a gun cabinet with two space rifles and a pistol, a noisemaker that was supposed to be an "atomic cannon," and a cheap views-cope with a picture of the moon in it. Gone was the table in the nose of the ship; in its place was a reclining swivel chair and a control stick. These improvements sparked excitement in Ricky's crowd and they played in the ship again — for how long, he can't say. Sifting through these memories is like stumbling through Venus fog. He knows that he received the prize in January 1954 and kept it until sometime in 1956.

"Was it hard to let go of it?" I ask.

"I can't remember any sadness or regret. By the time it got sold, it was like the old toy at the bottom of the chest. I'd gone beyond it to other things." His parents, seeing their son move on to girls and cars, sold the Rocket for $1,000 to an amusement park in Wichita, Kansas.[8] Ricky went along when his dad, a refrigeration truck driver, delivered it to the park, several hundred miles from their home. Not really interested in the Rocket's fate, he lost track of it after that. The last he heard, it was owned by "a private individual in Illinois."

I remind Walker that he lived out the fantasy of millions of space-happy "juves," some who still hate his guts. Winning the Rocket *had* to have changed his life ... right?

Walker sighs. "I'm sure it had effects that I'm not aware of," he offers.

"But wasn't it a fantastic dream come true?"

"It was!" he says, finally showing some emotion. "All of a sudden, you're in a different world and things don't seem the same." The media swarmed over the kid who'd won the Rocket, and his photo appeared in newspapers and magazines as far away as England. A few TV appearances followed, including Dave Garroway's popular morning show out of Chicago. Garroway gave him a television set, a huge Hallicrafter table model. It was the first set the Walker family had ever owned — Ricky had always watched *Space Patrol* at a neighbor's. But winning the Rocket did not give Ricky Walker a perfect life or even make him a better kid. He still got chosen last for the baseball team, he was still a Catholic (which some kids in town didn't like), and he admits to using his newfound celebrity to lord it over his pals. "I probably did figure I was something special because I had this rocketship. Nobody else had one. It was like, 'You're gonna play my way, 'cause I'm the kid who has the football.' But after a while, the other kids lost interest and it wasn't my football any more, you know what I mean?" At that point, says Walker, "like a movie star who ends up making soap commercials, I drifted into obscurity."

Somehow, Jack McKirgan missed the announcement that Walker had won the contest:

> It would be 40 years before I knew who won the ship. By then, my hatred for that kid had receded into a pool of low-level envy. The priorities in my life had changed. Yet, as I matured and came to realize the mortality of man and his inventions, the spirit of *Space Patrol* was rekindled in me as strong as ever. When I finally discovered that young Master Walker had won the Ralston Rocket, I was aghast to learn that he had sold it!

In the late '80s, it was rumored that Ricky's Rocket had been dismantled and sold for scrap metal, and credible evidence suggests that this is true. With that news, sadness

---

[8]*The Best of Starlog, Vol. II* (1981) reported this figure, though Walker can't confirm it.

swept through the space opera community. To these ex-kids, the Ralston Rocket — "the biggest prize ever offered any boy or girl" — was more than a dinosaur from the '50s. It was a piece of *Space Patrol* that had come to life, straight from the 30th century to a market parking lot in their town. But while Ricky's Rocket is space dust, the fate of the second rocket commissioned by the Gardner agency is still a mystery. To track it down, it's necessary to review a few significant events in 20th-century history.

The first of the two Ralston Rockets that ad man Ralph Hartnagel ordered landed on Earth in the winter of 1952 — a year and a half before the Name the Planet Contest was announced. The Rocket was unveiled on February 16 at a ceremony that drew nearly 10,000 people — including press, supermarket owners and reps from scientific and civic organizations — to the parking lot of ABC Television Center in Hollywood. A newsreel of that day shows a row of self-conscious dignitaries seated on a platform beneath a huge *Space Patrol* banner, staring out at the crowd of eager adults and kids, many in scouting and campfire uniforms. Popular radio and TV personality Al Jarvis introduced the guests of honor, who ranged from the television chairman of the local PTA (boos) to a PR guy from the Civil Air Patrol (big applause). Also present was Major Alexander de Seversky, an Air Force test pilot who had authored the wartime bestseller *Victory through Air Power*. In imperfect but poetic English, de Seversky captured the spirit of the day with a prophetic message:

> Kids understand me better than the men of my own generation because they have nothing to unlearn. They are not earthbound — they were born with wings. My generation provided pioneers in flying, but the new generation will guarantee us freedom of air navigation, which guarantees us all the freedoms and protection from all the dangers.

Finally Jarvis announced the arrival of "what you've been waiting for" and the crowd went wild as the *Space Patrol* cast bounded out of the Rocket, flashing official salutes as they dashed to the podium. A hush fell over the audience as Commander Buzz Corry stepped forward to deliver a proclamation to the children of Earth:

> It is hereby acknowledged that the children, the young boys and girls of today, will be the engineers and scientists of the future. In the interest of science, and in honor of the wonderful imaginations of the young at heart, the Commander-in-Chief of the Space Patrollers is hereby authorized to award to the children of the mother planet Earth for their own special enjoyment, the Ralston Rocket *Terra IV*, Commander Corry's own Space Patrol battlecruiser. As Commander-in-Chief of the Space Patrol, as authorized by the Secretary General, I hereby declare the Space Patrol battlecruiser, Ralston Rocket *Terra IV*, the property of the children of Earth and delegate Lieutenant Tessloff, our recruiting officer, to tour America with it so that all the children may visit it and see it.

"We've got 5,000 youngsters as happy and anxious as a bumblebee on the first day of spring," Jack Narz told the crowd. Then he ran through a checklist of raw materials ("Over 5,000 rivets, 5,000 screws, 25 gallons of paint and 50 sheets of 20-gauge steel") that had been used in the ship's construction, as the camera panned to a mob of kids and adults storming the landlocked metal hulk. This was the first and last time the cast appeared with the Rocket. Ed Kemmer notes that, contrary to what many kids believed, he and the other actors never traveled with the ship. "I can't remember an instance where we went where the damn thing was," he recalls.

Above: Commander Corry and Cadet Happy emerge from the first Ralston Rocket before 10,000 cheering Earthlings who gathered at ABC Television Center in Hollywood on February 16, 1952, to see the ship unveiled. (Author's collection)

Right: A postcard sent via "Rocket Mail" by Buzz Corry himself, inviting Space Patrollers to the Rocket ceremony.

Dear Space Patroller,

On February 16, 1952, we are going to land Terra IV, our "Space Patrol" Flagship, at the American Broadcasting Company's Television Studios, Prospect and Talmadge, Hollywood, California.

Since you have always upheld the code of the United Planets, I hereby invite you to be a guest of "Space Patrol" at 3 o'clock, February 16, 1952.

Terra IV and all the "Space Patrol" gang will be on hand to greet you.

Yours for Inter-Planetary Justice,

Buzz Corry

COMMANDER-IN-CHIEF • SPACE PATROL

The first Rocket was so successful touring parks, fairgrounds and store parking lots in the western states that a second ship was built to cover the eastern part of the country, recounts Beatrice Adams in her history of the Gardner agency. Both ships were 35 feet long, 8 wide and 12 high, mounted on truck trailers, and built by Standard Carriage Works of Los Angeles at a cost of $35,000 each, though columnist Barney Glazer set the price tag slightly higher. "*Space Patrol* has two rocket ships on the road which cost $40,000 apiece to build," he announced in January 1953, to the chagrin of the folks at Gardner.[9] The cat was out of the bag. That there were *two* ships was a secret closely guarded by Gardner's creative committee, whose ad copy referred to "the" Ralston Rocket. After all, it was Corry's own battlecruiser and to admit there were two would make it appear less unique. Often, at the end of the show, Jack Narz announced the Rocket's itinerary, and you held your breath because it might come to your town next.

Both touring ships were outfitted with space gear that delighted the juves who clambered aboard, but in the fall of 1953, the Gardner execs, in their wisdom, had the ship that was to become the grand prize in the contest stripped of its space gear and converted into a camper. Poor Ricky Walker. His Rocket was sissified and lacked the fabulous array of stuff it had once contained. According to a "top secret" memo (which somehow found its way into *TV Guide*), both touring Rockets sported an intercom system; munitions and weapons case full of "secret equipment"; porthole through which you could "see" Terra City (viewed from millions of DU's away); viewscope to track planets and stars flashing past; food locker stocked with Wheat Chex, Rice Chex and Instant Ralston; mass reaction generator for controlling atom-powered rocket engines; reaction generator control panel with 180 colored lights; astrogation and communication center equipped with Commun-l-Vision (displayed geographic scenes for navigation); a radarscope (space radar); and a Code-o-Graph to decode secret messages "by light and sound."

Eric Hogling got to see all this gear up close and live out a space-age fantasy when the rocket landed in a market parking lot in his town:

> I climbed aboard in absolute awe. There was a realistic pilot's control panel and a display of ray guns in a glass case. I suppose kids have more sophisticated entertainment today, but for the '50s, this was big time! Back then, TV was a new and strange medium. No one took it for granted. Through television, the heroes of *Space Patrol* could enter your living room and, through your imagination, your life. As a child of eight or nine, I would act out these roles with friends at playtime, so as I climbed aboard the *Terra IV* as it balanced precariously on the back of that truck, I *was* Buzz Corry, and for a brief moment the fantasy became a reality.

When Paul Subbie was seven years old, the Rocket landed in West Los Angeles. For the admission price of a Ralston cereal boxtop, Subbie climbed aboard and, "having been raised in the flight path of Santa Monica's Clover Field," even at that young age recognized the instrument panel as a slightly altered Douglas Aircraft design:

> Inside it was dark and lit with all manner of space-like instruments. What was most memorable, though, was the large table supporting the miniature city under glass, just the same as on the opening of the TV show. It was lit and had vehicles moving on roads as well as a glass tube above the city within which ran a monorail — very nicely done.

---

[9]"Televents" column (syndicated), *San Gabriel Valley Independent*. There's no date on the tearsheet, but it's grouped with clippings from January 1953 in Virginia Hewitt's files.

Today Captain Subbie, a former military and commercial pilot, identifies the rocket's shell as patterned after either the front fuselage of a DC-3 or its military counterpart, the C-47.

Norm Knights boarded the Rocket one summer day in the parking lot of Walgreen's drug store in Riverview, Illinois. "We were given just five minutes to look around," he recalls. "The cockpit had throttles, knobs and switches with a partial center console. It was heaven for a kid, with all those dials and gadgets."

Judd Lawson didn't even get five minutes. By the time Lawson, then 12, had figured out the Cleveland bus system enough to get to the corner of Detroit Avenue and 140th Street, there were several hundred kids ahead of him, waiting in line with their parents to board the Rocket on a summer day in August 1953. As he stood there clutching his Rice Chex admission boxtop, it seemed like forever until he was herded through the rear door at last, slowly inching his way to the front to worship at the shrine of the control panel. But when he got there, all did not go as planned:

> It's finally my turn. I sit down at the controls—and I'm there ten seconds and this guy dressed in a Buzz Corry uniform says, "OK!" And I said, "That's it?" And it was like, "Wait a minute—I haven't even killed a Martian yet." But he gives me the boot, like in *Christmas Story*, and I'm outta there. Geez, ten seconds wasn't enough. I mean, all you want to do is pretend for a minute, you know?

Lawson knew he had to get back on.

> I went into the grocery store, bought a box of Rice Chex for 19 cents, ripped the top off, threw the rest of the crap in the garbage can, got back in line and waited another hour. The second time, I hung on for about 30 seconds—white-knuckled and everything—until the guy made me go. But by that time, it was late in the day and I had my paper route to worry about, so I had to get out of there.

The Rockets crisscrossed the country from the winter of 1952 until September 1953, showing up in cities thousands of miles apart. The ad men still fostered the notion of a single Rocket, but unless you'd been drinking jet juice, you'd find that hard to believe. Take the touring schedule for August 1953: "The" Rocket hits New York, Pennsylvania and Ohio, swings back up to New York, over to the state of Washington, down to Texas, east to Virginia and west to Oregon. "It would take two ships to meet that crazy schedule," points out Jack McKirgan. "Besides being a logistical nightmare, the truck crews would have violated every commercial driving-time law on the books—and remember, this was before the Interstate Highway System."

Through the years, Galaxy Patrol fan club president Dale Ames and others called Ralston Purina to ask if the company had kept track of the Rockets and if anyone knew their fate, but it was like talking to Arcturians without a translator box; no one at the company knew what they were talking about or why they cared. Then, in January 1989, a story appeared in *Boxtop Bonanza* magazine that shed some light on the mystery. It tracked Ricky Walker's Rocket to the amusement park where his father had left it and reported that a Chevrolet dealer in Quincy, Illinois, bought the ship from the park. He stored the Rocket in a wrecking yard—and that's where Harry and Eleanor Nolin spotted it and decided it would make a great space museum. Their timing couldn't have been

Last photograph of Ricky Walker's Rocket in front of a construction company in Ghent, New York, 1985. Shortly after Dale Ames snapped this shot, the Rocket was destroyed. (Courtesy Dale Ames)

better. The day after the Nolins rescued the Rocket, severe flooding hit the area and the yard disappeared under 22 feet of water.

According to the article, the Nolins refurbished the ship but abandoned their dream of a museum and sold it to a cable TV company on the East Coast. That dovetailed with what I'd heard in 1985 from an engineer at USA Cable Network, which at that time was airing *Space Patrol* as a midnight fill-in. He said that a senior vice president of the company owned the Rocket and that the network had planned to use it in a made-for-TV sci-fi film, but had abandoned the project. Dale Ames learned that two fans had contacted the executive repeatedly, offering to buy and restore the ship, but he never returned their calls. Later that year, *Starlog* magazine launched a nationwide search for Ricky Walker's Rocket and reported that it had been sold (presumably by the USA Network exec) to a construction company in Ghent, New York. Ames rushed to the scene, where he found the Rocket, gutted and rusted, on the company's front lawn.[10] As he snapped photos of the once-sleek battlecruiser, a childhood dream now neglected and dying, his heart sank.

---

[10]The Rocket Ames found had blue trim, while the trim on Ricky's had been red. So was it really Ricky's Rocket — and not the *other* Ralston Rocket? Yes. The Ghent Rocket had no windows, like Ricky's. The other Rocket, still at large, kept its windows and showed up, eventually, windows intact. Someone had repainted Ricky's Rocket blue between the time his parents sold it and its destruction.

"I had the feeling of finding an old friend who needed help," says Ames, "and I couldn't do anything. I found it hard to drive home and leave this treasure behind."

Ames took his photos in the nick of time. A few months later, a construction worker stuck his foot through the rusted-out hull, and "for safety reasons" the company dismantled the ship and sold it for scrap salvage. "After all these years of searching, we lose a wonderful treasure," says Ames. "If only they had been aware of its history."[11]

It's tough to accept that a ship you love has been destroyed, but in *Space Patrol* episode 149 — which ran at the height of the Name the Planet Contest — Buzz Corry dealt with the same situation: the loss of his beloved *Terra V*. It happened when he and Hap cornered Prince Baccarratti in his fortress on Planet X but were overpowered by the castle guards.[12] After shoving the Commander and his cadet into the Tesseract Chamber — a diabolical device that will trap them in the fourth dimension forever — Baccarratti can't resist the chance to taunt Corry one last time:

> PRINCE B: *All right, Corry, you asked for it... I'm going to let you remain in contact with the third dimension. You can't say or do anything, but I want you to see everything that I do. I want you to see how I'll destroy your beloved spaceship,* Terra V — *how I'll blow it up!*

> While Buzz and Hap watch helplessly, one of Baccarratti's henchmen plants dynamite inside the battlecruiser.

> HAP: *Commander, your ship! He's really going to do it — he's going to blow up* Terra V!
> CORRY: *Would you rather not watch, Hap?*
> HAP: *I don't know, sir. It's such an awful feeling, not being able to do anything about it.*
> CORRY: *Don't let it get you down, Hap. This is exactly what Baccarratti wanted.*
> HAP: (tries to suppress feelings) *Who cares? Doesn't bother me. We wouldn't be able to use* Terra V *in the fourth dimension anyway...* (Sound of explosion as the ship blows up.) *Commander, he really did it! He blew up* Terra V!
> CORRY: (stoically) *Yes, Happy.* Terra V *is no more.*

But not all things are as they appear. Corry, thinking fast, as usual, found a way to travel back in time to before the explosion occurred and undo Baccarratti's mischief — though for a while, it *seemed* as if the *Terra V* had been destroyed. Likewise, when the news spread on Earth that Ricky Walker's Rocket had hit the scrap heap, it seemed to many ex-kids that a childhood dream was gone forever. Not true. Decades later, the secret the ad guys had carefully guarded — that there were *two* Rockets — came to light. And that's why it's possible that the second Rocket still exists in some forgotten hangar or warehouse; in fact, for a while it looked as if it had been found in the desert near Prescott, Arizona. For a brief period, hopes ran high that perhaps an important piece of space opera history — and many childhood memories — had survived.

In the early '60s, policeman Charles Chamberlin, walking the midnight beat in a suburb of St. Louis, Missouri, came across what looked like the Ralston Rocket on the front lawn of Riverview Senior High School. He could hardly believe his eyes:

> It was a real rocket! A couple of times, I went inside. It had started to deteriorate, but it was still a great memory — metal, with some TV screens and seats inside. It lay on its side, slightly angled upward as if poised for take off. It was very cool.

[11]In the mid-'80s, Ames set up the Galaxy Patrol fan club to honor space opera and its heroes. Contact Dale Ames, 144 Russell Street, Worcester MA 01609. E-mail: gpspace@msn.com.
[12]"The Tesseract Prison of Planet X," Episode 149, October 31, 1953.

Then suddenly one day the metal hulk was gone, taking with it a piece of his childhood. "I knew it was a contest prize that obviously the recipient's parents didn't know where to store," says Chamberlin, "but the Rocket was Buzz Corry's!" Just looking at it brought back a childhood fantasy: "If I was lucky, I might get to see Tonga climb up that ladder!!"

Chamberlin moved from St. Louis to become chief of police in a suburb of Chicago. Then one day, a friend casually mentioned that the Rocket had reappeared on the grounds of a hospital outside St. Louis. Chamberlin fired off a note to the hospital's administrator, who wrote back that the Rocket had been "dismantled into many pieces and junked from our facility." He added that when an official from the Missouri Department of Mental Health had inspected the hospital, he'd asked if the ship (which he mistook for a missile) was "pointed toward my office." It was the mid–'60s, when missiles with warheads and where they were aimed were on everyone's mind.

It was the first of many false sightings. Chamberlin, it turns out, had stumbled upon the Kraft Aerojet Training Space Ship, just one in a fleet of copycat rockets deployed by envious ad agencies in the wake of Gardner's successful Name the Planet promotion. Photos taken by officer Chamberlin clearly show the same ship pictured in an ad Kraft ran in 1959 to announce its Name the Rocket contest. (At least kids who entered *that* contest got to eat marshmallows instead of cereal.) Jack McKirgan, then 13, saw the Kraft contest as a second chance to compete for the glorious prize he'd lost to Ricky Walker when he was seven, but it was a tough sell to his parents. "I had a difficult time convincing my mother that 'just one more bag' of marshmallows was a necessary staple in the cupboard," he recalls.[13]

As the 20th century drew to a close, it seemed as if Earthlings were spotting rockets everywhere — at carnivals and grand openings, in shopping malls and junkyards.

One overcast afternoon in the summer of 1981, Doug Souter was driving down a country road in western Michigan when a flash of lightning lit up the hull of a rocketship silhouetted against the turbulent sky. "I made an anti-terrorist U-turn," he recalls; then he doubled back and searched desperately for the owners of the farm where the rocket had come to rest. "If I'd seen the 'Rocky Jones Space Ranger' logo on the other side of the ship," says Souter, "I would have pitched a tent on the property until they came back." Souter loves rocketships. "When I watched *Space Patrol, Tom Corbett* and *Rocky Jones*, I didn't see myself as one of the heroes, but as the guy who invented and built the rockets." In junior high, he built a five-stage rocket that zoomed 30 feet into the air before all the stages ignited at once and splattered all over the football field. When he heard that Ricky Walker's Rocket had been destroyed, he says, "I was crushed."

The ship he'd spotted turned out to be the Silvercup Bread Rocket, part of an advertising promotion once linked to *Rocky Jones*. The owner of the land (who Souter tracked down 19 years later) had hoped to restore it, but "never got around to it." For over two decades, the ship had been rusting out in a junk pile. Ironically, Rick Walker, who lives in the area, had spotted it, too, but knew it was not "his" Rocket. "It was neat to see it," he admits, owning up to some sentiment. "It would be nice to think that my rocket's still around, too."

In 1989, physicist Rory Coker was driving down a highway in Austin, Texas, when he saw a silvery rocketship from afar, mounted on a truck bed in the parking lot of a strip mall. For a moment, his heart leapt, thinking it might be Buzz Corry's ship, but he

---

[13]What do marshmallows have to do with spaceships? Ed Pippin, who hosts the Solar Guard Web page (*www.solarguard.com*), notes that Kraft Marshmallows had once sponsored *Tom Corbett, Space Cadet*, though the contest was not run in connection with *Corbett*.

couldn't stop because he was on his way to a meeting. When he came back later, the ship was gone. What Coker saw was probably one of the trailer-mounted Astro-Liners, built in the late '70s by Wisdom Manufacturing. The ships were popular carnival rides that bounced and swayed as wannabe space jockeys watched films depicting space flight and *Star Wars*–type battles. "About a hundred were built," says John Davis, who produced the films shown onboard. Davis, as a kid, had spent "nights lying awake picturing the Ralston Rocket in my backyard," so working on the Astro-Liner project was like fulfilling a childhood dream.

In the mid-'90s, access to cyberspace intensified the search for the missing Rocket. Now a fast-growing network of former "cadets" could pool information. Ed Pippin set up a Rocket forum on his Solar Guard Web page, and reports of sightings and theories about the fate of the Ralston Rocket poured in. It was a search-and-rescue mission whose target was a childhood memory.

In the fall of 2002, Doug Souter came across a photo of the Blakely Oil Rocket posted on Pippin's site by Bob Eisenhauer, who had visited it as a child. The ship, a tie-in with the company's brief sponsorship of *Rocky Jones, Space Ranger* in the mid–'50s, had toured Blakely-owned gas stations in Arizona and California, promoting "Rocket Gas" and entertaining customers with a movie about space flight. According to *In Advance of the Landing*, by Doug Curran, Blakely acquired the rocket in 1954.[14] Now who do you know who might have had a spare Rocket to unload in '54, right after "the" Ralston Rocket was awarded to Ricky Walker, hmmm? Souter laid Eisenhauer's photo of the Blakely Rocket next to one of the Ralston. The two ships were identical.

"It's clearly the 'other' Ralston Rocket," confirms film historian Steve Handzo, who spotted the similarity as soon as he saw Eisenhauer's photo. "It has the rectangular windows and tapered fin, and it looks just like the photo of the Rocket on a poster that announced 'Ricky Walker Day' when Ricky was awarded the prize."[15]

So where is the second Ralston (Blakely) Rocket today?

What happened to the ship after its tour of duty for Blakely is unclear. Prescott, Arizona, entrepreneur Rodney Welch told author Curran that he bought a rocketship for his theme park, Welch's Mountain Fantasy, from the Luer meatpacking company and that this rocket had previously been owned by Blakely Oil.[16] In 1955, Luer, a small company based in east Los Angeles, had attempted to link the Davy Crockett craze with the thing it helped kill—space opera—by launching a "Davey Rocket" promotion. ("Davey" was a comic-strip kid who took off on space-age adventures with his sidekick, "Frankie," a hot dog wearing a space helmet.)[17] So did Blakely sell its Ralston Rocket to Luer? Maybe.

---

[14]*In Advance of the Landing*, by Douglas Curran, a work that takes a non-judgmental look at the fringe element of the UFO crowd. Originally published in 1985 and reissued (updated) by Abbeville Press Publishers in 2001.

[15]Handzo notes that the photo on the Ricky Walker Day poster was an old promotional photo snapped *before* one of the Rockets was modified (side windows removed, top fin straightened, side fins eliminated, exhaust area blended into the fuselage) to become the Name the Planet grand prize. Some of these changes were functional, to make the vehicle into a camper; others, like the straightened fin, may have been an attempt to make the ship look more like Buzz Corry's. At any rate, the photo of the Ralston Rocket on the poster was taken at the same angle as Eisenhauer's shot of the Blakely and clearly shows the resemblance between the two ships.

[16]Curran's book falsely identifies the Blakely Rocket as being built for the film *Tobor the Great*. But "there is nothing in that movie that remotely resembles either the Blakely or [Welch's] rocket," says Steve Handzo. Curran also mistakenly identifies Rodney Welch as Ray.

[17]Though Curran does not state the name of the meatpacking company, the Luer logo can be seen in the photo of Welch's rocket (if you use your Space Binoculars).

The Luer/Prescott Rocket, docked on a hill behind the Coca-Cola plant in Prescott, Arizona. Under its streamlined façade, is it the missing Ralston Rocket? Someone better decide fast — before it's picked up with the trash. (Courtesy Herb Deeks)

Just one problem: At first glance, the Luer Rocket doesn't look much like the Ralston-Blakely — but it *does* look a lot like the *Terra IV*. In fact, it looks more like Buzz Corry's ship than the Ralston Rocket ever did. For a while, there seemed to be strong circumstantial evidence that the Luer Rocket in Prescott was the missing Ralston Rocket — but *if* Blakely sold its Ralston Rocket to Luer, then Luer had drastically altered its appearance, copying the *Terra IV* (for some reason we'll never know) by "re-skinning" the hull.

"Not likely," said Doug Souter, who works for a sheet metal component manufacturer. "I have some insight as to costs for this type of project, and it would be expensive." But legendary "Imagineer" Bob Gurr, who designed such Disneyland fixtures as the Matterhorn, Monorail and Autopia cars, disagrees. "It's not all that hard or expensive to re-skin a rocket," he explains. "You torch off the upper structure, put some sheet covering on the frame and pop-rivet or weld it into place."

Rodney Welch had big plans for the rocket he'd bought from Luer. He forked out $15,000 for a space flight movie you could watch inside while green-painted midgets

Opposite, top: Young Bob Eisenhauer surveys Earth from the Blakely Oil Rocket circa 1954–55. "My feelings about that rocket were, 'How can I get my folks to buy it from Blakely?'" he says. (Courtesy Bob Eisenhauer) *Bottom:* "Our own Ricky won it" sign displayed by a local merchant in Washington, Illinois. When Steve Handzo and Doug Souter compared this poster with Bob Eisenhauer's photograph of the Blakely Rocket, they knew the two ships were one and the same. (Courtesy Ed Pippin) dressed as space aliens served as hosts and ushers. When that didn't work out, he donated the rocket to the city of Prescott in 1983; they promptly unloaded it on the local rehab center. And that's where video producer Steve La Vigne found the once-grand ship a year later, rusting out in a field with a rattlesnake curled up in the back. He'd never seen *Space Patrol*, but he liked rockets. He bought it from the rehab folks for $100.

So, is the missing Ralston Rocket docked in Prescott, Arizona? Steve Handzo couldn't stop thinking about that possibility — especially since the ship resembles the *Terra IV*. "The Luer Rocket appears to be built by someone who had access to the design history of the *Space Patrol* ships," he notes, "and it's a professional job, not some backyard conversion nailed together over a weekend." He estimated the dimensions of the Luer and Ralston-Blakely Rockets, made rough scale drawings and overlaid them. They matched up pretty well, except for the elongated, pointed nose on the Luer, leading him to suspect that the Ralston-Blakely had, in fact, been re-skinned. Handzo figured that there could be only a few shops in the Los Angeles area capable of executing such a thing. Intrigued, he dug into the history of Luer Packing and unearthed an interesting fact: Remember Standard Carriage Works, the outfit that built the two Ralston Rockets? The Luer Packing Company was located on East Vernon Boulevard — *1200 feet away from Standard Carriage.*

Bob Gurr remembers Standard Carriage Works well. Unfortunately, the company was located in the meatpacking part of town, next to an animal rendering plant. "I never saw so many flies in my life," he recalls. But that didn't stop him and other Hollywood types from using the company's services. "They'd build anything for anyone. You'd walk in there with either a rough or final design and they'd give you a bid." While Gurr never saw the space opera rockets, he thinks that if Luer had wanted to re-skin the Ralston-Blakely, it would have been no big deal for their good neighbor, Standard Carriage.

Handzo made a timeline. He tracked down Carolyn Fuller, whose father owned Blakely Oil, based in Phoenix. She checked old scrapbooks. The last mention of the Blakely Rocket was in 1955; after that, it vanished. The earliest known photo of the Luer Rocket, taken in Sunland, California, shows it hitched to a 1956 Ford cab-over truck tractor, which would have gone on sale in late 1955 — about the time the Blakely (formerly Ralston) Rocket dropped out of sight. Both Rockets seemed to have existed within the same geographical space — Southern California and Central Arizona — but at different times.

Doug Souter began to think that maybe Handzo was on to something, but he was still skeptical. Comparing photos of the two rockets, by his scale calculations, the diameters were different. If that was true, it was unlikely that Luer had put a new skin over the old Ralston-Blakely framework. Besides, the front doors were not in the same place, and on the Luer rocket both front and rear doors were part of the trailer — not so on the Ralston-Blakely. But Handzo insisted that his scale calculations showed the diameters to be roughly the same. Besides, if the rocket had been re-skinned, the features — doors and fins — could easily have been repositioned.

Steve La Vigne wanted to believe Handzo was right, that his Luer Rocket was the missing Ralston-Blakely — but he sided with Souter. "The Ralston Rocket was bolted onto a regular flatbed trailer, while my rocket is integrated onto a low-boy semi-trailer chassis," he pointed out.

"The lower part of the Ralston appears to be integrated into its trailer, too," Handzo responded. And wouldn't it make sense, he added, for a small company like Luer to re-skin a rocket rather than build a new one from scratch at the huge cost of $35,000 — a stellar sum in the 1950s? "They'd save on the cost of design work and fabricating the inner structure."

Herb Deeks, an expert model maker who specializes in reproductions of space opera rocketships, agreed. He visited La Vigne's Prescott Rocket, took photos, and compared them with publicity shots of the Ralston-Blakely. "It's been re-skinned and re-skirted, too," he said.[18] "They flared the rocket into the trailer." His conclusion? "I think it's the Ralston Rocket — re-skinned."[19]

The re-skinning theory grew even more plausible when Jerry Cook noted that the interiors of the two ships were strikingly similar. Cook should know. He grew up in St. Louis about a mile from Ralston Purina's headquarters and played in the ship as a boy. "When it wasn't touring, they kept it right in the parking lot," he recalls. I'd ride my bike over, just raise the door and go in and have fun." (Young Cook was sure that Tom Mix and Buzz Corry lived inside the Ralston building.) Years later, he toured the rocket that Rodney Welch had purchased from Luer. "It was very similar inside to the Ralston," he confirmed.

But Souter was still not convinced. While he conceded that Handzo's timeline was compelling, "I still think the Ralston-Blakely Rocket was destroyed or is stored in some long-forgotten shed or country junkyard," he said. "Since there are no witnesses who can state what happened to the ship, I must take Carl Sagan's approach: 'I would like to believe, but there is no smoking gun.'"

And that's how it stood at the turn of the 21st century — until John Garrity showed up.

The case for the Ralston-Blakely lurking beneath a re-skinned Luer had been gaining momentum until the "witness" Souter had hoped for appeared. Garrity swears on Saturn's rings that he and his wife, Sandy, sighted the Ralston-Blakely Rocket in 1966 in the parking lot of Stovall's Inn of Tomorrow (now Space Age Lodge) in Anaheim, California. Garrity knew this rocket: He'd boarded the ship in awe at the age of nine, in the mid–'50s, at the Arizona State Fair. Dubbed "Flagship Arizona" back then by Blakely Oil, it still housed some *Space Patrol* artifacts, notably the model of Terra City — complete with miniature cars that moved — and a display case full of colorful, space-age weapons. Now, here was that childhood fantasy a decade later, looking old and weathered, docked next to Disneyland in the parking lot of an Orange County motel. Garrity and his wife moved in for a closer look:

> Sandy and I reached up and opened the rear hatch and got a brief look inside before a motel guard ran us off. The interior was full of trash — old rags, papers, cleaning materials — but it was the same as what I remembered from the Arizona State Fair! It was in poor shape, but not wrecked.

Bill O'Connell, a partner in the Stovall corporation, confirms that the company acquired the Blakely Rocket around 1966 for its motel with a space-age theme located a stone's throw from Disney's "Tomorrowland":

---

[18]Some researchers might argue Deeks's conclusion about the doors, which, in some photos, appear to be positioned differently in the two ships. But Deeks made his observations on the spot.

[19]Deeks offers a model kit called "Supermarket Rocket" which, he says carefully (in case anyone claims to still own the name), "looks a lot like" the Ralston Rocket.

When we bought it, it was in disrepair, so we used plywood and paint to fix it up. We set it up in the pool area, and it was a nice place for kids to play. We had pedals and controls—we made it look like a rocket inside. Then one day a kid fell and got hurt. It wasn't serious, but we decided it was risky to keep it.

O'Connell remembers that the motel chain donated the Rocket to "a Calvary Church."

"What church?" I ask.

"We have no idea. The pastor said he was going to use it for the kids to have Bible study." O'Connell wracks his brain to remember the name of the church, but draws a blank. He'll talk to his partner, Jim Stovall. "If we think of it, we'll let you know," he says politely.

I share this bombshell with Handzo and Deeks. We contact churches, historical societies. Handzo, tenacious researcher grasping at straws, tracks down the largest Calvary Church in Orange County, a guy who's written books about Southern California, a photographer who snapped shots of the Stovall Inn back in the 1950s. All dead ends. What's still bothering me is that Rodney Welch told author Doug Curran that his Luer Rocket had once been the Blakely. Why did he say that?

In the end, Handzo concedes defeat:

Any bona fide sighting of the Blakely Rocket after 1956—the year of that photo showing the Luer rocket hitched to the '56 Ford truck—blows the re-skinning theory. But the Luer is probably a close relative of the Ralston, most likely built by Standard Carriage Works from the same plans. You'd have all the dimensions—and we're talking about the '50s, before calculators and computers. Back then, everything had to be drawn by hand, so if the dimensions were already worked out, you were way ahead of the game. If they had the plans, they could just put a new exterior over it.

Besides, he adds, the Luer is a ringer for Corry's *Terra IV* and "that's more than a vague connection." Bottom line: If indeed the Ralston-Blakely ended up on the grounds of a church somewhere in Southern California, it has vanished into hyperspace.

Like Souter, Steve La Vigne had always been skeptical about whether the ship he rescued is a reincarnation of the Ralston. In any case, he'd like to restore it. Born in 1952, he understands the sentiment these rockets bear—aging hulks of metal that carry the resonance of a '50s childhood; a time when there were good guys and bad guys, you knew who was who and, in the end, good prevailed. And that, says Ed Pippin, is why the Rocket still matters:

Why does the Ralston Rocket trigger such special memories with the cadets? For me it revolves around a comfortable piece of the past that was a positive image to a young mind. The good guys win by honesty and forthright effort and the bad guys get caught—and, yes, character counts! Very basic, very simple. The Rocket was the means by which the good guys escaped the confines of Earth and pursued the evil that was in the universe. As a kid it represented a "safe" environment where I knew the rules of operation. There is more attachment to the Rocket as a symbol than as a piece of hardware.

But the hardware is important too, says Jack McKirgan, who doesn't want to see the artifacts of a 1950s childhood on Earth slip into a black hole. To dream of winning the Rocket, of having it in your own front yard, was to dwell in that nether land between imagination and reality where a kid lives:

It represents that portion of my life that was simple, hopeful, exciting and full of awe as I watched my *Space Patrol* "friends" perform heroically every week. That Rocket — an advertising prop — was the focus of attention for millions of kids and adults. To me, it was Buzz's ship and he was giving me a chance to win it. It's hardly a foolish symbol of the '50s, but rather an inspiration to an entire generation of kids who would use slide-rules to calculate the strengths, stresses, energy and voltages needed to build the St. Louis Arch, the World Trade Center, orbit a capsule and LEM around the moon — and then build the first pocket calculator that made those slide-rules obsolete.

"At this point in time," McKirgan vows, "my quest for the Ralston Rocket is tempered only by the restraints of my business and finances. I can imagine having the Rocket parked in a lot near my house and hearing the squeal of brakes as some former 'cadet' recognizes that wonderful symbol of his or her past."

For years, Rick Walker kept the Ralston Rocket banner that had been fastened to the side of the truck. "Going down the road would shred it," he remembers, "so you had to take it off." But somehow the banner, along with the Space Patrol uniform they gave him (which was too small), disappeared.

A couple of questions still bug Chuck Lassen half a century later: Was the Name the Planet Contest truly a test of skill? Was the winning entry carefully selected by *Space Patrol*'s producer and writers, or was it just a random drawing?

Ralph Hartnagel has the answers. "We hired a group of women from a church organization to come on down to the agency and open the mail," he recalls, putting a casual spin on what, for many kids, was a life-and-death situation. A university professor was brought in to eliminate common historic names that were not original. The church women were not given an office — they set up shop in a hallway for several days, weeding out lackluster names and sorting the entries by state. At that point, the ad men at Gardner and a couple of guys from Ralston Purina took over. "We'd take a handful from this state, then that one, and we just kept going through them till we got tired," says Hartnagel, a veteran of many name-the-whatever contests. One thing he'd noticed about the winners of Name the Pony contests on cowboy shows: "Most of the time when they won the pony, they lived in an apartment house." (So it was probably a safe bet that the kid who won the Rocket didn't live near a spaceport, right?) Battling fatigue and boredom, the judges tried their best to pick "a tricky name, something different," Hartnagel recalls. He insisted that Gardner publish the names of all contest winners — another advertising "first." "It proved to the public that someone really had won," he explains.

Of course, we ex-kids know that Hartnagel's account is not the way it really went down. In that magical place in our minds beyond the veil of adult life, we know what happened on that December day in 1953 when all the names arrived at Space Patrol Headquarters. The entries were placed on Buzz Corry's desk and a top-level meeting was called. This was something the Commander, Hap, Major Robertson, Captain Narz and even the Secretary General of the United Planets wouldn't miss for anything in the universe because, thanks to Earth's children, they would finally have a name for Planet X. You can imagine the excitement around that huge desk in the Commander's office as everyone tore open the envelopes and engaged in heated debate. This meeting took a long time — maybe days or weeks — but at last a decision was reached. A fantastic name had won, a grand name, the name *you* submitted. That's what happened — it *had* to. Because for months, we ate and slept that Rocket, eating the cereal to get to the Space Coins, falling asleep at night as we piloted it out to the stars.

CHAPTER 17

Landing

When the show ended, I was in shock for several days. It was as if an important part of my life had been torn away, leaving me stunned.

— Stan Kohls

On May 17, 1955, an ABC publicist named Dan sent a story idea to Hal Humphrey, TV-radio editor of the *Los Angeles Mirror-News*:

Dear Hal,
    I was passing by a corner of our lot that lies in front of the paint shop today and I saw some laborer doing a renovating job on a beat-up old cockpit section of the Terra V, the rocket ship that carried the Space Patrol through glorious adventure after adventure.
    I was surprised to see what he was doing and I asked him if Space Patrol was returning to the air. (The show has been extinct for about three months now since one of the participating sponsors failed to renew after its agency told it that it ought to buy into a newer-type of show.) The workman answered no, that he was getting the prop in shape to be rented out to somebody by ABC. This incident gave me the idea that you might be interested in doing a column on "The Rise and Fall of the Spacemen" or some such thing....[1]

By mid–1955, it was obvious that space opera was dead.

A week before Christmas, 1954, "Davy Crockett, Indian Fighter," the first of a three-part series, aired on the "Frontierland" segment of *Disneyland*—a popular ABC Wednesday night program hosted by Walt Disney himself. With Fess Parker in the title role, the series chronicled the adventures of Crockett, a real-life frontiersman who died heroically defending the Alamo, a Texas fortress, against Mexican attack. The ratings shot through the roof, the catchy theme song, "The Ballad of Davy Crockett," raced to the top of the charts, and overnight millions of juves developed a bloodthirst for coonskin caps. It seemed as if the country was back in the saddle again.

While it would be easy to say that Crockett killed *Space Patrol*, it's not that simple. In fact, The Gardner Advertising Company had already decided to drop the show in early December—before Davy ever shot his first b'ar. In a note penned December 9, 1954, director Dick Darley tells Gardner rep Jay Kacin, "We all regret your leaving the show and look forward to working again with your mighty fine agency." (To fulfill its contract, Ralston's spots continued to run, alternating weekly with Nestlé's EverReady Cocoa and candy bars, until the show went off the air on February 26, 1955.)

Could Gardner have been forewarned of Crockett's debut and figured that horse opera was set to kick space opera out of orbit? Not likely, says Darley, who notes that

---

[1]Letter found in the files on *Space Patrol* at the USC Cinema-Television Library, Los Angeles.

Crockett's rampaging success took everyone by surprise. And certainly *Space Patrol*'s ratings gave the ad agency no reason to drop the show, which seemed more popular than ever. "More adults than kids watch *Space Patrol*, according to the newly-released October media ratings," reported the November 1954 issue of *Radio-Film-Television* magazine:

> Flying high in the stratosphere, this space opera continues to soar ahead of its Saturday morning radio and television competition. With a near 60 percent adult audience share, the show continues to amaze its producers and delight its audience.

But even if Gardner foresaw the coming cowboy craze, or (as Dan told Humphrey) jumped ship because they wanted a "newer-type show," it's a good bet that *Space Patrol* could have weathered the storm had Mike Moser — or someone — been at the helm. But since the producer's death in April 1953, there had been no one on board to play hardball with sponsors, the all-powerful ad agencies, and the network. Rumors flew that a higher-up at ABC was willing to keep the show on the air, despite the loss of the sponsor, in return for a piece of the action — and Mike would have seized that opening in a heartbeat. But his wife, Helen, who'd stepped in when he died, had neither his passion for the show nor his killer instinct for greasing palms and cutting deals. In the end, it may be Helen Moser — not Davy Crockett — who killed *Space Patrol*.

"ABC wanted to own a piece of the show very badly — it was still popular and generating a fortune," associate producer Bela Kovacs confirmed in 1984, "but Helen didn't want to sell it to them."[2] In those days, he adds, TV stations were not that powerful, and it's likely that ABC would have been happy with a modest share. "They'd have taken whatever cut she'd wanted to pay them, but when she refused to sell, they canceled it. And she just didn't care." Ed Kemmer takes issue with that: "I don't think she wanted to be rid of it — it was an income." True, says Kovacs, but Helen may have had emotional reasons for dumping the show. When *Space Patrol* rocketed to success, Mike Moser started living it up, and it was no secret that the woman he died with in that dark West Hollywood intersection was his girlfriend. "I think Helen had a lot of bitterness," he points out.

Still, Mike's widow was fiscally savvy, says Frank Bresee, who syndicated the show in the mid-'60s. "Helen was a stickler for money. Every time I called her, I heard the clickity-click of an adding machine in the background as we talked. She was calculating things." Something else that Helen may have been calculating was the take from a rumored film deal announced in *Variety* in the spring of 1955:

> Whether the out-of-this-world vidshow continues or not, there's a feature film version in the works, and stet [same] characters in the TV series would be in it, with cast bulwarked by w.k. [well-known] names. Mrs. Moser won't be producer under deal being talked with a major [studio], but would act as advisor.[3]

That's news to Ed Kemmer, who never heard any talk of a movie deal, except from Mike Moser, back in 1953. But Mike was always spouting big plans. "I thought it was just

---

[2]"The mid-'50s saw the formula change for program ownership," says TV/film producer and *Space Patrol* fan Warren Chaney. "Until then, shows were owned by the producers and, in many instances, the sponsors. Networks were exhibitors only. As the medium began to expand, the networks saw the writing on the wall and began demanding 'pieces' of the programming. Most shows gave in and were eventually owned outright by the networks."

[3]"On All Channels" by Dave Kaufman, *Variety*, April 1955. (Month written on clipping from Dick Darley's files, but no date.)

Cadet Happy (left) and Commander Corry, in civilian clothes, visit a 20th-century supermarket with Helen Moser. (Author's collection)

pie in the sky," Kemmer recalls. And while he concedes that Helen was smart, he thought she was clearly in over her head when it came to the politics of keeping the show on the air. "She was not a producer—she was the wife of a producer, and she got bad advice." He agrees with Kovacs that a deal could have been struck with the network, had Helen played ball. "I think ABC would have bent a lot, if she had, too," he sums up. As he remembers it, the cast got a month's notice that the show would be dropped, and though they'd suspected that something was going on, they were powerless to intervene. "I wouldn't seek out Helen Moser and say, 'What are you doing about the show?'" says Kemmer. "I was an actor."

"How the mighty have fallen," the ABC publicist's note to Hal Humphrey continued:

The majestic Terra V, flagship of the Space Patrol, after gathering dust in the scene-storage room, is now being rented out for any purpose to whomever wants it. And all the members of the Space Patrol are now jobless. Joe Maggio, our director of publicity, says he ran into Ken Mayer, who played Major Robertson, in one of the local pizza parlors. Mayer was disconsolate. He said that he had just auditioned for a bit part on *You Asked for It*, but was turned down because he wasn't the type. This brings up the possibility that after five years in the same roles, all of the Space Patrollers are so damned "typed" they may not be able to get any kind of acting jobs. Bela Kovacs, associate producer and the chief villain in the cast, has gone to New York to look for work....

So why was Dan the Publicist so interested in *Space Patrol*'s demise? Because, like a vulture circling the hull of the Terra V, he spied grist for the Crockett publicity mill:

Now, to get back to the column. If you're interested in this "Whatever Happened to Outer Space?" idea, I'll give you whatever help I can in locating the *Space Patrol* cast for interviews, etc. But it will have to be unofficial help. The networks, as you know too well, are loath to admit that any shows ever go off their schedules. A column would draw attention to the fact that *Space Patrol* has. Somebody's liable to bitch that I'm doing more to publicize a dead show than I am to publicize our live ones.

BUT if you could put in a reference to how *Davy Crockett* has now succeeded the spacemen — maybe peg the column to that angle — and then take off on the sorrowful decline of *Space Patrol* from there, I'll put the tremendous brains and facilities of "The Third Network" at your disposal. This, you understand, would make your column a pro–ABC one and it would justify my efforts....

Riding a wave of success, Osborn (left) and Kemmer show their appreciation to Helen Moser, who inherited the show when Mike died. The cast never dreamed that she would not fight to keep it on the air. (Courtesy Beth Flood)

"Davy Crockett Goes to Congress," the second episode in the *Disneyland* series, ran on January 26, 1955, followed a month later by "Davy Crockett at the Alamo" on February 23. Three days later, *Space Patrol* blasted off for the last time. By the following year, *Gunsmoke* and a slew of adult westerns had sauntered into prime time, and it looked like Buster Crabbe had been right when he predicted that ultimately the cowboy would trump the spaceman as the true American hero. Then, on October 4, 1957, the Soviet Union did more for the future of space opera than any ex-cadet or rocket ranger could ever have hoped: It launched Sputnik I, the world's first artificial satellite, catching the U.S. totally off-guard.

Though it was only the size of a basketball, Sputnik had major political, military and technological impact. By January 1958, America had countered with its own satellite, Explorer I, and by the following October, Congress had chartered NASA.[4] All this got folks watching the skies again. The space race was on between the U.S. and the Union of Soviet Socialist Republics (USSR). CBS jumped on this bandwagon in September 1959, with the short-lived series *Men into Space*, an earnest but soapy blend of imagination and technology that one critic dubbed "Flash Gordon with facts." But now the U.S. had a real space program, and the race to the moon was on the national agenda. It was almost inevitable that, in 1966, Gene Roddenberry launched *Star Trek*, the first mega–space opera since the 1950s. Suddenly, TV viewers were dreaming again about the fantastic adventures to be had in the wild, vast reaches of space. Ironically, however, the pioneering shows that had mapped the space lanes for the starship *Enterprise—Captain Video*, *Tom Corbett* and *Space Patrol*—were forgotten, and few Trekkers knew that many of *Star Trek*'s plots echoed episodes of *Space Patrol*.

The launch of Sputnik was just fine with entrepreneur Michael Colin, who wanted to syndicate *Space Patrol* and figured the space race couldn't hurt. Colin was a Mike Moser type—a blend of dreamer and streetwise promoter. His daughter, Sybil Starr, remembers him watching *Space Patrol* with the family and getting excited about the show; when Sputnik was launched a few years later, he couldn't stop talking about it. In 1958, he cut a deal with Helen Moser to syndicate *Space Patrol* nationwide and formed Comet Distributing Corporation (CDC) to do the job. At a celebration party he hosted for the cast, he agreed (under pressure from the newly formed actors' union, AFTRA) to pay them residuals totaling $90,000, though Kemmer says that never happened. By the spring of '58, Colin had the show back on the air in Los Angeles on local station KTTV and in markets around the country.[5] He even sold it in Cuba, says his son (also Michael), who claims that the island nation, pre–Castro, had more television sets per capita than any western country, along with an insatiable thirst for American programming. Due to Colin's efforts, *Space Patrol* reruns were airing in many cities in August 1958, when Lyn Osborn suddenly died. It was a chilling, confusing experience for kids stunned by news reports of his death. There was Cadet Happy in their living rooms, on their TV screens: joking as usual; gone forever. For some children, it was truly traumatic—their first encounter with death.

As *Mirror-News* columnist Hal Humphrey read Dan's pitch about how Crockett had killed off space opera, he thought the story idea would work. Pretending it was he, not the publicist, who had come upon the once-mighty *Terra V* on the ABC lot, now no more than a spaceship-for-hire, he headlined his June 8, 1955, column "THE Z-O-O-M IS GONE!":

[4]Facts from NASA History Homepage, www.hq.nasa.gov.

[5]At one point in the show's spotty syndication history, the trademark "Spaaaaaaace Patrol!" intro done by Dick Tufeld was removed and the show was renamed *Satellite Police*. Whether this was done by Michael Colin to capitalize on the launch of the Sputnik satellite or by someone else to avoid annoying legal hassles (as when you're bootlegging kinescopes) is unclear. Frank Bresee of The Mack Agency, who syndicated the show in the mid-'60s, says Mack did not change the title. This supports Nina Bara's claim that it was done by Colin. Bara said that in 1957 she lent six kinnies to Helen Moser for syndication—even though Mike's widow had fired her during the last year of the show. "They were returned after a long time with 'Satellite Police' dubbed in," she recalled. Michael Colin's daughter, Sybil Starr, who worked in his office, is not sure if her dad used the alternate title but says it "rings a bell."

Are there any slightly-used space helmets, ray guns and interplanetary telephones lying around your house? If so, you may wish to unload them on the Salvation Army pickup man the next time he calls. You have probably discovered by now that Junior has lost interest in those rocket trips to Mars. He's either donned a coonskin cap and taken to hunting bears, or buckled on his six-guns and hit the trail again with Roy Rogers or Kit Carson....

This realization that Junior has hung up his spacesuit hit me the other day as I walked across the ABC studio lot here. In a remote corner was Terra V, the old rocket ship used on the network's "Space Patrol" TV show.... Dilapidated and deserted, it stood like a monument to the fickleness of young TV viewers. "Space Patrol" was the daddy of the space adventure shows on TV, getting its network start nearly five years ago. Lyn Osborn, who played Cadet Happy, was getting about $40,000 a year. He hasn't worked since....

One day in late 1963, Richard "Mack" McClain, head of The Mack Agency, a firm that specialized in TV advertising promotions, decided he needed more storage space, so he went downstairs to inspect the basement of the building that housed his office on North Ivar Street, across from the Hollywood Knickerbocker Hotel. The cellar was a mess, with reels of film, half-in and half-out of boxes, strewn across the floor. "Mack said, 'What are these?'" recalls Frank Bresee, who was working for McClain at the time. Bresee bent down to take a closer look:

> It was the *Space Patrol* kinescopes. They were scattered around and some were wet and damaged. And the owner of the building said, "We'll just throw these away," because our company had things we wanted to store in the basement. But I remembered the show from when I used to work at ABC, and I said, "I wonder if this is worth syndicating."

McClain liked the idea and phoned Helen Moser who, says Bresee, "was anxious to make a buck any way she could." A deal was cut, but it wasn't as profitable as McClain and Bresee had hoped. And there were other problems. Many of the kinescopes were poor quality and, in those days, could not be enhanced, creating some obstacles to syndication. "People just wouldn't stand for it next to the competition, which was good quality westerns on film," Bresee explains. By this time, video tape, which had made TV dramas virtually perfect, was on the scene, so if all you had to peddle was kinnies of a live show where an actor could flub a line or a special effect might fizzle, forget it. Syndicating *Space Patrol* "didn't turn out to be such a good idea after all," Bresee admits, though he and McClain did manage to sell it to three major markets—New York, Chicago and L.A. It ran for about a year, starting in May 1964, then dropped off the viewscope for the next two decades.[6]

In the mid–'80s, *Space Patrol* surfaced on USA Network as part of a camp, late-night potpourri called *Night Flight*. By this time, the baby boomers who'd grown up with the show were in their thirties and forties. Now they were discovering what their parents had known: *Space Patrol* was not just for kids. Seeing it as adults, they could catch the subtle overtones between the main characters, wince at the ineptness of guest actors and marvel at the skill of the regular cast, who were much better than they needed to be and kept the show going, no matter what. But how would this relic from the 1950s look to someone in their twenties who had not grown up with it? I phoned the production staff at USA Network, who put *Night Flight* together, to find out. "I'll tell you what," said a kid named Adam, "we're all hooked."

---

[6]Syndication by The Mack Agency began in Los Angeles on May 2, 1964, on independent station KTTV, according to *TV Guide*. Bresee says that WOR in New York and WGN in Chicago also came aboard.

When I first met the *Space Patrol* cast in 1984, they all said that when the show ended, they had been ready to move on. They'd had a dizzying ride to TV stardom and were eager to see what the future held. In private moments (as Dick Darley suspected) each must have envisioned starring in his or her own series, film offers pouring in, Hollywood awaiting the cast's release from the show with open arms. Back then, in 1955, the idea that they might slam into a typecasting wall as solid as Prince Baccarratti's Force Barrier would have been dismissed as so much space gas.

But while the actors looked expectantly toward the future, many kids were devastated by the show's sudden cancellation. They had no idea that squabbles among adults (sometimes called "politics") could destroy the United Planets faster than the Great Solar War. When the show crashed and burned, *Space Patrol*'s 60 percent adult audience was upset, but it was kids who took it the hardest. That Helen Moser had shrugged her shoulders in the face of ABC's demands, like a goddess sticking it to mere mortals, was incomprehensible—even had someone bothered to explain it to the juves. "We'd never heard of corporate takeovers, expanding media conglomerates, or financial blackmail," says Warren Chaney:

> We didn't know about any of that—to us, *Space Patrol* had just disappeared. There was no farewell, no good-bye to our trusted friends and "leaders." There was nothing. Even our quarters and boxtops were returned from Checkerboard Square, as if they didn't need us anymore. But we were all part of the club, and Commander Corry was our leader. Whether we were from rural Kentucky, like me, or suburban New York, we felt we belonged. Our 25¢ cereal premiums were more than coins and boxtops—they were marks of membership in a special club that taught leadership skills and saved the universe on a weekly basis. It just doesn't seem right that the greatest club on Earth, with the best mail order cereal premiums in the world, should have ended.

Chaney pauses. "I guess what I'm saying is that when the series was canceled, I couldn't get over it. I still haven't. If I'm candid with myself, I'm just a kid who grew taller."

CHAPTER 18

Spaceman's Luck

"I lay there for hours and I cried. It was just spontaneous, because Cadet Happy could not pass away — not in my life."

— Chris Darley

When *Space Patrol* crashlanded in February 1955, Lyn Osborn had no idea how hard it would be to get work. A reporter caught up with him as he stood in line at the state unemployment office in Hollywood, collecting his weekly check. The story, headlined "Crockett Puts Space Man in Jobless Line," went out over the *AP* wire:

> A few months ago, before Davy Crockett, Lyn Osborn was earning $900 a week as Cadet Happy in television's *Space Patrol*. Now each week, he waits in line to pick up a $30 jobless check. "I can't seem to convince casting offices that I am not really a man from outer space," he laughs.[1]

As usual, Lyn put up a brave front, joking about his predicament. It was reassuring, he told the reporter, to see bigger names than his in line with him (plus a few former villains from Jupiter and Saturn). To another newsman, he remarked that his problems would be solved "if a space helmet could grow fur," a snipe at the Davy Crockett craze that had gunned down space opera. In the few short months since Crockett had debuted on ABC's *Disneyland* in December 1954, legions of kids had swapped their space helmets for furry coonskin caps. Noting that he couldn't get a job on this planet, Osborn explained that he was "very big on Mars."[2]

He kept up a front for his parents, too:

> Dear Folks,
> Sorry I haven't written or called you, but just didn't seem to get around to it. Nothing much new here except for the show going off.... I got a new agent & he's looking for me at all the studios. I'm going to try and get a couple good parts in pictures before I look for another TV series.... I'll let you know as soon as something happens.
> P.S. I'm also collecting $30 a week unemployment insurance.
> P.P.S. All the movie stars not working do it too!

"My brother had it rough after *Space Patrol*—he had no idea of the trouble he would have getting work," says Beth Flood. There were bit parts in TV series like *Gunsmoke*, in movies like *Too Much Too Soon*. "But if you didn't watch close, you didn't see him," says Beth. Casting agents didn't see him either. When he made the rounds, they saw Cadet

---

[1] *AP* story circa 1955. No date on clipping in Osborn's pressbook.
[2] Bill Kennedy's column, *Herald Examiner*, May 10, 1956.

Celebrity astrologer Carroll Righter hosted a "Leo" party with a real lion — who took a liking to Lyn. "It adored him," says Rickey Barr. "It wanted to kiss him and play with him — it wouldn't leave him alone. He was terrified." (Author's collection)

Happy. "It's just like starting all over again," he told *Variety*.[3] By February 1956, a year after *Space Patrol's* demise, he had worked only twice — on *Private Secretary* and *The Lineup*, the only two shows that would give him interviews. "Everybody knew who he was, but they wouldn't give him work," says former Playhouse classmate John Buckley. "He used to say that he'd done over 1200 live TV shows — which was probably some kind of record — but he couldn't get arrested in this damn town."

[3] *Variety*, April 1, 1955.

He started preparing a nightclub act, but after catching Sammy Davis, Jr.'s, routine, he told *TV* magazine, "Who can top that talent? I think I'll just kill myself instead."[4] He'd lost some money in bad investments, but with his savings plus the unemployment check, he could pay the bills. He moved from the ritzy Sunset Plaza Apartments, shared bachelor pads with friends for a while, and finally leased a funky two-bedroom house in back of Harry Lewis' new restaurant, Hamburger Hamlet, on the Sunset Strip.[5]

In 1956, he met Rickey Barr, an aspiring agent who'd dyed her hair pink. Both strong personalities, they were a fiery match. After a brief fling, they decided they'd make better friends than lovers, and what they had, says Barr, was much deeper than romance; it was a profound spiritual connection. "We knew what the other one was thinking, and I could picture in my mind where he was at almost any given time. We loved each other very, very much — not just as a man and a woman, but as two human beings."

When I met Barr 30 years later, she was a hardened veteran of the Hollywood talent wars. But her turquoise eyes grew misty when she remembered Lyn:

> He couldn't stand it if you were mad at him. If we argued, he'd wake me up in the middle of the night, reading *Peanuts* on the phone. He didn't say hello — I'd just hear this voice telling me about Linus or Charlie Brown so I wouldn't be mad anymore. I'd say, "OK, Lyn, I'm not mad. Can I get some sleep?" He called at 1:00 A.M. once to let me know he was going to Las Vegas. He was so afraid I might need him and he wouldn't be there.

Rickey Barr used this photograph in Osborn's portfolio to convince casting directors to consider him for serious roles. (It was shots like this of Osborn smoking in public that infuriated Mike Moser during *Space Patrol*.) (Author's collection)

It was Osborn who encouraged Barr to follow her dream of becoming an agent. She took him on as a client and hammered casting directors nonstop. "They'd say, 'He's Cadet Happy,' and I'd say, 'No, he's Lyn Osborn, a trained actor.' Eventually they saw it, and he started to work quite a bit."

Things were definitely looking up. He got TV work on *The Thin Man*, *Life of Riley*, *Sugarfoot* and other series, and appeared in *Top Secret Affair*, *Too Much Too Soon*, *The Amazing Colossal Man* and other films. Though most of the parts were small ("second gunman" on the TV series *Jim Bowie*), he was delighted to get the work, say close friends Michael and Carol Hagen. Michael appeared with him in several little theater productions. "He was good to work with because he was consistent. He was an actor's actor, someone you could depend on."

[4]*TV*, July, 1955.
[5]Osborn was acquainted with Lewis, a former actor turned restaurateur, who had once been considered for the role of Commander Corry.

Rickey Barr celebrates Christmas, 1989. (Courtesy Diana Hale)

Lyn formed a bond with the Hagens, hanging out at their home to talk and watch TV. Here he could be himself. It was a respite from his wilder friends who partied and drank too much, says Carol. "We were a disgustingly square, normal couple. I think he felt safe with us." Osborn was well-read and knowledgeable about a lot of subjects and loved to discuss politics and philosophy. "He was a very deep thinker," Carol recalls, "and more fun than anyone else." Michael remembers the time on the golf course when a flock of blackbirds landed on the tee. "Without missing a beat, he snapped, 'All right, four and twenty of you mothers report to the bakery!' Everything struck him as funny. That was Lyn Osborn."

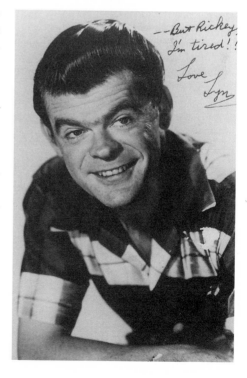

Lyn Osborn. "He couldn't stand it if you were mad at him," says Rickey Barr. "If we argued, he'd wake me up in the middle of the night, reading *Peanuts* on the phone. He didn't say hello — I'd just hear this voice telling me about Linus or Charlie Brown so I wouldn't be mad anymore." (Author's collection)

Michael Hagen as William S. Johnson in the Actors Incorporated production *Small Miracles*, in which Lyn played Tony Mako, a thug gunned down by police. (Courtesy Michael and Carol Hagen)

Hagen and Osborn shared a boundless intellectual curiosity. They talked for hours about controversial philosopher Immanuel Velikovsky as they built a telescope from scratch. "I think Lyn got interested in astronomy through *Space Patrol*," says Michael. When John Buckley came to live with Osborn in the last months of his life, Lyn had set up the telescope in the front yard of his house in West Hollywood. "He'd stay out there for hours, looking at the stars," Buckley recalls. Michael remembers Lyn's handshake. "It was strong — he had very strong hands." Says Carol: "He was always direct. You always knew what he felt."

By 1957, he was working more and got a meaty part in a teen thriller, *Invasion of the Saucer Men*. He was starting to break through the typecasting barrier, but he could still bask in his *Space Patrol* fame. When he'd cruise down the Sunset Strip in his spiffy Skylark convertible, people yelled, "Hey, Cadet Happy!" Later that year, when reruns of *Space Patrol* aired in L.A., he was mobbed by autograph seekers, just like old times. One day, he and Rickey went to Disneyland. "It was a really fun trip," Barr says, trying to sound annoyed. "I spent the whole day holding my purse so he could put a book on it and write his name. It was crazy — and he loved every second of it."

"Creeping horror from the depths of time and space" reads the tagline on a lobby card made from this photograph of Osborn attacked by an alien in *Invasion of the Saucer Men* (1957). Though the movie is B fare, Osborn turns in an A performance as Artie Shaw in his meatiest role since *Space Patrol*. (Courtesy *Filmfax* magazine)

John Buckley witnessed Lyn's first seizure. A crowd of actors was hanging out backstage at Actors Incorporated, a small theater on Vine Street, and as usual, Osborn was cutting up:

> He was doing this act, pretending he was some weird character. But then he looked kind of funny, his face turned white and he went blank for a second or two. And when he came out of it, he said, "I wasn't clowning. Something weird happened to me."

Suddenly Osborn plunged into a personal nightmare. A seizure could strike at any time. A strange, metallic taste gave him a few seconds' warning, but by that time it was too late — he'd be paralyzed for up to ten seconds. He hit on a way to mask the attacks. When he felt one coming on, he'd pull out a cigarette, quickly light it, and take a puff. If he did that, he told Beth, most people never noticed. But he couldn't speak during the "spell," and he lived in constant fear that an attack could hit while he was performing.

Abigail Shelton was with him when he blacked out backstage at Actors Incorporated again — this time just as he was set to go on. "He was kind of frozen for a few seconds, but somehow he managed to pull himself together and complete his performance. He had a lot of courage."

He had an attack once when he and Carol Hagen were at a movie. "He grabbed my arm and I looked at him," she recalls. "He was perfectly still." Osborn's deepest fear was that he had epilepsy, says Carol, because nobody was thinking "brain tumor."

Yes, they were, says John Buckley. People were whispering about what could be wrong with Lyn Osborn. His actor friends remembered the falls he'd taken in the past year and wondered if a crack on the head could trigger a brain tumor. "But," adds Buckley, "then someone else would say, 'How the hell do *you* know? You're not a doctor.'"

It got worse. The seizures were coming several times a day now and things were spiraling out of control. "He was terrified," says Virginia Hewitt. "He didn't fall down, but there would be a few seconds when he couldn't talk." Virginia and her husband, Ernst Meer, saw a lot of him during 1957, when he was starting to get some TV work. "He'd come to dinner from the studio and he'd say, 'Thank God we're doing this on film, because if it were live TV, I couldn't do it.'" Osborn confided that he'd been seeing a psychiatrist. "Has your doctor ruled out any medical problems?" demanded Virginia. "He said, 'Well, I guess so.' So I said, 'Look, Lyn, just go with it when it comes. Say to the blackout, *OK, I'm going with you.*' And he called the next day from the studio, so grateful, and said, 'It worked, Carol, it really worked!' You see, when he went with it, he wasn't so frightened. But he suffered — it was a rotten thing."

In the mid–'50s, psychiatry had taken Hollywood by storm, and everyone from Brando to bit players was "in treatment." Osborn had a shrink, too, who found plenty of things wrong with his offbeat personality and was rooting them out one by one. But when Lyn complained about the blackouts and the metallic taste that gave warning, his doctor, instead of ordering tests, called this "an emotional breakthrough in his psychosis," says Carol Hagen. Osborn wasn't so sure, but it was easier to buy that than the terrifying alternative — that something physical, such as a tumor, was causing his problems. "In those days," says Dr. Paul Crandall, the surgeon who later operated on him, "people regarded a brain tumor as almost a death sentence." But psychoanalysis wasn't so pleasant either. Lyn told Chuck Barkus that it was the worst thing he'd ever gone through:

> He said it was terrifying. They were breaking him down mentally, just ripping him apart — and it wasn't just one psychiatrist, it was several at a session. The poor guy had a brain tumor and they were trying to figure it out psychologically. It was really brutal.

Forty-five years later, Barkus is still upset. Ed Kemmer is angry, too. "I don't care much for those doctors," he says tersely, hearing the story.

Finally, in March 1958, Osborn consulted two neurologists. When an EEG detected irregular brain waves, the diagnosis was epilepsy. He was given drugs to control the seizures, but they made him drowsy and slurred his speech. He would not find out until five months later that the cause of the blackouts was, in fact, a deadly tumor — the same kind that cut down composer George Gershwin in his prime. Right now, the epilepsy sentence was bad enough and he struggled with whether to tell his folks. He didn't want to worry them, but felt that someone in the family should know, so he confided in Beth:

March 24, 1958

Dear Sis,

…There are a few things I want to say that I don't think [Mom and Dad] should know just yet…. I wouldn't want to see either of them get hurt or worry too much about me. Now that Dad has retired finally, I wouldn't want to get in the way or cause any change in anyone's plans….

…A year ago, I had my first attack of Petite Mal…. I've had a couple of attacks every other day for the past year. If you're not familiar with the term, I'll start by telling you that Grande Mal is the modern term for epilepsy…. You can imagine what something like that must feel like, and also how frustrating & confusing…. I don't have any fits or anything like that, and don't suffer from any loss of coordination. The main thing it does is scare me…. I've taken two electroencephalograms so far and the neurologists tell me that the condition is due to a blow on the head…. My psychiatrist thinks [it's] psychosomatic and is looking at it from that point of view…. In psychiatry they say you have to get worse before you get better. Well, right now I'm at my worst. The medication that they have me on now is sedatives, heavy ones, which is no medicine for an actor to be taking. It sorta stops the attacks, but sure makes me half-asleep all the time. The thing that makes me mad is that up 'til one year ago I never had anything wrong with me. I never even caught cold or anything. So much for all that….

P.S. Please don't think I wrote this for sympathy or anything like that. I just figure somebody in the family should know the story.

Despite his grim situation, Osborn, ever an optimist, figured he could beat it. He knew the power of hypnosis—he'd seen that when Kemmer had hypnotized him at a party once, planting the suggestion that he'd *have* to come back for a deck of cards before he could sleep. So in April 1958, he enrolled in TV hypnotist Emile Franchel's home-study course.[6] He still had plenty wrong with him, according to the psychiatrists, but perhaps he could overcome whatever deep flaw in his being was causing the blackouts with self-suggestion. Even if the seizures had a physical cause, maybe he could defeat them with the power of the mind.

But hypnosis didn't help much and even the drugs weren't doing the job—the following month he blacked out on the set of the movie *Torpedo Run*, in which he had a bit part. "He was practically in tears when he told me," says Rickey Barr. "He had no control over it; he didn't know what he was going to do." It was not only scary, he later told Kemmer, but embarrassing—not something you could easily explain to a director. Through it all, he never lost his sense of humor, recalls Carol Hagen. But "a notable change had come over him," says John Buckley. "He wasn't partying anymore or chasing women." In private moments, despair overwhelmed him. One day he hammered out a poem on the old typewriter he'd purchased a decade ago when he'd arrived in California to study at the Pasadena Playhouse. It contained a chilling line:

Why fight? Why worry? Maybe you'll get a pink slip in your next birthday card.

"Jesus, that hit me," says Kemmer, reading the poem years later. "A pink slip in a birthday card? It means you're fired—it's your last one, buddy. Sounds like a premonition."

By the spring of 1958, Rickey Barr was growing increasingly worried. With Lyn blacking out more and more, someone should be living with him. She convinced him that John

---

[6]Emile Franchel co-hosted the syndicated *Adventures in Hypnosis* TV show with Edward Cochran from 1956 to 1957. Shot in L.A., it used audience members as subjects to demonstrate hypnosis techniques and principles.

Last photograph of Lyn Osborn, taken one month before his death. John Buckley (left) moved in with Osborn to keep an eye on him because of his frequent blackouts. (Courtesy Beth Flood)

Buckley should move in, rent-free. It was a good deal for Buckley, who'd just quit his day job. John recalls Lyn, during the last months of his life, see-sawing between depression and lightheartedness. Sometimes he'd watch *Space Patrol*, then showing in reruns. "He'd chuckle at things and tell a little story about what took place behind the scenes. He always liked the show and the part of Cadet Happy." On the July 4th weekend, Lyn's cousin Morris came from Texas with his son, Tommy, to visit, and he showed them the famous tourist sites: the Rose Bowl, Farmer's Market, Forest Lawn Mortuary. Later, he had dinner with Chuck Barkus and said he was expecting a residual check for $30,000 for *Space Patrol* reruns. "I'm going to give it to you," he told Chuck. "You open a beauty salon and I'll be your silent partner. When the check comes, I'll call you and we'll get started." Barkus, whose dream was to have his own salon, was thrilled and began scouting locations. Later he, too, wondered if Osborn had harbored a premonition.

Things came to a head in early August when he was driving with Rickey and blacked out at the wheel. It was a moment of truth. "I could have killed you," he said, shaken. Rickey was more furious than scared:

I said, "Lyn, you're sick!" He'd been to a psychiatrist, a chiropractor and a hypnotist, and I begged him to see another M.D. I said, "Let's get married — at least I can live with you and take care of you," but he said, "No, I'm not sick." He would do anything in the world for me — except listen! But I demanded it. I told him I was going to push him out of the driver's seat if he didn't go to UCLA the next day. He did. But by then it was too late.

Preliminary screening at UCLA Medical Center suggested that Osborn should check into the hospital for a battery of tests. When he came home, says Buckley, he was not in a talkative mood. "He'd fall silent on the subject. I think he suspected it was serious." On August 7, Lyn wrote to his parents. At the bottom of the page, Bess scribbled, "Last letter from our Son."

Dear Folks,
    Sorry I've taken so long to write.... I'm still having those goofy attacks every day and I've checked with another doctor who has given me some more tests, trying to find out what the hell it is. It looks like I'll be checking into a hospital pretty soon for more extensive tests and things. As soon as I find out anything definite I'll let you know right away.... I start work tomorrow on another feature picture called "The Fire Bug" and I had a very small part in the first episode of Ann Sothern's new TV series....
    I really can't think of anything more to write. Things have been sorta dull for me and there's not much to talk about. I don't think I'll be doing anything in the business after this picture until I get rid of this condition and get back in the world and start living again. I'm really not worth much until I find out what it is and get it cleared up. Anyway, I'm going right ahead and doing whatever is necessary to beat it, and I won't stop until it's cured.
    Well, that's about it for now. I'll keep in touch and let you know how things are progressing. Keep writing and I'll try to do the same. Bye for now....

He called his friends to let them know he was checking into the hospital. Kemmer immediately phoned the *Space Patrol* cast. Though Osborn had not received a diagnosis yet, Kemmer put the pieces together and his heart sank:

He was going in the next day for the exploratory, so I invited the whole gang up to my house. Well, I'd just been through that with a director friend of mine with a brain tumor — five-day coma: dead. And, oh, I pushed that out of my mind, 'cause it was a very similar thing with Hap. At that time, it was horse and buggy days for brain stuff; going in to look meant death. But Hap was very "up" that night, in the best of spirits because he was finally doing something about this problem that had been bugging him. He went into the hospital with great hope.

The week Lyn Osborn checked into UCLA Hospital in West Los Angeles, toward summer's end in August 1958, he received three offers: Two movie roles, one to be filmed in Italy, and — at last — a show of his own. "I think it was a radio show," Beth Flood says, trying to remember.
    When what looked like a virulent glioblastoma showed up in Osborn's test results, says surgeon Paul Crandall, "I knew this tumor was going to be bad news." Lyn was quiet when he got the diagnosis and "very depressed." Crandall, aware of Lyn's talent and Cadet Happy fame, kept his emotions in check. More distraught was his colleague, neurologist

Abigail Shelton rushed to the hospital when she had a strong intuitive feeling that "if I didn't, I'd never see Lyn again." (Courtesy Abigail Shelton Baker)

William Oldendorf, who, several years later, would co-invent the CT scan. Oldendorf was a devoted *Space Patrol* fan. "That show was like a ritual to him," Crandall recalls. "I must say," he adds, "that [Osborn] had a lot of fans among medical colleagues of mine, who were quite shocked by this development." Lyn, says Crandall, was not a demanding patient. "I've treated a number of movie stars. Some are good and some are bad. He was one of the good ones."

Lyn's friends crowded into his hospital room — a dozen rowdy actors, laughing and talking loudly. Though his head was half-shaved, he joked around as usual and put up a good front, but "there was no question he was apprehensive," recalls Carol Hagen. The crowd grew noisier and hospital staffers asked them to leave. Abigail Shelton paused at the door. She'd been relaxing by a friend's pool earlier that afternoon, when suddenly she'd heard a voice in her head, saying, "*If you don't see Lyn today, you will never see him again.*" She rushed to the hospital. Now she turned back to look at him one more time. "He was sitting on the edge of the bed, sipping orange juice through a straw, and he said, 'Aren't you going to kiss me goodbye, Abby?' And I said, 'Oh sure, Lyn,' and went back and gave him a kiss on the cheek. I think he knew he was going to die. And the next day I got the phone call."

SCENE: The dense Cydonia jungle on Venus, ruled by a tall and powerful race of Amazon women. Three men are herded through the jungle at spearpoint, bound for slave labor — the fate of all male space travelers who chance upon this Venusian wilderness. Held captive with Hap and Buzz is their own prisoner, Johnson, a corrupt lab technician who has stolen a valuable formula for converting the deadly Cydonian foliage into edible food. One of the men staggers and falls.

CORRY: *Happy!*
HAP: *I'm sorry, Commander... I just can't make it.*
AMAZON: *What's wrong?*
CORRY: (angry) *You know what's wrong. Johnson shot Happy with a ray gun. Without care or rest, he won't live. He needs help right away!*
JOHNSON: *Yeah? Too bad I didn't do a better job when I had the chance.* (Corry, enraged, takes a swing at Johnson, but an Amazon restrains him.)
AMAZON: *Enough! We will go on. The little one is of no use to us as a man-slave. Leave him here.*
CORRY: *Leave him here in the jungle? Over my dead body!*
AMAZON: *As you wish.* (Three tall Amazons move forward, threatening Buzz with spears.)
JOHNSON: (snide) *It's your move, Corry.*

CORRY: (defiant) *All right… It's my move!* (Stoops down, ignoring spears; picks up Hap, now semi-conscious, and slings him over his shoulder. The Amazons move in, as if to attack.)
AMAZON LEADER: Halt! You're a fool, Commander, but a brave fool. Follow me!
CORRY: (voice low, in Hap's ear) *Hang on, Hap. All we need is time. Robbie's on his way…*
          —"The Men-Slaves of Cydonia," TV Episode 163, February 6, 1954

Osborn, 32, lingered in a coma for five days after surgery failed to remove the malignant brain tumor, never regaining consciousness. "They said if he did, he might be paralyzed on one side — a vegetable or something. He would have hated to live like that. He never wanted to be anything but whole, so … just five days." Beth Flood's voice trails off.

As Lyn lay in the hospital, the phone rang at his house. John Buckley took the call. "It was some producer saying, 'I have to talk to Lyn Osborn right away! I've got a good part for him in a picture — he starts in two weeks.' And I said 'He's not available.' It was a big break and he couldn't take advantage of it."

His parents flew out from Michigan and Bess kept watch at his bedside. Just as she had chronicled Lyn's childhood in her diary, now she recounted his last days in a letter to Beth:

> August 28, 1958
> …Our Bud has not gained consciousness or even moved since the operation and I don't think the doctor or nurse thinks he will be here long…. Ed Kemmer and his wife, Carol [Virginia Hewitt] and her husband, and Bud's gal Rickey were here for a while…. Doctor told me if he pulled through he probably wouldn't know anyone. He's paralyzed on the right side…. Can you imagine how Bud would feel about that? Rather never wake up. That's hard to say, but you know and I know it's true. There is no cure, and he was so proud of his well body and his bright mind. I think you know what I'm trying to say — we just have to face it, we are not going to have our Bud for long and never again as he was…. He has not moved since we came, just lying there so pitiful it breaks my heart.

Cadet Happy could always make the best of a terrible situation. Through harrowing close calls and near misses, you could count on Hap for comic relief. Osborn was, in his own words, "born with comedy timing," and he proved to millions of kids weekly that you could keep your sense of humor through the most unspeakable peril. In real life, he confided his frightening ordeal with the seizures to some friends, but not to others. He kept it from Kemmer — whom he didn't see that often after *Space Patrol* ended — until a few days before he died. Kemmer has some regrets:

> I was busy, but I could have paid more attention. Whenever I saw him, everything seemed fine — that was Hap, you know, making jokes. He'd never want to feel like a burden to anyone, and he never hinted that he was in any dire straits. He was very good at not showing anything he didn't want to show, and it never occurred to me to look deeper — and that was my limitation.

Kemmer sighs. "If he'd needed anything, I'd have been there, I'll tell you that."

In 1956, one year after *Space Patrol* blasted off for the last time, Osborn had put together a résumé in which he revealed his hopes for the future:

I'm in this business for the rest of my life, and I intend to progress and learn more about it every day. If a man has something to say to the world, the only place left where his voice can be heard is acting, writing, the affiliated arts. I have many things to say.... Through acting I hope to gain the courage to say them, and an audience to listen. It appears to me that the real successes in show business are those who dedicate their entire lives to it.

Which he did.

At 5:55 P.M. on August 30, 1958, Lyn's sister Beth, 2300 miles away in Michigan, was startled awake from a nap:

I worked from seven 'til midnight, so I used to lay down a while before work. And all of a sudden I came awake so fast, like I'd heard a noise or somebody had called or a bell rang. It was just like an alarm went off, but I didn't have an alarm — my husband was going to wake me up. I looked at the time because I had to get ready for work. And later that night, when I found out what time he died, it was right at that time. It was spooky.

"If you live to be one hundred," Lyn told brother-in-law Bill Flood, "you'll never do all the things and see all the things I have...."

"He was right," says Bill, suppressing the urge, under Beth's watchful eye, to light his cigar in the narrow kitchen of their motor home. "He lived more in his short life than I will, as long as I live."

"We remembered that when he died," Beth says matter-of-factly, "that at least he got to do the things he wanted. He had a full life, even though it was short."

When Dick Darley's son, Chris, came home from summer camp at the end of August 1958, his mom was strangely quiet:

She came into my bedroom and sat next to me and said, "I have to tell you something: Cadet Happy died." And it was just tears, because you can't say those two things in one sentence. It's just too incongruous. I lay there for hours and cried, because Cadet Happy could not pass away — not in my life. I took it so personally. It was the first person I knew who was mortal, who had passed away.

For many kids of the first, awestruck TV generation, Cadet Happy's death was scary and incomprehensible. "I was deeply depressed," recalls Jack McKirgan, then eleven years old. "I had no experience with death in my family. Cadet Happy's passing was like losing my best friend and I grieved for days."

Hap had come close to death many times in *Space Patrol*, but the Commander had always saved him. This time something had gone horribly wrong, and for some, it took years to comprehend. "Those people meant so much to us," says Chris Darley. "There was something so solid about them, even though the show had finished." Chris, who knew Osborn personally but had also bonded with his character, admits that he would think of Osborn and cry for the next 20 years. "Cadet Happy was so sweet. He was just a wonderful spirit in life."

Ed Kemmer made preliminary funeral arrangements. "His parents asked me to help. I went in to look at caskets," he says stoically. Abigail Shelton remembers Kemmer quietly stepping in to take charge. A group of Lyn's actor friends had gathered, stunned by his death, but Kemmer calmed everyone. "He was very soft-spoken; he just took over the whole thing," says Shelton." By the time the family arrived from Michigan, the Commander had things somewhat under control. "I got a beautiful lot, reasonably priced. Forest Lawn was marvelous," he says quietly. "It was all done very well." Though Kemmer held it together — even viewing Lyn's body first to make sure he looked OK — it was obvious that he was hurting. "Ed Kemmer is not the type to tear his hair or break into uncontrollable sobbing," says John Buckley, "but he was visibly upset."

Beth Flood noticed tears in her father's eyes. "It hit him really hard when Lyn died. It was the first time I ever saw him cry."

Chuck Barkus, who'd known Lyn longer than anyone else, except for the family, stood quietly in the large crowd at Forest Lawn's Church of the Recessional, pushed aside by those who had come into Osborn's life later on. He recalled the Playhouse days when he and Lyn had shared a bachelor pad, talking at night before sleep of their dreams of making it big in Hollywood. "It took me a long time to get over his death," Barkus admits. "I had plans of, 'Hey, when we get older, we'll get together.' I knew he'd still be my good buddy."

A month after the funeral, Osborn's parents received a letter from Geraldine Wall informing them that Lyn had a daughter he had never seen. "I wish I'd written this nine years ago," Wall began, dropping a bombshell:

> In the late fall and winter months of 1948, my seventeen-year-old sister and [Lyn] were very close friends. My niece Barbara was born as a result of their friendship. "Muggsy," as we called Lyn, was never told of Barbara's birth.... Her family had not intended to take her to visit with Lyn until such a time when she is older.... Now there no longer is a possibility of his ever knowing her, or her knowing him.... As her aunt, I worry that somewhere there may be grandparents or other relations who do not know of the existence of this wonderfully bright and beautiful little girl.... Learning that her real father is dead may be quite a shock for her, yet she is going to be told this week....

Bill Osborn refused to deal with this news, but Bess asked Beth to write Geraldine back. She did, and the two women corresponded for the next 12 years. Though Geraldine never divulged Barbara's last name or whereabouts, she sent photos that bore a definite resemblance to Lyn. It was enough for Bess. On the back of one of them, she penned: *Barbara Osborn — Bud's daughter — Born 1948.* "Please reassure your parents that my letter was no hoax," Geraldine told Beth. "At least that much of your brother still lives...." In 1970, the letters suddenly stopped.

Osborn's daughter, Barbara (Bobbi) Averell, one year old. The photograph was sent to Osborn's family after his death by the child's aunt, who informed them that Lyn had a daughter.

Postscript: Los Angeles: March 1986

I'm talking to Rickey Barr on the phone. This is our first conversation and she's wary, protective of Osborn's memory. I drop names from the past — Kemmer, Buckley, Hagen. Gradually she relaxes, then becomes disarmingly honest. Now she can't stop talking about Lyn — how he was the love of her life, how she was traumatized by his funeral and hasn't been to one since, how she has never watched an episode of *Space Patrol*. "It's too painful, because he was so alive," she says in a low, raspy voice. "I don't know if I could deal with it." The memories spill out, then suddenly she pauses. "I know I shouldn't be telling you this because you're gonna quote me in your book and I'm gonna feel like killing myself. But this really happened:

> I went to a psychic, years after he died. She was from Brazil and didn't speak great English, so there were a couple of guys in the room to translate. Suddenly she says, "You had two very serious illnesses and came close to death in both of them." Well, that was true. Then she says, "Oh, you had a friend who tried to take you!" I said, "What?" And she says, "You had this friend you were close to who died when he was very young. He never leaves your side. And she said, "I want you to say his name," so I just said "Lyn." She said, "Say it louder," so I said "Lyn" again. She said, "Say it one more time." And when I said "Lyn" the third time, there was a clap in the room that sounded like thunder. I didn't say a word, and she went right on with the reading. But the guys who were there to help translate said, "Did you hear something?" And I said, "Well, I heard something that sounded like a clap." And the psychic said, "That was him. He's just showing you he was here." She said, "He always shows you. You just haven't noticed."

At this point, I tell Barr about the candles that suddenly extinguished themselves during my own psychic reading. This common ground established, we decide to meet for lunch. "God," says Rickey, "the table will probably tip over!"

Two years later, when I tell Kemmer about the candles, I follow up by relating Barr's similar experience. Seems that Osborn, never one to let something as trivial as a dimensional barrier stand in his way, is still the prankster, I tell him.

"I'm glad he's found something interesting to do up there," Kemmer smiles.

"You wouldn't expect him to be idle, would you?" I ask.

"No," he says. "I would expect him to be getting a lot of laughs."

CHAPTER 19

Actors and Archetypes

At a supermarket, I heard a little kid saying, "Mommy, there's Commander Corry!"—
and it scared me to death because I did not want that to be my life. I thought, "I'm
not going to settle down and wear a white hat for the next 50 years."
— Franklin Mullen, AKA Glen Denning (the first Commander Corry)

I want to write to Ed Kemmer, but what can I say to a man who's been my hero for
50 years?

— Doug Moore

PASADENA, CALIFORNIA: MAY 2001

"I refuse to believe it," says Mike Guarino, raising his voice in frustration. "I can't believe that the stuff Kemmer got across as Corry was completely unconscious. He must have been trying to accomplish something." We're meeting for lunch at the Huntington Hotel — a Pasadena landmark even older than the Playhouse — and I've just told Guarino, the dean of a law school and an ardent *Space Patrol* fan, that while Kemmer has a fondness for Corry, he keeps a careful distance.

Guarino's not buying this. He's a prosecutor whose business is to bare people's deepest motivations, and he's convinced that Kemmer has bonded with Corry on some level that maybe he can't admit.

"Look," I say, "he's not like Clayton Moore, who never wanted to play anything but the Lone Ranger. Kemmer has never carried the mantle of Corry and he never talks about the character unless you press him. He thinks of himself as an actor first. He wants us to know that he also played villains."

"Nobody remembers those parts," Guarino shoots back, "but everyone remembers Corry. There was something right about him in that role that everyone understood. Ed Kemmer gets to you, right through your defenses. Maybe he has a gift he doesn't understand, but there was something in him that everyone could see — real courage, real virtue."

I toss out Kemmer's disclaimer: "He says that maybe another actor could have done just as well."

"Nothing doing! We all know that no one could have done it better and everyone would have done it worse. What the writers gave him, he pulled off beautifully. Doesn't he realize there was something magical about the way he played it? Doesn't he know he gave us something special and different — something that transcended American television?"

As extreme as that sounds, I see what Guarino is driving at. For 50 years, fans had drawn inspiration from the hero Moser and Jolley crafted and Kemmer and Darley made

Kemmer (right) was cast against type in *Sierra Stranger* (Columbia Pictures, 1957). "That's Howard Duff giving the nasty heavy his comeuppance," he says. "Ouch." (Author's collection)

real. And it did seem, somehow, that when *Space Patrol* disappeared, an era ended; that something left television forever. Over the years, I'd heard people say that they missed the straight-arrow heroes of the '50s; that Corry and others were archetypal — living blueprints for a good human being. Though Jolley had written the part, Kemmer embodied the magic. When he faded into the soaps (where most boomers never thought to look for him), it was as if he'd dropped off the planet. As I listened to Guarino, I heard the frustration of a generation weaned on courageous, compassionate heroes who had vanished into the sunset.

"So you're asking, 'Why did he leave us?'"

"That's it," Mike sighs. "Because the truth is, it didn't matter that the guy who played Sky King went away. Or Sergeant Preston — who cares? But Kemmer... What happened to Kemmer? Until he went the soap opera route, everyone pegged this guy as the ideal hero — not in some Schwarzenegger mode, but the old-fashioned do-or-die kind. Then he takes a different path — he makes a great living and does a lot of work that's not memorable. I guess, in a selfish way, we're wondering why he didn't give us another twenty years in a heroic role. Who knows what he could have done?"

"Maybe he wasn't offered those roles," I say. Or maybe, I think to myself, he didn't seek them out. For a moment, we're silent, letting the time between a '50s childhood and the 21st century comfortably blur. We're back in the twilight of yesteryear where our heroes are real and actors and archetypes merge. Here the line between Kemmer and Corry is thin. We're boomers, the first naïve TV generation. To us, Kemmer *is* Corry.

Mike breaks the silence. "Kemmer was special. In another dimension, another life, this guy could have *been* Commander Corry. He had all the right qualities. Compare him to others who have come and gone on the tube and they're light years apart. Kemmer was unique, and it must piss him off that America didn't single him out and idolize him, as it's done to other stars. He didn't just look good — he understood physicality. After *Space Patrol*, I saw him on *Perry Mason* where he has a fight scene and he throws an overhand right just perfectly. He's a warrior — that's what my age group saw in him." Mike pauses. "I think he understands that he had potential he did not actualize. Deep down, I think he knows that in a saner world he would have been huge."

Throughout his career as a prosecutor, Guarino grilled witnesses and studied their reactions, digging deeper, bent on shaking out the truth. He knows that, as a journalist, sometimes I do the same thing. He leans forward intently. "I want to know if the role meant something to Kemmer and if he understands what Corry meant to us."

"I've asked him that, but it's unclear. He doesn't want to go there."

"Look," says Guarino, "on cross-ex, you're never happy with the answer, so you ask a follow-up question, and then another. You force people to deal with their first causes — you just *make* them do it. Go back and ask him about it one more time."

CHAPTER 20

Carol and Tonga:
The Women of the Space Patrol

The United States had come out of a dreadful time — the Depression, and then five years tied up in a war. A lot of people were suffering from the loss of relatives, the loss of limbs. And then we came along — a daily soap opera, pure escapism, fantasy.
— Virginia Hewitt

During Space Patrol, it was a problem to visit a family with children because when they saw me, they'd run away, no matter how nice I was.

— Nina Bara

It was the skirts that fueled indelible memories. Never mind that Carol could build an atom bomb in less than an hour. Forget Tonga's startling transformation from the conniving "Lady of Diamonds" in early episodes to the trusted assistant security chief of the Space Patrol. It was the skirts that drew your attention. They were short — in fact, they were shorter than any skirts worn on civilized Earth in the 1950s, and they revealed more than most cadets had seen of a woman, especially when Carol and Tonga climbed the ladder that led up to Buzz Corry's sleek battlecruiser.

Whether good or evil, nearly all women portrayed on *Space Patrol* wore mini-skirts and were powerful. Carol and Tonga were expert pilots, and the commander sent each of them on occasional missions of daring. True, they usually got captured by the bad guys, but when that happened they were brave, defiant and clever, figuring out ingenious ways to communicate their whereabouts to Buzz so he could rescue them.

Even women who were not in the Space Patrol were entrusted with dangerous missions. Corry once asked famed scientist Lureen Harvey, who pioneered the Invisibility Transmitter, to infiltrate Ray Bolger's vicious gang. But what might have frightened Harvey more than space slime like Bolger was the plight of 20th-century women on Earth, who were still considered "the second sex" and lacked opportunities afforded men of that era. On that planet, in the mid–1950s, women had not achieved the status of their 30th-century sisters. Even in the United States, which some historians believe was the model for the freedom-loving United Planets, few — if any — women had attained a government post equal to Tonga's rank of assistant security chief.

Not that liberated 30th-century women always used their power for good. Crafty criminal Yula lured United Planets officials to her hideout, where she made lifelike android duplicates of them to do her bidding and advance her goal of conquering the solar system; and greedy Erika devised the infamous "Black Gauntlet" shake-down of innocent citizens — even trying to tempt Buzz Corry himself to join forces with her. In the *Space*

Showing off their 30th-century assets for publicity shots, Bara and Hewitt act like they've never seen a spaceship before; "Tonga" awaits take-off; "Carol" takes a break from building an atom bomb to get a leg up on the situation. (Photographs by David Sutton, courtesy Dick Darley)

Patrol universe, women, like men, could be heroic or evil, and in the staid 1950s—when the role model for girls in America was Donna Reed vacuuming the house in a cocktail dress and high heels—*Space Patrol* was ahead of its time. Young girls who envisioned a life of adventure, rather than doing the dishes in full makeup, identified as much with Buzz and Hap as Carol and Tonga, and role-played these heroes with their friends. To the sponsors' credit, girls were featured alongside boys in the commercials, and everyone was a "Space Patroller" (not a "Space Patrolman")—perhaps one of TV's first forays into political correctness. Of course the goal was to sell as many boxtop premiums as

Nina Bara fastens Virginia Hewitt's uniform before going on the air; the two women primp before airtime. (Photographs by David Sutton, courtesy Dick Darley)

possible to kids, so why exclude half of them? Still, some bright marketing genius could have come up with a Space Patrol Tea Set for girls—but that didn't happen. In the spirit of the 30th century, where daring women like Carol and Tonga flew spaceships solo, the show remained amazingly fair to women, who were allowed to be brainy, beautiful and brave.

LOS ANGELES, CALIFORNIA: MAY 1984

Before our first meeting, Virginia Hewitt, who played *Space Patrol*'s Carol, had gone down to the basement of her palatial home overlooking the Sunset Strip and brought up three dusty boxes filled with memorabilia from the show. Now, after an ice-breaking phone conversation the previous day—during which Hewitt had made it clear that she hardly ever talks about *Space Patrol* ("It was enjoyable, but something I did in my youth, and that's a long time ago"), we're sipping white wine in her white living room. Balancing a pile of newspaper clippings on her lap, she motions toward a silver platter of cheese.

"Won't you have a slice?"

The sun's waning rays slip in through ivory curtains. It's dusk in the spacious living room atop the Hollywood Hills. The phone rings again. "Excuse me," she apologizes for the third time. "My friends know I've been to the doctor today." It's a quick conversation. "No, darling, no change," she says in a voice still round and comforting like Carol's, though deeper from smoking and age. Her head is wrapped in a stylish scarf, turban-style, to conceal hair loss from "the chemotherapy bit." She has "this health problem with cancer," she explains, treating it as an annoyance, like a mild case of flu. She hangs up the phone and perches on the edge of a white sofa, strong and demure, forceful and sweet; if no longer the daughter of the Secretary General, then most certainly his sister.

Though *Space Patrol* was "centuries ago," as she puts it, it stalks her, showing up in the most unlikely places, such as the law firm she turned to recently when she divorced

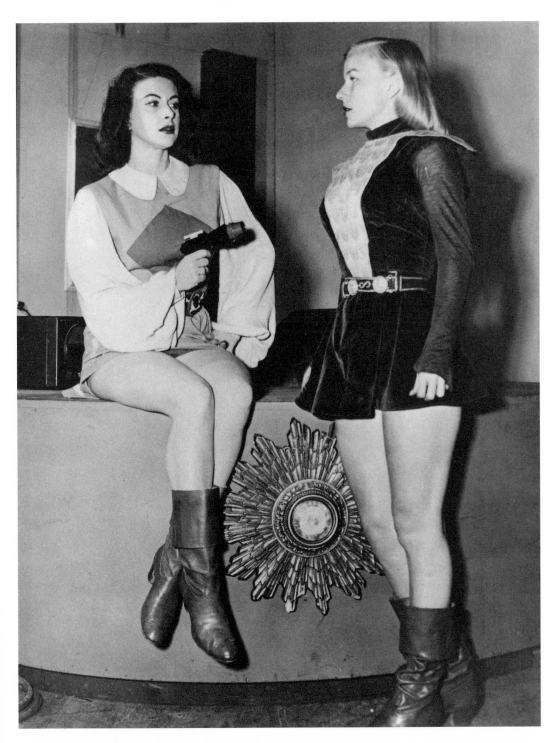

Carol (Virginia Hewitt, right) surprises the evil Tonga (Nina Bara) stealing Space Patrol documents, but the "Lady of Diamonds" gains the upper hand. Note the early uniforms from the local Los Angeles show. (Courtesy Joe Sarno)

Left: An agent spotted Hewitt playing the maid in *The Guardsman* at Hollywood's Masque Theatre. (Photograph by Jerome Robinson, author's collection) *Right:* Virginia Hewitt as charmer Felicia in *My Dear Secretary* (United Artists, 1948), starring Kirk Douglas and Laraine Day. (Author's collection)

Ernst Meer, her husband of 25 years. "Carol?" her new attorney exclaimed when she hit the door. "*Carol!* Omigod—I was so in love with you!"

She had no interest in acting when she came to Hollywood from Kansas in 1947 with her older sister, Penny, though she had dreams of being a writer. Born in Shreveport, Louisiana, in 1925, she grew up in Paola, Kansas, in agricultural Miami County, full of "splendid, shallow oil and gas fields and industrious, loyal citizens," according to the masthead of the local newspaper. Her father was an assistant superintendent for Panhandle Eastern Pipe Lines. Penny landed a job as a secretary at 20th Century–Fox and the two sisters rented an apartment in Hollywood. With her striking blond looks and figure (5'4", 117 pounds, 34-23-34), Virginia, then 22, soon landed modeling jobs. Pursued by talent scouts, she turned down their pleas to audition for film and TV parts and instead joined a little theater group, smart enough to know that she needed some acting experience before she embarked on a film career.

It wasn't long before an agent spotted her playing a maid in *The Guardsman* at Hollywood's Masque Theatre. More confident now, she agreed to audition for a supporting role in *My Dear Secretary* (1948) starring Kirk Douglas and Laraine Day. She got it, but rumors flew that Day was jealous of Hewitt's beauty and demanded the newcomer be fired, claiming she couldn't act and her presence would hurt the picture.[1] The produc-

---

[1]Jimmie Fidler in the *Wichita Beacon*; no date. Clipping found in Hewitt's files.

ers ignored Day's snipes, but columnists didn't, calling the feud "one of the hottest in Hollywood history."[2] Hewitt drew excellent reviews. "As a babe on the make [she's] a face and talent to remember," gushed *Los Angeles Daily News* critic Darr Smith. But *Secretary* didn't make Hewitt a star, though it led to featured roles in *The Flying Saucer* (1950) and *Bowery Battalion* (1951), and appearances on TV shows, including *You Be the Jury* and *Mystery Is My Hobby*. In the spring of 1950, her agent called about *Space Patrol*. "This doesn't sound like much," he told her. She showed up at the audition anyway because she wanted to keep busy and didn't have anything else lined up. Mike Moser signed her immediately and for the next five years, keeping busy wasn't a problem.

"How long my hair was in those days!" she says, rifling through publicity shots of a luminescent Carol. We stare at a headline in the *Los Angeles Times*, June 27, 1951: *30,000 Youngsters Visit TV Space Ship*. She recalls that day. "We doubted anyone would show up and when they did, we were so *relieved*," she smiles. For a moment, she lingers with this pleasant memory, then adds a disclaimer: "The only time I go through these clippings is when someone like you asks. Once in a while, to talk about *Space Patrol* is fun; then another ten years can go by without me even thinking about it."

"But Carol was a believable character," I tell her.

"Well, thank you. It really *does* make me feel good to hear that, because doing the same thing day after day, year after year, I thought, 'Oh heavens, this must be a bore for anyone to watch'—although, at the time, I was involved with people in the theatrical field who watched *Space Patrol* faithfully whenever they could. We had a little clique: Janet Leigh and Tony Curtis, Sammy Davis, Jr.—a few people like that. They *adored* it, they really did, thought it was high camp. Often I'd meet them for dinner at someone's apartment after I finished the show; they'd be patient, wait for me. A lot of people in the entertainment field got a big kick out of it." She jumps up to answer the phone.

"Who was Carol?" I ask when she returns.

"Well, I didn't create her in any special way, because there was really nothing there—the bland heroine of an adventure series. So I was just 'me'—my public self. Once in a while there was a chance to act, but that didn't come often. Generally, she was outgoing and warm, although businesslike when needed, and she could go to her lab and construct an atom bomb in about an hour. But the day-to-day routine was being me, and taking it from there."

She dreaded the scenes shot high on the catwalk, 40 feet above the studio floor. "Dick wanted me hanging over the edge. I'd be lying on my back, head and shoulders hanging out into the free air—I was terrified!" She suspected Darley had seen another Ava Gardner movie that week. "Someone, as usual, had kidnapped me, and I'd scream, 'Buzz, help me … please hurry!' It was like *The Perils of Pauline*."

"She was quiet, more reserved—a shyer kind of actress," Dick Darley remembers. "I think it was harder for her to do than for some of the others." Hewitt, he says, was private and complex, a mixture of coolness and unexpected warmth. Ed Kemmer agrees. "She never really opened up or allowed herself to become vulnerable in any way," he recalls, "but in spite of that, she was friendly and fun to be around. And she never complained." But if aloof and inscrutable at times, Hewitt was dependable, turning in a polished performance despite little training. Memorizing came easy, she says, so getting the lines down was seldom a problem. If she was anxious, then, like Kemmer, she concealed

[2]Newspaper clipping from Hewitt's scrapbook; no date or source.

Virginia Hewitt flashes a smile as she works the Automatic Astro-Navigator. Hewitt was surprised when this photograph became so popular. "Didn't anyone notice the tear in my uniform [upper left shoulder]?" she wondered. (Author's collection)

notes on the set — and she advised nervous guest actors to do the same. "Buzz would carry a clipboard with a script around, like he's doing some figuring on how many spacecraft he has," she recalls. "Or, we'd be in the cockpit, flying somewhere; I'd have my lines pasted up on one side and he'd have his on the other." Though she'd had little interest in acting, doing it nearly every day on *Space Patrol* got her excited about it, made her want to learn more. Watching Ed, Lyn and Bela, she wished that, like them, she'd trained at the Pasadena Playhouse. She debated whether to enroll in the school. "It would have been the smart thing to do," she says now. "But at that time it seemed like a waste of three years—which it wasn't, of course."

Instead, she got her training on the set. And while she was oblivious to many of the near-disasters that Kemmer staved off (such as leaning against teetering scenery to steady it), like him and Osborn, she covered for actors who panicked and forgot their lines. She did it for Gene Barry (who later gained fame as TV's "Bat Masterson") when he guest-starred as a heavy:

> He was a villain who'd kidnapped me—I was always being kidnapped—and the two of us were alone. So of course he went completely blank when he saw the red light go on, and I started feeding him his lines, saying, "So you're kidnapping me and taking me to Planet XX because…," praying that he'd pick up on it. But he didn't. He did not say one word in that whole scene. Finally, in the booth, Dick realized what was happening and quickly got the cameras into position for the next scene. But I got enough exposition out so people could understand the plot.

Hewitt has fond memories of the ABC crew:

> They were marvelous, always joking around, and they loved to tease me. Someone organized a "Beauty Contest," and they all went along with it. Everybody cast ballots to see who was prettier—Carol or Buzz. (Buzz was a very handsome young man!) It was all a big joke. It was supposed to work out 100 percent for Buzz—I found out later that's what they had planned. But one not-too-bright crew member—we used to call them "squares" in those days—took the whole thing seriously and refused to vote for Buzz. He was the only idiot that didn't go along with it; he had a crush on me.

She shoves the huge pile of clippings aside. "Why not arrange them in some order?" I ask.

"I wouldn't waste the time on it. Someone tried to start a scrapbook once, but the glue soaked through."

"What was the magic of *Space Patrol*?"

She settles into the plushness of the ivory sofa and considers the question. "I *do* know what you mean about that 'something' we had. Why did it work?" She's silent for a moment, sipping wine, then says softly:

> The United States had come out of a dreadful time—the Depression, and then five years tied up in a war. A lot of people were suffering from the loss of relatives, from the loss of limbs. And then we came along—a daily soap opera, pure escapism, fantasy. People loved the so-called relationship between Buzz and me. We could never kiss, but I was the only one in the show allowed to call him "Buzz" and be familiar with him. Sometimes he'd put his arm around my waist: "Careful, Carol." That's as far as we could go. People followed the continuing story of our lives, intertwined in the future, in space. Who would have dreamed, in those days, that in a few years there'd be Sputnik, and then somebody *really* up on the moon?

Suddenly she laughs, recalling one of the worst moments on camera. "We had this character actor playing a villain, and he had a huge stomach. Hap had just shot him with a ray gun and he was lying there on the floor, supposed to be knocked out and paralyzed—and for some reason he started laughing." And laughter in a tense situation, like when you're doing a TV show before millions of people, is contagious:

Carol gets set to either clean the spaceship or celebrate Halloween. (Author's collection)

That huge belly started shaking and Hap and I were just breaking up! There were some columns on the set in the background and Hap turned his face into one of them. His shoulders were shaking and I knew he was gone. Do you know how contagious that is? And so I had to do the same thing—I turned my back and talked into the next column. And it must have been the most ridiculous-looking show in the world because here we both were, talking into a column, our shoulders shaking—and this unconscious villain

Lyn and Virginia feign a rehearsal for a photo shoot. (Photograph by Richard Yale Plowman, courtesy Beth Flood)

with his stomach shaking. Naturally, up in the booth they could see what was happening, and it was one of the worst moments because it was uncontrollable and there was nowhere they could shoot to.

She doesn't talk about dating Lyn or their bitter breakup when she fell madly in love with Austrian interior design genius Ernst Meer, whom she married in 1953. Instead, she says only that "Hap and I spent a lot of time together because we were the two single people on the show," then fast-forwards to the year he died. By then, in 1958, Osborn had forgiven her for marrying Meer and confided in both of them about the blackouts he was having and how he was at his wit's end over how to deal with them. She felt help-less then; now, nearly three decades later, she's still furious at Osborn's psychiatrist, who failed to run tests to determine if Lyn's symptoms had a physical cause and thus missed the brain tumor that killed him. "I could have hung that doctor up by his toes, I was so angry!" she bursts out. "A psychiatrist is a medical doctor. If someone's having black-outs, you check the brain. Maybe, if it had been caught in time, he'd be alive today."

Thinking of Lyn's death triggers thoughts of her own; of how, from her vantage point at age 59, everything is relative. "I used to say, 'Dear God, if you'll let me live to be 35, I will be so happy—because after 35, who cares?' Now I say that if we're lucky, we get older. I don't worry about the wrinkles or the getting-older look. I just wish I were healthy, that's all. I'd be happy if that had happened to me, but it didn't." The chemotherapy, she explains, is just a way to buy time. "I ran out of luck."

I'm studying her as she talks. Though age has faded her once stunning beauty, I see a smooth, unlined face and Carol's lovely smile. "You haven't changed that much," I tell her.

She lights up for a second. "Well, thank you—that's nice to hear!" But the light quickly fades. "The fifties are not a good place to be in when you're alone and having health problems," she says. I tentatively mention alternative cancer therapies and she bristles. "I've told my friends that I don't want to hear about that. I have my own way of doing things." She throws that stubborn, defiant look at me that Carol used to give her kidnappers and says something so true that it sticks in my mind years later. "Look, I put a great deal of credence in how some of those therapies have worked for others, but you can only be successful at things if you really believe in them, right? And if you *don't* believe in them, what can you do?"

I change tactics. "The best thing people can do now is give you space, right?"

"That's it! You know, I'm alone; I'm not married. I have no men that I'm interested in, unfortunately. And as you get older, a woman alone in this society is excess: Forget it. People you've known for 20 or 30 years—suddenly, at dinner parties, they need an extra man, not another woman. It's rotten."

When *Space Patrol* ended in 1955, she and Ernst established Courant, a ritzy studio showroom on the Sunset Strip filled with spectacular crystal chandeliers that attracted the rich and famous. Hewitt adored this new life that whisked her out of SF fandom and into the society pages of the *Los Angeles Times*. For five years she'd been pursued by fans on the street, tailed by cars filled with high school girls when she left the studio. Most of these encounters were harmless, but some mail was "shady," and she turned at least one death threat over to the FBI. "It was a man in a mental institution in Texas who threatened to kill me when he got out," she recalls. It was a relief to leave that weirdness behind and throw herself into her husband's business. For years, she'd painted as a hobby; now, as a partner in Courant, she designed some of the shimmering crystal fixtures that graced the homes of the shop's stellar clientele. (Actor Laurence Harvey boasted that he had a chandelier from Courant in every room of his house—even the bathroom and kitchen.)[3]

Hewitt was not only artistically talented, but like *Space Patrol's* Carol, she was smart. Her witticisms ("A Hollywood parking lot is where you pay a quarter to have your car remodeled") were often quoted by columnists.[4] Strangely, one of her offhand quips in 1951 was eerily predictive of her future life with Meer. While donning a sequined costume for a film, she reportedly said: "I feel like a stand-in for a chandelier."[5]

She pulls a photo of "Carol" from the fragile pile of newspaper clippings on her lap. "The years go fast, and that's the trouble," she says softly, "especially when you're busy. They just zip by, and suddenly, there you are, the 'older woman'—and you can't believe it!" She stares at the photo. "And you think, 'Hey, *that's* me—not this thing.'"

That afternoon, in the spring of 1984, she was trying her best to live a full life—off

---

[3]*Los Angeles Herald Examiner*, August 2, 1978.
[4]Jimmy Starr, *The Evening Herald and Express* (Los Angeles), no date.
[5]*Ibid*, August 13, 1951.

Hewitt (center) greets clients in 1980 at Courant, the world-famous chandelier showroom that she and husband Ernst Meer created. (Courtesy Penny McFadden)

to London in two weeks, despite the chemo. "My *tumors* are healthy," she jokes. "Besides, what am I going to do—sit and cry? Life's too short. I believe in enjoying every minute you can." She sighs. "The happy ending would be that the prince and I ran away together and lived happily ever after, OK? But that didn't happen."

When she died two years later, she left me the boxes she'd dragged up from the basement for our first meeting. She had saved everything from the show—every scrap of paper, hundreds of fan letters, every card Lyn sent her, every photo they'd taken together, every teasing note he'd scribbled on her script. She'd saved the many thank-you notes for personal appearances at charity benefits and telethons and the driving directions for how to get there. She'd saved pitch sheets for her own interview show, *Roof Over Hollywood*, which never materialized but revealed a secret—if fleeting—wish for stardom. She'd saved *Space Patrol* merchandise too: the puzzle, the Chart of the Universe, party plates and napkins, the official handkerchiefs with Lyn's photo on the box. And she'd saved the piles of newspaper clippings that tracked her charmed life, from her childhood in rural Kansas to her stint as a TV star, her dream marriage to the talented Ernst Meer and their international success with Courant. Some of the articles noted that she liked to draw. Buried in one of the boxes among an array of publicity shots of herself looking pert, lovely, sexy, cool, vulnerable, casual, tough, hot, elegant, I found a caricature of a woman, mouth open, about to say something important. The caption in bold capital letters read:

RESOLUTION: TO MENTION SPACE PATROL OCCASIONALLY

"Resolution" found in Virginia Hewitt's files. (Author's collection)

LA CAÑADA-FLINTRIDGE, CALIFORNIA: APRIL 1984

"Did I mention that Happy unzipped my costume on network TV?" Nina Bara is saying, when she's interrupted by a loud clatter. Suddenly, a painting that's been minding its business on the wall has crashed to the floor. "What's that?" she asks, startled. I flash on the mysterious voice that had guided me to the nostalgia store where Bara had been hawking her *Space Patrol* memorabilia only a few days earlier. It's as if a portal to the past had opened in the gloom of that store; it's the reason I'm sitting opposite Bara now in the den of her home in this upscale Los Angeles suburb.

I do not mention the unseen friend who has awakened my interest in *Space Patrol*. Though kind and hospitable, Bara, who played Tonga, is edgy, excitable and self-absorbed; I have the impression that she skews reality the way she wants it. Tossing anything strange or other-worldly into that mindset could blow up in my face. To say that I was beginning to suspect that Lyn Osborn, long dead, was urging me to write about *Space Patrol* might have met with warm approval — or provoked a burst of temper that would get me thrown out of her house. So I say nothing about the synchronicity of the picture dropping from the wall at the sound of Hap's name.

Looking delicate and dangerous in a leopard-spotted velour pantsuit, she jumps up from her chair, replaces the picture securely on its hook, and resumes her story:

> We were doing the network TV show. The Commander had been lost somewhere in space and I was just saying how sorry I was when Happy hands me some files. I picked up the space-o-phone and while I was calling to find out news of the Commander, Happy unzipped my whole costume — and undid my bra too! I grabbed the files, put them in front of me, and said, "Thank you" to Happy as he left. I said my last line, "We'll find the Commander somehow" — and backed out the door. Then I went after Happy. Oh, God, I was out to *kill* him!

Her lilting, high-pitched voice is the same; she hasn't lost a trace of her melodious Argentine accent — though in *Missile to the Moon*, which she made in 1958, it seemed to have almost disappeared. She talks excitedly as we leaf through photos of the *Space Patrol* cast in piles of magazines and in the self-published books she has written about the show.[6] She loves reliving those days.

It was a late afternoon in February 1950 when Nina Bara, preoccupied with thoughts of quitting show business and returning to college, joined *Los Angeles Examiner* columnist Pat Hogan at Nickodell's for a drink.

"That's Tonga!" came a voice from behind her.

"Who the hell is that?" demanded Bara.

"Mike Moser," said Hogan.

Moser told her she was exactly what he had in mind for the villainess in his new TV space opera. The screen test was scheduled for the following day in a spaceship rigged up in the shadow of the imposing *Phantom of the Opera* set at the old Warner Bros. studios, now ABC Television Center.[7] "I sat in the back of a phony spaceship with two men rocking it up and down, and said: 'That'll be the end of Commander Corry. He doesn't know he's dealing with Tonga, Lady of Diamonds!'" She laughs heartily. "That was it." Moser said he'd call, but she forgot about it until the phone rang a month later. "We're on now," Mike told her. "Come on over and sign the contract." She turned on her TV set. "And sure enough, they *were* on, introducing the characters. And there I was, in the back compartment of the ship."

---

[6]In 1976, Bara published *Space Patrol*, a three-volume set of books, under her real name, Frances Linke. She ordered 250 sets, but due to a printer's error, only 225 were salable. (Bara's daughter, Cecillia, reports that the books sold out and there are no plans for a second printing.) Volumes 1 and 3 contain her memories of the show along with photos of the cast and promos for *Space Patrol* merchandise. Volume 2 is a black-and-white reprint of three *Space Patrol* comic books that originally appeared in color. The first two were offered in a much-touted, 12-issue subscription series distributed by Ziff-Davis. Issue 1 was released in July 1952, and dated "Summer"; issue 2 followed three months later, dated "October-November." Issues 3-12 never appeared, causing angst among kids who'd hurled their allowance at the $1.25 "yearly" subscription. The third reprint in Volume 2 is the rare *Space Patrol* "Blood Booster" comic book, part of a public relations campaign by Ralston Purina to get Americans to donate blood to replenish the national reserve during the Korean "conflict."

[7]The name was changed to The Prospect Studios in 2002.

She loved the role of the heavy, the evil Tonga, AKA "Lady of Diamonds," whose gang of thugs terrorized Buzz Corry. "My favorite is playing meanies. I've played Lady Macbeth — all the mean killers. There's lots more meat to a mean person, more complexity of character; it's *dull* to play an ordinary person. I like to play — it doesn't have to be a *bad* person, but someone who's suffering something." But Tonga's criminal tendencies, depicted in the early 15-minute episodes, were cleanly erased by the Brainograph, and by the time the show aired nationwide, she was Security Chief Major Robertson's trusted assistant.[8] Only one "flashback" episode revealed the ex-villainess involved in a rip-off scheme that targeted unsuspecting tourists just out to get away from it all on a trip to Earth's moon.

Nina slips that episode into the video recorder.

"This isn't my real bad Tonga — the *real* bad Tonga had agents, henchmen, the whole thing. In the early shows I was *so* bad."

On the screen, Buzz Corry hands Tonga a sheaf of confidential documents.

TONGA: Don't worry Commander, I will guard them with my life. (Smoothly exits.)
CORRY: (to Hap) She will, too.
HAP: Yeah, but there was a time when she couldn't be trusted.
CORRY: (confidently) Yes, but that was before Medical Science Center cured her of her criminal tendencies…
HAP: Do you remember the first time we ever ran into Tonga? (The flashback begins.)

"I get worse at the end of this thing, but they couldn't make me *much* worse because the P.T.A. had already complained. Some little girls were upsetting their parents by announcing they wanted to be just like me when they grew up." Bara sighs. "I'm much better as a heavy. Otherwise the lines are too dull: 'Yes, Commander; no, Commander.'" She settles wistfully into her overstuffed chair. "There are better episodes of the 'bad' Tonga. I wish I had them."

Bara goes to "paper conventions" — gatherings of collectors of paper keepsakes: old airline schedules, comics, picture postcards, stock certificates. And *Space Patrol* memorabilia. She appears as a guest star at science fiction conventions in her *Space Patrol* uniform, which she still wears well. She sits at a table, signing autographs and selling

Above: Bara, who bore a striking resemblance to movie star Hedy Lamarr, inscribed this photograph to Dick Darley, "To Dick, to whom I owe so much." (Courtesy Dick Darley)

Opposite: Tonga (Nina Bara) climbs the ladder to the Space Patrol battlecruiser. (Author's collection)

[8]Many viewers agreed with Bara that the evil Tonga was more exciting, and when she morphed into a "good" character, letters of protest poured in. On June 17, 1952, the *Los Angeles Daily News* offered some insight into her transformation. Producer Mike Moser (the paper reported) "changed her from a villainess to wearing a halo because small fry enthusiasts who eat up the science fiction program have plenty of time to find out about 'the other kind of woman.'"

her three-volume set of *Space Patrol* memories, written while she was battling cancer. "Writing those books kept me alive. I did it at a time when I was very ill, but I didn't want people to forget *Space Patrol*."

She was born Frances Bauer in Buenos Aires in 1920. Her mother, an Italian singer, dancer and actress, enrolled her in ballet school as soon as she learned to walk. The family moved to Germany when she was nine but fled when Hitler came to power. Her father was an American citizen, so she and her parents returned to the States and settled in Cincinnati, where Nina attended high school. Fluent in Spanish and German, she had yet to master English. Her dream was to be a doctor, but one day a friend with acting ambitions dragged her to a drama contest. "I didn't want anything to do with acting," Bara insists. "My mother had been an actress and I didn't want that kind of work." Nonetheless, she entered the contest, won a scholarship to an acting school, and was hooked. Roles in local radio dramas and summer stock tours followed; then she set out for Hollywood. She found bit parts in movies (*The Mummy's Curse*, *Adventure*, *The Gay Señorita*) but after five years of credits like "Cuban singer" and "Cajun girl," she was thinking of going back to school when Moser tapped her for *Space Patrol*.

As the 15-minute local show struggled to lift off in Los Angeles, Bara, who had an instinct for public relations, spent her off-hours plugging *Space Patrol* wherever she could. "I joined the Radio and TV Editors' Club so I could push the show; I placed items every day in one paper or another." She wrote a column called "Bara Facts" for *TV Times* magazine in which she gossiped about the cast, sparking curiosity about the show. She penned feature articles too, such as "That Gang of Mine" for *Tele-Views* (May 1952) in which she profiled the cast, both on and off screen. Moonlighting as a columnist boosted her own career. She schmoozed with celebs, got known around town. She was "Miss Emmy" of 1952, handing out the awards. From the day she'd set foot in Hollywood, she'd figured out that if you want to be seen, you court the press—or become one of them. "I was very friendly with newspaper people because they did a lot of favors for me," she admits. That's why she found herself in Nickodell's with the *Examiner's* Pat Hogan on that winter day in 1950, within eyeshot of Mike Moser. "I knew Pat would have some other guys from the paper there, so I went," she says candidly.

Considering that Bara did more than any other cast member to boost the show, it's ironic that she was fired from *Space Patrol* in December 1953. But that can happen, if you threaten to sue the producer.

When Mike Moser was hit by a car and killed in April of that year, Bara wondered what would happen to the merchandising agreement he'd signed with the cast just after the show went network. She remembers that meeting well:

> Mike called us all in and we sat on the floor of the stage. He wrote a piece of paper in which we agreed—and we got copies of it—to get 3 percent of the net profits which would be forthcoming from the merchandising.[9] Mike signed it and so did Mike Devery, who would be doing the promotion. Everybody signed it. That's how come we all took trips all over the United States to promote the show—we did it for nothing because we were supposed to get all this money.

Of course, as Ed Kemmer likes to say, the first thing you learn in a deal like that is to never accept a piece of the *net* profits "because there aren't any—ever." But the young

---

[9]Kemmer and Osborn were promised 5 percent.

cast, naïve and giddy with success, was unschooled in creative accounting, Hollywood style. It was soon evident that Mike wasn't living up to his word, but Bara had hopes that one day he would. Though she didn't trust him, she believed that, on some level, Mike cared. Like her, he knew that the show needed constant promotion; at least there was someone who gave a damn at the helm. But when Mike died and Helen Moser stepped in as producer, it was obvious that the show meant nothing to her. Passionate by nature, Bara was spoiling for a fight. She called Helen and reminded her of Mike's promise to share the merchandising profits with the cast:

> I said, "Helen, you know that before Mike died we signed those contracts and blah, blah, blah." She said, "It doesn't mean a thing. You might as well tear them up because I will never, ever give you a penny of merchandising." I said, "But Helen, we traveled all over. We did all this extra work for you." She said, "Not for me. You did it for Mike, and you got the publicity out of it." I said, "I'm not very happy, Helen. I'm going to see an attorney." And she said: "You see an attorney and you're fired." And that's exactly what happened.

Her friends in the press rushed to her aid, though it was too late. On December 8, 1953, *Daily News* columnist Paul Price wrote:

> Nina Bara, the Tonga of *Space Patrol*, is mighty unhappy over the way she's been treated by those running the program. No names today. Maybe later. After spending years to help build the show, Nina was suddenly dumped from the program.... According to Nina: "I just received a telephone call one day saying I wasn't to be used anymore. There could have been a nicer way to do it".... In the early days, Nina made personal appearances for nothing and was a real promotion-builder for the program. Now she's preparing a suit against the show to prevent use of her picture on packages of cereal, promotion gimmicks, etc.... Until there's reasonable rebuttal, I'm with Nina.

"Helen Moser was an accountant — she didn't know anything about show business," Bara says angrily. "But one thing she did know: she hated my guts." And though Mike was "a slippery character," Bara believes that "he would have seen the light, that we deserved better. If he'd been cornered by all five of us, he would have come across. He would never, ever have done what Helen Moser did."

Even though she was no longer officially "Tonga," it took a long time to shake the character. She finally landed a job on *Mr. Ed*, but when she arrived on the set, the director said, "I've seen her too many times on *Space Patrol*. Forget it." Finally, in 1958, she snagged the part of "Alpha" in the Richard Cunha B movie, *Missile to the Moon*—and got to play a villain again. "If you watch it, you'll see the evil," she says happily. In the Rhino Home Video release of the film, scream queen Elvira introduces it as "one small step for mankind; one giant step backwards for movie making," but if you like B movies in which the actors take everything seriously, heroically overcoming cheesy scripts and special effects, then *Missile to the Moon* is a treasure. Bara's cutthroat moon-woman, Alpha, makes "bad" Tonga look like a Girl Scout.[10] After *Space Patrol*, it was the highlight of her career.

Bara married ABC stage manager and assistant director Bob Sheldon in 1952, outraging young fans who expected her to wed Major Robertson. The union lasted a year. In 1956, she marched down the aisle again with actor-musician Dick Winslow, but the

[10]Rhino Home Video, 1992.

Nina Bara as conniving moon woman "Alpha" in Richard Cunha's *Missile to the Moon* (1958). Horror movie maven Elvira called the film "One small step for mankind; one giant step backwards for movie making." (Author's collection)

couple parted after six months.[11] In 1964, she married *Los Angeles Times Mirror* writer Ray Linke and they adopted a daughter, Cecillia. Bara finally went back to school, earning a master's degree in library science that led to a job as library administrator for Blue Cross; and she indulged her passion for breeding and showing pedigree Siamese cats, collecting dozens of ribbons and medallions for her national champions.

She curls up, catlike, in the big chair, lost, for a moment, in memories. Though she was fired from the show, she holds no bitterness— except toward Helen Moser. She talks affectionately of "the gang," as she calls the cast, as if their meteoric rise to fame was just a few years ago, not 30, and as if she had stayed with them until the end. She laughs, remembering how the "bad" Tonga scared little kids, who either ran from her or accused her of harming their idol, Cadet Happy. Other fans— mainly men — ran toward her, finding no fault with her figure (a well-publicized 36-24-36), emerald eyes or evil ways. "I watch *Space Patrol* every night and my father is nuts about you," wrote one kid who lived in Southern California, where the 15-minute show was broadcast on weekdays. A 30-year-old man in Michigan wrote, "You're the girl I'd most like to settle down with — on Mars."

To be fired had to be heartbreaking, though she'd brought it on herself. Bara glosses over that, recalling instead the closeness of the cast and the heady thrill as the show garnered big-time publicity:

> We weren't really aware of our impact until *Life* magazine ran this tremendous layout in 1952. Then every big star, director, producer in Hollywood started coming on this lousy set of ours to see this group of people. There was tremendous chemistry between us— a lot of bickering, but it was family bickering. Virginia and I used to fight a lot because of the color of her hair and my hair, stuff like that. Or the "boys" would come through our dressing room to get to theirs when we were in our underwear. We got so mad once, we nailed the door shut. They couldn't get through to their dressing room and we were all almost late for the show. But there wasn't a holiday— Christmas, New Year's— where we wouldn't all get together. We were a close-knit family.

The years have softened the blow of getting canned, as well as the competitiveness she felt with Virginia Hewitt. She remembers Hewitt flying into a rage when a publicity photo of Bara with Ed Kemmer appeared in the widely distributed *Hollywood Yearbook* for 1952:

> It was not my fault— it just so happened that the ABC publicity agent liked the look of danger in Commander Corry's face and mine, so they used it. But Carol was mad, and she and I got madder and madder until it got to be a real, rousing battle. We had a scene together in a 15-minute episode and we were fighting like cats and dogs. We went onstage and took our places, still fighting, until we heard, "You're on!" Then I said, "Oh, my dear Carol, don't worry," and she put her arms around me and we hugged each other. Everybody got hysterical!

"Ginny is very ill," Bara says softly, of Hewitt, "but I tell her, 'Just keep alive. I want to be able to do another show with you.'"

Like Hewitt, she compares her stage ordeals on *Space Patrol* to *The Perils of Pauline*. As the "good" Tonga, she was a famed scientist who invented devices like the Radurium

---

[11]She met Winslow on the set of *Easy to Wed* in 1946. He plays a bandleader; she's a rumba dancer.

Tonga shares a joke with Art Linkletter in 1952 on his popular *Life with Linkletter* show, which originated from ABC Television Center. (Author's collection)

Glove (which saved Hap's life once), but often the bad guys sabotaged her work and things literally blew up in her face. "I was in mine explosions. Sometimes the whole studio came down on me. It was balsa wood, but you had to be careful it missed you, you know?" Not only that, but, "I got beaten over the head and clobbered many times. The worst injury she ever suffered during a live show was from an exposed nail on a prop:

Nina Bara in December 1976. "This is one of my dad's favorite photos," says daughter Cecillia. (Courtesy Cecillia Pier)

> There were a lot of hazards. One of the villains hit me with a piece of equipment he had that was supposed to knock me out. It was nailed together, but a piece had fallen off and there was a raw nail exposed. He scraped it across my back and it went right through my costume. I was bleeding all through the show.

Her fondest memories are of Lyn Osborn, who teased her mercilessly. Bara believes that Osborn's death, three years after the show ended, traumatized the cast more than anyone could — or would — admit. "We were all so very close, and Happy was a great part of it. He was like our child, in a way. When he died, there were no more get-togethers. We avoided each other." Lyn, she says, "was good to everybody. He would help starving actors who begged for one-line roles on the show. He was a very good guy."

She's planning a comeback.

"I'm going to have a big kick in a year because I intend to retire from Blue Cross— and then I'll contact my old agents. Without an agent, forget it; you might as well go to a cattle call with a million actors. A friend of mine just got a part as a Southern belle on a soap. She's 69." Bara pauses. "Maybe I'll go with Carlos Alvarado — he got me parts in Spanish films. I did *The Gay Señorita* at Columbia and they gave me huge close-ups, the whole screen."[12]

---

[12]In *The Gay Señorita* (1945), Bara played "Lupita" (uncredited), according to the Internet Movie Database (www.IMDb.com).

Just six months ago, a disturbing incident occurred that nudged her to revive her acting career:

> The *Herald Examiner* ran a section right in the middle of their Sunday magazine about "nobodies" — people who'd never gotten anywhere in Hollywood — and there was my picture! Well, about ten or fifteen people called the editor, and my attorney, who loved *Space Patrol*, got angry and wrote them a letter. They thought they were going to be sued, but we said, "We don't want to sue; we want you to retract." They'd found the picture in the 5-cent bin in a Hollywood bookstore. If they'd known it was me, it would not have been there, but what are you going to do?

She's restless. She has to take a bath before dinner and everybody will be waiting for her. I swing the talk back to *Space Patrol* one last time. Why does she think the show (which, at the time of my visit, is currently airing on USA Cable Network) has endured?

"My books!" she says quickly. "My books brought it back. Let me tell you something: Before my books, nobody remembered anything — nobody except a few people sitting around and thinking about their childhood." For a moment, she's silent, a million DU's away. "We were a charmed group of people," she says slowly, "all five of us. It was our personalities, our directors, the people who dedicated their whole lives to it, back then. And it was the spirit of the times. It was not the kind of thing where they said 'We'll film it again.' We couldn't. It was a one-take thing."

CHAPTER 21

A Mission of Daring

Ed Kemmer didn't just act in a kiddie show for money, like he thinks; he had far more influence than he knows. The boomers were the first generation of kids brought up on TV. Every word, each innuendo made by the Commander or Happy was indelibly impressed.

— Arie Raymond

LOS ANGELES TO NEW YORK: JUNE 2001

I'd made a promise to Mike Guarino—to approach Kemmer again, dig deeper, see if at this point in his life he had any urge to move closer to Corry. I'd learned over the years that asking about his career path was touchy ground, a minefield where it didn't take much to make him annoyed or irritable. But like Guarino, I wanted him to understand his impact, embrace his legacy. For in the timeline of Earth, a strange thing had happened: A half-century had passed since our childhood heroes had visited our living rooms at twilight or on Saturday morning, and like time travelers rocketed into the future, we were suddenly older than them. Most of these icons had been 30-something when we'd bonded. Now we were old enough to be their parents—and with this maturity, this trick of time, came the urge to thank these actors who had given themselves so completely to their heroic roles that the roles had swallowed their careers.

Though Kemmer insisted he had not suffered typecasting after *Space Patrol*, he certainly had in the minds of many viewers, where he and Corry had merged forever. But unlike Captain Video, the Lone Ranger, Hoppy, Gene and Roy, he had not clung to the role that made him famous. Instead, he'd dropped off the viewscope and disappeared into the soap opera world. As I'd told him in 1988, that was a place most Space Patrollers, busy in the '60s with college and career, seldom visited. To which he'd replied: "I hope you weren't watching. I hope you had better things to do."

To some ex-kids, Kemmer's choice of a career in the soaps was only slightly less traumatic than if Corry had purchased a condo on Planet X. It was unthinkable that Hollywood had not teleported him into another heroic TV role, or better still, into memorable parts on the big screen. Since it hadn't, Corry was his legacy, and Guarino was typical of those who honored it by trying to apply the behavior he'd modeled in their daily lives. I knew many who did this and wanted Kemmer to know it. Their grateful letters—which he had read but not saved until Fran Kemmer stepped in — reflected the magic he'd turned loose in the world and that lived on in us. As Guarino put it: "Kemmer was an authentic hero, and those come few and far between." Now that we were older than our childhood idols had been on the screen, we had the right to speak up, to say, like proud parents: "Well done!" So I kept my promise to Mike. I called Kemmer with a mission in mind:

Ed Kemmer, as the heroic Buzz Corry, proudly displays a model of his battlecruiser, the *Terra V*. (Author's collection)

to find out if playing Corry had really meant something to him; and if he understood how much it had meant to us.

"We need more like him," Kemmer says quickly when I tell him about Guarino's work as a prosecutor and how he once ran for Los Angeles City Attorney because he wanted to make a difference.

"He was inspired by you," I point out. "He says: 'Kemmer was my first hero. I model a lot of my conduct after him in trial.'"

"That's powerful stuff," he says, taken aback.

"Mike thinks you were trying to accomplish something — that you believed strongly in what Corry stood for, that you wanted to get those values across."

"Well," he says cautiously, "he has some valid stuff there. When I went through cadet training, those principles were driven home through the code of honor. It forces you to be truthful, honest and compassionate, to never lie or cheat. Anyone who went through the cadets got that, and it stays with you. It's all the good things that Buzz Corry would be for."

"We missed that in television when *Space Patrol* went off the air. When you went to the soaps, it was as if you had left…"

"Left?" He's annoyed. "How the hell could I turn down a job? Whether a role is challenging or not, an actor needs money to live!"

"What people are saying is—"

"That they miss it." He's heard this before. "Nothing wrong with that. Hell, I didn't want *Space Patrol* to go off either. It was great while it lasted, and I wish it had gone on forever—though whether it would have lasted a lifetime and if I would have stuck with it, I don't know."

Whether he accepts it or not, Kemmer has an uncanny ability to inspire, even in real life. When Kim, the child he delivered himself, was 19, she had a boyfriend who knew of her dad's war experience and had watched several episodes of *Space Patrol.* One day they had a serious spat and he tore up all the photos she'd given him—except the one of her father. That one he needed. He was going on a long hike in the wilds and he always carried that photo of Ed in his backpack for inspiration. Stories like this make Kemmer uneasy; he knows his faults too well to be comfortable as a real-life hero. I know this but, for the moment, ignore it. "You seem to inspire people," I tell him.

"I don't dwell on that," he says sharply. "My God, I'm not such a heroic character that I go through life defending the innocent and beating up on the bad guys!"

"Of course not. But you brought a magic to Corry that seemed rooted in personal conviction. It reminds Mike Guarino of a scene from the movie *My Favorite Year*, where an actor known for heroic roles says to a fan: 'I'm *not* larger than life. I'm *not* those silly, goddamned heroes I played in the movies.' But the fan tells him: 'Yes you are! Nobody's *that* good an actor. There had to be something in you that convinced me of that courage, that virtue.'"[1]

"There may be a grain of truth in that," he says carefully. "A person who's not too nice wouldn't do well playing Corry. Even a good actor would have a hard time, if he wasn't a nice person—at least, he wouldn't get away with it for long." He hauls out the usual disclaimer, but this time adds a twist: "I like to think there were a lot of guys who would have played Corry just as well—but I played it, and if it meant so much to people, that's very good to hear." He coughs self-consciously. "I'm surprised at how much it *did* mean to people!"

"That's why we want to know if it meant something to you."

"Hell, yes!" he shoots back. "It's a great satisfaction. Making people believe in themselves is what it's about. And to know that you've had a good influence on young kids, that you've helped guide them forward in a decent manner. It gives me a warm feeling to know I was helpful—even in areas where I wasn't aware of *why* I was helpful." He pauses, still mystified by his impact. "It had to be strong stuff for them to remember it this long!"

"It was." I throw out a few examples to support my case: "Jon Rogers recalls that he 'wanted to grow up to be just like Commander Corry: cool under fire, brave in the face of danger, willing to stand up for what he believes.' Allan Cohen says: 'My big model was Kemmer. Commander Corry had compassion; he was gentle and treated everyone as an equal. I copied what he did.' And Elliott Swanson remembers that 'as a kid, I essentially raised myself, but Corry gave me something to hang onto.'"

He's listening.

"We know you liked to play bad guys, too," I say quickly, "but in our minds, you're

---

[1]*My Favorite Year*, Metro-Goldwyn-Mayer (1982)

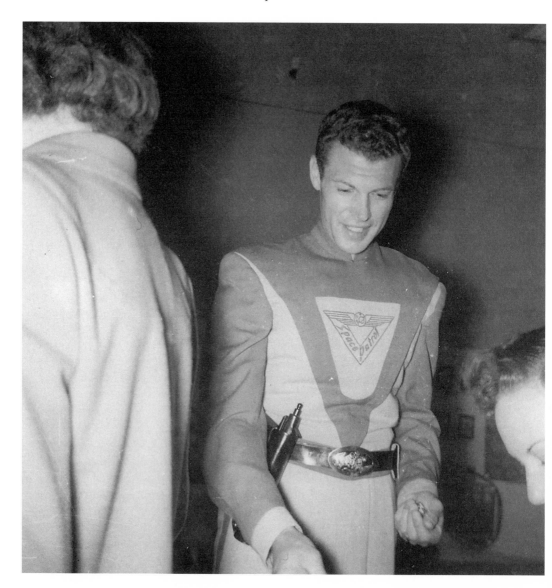

Kemmer makes a personal appearance in 1951 in dress uniform. (Author's collection)

Corry. You gave a lot of us kids our first glimpse of a truly good human being. Mike Guarino says, 'Kemmer was the first person I saw who modeled: Don't put yourself first; do whatever's necessary to do the right thing. That stays in a little boy's mind.'"

"Maybe that's it," he says, thinking it through. "Maybe it brought something to people's lives that they wanted badly but weren't getting in full measure."

"You did that."

"I'm sure happy I did! But I never thought of it in those terms before — that Corry gave them something they needed. That never occurred to me." He pauses. "That's heavy stuff. If it's true, then *Space Patrol* is obviously the most valuable thing I've done as an actor." Once again, he flashes back to his military experience. "It goes back to cadet training, to the code of honor. That's what the kids picked up: Corry being for the good things — not to cheat or be a bad person, but to be a good person, a kind person. I like to think I had those qualities. But to have kids remember that, to have this impact you're not even aware of, this effect on young minds — hell, you can't ask for more than that out of life." He's silent, letting it in. "I understand now," he says slowly. "I can see why that would have tremendous meaning — and it's very fulfilling. That's stuff you like to remember, that you can take with you wherever you go. And that includes the grave."

Kemmer, 79, shows off one of the family's eight cats. (Photograph by Jean-Noel Bassior)

Of all the interviews I did with Kemmer, the thing that struck me most was what he'd said in our first conversation when I'd asked what kept him going after he and two other men escaped during the forced P.O.W. march to Moosburg. In an heroic action right out of a *Space Patrol* script, Kemmer, too weak to keep up with his buddies, insists they go on without him, leaving him alone behind enemy lines. The weather is freezing, he has no food. How do you deal with a do-or-die situation like that? I'd asked. "It's doing what you have to do to accomplish something you think maybe you can't," he'd said quickly, not missing a beat. Perhaps that kind of raw focus and faith sparked the magic he brought to Corry five years later.

Sometimes an actor's destiny is to play a role that transcends his or her career. That happened in Ed Kemmer's case. Had he gone on to shine in a string of blockbuster films, perhaps Buzz Corry would be less memorable today. And though many felt Kemmer had star quality, by the late '60s, the industry had begun to change and people did business differently. In the old days, says actor Barry Newman, your track record counted:

> A producer would say, "I know this actor, I know Ed Kemmer. C'mon, Ed, do the show." But suddenly the networks took over and the producers were nothing but hired hands. The [network heads] wanted people to read who did less than five lines — just to show their power. I know guys who've won Academy Awards and some 25-year-old kid says, "Tell me what you've done." The business has changed.

Kemmer felt these changes. Talking once about auditions, he expressed anger and impatience at being kept waiting — something voiceover veteran Dick Beals, who played kids on *Space Patrol* radio spots, says is unavoidable when nobody cares what you've done. "You'd think that after doing 2,000 cartoon shows for Hanna-Barbera, they wouldn't call me in to audition — but they do. You gotta live with that or get out of the business. I'm angry and impatient, too, but if you want the work, you put up with it." If you've really got star quality, Beals adds, then once you get in, "you wow the director with a creative reading, even if you've waited an hour with 300 people. You do things that a star can do."

Some colleagues wonder if Kemmer's agent pushed hard enough to get him plum roles, pointing out that had he landed just one good part as an action hero, he could have defeated the link with *Space Patrol*. But TV was young — there weren't that many shows, and actors did not move as freely among them as they do today. And perhaps, says film producer Gary Shusett, who founded Sherwood Oaks Experimental College for aspiring screenwriters, Kemmer himself lacked the combo of blind ambition and tolerance for emotional abuse that might have propelled him to stardom. "Meeting him and realizing how much he was like his character, he didn't strike me as an actor who'd do anything to get ahead. He had the looks and the ability, but you have to be lethally ambitious to become a major star — push for the right parts, fire an agent who's been loyal to you, sacrifice personal relationships. I don't think he had that in him." Pasadena Playhouse classmate John Buckley agrees. He remembers that Kemmer was not particularly outgoing and doubts he had any desire to play the Hollywood game. "He wasn't the type to push his way into a booth at Ciro's, hobnob with the powers that be and kiss ass." And there's another reason Kemmer may not have sought out professional risks: Being a fighter pilot, says Dick Darley, can teach you to play it safe in other areas of life — if you survive:

> It was a crapshoot every time you took off. Being out alone in a fighter plane, you were screwing around with your life, but you took those risks because you were single, young and dumb. Since then, in my life, I've planned everything ahead of time — to have a place to land if the motor quit — and I think Ed was somewhat the same way. You appreciated security because you knew what it was like not to have it.

In the end, it may be Kemmer's diffidence, work ethic, pride and need for security — born of his war experience and a childhood touched by the Great Depression — that drove him to take steady work in the soaps, rather than gamble that fate would cast him in another extraordinary role.

While he seems closer to embracing his legacy, he remains modest about his place in TV history and reticent about his capacity to inspire. I mention Doug Moore, who wants to write him but wonders, "What can I say to a man who has been my hero for 50 years?"

"You can't even accept that statement, let alone think about it too much," he responds.

But others do.

"Goddamnit, Ed Kemmer *was* a hero," says Professor Richard Felnagle. "I mean, he wasn't Commander Corry, but he was, in essence, the man he played — morally, philosophically and ethically. That man went to war and believed in what he was doing; he got out of that prison camp, he did what he had to do. And then he got on that show and played the part that way because there wasn't any other way to do it. That's the way he believed it. It wasn't fake."

It's possible that the kudos that don't quit are a painful reminder to Kemmer of his genius for playing the true hero and a glorious career that might have been, but if that's true, he hides it well; in any case, he hasn't let 50 years of adulation swell his head. "It certainly doesn't get to his ego in any way," says Fran Kemmer. "I've had fights with this man, but I can tell you this: He truly is the kind and extraordinarily compassionate human being that people were inspired by. What people felt from him is true."

Perhaps Gary Shusett summed it up best in a letter he slipped Kemmer at an old-time radio convention in Los Angeles in 1995. Kemmer remembers the moment. "A man approached and handed me a note, saying, 'This is for you'— and walked away." Shusett wrote:

Dear Ed,

Somehow I feel you have tricked us all. For years I thought you were merely this adept actor who was playing the role of Commander Corry. The role called for someone to appear to be intelligent, honest and heroic. You filled the bill.

Now, years later, I find out the real truth: That was no act. In this modern world of dishonesty, greed and selfishness, you are the shining exception. You *are* Corry, but so much more. I found you to be gracious, patient, kind and humble. I know little about your parents, but I can tell you one thing about them: They have good reason to have been proud of their son.

Ed, I don't know what your personal goals in life are, but you couldn't possibly have done better than becoming the person you are. I heard you remark that you're retired. I beg to differ. You can't retire from being the remarkable role model and ambassador of good will that you embody.

You have done good, Ed.

CHAPTER 22

Where Have All the Heroes Gone?

I wonder if, 40 years from now, the kids of today will look back fondly on their violent video games and electronic mass killings.

— Rob Robinson

Each time I tuned in to Space Patrol, no matter what else had happened during the week, my faith in goodness was restored.

— Arie Raymond

FROM THE SPACE PATROL ARCHIVES:

Cruising in a stardrive ship beyond the orbit of Tyranna 15 — a hostile part of the galaxy — Commander Corry and his cadet, through their Space Patrol Periscope, observe the Tyrannians arming themselves for an all-out attack against the United Planets. Since space-o-phone signals won't travel through hyperspace, Buzz and Hap must rush back to the solar system and warn the Space Patrol. But as they're leaving the Tyrannian system, they spot a ship that has crash-landed on a meteor, and though the ship is sending no distress signal, they are overcome by a powerful, intuitive feeling that the pilot is gravely injured and needs help. They make a quick detour to rescue the man — but that act may prove fatal. As they bring him aboard their ship, Hap looks through the periscope and spots two deadly enemies, General Mognier and Matthew Sneed, racing toward them in a Tyrannian ship armed with a Null Ray that can disable their weapons. This pair is vicious; falling into their hands means certain death. As Corry tends to the injured pilot, he orders Hap to blast off, then stand by to fire torpedoes at the enemy ship. But just as Hap is about to obey, the pilot opens his eyes and, gasping for breath, pleads with Buzz:

> PILOT: *Please... listen to me... I'm hurt.... There's a medicine kit in my ship... I must have it or I'm finished.*
> HAP: (Looking through periscope) *Commander, Sneed isn't close enough to use his Null Ray on us. If we blast off now, we can keep the meteor between us and that ship until we get up to velocity again.*
> CORRY: (worried) *The Null Ray! If Sneed turns that on us, we're helpless.*
> PILOT: *Medicine... in my ship... Get it, please.*
> HAP: (anxious) *He's nearly within range, sir. Shall I blast off?*
> PILOT: *The medicine kit... Please...*
> CORRY: (hesitating) *He's nearly done for, Hap.*
> HAP: (panicking) *Sneed's reaching for the Null Ray controls, sir. What are we gonna do?*
> CORRY: (makes his decision) *We're going to save this man's life, Hap. Get the medicine kit.*[1]

---

[1]"Invasion from Tyranna," (Radio), September 25, 1954.

Three space heroes. From left: Major "Robbie" Robertson, Commander Buzz Corry, Cadet Happy. (Author's collection)

Moments like this when Buzz Corry put right action above his own life made a big impression on kids like Rob Robinson. "Children will learn the lessons you put in front of them. Show us heroes sacrificing themselves for their friends, showing calm and courage in the face of threats and standing for certain principles—and that is what we will learn." Robinson pauses. "I wonder if, 40 years from now, the kids of today will look back fondly on their violent video games and electronic mass killings."

Space Patrol was about dreaming, about the willingness to go courageously and vulnerably into the unknown. Watching the show, Bud Fraze, like Jon Rogers, was one of a future generation of aerospace engineers who caught the dream as a child and grew up determined to make it real. "I, along with every other kid, wanted to be out there exploring space, having adventures and experiencing danger," he admits. But besides instilling the urge for adventure in the souls of "juves," the TV space operas and other action shows of the day had something else — an element that appealed to viewers of any age. For on Earth, in the 1950s, the thoughtful, compassionate hero was still revered. "TV, comics and juvenile series books provided genuine heroes, with no sneering or mockery," says Rory Coker:

> Heroes, whether Hopalong Cassidy, Gene Autry, Roy Rogers, Tom Corbett, Captain Video or Buzz Corry — not to mention Joe Friday — were humble, dedicated, educated, competent men who treated their fight for justice, truth and freedom as just an ordinary job. And they had empathy. They were always sensitive to the plight of people around them, although in some cases (like *Dragnet's* Friday) they didn't display it overtly. The cowboys, especially, maintained stoic expressions — but their feelings showed in their eyes. Who wouldn't want to be like them? Who wouldn't want to do his part in the battle against intolerance, hatred and crime?

"Many fans," adds Coker, "remember Captain Video's public service announcements urging tolerance, social inclusion and sympathetic understanding of all races and ethnic groups."

Another thing about those old-fashioned heroes: Though willing to fight to the death, they respected life and spared it whenever they could. Space operas featured futuristic weapons that stunned but did not maim or kill. Software — the flesh and blood kind — was just as valued in these dramas as the hardware that made it possible to journey beyond the stars. In *Space Patrol*, it wasn't about how many bad guys you could shoot or blow up; it was about overpowering them so they could be captured and rehabilitated. Of course, you had villains like Prince Baccarratti, as treacherous and maniacal as Hitler (Baccarratti once planned to kill millions in Jupiter City, just to wipe out a few Space Patrol bases), and yet Buzz Corry — as much as he despised the evil Prince — once risked his life to drag the monarch from his castle as it collapsed around him. To these heroes, life — *any* life — was sacred; there was hope for every human being. To young Mike Guarino, Buzz Corry's concern for his enemies made a deep impression, reminding him of another childhood hero:

> When I was a kid, I got this book about Robin Hood — and he never killed anybody! He was this really compassionate hero who makes his enemies into friends. He'd defeat someone in battle, but then he'd prop him up and run down to the river and get water to bathe his head. It was so different from today's heroes — there was no slicing and dicing.

Like Robin, says Guarino, "Buzz Corry would give people sympathetic looks and a hand on the shoulder. That human thing was going on all the time in *Space Patrol*. It's a different approach to life. You don't see it on TV anymore." But for a brief, "naïve" period in Earth's 20th century, Corry, Robin and other fighter-protectors were mainstream role models, inspiring the hero within to awake and dream of adventure; transporting everyday folk, as they used to say on the radio show *Escape*, "beyond the four walls of today." And there was something else that made it easy to dream. Back then, when television was young, there was a quaint practice that died out as the infant medium morphed into a cool adolescent and later a suave adult: Actors threw heart and soul into roles that modeled decent behavior for both kids and their elders. Sometimes, they devoted their lives to those roles. Decades after his TV duty as Captain Midnight ended, actor Richard Webb spoke at schools. "I talk about the value of people helping one another, which Captain Midnight did all over the planet," Webb explained to a reporter.[2] Clayton Moore played the Lone Ranger for decades, but in 1978 a younger actor replaced him in a movie remake. When Moore continued to make personal appearances in character, the producers forbade him to wear the trademark mask. Moore fought back, launching a legal battle to continue wearing it. "I have been the Lone Ranger for the past thirty years," he told fans, "and I will not give up the fight."[3]

Norm Jolley says that it was in the mid–'60s that he and his colleagues (who had been in television from the beginning) noticed a strange trend sweeping the medium:

> The advertisers started slanting all their products toward kids. We couldn't understand why, but they were. And then, in a couple of years, the networks started slanting their shows toward kids, and we realized that they wanted to indoctrinate kids with their advertising so they'd buy their products when they grew up. And then they said, "Who knows more about kids than kids?" And they hired kids to run the shows—young kids who had not paid their dues, who had not learned their trade. And I would go down to the network to talk to these people about an idea for a new series—and they didn't know what the hell I was talking about. They'd come up with

The Space Patrol crew takes time to inspire young fans. (Author's collection)

[2]"Where Have You Gone, Captain Midnight?" by George Eldred Morgan, *Parade*, August 15, 1982.

[3]*www.celebhost.net*. Moore lost the initial battle and resorted to wearing sunglasses in the shape of a mask. But in 1984, the Wrather Corporation, who owned the rights to the character, relented and allowed him to don the real thing.

things we'd thrown away years ago. It just kept getting worse and worse, and it became the main topic of conversation through the '60s, '70s and '80s—and it wasn't just me. All of us guys, the adults, were saying, "What's happening to the business?"

Actor-director Larry Dobkin—like Jolley, a pioneer of early television—was asking himself the same question. He remembers the time when a director friend, Jack, came back "glowing" (he says, tongue in cheek) from a meeting with a young ad executive:

> He said: "I was taken to lunch by one of the agency's 22-year-old geniuses and this child said to me, 'I can't tell the difference between a 30-minute, 60-minute and 90-minute script, except for the number of pages.' And God kissed my tongue and I gave him a great answer. I said, 'Well, in 30 minutes I can tell you what happened; in 60, I can tell you what happened and to whom; and in 90 minutes I can maybe tell you why.'"

You'd think wisdom like this from seasoned veterans might be appreciated by what the old-timers over 40 were calling the "fetus-in-a-suit" crowd that had invaded the networks and ad agencies, but nothing doing.[4] "There was a perception that experienced people tend to repeat themselves and are less flexible," Dobkin explains. One day on the set, he'd just about had enough of a young, inexperienced producer who was critical of his directing:

> I said, "What exactly is bothering you? Do you want me to change my style, use the camera differently? All that is flexible. You want more close-ups? I may disagree with you there, but I'll give you what you want."

Then he drew the line:

> "But you want me to change the way I tell a story? You're dead in the water. You want me to talk to actors as if I don't know what their problems are? You're dead in the water. And if you want me to revise my pacing and timing, or the emotional content of the story, you're not gonna budge me. I was a storyteller when you were still wetting your pants."

Part of the magic of '50s TV, says Dobkin, was that "there was a phalanx of young writers who were given a chance. They would have died at the movie studios." Their fresh creativity, coupled with the raw excitement of live television, helped persuade millions of Americans to invest in pricey TV sets. (A 16-inch Admiral cost $300 in 1952, equivalent to about $3,000 today.) For some people, though, it was still a tough sell. Virginia Bach, wife of famed *Word-a-Day* syndicated cartoonist Mickey Bach, was not convinced that television was a worthy guest in her living room:

> When television appeared in 1948, I was apathetic. I said: "It has to prove itself before I'll have it in the house. It can teach great things. It can teach people how to think and how to act; it can teach history and geography, which is absolutely magnificent because it's fascinating to know what lies in other parts of the world; it can teach the classics and Shakespeare; it can teach people right action and the difference between right and wrong; it can educate people, stimulate thinking. Or," I said, "it can simply contribute to using up people's time."

---

[4]That's fetus in a *three-piece* suit, says *M*A*S*H* creator Larry Gelbart, who invented the term.

Mrs. Bach allowed television into her home in 1951, but by the end of the decade, big changes were underway in the industry as demographics grabbed center stage. As more households acquired TV sets, the fight for audience shares was the name of the game — and if you're going for numbers, it stands to reason that highbrow shows like *Playhouse 90* are not your best choice. Dobkin recalls attending a meeting at Warner Bros. in 1963 where *Dragnet* creator Jack Webb, who now headed up the television department, spelled out the new creative guidelines. "The word was simple," Dobkin recalls. "It was, 'Dumb it down.' Jack said: 'You are making a product that is too good for our audience. You're making dance slippers. Make tennis shoes.'"

To writer Lou Huston, the industry's newfound obsession with youth and numbers killed what broadcasting used to be all about: fun. When he'd started in radio in the 1930s, most stations had "an atmosphere of informal fun" in which even the top executives joined in. You used the term "big family" to describe your co-workers because that's what it felt like. Early TV was full of the same breezy spirit. "But as competition increased, people quit the experimental and began to take surveys," says Huston, noting that by the early '60s, ad agencies and sponsors wanted the tried and true. "Sure, the pay went up, but you got paid more for less fun," he recalls. And to cap it off, ageism appeared. "If you were anywhere near old enough to be the producer's father, you couldn't write for the show." A huge army of postwar juves now had money to buy records and shoes. How could a writer over 40 (reasoned the new, young execs) know how to appeal to the younger generation? "If *Sesame Street* hadn't been on Public Television," quips Huston, "they'd have been searching for three-year-olds to write for Big Bird."

In the '60s and '70s, agrees Dick Darley, everything turned toward youth:

> The most flamboyant things happening in the world were being done by rebellious youth, and people in the entertainment business know that dramatic things sell best, whether it's tragedy or Elton John. It was fascinating to watch this happen. Ageism? Nobody wanted to read your resume. If you had too much experience, they got scared to death. I lived through it and experienced it first-hand — and it was very, very discouraging, because you make your bones and then they're useless.

Darley saw other disturbing changes, too. As TV became wildly popular, everyone wanted a piece of the action. Creative decisions shifted from the soundstage and production office to the celebrities themselves, and then to an inner sanctum of business people, as agents and accountants discovered how much power they could wield in the new industry. "When television first arose, the engineers were in charge," says Bob Trachinger. "Then it was the directors and producers, and after that it was the lawyers. Then the bookkeepers took over, and it never recovered." Lethal cracks in the once-strong camaraderie on the stages appeared as studio employees unionized and pecking orders evolved. After a few nasty incidents in which hotheaded directors verbally abused crew members, NABET (then known as the National Association of Broadcast Engineers & Technicians) lobbied for industry rules that regulated communication between directors and technical crews — but what got lost in the shuffle was the easy, informal spirit that had once reigned on the set.[5] "Restrictions started on what you could do creatively," says Darley.

---

[5]According to Bob Trachinger, these NABET regulations affected the crews at ABC and NBC, but not at CBS because the technicians there belonged to a different union, the International Brotherhood of Electrical Workers (IBEW). In the late '70s, Trachinger, then part of ABC's management team, bargained with NABET to remove certain restrictions. (Note: "Employees" has replaced "Engineers" in the NABET name.)

I want to be
like BUZZ CORRY

I will help keep law and order

I believe in fair play

I want to be strong and healthy

I want to fly a space ship someday

(Color the picture)

Two Space Patrol Coloring Book kids remind you that if you brush your teeth, help your mother, get up on time, like your teacher, look both ways before crossing the street, and eat plenty of Instant Ralston, you'll make Buzz Corry proud. (Author's collection)

"When I was showing an actor how to do something, there were regulations that prevented me from picking up a prop. A crew member had to do it."

In a fast-paced show like *Space Patrol*, where Darley barked out camera shots at the speed of light, these new edicts spelled disaster. No longer could a director communicate with the cameramen; instead, Darley had to issue commands to his technical director (often Bob Trachinger), who relayed them to the crew.[6] In the pressure cooker of the control booth, where split seconds mattered, this was insanity and Trachinger knew it. Though this "TD System" was meant to protect his job, he defied it by turning his microphone slightly toward Darley so the cameramen could hear the director's instructions first-hand. As he did it, Trachinger knew he was putting his own job in jeopardy. "Every time I 'allowed' Dick to talk to the crew, I took the risk of being fired by the union," he admits today. These new rules that redefined roles and stifled communication not only distanced directors from crew members, but chipped away at the creativity that ran rampant at the dawn of television. Now tasks were divided and subdivided among hordes of specialized people. "Before," says Darley, "I could get three or four guys together and we could get a show on and go. Now, everyone needed assistants, and their assistants needed assistants. There were so many restrictions that after a while it got to be not much fun."

"Unions were necessary," says Trachinger, who later moved into ABC management but recalls the fledgling days of the industry before reasonable hours and adequate pay. "TV was glamorous, and getting a job in it was really prestigious. It was like a paradise up on some mountain." But when he landed a job in this Eden, he discovered that working conditions were brutal. "You worked split shifts, weekends and holidays because broadcasting activity was at its peak when people were home to see it. We had irregular eating and sleeping hours—our families broke up because we never saw them." Not only that, but the pay was poor. "Management took advantage of us because everybody wanted to be in the industry. They knew they could get people off the street." But once conditions improved, he says, "the pendulum swung in the opposite direction." A shipload of stringent regulations eroded the fellowship on the stage. Many electricians and prop men had come to TV from the film industry—where union traditions had been embedded for years—bringing heavy-handed practices with them that drove a wedge between crew members themselves. Trachinger got a taste of this early on as a young cameraman. "I had a shot, and there was a 'scoop'—a lamp that stands on the floor with a big reflector behind it—blocking it, so I leaned over and moved the scoop out of the way. And an electrician came over and said, 'If you ever do that again, we'll break your arm.' Just that explicit."

As this kind of static increased on production stages, Dick Darley watched the family feeling, once so strong, ebb away. "When TV was young, the crew, and I mean everyone—stage managers, costumers, painters—used to be close, like brothers. We boosted each other. You still had that World War II set of principles where everybody pitched in and pulled together because they wanted to. They felt part of it." But the new regulations fragmented that camaraderie. "They took the heart out of it," he says sadly. Bob Trachinger agrees. "It's the old story of unions contributing and unions suffocating," he sums up.

---

[6]When a show had been in rehearsal three times its on-air length, the TD (Technical Director) System kicked in, says Trachinger, forbidding the director from talking directly to the crew during the dress rehearsal and air show.

Dick Tufeld: "In the mid–'50s, when I was doing The Big News *on KNXT in Los Angeles, I'd come in, strip the teletype machine, and write the show. We didn't have camera crews, so I'd look at the Douglas Edwards CBS News— a feed that came in from New York— and take what kinescoped segments we could edit and use. Publicity guys would come in with film footage from things like* The Boat Show *that they wanted us to use, and I'd work that in. Then I would do the show. I never worked so hard in my life. I swear to God they have 200 people doing now what I used to do myself."*

As television left its gawky adolescence behind, a few watchdogs warned that its rapid growth, coupled with the increasing power of ad agencies and sponsors, might drain its vitality, kill the magic. Not that anyone wanted to go back to the days when TV was such a novelty that people sat around staring at the test pattern until something— anything—came on. But now that it had been welcomed into millions of homes, the industry's marketing potential was exploding and the commercialism of radio was invading the new medium. As early as 1951, in an article in *Tele-Views* titled "What's Wrong with TV," director Bob Finkel warned of the growing clout of ad agencies and begged them to stop trying to influence the content of programming. Leave that instead, he pleaded, to the new breed of professionals whose business it was to entertain:

> The men who buy into this medium to sell their products should take stock of the present trained producers and directors and be willing to place into their hands the responsibility for creating sound entertainment. Consideration of the audience is the first thought of the artists and craftsmen who devote their lives to filling the leisure hours of others.... When TV craftsmen are not bound by the desires of anyone except the viewing audience, television will come into its own with great entertainment.

"You sponsors who commercialize an audience into boredom — please take note!" chided *Tele-Views*.[7]

Commercialism, says Franklin Mullen (AKA Glen Denning), who starred as Commander Corry before Ed Kemmer took over the role, was exactly what he had worried about from the beginning. The bad attitude that got him fired from *Space Patrol* in 1950, he says today, stemmed from a distrust of the show's objectives. If it headed down the cops and robbers path of "cheap" entertainment, it would never live up to the lofty vision he held for television programming. Mullen and a small group of actor friends saw the new medium as a way to "raise the awareness level of the American public." As performers, they realized that TV's power to deliver images to millions of homes was staggering:

> We'd been living in the Radio Age, and we said, "My God, they're going to broadcast pictures into people's homes and *they'll see us while we're talking*!" It seemed so promising, and my friends and I, who were idealists, were hoping for a global conversation, global interaction, understanding, education. But then the same ad agencies that had corrupted radio took over and the dream died. They were concerned with tits and ass, with smashing fists and crashing cars and the excitement meter of the shows in terms of ratings. It was getting harder and harder to develop a purposeful story idea. We wanted to do the kind of shows that could now be expressed through this wonderful medium, but they told us, "What you want would only be of interest to people like you, and there aren't that many." So the dream faded. When Madison Avenue took over, television was stillborn.

[7]*Tele-Views*, August, 1951.

"GOTTA PATROL A PLANET, DAD!"

"I'D SAY you're equipped for the assignment, Son. With that modern gadget you'll handle any emergency, and your mission will be successful."

Emergencies in *business*, such as accidents on the job also require special "equipment." They call for workmen's compensation insurance placed with a reliable organization that assures quick, sympathetic service.

Hardware Mutuals rank among the leaders in promptness of paying workmen's compensation claims. This promptness helps speed recovery by relieving financial worry. With the help of Hardware Mutuals loss prevention specialists, employers can eliminate hazards *before* they cause accidents.

Among other benefits of Hardware Mutuals *policy back of the policy®* is friendly, nationwide, day-and-night service. More than $110,000,000 in dividend savings have been returned to policyholders.

For all the facts, simply *call Western Union, ask for Operator 25,* and say you'd like the name and address of your nearest Hardware Mutuals representative.

Insurance for your AUTOMOBILE...HOME...BUSINESS

Hardware Mutuals.

Stevens Point, Wisconsin · Offices Coast to Coast

HARDWARE MUTUAL CASUALTY COMPANY · HARDWARE DEALERS MUTUAL FIRE INSURANCE COMPANY

A big insurance company catches space fever. In the early '50s, Hardware Mutual Casualty used *Space Patrol*'s popularity to hawk workers' compensation insurance. (Courtesy *Filmfax* magazine)

But commercialism wasn't the only thing that sapped TV's vitality. "Video tape came in 1956," says Bob Trachinger, "and we thought it would be our savior, enable us to do things we'd never tried before. But all it's done, for the most part, is make television plastic, antiseptic and cover-your-ass." William O'Hallaren, a popular TV columnist of the day, agreed and railed against tape for killing TV's endearing spontaneity:

> Even the most carefully rehearsed of the live plays had their corpses that suddenly and delightfully crawled away, their electricians suddenly visible on stormy moors, their swinging doors that didn't swing, their guns that didn't fire and their animals unaware that there are certain things not done in 10 million living rooms. But tape, cursed tape, is the enemy of all this. It has made television a desert of arid perfection, revived only at the rarest intervals by an oasis of green and lovely flubbery.[8]

Tape spelled death to the raw, untamed energy that jumped off the screen in a show like *Space Patrol*, where both cast and crew were as high on adrenaline as you'd be in any life-threatening situation. Tape was like a giant safety net that stretched across the set and saved your life if you slipped and fell. It leveled the edginess that was, for a brief time, inherent in live TV, replacing it with predictable consistency. Today, says Trachinger, "TV is good if you like white bread that toasts evenly. But where do you get the bread that's hammered out in a Sicilian village? We want it perfect, we want it fast, and we're willing to give up everything in deference to that—but it's sterile." He sighs. "We walked a high wire with *Space Patrol* and we're proud of that fact. It manifested the very best of what could be done under the old system."

As nearly everyone bought a TV set and the medium became commonplace, so did the heroes it portrayed—in fact, the line between them and viewers, once so clear-cut, grew murky. Some champions now had shady pasts, parents who screwed them up, illicit affairs and vices. "Good guys used to have impeccable character traits. They set an example," recalls *Space Patrol* fan Ken Viall:

> They were polite and courteous, and they obeyed the rules of society—but now they're more in line with the accepted social standards of today. Having an affair, being married two or three times, running red lights, making a questionable living, not reporting all your earnings to the IRS and cleverly placing the blame on others are all accepted. Take Thomas Magnum of *Magnum, P.I.* He was basically a good guy, but a parasite. He never seemed to work or have money. Sure he caught the bad guys, but he set a bad example as a moral individual.

That's not to say that, back in the innocent '50s, Earthlings wanted their heroes to be pristine-pure. Carol Howard remembers being a pre-teen with an "outlandish crush on Kemmer and his voice," and thinking that "Virginia Hewitt was the most beautiful woman I'd ever seen." She wished that *Space Patrol's* producer and writer would push the romance more between Buzz and Carol. "Every once in a while they'd give the audience some little inkling of their relationship, but they never took it far enough to satisfy me. If it was today's market and demographics," says Howard, now retired from a career in casting and production, "they'd probably be sleeping together onscreen."

---

[8]Newspaper clipping in Lyn Osborn's files; no date or source. O'Hallaren was a well-known TV critic and sometime screenwriter who wrote newspaper columns and contributed to *TV Guide* until the early 1990s.

If it was *today's* market, says Jack McKirgan, "Buzz would spout obscenities to Robbie, Happy would be sent to the Cadet Corps in lieu of doing jail time for spray painting graffiti on the United Planets building, Carol would have a drinking problem and burst into Tonga's brothel to drag Buzz out — only to find her father, the Secretary General, engaged in a different type of 'political maneuver.'"

"I'm very upset about what's happened to television and movies," Norm Jolley tells me one afternoon as we sit in the small patio adjoining his motor home. "It's violence for the sake of violence, and it's totally unnecessary. There's no reason for it."

"It seems to me," I say, "that in your writing there was always a reason for violence. Heroes endured it to save someone they cared about, or were threatened with it because they defended some value or ideal. But it's not on that level anymore."

"No, it's not," Jolley sighs heavily. "And they just don't seem to understand it. Nobody in the picture business understands it."

Lou Huston remembers sitting in a movie theater during World War II and watching a Donald Duck cartoon:

> During the war years, everything was rationed. If you were lucky enough to have a car that ran, you knew it was going to have to run till the end of the war — *if* you could get gas for it. Well, a Donald Duck cartoon came out in the theaters where Donald is running a service station. He puts this car on the lift, and he raises it and loses control. He doesn't know how to stop it, and it crashes against the roof of the garage. And the audience groaned! Here was a cartoon car — a car that doesn't even exist, that's just some light on a screen — and when it's crashed by this silly cartoon duck, everybody gasped. You don't hear any gasps today when people are blown to bits.

Joseph Hogg: "My most poignant memory of Space Patrol *is watching an episode with my father. Buzz and Happy had come across a deserted spacecraft eons old with no one on board but a small robot caretaker. He said that the ship's crew was off visiting the third planet from the sun and exploring a group of islands in the western part of the planet's largest ocean. When asked when they had last contacted the mother ship, the robot replied: 'August 6, 1945.' I turned to my father, a World War II veteran, and asked him what had happened on that date. 'The atom bomb,' he said softly. Evidently the alien crew had been caught in Hiroshima. That memory has stayed with me all my life."*

"What happened to the action and character-based shows we grew up with?" repeats actor Slim Sweatmon in his easy Texas drawl. As "Mr. Boyd" on *Barney and Friends*, he's been talking to a purple dinosaur for nearly a decade and knows a little about kids' TV. He blames *The Howdy Doody Show*, in part, for the demise of the live action hero. Howdy hit the screen when shows like *Space Patrol, Hopalong Cassidy* and *The Lone Ranger* were at their zenith, Sweatmon points out, but there was one huge difference: budget.

> Compare the bills for producing *Space Patrol* with the expenses over at *Howdy Doody*. It's not hard to figure out why less expensive productions with benign and even simple-minded plots began to surface in the name of children's programming. Kids who had grown to love and identify with adventurous, honorable and courageous heroes were now watching eight-frame animated junk. Sure, some of the staples such as *The Lone Ranger* hung on, but for the most part, it was the Captain Kangaroos of the world who won out. "Keep it cheap, keep it simple, keep cranking it out" was the watchword of youth-oriented television. It was profitable — and disgusting to any kid with a brain.

There were a few bright spots in this wasteland, says Sweatmon, most notably Walt Disney, who introduced intelligent kids' programming such as *Disneyland*, *Zorro* and *The Mickey Mouse Club*, but the void those shows left was never filled. "There's a whole generation out there who have never 'come with us to those thrilling days of yesteryear.' They've never gone out to the backyard to play out the scenes they watched on TV that afternoon, holding the same ray gun as the *Space Patrol* crew." Sweatmon learned about the impact of TV role models on kids firsthand when a *Barney* viewer told him that her daughter, who had witnessed domestic violence, trusted only one man — his character, Mr. Boyd. "Using Boyd as a model, she began introducing the child to men who didn't hit first and ask questions later," says Sweatmon. It got him thinking about the life-changing power of television. "I am here to tell you that there are kids who are starved for heroes they trust tackling serious problems and coming out the winner."

Bruce David: "Buzz Corry is a hero and adventurer out of a mold that no longer exists. You trusted him to do the right thing because he was dedicated to something beyond himself: human decency. He was every kid's older brother — the guy who'd pick you up when you fell down, point you in the right direction when you were confused. It's easy to say the world was simpler back then, but I think it's more accurate to say that our values were purer."

*Mike Pahlow: "*Space Patrol *gave you the feeling that if you played fair and followed the rules, you were bound to come out on top. The fact that Buzz and company had to fight long and hard to win out in the end — but by being honorable and trustworthy, they did — sank into my mind and the minds of my friends. It was a terrific time to grow up. I would hate to have been a kid in the days of* South Park *and* Bevis and Butthead.*"*

You could count on Commander Corry to emerge with dignity and grace from the most harrowing situation. And once he'd defeated his enemies, he harbored little bitterness — like after that nasty time in the Cydonian jungle when a tribe of Amazon women forced him into slavery and nearly killed Hap. When Corry finally turns the tables and captures their leader, Queen Riva, he takes her back to Terra for Brainograph treatments and rehab so she can lose her criminal ways. On the voyage home, he pauses for a moment beside the sullen queen, who showed no mercy when he was her prisoner. "Don't be afraid to leave your homeland, Riva," he says gently. "No harm will come to you. When you arrive on Terra, you will discover that your rights will be respected. You will also discover that from now on you, too, must respect the rights of others."

Such was the compassionate hero, who breathed life into the precepts and platitudes taught in Sunday School. "Commander Corry provided for me what should have been provided by religion," says Arie Raymond:

> Each time I tuned in to *Space Patrol*, no matter what else had happened during the week, my faith in goodness was restored. My weekly failures, embarrassments and transgressions (through Commander Corry's treatment of Cadet Happy) were accepted and I was restored into grace — I didn't even have to confess or repent! At the time *Space Patrol* was broadcast, I was learning to ride a bike, do long division and accustom myself to wearing glasses. A few years later, the braces would come. I needed someone to affirm my worth, in spite of my awkwardness and abject failures. In short, the good Commander — I would never presume to call him Buzz — restored me to his side with each episode. He helped me to grow out of immaturity and into his strength.

Two happy cadets, Jay Chew (left), age six, and cousin Ken Linville, eight, brandish their new smoke guns for the camera on Christmas Day, 1952. Jay sports the official Space Patrol cap. (Courtesy Ken Linville)

Echoes of the 23rd psalm — and a kid's longing to see all that stuff adults preached about moral behavior made real. *Space Patrol* did just that, bringing right action smack into your living room. "TV was my window to the world, my mentor," says Paul Subbie. "*Space Patrol, Sky King, Rocky Jones, Hopalong Cassidy, The Cisco Kid*— all had danger, villains, role models, moral values, and respect. Each show taught a lesson you could relate to and learn from. I'm sure I got more training from those shows than from my parents."

"You taught us right from wrong," Brian Williams wrote to Ed Kemmer, 50 years later. In the late '90s, Williams purchased some *Space Patrol* tapes and watched them with his wife, who had never seen the show. Together they viewed "Revenge of the Black Falcon,"[9] in which Prince Baccarratti captures Corry and Hap, takes them back in time to Earth's 17th century, and dumps them in witch-hunting Salem, Massachusetts, knowing they'll be killed on sight. But Baccarratti gets stranded with them, and when the teaser for

[9]December 4, 1954.

next week's show came on, says Williams, "the announcer said, 'Tune in next week when Commander Corry and Cadet Happy keep Prince Baccarratti from being burned at the stake.'" Williams' wife turned to him in amazement. "Why would they want to go back and rescue a dirt bag like Baccarratti?" she asked. "He just tried to kill them!" Williams thought about that for a moment. "And all I could say was, 'That's just the way it was back then, and boy, do I miss it.'"

"*Space Patrol* is about love," sums up high school teacher Allan Cohen. "You either get it or you don't." Cohen figured his students, mostly seniors, would mock the show, but curiosity drove him to play a few episodes in class and find out. "Go ahead and laugh," he said as he set up the VCR. "Laugh at the special effects—and, by the way, they were the *best* special effects of that time." He explained the hazards of live TV, how actors jumped in and covered for each other when someone messed up. "Watch what happens when that actor loses a line," he instructed. "Watch Buzz recover." Cohen smiles. "And many of them got into it—they watched in a trance. After a few episodes, they were hooked." He had the kids write essays about the show. Some found it "amateurish," the "so-called commercials" and special effects "ridiculous." "It's for little kids," complained one teen. But most saw something else:

> Yes, the special effects were ridiculous, but that just adds to the character.
> It's not so predictable, like today's television.
> *Space Patrol* is much more interesting than *Space 1999*, *Flash Gordon* and even *Star Trek*.
> It was original and kept our interest.
> With the special effects of today, it would be an excellent show.
> *Space Patrol* is a part of American culture that influenced man's quest for the stars.

Theo Williams: "In the mid–'60s, I'd blossomed into a troubled adolescent when Space Patrol *re-emerged as filler material for children's afternoon television. The budding snob–Sophist in me noted the abundant technical crudities and gaffes preserved in those kinescopes, but at the same time, there was a little kid living next door in the same psyche who missed Buzz, Hap, Carol, Robbie and Tonga, and who dearly wanted to venture again aboard the mighty Terra V. Seen cynically, the show is too anachronistic to speak to modern audiences—a dusty curiosity. But nothing could be more wrong. There's a wild energy in any* Space Patrol *episode. It's still magical."*

Mike Marder: "As kids, we didn't care—or couldn't tell—if the special effects came off as planned. We cared more about the characters—we wanted to be *those characters. The neat thing was Buzz's inviolate sense of right and wrong. It taught me that without the initiative of the individual, nothing right is going to get done."*

Philip Allen Read, Jr.: "The extinction of live-action children's programming is one of the great tragedies of television. How difficult it must be for kids to aspire to the ideals of Ninja Turtles or Robot Transformers."

"High adventure in the wild, vast reaches of space... Missions of daring in the name of interplanetary justice...." Dick Tufeld had no idea that the intro he prerecorded in the bathroom off Studio A would stick in many kids' minds for over half a century. True, he'd grown up admiring those announcer guys who did famous title openings. "Like *The Lone Ranger*," he says excitedly, "*A fiery horse with the speed of light.... And Superman:*

'*Look! Up in the sky....*' I'd listen to guys like Fred Foy and Jackson Beck and think, 'God, I hope I can do something like that someday.'"

He broke into announcing at NBC when he was 18 — the youngest guy on the staff. Later he anchored the news and even had his own show, *Tufeld at Twelve*, on ABC. He was the announcer on *Hollywood Palace*, *Zorro*, *People Are Funny* and other classics, and was the voice of the robot in *Lost in Space* ("Danger, Will Robinson!"), which brought a baffling taste of fame. But people still ask him to do the *Space Patrol* opening. "That's one of the things I did pretty well," he admits. "People don't have to ask me to do it — I volunteer." Tufeld is a pleasant guy with a ready sense of humor: "I hope you had your good, Hot Ralston this morning, along with your Nestlé's Quik," he cracks.

Stan Kohls: "Each morning when I wake up, I feel like I'm taking off on another 'mission of daring in the name of interplanetary justice.' I can only relate my sense of excitement with the world to the excitement I felt as a kid of ten when Space Patrol *came on."*

One day I ask Ed Kemmer if he had any heroes when he was growing up. Who was *his* inspiration? He thinks about this. "I'm a fellow of the times," he says finally. "I didn't have a mentor." His character, he explains, was shaped by an era, not a role model:

> In those days, especially during the Depression years, there was more looking out for each other because everyone was in the same boat. You had good feelings for everyone, as opposed to every man for himself. The last thing you'd think of was trying to cheat someone or be other than as nice as possible. Life was bad enough in so many ways! That age of growing up was a kinder age, even though it was more painful in some areas — all needs weren't met and a lot of people suffered. But there was more decency. You did what was right — always. Why would you want to do it wrong? Why would you want to hurt someone — even hurt their feelings? That just never occurred to me. There was a sort of good fellowship — more than there is today.

Growing up in the same timeline as Kemmer, in small towns in Iowa a stone's throw apart, *Space Patrol*'s writers, Norm Jolley and Lou Huston, experienced the same thing. They, too, came of age in the 1930s and '40s, and while, in those days, surface civility was laced with racism and cultural mores that barred women from many careers, it was, in some ways, a kinder, gentler time. Baby boomers born in the '40s and '50s have one foot planted solidly in that era, the other in the quicksand of a less personal 21st century where the nature of human contact has changed. Dale Ames remembers growing up at a time when you could count on some things staying the same:

> You used to know who was working at the corner grocery store from one day to the next, who would deliver your mail — you got to know everybody in the world. Now, you go to a coffee shop and the waitress changes every month; the mailman changes every day. We've lost the glue that holds the world together.

Something else has changed, too, says Professor Rory Coker. It's the very concept of childhood:

> In 1950, childhood was a sanctuary, protected by parents and society and cherished by children. Kids, after school and through long summers, were left to their own ingenuity. They played self-invented games, rich in creative fantasy. If they wanted to turn a large, cardboard refrigerator box into the control deck of a spaceship, they just did it — with a

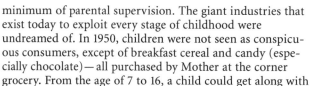

Above: Jim Scancarelli, who draws *Gasoline Alley*, featured *Space Patrol* Space-o-Phones in a five-part story that ran in summer 2002. "Buzz Corry," says Scancarelli, "has always been my hero." (Used by permission of Tribune Media Services ©2002) *Right:* Real Space-o-Phones in mint condition (Photograph © Ed Swift, courtesy Dale Ames)

minimum of parental supervision. The giant industries that exist today to exploit every stage of childhood were undreamed of. In 1950, children were not seen as conspicuous consumers, except of breakfast cereal and candy (especially chocolate)—all purchased by Mother at the corner grocery. From the age of 7 to 16, a child could get along with little supervision and was unlikely to run into any of the temptations and social problems that he or she would face later in life. Drugs, alcohol, sex, gangs, delinquency—these things were encountered only at the movies.

"There is more I could say," adds Coker, "but you guys who lived through it know it already."

When Coker, Ames and other space opera kids hit their fifties, a tsunami of nostalgia swept over them. "It was like a mechanism went off inside us and we wanted to recapture our childhood, the age of innocence," says Ames:

We suddenly had some free time; our families were grown and our salaries had grown, too. We had some money to collect those boyhood toys—the space helmets and ray guns—again. We were tired of fighting a hard battle with our jobs, sick and tired of seeing the dirty deeds out there. We knew there were good people, too, but it seemed that only the bad ones made headlines. And I was seeing my friends pass away. I was going to more wakes and funerals than I wanted to.

Enter the cyberspace revolution. Ames and his friends, former space cadets and rocket rangers, plugged in their modems and set out in search of yesteryear, back to the childhood promise of a utopian future.

Stephen Handzo: "Do you remember the coin-operated rocket rides that were on the sidewalk in front of stores? Do you remember sidewalks and stores—before everything moved to the mall?"

In 1996, former Air Force medic Ed Pippin set up a Web site "to act as a lighthouse" for space opera fans cruising the Internet. Its roots went back to 1951, when he'd seen his first space show on the DuMont television set down at the local garage. The screen was so small, the reception so poor, that sometimes it was hard to tell which show was on, but it didn't matter. At the age of six, Pippin was hooked on all of them. He named his Web site "Space Opera" but changed it to "Solar Guard" a couple years later, after the organization in *Tom Corbett, Space Cadet* that "safeguards the cause of universal peace in the age of the conquest of space." The site's purpose is "to honor the space heroes of the 1950s and preserve the heritage of the shows," Pippin explains.

A year later, Rory Coker got the same idea. Coker, who'd been searching the Web since 1990 for info on the space operas he'd watched as a child, finally decided to create his own site — but at first, while he tested the waters, he kept this mission top secret. He piggybacked a sample page, "Roaring Rockets," onto a friend's site devoted to helicopters in Vietnam, then asked several space buffs to check it out. The response was positive. Soon he was bombarded with grateful e-mails from strangers: "I thought I was the only person in the world who remembered these shows," wrote one space-happy Web surfer. "Thank you, thank you, thank you!"

The rush into cyberspace in the late 1990s sparked excitement akin to what kids of the '50s had experienced in front of the first TV sets. Once again you sat glued to a screen that brought endless possibilities into your living room (kitchen, office) — only this time, it was interactive: By tapping the keyboard, *you* steered the ship. Now, like a time-traveler, you could journey back to childhood. Pippin developed the theme on his Web site of a space academy (patterned after the training arm of the Solar Guard), where visitors are welcomed as fellow "cadets." "For me," says Elliott Swanson, "the Solar Guard and Roaring Rockets community is a place to dream; a place to sit around the stove in the country store on a winter day and tell stories; a place to remember childhood."

But becoming a "cadet" again in midlife, says Mike Elmo, is more than chasing pleasant childhood memories. "It's not so much to recapture good times from our childhood as to show our alignment with the values our heroes taught us: honor, trustworthiness, integrity, to name just a few. I try to emulate these qualities, and the cadets who have become my friends do the same." Elmo started making shirts and jackets sporting the colors and insignias of the old space opera shows. (No one on the planet had made a *Rocky Jones, Space Ranger* jacket since 1954.) As e-mails flowed into Coker's and Pippin's sites, it turned out that other fans, too — mostly men in their fifties and sixties — had been drawing, painting and modeling their space opera heroes, complete with ships and insignias, for decades. When Allan Cohen was a child, he sketched the *Tom Corbett* and *Space Patrol* actors as they flashed across the TV screen. His drawings kept the shows alive in his memory from one week to the next. He never stopped. Over the past 40 years, Cohen has done a series of acrylic paintings that depict his space heroes in their 30th-century settings. When he finishes one, he begins another, painting over the last one, never satisfied. Model kit maker Herb Deeks fills steady orders for replicas of Tom Corbett's flagship, *Polaris*, and Commander Corry's battlecruiser, *Terra V*. Tom Mason and his son, Chris, slapped a *Space Patrol* logo on a baseball cap. When Mason wore it during a trip to Las Vegas, he was stunned at the feedback it drew. "I can't tell you how many times I was stopped by people who remembered the show. I spent a lot of time scribbling the URLs of space opera sites on cocktail napkins," he reported.[10]

---

[10]Though Mason, an engineering supervisor who spent 36 years at ABC, passed away in 2003, his son, Chris, continues to host their Web site, *www.thecrimsoncollector.com*, which offers an array of current-day *Space Patrol* items — caps, mugs, shirts and more.

Allan Cohen began painting his space heroes as a child — and never stopped. From left: ***Tom Corbett, Space Cadet*** crew: Astro (Al Markim), Tom (Frankie Thomas), Roger Manning (Jan Merlin); Space Patrollers: Major Robertson (Ken Mayer), Buzz Corry (Ed Kemmer), Cadet Happy (Lyn Osborn); and ***Rocky Jones, Space Ranger*** (Richard Crane).

Ron Boucher: "I remember doodling Corry's ship, the Terra V, *all the time in first grade — as if it would take me to some adventure. I found myself doodling it again during a business meeting a few days ago."*

Mike Guarino: "I'd start drawing characters from Disney's Sleeping Beauty *in the middle of a trial I was prosecuting. Some people thought it was absurd, doing that in the middle of a double homicide trial, but it was my way of clearing my mind. Then someone told me that Ed Kemmer had modeled for Prince Philip and I said, 'My God, I loved him as Commander Corry, but I never noticed the resemblance!'"*

Just past midnight on July 18, 2001, Barbara ("Bobbi") Lynne Averell was surfing the Web when she came across the Solar Guard site. All her life, she'd been told that her father, whom she had never met, was the actor who played Cadet Happy on *Space Patrol*. I'd posted a notice that I was writing a book about the show on Pippin's site, so Averell sent me an e-mail:

> Do you know anyone who knew Lyn Osborn? Do you know anything about his family? I have a very important reason for asking.

Instantly, I thought of the shocking letter Osborn's family had received from Geraldine Wall the week of his death, informing them that Lyn had a child.

Smokin' rockets! I had a gut feeling that the e-mail I'd just received was from Lyn Osborn's daughter. I fired back questions that could only be answered by someone who knew Osborn had attended the Pasadena Playhouse in the late 1940s. The sender passed with flying colors, then confided that her mother and aunt claimed she was Lyn's child. She knew her Aunt Geraldine had corresponded with Osborn's sister, Beth Flood, for over a decade. "My middle name is Lynne," she added, "after him, so I've been told." The facts fit, but it was as if Averell needed a stranger — someone impartial — to voice what she believed in her heart. "He *is* your father," I wrote back. A few minutes later, my phone rang. We talked for nearly two hours. By morning, Bobbi had posted an essay on her Web site...

I Am My Father's Daughter

I never got a chance to meet my father in person.... I have known as far back as I can remember that he was an actor, that he and my mother didn't marry, that he died when I was a young child.... I have only seen two episodes of *Space Patrol* and I couldn't tell you much of anything about them. I was too busy staring at this fellow — my father. I was transfixed.... I felt something ... a scary feeling. I pushed it away.... My Aunt Gerry had offered to help me contact his family, but I declined. I was very angry.

Now I know he is my father.... I am going to contact his sister, Beth.... If she calls me, I will probably faint.... It's frightening but exhilarating.... I'm a nervous wreck.... I want to know all about my father, what he dreamed about, what he wanted to do with his life, what his favorite color was. I want to know his favorite foods, his favorite music. Did he like to read? Who were his idols? ... I do have roots. I have a connection now. I feel like climbing up onto the roof and shouting it to the world: "I am my father's daughter!"

Charles Drapo: "Lyn Osborn — we called him 'Buddy' then — was my second cousin. I watched him on Space Patrol *and it made me feel important to have a real movie star in the family. In fifth grade, Mrs. Toole had us do genealogies and he was pictured in mine, in his uniform. All through my life, I always looked for an adventure, whether hiking up a mountain, diving in the ocean or chasing bad guys, working undercover. To this day, I dream about other civilizations out there on some faraway world. I truly believe that Lyn and* Space Patrol *helped spark my desire for learning and dreaming."*

Joe Sarno pauses on a busy Saturday morning at his Comic Kingdom store in Chicago. "Did *Space Patrol* have any effect on my adult life? Oh, I think so. You try to be fair in your dealings. If I think *maybe* I've made a mistake, I'll double-check the price. Once a kid dropped a five-dollar bill on the floor. Another customer found it and I waited for the kid to show up again, to give it back. It gives you a good feeling, little things like that. I think we were all affected by those shows." In 1977, Sarno wrote a letter to Nina Bara:

I don't know what *Space Patrol* has meant to your career. I don't know if you think you might have been permanently typecast, but what made those early space shows was not the scripts or the sets. What made them an art form was the actors. You gave yourselves to your parts. Ed Kemmer *was* Buzz Corry to us, and we accepted him as Commander-in-Chief of the Space Patrol. He acted in the way we thought a Commander-in-Chief should act. And the same is true, right down the line, of all the actors and actresses we watched in our favorite shows in the 1950s. Maybe your careers were sacrificed to those parts, but you gave yourselves to us. You brought us — uncertain children in an uncertain time — safely to the here and now.

For Kemmer, Osborn, Mayer, Hewitt and Bara, their stardom was as ephemeral as the blinding flash of a supernova; but to kids of the 1950s, it was eternal. Baby boomers were the first generation weaned on television, points out Arie Raymond. "Those images displayed on the screen passed uncritically through our senses, became part of our life experience. Nowadays, kids are inundated with TV, computers, Nintendo—they're jaded."

"I like to think that our childhood heroes live on inside of us," says Eric Hogling. "All children need role models, and for the cast of *Space Patrol*, that may be their finest accomplishment."

Doug Moore: "Ed Kemmer wrote me and it was a real thrill. Just imagine getting a letter from your childhood hero! I got the feeling he's beginning to realize that the five years he spent with Space Patrol *may have been the most significant of his life. I wonder sometimes if anyone will remember any of the things I've done after 50 years."*

Slim Sweatmon: "The part of 'Mr. Boyd' has been a blessing and a curse. The longer I stay with Barney, *the less I get other roles. I admit I'd like to play a serious part, but that's OK. I would rather have made some mark in the lives of children than have been a great villain or dark character actor."*

On a visit with Norm Jolley, six months before he died, I ask him about the subtleties of *Space Patrol*, the extraordinary caring between the characters, the strange power the show had to inspire that has lasted more than 50 years. Once again, we're sitting outside his motor home, east of Palm Springs. A gentle breeze sweeps across the desert as daylight fades into dusk. I still want to know how he did it. "*Space Patrol* instilled a deep, unwavering belief in goodness, in heroic action to achieve the impossible, in good winning out in the end," I tell him. "As kids, we loved that stuff—the loyalty and trust between the characters, the self-sacrificing themes. It spoke to us because it was right. What was it that drove you to write it that way?"

Jolley falls silent, eyes half-shut. After a while he says softly, as if to himself. "It happened because … because … that's just the way it should go, is all. That's just the way it should go."

But that's not the way it goes today, says Richard Felnagle. "*Space Patrol, Roy Rogers, Rin Tin Tin*—the shows I grew up on—taught us that we had moral duties and responsibilities. It wasn't silly stuff that was part of the Boomer generation—it was a whole way of looking at life, a world view. Those shows taught us that by standing up, we could make things happen." But, adds Felnagle, other things happened, too—things we didn't count on, things that took us by surprise:

> Where have all the heroes gone? They started dying off—and not just in television shows. The heroes themselves have gone. It started with JFK and Martin Luther King—and we couldn't believe things like that could happen to people who were that good. And then we learned horrible things about them—and suddenly we couldn't believe in heroes anymore. And then, what's worse, we began to believe that the bad guys can win. All the heroes went away, and it changed us. And that's the saddest thing on the planet.

Felnagle pauses. "We've become cynical, blasé, accepting of evil because we feel we can't do anything about it. We've lost the sense that we can change the universe by doing the right thing. The right thing doesn't count anymore. It'll get you killed."

On a clear summer day in 2000, I visit the ABC studios at Prospect and Talmadge, where *Space Patrol* was shot. I search in vain for Studio A, but the stages have been renamed and are now identified with numbers instead of letters; no one who works here now remembers which ones housed ABC's live lineup of shows in the 1950s. Finally someone tells me that Studios A and B have been converted into office space and the set for the local news. The catwalks where Corry swung from the rafters as he battled Baccarratti in his castle have morphed into desk space where people shuffle papers. Outside the newsroom, I encounter the *Eyewitness News* team. (Local news and *General Hospital* are the only shows still shot here.[11]) I start talking about the lot's rich history; they listen politely. I ask a vice president in the legal department where the studio's archives are so that I can research *Space Patrol*. He looks at me strangely and says he'll do his best to find out. On the way out I pass the only trace of the lot's colorful past: a long corridor lined with photos of the network's hit shows, dating back to TV's "Golden Age." In one, a radiant Ed Kemmer and Lyn Osborn emerge from the Ralston Rocket on February 16, 1952, the date that Corry presented the ship to the children of Earth, right here on this lot before 10,000 people who had gathered to see it.

The VP doesn't call me back about the network's archives, so after a month, I call him. He's apologetic. "Even *we* have trouble trying to research the early shows," he says affably, shifting the focus ever so slightly away from my question about whether any record of *Space Patrol* exists at all. (In my mind's eye, I see a stately building labeled "ABC Archives" where historic scripts and kinescopes are carefully catalogued and preserved.) "It's hard to find data on these old shows," the VP is saying. "Our office hasn't had any success delving back to stuff from the '50s."

I'm catching on. "So the network didn't keep any records, scripts, kinnies or artifacts from those old shows?" I ask.

"They may exist someplace," he hedges, "but in those days, ABC was pretty much a mom-and-pop store. They weren't as organized as they are now." He's distancing himself, as if he's not part of this place where "they" threw everything out. "I don't hold much hope that we'll have very much in the way of accurate information," he says vaguely.

I'm tasting blood. "So ABC doesn't have any archives from the early days? They just don't exist, right?"

"They really don't... Right."

I run this bit by Norm Jolley, who understands my rage. "After the show was canceled, we got word that some executive at the network got rid of all the old scripts in their possession," he says. "We all thought it was a terrible thing for them to do—but they did it." Jolley adds that his first wife, What's-Her-Name, donated his personal set of scripts to a paper drive.

Fortunately, in late February 1955, meticulous technical director Irwin Stanton was thinking ahead, as usual. In the confusion of the show's demise, as models and props were distributed to cast and crew, he quietly gathered a complete set of scripts and presented them to Dick Darley along with a note:

> These are the original SP scripts. Thought you might like to keep them —for posterity or something.

---

[11]In 1996, Disney purchased ABC, and on November 1, 2002, ABC Television Center was renamed The Prospect Studios. Today, says Phil Angerhofer, Technical Manager, Studio Operations for ABC, it's primarily used for Disney productions and ABC soaps and pilots. In January 2001, *Eyewitness News* moved to KABC's new studios in Glendale.

"It seems funny, in retrospect," says Joe Sarno, "that the common people — the guys in little houses with big mortgages — were able to save the old comic books and toys of the space opera era. But the big, multimillion-dollar networks could do nothing to save the films and kinescopes of the heroes they created."

Lou Huston: "I was raised in a generation where you always knew who the good guy was. Tom Mix and Hoot Gibson stood up for right, but didn't preach. There was no religion brought into it, but there were no excuses for the bad guys, either, such as their mothers didn't treat them right or their fathers deserted them. That was never brought up. Both good guys and bad guys were judged by one thing: their behavior."

Jack McKirgan: "Time and reality bury youth under a mountain of education, employment, sweet and bitter loves, family bonds and tragedy. But youth is still with me, even if the youthful body is half a century away. Sometimes I want to be a kid again — shed the constraints and burdens of business, age, health problems and family responsibilities. If Commander Corry asked me to be his cadet, I'd jump into the right-hand seat of that ship and push the lever to fire the rockets as we head toward our next adventure."

Chris Darley: "There's a sweet, caring history about shows like Space Patrol. *Maybe, when we watch reruns, some of us just want to go back to that era and recreate how we felt when we first watched. Intellectually, we know we can't do that, but, emotionally, that's what we want."*

On a gray, winter day on the Oregon coast, Elliott Swanson relaxes in his office with a steaming cup of green tea ("which should be Nestlé's Quik," he explains, "but the ship's store was out") and stares at the brightly colored array of cardboard dials, gauges, switches and levers propped up on his desk:

> I'm looking at the Rocket Cockpit, which is more than a spaceship; it's a time ship. The Port Rocket Tubes are trimmed and the course is set on the Directional Indicator Outward. Thrust is set on the Anti Gravity Rockets and the Projectile Forward Rockets. Terra is on the Radarscope Strato Viewer. The two Time Computers are set — port computer at 19 within the Voohm System scale and the starboard computer at 1955 on the Erg System scale. Pressure and vacuum readings within normal operational parameters. Interior Lights at three-quarters and Exterior Landing Lights at one-quarter. Port and starboard Gravitational Range Corrections within standard range. Cosmic and Gamma Protective Shields active.

Swanson, director of a college library, has not managed to put childish things behind him and is not sure he should. "When the last of us who saw these programs in their original setting is gone, something will vanish from the collective unconscious," he maintains.

> And while future generations may recreate the setting of the 1950s, complete with vintage black-and-white TV sets, they will never duplicate the feel of that time — a world where we didn't know if there were Martians. To us, the space opera ships were not models or sets of wood and cloth; they flew to the planets on the fuel of imagination and hope — planets inhabited by people like ourselves. And for those of us who were there — children captured by the wonder — a small place of belief somehow survives. We are supposed to

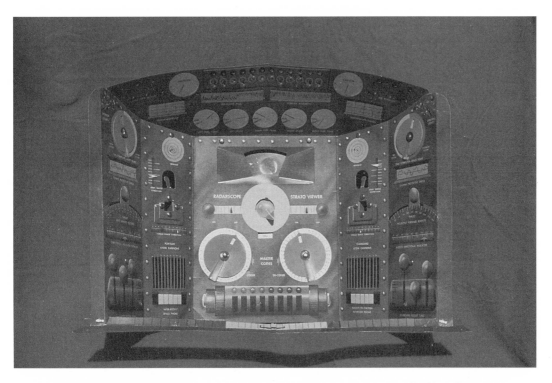

Space Patrol Rocket Ship Cockpit — a replica of the original premium, crafted by Elliott Swanson. (Courtesy Elliott Swanson)

give up childish things as adults, and probably to leave most of that in the past is for the best. But you give up all of it only at the peril of your soul.

Swanson leans back and takes a final sip of tea before blast-off. "Headed for dreamtime… Let the rockets roar!"

Appendix 1
Cadet Handzo's Guide to Space Patrol *Merchandising*

by Stephen Handzo

Boxtop Premiums

The *Space Patrol* experience involved more than passive enjoyment of the program. A Space Patroller had duties, chief among them to eat a big bowl of cereal every day. He or she was also expected to obtain "official" gear ("just like Buzz Corry uses"). This could require the consumption of even more cereal. When *Space Patrol* acquired Ralston as a sponsor, it got a company with nearly two decades' experience in kiddie marketing via the cowboy-themed trinkets on the *Tom Mix* radio show. From October 1951 to the middle of 1953, boxtop offers appeared regularly—a new one roughly every three months. After that, mail-in premiums became erratic, some offered jointly with co-sponsor Nestlé (as of 1954) and, in the show's final months, by Nestlé alone.

While it's common to see all *Space Patrol* merchandise referred to as "premiums," that term properly applies only to those items that required purchase of the sponsors' products. Most of the gear (and all of the better stuff) was sold by mail order or in retail stores.

Space Patrol "Jet-Glow" Code Belt

If *Consumer Reports* rated 1950s premiums, this inaugural offering would be a "best buy." Several radio and TV juvenile adventure shows had belts, and others had decoders—but who else had a decoder belt? The glow-in-the-dark plas-tic belt had a gold-plated metal buckle shaped like a rocket. The buckle alone was worth 25 cents. Mounted on a steel plate on the back of the buckle was a decoder wheel. "The Space Patrol Code Belt" was the first of many instances where a premium furnished an episode with its title and figured in the story. Kids were told that "*Space Patrol* radio and television broadcasts will give regular messages in code for Space Patrol members such as yourself to decode," although it's not clear if that ever happened. The white plastic belt had a greenish tinge. The reason it glowed in the dark was so you could wear it at night. I went into the closet to see if it really glowed—and it did! Surviving belts have generally turned brown and lost their phosphorescence.

Featured in Episode 43, "The Space Patrol Code Belt," October 20, 1951 (Live in Los Angeles; two-week delayed kinescope elsewhere). Production: 177,235.[1]

Cosmic Smoke Gun

Small plastic gun, about 4½" long, in "rocket-fire red," made by U.S. Plastics of Pasadena, California. (That company manufactured the full-size Rocket Dart Gun introduced in 1951, one version of which was in the same color. See below.) The Smoke Gun came pre-loaded but was supplied with a refill packet of talcum powder. Pressure on the trigger

---

[1]Production figures are from T.N. Tumbusch's *The Illustrated Radio Premium Catalog and Price Guide*, Tomart Publications (1989, Dayton, Ohio), as posted by Elliott Swanson on the space opera Web page www.solarguard.com.

squeezed an air bladder that forced a wisp of "cosmic smoke" out of the muzzle that the ads promised would "put someone instantly to sleep." On television, the pitchman (Jack Narz) reassured parents that while one puff of cosmic smoke would put someone to sleep for an hour and two puffs for 24 hours, the sleep-inducing agent had been removed, making the gun absolutely harmless. Size matters. The pooky little gun was barely visible on black-and-white TV, though when a Venusian miscreant fired it at Robbie, the bright white talcum powder that unloaded on the front of Ken Mayer's uniform was hard to miss. For a subsequent version, the manufacturer added spool-like segments to the barrel that extended the gun's length to 6 inches and the color was changed to the slimy metallic green that then denoted otherworldliness. Silly as it was, the Cosmic Smoke Gun is one of the best-remembered premiums and highly collectible today. It was also offered the longest, with the green version available as late as mid–1954.

Offer began with "Cosmic Smoke Guns," Episode 55, January 13, 1952 (first episode transmitted live, coast-to-coast) and continued through March.

Production: 147,456 (red version)

Lunar Fleet Base

A good one. A collection of punch-out structures with little plastic standee figures of the cast. The set contained 30 pieces (a figure inflated by counting the jetways as 10 pieces) and covered an area 6 feet square (2' × 3'). The central structure was Lunar Space Patrol Headquarters with an imposing Space-o-Phone tower topped by an antenna that resembled Bullwinkle on a bad day at electrician's school. A paper version of *Terra V* (4 pieces) was obviously designed during the *Terra IV* era with only the name updated. Included with the Fleet Base, and containing the assembly instructions, was the first edition of the Space Patrol Toy Catalog.

Offer began with "Mysterious Moon Quakes," Episode 67, April 6, 1952, and ran through May.

Production: 218,456

Space Patrol Balloon Kit

Sold in grocery stores for 10 cents with the purchase of a box of Ralston cereal. A blue rubber balloon with an illustration of the Ralston Rocket was packed in a checkerboard-motif cardboard folder that could be formed into a launching ramp. Although produced in great numbers, the survival rate is presumably low.

Membership Kit

A must-have! Included: plastic insignia badge, bluish Chart of the Universe, handbook rich in Space Patrol lore, membership card, photo of cast. A "two-for-one offer" combined the Membership Kit with the red plastic Cosmic Glow Rocket Ring, today a rare collectible. A generic rocket shape integral with the ring's setting had at its tip an "atomic glow chamber" that emitted a blue phosphorescent glow when viewed in darkness. The Glow Ring was seen in "Mission to Mercury," Episode 78, June 21, 1952.

Production: 664,751 (267,333 with ring; 397,418 without ring).

Space-o-Phone Set

A futuristic version of the tin can telephone that worked about as well; nevertheless, the best-selling plastic premium. Blue and yellow, about 3 inches high, 2 wide and ¾ deep. Made by J.V.Z. Co. of St. Louis, Missouri.

October 25–December 27, 1952.[2]

Production: 319,550

Space Binoculars

"Presenting the most unusual *Space Patrol* equipment you've ever had a chance to own! The biggest news for boys and girls in the history of *Space Patrol*! Greatest value ever offered on this program!" That was going a bit far, although the binoculars were one of the most popular premiums and even worked pretty much as promised. They were touted as "Big!" (5" × 5"), possibly to contrast with a smaller unit offered by Kellogg's cereals on their *Tom Corbett* show. A semi-circular plastic frame held four Lucite lenses with 4× magnification, compared with a lowly 3× for Tom's. The wider end fit to the face. If you looked through the

---

[2]Some premiums can be tracked through their use as TV episode titles, but where they can't, Handzo has relied on info from one of Jerry Haendiges' Vintage Radio Logs (compiled from a set of dated *Space Patrol* transcription discs) to determine the offering period. The same offers ran concurrently on both radio and TV, although the start and end dates may not always coincide. —JNB

other end, it "smallified." "Straps to your head so you can wear it like a mask," said the box copy, although the TV spots assured us that "it was not goggles, not a mask, not celluloid, not cardboard," but black plastic with "leather-like inserts." The leatherette-texture top and bottom panels *were* cardboard and didn't hold up too well. The original version came in black. A later version in metallic green was promoted on the back of cereal boxes in 1954. Available by mail for 25 cents and a boxtop, the binoculars were also packaged for sale in grocery stores for 35 cents—with the purchase of a box of Ralston cereal. For some reason, the original television spots specified an Instant Ralston boxtop instead of the usual Wheat Chex or Rice Chex. "If you don't agree that this is the greatest offer ever made on *Space Patrol*, return your binoculars and we'll return your money!" promised Jack Narz.

January 3–February 21, 1953. (A rare instance when a boxtop offer provided the title of a radio episode: "The Brain Bank and the Space Binoculars," January 3, 1953.)

Production: 168,718 (black version)

Project-O-Scope

Rocket-shaped, battery-powered film viewer with a yellow body, blue nose and fins; marked "Terra V." It was a diminutive cousin to the rocket-shaped Ray-O-Vac flashlight, and also capable of standing upright on its fins, but with the bulb at the small end. It was touted as a flashlight, a signal light, and a projector. A strip of sprocketed black-and-white 8mm film could be pulled through a slot in the tail. The film contained 24 minimally-detailed images showing the cast in four comic-strip adventures. Pressure on the nose cone's antenna activated the lamp. The lens in the exhaust port projected a cone of light in the area circumscribed by the fins. The recommended "throw" was one foot from a desktop or wall. This premium came at a premium: 35 cents instead of the customary "25 cents in coin."

April 25–May 30, 1953
Production: 97,616

Space Patrol Microscope

The small, all-plastic microscope ("not an inch of cardboard") stood about 4½" high with a black tube on a green base. The tube was removable for viewing large objects. This was demonstrated in the commercial by examination of a fence in the set, described as looking, under 15× magnification, like "icebergs in Alaska," should anyone ever need to inspect a fence for icebergs. It came with four clear slides and a pre-mounted "atomic particle" that glowed in the dark and was said to look "like a big purple planet with mysterious rays shooting out." Made by J.V.Z. Co.

Offered June 27–August 15, 1953.
Production: 56,672

[There were no boxtop offers between August l5, 1953, and January 2, 1954, although old premiums could be ordered from information on Ralston cereal boxes. The Magic Space Pictures (an in-box premium in Wheat Chex and Rice Chex packages) were promoted again in August and September, 1953. On October 2, focus shifted to the Interplanetary Space Coins, found only in packages of Regular and Instant Ralston. The coins, required to enter the Name the Planet Contest, were heavily promoted until December 26.]

"Mono-View" Outer Space Helmet

Scored cardboard with a glue seam, shipped flat. When opened up, it became a hexagonal space helmet secured at the top with a rubber band. A "silvery sheet" of semi-transparent, mirrored plastic covered the eyeholes. ("You can see out but no one can see in!") It was described as "what Commander Corry wears when he doesn't want anybody to know who he is." If Ed Kemmer felt any embarrassment at wearing a cardboard box on his head, he was a good enough actor not to show it. The helmet made its first appearance in Episode 157, "Mystery of the Missing Asteroids," Dec. 26, 1953. This was the last premium with "Captain" Jack Narz as pitchman. In a carry-over from the Name the Planet contest, boxtops from Regular Ralston and Instant Ralston were specified. During 1954, some premiums were offered in grocery stores with the purchase of a box of Ralston cereal. The Outer Space Helmet was promoted with a 5-foot cardboard standee figure of Buzz Corry in a spacesuit, holding a box of Ralston cereal (with Corry's picture on it). Instructions on the back showed the store manager how to flank the figure with artfully-stacked cereal boxes for an eye-catching display. The Binoculars and Cosmic Smoke Gun (both now in green) also made return engagements as in-store items.[3]

---

[3]One of these cardboard displays, auctioned on eBay in June, 2003, sold for $2052.77.—JNB

January 2, 1954–February 13, 1954
Production: 44,992

Cosmic Rocket Launcher

"Slick red-and-yellow plastic rocket with an unbreakable snap-on scout car! Stainless steel launching gun sends rocket whooshing over 33 feet of special break-proof nylon cord. Scout car drops down at end of trip. Use it for window-to-window communication with a pal next door. There's a special place in the scout car for secret messages!" A fan who posted to the space opera Web site "Solar Guard" described it differently: "The worst premium ever." The idea was that the cord would be tacked to a wall or board. On impact, the retractable rod on the nose of the rocket would release the scout car. When demonstrated on live TV, the scout car, instead of dropping, tended to fly upward or off to the side. In a scene out of *William Tell*, "Captain Barclay" (George Barclay, who filled in for Narz) aimed the primed rocket at a kid who held up a piece of wood. It was stressed that you could re-load the scout over and over again. (That assumed you could find it.) This was the first premium to be shared between Ralston and Nestlé after the latter had joined the show as co-sponsor. Although the address ("Box 812, St. Louis, Mo.") remained the same, the lid from a box of Nestlé's Quik (or "a tracing of the label") would be accepted as well as the usual Wheat Chex or Rice Chex boxtop. In another promo, Ed Kemmer was enlisted to declare that the "beautiful red and yellow rocket looks just like the big cosmic rocket that Hap and I used to blast off from Earth in today's episode." You couldn't be sure of that on black and white television, but episode 173, "Marooned in the Past," April 17, 1954, set in the Los Angeles of 1954, featured an experimental rocket and a scout car. The tradition of working premiums into the storyline was thus maintained. The Cosmic Rocket Launcher had the lowest production total of any premium.

April 17–May 22, 1954
Production: 22,682

Man-From-Mars Totem Head

How do you say "rip-off" in Martian? In 1954, that corner of Checkerboard Square (as Ralston dubbed its St. Louis headquarters) devoted to *Space Patrol* premiums) must have been in a state of confusion over the future of box-top offers. Perhaps because the Rocket Launcher was such a bomb, the Outer Space Helmet, offered just 15 weeks previously, was transformed via garish graphics, a beak, and earpieces into the "super-scary, super-spooky" Martian Totem Head. "A spook from outer space, that's you!" Remarkably, writer Norman Jolley managed to incorporate it into the storyline of a three-episode series about an ancient, totem-head-wearing tribe — the Carnacans — that Buzz and Hap encountered in an underground city on Mars. Kids were urged to order five or six heads — or more — to make a totem pole. Understandably so; the sponsors may have envisioned a pile of unsold totem heads. This was another joint effort between Ralston and Nestlé.

Episodes 179, "The Hidden Treasure of Mars," May 29, 1954; 180,"The Martian Totem Head," June 5, 1954; and 181,"Trapped in the Pyramid," June 12, 1954, comprised the story. The offer ran until Episode 184, "Marooned on the Ocean Floor," July 3, 1954 (the last show prior to the month-long "vacation," and the last show aired live).
Production: 32,681

Hydrogen Ray Gun Ring

Almost every adventure show that offered premiums touted a ring of some kind. The Hydrogen Ray Gun Ring was 1954's futuristic counterpart to the Lone Ranger's Six Gun Ring, introduced in 1948. A tiny plastic gun, about 1½" long, with a glow-in-the-dark chamber at the rear, sat atop an expandable metal setting. It rotated on the base so you could aim it at the person or thing to be destroyed. One of the lesser-known premiums, the ring may have been a casualty of the mid–1954 "vacation" when *Space Patrol* went off the air during July, as it does not appear to ever have been promoted on the show. The offer was made instead on boxes of Instant and Regular Ralston, double-billed with the periscope, though Buzz and Hap were no longer featured on the front of the package, as they had been during 1953's Name the Planet contest.[4]
Production: 35,227

---

[4]"And don't forget the Space Patrol Title Printer Plastic Ring," says Rich Gronquist, one of the few collectors to ever own the valuable Space Patrol Monorail. "The ring base was blue, and the circular top was yellow with the words Space Patrol printed backwards for stamping," he reports. "It also was circulated with a red base and green circular top. The stamp pad was hooked to the bottom part of the ring but could easily be broken or pulled off. Since the pad was not much bigger than a dime, it got easily lost, which makes this ring a hard one to find intact."—JNB

Space Patrol Periscope

"See over fences! Watch parades, see over crowds! Look around corners! Has a chart to identify people from other planets!" Another flat-packed, cardboard premium. When punched out and folded, it formed a tapered box 24 inches long "in neat colors of red, yellow, and blue" with dual-angled mirrors. The top had spaces for "name, address, and solar system," the latter two pre-printed: Planet Earth—Solar System/Sun Star "G" Yellow/ Galaxy—Spiral 279/Constellation OX34YL/ Intra-spatial ward PXL224. Above the eyepiece on the rear panel were circular pictures of (in descending order): Mercurian, Venetian [*sic*], Earthman, Martian, Jupiterman, Saturnian, Uranian, Neptuneman, and Plutoman. Buzz and Happy used the periscope to penetrate the defenses of the invisible creature Manza who ruled a planet by the same name. His security system could only identify electronic devices, which, as Corry explained to Happy, the periscope was not. This was one of the shortest offers—only four weeks—and was sponsored by Ralston.

Episode 186, "The Space Patrol Periscope," September 11, 1954, through 189, "The Giants of Pluto 3," October 3, 1954.

Production: 45,433

Rocket (Ship) Cockpit

"You can sit at the controls of your own ship and go up, up, up ... five ... fifty ... one hundred miles an hour. Past the moon, above Mars, through the starry rings of Saturn, even through the barrier of time!" exulted Ed Kemmer. This was another premium with roots in radio: Quaker Oats' *Captain Sparks and Orphan Annie* offered a "Captain Sparks Aircraft Cockpit" in 1942. *Space Patrol*'s final premium was the first to be offered exclusively by Nestlé. Even though Nestlé had a different ad agency (Cecil and Presby) from Ralston Purina, the premium was mailed from St. Louis in the same blue-and-red envelope as the Ralston paper items, which suggests that it may have been commissioned by Ralston before their decision to exit the premium business. The switch of sponsorship of premiums to Nestlé appears to have come abruptly, as the title card that showed the familiar "Box 812, St. Louis, Mo." to the TV camera was painted over to read "Box 54." Indeed, Ralston declined to renew its contract in December 1954, though its spots continued to run through the final episode, February 26, 1955.

"Mystery of the Stolen Rocket Ship," Episode 192, October 23, 1954, began a three-part story about the theft of the XRC, an experimental rocket ship. The Cockpit did not actually appear until the conclusion, Episode 194, "Danger: Radiation," November 6th.

The brightly-colored, creased cardboard punch-out of the Rocket Cockpit, when assembled, was 5" deep, 21" wide and 13" tall with an array of dials, gauges, switches, and controls that included "nine moving parts." Among its features were the Inter-Rocket Space Phone, Rocket-to-Station Intercom Phone, Directional Indicator, Cosmic Protective Shield, Gamma Protective Shield, Tracerscope and Magnetic Pull. There were 5 separate movable cardboard discs, including Master Codes Coder/Decoder, Time Computer for Light Years/Space Years (to program the "Secret Stardrive that lets you travel into the future"), and at the center a Radarscope Strato Viewer. In a die-cut screen above the viewer control were displayed images of 8 planets that could be changed by turning a knob. The names of the planets appeared in a smaller die-cut screen below. On each side, there were movable levers for Anti-Gravity Rockets/Forward Projectile Rockets. A separate pair of 2½" long cardboard tubes at the back served as Atomic Cannon Barrels. The barrel openings were matched on the front by places to attach rubber bands to propel projectiles, which the instruction folder suggested could be drinking straws. The 4-page assembly folder also included instructions for making "space phones" out of empty cocoa cans. In one of the TV spots, two boys, each seated at a Rocket Cockpit, communicate through cocoa box phones, though only about 10 feet apart. The Cockpit cost 25 cents along with the lid or a tracing of the label from Nestlé's EverReady Cocoa (not Quik).

Offered October 2–November 13, 1954.

Production: 40,000 (approximate)

A "Neddy Nestlé Space Jet" (a toy plane twirled on a string, 18 inches long with upturned fins at the tips of the wings) was announced in the trade press as both an on-air and "point of sale" (store) premium. It would have been Nestlé's second exclusive premium, had the show not gone off the air. (Neddy Nestlé was a cartoon strip that appeared as paid advertising in the comics pages of Sunday newspapers.)

In-Box Premiums

Not all premiums involved sending in boxtops and quarters. Ralston put three items right in the cereal box: Trading Cards, Magic Space Pictures, and the Interplanetary Space Coins needed to enter the Name the Planet contest and win the biggest prize ever awarded any kid: the gigantic, 35-foot Ralston Rocket. (See Chapter 16, "The Search for the Ralston Rocket.")

Space Patrol Trading Cards (40 in all)

When *Space Patrol* depicted other worlds, it was limited by the black-and-white technology of this one. The color trading cards, packed in Wheat Chex and Rice Chex boxes, had no such constraints. There were three sets: "Stars and Planets" (13), "Space Heroes" (13) and "Rockets, Jets and Weapons" (14). The "Stars and Planets" series, in particular, with its surrealistic landscapes and multicolored skies, typified the "space art" of the early 1950s that stirred childhood fantasies of interplanetary adventure.

Stars and Planets: Saturn, Terra City, Desert of Mars, Mars, Surface of Mercury, Operation Moon Crater, Galaxy S-33, Mira — Red Giant Sun, Multiple Sun System, Venus, Neptune, Expedition to Rhea, Rocket Over the Moon.

Space Heroes: Fleet Commander, Secret Code Master, Buzz Corry, Jet Car Trooper, Space Nurse, Clearing the Space Lanes, Cosmic Scientist, Cadet Happy, Interplanetary Guard, Rocket Astrogator, Rocket Test Pilot, Solar Space Race, Jetting Through Space.

Rockets, Jets and Weapons: Lunar Gyro Jet, Rocket Carrier Ship, Danger — Meteor Shower, Space Station, Space Refueling, Emergency in Space, Solar Disintegrator Ray, Monorail Liner, Saucer Attack, Rocket Over Canali, Stardrive, Ready for Action, Experimental Rocket, War of the Planets.

Magic Space Pictures

The art on the back of the cereal box showed an image beamed up to the sky as if it were Batman's Bat Signal projected onto the clouds over Gotham City, but what you got were flimsy paper rectangles with a reverse image in a "negative" format. Staring at a spot on the card for 40 seconds was supposed to produce a retinal after-image that would show up for about 10 seconds against a background of clouds or a light-colored wall. (Cracker Jack packages had a similar premium, but with figures from history.) The reverse side served up *Space Patrol* factoids. For example, the "Buzz Corry" card claimed he could "out-think giant brain-machines," while "Buzz Corry's Special Insignia" stated: "The space lightning insignia can be worn by only one man in the entire Universe [as] the symbol of his fast thinking and lightning-like action." The "Cadet Happy" card called Hap "the outstanding cadet of the Space Patrol Academy." (What could the competition have been like?)

The Space Pictures were furnished in boxes of Wheat Chex and Rice Chex (one to a box) in 1953 and promoted on the show at various times from March through September. "Magic Space Pictures" was the title of one of the rare radio episodes named for a premium; it aired March 14, 1953. There were 24 cards in all: Buzz Corry, Cadet Happy, Major Robertson, Tonga, Atmosphere Helmet, Tonga in Space Helmet, Robot Man, The Planet Saturn, Cosmic Ray Gun, Space Patrol Badge, Experimental Rocket Ship, Rocket Ship Blasts Off, Flying Saucer, Speeding Jet Car, Deadly Iron Fist, Trooper in Combat Helmet, Special Agent Jack Narz, Buzz in Space Patrol Cap, Happy in Space Helmet, Planetoid Prospector, Space Pirate Captain, Veteran Spaceliner Pilot, Buzz Corry's Special Insignia, Carol.

Interplanetary (Space) Coins (36 in all)[5]

These were your passport to enter the Name the Planet Contest and win the gargantuan Ralston Rocket. Elaborate contests where

---

[5]Were they "Interplanetary Coins" or "Swell Space Coins"? Though the Creative Committee at the Gardner Company wrote the ad copy for the show and informed the writers which premiums were to be worked into scripts and when, they failed to note that the names of some items differed slightly between the show, the spot, the cereal box and the shipping mailer. "It's hard to say what the 'official' name was, in some cases," notes Handzo. "Was it 'Space Patrol Decoder Belt' or 'Jet-Glow Decoder Belt,' 'Martian Totem Head' or 'Man-from-Mars Totem Head,' 'Rocket Cockpit' or 'Rocket Ship Cockpit'?"—JNB

you named things—like horses or spaceships—were a favorite ploy of the cereal-sponsored adventure shows. When Nabisco launched radio's *Straight Arrow* in 1948, the hero's horse was initially nameless to allow for a name-the-pony/win-the-pony contest. The winning entry was "Fury," the title of a later, unrelated TV series sponsored by Post, which hosted its own contest a few years later to name (and win) a palomino pony in conjunction with *The Roy Rogers Show*. And in 1950, the lucky winner of a Kix cereal contest to name a colt purportedly sired by the Lone Ranger's famous steed, Silver ("Silver has a SON!"), got to keep him.

Of course, no mere animal could compare to the *Terra IV*, AKA the Ralston Rocket. The possibility of winning Buzz Corry's former flagship was so unimaginably exciting that Ralston knew they could make entrants leap through hoops. While the trading cards and space pictures came only in Chex boxes, the coins needed to enter the Name the Planet contest were found only in boxes of Regular or Instant Ralston. Although the contest was described as "the simplest ever," it was anything but. You had to go to a Weather-Bird shoe store to get a coin album that contained the entry blank for the contest. (Why Weather-Bird got into it isn't clear, except it was based in St. Louis.) The "Weather-Bird man" gave you a starter set of three "Starlight Silver" coins" to be put in designated slots on a smaller, detachable part of the album. Next, you had to eat at least three boxes of cardboard-like cereal to acquire three more coins in a color other than "starlight silver." There was only one coin per box, and you had to make sure there was a picture of Buzz Corry or Cadet Happy on the package. (If you got an old box, you would endure the stuff for nothing.) The coins came in three colors: black, blue and gold. There were three series: Coins of Terra, Coins of Saturn, Coins of the Moon. Each series had four denominations: 10, 25, 50 and 100 credits. Mercifully, there was no specification as to which of these was needed to enter the contest. (This was obviously in the days before the Consumer Products Safety Commission. No sponsor today would take the chance that someone's little darling would swallow or choke on a plastic token.) When the

three additional coins were put into the slots on the entry blank, it was taken back to the Weather-Bird store to be "registered." The larger portion of the folder had slots for 12 coins in the four denominations from each of the six series. There were six "extra" slots. It's unlikely that many kids ever filled more than the six needed to enter the contest. On-air promotion began September 9, 1953, on television with the first "Planet X" episode, and September 26 on radio, continuing until December 26—way past the contest deadline of December 1.

Toy Catalogs

Space Patrollers who ordered the Lunar Fleet Base in 1952 received a highly decorated mailer from glamorous Hollywood, where the show originated, instead of the usual brown box from St. Louis. Along with their premium came the "First Edition" of the Official Space Patrol Catalog. While some items would make but a single appearance, a few were mainstays through several editions issued from 1952 to 1953, such as the Rocket Dart Gun (called a "ray gun" in the show, where it served as the basic sidearm) and the clear, bubble-type Space Helmet emblematic of annoying, space-addicted juveniles in 1950s movies such as *The Rocket Man* and *The Seven Year Itch*.[6]

Ralston had plenty of experience in merchandising. Their early premiums, first offered on the *Tom Mix* radio show (1933–1950), were so numerous that they were contained in catalogues published from 1936 to 1940. The 1938 catalogue offered eight items at two price levels: one boxtop for lesser trinkets; one boxtop plus 10 cents for the better ones (though Depression-era kids who couldn't spare a dime could send in two boxtops). By the time *Space Patrol* came along in the 1950s, Ralston had brought the price of their premiums up to 25 cents, but even in the early 1950s a quarter didn't buy much. With more money around than ever before, the time was ripe for a *Space Patrol* catalogue with better-quality merchandise at a variety of price points. Here's a rundown of *Space Patrol* gear that could be purchased by catalogue:

---

[6]The get-up of Tom Ewell's son in *The Seven Year Itch* (1955) combines a *Space Patrol* helmet with a *Tom Corbett* spacesuit. The boy holds a "Buck Rogers Sonic Ray" flashlight pistol, making for maximum visual impact on an adult audience but bewilderment for juvenile fans.

Rocket Gun

Made by U.S. Plastics of Pasadena, California, it was issued under the "Toy Time" label. U.S. Plastics offered a variety of space-themed toy guns and water pistols and was one of the few *Space Patrol* vendors able to get into toy counters outside of the Los Angeles area. The gun could be bought for a mere 98 cents and came in a cellophane package designed to dangle from a display rack; a boxed version sold for $1.49 in better retail stores and through the toy catalogue. Both red and black versions were sold in stores, but the less popular black version, with red trigger and (non-functional) knob, was sold only in stores—not in the catalogue. The catalogue offered the same gun used on the show: red with black details.

To baby boomers who saw *The Graduate* in 1968, "plastics" stood for everything conformist and inauthentic in American life, yet as kids in the early '50s, they had delighted in futuristic playthings made of wondrous polystyrene in a cornucopia of shapes and colors. The Rocket Gun, the signature *Space Patrol* artifact, had a sculpted-by-the-wind quality that Zeus himself might have coveted. Made of thin plastic and unexpectedly light, it fit beautifully into little hands. It came with two red-and-yellow finned plastic darts: one had a "Captomatic" warhead ("loud and pleasantly effective as a real guided missile") into which a paper cap could be inserted to detonate on impact. This never worked very well, even when fired straight down at the sidewalk. The other dart had a removable suction cup that exposed a hollow chamber suitable for microfilm or secret messages. In the 1953 movie *The Caddy,* Jerry Lewis plays an inept toy counter clerk, who, while playing with the Rocket Gun (modified so he could twirl it on his finger), plants a rubber-tipped dart on the forehead of his manager (Fred Clark).

Outer Space Plastic Helmet

The 12" diameter, clear acetate space helmet created work for Beemak Plastics of Los Angeles, founded in 1951 with four employees and still in existence. Southern California emerged as a manufacturing center after World War II, so Space Patrol Enterprises, set up by Mike Moser as his merchandising arm, didn't have to venture far from home to find production lines. The helmet's two hemispheres were welded together and the seam concealed by a red plastic strip. The front and back had 6" × 6" openings that even a child might find at odds with the retention of oxygen in space. The collar, oxygen tanks and tubes were a single, inflatable vinyl unit resembling a beach toy and thus prone to punctures and split seams. Although an intact helmet occasionally turns up in the original box, most often it's the "bubble" alone that has survived, little the worse for wear, except for fading and scratches on the decal, which—on every helmet—said "Commander." (Purchase of a helmet was a quick way to make rank, as the maker seemed oblivious to the threat to Buzz Corry's singular authority.) It was also offered through the "Carol Beatty" catalogue, a Los Angeles mail-order house that advertised in women's magazines.

Uniforms and Clothing

The first catalogue was heavy on haberdashery: Space Patrol ties, scarves, T-shirts, flight suits, boys' cadet shirts and girls' "space blouses," mufflers, handkerchiefs, and even suspenders. A "boys' and girls' Cosmic Cap" with built-in goggles was made by Bailey of Hollywood. Hidden features were common in Space Patrol mufti. The leather gauntlets, or "Cosmic Gloves," offered in the initial catalogue had a Magic Message Pad and stylus built into the cuff.

Aquajet

Another item making a single appearance was the "Aquajet," an inflatable 36-inch-long device that could float or be used as a cushion in front of the TV while watching *Space Patrol.*

Comic Books

"12 big issues" of the Space Patrol Comic Book were offered for a subscription price of $1.25 (10 cents singly), but only two were produced. This would be the first of at least two broken promises. The books were published by Approved Comics, Inc. (Chicago and Bridgeport, Conn.) and distributed by Ziff-Davis. Issue 1 was released in July, 1952, and dated "Summer"; issue 2 followed three months later, dated "October-November."[7]

[7]For a brief time, Ralston Purina offered "Space Patrol's Special Mission," a comic book in which Buzz, Hap and Tonga travel back to Earth's 20th century to urge kids to alert adults to the nation's dwindling blood supply. The comic was offered as a Chex premium for a boxtop and 25 cents, along with a Blood Booster Badge, but had nothing to do with the Approved Comics/Ziff Davis series.

Watch

A 6-in-1 Space Patrol Watch was offered for $7.95. The watch ("a jeweled, precision timepiece, not a toy") was an early variation of the classic Timex introduced in 1950 by U.S. Time, the leading purveyor of character watches, including Hopalong Cassidy, Disney's Cinderella, and later, Zorro. (U.S. Time had been the exclusive Disney licensee since 1933, when Mickey Mouse watches and clocks hit the market.) Only three of the six functions—seconds, hours, hours in military time—were on the watch itself; the others were on the dome compass packed with it. The first version of the watch was sold in a display box with a lid in the shape of the *Terra V*. This carried the imprint Toys of Tomorrow ("for the children of today"), which appears to have been an offshoot of Space Patrol Enterprises. The watch was later dropped from the catalogue and sold by U.S. Time under its own name in a simpler box with a picture of Ed Kemmer as Buzz Corry.

Monorail and City of Terra

Another high-end Toys of Tomorrow contribution was the Monorail. A single car with a battery-powered motor traveled on a track supported by pylons. In the "First Edition" (Spring 1952) of the toy catalogue, the price was $7.95, but by the end of the year it had climbed to $12.95—the most expensive *Space Patrol* toy then and the most prized today. To make up for the escalating price, a punch-out City of Terra was included to provide a suitable backdrop. The 'City' was similar to the Lunar Fleet Base but more elaborate (50 pieces). It also cost four times as much, as it could be purchased separately for $1.00 and thus only thinly concealed the fact that the price of the Monorail had jumped about 50 percent. To replicate the structures of the Space Patrol's home base in tab and slot paper was no easy task, but to the toymaker's credit, they tried.

As the toy operation approached its first Christmas, the Fall 1952 catalogue offered seventeen items, several of them new. It was sent out with the Space-o-Phone premium and contained the operating instructions.

Space-a-Phones (Space-o-Phones)

For the catalogue, Toys of Tomorrow offered "Space-a-Phones" (misspelled on the box or possibly renamed to avoid confusion with the cereal premium). These were much nicer aesthetically and ergonomically than the Ralston Space-o-Phones. Though they cost more ($1.00), they didn't work better and were more awkward to use because the cord was permanently attached. In subsequent catalogues they were called "walkie-talkies."

Coin and Stamp Set (Courier Pouch)

Toys of Tomorrow also offered the first edition of Space Patrol Interplanetary Coins and Stamps, better known as the Diplomatic Courier Pouch. Included were 200 stamps (many of which repeated art work from the trading cards) and a stamp album, plus 12 colored plastic coins (also with album). Twelve pieces of green and magenta paper currency, in denominations of 500 to 5000 United Planets credits, all had the same picture: Buzz Corry in a space helmet. His signature was on the money too. (Buzz's signature on the bills differed from that on the membership card, but then, he couldn't very well defend the universe and handle the money too.) A later version of the Courier Pouch came with a ballpoint pen in the shape of the *Terra V*—the only representation, in all the toys and premiums, of Buzz Corry's flagship that actually resembled the one on the show.

Flight Suit

One-piece cotton twill body suit with zippered front and ribbed neck, cuffs, and ankles. A blue triangular panel in the front contrasted with a gray background. Nice-looking but relatively expensive ($4.95).

Holster and Belt

The ray gun got a companion holster that cost more than the gun itself. The black leather belt and holster with "Space Patrol" on the belt and an emblem on the holster, both in silvery paint, went for $2.30 alone. A "Gun and Holster" set cost $3.79 (reduced to $2.98 in one ad). In later catalogues, the gun and holster were only sold as a set. Little straps on the holster to hold a second dart while the first was loaded were a nice detail.

Space Patrol Belt

Not to be confused with the belt from the holster, the Space Patrol belt had a compartment that sported a chrome-plated oval buckle on the outside. On the inside, it concealed a membership card (different from the one in the Membership Kit cereal premium) signed, of course, by Buzz Corry. $1.00.

Also offered were a boy's broadcloth cadet shirt in red and gray with a triangular insignia on the chest like that on the "dress" uniform worn by male cast members in personal appearances, and a "dress" cap (different from the Cosmic Cap).

In the four catalogues between the first edition in the spring of 1952 and the last in December 1953, and supplemental flyers, some 30 distinct items were offered.[8] They included some oddities connected tenuously — if at all — to the show. A 1952 Flying Saucer Gun spun propeller-like discs into the air. (George "Superman" Reeves hawked a similar item as a Kellogg's premium in 1955, and variations were produced in the U.S. and Britain into the 1960s.) A space-age hobbyhorse in the form of a 4-foot-long inflatable rocketship (marked *Terra V*, though hardly worthy of it) appeared in 1953. Taking honors in the "What *were* they thinking?" category were Cosmo and His Pals, a 2-foot-high rabbit flanked by a 1-foot rabbit and two 1-foot ducks— all wearing space helmets. They appeared only once, in the Christmas 1953, edition. The ad copy explained that Buzz Corry brought the foursome back from interplanetary space but it did not account for their Space Patrol uniforms.

The mid–1953 catalogue, under the auspices of a new entity, "Space Products," had only eight items but included several new and interesting ones.

Space Patrol Bank

"Shaped like a space station." You made deposits by putting a coin into a rocketship that could be moved in and out of a docking bay. The plastic, basketball-size bank resembled the spacecraft depicted on the "Rocket Carrier Ship" trading card and served as a prop in "The Man Who Stole a City" (Episode 129, June 13, 1953) as a shrunken version of the "real" Bank of Terra, reduced in size by a fiendish device

that compressed molecular structure.

Auto-Sonic Rifle

"Long promised to all Space Patrollers," but, alas, another (partially) broken promise, as those who ordered it from Space Products' next (and last) catalogue never got it. The slim, finned tubular rifle with double-grip design, executed in red-and-yellow plastic (by U.S. Plastics, makers of the Rocket Dart and Cosmic Smoke guns), was a "yesterday's future" precursor of the sleek underwater guns favored by James Bond (*Thunderball*) and Lara Croft (*Tomb Raider*), but instead of harpoons, it fired up to six sponge rubber balls. (A popular toy of the era was a "burp gun" that fired Ping-Pong balls through an aluminum barrel.)

Emergency Kit

A handsome item featured in the final catalogues, this plastic first-aid kit, made by Regis Space Toys, had a carrying case with a flashlight handle and compass rose design on the lid. When the contents— tape, bandages, "Space Sickness Pills," "Cosmic Ray Pills" and "Space Rations"— were depleted, the kit could be used as a lunch box. (Character lunch boxes were just coming into vogue in the early 1950s. There was a Tom Corbett lunch box, but the art was a decal, not the lithographed lid given icons like Hopalong Cassidy and Roy Rogers.) Unfortunately, very few of us got to be the coolest kid in the cafeteria, as anyone who ordered the Emergency Kit — or the Auto-Sonic Rifle —from the Christmas 1953 catalogue came up empty-handed. Among the few kids who may have received these items were third-prize winners of the Name the Planet contest, where 250 of each were awarded, along with 250 each of the more common Space Helmets and wrist watches.

By 1953, even a child might have suspected that there was trouble in Toyland. While the first catalogue emanated from "Space Headquarters" (a post office box on Hollywood Boulevard), subsequent flyers and multi-item order blanks gave the vendor as "Space Patrol Toys." But the 1953 catalogues listed the more

---

[8]The total would be more than 30 if the different versions of items are counted, such as the Stamp and Coin Set with and without the ballpoint pen; the Monorail with and without the City of Terra; and the "combo" offers, such as the gun and holster set.

ambiguous "Space Products" as the vendor, and there was a hint of desperation in the Christmas 1953 edition's "Space Products Special": a set of Space-o-Phones (now just called "walkie-talkies") was tossed in free if you bought the cotton twill Flight Suit, Space Helmet, and Gun and Holster Set at the regular price. The Flight Suit was described as "going to be rather scarce this year." That it was part of a discount package made no sense — unless the vendor was planning to exit the business permanently. A retail outlet was listed at 1641 N. Las Palmas in Hollywood. Did disappointed kids, stiffed on their Christmas presents, come pounding at the door?

Other Licensed Merchandise

Life magazine's September 1, 1952, spread devoted to *Space Patrol* displayed 80 items predicted to bring "$40 million this year in sales." The first number seems plausible; the second figure should be taken with a large (Kosher-sized) grain of salt, given the sudden, ignominious demise of the toy operation a year later. (Also, $40 million would have equaled or exceeded that year's revenue from Ralston's entire cereal business!)

Space Patrol merchandise peaked in 1952 as a number of "big-name" deals were cut with Marx Toys, Milton Bradley, Decca Records and U.S. Time/Timex. Far fewer items debuted in 1953, and they came mainly from smaller companies like Regis Space Toys. For 1954, with the toy catalogue gone, the only new items were premium offers, including revivals of the Space Binoculars and Cosmic Smoke Gun in green, while most of what had been available vanished from the marketplace. The bubble Space Helmet was still in the F.A.O. Schwarz catalogue for Christmas of that year. The Rocket Dart Gun outlasted the show itself; highly "unofficial" yellow, blue and green versions appeared in 1955.

When Space Products failed to ship the merchandise ordered for Christmas 1953, and weeks, then months, went by with no explanation or apology, inquiries to the postal authorities produced the revelation that the company was in receivership. There would never be toys for the kids, as promised, nor refunds for their parents, last and least in a long line of creditors.

Without access to the legal files of Space Patrol Enterprises, it's not possible to compile a definitive list of licensed merchandise. Nev-

ertheless, we can cite some additional items that were sold in retail stores. While most *Space Patrol* toys were made by small companies in California rather than big toy outfits based in the East, Space Patrol Enterprises did have some dealings with the largest of them all: Louis Marx Co. of New York. Marx's contribution to the *Space Patrol* oeuvre was limited, compromised by their use of the same basic design for multiple products. The Marx Space Patrol Atomic Disintegrator Pistol was, except in name, the same as the Tom Corbett, Space Cadet Atomic Pistol, both derived from a weapon labeled "Rex Mars Planet Patrol," a Marx house brand. And Marx's "official" Space Patrol Rocket Port Set was nearly identical to their Tom Corbett Space Academy playset. Among the little 2" high figures, some wearing pea-sized space helmets, were characters from both shows.

The Ray-O-Vac Rocket Lite, sold primarily in hardware stores, was strikingly designed with a stainless steel fuselage, a clear plastic nose cone over the lens, red bands and blue plastic fins that carried the *Space Patrol* logo and Buzz Corry's signature. The fins made it easy to park the flashlight upright, but not the most user-friendly to handle. One of the most widely circulated items, it was also produced under the manufacturer's own brand, "Captain Ray-O-Vac."

Milton Bradley produced a 1952 jigsaw puzzle with a stylized Terra IV flying above a very accurate rendition of the City of Terra and with circular portraits of Buzz, Happy and Carol. This was issued under license from Mike Moser Enterprises.

The 1950s vogue for stereo photography resulted in the *Space Patrol* cast's appearance in 3-D for Stori-Views in 1952, a St. Louis company best known for Bible scenes for children, seen through their "Pixie Viewer." Unlike the more familiar View-Master reels, Stori-Views used stereo pairs of transparencies mounted on individual cards. There was descriptive text between the images. (View-Master is still around, just barely, and its viewer can show the old reels, but Stori-Views used a different and long-defunct format. For *Space Patrol*, there were three sets of cards: Terra, the Land in Space — shots of the actual miniature used on the show (6 images); The Space Patrol Crew — waxworks-like tableaux, all taken on the set, that show each of the five principals, plus a group shot, for a rare view of the cast's costumes in color (6 images); and Testing Space Ship *Terra IV*—some narrative with a rare glimpse, in color, of a model of Buzz Corry's battlecruiser, the *Terra IV* (12 images).[9]

You could throw a *Space Patrol* theme birthday party with a set of eight paper plates and napkins plus party favors (five to a box) produced by C.A. Reed Company. The Ben-Hur Company made barrettes with rocket, jet plane, and ray gun designs. You could cover your head, rain or shine, with a "Commander" vinyl rain hat made by Marketon or a solar helmet from Bailey of Hollywood (makers of the Cosmic Cap).

Pre-dating the toy catalogues were Space Patrol dresses sold by May Company department stores in California in 1951, and a set of five bracelet charms with pictures of the cast.

Unlicensed Merchandise

Unlicensed "Space Patrol" merchandise appeared even after the show left the air. Without ownership interest, neither Ralston nor ABC had any stake in defending the franchise, and "Space Patrol" became a generic name, if not in legal fact, then in practice. A "Space Patrol" drink mixer in the shape of a rocket ship with an opening in the nose for a straw was produced in pink translucent plastic by SteriLite (United Plastic Co. of Fitchburg, Mass). This may have been designed during the period when Nestlé was a co-sponsor. (Rival Ovaltine had long offered *Captain Midnight* shake-up mugs.) The drink mixer was marketed without the distinctive logotype of the "official" *Space Patrol* merchandise. The box art made no reference to the show and suggested the product be used for fruit juice and (un–Buzz Corry–like) cocktails.

In the mid–1950s, Nomura and other Japanese manufacturers produced "Space Patrol" friction toys (tin rockets and space cars). They were not related to the U.S. show, but they are collectibles in their own right. There were also Asian knock-offs of the knock-offs, e.g. "Space *Control*" toys. To confuse things further, there was a 39-episode series titled *Space Patrol* on British television in 1963 (later shown in the U.S. as *Planet Patrol*) with a cast of puppets and its own line of licensed merchandise sporting similar items to the U.S. show: a jigsaw puzzle; trading cards (50 in all, collected one at a time in packages of chocolate cigarettes); a walkie-talkie (common on eBay); and a flying saucer gun like the one in the 1952 *Space Patrol* catalogue, selling here under the *Planet Patrol* logo. In addition to "Space Patrol" merchandise that (for present purposes) wasn't, Britain produced incognito one item that *was*: The Rocket Dart Gun, shorn of *Space Patrol* identifiers, resurfaced overseas well after the U.S. show went off the air. Reproduced by Merit from the original tooling, it was one of a series of ray guns associated with Dan Dare, "pilot of the future," a British Buck Rogers character that had debuted in 1950 in *Eagle*, a weekly cartoon book. *Uchu Patrol Hopper (Space Patrol Hopper*, AKA *Space Boy Jun)*, a 44-episode animated Japanese series, appeared in 1965, and West Germany had their own live-action "*Space Patrol*" (*Raumpatrouille*) for just seven black-and-white filmed episodes in 1966, but neither show seems to have yielded any merchandise. In the mid–1960s, Radio Shack used the tag "Space Patrol" as part of its Archer line of electronic items (which included walkie-talkies), the name having descended into the realm of nostalgic camp.

---

[9]The Stori-Views images captured the cast's costumes in color for future historians.—JNB

Appendix 2
Space Patrol *Television Episode Guide: Network Shows*

by Frank Bresee with additions
by Cadets Nancy Heck and Joe Sarno

History of the Guide

The first version of this guide to the 210 half-hour network shows was prepared in 1964 on Planet Earth by Frank Bresee, then an account executive at The Mack Agency in Hollywood, which syndicated *Space Patrol* in the mid–'60s. Bresee watched all the shows, took notes and passed them along to his secretary, who wrote a brief summary of each episode.[1] These synopses were sent to TV stations airing *Space Patrol* reruns. The stations passed them along to the press, where they served as source material for TV listings in local newspapers and magazines. Only the regular cast was credited in The Mack Agency's writeups; the names of guest actors were not included.

In the early '80s, Bresee gave Nina Bara a copy of the summaries. She included it in Volume III of her self-published books on the show and it became the "official" TV Episode Guide. In the late '90s, space opera historian Joe Sarno improved the guide, adding relevant plot details and factual notes (such as the episode in which a ship or costume first appeared), and posted it on the Web. Now, for the first time, the guide was available to every citizen of the United Planets.

In 2001, director Dick Darley made his

personal files from the show available, which included detailed descriptions of many episodes, the original titles (Some had been changed by The Mack Agency to sound more commercial), and the names of most of the players. Researcher Nancy Heck used this new data to flesh out and correct the text; she also added the names of guest actors, when available.[2] I did an edit, filled in some gaps, and have dispatched this updated version to Space Patrol Archives.—JNB

Regular Cast Members

Commander Buzz Corry . . . . Ed Kemmer
Cadet Happy . . . . Lyn Osborn
Major Robertson . . . . Ken Mayer
Carol Carlisle . . . . Virginia Hewitt
Tonga . . . . Nina Bara

1950, 1951

#1 *"Treachery on Mars"*
December 30, 1950

Buzz Corry, commander-in-chief of the Space Patrol, is returning to Terra from Earth, accompanied by his new cadet, Happy, winner

---

[1]The Mack Agency syndicated only the 210 network shows—not the 15-minute shows that originally aired in Los Angeles.

[2]Darley's papers describe some episodes in great detail, while others have only a line or two. 1–14 and 38–49 are marked "no record"; thus the names of guest actors are unavailable.

of the Corry Scholarship, when he spots what he believes to be a derelict guided missile floating in space. As the Space Patrol battlecruiser closes in to destroy it, the missile heads for the ship, narrowly missing it — then turns and strikes again. The missile is in reality a cosmic bomb controlled by Major Gorla from his fortress on Mars. The major, with the help of Marta — who has landed a job as the secretary general's assistant — plots to conquer the United Planets, beginning with the murder of Buzz.

#2 "The Lethal Lady" January 6, 1951

Marta attempts the theft of top-secret plans and plots Buzz's destruction. She enlists the aid of a Space Patrol officer, Lt. Krasnoff, who carries a grudge against Major Robertson, United Planets security chief. Marta imprisons Carol Carlisle, daughter of the secretary general, behind a secret panel when Carol begins to suspect the plot. Meanwhile, Lt. Krasnoff paralyzes Robbie with a ray gun and releases Magnetic Force Control, throwing Buzz and Happy's ship into free fall only seconds from the ground.

#3 "Intrigue in the Cabinet" January 13, 1951

Baron Von Kreitz, a member of the cabinet of the United Planets, is scheming to overthrow the secretary general. The Baron instructs Lt. Groat to prevent Buzz from delivering damaging information to the secretary, who's on Venus. Tonga, assistant to the security chief, is entrusted with a top-secret audiogram, but she's partially paralyzed by Lt. Groat while en route to Venus in her space car. Left in the aft compartment, she bravely risks a cosmic burn to turn on the ship's magnetizer. The resulting cosmic static trail aids Buzz and Cadet Happy in tracking her to Earth's moon — and the headquarters of Baron Von Kreitz. *(Commander Corry's ship is referred to as "Battlecruiser 100"— fastest ship in the universe.)*[3]

#4 "The Agra Ray" January 20, 1951

Carol is testing her most recent invention at the Science Academy, with the help of her lab assistant. The invention is called the Agra Ray, a device which speeds up the growth of plants, enabling them to reach their full growth in a matter of hours, thus eliminating food shortages. However, it's also discovered that when the ray is inverted, it is capable of turning entire cities into stone. The lab assistant is secretly in the employ of Prince Greegor of Mercury, who desires the Agra Ray in order to threaten Terra, capital of the United Planets. The lab assistant kidnaps Carol and takes her and the Agra Ray to Mercury — but she leaves a clue for Buzz and Happy, who speed through space to save her and Terra before the prince can make good his threat.

#5 "The Ivy of Death" January 27, 1951

Robbie and Tonga have been assigned the duty of taking the Agra Ray to Jupiter to allay the food shortage there. They are met by the sinister Gorgon, who pretends to be Jupiter's minister of agriculture. He takes them to his headquarters at the foot of the crater Cornicus, where he plans to steal the Agra Ray and use it to grow the Ivy of Death, a plant that gives off a suffocating dioxide and produces seeds capable of poisoning the atmosphere of the United Planets. When Robbie and Tonga fail to report in, Buzz and Happy begin a search for them. *(Universal Star Time mentioned for the first time.)*

#6 "Trouble on Saturn's Third Moon" February 3, 1951

Tonga is sent to investigate reports of trouble at Cosmic Radiation Plant No. 1, located on Saturn's third moon. She dismisses the hot-tempered Captain Kronk for mismanagement and Kronk vows to get even. Tonga is mysteriously shot with a shock rifle, but when Buzz and Happy arrive they can find no trace of Kronk, though they do catch his assistant absconding with embezzled payroll funds. *(Distant Units mentioned for first time.)*

#7 "Solo Flight to Jupiter" February 10, 1951

While on his first solo flight from Terra to Jupiter, Happy acquires an unwelcome passenger at the Jupiter Spaceport — a fellow named

[3]Note that this is a call sign, not the actual name of the ship, which is believed by historians to be *Terra I.*—JNB

Lucky, who is making off with the Jupiter Trust Company's funds. To ensure Happy's silence, Lucky threatens the lives of Carol and Buzz. When asked to explain his strange behavior on the "solo" trip, Happy is unable to give any reason — to the great disappointment of both Carol and the commander.

#8 "Cosmic Debris Warning" February 17, 1951

Robbie, at Space Control on Earth, receives a report from the chief astronomer that a planetoid has exploded nearby and all spaceships in the vicinity should watch for danger from cosmic debris. Buzz, Happy and Carol are returning to Terra from Earth when they are hit by a meteor. They are rendered helpless in space, rapidly losing oxygen and unable to communicate.

#9 "The Planos Epidemic" February 24, 1951

Burger, owner of six lead mines on the moon Planos, reports that an epidemic caused by a deadly bacteria is spreading through the mines. Tonga joins Buzz and Happy in space with the precious serum needed to combat the disease. But Burger and his accomplice, Leckner, wish to frighten everyone away in order to keep secret their discovery of a rich deposit of Exonium. When Happy catches Leckner in the process of tampering with the atmosphere system of one of the mines, they struggle, and Happy unknowingly inhales a lethal dose of the concentrated bacteria.

#10 "Tunnel of Escape" or "Tunnel of Death" March 3, 1951

Warden Sovak of the Mars Detention Quarters and his head trustee, Erik, have arranged for the escape of prisoners who are able to pay. The prisoners exit through a tunnel that runs underneath one of the irrigation canals. When Buzz learns of the escape of three prisoners in one month from the "escape-proof" prison, he decides to investigate with the help of Robbie and Happy. Erik leads the Space Patrollers to the tunnel and traps them inside — and soon the ceiling separating them from the canal above begins to give way.

#11 "The Perilous Sleep" March 10, 1951

Happy, suffering from lack of sleep due to a heavy study workload, falls victim to the beautiful Mara and her accomplice, who have recently stolen the Brainograph from Medical Science Center. Aboard her laboratory ship, Mara decides to use Happy as a guinea pig to help her learn how to use the device. Hearing of the cadet's plight, Buzz rushes to rescue the hapless Happy before he succumbs to the Brainograph.

#12 "The Sea-Car Sabotage" or "A Vacation at Lake Azure" March 17, 1951

Superintendent Brand of the spaceport at Lake Azure on the planet Venus informs Buzz that his Aqua jet car is ready. Buzz decides to take a vacation at the lake and test the new vehicle with Tonga and Happy — but Zurach, an escaped convict who has vowed revenge against Buzz, bullies the superintendent into helping him sabotage the new sea-car.
Brand . . . . Perry Evans
Zurach . . . . Peter Foster

#13 "Theft of the Zeta Ray" March 24, 1951

Robbie completes the formula for the Zeta Ray, an amazing machine that cures any illness and halts infection. But before he can transport it from Earth to Terra Medical Science Center, his former lab assistants kidnap him, abscond with the Zeta Ray, and leave Robbie helplessly floating in space around Earth's moon.

#14 "Blackmail on Saturn" March 31, 1951

Buzz, Happy and Carol are embroiled in a sinister plot with a mysterious universal blackmail ring run by Professors Garson and Sheldon, who have devised an ingenious scheme to force Happy into serving their evil purposes.

#15 "The Man in the Radurium Glove" or "Race Against Radurium" April 7, 1951

Kessler, one of the most dangerous criminals in the United Planets, escapes from the

rehabilitation room of Medical Science Center after being rematerialized from suspended animation by Robbie and Tonga. He kidnaps Happy, who is a patient at the center. Happy is wearing a Radurium glove to treat a serious cosmic burn, but the treatment will be fatal if the glove is worn for too long. Buzz searches frantically for Happy and the vicious Kessler, knowing he must find them before the cadet's time runs out.
Kessler . . . . Crane Whitley

#16 "Under the Red Lake of Jupiter" or "Menace of the Red Lake" April 14, 1951

After blasting off from the Red Lake Winter Resort on Jupiter, Carol and Tonga suddenly develop rocket trouble, causing them to crash land at the bottom of the great Red Lake. Buzz, in space-o-phone contact with them at the time of the crash, rushes to their rescue along with Robbie and Happy. However, the lake has frozen over for the night and Carol and Tonga's oxygen is almost exhausted.
Regular cast members only.

#17 "The Counterfeit Commander" April 21, 1951

Dr. Smatka throws the Space Patrol into chaos when he creates a duplicate of Buzz by using plastic surgery on an interplanetary criminal. As a result of the pretender's orders, Robbie abandons his post on Saturn, allowing enemy ships to raid the city, and all Space Patrol ships leave Terra for a phony uprising on Pluto, leaving the capital unprotected.
Dr. Smatka. . . . . George Demetrios
Kayjan . . . . Ed Kemmer

#18 "Mysterious Mission to Canali" April 28, 1951

Buzz and Happy embark on a highly secret and mysterious mission to the City of Canali, capital of Mars. They are to pick up 100,000,000 credits worth of Tellurium and transport it to Terra. However, Alicia, the trusted and beautiful confidential secretary to the governor of Mars, and her accomplice, Ghent, execute a sinister plot to steal the Tellurium and destroy Buzz and Happy in the process.
Alicia . . . . Anne Diamond
Ghent . . . . James Clay

#19 "The Major's Dilemma" May 5, 1951

During a routine inspection of the Space Patrol maintenance shop, Robbie discovers a heavy purchase of surplus battlecruisers by the Pluto Transport Company. Suspicious, he tells the owner of the company that he can no longer buy these ships—and immediately "accidents" begin happening in the shop. When Buzz and Happy attempt to test-fly the secretary general's new ship, they nearly crash as a result of sabotage.
Mr. Brecker . . . . Jack Reitzen
Lt. Conway. . . . . Stephen Coit

#20 "Isolation in Space" May 12, 1951

When Buzz, Happy and Carol attempt to apprehend a pair of dangerous criminals smuggling valuable parasonic crystals from the Synthetic Crystal Company, they find themselves in a virtually isolated space relay station orbiting Terra with only 1½ hours of oxygen left. Their only hope is that an alert Space Patrol unit will spot them.

#21 "The Tourist Trap" May 19, 1951

A flashback episode showing Tonga's venture into crime before she was rehabilitated. Buzz and Happy are called to investigate robberies on a tourist sightseeing ship traveling to Earth's moon. Tonga, acting as tour guide, is in league with the ship's pilot, Captain Holt. First the pair blinds the passengers with a photon bomb; then they relieve them of their valuables. Buzz and Happy confront the evil duo and figure out how they're disposing of the loot.

#22 "The Defeat of Dr. Owen" or "Dangerous Intrigue" May 26, 1951

Major Robertson is on the planet Neptune. After memorizing and destroying the plans for a powerful new rocket engine, he is overpowered and rendered unconscious by his physician, Dr. Owen. The doctor takes Robbie to his private sanatorium, where he intends to force him to divulge the secret plans. When Buzz and Happy discover the treachery, the cadet embarks on a scheme to rescue the major, without the commander's knowledge. Unfortunately, this results in Buzz using a cosmic missile to blast a radio-controlled space car—unaware that Happy and Robbie are in it!

Dr. Owen . . . . Jerome Sheldon
Purves . . . . Bela Kovacs

#23 "The Secret Injection" June 2, 1951

Buzz and Happy apprehend two dangerous criminals—the renegade Dr. Phillips and his confederate, Dixon. While captive aboard the Space Patrol battlecruiser, the doctor slyly injects Happy with a solution from a concealed Narco injector, subjecting the cadet's will to the doctor's evil control. Answering a distress call in space with Buzz, Happy attempts to carry out Dr. Phillips' command to attack the Commander, while the doctor and his henchman threaten Carol aboard the ship.

#24 "The Treacherous Technicians" June 9, 1951

In the course of an experiment in the Terra Research Lab, Tonga orders two grams of precious Tritonium from the Space Patrol Research Laboratory on Earth. Buzz and Happy, on a training flight near Earth, agree to transport the 2,000,000 credits worth of Tritonium to Terra. However the lab technicians on Earth, Lisa and Chaney, plot to steal the Tritonium. They follow the commander's ship and blast it with a missile, knocking out its power. Then they threaten to fire another missile unless Buzz and Happy abandon the ship.

Lisa . . . . Lisa Howard
Chaney . . . . Pierce Lyden

#25 "The Disastrous Flight to Pluto" or "Beyond the Rim of Space" June 16, 1951

Buzz and the Space Patrol crew are on a pleasure trip to the planet Pluto aboard a luxury space yacht. A fault in the engine causes the ship to go off course, sending them into the uncharted Outer Galaxy. To make matters worse, radiation is spreading throughout the ship and all communications have been cut off due to engine failure. Buzz puts Carol and Tonga to work constructing an atomic device, while he, Robbie and Happy attempt to cut the ship in two. The plan is to blow up the dam-

aged half to attract attention—before they travel out of sight forever.

#26 "Perilous Chase Through Space" or "Race Against Death" June 23, 1951

During an official reception at the governor's mansion on the planet Mars, the governor's son pressures Tonga into taking a space ride with him, but she is unaware that he has stolen his father's space coupe. When Buzz and Happy set out in pursuit, all of them end up being buried alive in a crystallized cave with little hope for escape.

Governor's son . . . . David Bair

#27 "The Lost City of the Carnacans" June 30, 1951

The United Planets Communications Commission receives a message that the underground city of Temphi, capital of the lost civilization of the Carnacans, has been discovered in the Martian Desert. Buzz, always fascinated by Carnacan history, goes exploring with Happy and Carol to learn who or what is transmitting radio messages with a 1,000-year-old transmitter from the ancient city.

Terry . . . . Sue England
Paul . . . . Dabbs Greer

#28 "The Deadly Weapon" July 7, 1951

A 20th-century weapon is stolen from the United Planets Museum and turns up in the hands of a dangerous convict escaping from the Terra Honor Farm. Buzz and Happy lead an exciting chase on the speedways at daredevil velocities to recapture the fugitive and recover the antique weapon—but they face a treacherous surprise when their foe is finally cornered.

Wenzel . . . . Bela Kovacs
Thutmon . . . . John Mel

#29 "The Wild Man of the Ridge" or "The Legend of Wild Man's Ridge" July 14, 1951

Buzz, Happy and Tonga are forced to crash land in the barren Wastelands of Kralic on the planet Mars. They have to leave the spaceship and the precious Space-o-Phone — their only hope of rescue — due to lethal radiation spreading from the engine room. Soon lost in the wilderness, they are stalked by the Wild Man of the Ridge.

MacCarin . . Bela Kovacs   Sara . . Sara Berner

#30 *"The Magnetic Charm of Pluto"* or *"Way Station to the Stars"* *July 21, 1951*

Buzz, Happy, and Carol, accompanied by two engineers, are on their way to the outermost planet, Pluto, to plan the construction of a new Space Patrol way station. However, a mysterious magnetic force interferes with their landing, disrupting all power in their spaceship and leaving them stranded in a desolate area of the planet. The engineers make a discovery that puts their lives in jeopardy.

Frank Hanford. . . . . Henry Corden
Gerald Mazzman . . . . Wayne Winton

#31 *"The Hidden Reflector"* *July 28, 1951*

Baffled by the mysterious hijacking of the Procyne Transport Company's cargo-carrying spaceships, Buzz, Happy and Robbie must endure constant badgering by the disagreeable owner of the transport company as they investigate the latest occurrence. After narrowly escaping a collision with Jupiter's fourth moon, the Space Patrol trio faces an unexpected challenge aboard one of the pirated ships.

Fairhorn. . . . . Jack Wilson
Craig. . . . . William Schallert

#32 *"The Dangerous Discovery"* *August 4, 1951*

Buzz, Happy and Tonga are called upon to help Pop Hanson, a top archeologist on Higgins' Planetoid, who has been overpowered by his assistant after finding a weapon capable of destroying the entire solar system. The weapon was invented by the ancient Carnacans and is so dangerous that it caused them to leave this galaxy. The Space Patrollers face the threat of utter holocaust as the assistant threatens to push the button triggering the mutation bomb if Buzz and Happy attempt to recover it.

Pop Hanson. . . . . Fred Howard
Pete . . . . Emil Sitka

#33 *"The Mysterious Spaceship"* or *"Spaceship on the Edge of Forever"* *August 11, 1951*

Drs. Marston and Hillier, chief astronomers at the Morehouse Observatory, sight an unidentifiable object in the dim ranges of the universal perimeter. They call in Buzz, along with Happy and Carol, to investigate. The trio discovers that the object is a spaceship from a highly advanced civilization, which has been orbiting the solar system for hundreds of years. The robot operating the mysterious ship gives Buzz and his comrades the horrifying answer to what became of its crew.

#34 *"The Underwater Hideout"* *August 18, 1951*

What starts out as a routine flight to Earth for Buzz, Happy and Robbie turns into a terrifying adventure on the bottom of the Pacific Ocean, as the three Space Patrollers are trapped by two vicious accomplices of the captured payroll robber, Sobia. After nearly ramming the commander's ship in space, the two criminals lead Buzz and his comrades to their underwater hideout, where they attempt to force Buzz to order Sobia's release by brutally attacking Happy.

Farlon . . Ward Wood   Ben . . Jim Nusser

#35 *"A Big Wheel Named Ferris"* *August 25, 1951*

Happy is assigned to greet a future cadet in the Space Patrol, Ferris Macklin, son of the governor of Triton. Ferris, a spoiled smart aleck, shows his true self to Happy, but presents the façade of a serious, respectful young man to Buzz. Accompanied by Tonga and Jo Vance, a beautiful young cadet, the group blasts off for Saturn where Ferris pilots them into the middle of a ring of meteoric debris and then blames their predicament on Happy.

Ferris Macklin . . . . Alvy Moore
Jo Vance. . . . . Jane Davids

#36 *"The Vindictive Brother"* *September 1, 1951*

Buzz's old school pal, Fred Masterson of Masterson Aircar Company, is nearly killed in a bombing attempt on his office. Thinking it is the work of rival aircar manufacturers who resent his development of a new power plant which will lower the price of aircars, he retires to his lodge to complete work in secret. When Buzz, accompanied by Happy and Carol, pays a visit to Masterson, he meets Fred's younger brother, Sam, and learns — almost too late — that Sam has his reasons for wanting Fred out of the way.

Fred Masterson . . . . George Chandler
Sam Masterson . . . . Bill Baldwin

#37 "Photograph of a Traitor" September 8, 1951

Happy's hobby of photography plays an important part in the apprehension of two wily criminals committing space robberies of pay-roll ships. When Tonga and Hap are kidnapped, Buzz and Robbie find a photo clue left by the cadet that points to a Space Patrol officer involved in the crimes and enables them to rescue Tonga and Happy from the vicious pair in the nick of time.

Lt. Gethard . . . . Richard Bergren
Brewer . . . . Hans Schumm

#38 "The Courageous Coward" September 15, 1951

On their way from Terra to Earth to deliver 50,000 credits for the Terra Awards, Buzz, Happy and Carol are held up by an interplanetary gangster. The gangster has bullied an old friend — recently released from Terra Detention — into smuggling him on board the *Terra IV.* However the ex-con comes through and bravely prevents his pal from leaving the Space Patrollers on Earth's moon to die.

#39 "The Theft of the Scrambler" September 22, 1951

Carol and her laboratory assistant, Selma, complete their work on the "Scrambler," a transmitter-receiver designed to decode secret messages sent between Space Patrol ships and Headquarters. When Carol surprises Selma and her boyfriend stealing the decoder, the couple kidnaps her — but they get caught in a cloud of meteoric debris that cripples their ship, forcing them to signal the Space Patrol for help. Buzz, Robbie and Happy come to the rescue and transport them to the *Terra IV,* unaware that they have stolen the Scrambler

and abducted Carol. Buzz prepares to blast the damaged ship with a cosmic missile, never suspecting that Carol is still on board.

#40 "Prometheus Bound for Destruction" September 29, 1951

Buzz, Tonga and Happy blast off to explore an obsolete space station called Prometheus, which is orbiting Ganymede, Jupiter's fourth moon. Prometheus is scheduled for destruction by Space Safety. Boarding the station, the Space Patrollers are threatened by an old space criminal who has hidden there for forty years and resists their efforts to remove him. Preoccupied, they fail to hear the broadcast warning all ships in the vicinity that hydrogen torpedoes will destroy the station within minutes.

#41 "Blood Brother" or "Immediate Disaster" October 6, 1951

The *Terra Express* flagship with one thousand passengers on board, including Carol, is hit broadside by a derelict cosmic missile, but does not explode. Buzz and Happy risk their lives to save the passengers as they successfully disarm the warhead. But Happy is knocked unconscious and Buzz receives serious gamma radiation burns, requiring a blood transfusion to save his life.

#42 "Lunatics from the Future" October 13, 1951

Testing a new stardrive, Buzz and Happy travel faster than the speed of light and backwards in time to the 20th century and a New England farm in the year 1950. Unaware that they have been transported in time, a farmer and his wife hold the Space Patrollers at gunpoint, believing that Buzz and Happy have escaped from the local asylum.

#43 "The Space Patrol Code Belt" October 20, 1951

A trio of space criminals evade Buzz and his cadet and steal the payrolls from the Ursa Transport Company's ships. One is a company pilot, one works in the Space Patrol Code Room (giving the crooks the code of the day) and one is a beautiful but ruthless woman who foils both Happy and Buzz.

#44 "The Floating Image in Space" October 27, 1951

Buzz and Happy find strange reports of the image of a man floating in space difficult to believe — until they receive a firsthand report from the secretary general's daughter, Carol. She sees the image of a man in flowing robes, holding a torch, and is blinded by a brilliant flash of light that cuts off the power in her spaceship. An ominous voice proclaims the invasion of the United Planets by a superior intelligence.

#45 "The Laboratory Ship Sabotage" or "Secret Peril" November 3, 1951

While investigating the sabotage of a top-secret laboratory ship on the planet Venus, Buzz, Robbie, Happy and Carol unravel an unscrupulous scheme and find themselves seconds away from being at the center of an atomic explosion.

#46 "The Parasite Disc" November 10, 1951

Caught in a terrifying and sinister scheme, the Space Patrol crew find themselves fighting each other as both Carol and Tonga are taken over by a fiendish professor who turns them into zombies. Using an insidious device concealed beneath a surgical bandage taped to the backs of their necks, the professor has gained complete control over the will of the women. To make matters worse, removal of the tape would send an electronic shock through the brain, causing instant death. Thus armed, the treacherous professor aims to control all persons of authority in the United Planets.

#47 "The Secret of Terra" November 17, 1951

A power-mad renegade from the Space Patrol, Major Gruell, and his confederate, Lt. Barin, plot the destruction of the United Planets from a hidden fortress on the planet Mars. To accomplish their aim, they steal a locket worn by the secretary general which contains the "secret of Terra." After brutally carrying off the theft, the lieutenant escapes to Mars with Buzz and Happy in pursuit. (*This was the demo show, penned by Mike Moser, that convinced ABC to put* Space Patrol *in its network line-up. Norm Jolley later rewrote it, and it became Episode 47.* — JNB)

#48 "Captive in the Jungle" or "Jungle of No Return" November 24, 1951

On a routine inspection of his security posts on Venus, Robbie crash lands in the savage Mogi Jungle, from which no man has ever returned. While signaling for help, he is captured by the uncivilized, hostile natives. Buzz and Happy come to his aid but are also captured and taken to Pago, a brutal, half-mad scoundrel who believes the Space Patrollers are after the jewels he has stolen from the Mogi natives. Pago tells them they will not leave the jungle alive.

#49 "Prison of Deadly Gas" December 1, 1951

An Endurium mill located inside one of Jupiter's moons, which processes the metal from which the hulls of spaceships are fashioned, becomes a trouble spot when successive quakes endanger the atomic pile needed for its operation. Captain Doherty, who is in charge, calls the Space Patrol for help. While investigating the damage caused by the quakes, Buzz, Happy, Robbie and Tonga are overcome by Nagrom, a deadly gas.

#50 "The Sacrifice" December 8, 1951

Tonga and Carol are at the Morehouse Observatory on the planet Pluto when they receive word from Security Communications that a cloud of meteoric debris is rapidly approaching the solar system. They communicate the news to Buzz, on a training flight with Happy, who scatters the cloud with a cosmic missile. However, a meteoric particle hits their ship, cutting off the power and causing a dangerous loss of pressure. With great courage, Buzz knocks out Happy and ejects him into outer space, then blows up the ship, exposing himself to lethal radiation in the hope that the explosion will bring someone to rescue the cadet.

Capt. Hayward . . . . Maury Hill

#51 "Test Flight of the Galaxy" December 15, 1951

Carol has designed a magnetic ship shaped like a metal sphere and capable of traveling at the speed of light. While on a test flight with Buzz and Happy, she's overpowered by two workmen who force her to pilot the ship after ditching Buzz and Hap on one of Jupiter's moons. Carol craftily manages to alert Robbie, who comes to their rescue.

Pete Kovach . . . . Peter Mamakos
Pop Stanton. . . . . William E. Green

#52 "The Brothers Krone" or "Fair Exchange" December 22, 1951

A convicted criminal, Karl Krone, vows he will be freed by his brother, Vito, despite the fact that all his thoughts have been read by the Space Patrol's Brainograph. Sure enough, the wily Vito kidnaps Happy and offers the cadet's life for Karl's freedom. Buzz, powerless to rescue Hap without Vito's cooperation, is forced to agree to the illegal trade. He is promptly double-crossed by the brothers, who leave Happy stranded on a moon with a limited supply of oxygen.

Vito Krone . . . . Don Gordon
Karl Krone . . . . Dick Bartlett

#53 "The Counterfeiting Puzzle" December 29, 1951

Buzz and Happy blast off on a routine inspection flight to several planets, leaving Carol, Tonga and Robbie to apprehend a counterfeiting ring operating on Terra. As Tonga reports that despite strict security precautions, the counterfeit money is appearing on one planet after another, Buzz and Happy never suspect that they are carrying the bogus money aboard the *Terra IV*. When Carol is reported missing, Buzz begins to put two and two together.

Eric Werner. . . . . Sam Edwards
Adolph Werner . . . . Bela Kovacs

1952

#54 "The Flowers with the Fatal Fragrance" or "Flowers of Death" January 5, 1952

A prisoner scheduled to be dematerialized into suspended animation issues a threat against the lives of Buzz, Happy, Robbie and a Space Patrol lieutenant. Soon a bouquet of deadly Narcola flowers is delivered to each of the four intended victims. The illegal, innocent-appearing flowers give off a fatal fragrance and Buzz and Happy are caught in a room full of the deadly blooms.

#55 "Cosmic Smoke Guns" January 12, 1952

A shipment of eight crates of a brand new weapon, a cosmic smoke gun which puts its victims to sleep instantly, arrives at Space Patrol Headquarters—minus the guns! As he discovers the theft, Robbie is shot by the deliveryman, who escapes with the guns and returns to his employer on Venus. When Robbie and Tonga attempt to arrest the two culprits, they are shot and placed, unconscious, aboard their ship. The ship is on a collision course with the moon Deimos, and Buzz has only a few minutes to board it in flight and change its course.

Brooks . . . . Henry Cordon
Stanton . . . . Thomas Brown Henry

#56 "Lost in the Snow-Cap Region of Mars" January 19, 1952

Carol follows a wanted criminal from the Mercury Spaceport to Mars, where he and his accomplice have a cave hideout in the snowcap region. Having ignored Buzz's warning not to land, Carol is taken hostage by the two criminals, who then booby-trap her ship so that if the hatch is lifted, the ship will explode. Buzz and Happy are captured when they arrive to rescue her. Meanwhile, Carol, under the effects of the cosmic smoke gun, wanders out of the cave and gets lost in the snow-covered terrain. Buzz and Happy must escape being thrown into an active volcano in the cave and find Carol before she either freezes or tries to open the rigged hatch.

Phelps . . . . Ward Wood
Stuart . . . . William Schallert

#57 "Explosion on Morehouse Five" January 26, 1952

An explosion occurs on a newly colonized planetoid, Morehouse Five, causing it to move into a new orbit that will pass so close to the sun that no one on the planetoid will survive.

Buzz and Happy face great peril in their attempt to rescue a space prospector and his granddaughter on the threatened planetoid.
Andrews. . . . . Fred Howard
Teddy. . . . . Claudia Barrett

#58 "The Evil Guardian of Harpola" February 2, 1952

While Tonga is working in a Security Department ordnance lab located on a tiny asteroid in space, she accidentally uncovers a hidden passageway to an underground city of the lost civilization of the Carnacans. Buzz, puzzled by the recent appearance of an ancient Carnacan deadly weapon, goes to the asteroid with Happy to investigate Tonga's discovery. All three fall victim to a robot brandishing a paralyzing whip antenna. The robot is controlled by a nefarious character who says he is a member of the lost race of Carnacans that disappeared a thousand years ago.

#59 "Hit by a Meteorite" February 9, 1952

While on a pleasure trip from Terra to Earth, Buzz and the Space Patrol crew are caught in a storm of meteorites brought about by the appearance of Trachinger's comet.[4] Disabled by a meteorite lodged in the hull of their ship, they have no power to alert Space Control on Earth to their condition. Unless the meteorite can be dislodged it will burst into flame and set the *Terra IV* on fire when it enters Earth's atmosphere. Even if the Space Patrollers are able to avoid that danger, they will still crash into Earth unless Space Control headquarters is sharp enough to note their speed and use Magnetic Force Control to land their crippled ship.
Cam . . . . Joel Marston

#60 "Flying Blind" or "Planetoid Plot" February 16, 1952

In a fiendish plot to rob payroll ships flying within range of their planetoid, two interplanetary thieves blind Buzz and Happy with a hidden photon bomb as they travel from Terra to Jupiter carrying a 75,000-credit payroll. Their battlecruiser is then hit with a mag-

netic disrupter, which cuts all power, including communications with Robbie, and the ship is landed with Magnetic Force Control at the villains' hideout. Buzz and Happy are imprisoned and, still blind, directed to walk forward—into a deep chasm!
Layman . . . . Jeff Donovan
Harpell . . . . Leo V. Matranga

#61 "Victim of Amnesia" February 23, 1952

Preparing to blast off on a routine mission to Venus, Tonga suffers a life-threatening radiation burn that must be treated promptly. However, she trips while disembarking from the space car, hits her head and becomes a victim of amnesia. Meanwhile, two prisoners have escaped from detention quarters and choose Tonga's space car as their getaway vehicle, taking the bewildered Tonga along with them. Discovering Tonga's absence, Robbie, Buzz and Happy follow her trail to Mars. The thugs have abandoned her on one of the moons and the Space Patrollers must find her.
Bradford . . . . Keith Larsen
Franklin . . . . Bela Kovacs

#62 "The Lieutenant's Revenge" March 1, 1952

Seeking revenge against the Space Patrol and Buzz for dismissing him from its ranks, ex-lieutenant Graham manages to get hired as a mechanic in the Space Patrol maintenance shop. Thus employed, he sabotages spaceships, causing three to crash—including the *Terra IV* with Buzz aboard. Buzz and Happy track down the disgruntled ex-officer, but not before he arranges for Carol to have an "accident."
Graham. . . . . Howard Price
Forman . . . . Phil Chambers

#63 "The Mind Readers" March 8, 1952

Surveying a runaway planet passing through the solar system, Buzz, Happy, Robbie and Carol land on it to investigate a light coming from the dark side of the strange orb. There they discover two weird outcasts from an alien star system who communicate solely by mental

[4]Writer Norm Jolley named the comet after ABC technical director Bob Trachinger.—JNB

telepathy. Possessing the ability to read the minds of the Space Patrollers, the menacing aliens prevent any successful resistance. They threaten Carol and force Buzz to blast off, leaving Happy and Robbie on the doomed planet.

Roc . . Bela Kovacs   Gar . .Walter Beecher

#64 "Slaves of the Exonium Mine" March 15, 1952

Three citizens disappear after leaving Terra for Earth in their spaceship. Buzz, Tonga and Happy receive an anonymous call directing them to fly over the Dust Bowl of Venus if they wish to learn the fate of the missing men. However, they are taken prisoner by the ruthless Brunner, who has stowed away on their ship and forces them to work as slave laborers in the Exonium mine on Venus.

Brunner . . . . Paul Guilfoyle

#65 "Abandoned in Outer Space" March 22, 1952

In a research laboratory on the planet Mars, Carol and Tonga create a synthetic form of Radurium, an invaluable and rare drug used in the treatment of cosmic and radiation burns. But before they can deliver the formula to Terra, they are kidnapped by two desperate killers who steal it and abandon the women in space. Buzz and Happy capture the villains, who lead them to where they deserted the women, only to find no trace of Carol or Tonga an hour after their oxygen supply would have run out.

Bender . . . . Fred Berest
Willie. . . . . Jerry O'Sullivan

#66 "The Great Bank Robbery" March 29, 1952

After personally installing an alarm system in the Terra Interplanetary Reserve Bank, Major Robertson is forced to assist in a robbery of two million credits. Buzz and Happy investigate and track Robbie and his captor to Asteroid 41. They find the grim remains of their space car, which appears to have fatally crashed. Trying to clear the major of the robbery, Buzz and Happy learn that McNeill, the president of the bank, plotted the crime — and now plans to drop them 20 floors down an elevator shaft.

McNeill . . . . Jack Reitzen
Moss . . . . Bela Kovacs

#67 "The Mysterious Moonquakes" April 5, 1952

While surveying the site of a new Lunar Fleet Base on the Earth's moon, the chief engineer, Lt. Bruce, discovers a rich surface deposit of rare Exonium. Keeping the discovery secret, he recommends that the base be constructed elsewhere due to tremors that he reports having felt. Buzz rejects his recommendation and the base is constructed. Robbie and Tonga are in charge of selecting personnel and opening operations. Securing the position of maintenance engineer, Lt. Bruce then creates his own, contrived moonquakes, damaging several buildings and endangering the lives of the Space Patrollers until Buzz uncovers the officer's greedy scheme.

Lt. Bruce. . . . . Robert Knapp

#68 "The Phantom Fleet" April 12, 1952

Buzz, Happy and Carol receive an emergency report from Professor Bradshaw aboard a laboratory ship orbiting Pluto: Unknown objects are rapidly approaching the solar system from the Outer Galaxy. The ship's radarscope shows what they assume to be a fleet of ships invading the United Planets. A voice broadcasts a warning about a hostile, phantom fleet from the planet Maxim and indicates that resistance is futile. When met by the Space Patrol, the enemy ships seem to disappear, yet succeed in carrying out their threat to attack Earth. Then the voice announces that Terra is their next target.

Prof. Bradshaw. . . . . Ludwig Donath
Prof. Henry. . . . . Jan Arvan

#69 "Crisis on Titan" or "Trouble on Titan" April 19, 1952

While accompanying Robbie in his inspection of the Security Detention Colony on Titan, Carol is taken hostage by an escaping criminal brandishing a hand-fashioned weapon similar to a heat ray. Retreating into the rocks and threatening to kill Carol if anyone approaches, he seriously wounds Robbie. Buzz and Happy are summoned to aid in Carol's rescue. They relieve Robbie and his guards and go after the desperate killer alone.

Wessler. . . . . Bela Kovacs

#70 "Sacrifice to the Moon God" *April 26, 1952*

Buzz, Happy, Carol and Tonga are again experimenting with the new faster-than-light stardrive when the relays freeze and send them rocketing into the past to the era of the Aztecs on the planet Earth. Exploring alone, Carol is taken captive and prepared for sacrifice to the Moon God. Buzz and Happy, disguised as Aztec priests, must prevent her death in the presence of hundreds of Indians, as the high priest ceremoniously raises the sacrificial knife over the helpless Carol.

Regular cast members only.

#71 "Flight of Doom" or "Uncertain Death" *May 3, 1952*

Happy takes a novice cadet on his first space flight but neglects to make a mandatory equipment check to ensure that spacesuits are aboard. A leak develops and the ship loses air pressure, forcing the cadets into the airlock with a limited supply of air that is fast running out. When Happy fails to respond to a routine call, Buzz and Tonga rush to the rescue — but opening the hatch to save the cadets might cause a sudden loss of pressure that spells certain death.

Cadet Cramer. . . . . James Dobson
Mechanic. . . . . Tony Michaels

#72 "The Alien Invasion" or "Invasion" *May 10, 1952*

Tracking a "meteor" from the Outer Galaxy that has suddenly broken from its orbit just outside the solar system and crashed into one of Saturn's moons, Buzz confirms his suspicion that it's an alien spaceship in disguise. He and Hap set out to investigate, but to ensure the safety of the United Planets, he orders Robbie to destroy the moon with a cosmic missile if he doesn't contact him within an hour. Inside the meteor, Buzz and Hap find a teleportation receiving station for aliens planning to infiltrate and colonize the United Planets. Two aliens materialize and try to transport them to their overcrowded planet. Buzz and Hap overpower them, but time is running out. Robbie is set to blow up the meteor in seconds and there's no time to escape!

Tharl. . . . . Will White

#73 "The Cunning Captain Quick" or "A Threat to the United Planets" *May 17, 1952*

Facing an invasion of the United Planets by the Thormans (an alien race), Buzz, Happy and Tonga are en route to Terra when they rescue Captain Quick, who claims he was left floating in space, abandoned by his first mate. Tracking down his ship, an ore carrier, the *Terra IV* is swallowed up by it and the three friends are taken prisoner by Therma, a Thorman, who's Captain Quick's evil accomplice. The two criminals demand a ransom of 50,000 credits for the release of the Space Patrollers. Repeatedly foiled by Captain Quick's knowledge of human nature, Buzz turns the tables by using it to his advantage when he instructs Robbie to deliver the "ransom."

Captain Quick . . . . Marvin Miller
Therma . . . . Tracey Roberts

#74 "The Threat of the Thormanoids" *May 24, 1952*

The Space Patrol is alerted to the sinister fact that aliens from the deep Outer Galaxy are penetrating the United Planets. The Thormanoids (called Thormans in the previous episode) may have already infiltrated important posts in the United Planets because they look exactly like humans. However, Thormanoids are able to walk through walls and because of their low body temperature must wear insulators to live in a human climate. These telltale signs help Buzz and Happy track them down — but they nearly meet their end beneath the Terra Express when they attempt to capture two of the aliens masquerading as Space Patrol officers.

Capt. Sackett . . . . Keith Larsen
Loren . . . . Lee Van Cleef

#75 "Jungle Jeopardy" *May 31, 1952*

Robbie and Carol follow two of the Thormanoids to the Venusian jungle. When Robbie is knocked unconscious and Carol taken captive by hostile natives, Buzz is alerted by space-o-phone and comes to the rescue with Happy. They uncover one of the secret teleportation stations of the Thormanoids hidden in the jungle.

Regular cast members only.

#76 "The Scheming Sibling" June 7, 1952

Buzz's young secretary, Lois, is held hostage along with Happy by her vicious brother, who is being sought for the theft of secret documents. Trapped into promising to turn himself in, the brother almost succeeds in ambushing Buzz.
Lois . . . . Gloria Saunders
George . . . . Bela Kovacs
Other cast: Byron Foulger, Stephen Chase

#77 "Danger on Mars" or "Treachery Under the Kralic Mountains" June 14, 1952

Two old prospectors stumble over an opening in the foothills of the Kralic mountains and discover evidence that it once served as a shelter for Earth's first settlers on Mars. Buzz joins the men at the scene, which becomes cloaked in mystery and danger when they find themselves pinned down by a hidden barrage of gunfire.

#78 "Mission to Mercury" June 21, 1952

Happy is sent on an important mission to Mercury with a briefcase full of papers which puts the finger on an interplanetary official involved in a bribery scandal. But when the cadet is off-guard, the suspect replaces the contents of the case with a time bomb!
Lennan . . . . Stanley Farrar
Barrow . . . . Stanley Andrews

#79 "The Deadly Ray Gun" or "Interplanetary Smugglers" June 28, 1952

Buzz investigates a report that ray guns have been adapted to fire deadly missiles and are being smuggled onto the man-made planet Terra in large numbers. A series of attempts made on his life in the course of the investigation points up the danger of his mission and also convinces Buzz that he is on the right track.
Max . . . . Henry Rowland

#80 "The Force Barrier" or "Stolen Barrier" July 5, 1952

A scientist who has developed a force field barrier in a Space Patrol research laboratory on Earth suddenly decides to make off with the powerful invention and use it to suit his own purposes. Employing the barrier as a shield to protect himself, he makes his getaway with Buzz in hot pursuit.
Squeaky . . . . Leo V. Matranga
Moore . . . . Bela Kovacs

#81 "The Black Gauntlet" or "The Iron Fist" July 12, 1952

A 20th-century Earth "protection" shakedown racket becomes a 30th-century problem for Buzz. An organization known as the Black Gauntlet terrorizes and blackmails its victims by leaving a calling card—a "black gauntlet"—followed by a beating, and then a shakedown to prevent further beatings. Buzz falls victim when he is badly beaten and then guaranteed that it will not happen again if he pays for "protection." Little does he know that the Black Gauntlet is a woman—and also the head of the Women's League for the Prevention of Crime!
Erika . . . . Inga Borg
Igor . . . . Lou Nova

#82 "The Derelict Space Station" July 19, 1952

Buzz, Happy and Tonga become involved in a harrowing adventure when two dangerous criminals overcome the trio in a spaceship which goes out of control and hurtles toward the planet Earth.
Herrick. . . . . Peter Mamakos
Klinger . . . . Tom Daly

#83 "The Mystery of Ancient Egypt" July 26, 1952

Buzz, Happy, Carol and Tonga are aboard the commander's ship, the *Terra V*, testing its powerful stardrive. The new ship accelerates them beyond the speed of light—6,000 years into the past to ancient Egypt in the year 2700 BC. Their mission: to discover how a piece of 30th-century metal could have gotten into the ruins of ancient Egypt.
Regular cast members plus four extras

#84 "Mystery of the Flying Pirate Ship" August 2, 1952

Robbie and Happy are on a routine space flight when they sight a square-rigged sailing vessel flying the Jolly Roger floating in space. Walking the deck are two men — without spacesuits!

Capt. Jonas. . . . . Glenn Strange
Davy . . . . Bela Kovacs

#85 *"Emergency Flight to Mercury"* *August 9, 1952*

Happy is scheduled to join Buzz on an emergency flight to carry Radurium to epidemic-stricken Mercury. But the cadet is kidnapped by two adventurers who plan to steal the valuable serum. Only Buzz's skill and daring outwit the criminals and save the precious substance.

Harris . . . . Ward Wood
Manson . . . . Clark Howat

#86 *"Blackmail at Lake Azure"* *August 16, 1952*

A pair of villainous characters living at Lake Azure, a 30th-century resort, frame a gullible Happy in a blackmail plot to spring a criminal out of suspended animation.

Hislop . . . . Ben Welden
Benson. . . . . Douglas Grange

#87 *"The Hidden Map"* *August 23, 1952*

The 12-year-old son of a space prospector is led to believe by his self-styled guardian that his father has perished in his quest for a precious metal. The boy's "guardian" then seizes possession of a map the prospector has left his son. The map reveals the location of a valuable mine.

Jimmy. . . . . Jimmy Boyd
Wells . . . . Stephen Chase

#88 *"The Green Mold of Mars"* *August 30, 1952*

Thorgan, an enemy of Terra, seizes Tonga and takes her to Mars, where he brainwashes her, then uses her as an agent in a treacherous scheme against the United Planets in revenge for being expelled from the United Planets Scientific League.

Thorgan. . . . . Marvin Miller
Harris . . . . Richard Bartlett

#89 *"The Galactic War"* *September 9, 1952*

A patrol flight into the Outer Galaxy almost ends in disaster when Buzz and his crew encounter a huge radioactive cloud that overloads the circuits and burns out the wiring of their ship, forcing Buzz to crash land. Meanwhile, the deadly haze heads for the United Planets, leaving destruction in its wake.

Jana. . . . . Liba Petrova
Graff. . . . . Bela Kovacs

#90 *"The Energy Thief"* *September 13, 1952*

Tonga is sent to investigate an enigmatic force operating in the twilight belt of the planet Mercury. After discovering the force, which is greater than atomic power and robs human beings of their energy, she mysteriously disappears. Meanwhile, en route to the danger zone, Buzz, Happy and Robbie find their spaceship disabled by an inexplicable magnetic disruption.

Hefler . . . . Jerry O'Sullivan

#91 *"Sabotage of the Jupiter Run"* *September 20, 1952*

A traveler found floating in space between Venus and Mars provides a clue to saboteurs seeking to wreck the famous "Jupiter Run." Buzz impersonates the traveler and continues on to Mars. He is soon involved in a series of incidents that place him in the midst of a conspiracy — and in mortal danger.

Lola. . . . . Joyce Craig
Malcolm . . . . James Bronte

#92 *"The Star Raiders"* *September 27, 1952*

Buzz, in his search for the Star Raiders deep in galactic space, encounters this little-known race of primitive people. He soon learns that, though backwards in many respects, they live in a civilization far in advance of any in recorded history. Moreover, the Raiders, gifted with a tremendous power of destruction, have decided to invade the solar system. Buzz fights a sword duel with their leader, Kavel, to determine the fate of the United Planets. (*This episode was directed by Larry Robertson.*)

Maleeva. . . . . Elaine Williams
Kavel . . . . Joel Smith

#93 "The Code Breakers"
October 4, 1952

Buzz and his crew face the loss of the powerful and top secret Proton Gun when plotters against universal peace crack the code describing the secret elements of the weapon. *(Ken Mayer stars in this episode — the only network show in which Ed Kemmer did not appear, due to the death of his father.)*

Cadwalader. . . . . Lyle Talbot
Capt. Hayward . . . . Maury Hill
Hoag. Robert Dane

#94 "Errand of Mercy"
October 11, 1952

Buzz, Hap and Tonga journey a thousand years into the past to launch a Blood Boosters Campaign on present-day Earth to replenish Red Cross blood banks depleted by the Korean conflict. But their time-drive malfunctions and instead of hitting their mark in 1952, they land in the 1940s— right in the middle of World War II. A vicious Nazi officer captures the crew and, convinced they're spies, tries to force Buzz to reveal their "real" mission.

Nazi Major. . . . . Bela Kovacs
Nazi Lt.. . . . . Albert Taylor

#95 "Underwater Treachery"
October 18, 1952

The strange elliptical orbit of Planetoid 91 on the fringes of the solar system engages the attention of Buzz. Stranger yet is the fact that the planetoid has industrial complexes that are operated entirely underwater.

Kemper . . . . Peter Mamakos
Todd. . . . . James Logan

#96 "The Electronic Man"
October 25, 1952

Buzz finds an electronic transmitter planted on Terra by an alien race and set to automatically transmit information about the United Planets back to their planet. He and Happy follow the directional beam of the transmitter to the home planet of the aliens in the Outer Galaxy.

Mr. Smith. . . . . Joel Smith
Yasma . . . . Dan Seymour

#97 "Treachery on Terra Five"
November 11, 1952

Buzz, Hap and Tonga corner two dangerous criminals, Lantz and Freddie, who are on their way to rendezvous with their accomplice, Wallace, for their share of stolen loot. But once aboard the *Terra V*, the thugs overpower the Space Patrollers. Freddie beats up Hap, who does not revive, and Lantz roughs up Buzz when he battles for control of the ship so he can save Hap's life. Lantz steers the ship into the asteroid belt where it's hit by debris that damages the air purifier. Buzz passes out from lack of oxygen before he can complete a space-o-phone call for help.

Lantz . . . . Charles Horvath
Freddie . . . . Leo V. Matranga

#98 "Frontier Epidemic"
November 8, 1952

Buzz, Happy and members of their crew are exposed to a lethal virus on a strange, unknown planet. In order to prevent the virus from spreading throughout the United Planets they are forced to remain on the planet until they overcome it.

Doc. . . . . Roland Varno
Butler . . . . John Anderson
Andy . . . . Gordon Grange

#99 "Powerdive" November 15, 1952

Colonization has begun on the most remote outpost of the United Planets, a strange uninhabited planet in the solar system of the great double star Sirius. When the Space Patrol learns that cargo ships are being sabotaged, they investigate — but their ship is rigged to crash so that an unscrupulous firm can collect insurance.

Harvey. . . . . Ben Welden
Ward. . . . . Lee Van Cleef

#100 "Three Exiles"
November 22, 1952

Buzz and members of the Space Patrol land on the planet Sirius Four, the first outpost of the United Planets, where they are confronted with the gigantic task of preparing the planet for colonists. Their work is interrupted, however, by an amazing encounter: The scientist who discovered atomic power is living there in primitive surroundings, determined to shelter his awesome secret from the world so that it can never use his invention for self-destruction.

Lanya . . . . Mona Knox
Bruta . . . . John Roth
Abra . . . . Bela Kovacs

#101 "The Shakedown"
November 29, 1952

Buzz uncovers a gigantic blackmail racket that seriously hampers work on the planet Sirius Four. The racket immobilizes thousands of laborers imported to the planet by the Space Patrol, who refuse to carry out the vast construction program. It's soon discovered that important electronic devices and formulas are being stolen from Terra, endangering the lives of the colonists on Sirius Four.

Parvell . . . . Marvin Miller
Miss Wagner . . . . Evelyn Eaton

#102 "The Human Trap"
December 6, 1952

A mysterious guided missile breaks through the radar system without alerting Earth Space Control in time for the Space Patrol defense system to stop it. Buzz and Happy, cruising in the same space sector, are sent to intercept the missile and thus prevent widespread destruction on planet Earth.

Sandor . . . . Harold Dyrenforth
2 extras

#103 "The Chase in Time"
December 13, 1952

An old prospector accidentally finds a rich vein of Exonium and his dying wish is to give the precious compound to the United Planets. A mysterious gang of thieves thwarts the old man's plans— and the map leading to the rich discovery suddenly disappears.

Henry . . . . Fred Howard
Fred . . . . George Pembroke
Kirk . . . . Alvy Moore

#104 "The Deadly Sunbeam"
December 20, 1952

A scientist accidentally discovers the deadly Iota Ray. High-handed mobsters from the planet Mars, capitalizing on the new discovery, take control of the United Planet's Security Council. But the mobsters' plans fail to take into account the efficiency and loyalty of Buzz Corry and the Space Patrol.

Marshall Krone . . . . Robert Carson
Rita Kova . . . . Jean Howell
Prof. Kress . . . . Bruce Payne

#105 "The Conspiracy"
December 27, 1952

A top-level scientist, working at the Terra Experimental Laboratories, disappears in a stolen spaceship. Buzz, Happy and the members of the Space Patrol launch a search for the missing scientist. Gone with the scientist and the ship is a briefcase full of top-secret documents. Buzz considers the possibility that the scientist may have been spirited away, and that others— not the scientist — may have stolen the spaceship.

Wehrmut . . . . Tom Daly
Hatcher . . . . Bela Kovacs

1953

#106 "The Human Targets"
January 3, 1953

Buzz, Robbie and Happy complete a mission and turn their prisoners over to the guards. However, before the guards can deliver them to the prison, they escape and plan to take revenge on the Space Patrol trio. Derelict ships are being used as target practice and Hap goes out to blast the ships, unaware that Buzz and Robbie have been captured and put aboard one of them.

Danton . . . . John Alderson
Kazer . . . . Lee Morgan

#107 "The Rifled Arsenal"
January 10, 1953

A group of conspirators have stolen 3,000 paralyzer ray guns and set themselves up in the Space Patrol arsenal. At zero hour, they plan to take Terra by force and assume command of the capital city, but Buzz, Happy and Carol spoil the plans of the power-hungry adventurers to control the United Planets.

Brenner . . . . Hal Gerard
Galen . . . . Michael Colgan

#108 "The Stolen Prisoner"
January 17, 1953

Buzz and Happy, cross-examining Shrager — a stubborn and silent witness — with the use of the Brainograph, learn of a secret plot that menaces the peace and security of the United Planets. But before Buzz can set up proper safeguards, Shrager is handed over to the plotters operating out of Cole's Sanitarium. Buzz gets himself committed to the sanitarium so he can gather inside information, but the situation becomes dangerous when his identity is discovered.

Cole . . . . Gene Roth
Shrager . . . . William Justine

#109 "The Deadly Flower"
January 24, 1953

The mass exodus by thousands of citizens from the planet Neptune, without any logical explanation, poses a security problem of the first magnitude for the Space Patrol. More and more people join the ranks of those deserting the planet — with no apparent clue to the mass hysteria. Meanwhile, it comes to the attention of the Space Patrol that two nefarious characters in a jungle on Venus are cultivating a field of the plant that yields the deadly drug Narcol. Buzz and Hap, followed by Carol and Tonga, set off to investigate the situation.

Keller. . . . . Jack Reitzen
Hargis. . . . . Charles Horvath

#110 "Runaway Planetoid"
January 31, 1953

While on a routine flight, Carol is forced to make an emergency landing on a small planetoid, where she contacts Buzz and Hap on Terra for assistance. What she doesn't know is that the planetoid is occupied by a man wanted by the Space Patrol. When the fugitive learns that Carol has given out her position in space, he blows up her ship to prevent Buzz and Hap from identifying the planetoid, hoping to keep his hiding place a secret. However, the explosion jars the little planetoid, throwing it off its normal orbit into a collision course with Terra, and Buzz and Hap are thrown into a harrowing encounter with the runaway planetoid.

Stander. . . . . Bela Kovacs
Ronald. . . . . Eddie Ryder
Pilot . . . . William Boyett

#111 "Radioactive Cave"
February 7, 1953

The initial inspection of a proposed site for the new Space Patrol way station in Mercury's Twilight Belt sends Buzz, Happy and Robbie on a strange adventure. Robbie is overcome by radiation from an unknown rock formation, and the engineer and his assistant at the site, realizing it might contain valuable ore, quickly decide to let Buzz and Hap also expose themselves to the radiation. They figure that by eliminating all three men, they can keep the cave's value a secret and sell it later for a huge profit.

Korwin . . . . John Larch
Irene . . . . Jean Howard
Todd . . . . William Green

#112 "Trip to Deimos"
February 14, 1953

A pilot en route to the moon Deimos, carrying a payroll of 30,000 credits aboard his spaceship, is knocked out by a paralyzer ray device planted in his space-o-phone, robbed of his payroll, and left with an unbelievable story to report to the Space Patrol. Happy poses as a payroll pilot traveling the same route in an attempt to find out if the robberies are really taking place. He gets "special treatment" when the villains discover he belongs to the Space Patrol: They leave him on one of Pluto's moons with a limited air supply.

Miller. . . . . Charles Victor
Craig. . . . . Gil Warren
Harkins. . . . . Edward Clark

#113 "Operation Rescue"
February 21, 1953

A businessman, Henderson, pays a pilot to fly him and his secretary to Jupiter via a forbidden shortcut — through the Asteroid Belt, which lies between the planets Mars and Jupiter. Their ship is hit and damaged by an irregularly shaped object in the belt. Buzz and Happy answer their emergency call and fly into danger to rescue the errant ship.

Malin . . . . Art Marshall
Henderson . . . . Richard Karlan
Lowell . . . . Earl Lee

#114 "Survival in the Ice Desert" February 28, 1953

While on a routine inspection of Space Patrol security posts, Robbie spots a stolen spacecraft on Mars, but is soon kidnapped by two criminals — the Redrow brothers. Buzz and Happy fly to Mars to initiate a search for the major, but when they leave their own ship, the brothers steal it and hide it in an ice crevice, leaving Buzz and Happy stranded miles from civilization in the dreaded Ice Desert of Mars. They investigate the charred wreckage of Robbie's ship in an attempt to find a means of escape. Fighting the bitter cold, Buzz and Happy realize that they must take immediate action before this region of ice becomes their tomb.

Bill Redrow . . . . Joel Marston
Ed Redrow . . . . Paul Guilfoyle

#115 "Space Fatigue" March 7, 1953

A vicious conspiracy to remove Buzz from his office as commander-in-chief of the Space Patrol has been carefully devised. Buzz is baffled by his inability to perform routine tests and doctors at Medical Science Center inform him that he must be grounded. Realizing the seriousness of his situation, Buzz signs papers that relieve him of his post due to his "illness." The real cause of his problems is that he's being slowly poisoned during his hospital stay by a nurse — the evil twin sister of the real nurse on duty. Meanwhile, Robbie and Happy, suspicious of Buzz's symptoms, conduct an investigation of their own — at the risk of their lives.

Dr. S. Buehl . . . . Roland Vargo
Miss Gordon . . . . Dran Seitz
Sara . . . . Toni Seitz

#116 "The Magic Space Pictures" or "Threat to Terra" March 14, 1953

Somewhere in the City of Terra, a raving maniac has planted a bomb and is threatening to blow the Space Patrol out of existence. Tracking the madman with the help of the Brainograph and Magic Space Picture technology, Buzz, Happy, and Robbie find themselves in a race against time as they attempt to apprehend the criminal before he sets off the bomb and destroys the man-made planet.

Stone . . . . Lennie Bremen
Bolen . . . . Bela Kovacs

#117 "Jail Break" March 21, 1953

Happy is planted as a prisoner in the new "escape-proof" detention quarters to learn how some prisoners are managing to break out. The cadet is included in plans for the next "break," but his identity is discovered by another prisoner while he is trying to get word of the plot to Buzz. Happy is taken by gunpoint to the uninhabitable satellite, Titan, where he must use his wits to stay alive long enough to be rescued by the commander.

Murdok . . . . Bela Kovacs
Fredericks . . . . Michael Colgan
Guard . . . . Edward Taylor

#118 "The Laughing Alien" March 28, 1953

An alien arrives on Terra, judges its inhabitants an inferior race, and resolves to take a few specimens back to his star system for experimentation. He uses mental telepathy to project continuous images to Buzz of Happy in danger. Buzz issues a bulletin to all members of the United Planets to be on the lookout for the alien intruder. His fears for Hap's safety are confirmed when the cadet disappears and Robbie sends an alert that Space Patrol Headquarters is on fire.

Muzak . . . . Norbert Schiller

#119 "The Space Doctor" or "The Vital Factor" April 4, 1953

While on a routine flight with Buzz and Happy, Carol spills a deadly poison on her hand. Since they are too far from Medical Science Center to reach it in time to save her, Buzz contacts a nearby dispensary ship requesting the Space Patrol doctor on board to expedite prompt treatment. But when Buzz reaches the ship he learns that a dangerous criminal has kidnapped the doctor. Time is of the essence, and Buzz must apprehend the villain and find the doctor who can save Carol's life.

Dr. Jerry Taylor . . . . Charles Victor
Benjamin . . . . William Justine
Durk . . . . Karl Davis

#120 "Space Mail Robbery" April 11, 1953

An unprincipled criminal tricks his young nephew into helping him commit a robbery, thinking that once implicated, the boy will be useful as a decoy in future jobs. The boy tries to turn his uncle in, but is caught in the act — and now his uncle sets out to do away with him. Buzz is incensed by the idea of a man leading a 16-year-old into a life of crime and personally determines to hunt the man down.

Carl Marsden . . . . George Pembroke
Rudy. . . . . Jeff Silvers
Reynolds . . . . Marshall Bradford

#121 "The Space Wanderer" April 18, 1953

A strange new planet, known as a space wanderer, is attracted to the solar system. Fearing that the visiting body may disappear as quickly as it appeared, an Earth scientist and his daughter set out to investigate. What they do not know is that the alien planet has an atmosphere that decomposes metal in a matter of minutes— including spaceships. Buzz, having failed in his attempt to thwart their mission, flies to their aid. But it isn't long before the *Terra V* begins to weaken and decompose, putting him, Hap and Tonga in danger of being stranded forever on the wandering planet.

Dr. Beck. . . . . Fred Howard
Judy . . . . Jeanne Gail

#122 "The Big Impersonation" April 25, 1953

There appears to be conclusive evidence that Buzz is secretly involved in a plot to undermine the activities of the Security Council. Infuriated by the accusation, Buzz breaks free from the guards who are escorting him to detention quarters. Much to their consternation, Happy and Robbie are assigned the duty of capturing Buzz and returning him to prison.

Gov. Willis. . . . . Robert S. Carson
Dr. Brockway. . . . . Michael Hale
Croner . . . . Bela Kovacs
2 Guards. . . . . Paul Richards, Lee Millar

#123 "The Electronic Space Storm" May 2, 1953

A space storm of contraterrene, a complex composite of inside-out matter, is headed for the solar system. Due to its makeup, the storm is capable of reducing everything in the United Planets system to cinders. In an attempt to divert the course of the storm, Buzz and Happy undertake the dangerous assignment of plotting the progress of the storm and analyzing its characteristics— at close range.

#124 "The Mutation Bomb" May 16, 1953

While studying a new translation of a Carnacan manuscript, Professor Walton, curator of the Museum of Carnacan History, discovers that the ancient Martian treasure is guarded by a Mutation Bomb rigged to detonate if the treasure is disturbed. Walton calls in the Space Patrol, realizing that as long as people know there is a hidden treasure, they will try to find it — which is just what his crafty helpers, unaware of the bomb, have in mind. A race ensues to find the treasure before the professor's unsuspecting staff sets off the bomb — which could wipe out the entire population of the planet Mars.

Prof. Walton. . . . . Robert Shafto
Gregor . . . . Lawrence Dobkin
Nils. George Meader

#125 "The Deadly Glacier" May 9, 1953

Scientists fear that an accumulation of ice on a huge glacier near the North Pole could cause the Earth's axis to shift. Already the glacier has caused earthquakes that are felt around the world. Professor Gordon and Happy travel to the Polar region to conduct an investigation. Meanwhile, Captain Smith has received orders to bomb the glacier to set up a force to offset the quakes, unaware that Happy and Gordon are conducting their investigation right on top of the glacier that is scheduled for disintegration. Buzz finds out at the last minute that his cadet and the professor are in peril.

Prof. Kurzen . . . . Edward Clark
Prof. Gordon. . . . . Ramsay Hill
Capt. Smith. . . . . John Larch

#126 "The Space Derelict" or "Phantom Space Ship" May 23, 1953

Holliday, the bank president, finds himself in a predicament when the bank examiners are due to arrive and realizes he must cover up his recent embezzling before they discover it. He hires two thugs to rob his bank — and share the loot with him. In a complex plot to pass the security station at the bank, they trap Happy and use him as a decoy in a derelict spaceship which appears to be floating aimlessly, posing the threat of collision in an open space lane. Buzz and Robbie are lured to the ship, where the thugs plan to drug them with Narco so they can carry off the bank heist and avoid pursuit by the Space Patrol.

Holliday . . . . Tom Browne Henry
Duval. . . . . Tom McKee
Hackman . . . . Joe Cranston
2 Guards . . . . Bill Boyett, Bela Kovacs

#127 "The Green Plague" May 30, 1953

Inhabitants of Mars are thrown into a panic when the "Green Plague" strikes the city of Canali and threatens the entire planet with famine. The plague has been caused by a businessman named Crandall, who had a scientist develop a white plant that grows at night. When Crandall discovers that it drains all the elements from the soil that green plants need, he utilizes this knowledge for his own selfish purposes. Using a secret process, he plans to turn the white plant into food and create a complete food monopoly, forcing the citizens of Mars to buy their food from him. Buzz and the Space Patrol step in to thwart his plans and prevent a disastrous famine.

Crandall . . . . Richard Karlan
Attarian . . . . Fred Howard
Man. . . . . Phil Chambers
Woman . . . . Elizabeth Harrower

#128 "Fraud on Titan" or "The Fraud of Titan" June 6, 1953

Stanton is suspected of shady real estate dealings, so the Space Patrol sets a trap for him. They get him to act as the liaison for the purchase of Todd's Way Station, a privately owned spaceport located on Saturn's sixth moon. The station is to be used as a refueling area for Space Patrol ships. Stanton discovers that Mr. Todd's nephew, Truck, is a discontented young man, so he uses him to help force the elder Todd into selling at a low price; he then plans to charge the Space Patrol a much higher sum and pocket the difference.

Jim Todd . . . . I. Stanford Jolley
Aunt Sybil Todd . . . . Edith Evanson
Truck Todd. . . . . Wayne Taylor
Arch Stanton . . . . Marvin Miller

#129 "The Man Who Stole a City" June 13, 1953

A leading scientist perfects an Atom Harmonizer that can shrink buildings and ships, but not people. His intentions for the use of the harmonizer are noble, and he plans to give it to the Space Patrol. But before the transaction can take place, villains steal the harmonizer and use it to transport key buildings from Terra to an asteroid they own, where they are constructing a city. They even plan to steal Space Patrol headquarters! Buzz summons the assistance of the top scientist, only to discover that he, too, has disappeared.

Kovel. . . . . Dan Seymour
Lesser . . . . Lee Van Cleef
Dr. Getlin. . . . . Bela Kovacs

#130 "The Gigantic Space Knife" June 20, 1953

A well-traveled space lane becomes the scene for a series of daring interplanetary hijackings. Buzz and the Space Patrol prepare a trap which will catch the bandits in action, planting Robbie at the controls of the next scheduled flight of a space freighter. The plan goes awry when Robbie's freighter is attacked and neatly cut in two. The fiendish villains have devised a space knife that can sever a ship, using a pencil-thin ray beam. They use magnetism to draw the portion of Robbie's ship holding valuable mineral deposits to an unknown destination; but the cockpit in which the major is seated is left floating aimlessly in space.

Barrow . . . . Donald Lawton
Hendrix . . . . Kem Dibbs
Perry . . . . Marshall Bradford
(Kem Dibbs starred in ABC's short-lived television version of Buck Rogers in the 25th Century *in April 1950 before Robert Pastene took over the role.)*

#131 "The Space Patrol Microscope" June 27, 1953

After a series of thefts of money boxes, the president of a bank on Mars— secretly the ringleader of the thieves—calls on the Space Patrol for assistance. It seems that boxes of cash are being replaced by fake ones somewhere in transit. The Space Patrol sends Happy aboard the ship as a stowaway to find out what's happening, but when he discovers the ruse, the criminals leave the cadet adrift in space. With the aid of a powerful microscope, the Space Patrol is able to decipher a message written on a coin and thus stop the theft of the money boxes; meanwhile Buzz and Carol set out to rescue Happy.

Bolen . . . . John Alderson
Harper . . . . Marvin Press
White . . . . Paul Keast

#132 "The Theft of Terra Five" July 4, 1953

Buzz's own ship, the *Terra V*—the most powerful in the United Planets—has been stolen. When all the evidence points to Happy and the young cadet is unable to account for his whereabouts at the time of the theft, Buzz has no alternative but to order his arrest. However, Happy has been the victim of a frame-up by two repairmen at the shop where the *Terra V* was recently serviced, who, after stealing the ship, turned it over to Croner, Public Enemy #1.

Joe . . . . Ben Welden
Lud. . . . . Joel Smith
Walk-ons . . . . . George Douglas, Bela Kovacs

#133 "The Mysterious Ocean in Space" July 11, 1953

On a routine flight, Buzz and the Space Patrol crew plunge headlong into the middle of an ocean in outer space and the *Terra V* is submerged underwater. Meanwhile, communications from Earth report that an unknown force is draining the Earth's oceans, lakes and rivers. Villains have set up headquarters at the foot of the Kralic Mountain Basin on Mars, and by utilizing a tremendous force field that is hollow like a pipeline, they start to drain the water from Earth's Great Lakes. They plan to blackmail the United Planets government, threatening to drain all water off of Earth.

Mr. Flagg. . . . . Jack Reitzen
Burger . . . . Henry Corden

#134 "The Stolen Evidence" July 18, 1953

The governor of Mars is convinced that government officials are selling important state secrets. When Buzz arrives to investigate, the governor's daughter is kidnapped, and an envelope containing documented evidence against the crooked officials also disappears.

Governor Marin . . . . Ramsay Hill
Linda . . . . Sally Fraser
Gregory. . . . . Larry Dobkin

#135 "The Traitorous Triangle" July 25, 1953

The secretary general discovers a powerful movement called the Traitorous Triangle that is slowly taking control of agencies at the top level of government. He puts in a call to Buzz and Happy, away on a mission, and orders them home. Three members of the Triangle, wearing hoods to disguise themselves, force entrance into the capitol of the United Planets, take the secretary general prisoner, and threaten Carol at gunpoint unless the leader turns over his secret files. Once they gain access to the files, the hooded agents can immediately place the United Planets under dictatorial powers and force the people of the solar system into slavery. So cleverly devised is the plot that Buzz cannot make a move without risking the lives of the entire capitol representative body.

Sec. General. . . . . Bob Carson
Governor from Mercury & #1 . . . . Gene Roth
#2 . . . . John Damler
#3 Doss Markham . . . . Bela Kovacs

#136 "The Desert Crash Helmet" or "Crash Landing" August 1, 1953

Buzz and Happy are taking a ship on a trial run, unaware that eight-year-old Danny has hidden himself aboard in order to give Buzz the three desert crash helmets he has made. The ship encounters radiation trouble and is forced to crash-land in the middle of a desert sandstorm. Danny slips away to find help, but ends up lost in the sandstorm and is snatched by two criminals who were hiding out in the wastelands. Using the crash helmets, Buzz contacts Danny, helps the boy escape, and eventually apprehends the criminals.

Danny . . . . Mickey Little
Sloan . . . . Stephen Chase
Gates. . . . . Jan Arvan

#137 "Slaves of the Mind Pirate" or "The Brain Machine" August 8, 1953

A mad scientist constructs a computer containing all the brilliance and reasoning power of the greatest minds in the solar system,

then uses a teleportation machine to go after his "selected" subjects—including Buzz—and bring them to his control room. He hooks the men up to the machine, and it falls to Buzz to figure out how to free himself and the others.
Breckrenridge . . . . Bruce Payne
Casullo . . . . Tom McKee
Brokaw. . . . . Marvin Miller

#138 "The Alien Invasion" or "A Dangerous Smoke Cloud" August 15, 1953

Buzz, Happy and Robbie head for Mars after receiving a call for help via mental telepathy. They meet two aliens who tell them of a super-intelligent life form that looks like a cloud of smoke and invaded their planet long ago, capturing the mind of every being. While the cloud of smoke surrounds them, they are under its control; when it leaves, they can think for themselves. Happy and Robbie fall victim to the cloud, and it's up to Buzz to combat the menace and save the people of the United Planets.
Riva . . . . Ruth Gur
Mandra . . . . Norbert Schiller

#139 "The Black Falcon's Return" August 22, 1953

The cunning and ruthless Prince Baccarratti, AKA "The Black Falcon," reaches out from his lair to spread death and destruction. Possessed with a burning desire to rule the United Planets, the evil prince devises a plan which will place the Falcon's throne at the head of every planet in the solar system.
Prince Baccarratti . . . . Bela Kovacs

#140 "The Mystery of Planet X" August 29, 1953

A mysterious new planet, Planet X, estimated to be five thousand times the size of Earth, has affixed itself to the outer edge of the solar system and Buzz is ordered to investigate. In short order, a strange "sun" appears and is burning a swath a mile wide on Earth at the rate of 1,000 miles per hour. Buzz quickly orders an evacuation of inhabitants in its path and concludes that the "sun" is actually a giant solar mirror connected somehow to Planet X. Buzz and Happy set out for the evil planet to destroy the mirror.

Dr. Gruber . . . . Gabriel Curtiz
Savant . . . . Joe Cranston
Prince Baccarratti . . . . Bela Kovacs

#141 "The Trap on Planet X" September 5, 1953

Robbie and Tonga are circling Planet X in a fixed orbit, equipped with an infrared camera which is making a photographic reproduction of every square mile of the planet's surface. Meanwhile, the tyrant Prince Baccarratti, from his castle stronghold, devises a scheme to trap them in order to force his archenemy, Buzz Corry, to come to their rescue. Hearing a distress signal coming from the surface of the planet, Robbie and Tonga approach and crash into a jungle filled with prehistoric dinosaurs. They manage to escape the ship before one of the monsters takes a bite out of it. Robbie calls Buzz for help, while Baccarratti's minions are hunting them down.
Salvo . . . . Jack Halloran
Prince Baccarratti . . . . Bela Kovacs

#142 "The Primitive Men of Planet X" September 12, 1953

Buzz goes to Planet X in search of Happy, who has been lured there by an old prospector. He and Hap become trapped in a gigantic underground cavern where, although safe from the prehistoric dinosaurs roaming the surface of the planet, they are held at the mercy of a tribe of primitive men. While fighting off these natives, Buzz observes that Happy is acting strangely, as if under a spell—and his suspicions are confirmed when the cadet tries to shoot him! Now he knows that it's his enemy Prince Baccarratti who resides in the castle, and who has been behind the fiendish attempts on his life—but the immediate problem is escaping from the planet.
Prince Baccarratti . . . . Bela Kovacs
Extras as primitive men

#143 "The Hate Machine of Planet X" September 19, 1953

The Hate Machine is a diabolical mechanical invention created by Prince Baccarratti to foster bitterness, resentment and dissension within the Space Patrol and among the people of the United Planets. When Buzz and Happy are taken captive on Planet X, the crazed ruler tries the device out on them — and Buzz and his cadet fight with each other. In the meantime, Baccarratti aims the Hate Machine at Terra.

Malengro . . . . Gabriel Curtiz
Two guards . . . . Joel Smith, Bill Boyett
Prince Baccarratti . . . . Bela Kovacs

#144 "Black Falcon's Escape from Planet X" September 26, 1953

Buzz, Robbie and Happy attempt to capture Prince Baccarratti and bring him to justice by hunting him down in his castle. However, Baccarratti has many evil surprises in store for the Space Patrollers. We find Buzz dangling helplessly at the end of a rope over a vapor pit while Robbie is caught in the iron grip of a man-eating wolf plant. The treacherous Prince Baccarratti cheers triumphantly as he observes the two men struggling for their lives.

Malengro . . . . Gabriel Curtiz
Two guards . . . . Joe Smith, Bill Boyett
Prince Baccarratti . . . . Bela Kovacs

#145 "Destruction from Planet X" or "Resonance Impeller" October 3, 1953

Prince Baccarratti shocks the people of Terra with the news that Buzz, Happy and Robbie have succumbed to the wolf plant on Planet X. The "deaths" of Buzz and his crew clear the way for the ruthless Baccarratti to become the supreme ruler of the United Planets. To demonstrate his power, Baccarratti beams the Resonance Impeller toward Terra. The man-made capitol quakes under the powerful ray's vibrations, and the terrified inhabitants send a plea for mercy to Planet X.

Sec. General. . . . . Robert Carson
Prince Baccarratti . . . . Bela Kovacs

#146 "The Ice Demon of Planet X" October 10, 1953

Having disabled Baccarratti's Resonance Impeller, located in the freezing polar region of Planet X, Buzz and Happy return to their ship and put in a call to Robbie to come pick them up. However, the treacherous Prince is not about to let them go so easily, and he sics the Ice Demon, who lives in the polar area, on their ship. Although the demon is unable to crush the battlecruiser, he cracks the hull, causing it to lose heat. Buzz and Hap pour every bit of available electrical power into the outer hull, hoping to make it so hot that the monster will drop it.

Prince Baccarratti . . . . Bela Kovacs

#147 "The Slaves of Planet X" October 17, 1953

Still marooned on Planet X, Buzz and Happy abandon their spaceship and search for a safe hiding place. They enter a narrow shaft in the side of a rock that leads to a valuable mineral ore mine but are captured by a band of little people whom Baccarratti has enslaved. The prisoners are convinced that the Space Patrollers are agents of the evil prince. Baccarratti seals the mine entrance and the group discovers they have company: two brilliant scientists whom the prince kidnapped long ago.

Gino . Bill Curtis   Mario . Harry Monty
Dr. MacNeil . . . . Fred Berest
Dr. Owen . Tom McKee   Rollo . Paul Klatt, Jr.
Prince Baccarratti . . . . Bela Kovacs

#148 "The Giant of Planet X" October 24, 1953

Buzz devises a plan to destroy Baccarratti's castle: He removes the damper rods that were the only controlling factor limiting the amount of radiation released by the castle's atomic pile. It is just a matter of time before the pile reaches critical mass and becomes an atom bomb. Unaware that this has happened, Prince Baccarratti turns his diabolical Diminisher Machine on Buzz and Happy, reducing them to only inches tall. They try to turn off the damper rods, but their small size makes this impossible. Their only hope is to get control of the Diminisher, reverse it, return themselves to normal size and replace the damper rods in time to prevent an atomic explosion![5]

Malengro . . . . Gabriel Curtiz
Guard. Joe Cranston
Prince Baccarratti . . . . Bela Kovacs

[5]This show, in which Buzz and Hap were reduced in size to only a few inches tall, was a risky undertaking for live TV. Ed Kemmer says two matching sets were used. One showed the furniture in Baccarratti's castle; the other was black. "Hap and I worked in a completely black set so that only our bodies were visible; we were photographed from a distance, so that, when superimposed, we looked much smaller than the objects on the main set." — JNB

#149 *"Tesseract Prison of Planet X"* October 31, 1953

Once again the Space Patrollers face deadly peril on Planet X. Tonga is captured, shot with a ray gun and left to die. In the meantime, Prince Baccarratti imprisons Buzz and Happy in the Tesseract Chamber, where they are trapped in the Fourth Dimension, able to observe events in physical reality yet powerless to change them. From the chamber, they watch Baccarratti's henchmen blow up the *Terra V* and leave Tonga to die in the Valley of the Dinosaurs.
Malengro . . . . Gabriel Curtiz
Guards . . . . Joe Cranston, Ron Sha'an
Prince Baccarratti . . . . Bela Kovacs

#150 *"The Falcon's Web on Planet X"* November 7, 1953

In an attempt to learn more about Prince Baccarratti's castle stronghold, Buzz and Happy capture his captain of the guard and bring him back to Terra in order to use the Brainograph on him. However, the guard collapses after swallowing a capsule that he carried for just such an emergency and is sent to Medical Science Center where he's placed under the care of Dr. Svetka — who is really Prince Baccarratti in disguise. Through the guard, Baccarratti lays a devilish trap to destroy the Space Patrol and sends Buzz and Happy zooming headlong into a force barrier.
Malengro . . . . Gabriel Curtiz
Captain of the Guards . . . . Ron Sha'an
Prince Baccarratti . . . . Bela Kovacs

#151 *"The Castle's Destruction on Planet X"* November 14, 1953

Just as Prince Baccarratti captures Buzz and Hap, he discovers that Carol and a Space Patrol squadron have located his castle. He decides the castle will never again be a safe place and puts Plan Z-1 into effect. Activating a prearranged time mechanism designed to blow up the castle — and Buzz and Hap with it — the Black Falcon flees his stronghold through an escape tube that houses a magnetic car.
Malengro . . . . Gabriel Curtiz
Guards . . . . Tom McKee, Joel Smith
Prince Baccarratti . . . . Bela Kovacs

#152 *"The Valley of Illusion on Planet X"* November 21, 1953

Prince Baccarratti flees from his castle to the Valley of Illusion. Buzz and Happy follow and find themselves in a surrealistic land where nothing is what it seems to be. The prince's evil engineers have constructed a mechanism which uses the atmosphere of the valley as a giant screen upon which a three-dimensional scene can be projected, completely obscuring the valley as it really is and making unwanted visitors see anything Baccarratti wants them to see. The images of guards are projected in front of Buzz and Hap, confusing them while the real guards sneak up behind them and knock them out.
Malengro . . . . Gabriel Curtiz
Two Guards . . . . Tom McKee, Joel Smith
Prince Baccarratti . . . . Bela Kovacs

#153 *"The Doom of Planet X"* November 28, 1953

Buzz and Happy are seeking the entrance to Prince Baccarratti's hideout when they are threatened by a charging dinosaur. Buzz turns this into an advantage as they duck out of the way at the last second and the beast creates an entrance to the hideout. Leaving word for Robbie to join them on Planet X with the *Terra V*, Buzz and Hap go inside to hunt the prince. However, Robbie is captured and Baccarratti once again has the upper hand. The evil Black Falcon plans to use the Time Warp Machine on the Space Patrollers, who will be doomed to spend eternity on Planet X in the Fourth Dimension.
Malengro . . . . Gabriel Curtiz
Guards . . . . Tom McKee, Joel Smith, Joe Cranston, Fred Berest
Prince Baccarratti . . . . Bela Kovacs

#154 *"The Alien and the Robot"* December 5, 1953

Investigating the mysterious theft of electronics equipment from laboratories on Mars, Buzz, Robbie and Happy meet Letha, a gorgeous exile from outer space. She's accompanied by a brutish robot and uses a fiendish Retardo-Ray machine that turns people into mental vegetables. Letha has already paralyzed Dr. Cameron Stanton with the Retardo-Ray and deals with Robbie and Happy in the same manner. She hopes that using the Ray on them will serve as an example to others in a "payoff-or-else" shakedown scheme. Meanwhile, Buzz has been given an ultimatum: Join her in the racket or become the Retardo-Ray's fourth victim.

Letha . . . . Ann Dore
Robot "Five" . . . . Joel Smith

#155 "The Robot's Escape" December 12, 1953

Although Buzz has captured Letha's human-like robot and Retardo-Ray, Letha herself has escaped. In Space Patrol headquarters, Buzz and Hap stand by while Carol tries to imitate the voice of the alien woman in an attempt to fool the robot into answering questions. In the meantime, Letha returns to a secluded spot on Canali where she is able to activate her robot by remote control. The robot knocks out Buzz and Happy, then, at Letha's command, returns to the ship with Carol as a hostage.

Letha . . . . Ann Dore
Robot "Five" . . . . Joel Smith
Secretary General . . . . Marshall Bradford

#156 "The City of Living Statues" December 19, 1953

Tall blonde alien Letha, from deep in the Outer Galaxy, and her human-appearing robot, "Five," escape from Mars Space Headquarters with the Retardo-Ray and proceed to turn Canali into the City of Living Statues. Meanwhile, Letha tries to interest Buzz in joining forces with her. For a while, it looks as if Buzz may accept her offer — much to the horror of Hap and Robbie.

Letha . . . . Ann Dore
Two Guards . . . . Joel Smith, Joe Cranston

#157 "The Mystery of the Missing Asteroids" December 26, 1953

Two unscrupulous miners use a Gravi-Magnet device to pull mineral-rich asteroids out of their orbits and stake claims on them, planning to make themselves rich. Buzz and Happy encounter a storm of "flying" rocks before they can bring the two outlaws to justice.

Grandpa . . . . Fred Howard
Millie . . . . Isa Ashdown
Horner . . . . Larry Dobkin
Kruse . . . . Jan Arvan

1954

#158 "The Phantom Space Pirate" January 2, 1954

Captain Dagger, space pirate, has developed a unique method of looting payroll ships. Using the Visi-Shield, a device he has perfected, he sets up a field around his ship that absorbs radar signals and makes viewscopes ineffective. Then, invisible, he stalks payroll ships, blasts them with an Inertia Bomb and boards them. An expert fencer, he always offers to duel the captain of the ship he is looting — and he always wins.

Captain Dagger . . . . Richard Karlan
Johnson . . . . Charles Victor

#159 "The Space Vault Robbery" January 9, 1954

Captain Dagger and his first mate, Dr. Maddox, a renegade scientist, use the Phobia Ray to rob banks. The ray induces claustrophobia, causing people to feel so closed in and emotionally upset that they must leave the premises — allowing the villains to walk in and clean out the safes. At one point, the captain nearly succeeds in stealing the entire treasury reserve of the United Planets. A public furor erupts, and people demand that the Security Council investigate the inability of Buzz and the Space Patrol to stop the looting.

Captain Dagger . . . . Richard Karlan
Dr. Maddox . . . . Harold Gordon
Harris. Richard Weil

#160 "The Pirate's Escape" January 16, 1954

Captain Dagger and his henchman, Dr. Maddox, have been captured, and Buzz and Happy must force Dagger to reveal the location of his hideout in order to recover the property stolen by the pirate. While being guarded by Happy, Dagger uses his Phobia Ray, forcing Hap to leave the ship, but also subjecting Dagger, while still tied up, to its horrible effects. Dagger withstands it and is able to switch off the controls and free himself and Dr. Maddox. The two pirates escape, using the Visi-Shield to obscure their ship. However, Buzz is one step ahead of them — he has secured a crate of Tellurium to their ship, hanging down far enough to be out of range of the Visi-Shield. The Space Patrollers follow the pair as they head for their hideout in an inactive volcano in the Kralic Wastelands on Mars.

Captain Dagger . . . . Richard Karlan
2 Guards . . . . Bill Justine, Bill Bryar

#161 "The Amazons of Cydonia" January 23, 1954

Dr. Oliver Tuttle and his assistant, Johnson, have established a laboratory in the Cydonian Jungle on Venus where they are experimenting on plant life to use as the basis for synthetic food. When their daily report fails to reach Space Patrol Headquarters, Buzz, Happy and Robbie investigate. Arriving in Cydonia, they find that it's ruled by a tribe of Amazon women who make slaves of all strong men and destroy the weak ones. Buzz rescues Dr. Tuttle and sends him back to Terra with Robbie, but he and Hap are trapped by the Amazons.

Queen Riva . . . . Dorothy Ford
Dr. Tuttle . . . . Jerome Courtland
Zamba . . . . Gloria Pall
Calva . . . . Frances Farwell
Man Slave . . . . Jack Carroll

#162 "The Monsoon Trap on Cydonia" January 30, 1954

After helping Dr. Tuttle escape the Amazons, Buzz and Happy continue their search for Tuttle's assistant, Johnson, who is now working in league with the Amazons and has possession of Tuttle's valuable micro-tape which contains all his research. Buzz gets ahold of the tape and manages to send it by "space jet" to Hap. But Johnson gets the upper hand and orders two of the Amazons to tie Buzz to a tree facing a cross-bow rigged to go off when the monsoon wind strikes. The commander escapes with the aid of Happy, but the pair are captured and held hostage by the Amazons.

Johnson . . . . Ben Welden
Queen Riva . . . . Dorothy Ford
Calva . . . . Frances Farwell
Zamba . . . . Gloria Pall

#163 "The Men Slaves of Cydonia" February 6, 1954

Having been captured by the Amazons in the previous episode, Buzz and Happy are at the mercy of Queen Riva, who is determined to make them men-slaves. In a scuffle with Johnson, Hap is seriously wounded. Buzz works as a slave and cares for Hap, all the while planning an escape. Johnson talks Riva into making him her slave master and attempts to force Buzz to reveal the whereabouts of the valuable micro-tape by hiding Hap, now extremely ill, in the jungle where Buzz can no longer take care of him. Learning that Johnson cannot be trusted, the Amazons wound him with a ray gun. Meanwhile, when Robbie has not heard from Buzz and Hap, he returns to Cydonia to look for them.

Johnson . . . . Ben Welden
Queen Riva . . . . Dorothy Ford
Calva . . . . Frances Farwell
Zamba . . . . Gloria Pall

#164 "The Deadly Radiation Chamber" February 13, 1954

Three nuclear fission plants suddenly declare their factories unsafe and shut down—throwing the United Planets into an unprecedented energy crisis. Buzz and Happy, called to investigate by the Security Council, are thwarted by Mr. Halifax in their attempt to inspect his company. They force their way into the plant, but once inside, they find themselves trapped in a deadly radiation chamber.

Mr. Proteus . . . . Marvin Miller
Tyler . . . . Ed Hinton

#165 "The Plot in the Atomic Plant" February 20, 1954

Buzz and Happy's investigation reveals that the power plants' shortage threatens the entire solar system with total destruction. More attempts are made upon their lives. Though they know Mr. Proteus as the director of the United Planets Fissionable Materials Commission, they see no reason to distrust him and are unaware that it is he—impersonating the heads of the three major nuclear power plants—who is plotting against them and trying to corner the market on atomic power units.

Proteus. . . . . Marvin Miller
Tyler . . . . Ed Hinton
Dr. Lorenz. . . . . Robert Nash

#166 "The Blazing Sun of Mercury" February 27, 1954

Buzz learns that the chameleon-like master of disguise, Mr. Proteus, is the man who is trying to gain sole control of the atomic energy of the United Planets. Proteus lures Buzz, Happy and Robbie to Mercury, where he imprisons them along with the real heads of the power plants— Halifax, Matsoong and Justin— and all nearly perish from the intense heat. Proteus blasts off in his ship for Terra — but he underestimates Buzz and is in for a startling surprise.

Mr. Proteus . . . . Marvin Miller
Marco . . . . Larry Dobkin
Justin. . . . . Bill Justine
4 Guards . . . . . . Lloyd Nelson, Rand Brooks,
                    Don Hicks, Bela Kovacs

#167 "The Big Proteus Swindle" March 6, 1954

As director of the Security Council, the ruthless Mr. Proteus has authorized the purchase of 6,000 power units for the outrageous, black market price of 6 billion credits. The transaction will be in cash and will be paid to Mr. Halifax. Proteus, disguised as Halifax, accepts the money and travels to Venus, where he attempts to pose as Mr. Matsoong and swindle the United Planets out of even more credits. The Space Patrol crew catches him in the act, but Proteus deals the Space Patrollers an unexpected blow.

Mr. Proteus . . . . Marvin Miller
Marco . . . . Larry Dobkin
Major Caldwell. . . . . Kerwin Matthews
2 Guards. . . . . Jack Lynn, Bela Kovacs

#168 "The Escape of Mr. Proteus" March 13, 1954

Buzz, Happy and Robbie follow Mr. Proteus and Marco to Venus, where they have fled with the 6 billion credits, and are trapped in the Matsoong Plant. Believing that they have at last stopped him in his unscrupulous plan, the Space Patrollers are momentarily caught off guard when Mr. Proteus uses another of his clever disguises and once again escapes.

Mr. Proteus . . . . Marvin Miller
Marco . . . . Larry Dobkin
2 Guards. . . . . Jack Lynn, Bela Kovacs

#169 "Mr. Proteus and the Poison Gas" March 20, 1954

Buzz and Happy recover the 6 billion credits from Mr. Proteus, but the unscrupulous villain eludes them once again. Through a diabolical ruse, he lures Buzz and Happy into his spaceship and nearly succeeds in ending their lives with poison gas. Although the Space Patrollers turn the tables on their adversary, the cunning Mr. Proteus manages to escape once more.

Mr. Proteus . . . . Marvin Miller
Esteban . . . . Tom McKee

#170 "The Revenge of Mr. Proteus" March 27, 1954

Having recovered all of the money Mr. Proteus swindled from the United Planets and returned it to Terra, Buzz and Happy renew their search for the criminal. Seeking revenge against Buzz, Proteus disguises himself as "Captain Quick," whose treacherous shipmate has set him adrift in space, and calls for help from the Asteroid Belt. Buzz and Hap come to his rescue, but the phony Quick pulls a gun on the Space Patrollers, ties them up, and sets the *Terra V* on a collision course with an asteroid.

Mr. Proteus . . . . Marvin Miller
Esteban . . . . Tom McKee
Bela Kovacs doubles for both Marvin Miller and Buzz

#171 "The Capture of Mr. Proteus" April 3, 1954

Buzz and Happy, having escaped the near-fatal collision with an asteroid orchestrated by Mr. Proteus, call Carol for assistance. Then they set about repairing the ship. When Proteus discovers that they haven't crashed, he fires at them. In order to avoid being hit by one of the missiles, they are forced to blast off with Buzz holding the main power cables together in his hands. Carol overtakes Proteus' ship and tries to place him and Esteban under arrest, but they turn the tables and take her prisoner. They spirit Carol back to their hideout, where they set a trap for Buzz and Hap, knowing they will come to her rescue.

Mr. Proteus . . . . Marvin Miller
Esteban . . . . Tom McKee
Hendrix . . . . Kerwin Matthews

#172 "Baccarratti's 'Z' Ray" April 10, 1954

Groata comes to Terra asking to see Buzz and Happy's prisoner, Prince Baccarratti — and announcing that he wants to kill him. Buzz and Hap learn that Baccarratti has a twin brother, Zarra, and that Groata is his guardian. Groata believes that Zarra — not Baccarratti — is the real heir to the throne of the House of Venus, and that the evil prince must be eliminated. He has kept Zarra hidden in the 20th century, tutoring him in the traditions of his forefathers, awaiting the proper time for him to seize the throne. As the pair escapes back to their refuge in time, Buzz vows to follow them.

Bela Kovacs plays a duel role as Prince Baccarratti and Zarra.

Groata . . . . Robert Shayne
2 Clerks . . . . Joe Cranston, Ed Taylor
Bank Officer . . . . Chris O'Brien

#173 "Marooned in the Past" April 17, 1954

Buzz and Happy, in a desperate effort to capture Prince Baccarratti's twin brother, Zarra, follow him and his evil guardian, Groata, back in time to Earth's 20th century and a bookstore in Hollywood, California. Groata has hidden the twin in this timeline for the past 30 years, and now he and Zarra, using their powerful Z-Ray weapon, try to trap the Space Patrollers in the 20th century forever. Fortunately, Earth is getting set to launch its first experimental rocket, and Buzz and Hap enlist the test pilot's help to get back to their ship and escape.

Carson. . . . . LeRoy Lennart
Groata . . . . Robert Shayne
King . . . . Frank Richards
The Girl . . . . Janet Dascher
Nick . . . . John Larch

#174 "Evil Spirits of the Great Thunderbird" April 24, 1954

When Buzz and Hap return to the 30th century, they learn that Zarra, with the help of Groata, has already begun a devastating attack upon the United Planets in his effort to re-establish himself on the throne of Venus. Buzz must stop them before they can cause irreparable damage with the treacherous Z-Ray. Zarra realizes he doesn't stand a chance in open combat against Buzz's battlecruiser, so he lures the Space Patrollers back into the past among a tribe of Indians, where they will be burned at the stake as evil spirits.

Groata . . . . Robert Shayne
Yellow Feather . . . . Joel Smith
Chief Eagle Claw. . . . . Ron Sha'an
5 Indian extras. . Joe Cranston, Marvin Press,
Ed Taylor, Bill Justine,
Ken Mayer

#175 "The Fall of the Kingdom of Zarra" April 30, 1954

Under the impression that Buzz and Hap have been done in by the Indians, Zarra returns to Venus, where he sets up his castle as a stronghold, installing the Z-Ray as a line of defense. Meanwhile, Buzz releases the information that Prince Baccarratti is alive, thus setting a trap for Zarra and Groata, who, upon hearing the news, attempt to kill the prince. Zarra uses the Z-Ray to take Happy and Robbie prisoner and make them his "loyal subjects"— then orders them to do away with Buzz!

Prince Baccarratti and Zarra . . . . Bela Kovacs
Groata . . . . Robert Shayne
Man #1. . . . . Marvin Press
Man #2 . . . . Richard Tufeld
Rudolph Horavatik . . . . . . Prince Baccarratti
for 2 scenes

#176 "Prisoners of the Giant Comet" May 7, 1954

A giant comet enters the solar system from outer space and threatens everything in its path with total destruction. Carol, flying a ship en route to Terra, is caught in the comet's tail and faces certain death. Buzz, Happy and Robbie blast off in the *Terra V* to come to her rescue, but the gravitational pull of the comet imprisons them, too.

Regular cast only.

#177 "The Demon Planet" May 14, 1954

After escaping from the magnetic pull of the giant comet, the *Terra V* drifts toward the surface of a mysterious unknown planet. Buzz, Happy, Robbie and Carol land on the planet to repair their damaged ship. Hap spies a rock that mysteriously moves by itself, and he, Buzz and Robbie investigate while Carol stays aboard the ship. They follow the rock to a crater, which seems to be swallowing it — and they realize that they have landed not on a planet, but on a huge monstrous life form that feeds on whatever happens to get caught in one of its "mouths" or craters. Meanwhile, Carol discovers to her horror that the crater in which they have landed is slowly enveloping the ship.

Regular cast only.

#178 "Lost in Galactic Space" May 21, 1954

Buzz, Hap, Carol and Robbie have just narrowly escaped death on the Demon Planet when a group of its satellite moons breaks free from their orbit and hits the ship with glancing blows. The air purifier is damaged beyond repair and the air is growing stale. As if things weren't bad enough, it seems as if the *Terra V* has been severed in two! Buzz suspects this is an illusion caused by space warp when he put the ship in timedrive to outrun the moons, and to prove his point, he steps into what appears to be outer space — without a spacesuit.

Regular cast only.

#179 "The Hidden Treasure of Mars" May 28, 1954

Buzz and Happy blast off for Mars to join the famous archeologist Dr. Lambert, who has just discovered the underground city of the ancient Carnacans, a race that disappeared from the planet a thousand years ago. Once there, Buzz and his cadet incur the wrath of some "Carnacans" who claim they've come back to their native planet to search for treasure they left long ago. Soon Buzz suspects that the so-called Carnacans are a gang of thugs. The criminals overpower Dr. Lambert and throw him in the "trial chamber," a fiendish device that crushes prisoners to death.

Dr. Lambert . . . . I. Stanford Jolley
Carnacan . . . . Nestor Paiva
Sollum . . . . Ben Welden
Axel . . . . Ron Sha'an
Other cast: John Halloran, Bill Justine, Joseph Barker, Fortune Gordien

#180 "The Martian Totem Head" June 4, 1954

Buzz and Happy, in their efforts to rescue Dr. Lambert, find themselves trapped once again by the ruthless men posing as ancient Carnacans. The villains have a chance to shoot the Space Patrollers, but decide not to — not until Buzz deciphers the clues left by the real Carnacans in a series of maps and poems and leads them to the hidden treasure.

Sollum . . . . Ben Welden
Axel . . . . Ron Sha'an

#181 "Trapped in the Pyramid" June 11, 1954

Having survived the collapse of the ancient underground Carnacan city on Mars, Buzz and Happy are trapped with the bogus Carnacans in the secret pyramid chamber. Buzz wracks his brain to find a way out of the "safe" room that could become their tomb.

Sollum . . . . Ben Welden
Axel . . . . Ron Sha'an
Dr. Lambert . . . . I. Stanford Jolley

#182 "The Underwater Space Ship Graveyard" June 18, 1954

A vacation for Buzz, Happy, Carol and Robbie ends as a nightmare on the floor of Venus' Caloric Ocean when they're trapped in an underwater spaceship graveyard that belongs to Agent X, a super-criminal whom they believed to be dead. But X, who lures payroll ships to his ocean stronghold, reappears and maneuvers the Space Patrol crew to his hideaway, where they face almost certain death.

Agent X . . . . Norman Jolley

#183 "The Giant Marine Clam" June 25, 1954

Buzz, Robbie, Happy and Carol have captured Agent X — but he gets a gun and turns the tables, overpowering the Space Patrol crew. Aided by his brutal robot, Junior, the vicious Agent X tries to force Buzz and Robbie to reveal top secret information regarding the movement of payroll ships by holding Hap and Carol hostage — without space helmets — in an airlock that is slowly filling with water.

Agent X . . . . Norman Jolley

#184 "Marooned on the Ocean Floor" July 2, 1954

Agent X escapes and succeeds in burning a hole in the *Terra V*, forcing Buzz, Hap, Carol and Robbie to seek refuge in his undersea hideout. Then he blasts off in his hydro-jet, from which he plans to destroy his stonghold with deadly depth charges— and the Space Patrollers along with it. It's up to Buzz to find a way to repair their waterlogged ship and blast off before X makes good on his promise.

Agent X . . . . Norman Jolley
Junior [robot] . . . . Bela Kovacs

#185 "Mystery of the Disappearing Space Patrolmen" September 4, 1954

The baffling disappearance of Major Robertson and a pair of young Space Patrol cadets named Clay and Victor sends Buzz and Happy on one of their strangest adventures. Buzz learns that they have been abducted to the planet Manza via a force field controlled by an invisible creature who bears the same name as his remote lair.

Manza . . . . Tom McKee
Clay . . . . Gene Reynolds
Victor . . . . Ted Donaldson

#186 "The Space Patrol Periscope" September 11, 1954

The invisible creature Manza intends to use his Space Patrol captives as gunners in a war against the Icarians. Manza long ago drove the Icarians from the planet on which his stronghold is located and where he is now master. Buzz and Happy arrive on the planet and are captured by Manza, who wields a "pain whip" to force them to do his bidding. Meanwhile, the Icarians give Manza an ultimatum: Surrender or be destroyed by their heat ray.

General Nardo . . . . Carleton Young
Manza . . . . Tom McKee
Robot . . . . Bela Kovacs

#187 "The Space War" September 18, 1954

Buzz and Happy are helpless as the Icarians attack and their heat ray intensifies. Buzz makes a desperate plea to their leader, General Nardo, to withdraw. Escaping from Manza's stronghold, he boards Nardo's ship and briefs him on the perilous situation of Happy and the other Space Patrolmen. Then, as Buzz and Nardo plot Manza's downfall, their foe retaliates by kidnapping Carol and demanding that Buzz return to the fortress at once — alone.

General Nardo . . . . Carleton Young
Manza . . . . Tom McKee
Griff . . . . Joel Marston
Clay . . . . Gene Reynolds

#188 "The Defeat of Manza" September 25, 1954

While plotting Manza's downfall with General Nardo, Buzz is forced to surrender his freedom and become Manza's prisoner again. He takes this drastic step when he learns that the invisible tyrant has captured Carol and is holding her hostage for his return. But Manza accidentally imprisons himself, allowing Buzz and Hap to invade the heart of his stronghold and learn the secret of his destruction.

General Nardo . . . . Carleton Young
Manza . . . . Tom McKee
Griff . . . . Joel Marston

#189 "The Giants of Pluto #3" October 2, 1954

Suspicious happenings on Pluto's third moon have come under the scrutiny of the Space Patrol. Buzz and Happy soon meet with trouble at the hands of Dr. Frederic Kurt, the undersize operator of a sanitarium for run-down citizens of the universe who the evil doctor turns into mindless giants to do his bidding. Buzz and Hap learn that Major Robertson, sent to investigate, has fallen under the doctor's influence.

Dr. Kurt . . . . Hannes Lutz
Mrs. Gordon . . . . Lyn Guild
Other cast . . . . Michael Ross, William Dalzell

#190 "The Fiery Pit of Pluto #3" October 9, 1954

Determined to bring the evil Dr. Kurt to justice because of his practice of converting his patients into giant, robot-like slaves, Buzz and Happy are hampered by the very zombie-like creatures they are trying to save. The two Space Patrollers attempt to overcome the zombies without harming them, only to wind up as candidates for a bath in a pool of molten lava!

Dr. Kurt . . . . Hannes Lutz
Atlas . . . . Michael Ross
Colossus . . . . William Dalzell

#191 "The Man-Hunt on Pluto #3" October 16, 1954

Having reconverted all but one of Dr. Kurt's zombies into the normal humans they once were, Buzz and Happy turn their attention to the task of corralling the evil scientist. But thanks to Atlas, his one remaining giant slave, Kurt escapes and the two Space Patrolmen become the hunted, instead of the hunters. Their plight appears hopeless when Kurt and Atlas trap them in a deep canyon that offers no means of escape.

Dr. Kurt . . . . Hannes Lutz
Atlas. . . . . Michael Ross

#192 *"The Theft of the Rocket Cockpit" or "Mystery of the Stolen Rocket Ship" October 23, 1954*

The top-secret timedrive XRC, experimental model for a fleet of sensational new spaceships ticketed for Space Patrol service, falls into the hands of interplanetary gangsters. After taking Carol hostage, the ruthless Gart Stanger forces Happy to take him aboard the new ship and pilot him back through space and time to Earth in the year 1954. There, Stanger intends to construct duplicates of the XRC with which he will equip his henchmen when he returns to the 30th century. Unfortunately, the pair arrives on Earth to find themselves imminent targets for an atomic bomb test.

Col. Henderson. . . . . Paul Cavanaugh
Gart Stanger. . . . . George Baxter
Gregory . . . . Bill Haade
Sgt. Novak. . . . . Richard Thorne

#193 *"The Space Patrol, the Army, and the Atom Bomb" or "The Atom Bomb" October 30, 1954*

While the top brass at the military base in New Mexico are discussing why the atom bomb test did not go off on schedule, Buzz and Hap conceal the XRC in a livery stable. Meanwhile, Stanger and his accomplice, Gregory, disguised as military police officers, plan to steal the powerful new space cruiser. They blast off, hoping to locate the XRC from the air. Realizing that the villains will probably send a missile down, hit the atom bomb, and blow everyone up, Buzz sets off the bomb while he, Hap and the ground forces are safe in the shelter house. The villains fly through a deadly radioactive cloud and must land to seek medical attention.

Col. Henderson. . . . . Paul Cavanaugh
Gart Stanger. . . . . George Baxter
Gregory . . . . Bill Haade
Lt. Marshall . . . . Maury Hill
Sgt. Novak . . . . Russell Whitney

#194 *"Danger: Radiation" November 6, 1954*

Contaminated with a lethal dose of radioactivity from an atomic bomb, Stanger and Gregory seek aid from a small-town doctor on 20th-century Earth. Buzz and Happy track the villains to the doctor's office, but now they, too, are contaminated and face death from radiation poisoning.

Gart Stanger . . . . George D. Baxter
Gregory . . . . Bill Haade
Dr. Paul Yates . . . . Peter Hansen
Fern [nurse] . . . . Jean Howell

#195 *"The Exploding Stars" November 13, 1954*

Buzz and Happy are summoned by Dr. Van Meter from a new type of observatory stationed in outer space to halt the imminent explosions of a series of stars near the solar system. All indicators point to an organized pattern of destruction in a path that leads straight to the United Planets. The pattern indicates that the sun will be the next to go.

Dr. Van Meter. . . . . Rudolph Anders

#196 *"Dwellers of the Prime Galaxy" November 20, 1954*

Buzz and Happy venture into deep space to learn what's causing the explosions of suns near the solar system. They discover that a race of advanced beings is to blame for the deliberate pattern of exploding stars and are captured by one of them, Ahyo— an alien who shoots his foes to the ceiling with a gravity-inverter, then knocks them cold by dropping them to the floor.

Ahyo . . . . Tom McKee

#197 *"Terra, the Doomed Planet" November 27, 1954*

Ahyo, the super-intelligent alien whose mission is to destroy the entire galaxy, employs his advanced knowledge of force fields to deal a crushing blow to Buzz's battlecruiser and capture Buzz, Hap and Robbie. Holding the Space Patrollers helpless in a force field aboard his ship, Ahyo activates his deadly Sphere, which "force rams" the planet Terra, triggering floods and fires. But Ahyo's advanced weapons prove worthless against the fury of Buzz's fists

when the alien attempts to destroy the solar system by making Terra collide with the sun.
Ahyo . . . . Tom McKee
Sec. General . . . . Hal Forrest

#198 "Revenge of the Black Falcon" December 4, 1954

Prince Baccarratti, false pretender to the throne of Venus, once again returns to haunt his foe, Buzz Corry. Thought to be on the road to rehabilitation with the use of the Braino-graph, the evil prince springs a trap which sends Buzz and Hap back to 17th-century Salem to be burned at the stake for the crime of witchcraft.
Prince Baccarratti . . . . Bela Kovacs
Barti . . . . Bill Baldwin
Ezekial Martin . . . . Oliver Blake
Josiah . . . . Jack Brown
Goodwife Martin . . . . Gail Bonney

#199 "Sorcerers from Outer Space" December 11, 1954

Having been shanghaied by Prince Bac-carratti to 17th-century America, Buzz and Happy continue to outwit the superstitious colonists, who think they are sorcerers and want to burn them at the stake. But Baccarratti falls under suspicion, too — and he's dependent on the Space Patrollers to rescue him from the angry mob.
Prince Baccarratti . . . . Bela Kovacs
Barti . . . . Bill Baldwin
Ezekial Martin . . . . Oliver Blake
Josiah . . . . Jack Brown
Goodwife Martin . . . . Gail Bonney

#200 "Baccarratti and Black Magic" or "The Defeat of Baccarratti" December 18 1954

After recapturing Prince Baccarratti and his pal, Barti, Buzz and Happy have one more task to complete before returning to the 30th century. Goodwife Martin, a woman who helped Buzz and Happy, has been accused of witchcraft by her own husband and son. Some-how the Space Patrolmen must save the woman from death before they return to their own timeline. The two comrades take a drastic step to clear her — only to find that through an over-sight they may spend the rest of their lives trapped in the 17th century.

Prince Baccarratti . . . . Bela Kovacs
Barti . . . . Bill Baldwin
Ezekial Martin . . . . Oliver Blake
Josiah . . . . Jack Brown
Goodwife Martin . . . . Gail Bonney

#201 "A Christmas Present for Happy" December 25, 1954

Christmas on the planet Terra is a dismal date for Happy. He has good reason to think that he has not a friend in the universe until some special people from Earth, Happy's native planet, arrive and make Christmas a joyous occasion and a day to remember for the young cadet.
Bill Osborn. . . . . Charles Calvert
Bess Osborn . . . . Jean Inness

1955

#202 "Lair of the Space Spider" January 1, 1955

A search for a vanished spaceship leads Buzz, Happy and Robbie into the clutches of Arachna, the Space Spider. Arachna is the mer-ciless human ruler of a doughnut-shaped planet who kidnaps space travelers, capturing them in a web of force rays. He puts his pris-oners to work at slave labor and turns their ships into raw materials for the construction of his escape-proof domain.
Arachna . . . . Kurt Katch
Guard #1. . . . . Joel Smith
Guard #2. . . . . Phil Sutton
2 extras. . . . . . . Norbert Schiller, Bela Kovacs

#203 "The Web of Arachna" January 8, 1955

Having escaped once from Arachna's clutches, Buzz, Happy and Robbie employ clever deception and the help of a fugitive from Arachna's slave ranks to bluff their way back into the villainous Space Spider's lair and free his prisoners. But Arachna sees through Buzz's disguise as an old prospector and captures him again.
Arachna . . . . Kurt Katch
Guard #1. . . . . Joel Smith
Man . . . . Charles Victor

#204 *"Collapse of the Spider's Web"*
January 15, 1955

Buzz learns the secret of Arachna's invisible "web": He's been using an artificial gravity-booster to trap unsuspecting space travelers. As Robbie and Hap deal with the Space Spider's debilitated prisoners, Buzz pursues Arachna, who has escaped with a block of Neutronium — essential to the stability of the planet. As the doughnut-shaped ring grows increasingly unstable, Buzz orders a reluctant Robbie and Hap to blast off, leaving him behind to capture Arachna and escape — if there's time — in the villain's space car.
Arachna . . . . Kurt Katch
Woman. . . . . Valerie Bales
3 extras. . . . Howard Culver, Jerome Sheldon,
Bela Kovacs

#205 *"The Androids of Algol"*
January 22, 1955

Raymo and Yula inhabit a barren planet in the star system Algol, but the couple is busy. They're fashioning lifelike duplicates of key United Planets officials out of jelly-like protoplasm so they can take over the government with these puppets or "androids." They capture Buzz and create a duplicate of him, then send his robot-like twin back to Terra to command the Space Patrol as their secret puppet.
Raymo . . . . Larry Dobkin
Yula . . . . Valerie Bales
Secretary General . . . . Paul Cavanaugh
Android . . . . Joel Smith

#206 *"Double Trouble"*
January 29, 1955

Yula and Raymo trap Buzz and Hap behind an electric barrier in their hideout, rendering them helpless to prevent their manufacture of androids and scheme to take over the United Planets. Buzz wracks his brain for a way to break through the deadly barrier and get back to Terra, where androids are rapidly taking over the government.
Sec. General . . . . Paul Cavanaugh
Yula . . . . Valerie Bales
Raymo . . . . Larry Dobkin
Sec. of Interplanetary Relations . Pierce Lyden
Sec. of Communications. . . . George Douglas

#207 *"The Android Invasion"*
February 5, 1955

Terra City, capital of the United Planets, is thrown into an uproar by the androids planted in key government posts by Raymo and Yula. Meanwhile, Buzz and Hap have returned to the city, where an android duplicate of the secretary general promptly orders Major Robertson to arrest them for "treason." As they battle to regain control of the government, Buzz, Robbie, and the secretary general come face to face with their own android counterparts.
Sec. General . . . . Paul Cavanaugh
Yula . . . . Valerie Bales
2 Guards. . . . . Bela Kovacs, Lloyd Nelson

#208 *"The Wild Men of Procyon"*
February 12, 1955

When Buzz, Happy, Robbie and Carol land the *Terra V* on a planet that has been scorched by atomic war, they are given a savage greeting by the two remaining members of the planet's demolished civilization. These sole survivors of nations that have committed atomic suicide have been converted into maniacs by the desolation that surrounds them, and they are determined to destroy the Space Patrol crew and escape on the *Terra V* to a better world.
The General . . . . Bert Holland
Corporal. . . . . Charles Horvath

#209 *"Marooned on Procyon Four"*
February 19, 1955

The general and the corporal, two crazed survivors of a devastating atomic war, take Robbie and Carol prisoner and continue their efforts to hijack the *Terra V* and escape the planet. The general, skilled in military strategy, proves a worthy opponent for Buzz.
The General . . . . Bert Holland
Corporal. . . . . Charles Horvath

#210 *"The Atomic Vault"*
February 26, 1955

The mysterious disappearance of Happy and Carol prevents the Space Patrollers from blasting off from the desolate Procyon IV. Buzz and Robbie discover the pair has been kidnapped by Menzo and Rayzo, two soldiers from the enemy forces that destroyed the planet. The men have returned to search the ruins for a microtape containing the valuable Duration Formula. Robbie and Buzz are captured, too—and Buzz risks a deadly overdose of radiation to free his comrades.

Rayzo . . . . Robert Boon
Menzo . . . . Bela Kovacs

Appendix 3
Major Chuck's Space Patrol Radio Episode Log

by Charles S. Lassen
United Planets Space Patrol (Retired)[1]

10/25/52 — The Hole in Empty Space. *Premiums/Spots:* Space-o-Phones, Blood Boosters. The Cycloplex, a force intruding from another dimension, threatens the solar system, prompting Buzz and Happy to rescue Professor Jelka from the space observatory orbiting Saturn. The concept of a black hole is introduced, and the Brainograph makes an appearance. Superconductivity of material at extremely low temperatures plays a role in destroying the Cycloplex. Buzz Corry: Ed Kemmer, Cadet Happy: Lyn Osborn,[2] Major Robertson: Ken Mayer, Prof. Jelka: Bela Kovacs, Lt. Grayson: Norman Jolley.

11/8/52 — The City of the Sun. *Premiums/Spots:* Space-o-Phones, Blood Boosters. A huge mobile atomic drilling machine runs amok on the planet Mercury while Buzz and Happy search for Prof. Mallison, whose spaceship disappeared on the dark side of the planet. Solaria Base is endangered by a mysterious disruption in its water supply. Burdock: Bela Kovacs, Prof. Mallison: Ken Mayer, Henchman: Norman Jolley.

11/15/52 — The Queen of Space. *Premiums/Spots:* Space-o-Phones (Time is "*really* running out!*"), Blood Boosters. A power-hungry woman who owns a transorbital shipping company destroys her competition in the Uranus/Neptune/Pluto space lanes. Buzz sends Tonga off to Neptune as an undercover investigator disguised as a journalist. Tonga is kidnapped and held hostage; Buzz and Happy rocket to the rescue. Tonga: Nina Bara, Jelna Fanton: Virginia Hewitt, Brox Cardo: Norman Jolley.

11/22/52 — The Giant Bubble. *Premiums/Spots:* Space-o-Phones. ("Positively the *last time!*") Unidentified space-o-phone signals from Saturn puzzle Corry and his cadet. Dr. Berman invents the electroplast system for constructing atmosphere shells to enclose Space Patrol bases on airless worlds, which prompts sabotage and thievery from some unsavory space crawlers. Next week: "Buzz and Happy come across a huge expanse of tiny green plants on Mars, CRAPETTING the desert for miles!" (Well, that's what announcer Dick Tufeld said!) Dr. Berman: Norman Jolley, Colgar: Bela Kovacs, Drovic: Ken Mayer.

11/29/52 — The Electronic Burglar. *Premiums/Spots:* Blood Boosters. A major electronic

---

[1]"Major" Chuck Lassen has logged the shows available on CD, and William F. Drish, Jr., has added some hard-to-find episodes from his private (taped) collection. According to collector Jerry Haendiges, at least 129 radio shows were transcribed; radio historian David Goldin puts the number at 166 (see www.radiogoldindex.com). Some of these shows survive because they were dubbed from broadcasts over the Armed Forces Radio Service to troops in Korea. In these episodes, cast credits were deleted, resulting in some confusion over who played what part. Norman Jolley and Ken Mayer appear in nearly every show, sometimes (notes Lassen) disguising their voices so well that it's hard to tell who's who. Occasionally, Jolley and Mayer switch characters from one week to the next or play two characters in the same episode.—JNB

[2]Kemmer and Osborn appear in every show.

R & D firm is burglarized, and a valuable device used for detecting underground mineral deposits is stolen. Corry and Happy are marooned on the Martian desert with one of the thieves and suffer the effects of poisonous plant spores. Bela Kovacs "hams it up" in fine form as a cowardly crook. Marist: Norman Jolley, Boucher: Bela Kovacs, Stokes: Ken Mayer.

12/6/52 — The Space Shark. *Premiums/ Spots:* Blood Boosters. Buzz and Happy infiltrate a hydroponics farm on Venus to rescue undercover agent Tonga, who has identified blackmailers bribing farm workers to poison the chemically-grown crops. An accurate educational description of Saturn's rings is somewhat compromised by the *Terra V*'s three and one-half hour trip from Saturn to Venus. Tonga: Nina Bara, Baxter: Ken Mayer, Agle: Bela Kovacs.

12/13/52 — The Search for Asteroid X. *Premiums/Spots:* Blood Boosters, Christmas Seals. An organized crime syndicate on Saturn victimizes businessmen operating in the outer planet regions. Posing as Space Patrol agents, Chura and Hundley accidentally leave a stolen Space Patrol evidence microfilm at the solitary Martian outpost of a prospector, Marty Noonan. Happy flies an atmosphere ship to Noonan's isolated dwelling on the plains of Mars to retrieve the microfilm and gets shanghaied by the racketeers trying to repossess the evidence. Buzz flies the *Terra V* to Ganymede to rescue Happy and reclaim the microfilm, now stashed on Asteroid X. Steve Chura: Bela Kovacs, Wally Hundley: Ken Mayer, Marty Noonan: Norman Jolley.

12/20/52 — The Lady from Venus. *Premiums/Spots:* Blood Boosters. A woman extorts illegal shipments of plutonium from an authorized atomic reactor plant manager on Venus. Buzz and Happy are doused with dangerous sodium-potassium coolant as the villainess and her partner attempt to elude capture. Edward Stratton: Ken Mayer, Elsie Bennett: Virginia Hewitt, Ivan Elvin: Bela Kovacs.

12/27/52 — The Last Voyage of the *Lonesome Lena*. *Premiums/Spots:* Blood Boosters. A callium-seed-chewing, grizzled old space captain deals in black market processed food and antibiotics using his ancient cargo ship based on Saturn's moon, Titan. Tonga uncovers a plot to tunnel into a Uranium mine to steal ore, and Buzz and Happy are nearly drowned in the mine when the crooks reverse the scavenger pumps. The medically-grounded Captain

Kruger saves the day with his condemned ship, the *Lonesome Lena*. Tonga: Nina Bara, Gustav Kruger: Marvin Miller, Sherwin McKurdy: Norman Jolley.

1/3/53 — The Brain Bank and the Space Binoculars. *Premiums/Spots:* Space Binoculars. The evil director of a conglomerate technology firm, John Kroser, attempts to force a brilliant professor to continue his work in opposition to his doctor's order to retire. A plot to put the professor's brain in suspended animation ensues. Meanwhile, Buzz and Happy work several not-too-subtle commercials for the Ralston "Space Binoculars" into the plot. The Commander chases down Kroser's ship in the *Terra V* and rescues the "suspended" Prof. Hegman in the nick of time — after he's been deep-sixed into space. Erla Becker: Virginia Hewitt, Professor Hegman: Bela Kovacs, John Kroser: Ken Mayer.

1/10/53 — The Sleepwalker. *Premiums/ Spots:* Space Binoculars. Interplanetary Transport Control, Neptune Base, reports an overdue spaceship. The passengers and crew have been mysteriously put to sleep by a thieving space construction contractor. Looks like the work of "The Sleepwalker," the crook who had been stealing plant payrolls by knocking out the workers. Carol has been kidnapped from the passenger ship — Buzz and Happy rocket off to the rescue, and are nearly done in by an ultrasonic paralyzing ray! Ron Morgan: Ken Mayer, Woody Knorr: Bela Kovacs, Carol Carlisle: Virginia Hewitt.

1/24/53 — The Scavenger of Space. *Premiums/Spots:* Space Binoculars. ("Limited time!") The brother of the owner of a metal and chemical reclaiming company in Lowell City on Mars steals sensitive documents to give business a boost. Buzz and Happy hit the trail to track down the thieves. Larry MacRae: Norman Jolley, Carlyle MacRae: Ken Mayer, Donald Hall: Bela Kovacs.

1/31/53 — The Top-Secret D-Ray. *Premiums/Spots:* Space Binoculars. ("Offer ends soon, so don't miss out!") Corry and Happy visit the Lunar Fleet Base for a visitors' week "open house." Tonga discovers a security breach of the top-secret D-Ray design at the base, and the search is on for the stolen microfilm! She personally reviews all photos carried by passengers leaving the spaceport: "So, are these pictures of your family, Mr. Morgan?" (And we thought 21st-century airport security was a pain.) The microfilm thieves escape to Venus

City with the plans, and are found by Tonga, whom they promptly "bag" in the cellar of a downtown skyscraper! Tonga: Nina Bara, Bob Morgan: Ken Mayer, Art Robertson: Norman Jolley.

2/7/53 — Crash Landing. *Premiums/Spots:* Space Binoculars. ("They stand out from your eyes 3.5 inches! Offer may be withdrawn at any time!!!") Boy Scouts of America. Buzz and Happy devise a daring and dangerous plan to rescue Carol, who is being held by criminals in the hills of Mars. Their entrance is made by subtly staging a crash landing of their spaceship. A Stimutron, a rare medical device used for treating Venus Fever, has been stolen, setting the stage for the Martian rescue. Bela Kovacs gives a priceless performance as a victim of Venus Fever. Don Veo: Bela Kovacs, Bob Henry: Ken Mayer, Carol Carlisle: Virginia Hewitt.

2/14/53 — The Mysterious Meteor. *Premiums/Spots:* Space Binoculars. During a meteor shower, Buzz and Happy observe a meteor hit near New Arcadia City, Arizona, a fertile farmland recently created from desert wasteland. The characteristics of the meteorite lead to a description of the possible existence of anti-matter, a painless science lesson for young listeners. Bela Kovacs, usually cast as a villain, plays a rare role as a "good guy." Major Robertson: Ken Mayer, Prof. James King: Bela Kovacs, Phil Craig: Norman Jolley.

2/21/53 — The Moon Beetles. *Premiums/Spots:* Space Binoculars. ("Last chance!") The competing *Tom Corbett* space goggles are slammed in this commercial: "These are NOT flimsy goggles!" On Jupiter, Commander Corry, Major Robertson and Cadet Happy are endangered by swarms of strange insects that cover the atmosphere dome of a research station, threatening to destroy it. The Space Patrollers try their hand at exterminating the critters. (Fortunately, no complaints are received from environmentalists.) Another "good guy" role for Bela. Major Robertson: Ken Mayer, Dr. Conrad: Bela Kovacs.

2/28/53 — The Strange Gift of the New Star. A peculiar object has been detected far beyond the orbit of Pluto, approaching the commercial space lanes. Buzz and Happy discover it to be an old, disabled spaceship with a lone survivor, drifting back from uncharted regions of space. A million credits worth of stolen uranium is found on board, and the Space Patrollers try to unravel the mystery of the missing ship's owner and the survivor, who had previously been reported murdered. Wes Pence: Bela Kovacs, Joe O'Malley: Ken Mayer.

3/7/53 — The Seed Crystals of Zeldebran. Animosity brews among the crew of a communications relay space station orbiting Saturn. Invading beings from Zeldebran, in another universe, use telepathic communications via meteorite crystals to coerce two of the space station crew members to guide the hostile Zeldebran ships to the solar system. Buzz and Happy fall under the power of the crystals, and struggle to resist the alien orders to destroy themselves. Kohlmar: Bela Kovacs, Jack Perkins: Norman Jolley, Major Robertson: Ken Mayer.

3/13/53 — The Magic Space Pictures. *Premiums/Spots:* Magic Space Patrol Space Pictures, in new packages of Chex with pictures of Buzz or Happy on the front. Corry tests an experimental rocketship, the XR5-1, containing top-secret equipment while Happy goes to school to learn how to use the Magic Space Pictures and control the XR5-1 telepathically. The chase is on when an impostor steals some of the telepathic control devices and rockets off to his planetoid hideout. Todd Barrett: Norman Jolley, Juro Vanek: Bela Kovacs.

3/21/53 — The Caverns of Venus. *Premiums/Spots:* Magic Space Pictures. ("Yessir, gang, there's 24 different pictures!") Working undercover, Tonga investigates the theft of valuable materials on Mars. Buzz and Happy are trapped aboard the criminals' robot rocketship, stocked up with the stolen goods. Upon reaching Venus, the Space Patrollers are captured and held in the underground mine storage facilities of the crime ring. Buzz and Happy escape in a magnetically powered tunnel car. (Shades of Flash Gordon!) Tonga: Nina Bara, Morton: Ken Mayer, Dratcher: Bela Kovacs.

3/28/53 — The Forgotten City. *Premiums/Spots:* Magic Space Pictures. On the planet Saturn, Buzz and Happy, searching for a missing scientist, find a deserted city filled with old and precious gems — and a modern vaccine for space sickness. Best lines: Kemmer: "Hold your fire! We're Space Patrolmen!" Kovacs: "That's why I'm shooting!" Shefka: Bela Kovacs, Arlana Lubeck: Virginia Hewitt.

4/25/53 — The Prisoners of Pluto. *Premiums/Spots:* Project-O-Scope: Film strips include "Mighty Meteor," "Space Pirates," "Men from Mars," and "Robot Invasion." The Project-O-Scope proves to be an invaluable rescue tool for a stranded professor who crash-landed on Pluto. Corry homes in on its signal light to track down Prof. Walker, imprisoned in a cave hideout by Hagle, an habitual criminal. Most of this program is a not-too-subtle commercial for the "Project-O-Scope" premium, very rare and valuable to 21st-century collectors. Prof. Malcolm Walker: Norman Jolley, Hagle: Bela Kovacs, Rorman: Ken Mayer.

5/2/53 — The Venus Space Factory. *Premiums/Spots:* Space Binoculars. Space factories, privately owned, orbit Venus. A Space Patrol inspector invests a substantial amount in the business dealings of a factory owner and gets into a bad loan deal trying to recoup his losses. The orbiting factory is found to have safety deficiencies. Apparently, OSHA has survived into the 30th century! (A rather boring plot for ten-year-old kids.) Trowbridge: Bela Kovacs, Curtis: Ken Mayer.

5/9/53 — The Cosmic Ray Detector. *Premiums/Spots:* Project-O-Scope. Jewel smugglers attempt to evade detection by the Space Patrol. They slip the jewels into the unwitting Carol's luggage as she checks into a commercial spaceship. When Carol opens her luggage and finds the necklace made of special "ray detector crystals," she assumes they are a gift from her father, the secretary general of the United Planets, and walks off wearing them in Jupiter City. The smugglers freak out and try to get them back. Carol Carlisle: Virginia Hewitt, Dolf Rambo: Ken Mayer, Burton Hensley: Bela Kovacs.

5/16/53 — The Secret of Sublevel 7. *Premiums/Spots:* Magic Space Pictures, Project-O-Scope. Ralston Rocket will be in Dayton and Columbus, OH, and Baltimore, MD, next week! On Terra, an exhibition of new improvements in spaceship equipment and household devices draws huge crowds to the Hall of Science. There, Happy receives a tip about a massive plutonium heist from a reactor plant on Jupiter's third moon. Investigating the lead, Buzz and Happy travel to the crooks' hideout in the tunnels beneath Saturn City. The thieves reverse the ventilation fans, drawing the planet's deadly methane atmosphere into the tunnel system, and threaten to blow up the entire city. Victor Drummond: Bela Kovacs, Edmund Vogel: Ken Mayer.

5/23/53 — Treachery in Outer Space. *Premiums/Spots:* Magic Space Pictures; Project-O-Scope. Ralston Rocket coming to Columbus and Dayton, OH, and Wilkes-Barre, PA, next week! On a diplomatic mission to meet with the governor of Jupiter, the Space Patrollers change course to investigate reports of a bandit spaceship operating around the Jovian moons. Flying a private cruiser, Corry is mistaken for one of the pirates and is torpedoed by a double-crossing crook. Loring: Norman Jolley, Scranner: Ken Mayer, Rackman: Bela Kovacs.

5/30/53 — The Immortal Brain. *Premiums/Spots:* "Last day to order your Project-O-Scope!" With amazing foresight, writer Lou Huston predicts the application of *electronic computers* to the technology and economics of the 30th century. Portable electronic check writers are also predicted. (Lou envisioned today's handheld computers in 1953!) This episode is an outstanding example of a great writer's intuitive imagining of things that became reality in the 21st century. Anton McDermott, running "Future, Inc." in Venus City, has scanned his late father's financial acumen (using Brainograph records) into a supercomputer and is using the data to benefit unethical investors. McDermott plots to destroy the main Space Patrol computer on Terra to gain a monopoly on crucial economic theories. Meanwhile, the misguided super-computer that has been programmed with his father's intelligence prompts McDermott to "cancel" Buzz Corry, whom it believes to be a threat to its survival. Anton McDermott: Ken Mayer, Mr. Fergus: Bela Kovacs.

6/20/53 — The Indestructible Germ. *Premiums/Spots:* Magic Space Pictures — 24, all different, in packages of Chex. Ralston Rocket will be in Boston and Louisville next week. In the city of Euphoria on Venus, illness has been unknown — until now, when citizens are beginning to feel a strange weakness. The Space Patrol investigates medical security and finds that jealous scientists have engineered a deadly bacteria, blaming it on an upstanding doctor. Waiting for an epidemic to develop, they plan to take credit for discovering a cure. Miss Kraven: Virginia Hewitt, Mondo Skarn: Bela Kovacs, Lyle Vosper: Ken Mayer.

6/27/53 — The Treasure of Planetoid 60. *Premiums/Spots:* Space Patrol Microscope. ("The lens tube is not cheap cardboard — it's REAL PLASTIC!") Ralston Rocket visits four cities next week! Transplutite, a rare gem containing radioactive Arcturium, suddenly appears on Neptune, and Buzz and Happy investigate the possibility of museum theft. Writer Lou Huston hits right on with another prediction in this episode: Buzz and Happy remove the "vector computer" from the crooks' spaceship, which contains navigation information from their last flight. Huston foresaw today's "black boxes" on commercial aircraft! Frank Rupp: Norman Jolley, Kent Corpo: Ken Mayer.

8/1/53 — The Sleeping Demon of Saturn. *Premiums/Spots:* Magic Space Pictures; Space Patrol Microscope. ("Insects look like men from Mars!") Solid plastic lens, optically ground! (Yeah, right!) *Woman's Day* magazine for August contains plans for making *Space Patrol* helmets! (*Captain Video* helmets, too!) A quake occurs on Mercury, exactly as predicted eight years before. Quake expert Dr. Ramsey insists that a similar disaster is unlikely in Keppler City on Saturn. But criminals force Ramsey to falsely predict quakes from the dormant Sleeping Demon volcano in the area, creating panic selling of spaceships and other assets upon which the crooks plan to profit. Tonga: Nina Bara, Gresham: Ken Mayer.

8/8/53 — Trouble Aboard the Supernova. *Premiums/Spots:* Magic Space Picture; Space Patrol Microscope. Industrial research firm SolarTechnic provides technical innovations and humanitarian benefits to the solar system. Tracking down vital process documents, stolen from SolarTechnic and hidden as microfilmed copies in a ring with a secret compartment, Buzz and Happy end up in a waste disposal chute aboard the Luxury Space Liner *Supernova*, where at any moment they may be dumped into space! Clarence Wobat: Bela Kovacs, Greyson: Ken Mayer.

8/15/53 — Peril Over Jupiter. *Premiums/Spots:* Microscope. ("Last time we can make this offer!") A woman inherits a lucrative metal processing plant on a Jupiter moon and is victimized by two extortionists, who threaten to sabotage the plant and take her life. Corry and Happy brave Endurium beams and magnetic force fields as they investigate the woman's kidnapping. Carla Markim: Virginia Hewitt, Nelson Sprague: Norman Jolley, Duke Dortsch: Ken Mayer.

8/22/53 — The Menace of Planet X. *Premiums/Spots:* "Space Talk" definitions by Dick Tufeld. This is the first in the "Planet X" series, in which Buzz Corry battles his archenemy, Prince Baccarratti, for 16 consecutive episodes. Dinosaurs abound and threaten Commander Corry and Cadet Happy as they explore this hostile, gigantic planet. Priority: investigate the strange disappearances of spaceships in the proximity of the planet. Self-imposed ruler Prince Baccarratti (the "Black Falcon") orchestrates general mayhem for the United Planets from his castle fortress. Prince Baccarratti: Bela Kovacs, Dr. Malengro: Norman Jolley, Others: Ken Mayer, Steven Robertson.

8/29/53 — The Trap on Planet X. *Premiums/Spots:* More "Space Talk." Buzz and Happy plan to infiltrate Baccarratti's stronghold on Planet X to free his captive laborers and thwart his agenda to enslave the United Planets. They wind up imprisoned in Baccarratti's dungeon, where they befriend the giant native "Goro," who helps them escape. Prince Baccarratti: Bela Kovacs, Dr. Malengro: Norman Jolley, Goro: Ken Mayer.

9/5/53 — The Valley of Dread. Robot spaceships disguised as meteorites are sent to map Planet X with their viewscopes. The Space Patrollers tangle with man-eating plants after Baccarratti bombs their armored tank. Prince Baccarratti: Bela Kovacs, Dr. Malengro: Norman Jolley, Captain Jecker: Ken Mayer.

9/12/53 — Escape from Planet X. Prince Baccarratti has been captured by Commander Corry and is being held in his own prison camp, where he had forced 130 captives to work in the Arctite mines. Corry prepares to return the captives to their home worlds, but Baccarratti's henchmen try to thwart Buzz's plans. Prince Baccarratti: Bela Kovacs, Dr. Malengro: Norman Jolley.

9/19/53 — The Spies from Planet X. *Premiums/Spots:* A fighter pilot describes his F-86 Sabre Jet in a cereal commercial. Buzz and Happy travel to Saturn on a tip that Baccarratti has been sighted there. His recent business dealings with Zachra Trading Company are investigated, along with a man who claims to be Baccarratti's cousin from Neptune. Prince Baccarratti: Bela Kovacs, Dr. Malengro: Norman Jolley, Mr. Benson: Ken Mayer.

9/26/53 — Target: Jupiter. Corry subjects the captured Malengro to a Brainograph test to learn what Baccarratti might be up to next. Baccarratti threatens to destroy the man-made planet Terra with a missile to gain Malengro's release. Corry complies — but then Baccarratti proceeds with plans to launch a major attack on Jupiter's cities, using missiles wrapped in "radar foil," which makes them invisible to tracking systems. (Writer Lou Huston had predicted our current "stealth aircraft" technology — 50 years before it came to be!) Prince Baccarratti: Bela Kovacs, Dr.

Malengro: Norman Jolley, Major Robertson: Ken Mayer.

10/3/53 — Rescue from Planet X. *Premiums/Spots:* Initial announcement of the Ralston Rocket giveaway contest! 10,000 lbs and 35 feet long, with a truck to pull it! Plus $1500 in cash for Dad to buy gasoline! Baccarratti's camouflaged launching base on Jupiter's moon #4 is blasted into rubble by the Space Patrol after missiles are launched at two key cities on Jupiter. Searching for survivors, Buzz and Happy find Malengro and Baccarratti hiding in an underground fortification. Prince Baccarratti: Bela Kovacs, Dr. Malengro: Norman Jolley, Major Robertson: Ken Mayer, Carol: Virginia Hewitt.

10/10/53 — On the Icecap of Planet X. *Premiums/Spots:* "Get your space coins at the Weather-Bird Shoe Store, along with the official entry blank to enter the Name the Planet Contest." Granu, a huge giant native of Planet X, befriends Buzz and Happy, and helps them escape captivity in the frozen Endurium mines beneath the polar icecap of Planet X. Prince Baccarratti: Bela Kovacs, Dr. Malengro: Norman Jolley.

10/17/53 — Rescue from Planet X. *Premiums/Spots:* More about Name the Planet Contest. Buzz forces the captured Baccarratti to escort him past the defenses, into the castle stronghold, where they encounter a race of non-corporeal, thought-projecting aliens. Prince Baccarratti: Bela Kovacs, Dr. Malengro: Norman Jolley.

10/24/53 — The Secret of the Dargo Ruins. *Premiums/Spots:* More "Ralston Rocket Name the Planet" contest info. (The Ralston Rocket is a worthless pile of scrap today, but those third-prize Autosonic Rifles are $1500 collector items!) The mysterious alien, Ortho, guides Buzz and Happy to a desert landing on Planet X via telepathic communication. The usual confrontation with Baccarratti and his henchmen is inevitable. Prince Baccarratti: Bela Kovacs, Dr. Malengro: Norman Jolley, Major Robertson: Ken Mayer.

10/31/53 — Iron Eaters of Planet X. *Premiums/Spots:* Name the Planet Contest continues. An imaginative episode, featuring giant worms that eat through spaceship hulls! Prince Baccarratti: Bela Kovacs, Dr. Malengro: Norman Jolley.

11/7/53 — Cyclone in Outer Space. *Premiums/Spots:* Name the Planet Contest continues. Buzz and Hap pursue the evil Prince while Dr.

Malengro invents a new weapon, the Torque Ray, which twists matter like a cyclone at the speed of light. Baccarratti soon becomes the "Torque of the Town." Prince Baccarratti: Bela Kovacs, Dr. Malengro: Norman Jolley.

11/14/53 — Under the Sea of Planet X. *Premiums/Spots:* Name the Planet Contest continues. Weather-Bird Shoes co-sponsors the Ralston Rocket giveaway. A mysterious distress signal from Planet X and an ancient jeweled medallion set the stage for this adventure. Baccarratti threatens to destroy a civilization of primitive cliff dwellers in his quest for the source of the medallion jewels. Prince Baccarratti: Bela Kovacs, Dr. Malengro: Norman Jolley.

11/21/53 — Sea Monster of Planet X. *Premiums/Spots:* Name the Planet Contest continues. In a continuation of the previous episode, Buzz and Happy's submarine is pursued by Baccarratti's atmosphere ship. Prince Baccarratti: Bela Kovacs, Dr. Malengro: Norman Jolley.

11/28/53 — The Revolt of the Space Rats. *Premiums/Spots:* Name the Planet Contest winds up. Transporting the captive Baccarratti and Dr. Malengro back to Terra for rehabilitation, Buzz and Happy take time to rescue an ill space prospector on the third moon of Pluto. Malengro, under the ruse of treating the space fever victim, overpowers Cadet Happy and captures Buzz and the prospector's partner, Skiller. Baccarratti heads back to Planet X with Buzz, where he plots to destroy Pluto City and its Space Patrol base, leaving Happy marooned on Pluto's moon. Prince Baccarratti: Bela Kovacs, Dr. Malengro: Norman Jolley, Pete Skiller: Ken Mayer.

12/05/53 — Baccarratti's Secret Weapon. *Premiums/Spots:* Space Coins. Baccarratti turns a scientist's invention into deadly weapons to destroy ten major cities throughout the United Planets. Fearing for his daughter's life, famed scientist Dr. Crocken is blackmailed into providing material to arm the bombs. Prince Baccarratti: Bela Kovacs, Dr. Malengro: Norman Jolley, Dr. Croken: Steven Robertson.

12/12/53 — The Lost Condor. *Premiums/Spots:* Space Coins. An ex-criminal, Don Blake, reformed by the Brainograph, is coerced to turn over his diary with details of his crimes to a corrupt official, criminal mastermind Reese *Corbett*(!). Stubby Sykes, mechanic and owner of the old spaceship *Condor*, leads Buzz to the site of a wrecked ship on Saturn's fifth moon, where they recover millions of space credits stolen in a complex scheme engineered by Corbett. Blake: Joe Penson, Reese Corbett: Ken Mayer, Sykes: Steven Robertson.

12/19/53 — Venus Tulanium Mystery. *Premiums/Spots:* Space Coins. Deep in the heart of a Venusian jungle, space claim-jumpers kidnap a mining company official in hopes of forcing him to lead them to vast deposits of the valuable ore Tulanium. Buzz and Happy conduct an undercover investigation and find themselves suddenly in grave danger. Frank Michaelson: Ken Mayer.

12/26/53 — The Lost Dimension. *Premiums/Spots:* MonoView Outer Space Helmet, with one-way "strato-viewer." Shyster Boris Gambine uses a scientist's invention to teleport credits out of the Terra City bank. Introducing the "N-Ray"—a transporter beam that relocates people and objects through solid walls and across hyperspace; another creative concept from writer Lou Huston, later forwarded to *Star Trek*. Major Robertson: Ken Mayer, Boris Gambine: Lawrence Dobkin, Mark Duncan: Norman Jolley.

1/2/54 — Wistful Wizard of Neptune's Moon. *Premiums/Spots:* MonoView Outer Space Helmet. The possibility of telekinesis is explored. An unsuspecting theatrical magician is exploited by shady characters who trick him into using his abilities to obtain sensitive materials. Wistful Wilbur Crawford: Bela Kovacs.

1/9/54 — In the Claw of Venus. *Premiums/Spots:* MonoView Outer Space Helmet; Winner of Name the Planet Contest is announced by Commander Corry. Corry searches for 100 pounds of stolen Zolonite (a rare element capable of neutralizing gravity), leading him to the research tower of Gaston Sharn. Bela Kovacs, as lab assistant Durant, gives a comical portrayal of a man with thunderstorm phobia! Later, a disc-shaped UFO hovering over Venus City is investigated by Buzz and Happy. Boarding the UFO, Happy is taken on an unexpected ride. Richard Durant: Bela Kovacs, Gaston Sharn: Ken Mayer.

1/23/54 — Martian Masquerade. *Premiums/Spots:* Last call for Space Helmet! Virginia Hewitt plays a dual role as Carol Carlisle and her evil look-alike, Xyla Carmandy. Xyla conspires with her husband to steal secret plans for a new weapon from Captain Halcroft. All ships are grounded while a search is conducted for a woman resembling Carol Carlisle. Carol, posing as Xyla, infiltrates the criminal clique.

Carol/Xyla Carmandy: Virginia Hewitt, Capt. Halcroft: Norman Jolley.

1/30/54 — Treasure of Mt. Rolcab. *Premiums/Spots:* Space Patrol Trading Cards, in Chex boxes. Buzz and Happy go hunting with weapons that "cause no pain" to any animal they may hit! Still, they are shooting and eating the critters at will. A confusing story of claim-jumping and double-crossing ensues. Endacott: Bela Kovacs, Hoke: Norman Jolley.

2/13/54 — Revenge of Dr. Yaeger. *Premiums/Spots:* Space Patrol Trading Cards, in Chex boxes. Lorna Stark, who holds the key to important weapons hidden away for 30 years after the death of the inventor, is kidnapped by an instrument repair technician seeking to steal the inventions, which include the deadly Letha-Ray. Buzz and Happy travel to Dr. Yaeger's hidden castle on Mars to rescue Lorna and thwart the theft of the sinister weapons. Lorna Stark: Virginia Hewitt, Carl Bracker: Ken Mayer, Merton Yost: Norman Jolley.

2/20/54 — Visitor from Galaxy 9. Westfall, head of Planetoid Mineral Corporation, reports the disappearance of Cronin, a mining engineer, to Commander Corry. Cronin was grabbed by a giant robot and taken aboard an intergalactic spaceship operated by the tiny creature Zurbok, a member of the Krawlni race from Galaxy 9, who has been sent on a scouting mission to the United Planets. To save Cronin, Buzz and Happy agree to meet the Krawlni ship on Jupiter's fourth moon. When Cronin fails to appear, Buzz and Happy board the craft, where they learn that Zurbok plans to obtain information on weapons and defenses from them. The giant Krawlni robot seizes Buzz and takes him to an alien Brainograph, where Buzz will be forced to provide vital information that will help the invaders destroy the United Planets! Zurbok: Ken Mayer, Cronin: Norman Jolley, Westfall: Bela Kovacs. [*Summary by Bill Drish*]

2/27/54 — The Serpent of Saturn. *Premiums/Spots:* Rice Chex claimed to make you "a whizzer on rollers." What a mental image! This episode introduces a nifty new weapon, the Black-out Beam. Space Patrol agents are victims of a gang of thugs—they're being beaten and robbed all over the solar system. Buzz and Happy track down the ringleader with help from an informant. Thad Wogen: Norman Jolley, Gargoth: Ken Mayer, Walter Reiner: Bela Kovacs.

3/13/54 — Test for Survival. *Premiums/Spots:* Space Patrol Trading Cards, in Chex boxes. A thousand cadets participate in training simulations. Happy is assigned to a survival testing situation. The Cobra Gang captures Happy, armed only with a harmless training rifle, during the exercise. Buzz goes incognito to infiltrate the gang leadership. Gargoth: Ken Mayer, Steve Hegdorn: Bela Kovacs.

3/20/54 — The Secret of Dr. Borodeck. *Premiums/Spots:* Happy hawks Ry-Krisp and salad recipes. A robot suit proves to be a nifty crime tool, as it allows Gargoth to control the actions of whoever wears it. A wealthy old man is targeted to be swindled out of his fortune via a phony longevity elixir, which is actually deadly poison. Trapped in a robot suit, Happy is controlled like a puppet and forced to attack Corry. Clement Borodeck: Norman Jolley, Andrew Means: Bela Kovacs, Gargoth: Ken Mayer.

3/27/54 — The Zero Ray. *Premiums/Spots:* Space Patrol Trading Cards, in Chex boxes. The Cobra Gang continues to wreak havoc on the Space Patrollers with another unique weapon, the Zero Ray, which projects invisible beams that freeze everything they touch. Corry continues his pursuit of the elusive Gargoth, head of the Cobra Gang. Gargoth: Ken Mayer, Dr. Arnold: Norman Jolley, Ulrich Renssler: Bela Kovacs.

4/3/54 — The Super Brain of Volmer Castro. *Premiums/Spots:* Nestlé is new sponsor, along with Ralston. A new invention, the Cerebrescope, is intended to increase human intelligence, but requires further testing. Castro uses the device to turn himself from an ordinary crook into a super swindler with the help of Blake's errant assistant, Rhoda. Dr. Ernest Blake: Ken Mayer, Volmer Castro: Norman Jolley, Rhoda Nexon: Virginia Hewitt.

4/10/54 — The Test of the XK-3. *Premiums/Spots:* Trading cards. The hunt for Volmer Castro continues, while a race to test a new interplanetary space drive takes priority. Castro plants a stowaway on the robot-controlled XK-3 to sabotage the test. Volmer Castro: Norman Jolley, Grant Halcorn: Ken Mayer.

4/17/54 — The Image of Evil. *Premiums/Spots:* Cosmic Rocket Launcher. (Probably the most disappointing premium of all.) Baccarratti escapes from the Venus Rehabilitation Center. Carrying the premium Cosmic Rocket Launcher into the storyline, Buzz and Happy are test pilots for the real thing. (Apparently, the real prototype worked a lot better than the toy replica.) Baccarratti: Bela Kovacs.

5/8/54 — Captain Hackett's Planetoid. *Premiums/Spots:* Cosmic Rocket Launcher. Captain Hackett, an old space prospector, makes his living mining asteroids and planetoids. Buzz warns him that his planetoid is on an errant orbit and will be blasted by the Space Patrol before it becomes a hazard in the space lanes and ultimately crashes into the sun. Conspiring with Borzack (AKA Baccarratti), Hackett plots to thwart the Space Patrol's plans. Paul Borzack (Baccarratti): Bela Kovacs, Captain Hackett: Ken Mayer.

5/22/54 — The Strange Voyager. *Premiums/Spots:* Last time for Rocket Launcher offer! Buzz and Happy travel to Earth to assist relief operations following an earthquake near the major trade city of Amazonia. A man in a state of suspended animation, believed to be from 1954, is rescued. Harrison: Bela Kovacs.

5/29/54 — The Red Demon of Venus. *Premiums/Spots:* Nestlé's candy bars and Quik chocolate milk powder. A Space Patrol undercover agent's investigation of a criminal gang is interrupted by a deadly spider bite. Coincidentally, the gang leader carries the rare antibodies in his blood that can save the agent's life. A trap is laid for Buzz and Happy as they offer to meet with the criminal for a sample of his blood. Nelson Tenagrew: Ken Mayer, Theodore Rorschat: Bela Kovacs.

6/5/54 — The Mystery of the Masked Martians. *Premiums/Spots:* Man from Mars Totem Head with magic forehead vision, from Nestlé. On Mars, men in strange, primitive masks, armed with spears, hold a girl captive. The script is written to showcase the new premium, the Man from Mars Totem Head. Buzz and Happy search the Martian desert for the kidnappers, who should be pretty easy to spot, wearing those totem heads! (Interesting to note that the Martians speak like the Lone Ranger's sidekick, Tonto. Best line: "Hmmmmm ... heap big noise!") Ed Hicks and Strack: Ken Mayer, Dr. Thana Loring: Virginia Hewitt, Zolton: Bela Kovacs.

6/12/54 — The Tattooed Atom. *Premiums/Spots:* Man from Mars Totem Head. ("You can see out, but no one can see in!") Thinking that missing scientist Gene Satterly might try to contact family or friends in Jupiter City, Buzz and Happy go to the home of his fiancé, where they are overcome by a hidden Fatigue Ray device. Satterly's technique for electronically coding atoms is hidden within a container of ordinary-appearing mercury which is stolen, leading the Space Patrollers on a search and rescue mission. Gene Satterly/Joseph Satterly: Norman Jolley, Polidor: Bela Kovacs, Ed Lorimor: Ken Mayer.

6/19/54 — The Cavern of Fear. *Premiums/Spots:* Man from Mars Totem Head. Buzz and Happy are lured into a supply room in the Terra Hotel by one of Polidor's henchmen, where Corry discovers Polidor's "Detecto-Scope," a system for transmitting his evil presence across vast distances. In a dark cavern on Neptune, Happy is psychologically tormented by Polidor, via the Detecto-Scope. Polidor: Bela Kovacs, Sam Grady: Norman Jolley, Blanchard: Ken Mayer, Pete Vorchek: Ken Mayer.

6/26/54 — Race Against Time. *Premiums/Spots:* Man from Mars Totem Head. A small chemical company supplies Corry with a sample of a new substance, Lumiplex, said to amplify light. An amateur astronomer sabotages Corry's surface car with a hidden Detecto-Scope, and the Commander finally determines the identity of the infamous Polidor. Corry races to Terra to defuse Polidor's Omicron bomb, set to destroy the crucial Communications Center. Neal Channing: Ken Mayer, Rudolf Gannett: Bela Kovacs, Chad Thessig: Steven Robertson, Polidor: Bela Kovacs.

7/3/54 — The Robot of Bor Kenna. *Premiums/Spots:* Man from Mars Totem Head: Last time for this offer! More hi-jinks from Polidor with his Detecto-Scope. Carol is hijacked from a diplomatic mission and imprisoned by Polidor in the castle of Bor Kenna while he plots Corry's demise. Corry disables Polidor's superhuman robot by dumping a can of paint over its head! Carol: Virginia Hewitt, Jedro: Norman Jolley.

7/10/54 — Trial by Terror. *Premiums/Spots:* Real-life military test pilot testimonials for Chex cereals. Buzz and Happy are still chasing Polidor across the Martian desert. (He has eluded them so many times, they should be embarrassed by now.) Meanwhile, a heist at the Zenith Microfilm Lab on Terra nets Polidor's gang two million space credits. Graham Slazer: Norman Jolley, Polidor: Bela Kovacs, Harnung: Ken Mayer.

8/14/54 — The Counterfeit Atom. *Premiums/Spots:* Real-life military test pilot testimonials for Chex cereals. Counterfeit gems take precedence over counterfeit paper money in this episode, because, as it is explained, the gems are not "biodegradable" like paper.

Sounds logical. Edwards: Norman Jolley, James Kent: Ken Mayer, Ferris: Bela Kovacs.

8/21/54 — Formula for Crime. *Premiums/Spots:* Ralston invents the "loud, screaming, annoying commercial" concept on this show. Thanks. "Are you in the market for Jupiter jade? Are you trying to locate a set of Martian silverware? Do you need a pair of horns from a Venus water buffalo?" Step right up, folks…. Unscrupulous traders attract the Space Patrol's attention. Erik Zankar: Bela Kovacs, Gant Carman: Ken Mayer, Marta Crandall: Virginia Hewitt.

9/11/54 — Design for Disaster. *Premiums/Spots:* Space Patrol Periscope, with "magic mirrors!" A distant solar system, Tyranna, plans to attack the United Planets. A captured agent is subjected to a Brainograph test in an attempt to acquire tactical defense information. The official Space Patrol Periscope is written into the plot to help Buzz and Happy defeat a plan to destroy an atmosphere plant. Corry's description of how the periscope works borders on total fantasy, rather than the simple principle of two mirrors. Matthew Sneed: Bela Kovacs, Max Targo: Norman Jolley.

9/18/54 — Prisoners of Tyranna. *Premiums/Spots:* Space Patrol Periscope. More spies from Tyranna have been captured, but the search for chief spy Matthew Sneed continues. The hyperspace drive is used to propel the *Terra V* to the planet Tyranna 7, 80 light years away, in the constellation Pegasus. Matthew Sneed: Bela Kovacs.

9/25/54 — Invasion from Tyranna. *Premiums/Spots:* Space Patrol Periscope: Last time for offer! Buzz and Happy use the *Terra V*'s stardrive to travel to Tyranna and gather intelligence about preparations for an invasion of the United Planets. While being chased by Tyrannian agents, the Space Patrollers land on an asteroid to answer a distress call from a wrecked spaceship. The rescued pilot, from another targeted planetary system, provides valuable assistance in thwarting the Tyrannian invasion. Matthew Sneed: Bela Kovacs, General Mognier: Ken Mayer, Ohmra: Norman Jolley.

10/2/54 — The Voice from the Future. *Premiums/Spots:* "X-RC Rocket Cockpit," a cardboard replica of the control panel of the newest stardrive ship, with moving controls, is a fine new premium for 25 cents from Nestlé. At the Lunar Fleet Base, Buzz and Happy test a prototype stardrive system in a top-secret ship, the SD-1, starting with a rocket cockpit simulator. Ousted renegades from a space cargo company tinker with a plan to steal the new stardrive and embark on a career of piracy. The time-travel capability of the new stardrive opens fascinating new adventure possibilities. In hyperspace, Buzz and Happy pick up a news broadcast from Earth, a thousand years old, announcing the first manned moon landing in 1972. Writer Lou Huston's prediction missed the actual date of 1969 by only three years! Rork Dexter: Bela Kovacs, Nate Sorens: Ken Mayer.

10/30/54 — The Realm of the Robots. *Premiums/Spots:* Rocket Cockpit. Testing the new stardrive, Corry and Happy embark on an exploration mission to Orion 14, 50,000 light years from our solar system where scientists have detected evidence of a super radioactive element in the distant star. There they discover a habitable planet, complete with robot aggressors who have enslaved the natives. Mono: Ken Mayer.

11/6/54 — The Watchman of Warmok. *Premiums/Spots:* Space-o-Phones. On a voyage to Orion 14, Buzz and Happy discover the deserted planet Warmok, where robot spaceships dump half the industrial output of the nearby planet Gobonik, which is populated by human beings enslaved by a robot-controlled government. Buzz and Happy supply two freedom fighters with space-o-phones, so that they can organize a revolt against the robots, but the devices are intercepted by Administrator Roaknar and his robot patrol. Buzz and Happy come to the rescue and, at the spaceport on Warmok, they are attacked by a giant, insect-like robot! (Don't touch that dial!) Mono: Ken Mayer, Aneela: Virginia Hewitt, Roaknar: Bela Kovacs. [*Summary by Bill Drish*]

11/13/54 — The Frightened Robots. *Premiums/Spots:* More fantastic qualities are attributed to the Space Patrol periscope. Hope the kids weren't disappointed when they found all they could do with it was look over fences! Five hundred workers are forced by robots to dig in the deadly Kaelite mines, deemed by Corry to be "cruel and unusual punishment." A tricky decision on how to intercede without violating the prime directive of non-interference faces the Commander. Roknar: Bela Kovacs, Daruga: Norman Jolley.

12/4/54 — The Invisible Enemy. *Premiums/Spots:* Public service announcements for Christmas Seals, and National Guard recruiting. No commercial sponsors for this episode.

A secret device allows criminals to walk through solid matter. Writer Lou Huston also introduces a means of making spaceships and people invisible, foreshadowing *Star Trek*'s "cloaking device," which came along years later. And would you believe the "food replicator" also appears in this episode? Seems like *Star Trek* borrowed many ideas from *Space Patrol* and the other early space operas. Rolf Bolger: Bela Kovacs, Gart: Ken Mayer, Slake: Norman Jolley.

12/11/54 — The City of Hidden Doom. *Premiums/Spots:* Nestlé Hot Chocolate, hawked by Commander Corry and youngster-huckster Tony Sides. Buzz and Happy search the Jupiter atmosphere plant for a bomb hidden by the criminal Bolger, who continues to worry the Space Patrol with his cloaking device. Rolf Bolger: Bela Kovacs, Rubeck: Ken Mayer.

12/18/54 — Escape from Neptune. *Premiums/Spots:* Public service announcements for C.A.R.E. and government propaganda booklet "The Future of America." This is getting old. Bolger continues to wreak havoc as an invisible man, using his cloaking device. Rolf Bolger: Bela Kovacs, Jeannine Harvey: Virginia Hewitt.

12/25/54 — The Lost Galaxy. *Premiums/Spots:* Nestlé chocolate products. Radio signals from intelligent beings in an uncharted region of space are picked up by an observation station beyond Pluto's orbit. The aliens are equally surprised to pick up space-o-phone transmissions from the United Planets. Afraid of being conquered, the aliens launch a first assault. Buzz fires up the *Terra V*'s hyperdrive to investigate the situation. Macor: Bela Kovacs, Lt. Norfield: Ken Mayer.

1/1/55 — Ambush in Space. *Premiums/Spots:* U.S. Savings Bonds and public safety messages. Buzz and Happy continue their search for "Expedition Enigma," the missing patrol fleet sent to investigate the mysterious signals from a distant galaxy. Lt. Norfield: Ken Mayer, Lt. Marsden: Norman Jolley, Macor: Bela Kovacs.

1/8/55 — Prison Planet. *Premiums/Spots:* Nestlé chocolate products. Macor threatens to destroy Corry and the United Planets fleet. He tricks Space Patrol Lt. Skitter into landing on a prison planet, where he is captured and held as bait to trap Buzz and Happy. Macor: Bela Kovacs, Lt. Skitter: Norman Jolley.

1/15/55 — The Crown of Darjeda. *Premiums/Spots:* Public service announcements for C.A.R.E. and "Future of America" booklet. An alien spy hunts for a jeweled crown hidden on Earth centuries earlier. A "wild west" adventure follows with Buzz and Happy chasing the spy through ancient ruins in Earth's Southwest desert region. Shardu: Tom McKee, Hank Hodges: Norman Jolley, Orcon: Ken Mayer.

1/22/55 — The Shadow of Shardu. *Premiums/Spots:* Nestlé chocolate products. Apparently, the days of neat premium offers are over. The agents from Darjeda are still skulking about, looking for the jeweled crown. Their superhuman strength and intelligence make them difficult to outwit. The search now moves to Venus. Howard Sterndorf: Bela Kovacs, Orcon: Norman Jolley, Voder: Ken Mayer.

1/29/55 — The Planet of Discord. *Premiums/Spots:* March of Dimes. Shardu's henchmen kidnap Happy, then leave him alone with a space-o-phone. When Hap calls Buzz to alert him to his predicament, he doesn't realize that he is unintentionally leading the Commander into a trap. Borbane: Norman Jolley, Rog: Ken Mayer, Kleto: Bela Kovacs.

2/5/55 — The Conquest of Darjeda. *Premiums/Spots:* Nestlé chocolate products. No more neat stuff to send for; the "Fat Lady" is about to sing. Shardu is still chasing the jeweled crown, eluding Buzz and Happy, but fortunately failing to destroy them. Now the chase moves to Saturn. Shardu: Tom McKee, Borbane: Norman Jolley.

2/12/55 — The Hermit of Pluto. *Premiums/Spots:* "Future of America" booklet; U.S. Savings Bonds. Buzz and Happy are trapped inside a small city atmosphere shell on Pluto by a gang of criminals. Claim jumpers attempt to steal rights to a rare deposit of the mineral Plutolite from a prospector. Savage: Bela Kovacs, John Harbock: Ken Mayer, Morris: Norman Jolley.

2/19/55 — The Time Pirates. *Premiums/Spots:* Nestlé chocolate products. A criminal scientist travels 14 centuries back in time. (Bela Kovacs performs a nice characterization as a cowardly henchman.) Dr. Skarno: Ken Mayer, Hugo: Bela Kovacs.

2/26/55 — Voyage to the Future. *Premiums/Spots:* National Guard recruiting opportunities pitched to ten-year-old kids! Also, a condescending message for kids who don't understand the dangers of "jaywalking." Dr. Skarno figures out how to use the hyperspace mechanism to bring back valuable objects from the past. (Illegally, of course.) Fighting black market contraband transported through time makes for an interesting plot, putting Buzz and Happy in peril in the sixteenth century. Dr. Skarno: Ken Mayer, Bill Bristoe: Tom McKee, Norman Vetson: Norman Jolley.

3/5/55 — The Monster from the Past. *Premiums/Spots:* Nestlé chocolate products. Buzz and Happy are taken back millions of years in time and forced out of Skarno's spaceship on the planet Earth. Great dinosaur episode to fire the imaginations of young radio listeners. Dr. Skarno: Norman Jolley, Dr. Dawson: Bela Kovacs.

3/12/55 — The Weed of Despair. *Premiums/Spots:* Government public service announcements, re school improvement civic groups. Buzz and Happy investigate the destruction of a ship from another solar system on Titan, Saturn's sixth moon.

3/19/55 — The Fugitive from Telarma. *Premiums/Spots:* Nestlé chocolate products. Buzz and Happy are infected with a dangerous sickness on Venus and seek medical treatment. It seems that Brokoff, an alien criminal, has unleashed deadly spores from another solar system in a terrorist attack on the United Planets. Brokoff: Bela Kovacs, Carol Carlisle: Virginia Hewitt.

No Date — "Baccarratti's Family Treasure."[3] Zolton, in an attempt to rebuild the crime empire of his twin brother, Prince Baccarratti, plans to use the Baccarratti family treasure to finance his scheme. The location of the treasure — a secret castle in the Storm Belt region of Venus — is known only to the rehabilitated Prince, who wants to turn over the treasure to the United Planets. He divulges the location to Buzz. Zolton and his henchmen, Druga and Liggett, follow Corry to the castle, subdue Buzz and Happy with a heat ray, retrieve the treasure map — and leave the Space Patrollers to die in a storm. Druga: Ken Mayer, Liggett: Norman Jolley, Baccarratti: Bela Kovacs, Zolton: Bela Kovacs. [*Summary by Bill Drish*]

No Date — "The Radioactive Bees." *Premiums/Spots:* Space Patrol Microscope. On the

---

[3]Titles appearing in quotes were created by Bill Drish because the shows he summarizes, dubbed from Armed Forces Radio Service broadcasts, often lacked titles, commercials and credits. Thanks to these AFRS broadcasts, many *Space Patrol* radio shows survived. — JNB

trail of space bandits, Commander Corry visits an experimental bee farm on Venus, run by Brother John, to find out if any suspicious spaceships have landed in the valley below. While at the farm, Buzz receives a space-o-phone message informing him that the gang has looted a space platform in Mars' orbit and that an automatic camera will reveal the identity of the thieves. One of the beekeepers, a spy for the gang, places a microfilm on the wing of a radioactive bee that flies down to a gang hideout in the valley. Two gang members locate the message bee with a Geiger counter and recover the microfilm with the message that Corry is on the way to obtain evidence against them. They pursue *Terra V* to Mars and, on arriving, launch a missile at the space platform, hoping to destroy the evidence — and Corry! Brother John: Ken Mayer, Prentice: Norman Jolley, Sorenson: Bela Kovacs. [*Summary by Bill Drish*]

No Date — "The Disappearing Lake." Tarnhelm Industries supplies the United Planets with Vita-plast, made from the unique clay scooped from Jupiter's Lake Tarnhelm. But the lake is drying up, causing a shortage of the vital material. Because of the strategic importance of Vita-plast, Buzz and Happy visit Director Purvent to determine whether the United Planets should provide financial aid to the failing operation. The disappearing lake — and sabotage at the plant — is the work of Purvent's assistant, Drover, and a mining engineer, Halstead, who are running a fake mining operation to drain the lake. Drover (to prevent Corry from finding out about the scheme) pretends to see a suspicious character in the plant and tricks Buzz and Happy into searching among the Vita-plast vats, where pipes carrying poisonous gas burst, causing the pair to inhale the deadly fumes. Drover: Ken Mayer, Halstead: Norman Jolley, Purvent: Bela Kovacs. [*Summary by Bill Drish*]

No Date — "The Heliophobic Space Pilot." Cutler, president of Tri-Orbit Lines, and his assistant, Van Dorn, are using the company's ships to transport stolen material via space lanes inside the orbit of Mercury. One of their pilots, Prentice, has made flights close to the sun and has come down with "heliophobia," which increases telepathic ability. Using this power, Prentice knows when Commander Corry and Happy are about to visit Cutler's office to investigate suspicious activities. Buzz and Happy stow away on a freighter hauling stolen goods, piloted by Prentice, who becomes aware of their presence in a hold containing canisters of deadly gas. But Prentice blacks out and, as the freighter plunges toward the sun, the gas canisters become dangerously hot, threatening to explode and blow Buzz and Happy to atoms! Cutler: Ken Mayer, Prentice: Norman Jolley, Van Dorn: Bela Kovacs. [*Summary by Bill Drish*]

No Date — "The Missing Stardrive Spaceship." At the Lunar Fleet Base, Buzz, Happy and Meyerhoff, the scientist believed to be the inventor of stardrive, plan to inspect the first spaceship with that feature before its maiden flight — but when they enter the hanger, the ship is not there. Buzz and Happy learn that the actual inventor, Jano Kalmyr, has escaped from a rehabilitation center on Mars. The Space Patrollers and Meyerhoff blast off for Mars, but stop to aid a freighter, piloted by Kalmyr, which sheds its hull, revealing the missing stardrive ship. Buzz and Happy are taken prisoner and learn that they will never be able to return to the solar system! Dargo: Ken Mayer, Jano Kalmyr: Norman Jolley, Meyerhoff: Bela Kovacs [*Summary by Bill Drish*]

No Date — "Sabotage of the Stardrive." Buzz and Happy visit Space Observatory No. 2 to confer with Dr. Dinsmore. The sun is emitting a new type of radiation that has been detected from only one other star, Trogonak, which is similar to the sun; information about Trogonak's present condition would help predict the sun's future behavior. Buzz and Happy agree to go to Troganok to gather data. What they don't know is that the criminal Baxon has bribed an engineer, Niblow, to sabotage the stardrive on their ship. When they reach Trogonak, their tests prove the star is not emitting harmful radiation, and they prepare to return to the solar system with the good news. But, when Buzz sets the controls, the stardrive fails to work! Dr. Dinsmore: Ken Mayer, Niblow: Norman Jolley, Baxon: Bela Kovacs [*Summary by Bill Drish*]

No Date — The Galaxy Trade Association. Exploring near Vega, Buzz and Happy encounter a strange craft and a space-suited man. Once aboard, Errdu tells Buzz and Happy about the "Galaxy Trade Association" and urges the Commander to enter an agreement to supply raw materials to the United Planets in exchange for production of goods for export. Buzz refuses, and Errdu admits that the Association plans to enslave all the planets in the galaxy. Buzz and Happy return Errdu to his home planet, but the head of the Trade Association, master criminal Krexor, tries to force the Space Patrolmen to reveal the location of the solar system, dooming all the people of the United Planets to live as slaves! Krexor: Bela Kovacs. [*Summary by Bill Drish*]

No Date — The Forbidden Planet. With the permission of an Arctronian official named Vorbol, Commander Corry and Cadet Happy pursue the criminals Spangler and Rem to the Arctronian System, where Spangler expects to "unload" a cargo of Litronium. To travel freely in the Arctronian System, the criminals plan to steal the Space Patrol stardrive ship. Using a fake space-o-phone message, they lure Buzz and Happy to the planet Gazyr. Unaware that the atmosphere is filled with deadly poison, Buzz and Happy leave their spaceship without spacesuits. As they creep toward the dome, where they believe Spangler and Rem to be hiding, their ship is hijacked. Watching the ship blast off, they are overcome by the poisonous atmosphere of the "forbidden planet." [*Summary by Bill Drish*]

No Date — "Wreck of the *Black Star*." Zolton Baccarratti and his henchman, Strack, kidnap anthropologist Dr. Thana Loring and force her to lead them to the treasure-laden wreck of the 900-year-old pirate spaceship *Black Star* on Mars, threatening to harm her if they are pursued. Nevertheless, Buzz and Happy track Baccarratti's spaceship to the *Black Star*'s location. While stealthily approaching the site of the wreck in a scout tank, they happen upon a strange rock formation and a hideous-looking bejeweled "war mask" with glaring eyes that seems to be watching them! Strack: Ken Mayer, Dr. Thana Loring: Virginia Hewitt, Zolton: Bela Kovacs. [*Summary by Bill Drish*]

Appendix 4
The Ships and Miniature Sets
of Space Patrol

by Jack McKirgan II

Space Patrol was among the most innovative of early television programs. During the course of each episode, a few seconds were devoted to giving mid–20th-century young people a glimpse into the future — a distant future. One thousand years into time yet to come, the universe would become humanity's playground. Fabulous cities connected by highways for jet-powered cars and monorail systems would be built. Architecture would be aided by new construction methods and materials, giving free form to buildings in which the populace lived and worked. New worlds would provide a clean slate to begin building the shops, factories, homes and offices that would become the cities and outposts of space exploration. Inter-planet travel would be accomplished by a variety of nuclear-powered spacecraft, ranging from tiny one-person rocket coupes to commercial liners that would cater to over a thousand passengers in comfort and style. People would be protected and commerce conducted by the manned fleet of the Space Patrol. Depicting this space-age society in sets and miniature models was the challenge faced by the art directors at ABC and property master Al Teaney in the early 1950s.

Building miniatures for use in films is an expensive process. However, it is much less expensive and more practical than building full-sized replicas of the same objects. Perhaps the most artful and dramatic use of miniature architecture up to the time of *Space Patrol*'s production was in David O. Selznick's *Gone with the Wind*. The burning of Atlanta would have been impossible to produce without the use of miniatures. During World War II, miniature aircraft and ships were often used in war films in order to reduce the budget and also to keep vital war materials available for use in the conflict. The War Department would supply war-weary and disabled craft for some sequences, but the studio effects departments had the job of integrating reality with illusion. The wonderful models used in Warner Bros.' *Captains of the Clouds* demonstrate the height to which this art could be carried.

I began my survey of the miniature ships used in *Space Patrol* in an effort to document them for posterity before everybody forgot about them. Most of what is written about the show focuses on the characters and their personalities, but hardware is my forte, and I believe it deserves some recognition too! I have a great affinity and admiration for any kind of craftwork, and the woodworkers at ABC did amazing things on small budgets and with limited materials. I guess it's important to me because it was important to them!

In the very first 15-minute episodes of *Space Patrol*, there were no miniatures at all. The spark of the evolutionary process began when Lyn Osborn, passing by a window in Commander Kit Corry's office, looked out on a panoramic view of Terra City. The "city" was nothing more than a hasty airbrush rendering of a few globe-like structures with interconnecting pipes, but Lyn's lines and delivery conveyed his awe, convincing youngsters that the future was exciting and full of wonder. His description made us want to see more. It would be up to the studio to provide that vision.

Like all cities, Terra City, the capital of the United Planets, started out with very few buildings. In fact, most of the model structures were not residential or office buildings at all; they were support facilities for the ships of the Space Patrol. For the first year of its run, the spaceport at Terra City seemed to grow with each episode. The show's opening was a mixture of shots taken from several angles and featuring the visually exciting launch of an interceptor spaceship, which I've dubbed the *Vindicator*, from a catapult-like ramp. Close study of this sequence shows several launch ramps, launch pads, a communications tower shaped much like a fishing bobber, a few factory-type buildings and a maintenance hanger. There are also several tank-like structures similar to those found at an oil refinery, a large, finned globular structure and a straight two-lane highway. The spaceport is on the edge of a body of water, presumably a lake, and a rocket-propelled watercraft cruises swiftly past the spaceport.

With all of the visual excitement in this opening sequence, the most-remembered scene seems to be the launch of the *Vindicator*. Though a simple shot by today's standards, the impression created as the camera moved in tightly upon this sleek rocket with large ovate wings, smoke billowing from its exhausts, and the sensation of sudden, bone-crushing acceleration one felt as the ship smoothly shot into the darkness, trailing pulses of smoke, would cause even today's youngsters to sit up and take notice. Such is the power of a miniature.

The ships of the Space Patrol were the means by which most of the show's adventures took place. The primary mission of the Space Patrol, like today's counterpart organizations, was to enforce the laws, capture lawbreakers, protect commerce and keep the space lanes clear for the safety of the citizens of the United Planets of the Universe. Considering the distances involved, this was not an easy task. A fleet of spaceships was developed for use by the Space Patrol. The implementation and visualization of each type of ship was a lengthy one. Usually several episodes were aired before an existing ship was revised or a new one introduced.

Terra I

Perhaps the best example of the evolutionary process would be with the personal ship of the commander-in-chief of the Space Patrol. Originally the character was Kit Corry, played by Glen Denning. Kit's ship was never a miniature, but was first seen as an airbrush painting at the end of the second show, a 15-minute episode aired locally in Los Angeles. The design could best be described as "interesting." Overall, the ship had a shape similar to the World War II–born German V-2 (A4) rocket that was being used as a test bed for the infant rocket program in the United States. Kit's ship was stubbier, yet still retained the classic double-tapered fuselage of the V-2. The nose was extended into a needle-like probe, no doubt inspired by the test probes that were fitted to the many new jet aircraft that were under development at that time. The rest of the ship was decidedly "retro" in appearance. Scallop-shaped fins in vertical and horizontal planes were sandwiched between a pair of blunt-ended rocket tubes that resemble the solid rocket boosters (SRBS) found on today's space shuttle. Since the painting was essentially a still-life, the artist brushed in fine lines in the ship's wake to give the impression of speed. Overall, this was not a bad effort, but it was obvious that more would be required if the show was to develop into a long-term venture. In these early episodes, the Commander's ship was never mentioned by name, but for reasons of historical continuity and consistency, this ship shall be referred to as the *Terra I*.[1] It is sometimes mistakenly called *Darkness I* by fans because of a scene in the show's second episode in which Happy, instructed in approach procedures, uses that name as a call-sign. As a contemporary example, at one point the United States president's transport was named *The Columbine*, but the flight call-sign was, and remains, *Air Force One*.

Terra II

Like the *Terra I*, the *Terra II* was not referred to as such in the script of the television program. It was, however, prominently

---

[1] Possibly the only reference to this ship is on the second Decca "prequel," *Cadet Happy Joins Commander Corry*, in which Corry assigns Hap to permanent duty aboard the *Terra I*. The script was written by Lou Huston, and the 78 rpm record was released in November 1954.—JNB

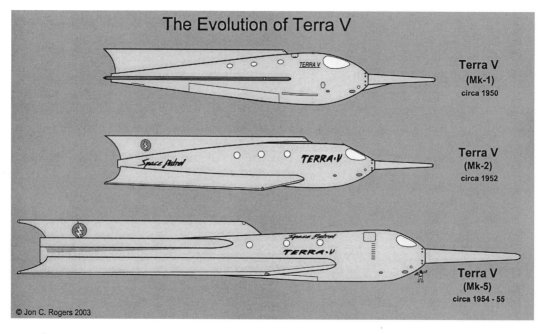

The evolution of the *Terra V* (courtesy Jon Rogers, co-author with Jack Hagerty of *Spaceship Handbook*, ARA Press, Livermore, CA, 2001, and *The Saucer Fleet*, 2005).

named in several episodes of the weekly radio show on the ABC radio network. The *Terra II* was also presented as a painting in early TV episodes, usually superimposed on a background of clouds or planets. It retained the same basic fuselage as the *Terra I*, but the tail fin was replaced with a more conventional surface and the starboard and port rocket tubes were replaced by narrow wings that extended three-quarters of the length of the fuselage. The integrated cockpit of the *Terra I* was now enclosed in an extended bubble-like canopy at the top of the fuselage. Although no markings can be seen on surviving prints, it is known from script lines that the marking "100" is supposed to appear on the ship as a registry number. Color of the ship is uncertain, but it appears to be natural metal.

Terra III

At this point in the chronology of the commander-in-chief's ships, the *Terra III* would be the logical ship of reference. However, study of many available radio and televi-

sion transcriptions reveals no mention of this ship.[2]

Terra IV

The *Terra IV* was the first Space Patrol flagship to enjoy a long life, both as a full-sized set and as a miniature prop. This was a ship that a person would feel confident in during a flight around the solar system! The *Terra IV* boasted a sleek, double-tapered fuselage which terminated at the front in a needle-like probe. Three long fins extended from the front third of the fuselage to well behind the rocket exhaust. The tips of the fins' trailing edges curbed gracefully into the fuselage. The rocket exhaust consisted of a larger central chamber surrounded by a number of smaller rocket tubes, which was a common design concept of the rocket pioneers of the 1920s and 1930s. At this point in its evolution, the *Terra IV* could be truly considered an elegant spaceship — but the designer decided to include one additional feature, which many people believe spoiled its appearance: a pair of stubby winglets protrud-

[2]References to "Terra the Third" appear in the radio scripts penned by Mike Moser in the summer of 1950. He also mentioned this ship in his demo show, "Secret of Terra," sent to the ABC network that fall. The show was later rewritten by Norm Jolley and aired as Episode 47 (half-hour).—JNB

ing from the mid-point of the fuselage. It is unclear whether these were supposed to be functional or an homage to the similar design seen on Emperor Ming's ships from the *Flash Gordon* serials produced in the 1930s. Most likely the average viewer did not even realize that these winglets were present because the minimal lighting, made necessary by the need to disguise the support wires and other fixtures used in presenting the miniatures, usually hid the stubby protrusions. There were only a few times when these wings could be seen, usually when the model was at rest on the surface of a planet. Fortunately, a few well-composed and well-illuminated photographs of this model have survived.

Two important and previously unknown photographs of the *Terra IV* surfaced in 1999. In these photos, the winglets are seen to be supports for three missile rails, missile tubes or pitot-tube assemblies, very similar in function to the stub wings used on modern attack helicopters. One photo is slightly suspect because even though it is a frame from an episode, it may be a matte-painting, rather than the actual model. The other photo is a colorized view of the model from an original black-and-white print. If either photo is authentic, it demonstrates a military concept that was not actually implemented for another 15 years.

Although daily transmission of color television broadcasts was still over 10 years away at the end of *Space Patrol*'s run, many of the miniatures did, in fact, exhibit the use of color as a necessity for a number of reasons. The *Terra IV* was featured in a series of *Stori-Views* 3-D slide sets that were photographed on color transparency film. The few surviving sets of these slides give a good indication of the colors used on the miniatures during the filming of the episodes. However, dyes, particularly in color transparency films of the day, have a tendency to shift color, usually with a loss or darkening of various shades of green and blue. Using the best examples available, it has been determined that the *Terra IV* was painted in a glossy dark teal overall with the ship's name painted in a light blue shade. Rocket exhausts were a metallic silver color and the windscreen was a shade of blue, although some photos indicate that this may have been repainted from an original black for the purpose of color photography.

Terra V

The *Terra V* was the longest-lived of the *Space Patrol* flagships. During the course of the program, it underwent at least two major overhauls and a few minor refits. Its design was also a departure from the previous ships of the commander-in-chief.

Departing from the double-tapered fuselage of the *Terra IV* and earlier ships, the *Terra V* employed a tadpole shape, reminiscent of designs that were popular in 1920s and 1930s pulp magazine illustrations. However, instead of large bat-like fins or airplane wings, the *Terra V* was given a more rakish look with long graceful wings and a vertical fin, both of which created a "leveling" effect on the shape of the fuselage. The ship also sported a prominent nose-boom in place of the previous needle-nose designs. Because of the number of variations on the *Terra V*, each version will be described in chronological order, the variants labeled with a "Mark" number. The first variant will be called the Mk. 1; the second version, the Mk. 2; and so on.

Terra V, *Mk. 1*

The *Terra V*, Mk. 1, was a slightly smaller ship than its refitted later incarnations. Using various scaling techniques, one can estimate that the full-sized ship would have been approximately 216 feet long from the tip of the nose-boom to the trailing edge of the wings. While these dimensions could easily be disputed by someone who used only sets of the exterior of the ship for size comparison, the dimensions used here were extrapolated from comparisons of Ed Kemmer's height of approximately six feet with the scale of the cockpit area in the full-sized set. These data were then applied to the cockpit area of the miniature in order to arrive at the dimensions.

The Mk.1's large nose-boom was given additional structural support by the use of a triangular "strake" that ran about one-quarter of the length of the boom and was faired into the nose of the craft. This feature was removed after a few episodes, and most photos of the Mk. 1 do not show the boom strake at all. Just behind the nose-boom was the cockpit area, occupying the upper level of the forward fuselage. The rear of the cockpit area also contained a periscope-like instrument that presumably controlled a camera mounted beneath a small blister on the top of the cabin. Behind the cockpit was a small cabin containing an air-lock. The exterior of the miniature indicates a single rectangular hatch in the top-center of the fuselage with a series of ladder-like rungs and hand-holds extending downward approximately one-sixth of the circumference of the fuselage. The Mk. 1 featured a pair of relatively wide wings located at the midpoint of the fuselage beginning about one-fourth of the distance from the nose of the ship and extending slightly behind the exhaust. The trailing edge of the wings were radius-cut, giving the ship a very sleek look. The plane of the wings was at 90 degrees from the vertical tail of the ship. The tail fin's leading edge was shorter than those of the wings and begins slightly farther back on the fuselage than did the wings, extending slightly behind the exhaust. Three portholes were located, evenly spaced, at about 45 degrees down the fuselage from the tail fin. In one publicity photo of the model, the portholes appear to be slightly oval in shape, but with the heavy lighting on the kinescopes, they seem to be round. A medium-sized model, probably about two feet long, has the portholes spaced slightly unevenly with the rearmost porthole being slightly wider spaced than the first opening to the second. The ship's name appeared in the highly stylized Space Patrol font just behind the windscreen and was underlined with a very thin lightning bolt. The Space Patrol logo was located between the wings and tail fin, near the exhaust. The underside of the *Terra V*, Mk. 1, has never been documented in an episode, but extrapolating from script information and depiction onscreen, it may be assumed that in the 30th century ships of this type employed a system of levitation, usually with the ship in a horizontal position, in which it would accelerate along a launch ramp during takeoff and hover straight downward for landing. For this reason, an aircraft-type undercarriage was not necessary, and it is believed that retractable skids were used to support the ship at rest.

Available photos and video clips disagree somewhat on the use of a fin-flash on the tail. Part of this discrepancy may be caused by the dark lighting that was used, particularly on the aft part of the model.

Terra V, *Mk. 2*

The *Terra V*, Mk. 2, was virtually the same as the Mk. 1, except that the wings were slightly narrower and angled downward at approximately 105 degrees relative to the vertical fin. Although there is no official explanation for the change in design, it is likely that the wings were angled downward in order to facilitate keeping the model level when placed on a flat surface, such as a launch ramp. Previous landing sequences with the Mk. 1 usually displayed the ship landing at the Terra City Spaceport on a form-fitting cradle, which kept the model in a level position without the need for an undercarriage. The boom strake was also deleted permanently on this mark. The color of the ship remained an overall metallic shade and there was a slight variation in the shape of the trailing edge of the wings, which enabled the model to sit precariously on its tail for vertical takeoff and landing. The Space Patrol service logo remained on the fuselage in front of the exhaust opening, and the ship name was placed just behind the windscreen. A commander's flash can be seen on the vertical tail surface. Unlike the Mk. 1, there appears to be no stylized lightning bolt under the ship name. All markings were in black on the metallic background.

Terra V, *Mk. 3*

The *Terra V*, Mk. 3, marked the beginning of a new concept for the commander's ship. It is interesting to note that the scripts and continuing storyline made no mention of a new ship, but only of "extensive repairs," when this model was introduced. By all measures, this ship probably should have been dubbed the *Terra VI*, but the writer and production crew probably saw the need for continuity since the *Terra V* had become an established icon of the program. The Mk. 3 was extensively longer than the Mk. 2. With scaling techniques, one can estimate that the ship was about 30 feet longer and the fuselage taper slightly less than the earlier models. The nose of the ship was somewhat more rounded than the previous models, and some photos suggest that the model was not totally finished when pressed into production sequences. The portholes were now located at the centerline of the fuselage and the wings were as long as the vertical fin, making them appear a bit narrower. The height of the vertical fin's leading edge was reduced somewhat, again making the entire unit appear much narrower, although the overall height remained the same. The ingress/egress hatch was still centered at the top of the fuselage, just

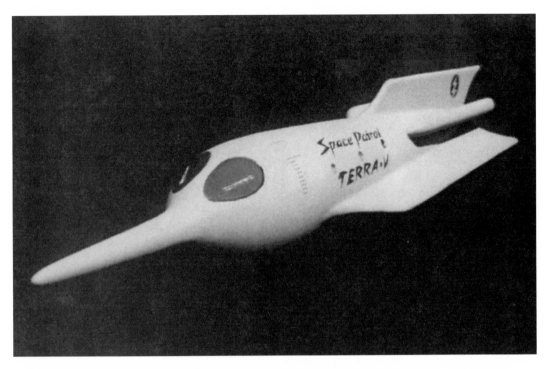

Jack McKirgan's restoration of Beth Flood's Terra V, Mk. 6, the only known surviving ship model from the show (courtesy Jack McKirgan).

ahead to the vertical fin. The ship's markings changed in position somewhat: The Space Patrol service name was relocated above the three portholes and the ship name, *Terra V*, was located below the apertures. The still-ambiguous fin flash was located on the vertical fin and the ship's overall color was still metallic in appearance.

Terra V, *Mk. 4*

The *Terra V*, Mk. 4, was perhaps the most ambitious design change of the entire series of commander's vessels. It was introduced with the "extensive repairs" script notation; no mention was made of the very obvious changes to the ship. The ship was based on the existing Mk. 3, but a pair of thrust-augmenting "plasma tubes" were located halfway between the vertical fin and the wings. Supported on tapered finlets to keep the thrust line parallel with the center of the fuselage, these long tubes extended from just behind the portholes to slightly behind the main exhaust. The addition

of this feature was probably due to the development of similar-looking rocket boosters on the experimental and operational military missiles that were in development in the early 1950s. Unfortunately, most of the kinescopes of this ship are poorly lit, and many fans of the program still believe that these tubes are narrow wings that were attached to the ship.

The introduction of the Mk. 4 also heralded another major change in the production values of the program: extensive use of color on the ships. Without eyewitness confirmation of the color schemes that were used, actual colors can only be guessed at, using hue intensity on the black-and-white images as a guide. However, these can be somewhat misleading due to the variation in shades of a specific color. The colors presented here are only a best guess and are to be considered as guidelines. It's possible that the production designers introduced color to the miniatures in anticipation of the introduction of color network broadcasts.[3] Other programs, such as *The Lone Ranger, Roy Rogers* and *Superman*, were already filming

[3]Director Dick Darley's son, Chris (who was a child at the time), recalls that the ship models would be produced in several colors "so they could light them differently." He remembers white and silver models of the *Terra V.*—JNB

episodes in color, even though it would be almost 15 years before reruns of these programs would be shown on home television screens in color. *Space Patrol* was handicapped in the implementation of color by the network's use of kinescopes instead of direct-to-film photography. Rather than blame the network or production company for being tight-fisted, one should note that at that time most episodic TV programs were filming 26 to 40 episodes of a half-hour program during each production year, and *Space Patrol* was producing 52 half-hour episodes. This was certainly an impossible set of circumstances to contend with in terms of the necessary producing, editing and post-production services for a program to be filmed in color. Had it not been for the untimely death of producer-creator Mike Moser, it's possible that necessary changes in the show's production schedule would have been made to facilitate the continuation of *Space Patrol* in the full spectrum of color.

The nose of the *Terra V*, Mk. 4, was painted red. The paint scheme extended behind the cockpit in a scalloped pattern, the peaks of which were located, pointing rearward, at the vertical fin and repeating at 90-degree spacing around the fuselage. The vertical fin was also painted red and, although it is difficult to make a firm determination, it appears that the wings were red as well. The color of the remainder of the fuselage is somewhat of an enigma. The best guess is that it was painted a neutral gray, rather than the yellow that had been used in the past. Another possible fuselage color, though unlikely, would be green. This would coordinate with the *Space Patrol* service uniforms, which were green with red panels. One clue shows up on video tapes to indicate that the color scheme of this ship was darker than previous models: The service and ship names are a lighter hue than the fuselage. Repeated study makes it apparent that the difference is not caused by a reflection of the studio lights on the paint of the lettering, but is a real artifact of the paint scheme. The difference in shades suggests that the lettering may have been painted in a light gray, yellow or even in metallic silver. The fin-flash appears to be black, but there are white or light shades in the interior of the shield, which would indicate that the lightning bolt or commander's insignia is in a contrasting color.

Terra V, *Mk. 5*

The *Terra V*, Mk. 5, was a refined version of the Mk. 4. Fuselage dimensions were approximately the same as the earlier version, but the cockpit area was less rounded, with a more streamlined appearance. The vertical fin was much taller at the leading edge and the fin began farther back on the spine of the fuselage. The plasma tubes were larger in diameter and better defined on the kinescopes. During the course of the "Theft of the Rocket Cockpit" series of episodes, another new feature was depicted: A pair of cargo bay doors, similar to the bomb bay doors on a contemporary bombing plane, were shown in operation as the ship withdrew a stolen vessel from the ground into its hold. The entry hatch was still located in the center of the fuselage, but the windscreen was slightly larger, adding to the more streamlined appearance of the ship; the color had reverted back to the natural metal appearance and all markings were in black. This is, by far, the most memorable version of the *Terra V* to be seen on the series.

Terra V, *Mk. 6*

The *Terra V*, Mk. 6, was similar in appearance to the Mk. 5, except that it appears to have been a modified version of the Mk. 2 model. The ship was shorter, but the plasma tubes had been added and the vertical fin was shortened at the fore-end in order to assume the profile of the Mk. 5. It is easily identified because the leading edge of the vertical fin is slightly concave in appearance. Another major departure from the previous designs was that the boarding hatch was no longer located on the center line of the fuselage, but was, in fact, two hatches, left and right, with hand-hold or ladder-like rungs extending from the front edge of each hatch. This model has only been seen in extremely rare close-up shots of the *Terra V* sitting or landing at the Terra City Spaceport set. The windscreen area was, again, enlarged to better define the area in the close-up views. This is the only model on which the tail markings can be confirmed. The fin-flash was the double-jagged lightning bolt, rather than the commander's insignia. This version of the *Terra V*, while given less screen time than the other models, is the easiest to document because it has survived to the present.

Variations on Variations

Often the production crew had to work with models of different sizes in order to keep them in scale with other miniature set pieces, which ranged from simple clumps of foliage to complex cityscapes requiring forced-perspective views to give the illusion of added depth. There were at least three different scales of models used in the *Space Patrol* sets — and possibly more. These ranged from large "hero" models of about four feet in length to intermediate models (two feet) and smaller models (six to eight inches). The intermediate models seem to be the most commonly used, probably because of the ease with which they could be set up for a particular shot. In addition to the different scales, there seem to have been some differences in the features of these models. Most of the variations are differences on the glazed portions of the ships. Windscreen shapes, porthole location and spacing varied, depending on the model used. It must be remembered that each model was unique — there were no computer-controlled tools to cut out fleets of identical ships. Because of the less sophisticated nature of the television recording process, these anomalies usually went unnoticed or were not discernible to the viewer. While they are of little importance to the overall enjoyment of the program, they are noted here for historical reference.

Other Ships of the Space Patrol

Although the *Terra*-series craft were the featured ships of *Space Patrol*, it would be difficult for any police force to patrol and maintain security in the solar system with only one ship. Constant reference was made — particularly in the 1953-54 season — to other Patrol vessels which relayed reports and needed occasional help and support from Commander Corry and his crew. Usually there were no visuals of these ships, probably because of budget constraints, but beginning in the 1953 season, a few other craft of the Space Patrol were seen onscreen. The most recognized ships of the Space Patrol (other than the *Terra V*) were the three shown in the filmed opening sequence used as the show's intro, beginning in 1952. While there were no "official" names for these ships, I've dubbed two for their physical attributes and the third with what I feel is an appropriate title.

Bullet Rocket

This ship was originally used in a filmed intro scene in which the rocket was supposed to zoom across the screen, leaving a plume of smoke trailing behind a pillar of flame. Unfortunately, the effect was less than desirable — in fact, it was unconvincing — so this stubby, bullet-shaped ship was quickly re-shot in a wipe-effect for a second version of the intro. As the opening sequence begins, the hull of this ship blocks the lens from capturing anything beyond it, and as it zooms out of the frame, the spaceport at Terra City is revealed. Details other than the Space Patrol service name are hard to pick out as it sweeps by in the foreground, but its earlier use as a fly-by model in the original filmed intro make it easy to recognize. This ship was also used in a publicity photo, which provides a good record of its shape and size. It was painted yellow to provide a metallic look on the kinescopes.

Biscuit Rocket

The "Biscuit Rocket" was the ship that replaced the "Bullet Rocket" in the intro's fly-by sequence. The "biscuit" reference relates to the shape of the fins, which look like carpenter's biscuits — pieces of wood used to lock together two joined pieces of wood. In fact, the fins may have originally been these joinery items from the studio workshop. In the fly-by sequence, the Biscuit Rocket produces a much more convincing exhaust. The rocket plume appears to be provided by a fusee or emergency flare that is neatly tucked into the tubular fuselage. This ship displayed no markings that can be detected. The overall color is represented as natural metal.

Vindicator

The wonderfully designed ship that I call the "Vindicator" was probably influenced by the development of the Vought XF-7U fighter for the U.S. Navy at the time. The overall design is that of a rocket-powered aircraft rather than a spacecraft. The large teardrop-shaped wing-plane provided a very high weight/lift ratio which would make the Vindicator extremely maneuverable at low altitudes. Vertical stabilization and yaw control were provided by a pair of bisected teardrop-shaped vertical surfaces, located approximately two-thirds of the distance from the root to the tip of each wing.

The one piece canopy covered a cockpit designed for side-by-side seating of the pilot and co-pilot. The rocket motors were twin units, mounted side by side in the aft of the fuselage. Exhaust nozzles ended in a hexagon shape, rather than a perfect circle. Actual color of the Vindicator is difficult to determine due to the high-contrast photography, but it is a light color, possibly represented as natural metal.

X-100 Class Battlecruiser

Other than the *Terra*-series ships, the X-100 class vessels were the only other capital ships in the known Space Patrol fleet. In order to visually demonstrate that the *Terra V* was a unique vessel, prop master Al Teaney and his assistants decided that Major Robertson and other high-ranking Space Patrol officers should be in command of a battlecruiser with many of the same characteristics as the *Terra V*, yet distinctly different enough to allow the audience to realize which ship interior they were about to be shown. (In most instances the same interior set was used for the *Terra V* as well as other ships.) The X-100 class vessel design was an evolution from previous *Terra V*–style ships. The vessel had the same nose profile as the *Terra V*, but the fuselage was a bit longer than the command ship. The longer fuselage provided a different arrangement for the portholes as well. Instead of three portholes per side on the fuselage, there were six and sometimes eight per side, arranged on two levels, which reinforces the assumption that there were two decks on these ships. The most radical departure from the *Terra* design was the use of four equally-sized fins or wings on the models. These were arranged in an "X" configuration with a wider spacing on the sides than on the top and bottom. Paint schemes for this ship varied somewhat, depending on its function. Early depictions of the ship represent the finish as overall natural metal, but it was also used as a villain's ship early in its career. Hue intensity interpretations show it to have been painted, at various times, in black, red and possibly green. In a series of programs that were presented late in the show's run, an X-100 is seen on the surface of a planet that was laid to ruin by a nuclear war. The video engineer inverted the hues, producing a negative image to give an eerie appearance to the barren planet. A result of this process was to present the viewer with an X-100 in black finish with a boiling post-holocaust sun reflecting off of the windscreens.

Probably the most interesting variation was Robbie's personal ship, which displayed a distinctive striped pattern during the final full season. This ship had a natural metal nose with the remainder of the fuselage and wings painted orange with black diagonal stripes and trim. Perhaps the paint shop decided to pay homage to the famed "Flying Tigers" of World War II. Whether launched on a whim or with deliberation, the paint scheme had staying power. During the late 1950s and well into the 1980s, international aerial gunnery competitions between NATO air forces frequently featured aircraft painted in this same type of color scheme.

One other variation of the X-100 class battlecruiser must be noted: The Planetoid Payroll Ship that was attacked in the series of episodes featuring the space pirate Captain Dagger was an X-100 ship with three portholes per side of the fuselage and "PPS" painted in huge letters across the fuselage and wings. According to the script, any vessel encountering a ship carrying these markings was required to stay at a great distance or risk having a cosmic missile fired at it. Color scheme of the PPS ship appears to be light blue with white or yellow lettering.

Space Cars

Space Cars, small personal transports, came in several versions and with many variations. They were used by the Space Patrol as well as by civilians and were a favorite transport for villains.

One of the first space cars seen on the series was dispatched from the Mars spaceport. The Mars space car was a bullet-shaped ship with three short fins which terminated with pods on the tips of the appendages. The cockpit area was huge in relation to the remainder of the ship and served to indicate that the ship was, indeed, relatively small. Overall color appears to be white and there is no indication in the surviving kinescopes that there were any other markings. Because of the civilian nature of this ship, it is easy to speculate that the scene in the Martian spaceport would include a large number of these ships with a wide range of trim and color schemes.

The most used type of space car was what

we might call the Type II. This type of ship was about half the size of the *Terra V* and roughly the same fuselage shape. The cockpit area was sometimes asymmetrical, sometimes symmetrical, and the fins and wings have been seen with at least two distinct shapes on the trailing edge. Typical of this ship are Baccarratti's space car, Space Car 127, Space Car CNY-801, Garth Stanger's space car and others. One other notable variation on the design of this ship is the placement and number of observation blisters and portholes. Changes to these features could allow a large number of ships to be represented by a relatively small number of models. Paint schemes also varied somewhat; the most evocative was seen in the early "Planet X" episodes on Prince Baccarratti's space car, which sported black stripes extending over the cockpit area, suggesting banditry. The cockpit windscreens were shaped much like a stylized hawk's eye, giving the ship a predatory look.

Since these features were painted onto the wooden models, it was relatively easy to make changes in the appearance. One of the Type II models was used in several episodes. It appears that this ship was intended to become Cadet Happy's personal transport. It carried the large marking "A3" on the fuselage and was seen in at least two scales. The larger, close-up model, featured a transparent canopy bubble and a transparent observation dome on the top of the fuselage. Although no center brace is noticeable on the model, the full-sized nose-section set does show the canopy windscreen with a divider that sectioned off the port and starboard sides of the bubble.

Villains' Ships

Most of the criminals who began their careers within the solar system used "off-the-lot" vehicles or even stolen Space Patrol ships in order to perform their misdeeds. During the course of the program, three master criminals gave the studio woodworking department the opportunity to be creative. It is interesting to note that all three of the masterminds employed ships that drew from nature for their inspiration.

Prince Baccarratti

Prince Baccarratti, the self-proclaimed Black Falcon, was *the* most tenacious criminal

to face, confound and be confounded by Buzz Corry and the Space Patrol. At first, Baccarratti used the modified Type II space car described above. However, after only a couple of "Planet X" episodes, his personal ship was introduced. True to his title, the ship was shaped like a hawk in diving position and is an impressive sight even on grainy kinescopes.

Captain Dagger

Captain Dagger's pirate ship retained the classic double-tapered fuselage, but the addition of a large dorsal fin and wings resembling pectoral fins gave the ship a decidedly shark-like appearance. The pectoral wings were angled downward, as on the predatory fish, and the ship looked as if it could swim through space. Were it not for the addition of an unexplained clear dome just ahead of the dorsal fin, the design would have been perfect. The ship was painted in contrasting colors on the fuselage and appendages, probably blue on the fuselage with yellow fins. The paint scheme was scalloped at the interstices of the colors, giving the viewer a glimpse of Captain Dagger's humor. The peaks of the scallops were arranged so that the tail looked like the dorsal fin of a shark sticking out of a blue ocean. The light-colored tail fin was decorated with a pirate's "Jolly Roger" skull and crossbones in black, and a white version of the emblem was painted on the darker fuselage, just ahead of the pectoral fins.

Arachna

The episodes featuring Arachna, the "Space Spider," depicted a ring-shaped rogue planet that harnessed gravitational forces to travel the galaxy and pique the curiosity of innocent spacefarers. When a ship moved in to investigate the enigmatic planet, Arachna would capture it in a magnetic field; then he'd dispatch a remote-controlled, gravity-propelled ship to disable the crew and retrieve their vessel for smelting into raw materials to further his plans of conquest. Oddly, Arachna's small ship, called a "gravity pod," was not based on a spider's design, but was more like an aphid. The pod would be maneuvered over the captured ship and attach itself to the hull over the cockpit. A "stinger" would then be extended from the pod, penetrate the hull and inject a sleep gas into the larger ship, disabling the crew. Then the gravity drive would bring both the host ship and the parasitic drone back to Arachna's lair.

Cityscapes

Terra City was the first city of the future that most television viewers had seen. In the first 15-minute episode that aired locally in Los Angeles, it was represented as a simple airbrush drawing of a series of tanks and pipes similar to the structures in a refinery. A few episodes later, it appeared as an airbrush painting with the same buildings and support facilities that were later seen as miniature set pieces. It's quite possible that the airbrush painting was an artist's conception of the Terra City spaceport used while woodworkers created models of the same subject. The miniature set was first seen in the opening (national) half-hour episode, and its construction was, without doubt, due to the increased budget provided for the network production.

Over the years, the model of the spaceport was augmented by additional set pieces of new buildings, some of which appeared to be designed by professional architects. Terra City proper was usually depicted as a separate set from the spaceport, but during the 1954 and 1955 seasons, the sets merged and many of the pieces were integrated. Downtown Terra City was frequently the landing site of the *Terra V*, and the rooftops of many buildings were adorned with spaceships and launch ramps. In one version of the set, a monorail track can be seen winding through the buildings, and a multilane freeway system, complete with entry and exit ramps, appears to be handling a high volume of ground transportation. In all, it appeared that the city grew up around the spaceport.

Most of the buildings in the Terra City set were generic skyscraper types, often with spinning radar antennae and blinking lights on their roofs. One of the first buildings identified specifically in the show was the headquarters of the United Planets. As befitted the spirit of the age, it was obviously modeled after the United Nations building in New York. Probably because of its relatively large scale, this building was always depicted in a stand-alone set or in the foreground of a forced-perspective view of Terra City; the size of the model also allowed the addition of details that were not present on other set pieces.

Other structures were made from a wide range of shapes, some of which seemed to be whimsical, yet conveyed a sense of purpose, especially when depicting an industrial complex or a spaceport structure. Occasionally, buildings reflected the architecture of the early 1950s. An excellent example of this style of architecture is the laboratory on Pluto's moon in the "Giants of Pluto #3" series of episodes. The combination of round and angular shapes is very similar to those used at that time in the design of hospitals and research facilities.

Construction Materials

Much of the following is speculation, but it is based on known examples and observation of the actual sets in still photos and video frames. It is known that the spacecraft models used in the series were made of mahogany. The fuselages were turned out on a lathe and the fins were cut on a band saw. The construction was top-notch, with milled attachment channels for the fins and precise alignment of the windows and portholes. The only known surviving example of the *Terra V* models is a two-foot-long version of the Mk. 6, belonging to Lyn Osborn's sister, Beth Flood. I had the privilege of restoring this model, and the project confirmed many of my assumptions about construction practices. It is evident that when the ABC TV Network began producing the program, skilled woodcrafters were used to construct the miniature set pieces. All wood used on the miniatures was clear, dense-grained and very well finished with a minimum of filler on adjoining surfaces. The finish consisted of at least one coat of grain sealer, a primer coat and a finish coat, with lettering and details applied using a liner brush and stabilo pen. There was no protective overcoat applied over the details. It appears that all of the models used on the program were made entirely of wood, with three exceptions: Captain Dagger's ship, one space car and one of the *Terra V*, Mk. 4. All had canopies or windscreens made of clear plastic or formed Plexiglas.

The architectural models used in miniature sets were, for the most part, much simpler to produce than the spaceships. Most of the spaceport buildings began as simple geometric shapes, relatively easy to find in those days because large hardware stores and lumber yards stocked a wide variety of shaped wood pieces:

finials, dowel rods, spheres, bowls, domes, plaques and any number of odd shapes in various sizes. Also, specialty shapes could be easily made with standard shop tools and assembled in various combinations to arrive at the required "futuristic" designs for 30th-century buildings. Larger scale buildings were used in close-ups as part of forced-perspective views of the city, and some of these had window moldings and other details which were absent on the smaller set pieces. As the Terra City set expanded, new pieces were added from a most reasonable source: toy sets. Some of the items from the popular Marx playsets were seen in *Space Patrol* episodes. Most notable, in the cityscapes, were three connected vertical fuel tanks which were used at the spaceport in Terra City, the Venus spaceport, and as part of various industrial miniatures. Another widely used piece was a power generator, which looked like a large, domed structure with six vertical fins evenly spaced around the perimeter.

As the popularity of *Space Patrol* grew, so did the demand for children's toys based on the program. Marx, the leading manufacturer of children's playsets, produced plastic and metal fixtures and tinplate buildings that imaginative youngsters could assemble as part of role-playing their favorite heroes. Marx produced a number of playsets through the 1950s and 1960s, including sets for *Space Patrol* and *Tom Corbett, Space Cadet*; the Cape Canaveral Space Center set; and the International Geophysical Year exploration set. Less complete playsets were produced in the 1970s, and even today, some of the same components used in the original set are available in the Marx Cape Canaveral Space Center, Limited Collector's Edition, found in specialty or nostalgia shops. The use of these toys as props offers a reliable way to establish the physical size of the miniature sets. For example: The laboratory on Pluto # 3 scales out to about 24 inches at its longest part because the effects department used the Marx playset power generator on its roof to conceal an antenna that disabled space ships. The same power generator is used in Terra City and as the observation dome on a space station. Using these objects, which have known dimensions, it is easy to conclude that the Terra City set was probably no more than 10 feet wide and eight feet deep.

While most of the structures were static, some animation was used — often with good effect. Most of this movement was accomplished by using small motors, most likely from Lionel model railroad equipment, to turn antennae on the rooftops of buildings — but probably the most effective and impressive motion came from Terra City's freeway system. The miniature cars were attached to thin strips of rubber material which were painted the same color as the pavement of the freeway. The "pavement" had a groove in which the rubber strip would lie and guide the stream of cars as a chain was pulled along. The movement of the cars was quite smooth, which suggests that the chain was pulled by an electric motor. Different "lanes" ran at different speeds, which added to the realism of the effect. Although it is unlikely, it's possible that this was the same or similar system used in the "City of Tomorrow" exhibition at the 1939 New York World's Fair.

Miniature lights were also used in the models and sets, although sometimes not very convincingly. Even with the low resolution of the kinescopes of the day, on at least one episode, the *Terra V*'s navigation lights and their wires could be seen dangling below the wings. Apparently the gaffer's tape had lost its adhesive properties just before the live scene was shot. Many of the large-scale buildings in Terra City were adorned with flashing clearance lights attached to radio masts or directly to the buildings. While these lights were motionless, they did impart a sense of reality to the set by making it look "alive"; however, the flashes produced a problem for the video engineer. Early television cameras used a vidicon tube to capture the images that were focused onto it by the lens. These tubes were unable to handle large differences in light intensity within the same scene, and the bright spot of a light bulb would produce a dark eyebrow-shaped halo around the source. While this was annoying to the video engineer, the fans of the day did not seem to mind. It should be noted that this effect can also be seen in many of the early episodes in which the high-contrast lighting would cause smearing of the areas between portholes or other details on the models.

Conclusions

The ships of *Space Patrol* drew their designs from many avenues, ranging from the futuristic to the fanciful and fantastic. Pulp magazine cover art of the 1920s and 1930s, con-

The *Terra V* departs on another mission of daring.

temporary experimental aircraft designs and the latest ideas in spacecraft design were all represented by the studio woodcrafters and artists. Taken together, these elements offer a somewhat naïve vision of the future of space travel. *Space Patrol*'s miniatures were created at a time when Willy Ley and Werner Von Braun were designing beautiful ships to do wonderful things. In less than 10 years, the reality and cost of space travel would replace aesthetic appeal with functionality. The vision of sleek spacecraft zooming to Pluto at the whim of the pilot was replaced with tiny capsules on the end of a large firecracker. In the late 20th century, an army of technicians, bureaucrats, politicians and scientists replaced the individualistic adventurers on whom we had modeled our young lives. Those born too late to experience the wonder and hope that was generated in those post–World War II years have been deprived of a gift to the imagination. These wonderful ships took us "where no man has gone before" long before Leonard Nimoy donned his ears and entered the bridge of the *Enterprise* for the first time.

Bibliography

Books

Adams, Beatrice. *Let's Not Mince Any Bones*. St. Louis: Western, 1972.

Alexander, David. *Star Trek Creator: The Authorized Biography of Gene Roddenberry*. New York: Penguin, 1994.

Curran, Douglas. *In Advance of the Landing: Folk Concepts of Outer Space*. 1985; reissued (updated), New York: Abbeville, 2001.

Dunning, John. *On the Air: The Encyclopedia of Old-Time Radio*. New York: Oxford University Press, 1998.

Hagerty, Jack, and Rogers, Jon C. *Spaceship Handbook*. Livermore, CA: ARA, 2001.

Jameson, Malcolm. *Bullard of the Space Patrol*. New York and Cleveland: World, 1951.

Linke, Frances. *Space Patrol Memories by Tonga*. Vols. 1–3. Los Angeles: Nin-Ra Enterprises, 1966, 1976, 1977.

Miller, Kent D. *Seven Months over Europe: the 363rd Fighter Group in World War II*. Hicksville, NY: Schiffer, 1989.

Thomas, Bob. *Walt Disney: The Art of Animation*. New York: Golden, 1958. P. 129.

Tumbusch, Tom N. *The Illustrated Radio Premium Catalog and Price Guide*. Dayton, OH: Tomart, 1989.

Young, S. Mark; Duin, Steve; and Richardson, Mike. *Blast Off! Rockets, Robots, Rayguns and Rarities from the Golden Age of Space Toys*. Milwaukie, OR: Dark Horse, 2001.

Zicree, Marc Scott. *The Twilight Zone Companion*. Los Angeles: Silman-James, 1992.

Articles

Ames, Walter. "Reader Rates Jeffrey Jones as Top Video Private Eye; Lyn Osborn Happy as Happy." *Los Angeles Times*, 17 July 1952.

Bassior, Jean-Noel. "Space Patrol: Missions of Daring in the Name of Early Television." *Filmfax*, Issue #1, January–February 1986, and Issue #2, April 1986; reprinted in Issue #9, February–March 1988, and Issue #10, April–May 1988.

Crane, Ellen. "Out of This World." *TV Show*, February 1952.

Danson, Tom E. "Involved Story Endings Excite Virginia Hewitt." *TV Radio Logic*, month unknown (clipping undated), 1952.

"Fans Dislike Halo Role of TV's Tonga." *Los Angeles Daily News*, 17 June 1952, p. 29.

Fighter Pilots in Aerial Combat, Issues #9 and 11. (Articles by Steve Blake.).

Fishberg, Herbert. "The First 500 Shows are the Toughest." *Afternoon TV Stars*, December 1977.

Glazer, Barney. "Television Topics of Current Week." *The Beverly Hills Bulletin*, 14 December 1952.

Hewitt, Virginia. "So You Want to Be Sexy!" *TV People*, June 1954.

Hogan, Pat. "Stop-Look-Listen." *Los Angeles Examiner*, 30 March 1950; *Los Angeles Examiner*, circa 1951 (clipping undated).

The Hollywood Reporter, 31 January 1952.

Hope, Gwen. "Space Patrol." *Tele-Views*, November 1950, p. 24.

Humphrey, Hal. "Marital Status: None." *Los Angeles Mirror*, 13 April 1953.

"Interplanetary Cop." *Time*, 11 August 1952, pp. 46–47.

Kaufman, Dave. "On All Channels." *Variety*, 1 April 1955.

Kennedy, Bill. "Our Home Town." *Los Angeles Herald Examiner*, 10 May 1956.

_____. "Our Home Town." *Los Angeles Herald Express*, 17 June 1952.

Lait, Jack Jr. "Stop-Look-Listen." *Los Angeles Examiner*, 4 December 1954.

Los Angeles Daily News, 3 July 1953.

Los Angeles Mirror, 17 March 1952.

Los Angeles Times, 8 April 1952, p. A-10.

Maxberry, Earlene. "Buzz Corry's Girl of Tomorrow." *TV Time*, February 1953.

"Missiles and Miseries." *TV Guide*, 25 February 1961.

"Missing: One 35-Foot Rocketship." *The Best of Starlog, Vol. II*. Starlog, 1981, p. 11.

"A Mission with the Space Patrol." *TV-Radio Mirror*.

Morgan, George Eldred. "Where Have You Gone, Captain Midnight?" *Parade*, 15 August 1982.

Newsweek, 25 January 1954.

"On the Air." *The Hollywood Reporter*, 12 February 1953.

"On the Air." *The Hollywood Reporter*, 6 October 1953.

Osborn, Lyn. "Don't Be a Problem Pal." *TV Fan*, June 1954.

_____. "Why I'm Unhappy." *TV-Radio Life*, 27 June 1952.

"The Playboy Interview: Roone Arledge." *Playboy*, October 1976.

"Poolside Patrol." *TV Star Parade,* October 1953.

Price, Paul. [Column.] *Los Angeles Daily News*, 14 August 1951.

Radio-Film-Television, November 1954.

Rich, Allen. "Listening Post and TV Review." *Valley Times*, 26 August 1952.

"Ricky Walker Has His Day Here Thursday...." *Tazewell County Reporter*, 14 January 1954.

Ripley, Austin. "Photocrime: Death Points the Finger." *Look*, 2 January 1951.

Robinson, Murray. "Planet Parenthood." *Collier's*, 5 January 1952, p. 31.

"A Romance for 'Happy.'" *TV Time*, 7 March 1953.

Snyder, Camilla. "Let There Be Light ... Chandeliers Are Still Hanging in There." *Los Angeles Herald Examiner*, 2 August 1978.

"Space Happy! And at $45,000 a year Lyn Osborn Should Be." *TV Guide*, 25 December 1954.

"'Space Patrol' Being Cut to Half-hour Weekly Show." *The Hollywood Reporter*, 9 June 1953.

"'Space Patrol' Cast to Aid 'Time Capsule' Rite." *Los Angeles Herald Express*, 8 April 1952.

"Space Patrol Conquers Kids." *Life*, 1 September 1952, pp. 79–83.

"'Space Patrol' in Albums by Decca." *The Hollywood Reporter*, 10 November 1954.

"Space Patrol Zooms 2 Thesps from $40 to $500 Per Week." *Variety*, 29 April 1952.

"Space Patrolman's Pay Soars 700%, But He Misses Those $8 Laughs." *Variety*, 20 January 1954.

Starr, Jimmy. "Lisa Kirk Signs for Filmusical in Rome." *Los Angeles Herald & Express*, 11 November 1954.

_____. "M-G-M's 'Young Bess' Stars Stewart Granger." *Los Angeles Evening Herald and Express*, 13 August 1951.

Tattletale. "Behind the Screen." *TV Show*, November 1953.

"Televents" column (syndicated), *San Gabriel Valley Independent*. Undated tearsheet grouped with clippings from January 1953 in Lyn Osborn's pressbook.

"Television Chatter." *Variety*, 3 June 1953.

Terrell, Maurice. "Photocrime: Death in a Flash." *Look*, 10 October 1950.

_____. "Photocrime: The Murder Ray." *Look*, 2 December 1952.

TV, July 1955.

TV, September 1954.

"TV Pair's Death Witnesses Sought." *Los Angeles Times*, 25 April 1953.

Variety, 29 April 1953.

"What's Wrong." *Tele-Views*, August 1951.

"Will Television Costume Become Custom?" *Tele-Views*, September 1950.

The Wilshire Press, 21 May 1953.

"[Writer] Tells How Pressure Censors TV." *Des Moines Sunday Register*, 4 June 1967, p. 9-L.

Films

Earth vs. the Spider. Creature Feature Productions, LLC, 2001.

Missile to the Moon. Rhino Home Video release, 1992 (film originally released in 1959).

My Favorite Year. Metro-Goldwyn-Mayer, 1982.

Sleeping Beauty (Fully Restored Limited Edition). Buena Vista Home Video, Burbank, CA, 1997.

Recordings

Adventures of Superman. 78 rpm records. Varése Sarabande, 2000.

The Airport Boys. "You Are My Sunshine" and

"Bad Girl" *Away Back West Again!* Collector Series Tape #89. Victor Bluebird Records; available from American Gramophone and Wireless Co., Orting, WA

Huston, Lou. *Buzz Corry Becomes Commander-in-Chief.* 78 rpm record. Decca, November 1954.

_____. *Cadet Happy Joins Commander Corry.* 78 rpm record. Decca circa November 1954.

Spear, Eric. *Stratosphere.* From the Francis, Day and Hunter Music Library (a collection of British production music), available on CD in *The Sci-Fi Channel Presents Sci-Fi's Greatest Hits*, Volume 4, "Defenders of Justice." TVT Records, 1998.

Web Sites

www.bbc.co.uk
www.celebhost.net
www.hq.nasa.gov
www.IMDb.com (Internet Movie Database).
www.joepierre.com
www.osia.org (Order Sons of Italy in America).
www.otrsite.com (Jerry's Vintage Radio Logs).
www.radiogoldindex.com
www.slick-net.com/space/ ("Roaring Rockets" Web page created by Dr. Rory Coker).
www.solarguard.com (created by Ed Pippin)
www.tech-notes.tv

Interviews

Akins, Glen and Alice. 27 May 1999.
Aldrin, Buzz. January 2002.
Ames, Dale. June 2001.
Bailey, Ellen. 27 November 2001.
Baker, Abigail Shelton. 2 March 2002.
Bara, Nina. 29 March 1984.
Barkus, Charles. August 2001 through 9 August 2002.
Barr, Rickey. 4 March 1986.
Beals, Dick. 18 May 2002 through 20 May 2002.
Bresee, Frank. June 1998 through 16 April 2002.
Buckley, John. 13 March 1993 through August 2000.
Clifton, Marg. 13 March 1999.
Cohen, Allan. January 1989 through November 2000.
Crandall, Paul. 22 February 2002.
Darley, Chris. 1 December 2000.
Darley, Dick. 3 April 1985 through 14 August 2002.

Davis, Greg. May 2001.
De Mots, Maury. 7 December 1998 through 14 March 2000.
Denning, Glen. 6 January 2002.
Dobkin, Larry. 2 May 2000.
Doshna, Al. February 2002.
Flood, Beth. 14 June 1984 through 28 November 2002.
Gelbart, Larry. 8 May 2003.
Gerrold, David. February 2003.
Grant, Stuart. 1 October 2002.
Guarino, Michael. 5 May 2001 through 20 January 2002.
Gurr, Bob. 5 December 2002.
Haendiges, Jerry. June 2002.
Hagen, Michael and Carol. 11 March 2002.
Hartnagel, Ralph. 18 November 2000.
Hewitt, Virginia. 30 April 1984 through 19 January 1986.
Higgins, Clair. 5 August 2002.
Hill, Maury. August 1984.
Huston, Lou. November 1997 through 15 July 2000.
Jolley, Norman. 21 November 1991 through 2 April 2000.
Kemmer, Ed. 31 July 1984 through 24 March 2003.
Fran Kemmer, February 1988 through January 2003.
Kovacs, Bela. July 1984.
Krone, Truck. 5 February 1999.
Lewis, Charles. 4 September 2001 through 2 March 2003.
Lynes, Bobb. 26 February 2001.
MacDuff, Tyler. August 2001.
Mayer, Ken. 30 April 1984.
Mayer, Ruth. 28 January 1999.
McCroskey, Don. 27 May 1999.
Miller, Darla. 3 April 2002 through 10 May 2002.
Montreys, Margaret. 30 March 1999.
Musgrave, Story. 15 October 2001.
Narz, Jack. December 2000.
Newman, Barry. February 2000.
Teaney, Alyce. 27 May 1999.
Trachinger, Bob. 31 October 1999 through 1 January 2001.
Tufeld, Dick. 14 December 2000.
Walker, Rick. 1 November 1999 through 9 November 2002.

Letters and Personal Papers

Darley, Dick. "ABC Work Schedule." 23 February 1950 through 19 February 1955; personal letters and documents, 1950–1999.

Fan letters to cast, July 1950 through February 1955.

Hewitt, Virginia. Personal letters and documents, 1947–1985.

Moser, Mike. Character fact sheets for *Space Patrol*, circa February 1950.

Osborn, Lyn. Letters to family, 25 December 1947 through 7 August 1958.

Memorabilia

Space Patrol Handbook from Space Patrol Membership Kit.

Index

*Numbers in **bold** represent photographs.*